The Reading Process

The Reading Process

The Teacher and The Learner

MILES V. ZINTZ
University of New Mexico

WM. C. BROWN COMPANY PUBLISHERS
Dubuque, Iowa

ISBN 0–697–06169–8

Library of Congress Catalog Card Number:79-105519

Second Printing, 1970

Printed in the United States of America

Contents

v

PART V — PROVISION FOR ALL THE CHILDREN

Preface

The primary purpose of this text is to help the classroom teacher to be a *diagnostic teacher of reading* every day—from the very first day of school.

After an initial overview about the place of reading in the elementary school, the teacher inventories the reading abilities of a number of children who are able to perform at various levels. Thus, even before the teacher becomes concerned about the course of study in reading in the classroom, he learns something about *how children read* by listening to them. He has just enough techniques to evaluate the four levels of performance: independent, instructional, frustration, and capacity. Since he can then approach Chapter 4 with the basic principles of learning and some observation of how well children read, he is better able to understand the reading needs in a classroom enrolling children of varying abilities. Programming for each child then becomes primary as he learns in Chapters 7-12, the scope of word recognition, comprehension, study skills, critical reading, oral reading, and permanent reading interests.

Oral reading serves many purposes in everyday life. It, too, can be useful to the classroom teacher in continuous evaluation of developmental reading skills in his diagnostic teaching.

Throughout the text, also, the emphasis on the affective values in learning have been expressed and often reinforced. Developing permanent interests in reading and reacting critically and constructively to material read is as much *affect* as *cognition*. Teachers have sometimes failed in the past to establish this value in teaching reading in the elementary school.

Readiness is also approached as a diagnostic problem in the first grade. Diagnostic evaluation of abilities and disabilities in the readiness area enables those who are *ready to proceed* to move as far and as fast as they can go in the reading program. It prevents failure for those who need to build on strengths and overcome weaknesses.

Good diagnostic teaching of reading in any classroom requires an eclectic approach to methodology. For some, individualized reading with programmed lessons to teach and reinforce the skills will be appropriate; for some, sequenced basal reader lessons with long periods of practice on plateaus of learning, seasoned with the patience of Job, will work best.

The gifted, the retarded, the bilingual, the gifted bilingual, the non-lingual, the child with specific learning disability . . . each one has a place in the classroom reading program that is completely diagnostic in its operation.

Finally, the text concludes with a number of questions concerned with reading in perspective in the total elementary curriculum. How can *each teacher* increase the functional level of reading ability that each child brings to the classroom? This is diagnostic teaching.

Diagnostic teaching is a methodology which requires that the teacher ascertain the functional level of skills and abilities of *each child* in his classroom. It will never be possible for all of the children in a group to learn the same thing, at the same time, with the same amount of practice. To teach diagnostically, teachers utilize valuable psychological concepts regarding (1) variations in innate abilities of children in all skills, abilities, and appreciations; (2) the role of practice in learning; (3) motivation of school work for efficient learning; (4) development of understanding; (5) the place of transfer of learning where common elements exist; and (6) the problem of forgetting. Finally, diagnostic teaching provides for the deviant child and his learning needs, whether he is gifted, retarded, emotionally disturbed, or neurologically impaired.

It is hoped that the references at the end of each chapter will provide extensive reading in any of the many phases of the program which a specific teacher finds most meaningful or necessary in his day-to-day work.

Miles V. Zintz

Acknowledgments

It is a truism that one learns more about his subject when he teaches it than when he studies it. During the past twenty years students have raised many questions for which both professor and student needed to search out answers. I am grateful to all those teachers who have introduced me to new problems and have helped search for answers.

Dr. Joyce Morris and Dr. Margaret Greer read the total manuscript in rough draft form and offered their comments. Dr. Judith Dettre read chapters 19 and 20 critically and helped select the readings for the ends of the chapters. Dr. Robert Hanny read Chapter 5 and offered constructive suggestions about interaction analysis as a process. Dr. Bernard Spolsky, a linguist on the staff of the University of New Mexico, read Chapter 13 on linquistics and the reading teacher. I am especially indebted to these people for their efforts in adding to the quality of the manuscript.

PART I

THE OVERVIEW

Chapter 1 defines reading as a continuous developmental process and Chapter 2 discusses the psychological foundations on which learning in school children is based. The reader then immerses himself in the task of analyzing how well or how poorly each person reads and understands what he reads. This sampling of an individual's oral and silent reading abilities, through the use of the informal reading inventory, should demonstrate how disparate the varying abilities are in a given class.

Chapter 4 describes how the teacher plans a reading program to meet the varying needs and abilities of the students in the class. Chapter 5 presents concepts in interaction analysis to provide the teacher concrete help in measuring teacher-student and student-student interaction in the classroom. Chapter 6, Parent-Teacher Cooperation, emphasizes the need for the school and the home to work together: for each to understand the part the other plays in the life of the child, and to keep channels of communication sufficiently open to serve the child's best interests.

Such an introduction prepares the reader for the next section which is devoted to the skills to be developed in a complete reading program.

1

What is Reading?

Jack in the first grade. Jack is a happy little boy who happened to be born into a comfortable middle-class family early in May. He had only one brother and no sisters. His father was past thirty and already a junior executive when Jack was born. His father often brought his briefcase home and worked at a desk in the extra bedroom. Jack's mother had graduated from a two-year college course with an A. A. degree and had been working for a few years as an efficient secretary in a large telephone company office before she married. Jack's father was a very curious, interested, "always learning" kind of man and read a great deal. His wife read too, but more often things related to helping her with what was more practical. When Jack was an infant his mother spent all her time with him when his father was at work and they laughed and played and she *talked to him* a great deal. By the time he was able to walk around a bit, his mother was pregnant a second time. During her pregnancy she continued to spend a great deal of time *talking to Jack.* When he was eleven months old he was saying *mama* and *daddy* and *go, come,* and a few other words in clearly intelligible language. His mother explained to Jack about going to the hospital when his little brother was born and his grandmother came and lived in the house and assumed full responsibility during the mother's absence. The grandmother bought books of the *Baby's First Book* variety and shared them with Jack. By the time Jack was 18 months old, his mother was holding him on her lap reading *Mother Goose* to him for relatively long periods of time in the afternoon while his brother slept or in the evenings while they waited for daddy to come home. By the time Jack was three, he was "demanding" a story hour at bedtime and using language confidently and in complicated language structures.

His growth in language skills was constant and he developed a *broad vocabulary* with concepts and thinking in problem-solving situations.

3

Even though he lived in a state that did not provide kindergarten classes for five-year-olds, he enjoyed many of the experiences of five-year-olds with his mother and brother 16 months younger. He learned how to *sequence ideas,* how to *explain* simply and carefully, teaching his little brother many things "big" boys had already mastered.

Jack entered first grade with *highly developed verbal* skills. He could *listen well with understanding, understand* many of the *simple jokes* his mother and father told largely for his benefit. He went most *willingly to school* because he felt he was getting very grown up by the time he was *six years and four months old.* When he asked his mother about words, she had always answered his questions. He usually recognized his own, his father's, and his mother's names on letters that came in the mail. He could distinguish many of his books by the pictures on the covers but he was probably also noticing distinguishing features in the titles, too. By the time he entered school, he and his brother had a little library of nearly 200 books, mostly the sixty-nine cent or less, supermarket variety.

Needless to add, Jack entered first grade *confident and secure.* He was anxious to learn to read and, as long as his teacher was gentle and understanding and efficient in the teaching of reading, he would likely read by almost any method available. The teacher, fortunately, did know that all children grow at different rates, all children have varying needs for emotional response and security, and that all children have different levels of maturity in mastery of language as a communication process. She encouraged all the children to talk, to discuss, to explain, and to have fun at school. By the end of one month, she had divided her total group into those who were really ready for formal reading, those who needed readiness activities and a gradual introduction to formal reading, and those who would not show a great deal of interest in the printed word for several months.

She continued to study them carefully, discuss them with her supervisor, refer one to the school nurse, the school psychologist, or the school social worker, as problems in their learning arose, but her goal was to keep everybody learning something.

When Jack dictated an especially good experience story, she encouraged him to take it home and read it to his father and mother; when he finished each of the pre-primers, she encouraged him to carry them home and read aloud to whichever *parent* would *really listen.*

Phonics, spelling, and writing developed naturally and smoothly for Jack. His manuscript writing was very legible almost from the beginning. Jack will finish first grade able to read fluently and smoothly from books more difficult than first grade readers. He may have read the stories in a first semester, second grade book, or he may have read many trade books of interest to him. He will also have written at least one book of his own in which his stories (dictated) will have been bound together, have a table of contents, and have his name visibly displayed on the cover as the author.

How fortunate Jack was to have six excellent *years of readiness* for the academic job of going to school!

Now contrast Jack's successes with the problems confronting Ernesto.

Ernesto in the fifth grade. Ernesto's grandparents speak Spanish. Ernesto's parents speak Spanish well but attended only English language schools. They were never taught the structure of English as a second language and never learned to speak it confidently. As a result Ernesto and all his brothers and sisters have difficulty with English syntax and depth of vocabulary. While they use the superficial, everyday expressions, "Good morning, Miss Smith," or "How're things?" with ease, they lack both ability and confidence to compose essays in class or give good oral reports.

Neither did Ernesto study Spanish, nor learn to read or write it. Consequently, in fifth grade he has confidence and understanding with the sound patterns of commonly used Spanish vernacular and he "gets along" with the minimum amount of English language. He is illiterate in Spanish and considerably sub-standard for fifth grade in reading and writing English. He is well on his way to finishing school more non-lingual than either mono- or bi-lingual. As Knowlton said, he may graduate from high school illiterate in two languages![1]

These children, Jack and Ernesto, represent only two of the myriad children any classroom teacher in the elementary school must be prepared to meet and guide through a school year. While all children are probably like each other in more ways than they are different from each other, it is the understanding, and acceptance of these degrees of difference that enable each child to grow from his place on the long continuum.

Reading has been defined as a process of thinking, evaluating, judging, imagining, reasoning, and problem-solving.[2] Gray identifies four steps in the reading act: perception, comprehension, reaction, and integration.[3] Perception is the ability to pronounce the word as a meaningful unit; comprehension is the ability to make individual words construct

---

[1]Clark S. Knowlton, "Spanish-American Schools in the 1970's," *Newsletter,* General Department of Mission Strategy and Evangelism, Board of National Missions, United Presbyterian Church in the U. S. A., 475 Riverside Drive, New York, New York, 10027, July, 1968, p. 4.

[2]*Reading in the Elementary School,* 48th Yearbook of the National Society for the Study of Education, Part II, (Chicago: University of Chicago Press, 1949), p. 3.

[3]William S. Gray, *On Their Own in Reading,* (Chicago, Scott Foresman, 1948), pp. 35-37.

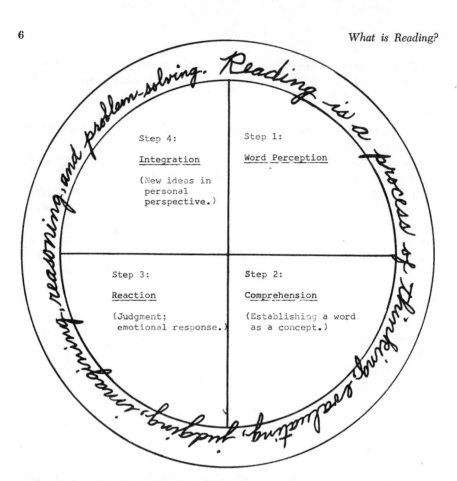

Figure 1.1. Reading Defined. This diagram is adapted from one written in Spanish in one of the language bulletins prepared for elementary teachers by Senora Consuelo de Escorcia, Tegucigalpa, Honduras.

useful ideas as they are read in context; reaction requires judgmental action—a feeling about what the author has said—and the final step is the ability to assimilate the idea or concept into one's background of experience so that it is useful as a part of the total experience of the individual. Of course these four steps are completely interdependent in a meaningful use of reading as a tool in the solution of problems. (See Figure 1.1.)

I. READING AS A NECESSITY IN TODAY'S WORLD

The people who become teachers in the United States probably have been fortunate enough all their lives to live in a world where reading is encouraged, respected, and expected. They have developed reading habits sufficiently mature to succeed in courses in general education in college. In this environment, it is easy to overlook the fact that many people in this country grow up and live out their lives without learning to read.

The drop-out rates in high schools over the country may run as high as 50 percent of the first grade populations. In inner-city slums, in deprived areas, and in schools with high percentages of minority ethnic groups, the total social structure has responded to the inadequacy of the academic high school, and has recently created alternate choices for teen-agers in Job Corps, Vocational training, special GED programs,[4] and MDTA training programs.[5] According to the 1960 U. S. Census, 2.3 percent of the population had no education; 6.1 percent had from one to four years; 7.5 percent had five or six years in school. This constitutes an adult population of about 16,000,000.[6]

In studies surveying populations in adult basic education programs, evidence is revealing that the person over twenty-five who attended school for seven years is more apt to perform on an achievement test currently at about the fourth grade level; and if he attended four years of school, he is likely to perform more nearly at the second grade level.

It is obvious that the efforts of the Office of Economic Opportunity currently under way are long overdue if the adult population is to acquire the minimum essential skills for literacy.

One of the objectives of reading instruction has been the development of life-long reading habits for the population of boys and girls going through school. To build such habits, to instill constructive attitudes, and to ensure success in the efforts of students during their school attendance, *is a sacred trust of classroom teachers.*

The inadequacy with which the schools have met this objective is made baldly clear in a statement by Asheim:

> . . . Not only is reading the occupation of a small segment of the population but serious and continued reading is limited to a smaller segment within that one. This is most clearly shown in the figures we have for library use. About twenty-five per cent of the adult population of a library community is registered with the public library, but actually only about eighteen per cent use the library at least once a year, and only about ten per cent use it as often as once a month. This concentration of library use is typical of reading activity generally; it is probably safe to say—borrowing figures from library studies—that about three-fourths of the books that are read are read by less than five per cent of the adult population.[7]

---

[4]General Educational Development or High School Graduation Equivalency.
[5]Manpower Development Training Authority.
[6]U. S. Department of Commerce, Bureau of the Census, U. S. Census of Population: 1960, General, Social, and Economic Characteristics, PC Series.
[7]Lester Asheim, "What Do Adults Read?" *Adult Reading,* (ed. Nelson B. Henry, The National Society for the Study of Education. Chicago: University of Chicago Press, 1959), p. 19.

II. READING AROUND THE WORLD

High rates of illiteracy have been reported through UNESCO publications for a quarter of a century. How can social groups in any of the small countries of the world make "intelligent" decisions when the nation's majority is illiterate and living in poverty? Political ideologies in direct contradiction to the American Democracy most middle-class Americans take for granted will surely find their most fertile seed-beds where there are hungry, ignorant people with little hope.

In Colombia, where the elementary school is a five-year program, only eight of each one hundred children who start to school in first grade actually complete the work of the elementary school. While many of this 8 percent enter secondary schools, the attrition continues through the university. In Ecuador, of one hundred children who start to school in first grade, only five may be expected to finish the six-year elementary school program. With such drastic attrition rates, it is apparent that those countries cannot now meet the demands of any kind of a technological society with its requirement of technical, academic knowledge. Yet, the only escape for the masses from marginal existence in poverty is some kind of social and economic revolution to industrialize their countries with modern equipment. Such a possibility is predicated on first educating the masses to as high a literacy level as is possible.

III. THE TEACHING OF READING AS A DEVELOPMENTAL PROCESS

Readiness for reading is probably most closely related to language facility in young children. In most of the research relating reading success at the end of first grade and performance to standardized reading readiness tests administered early in the year, the relationship is very low. Karlin found that

> The confidence which teachers place in the concept of reading readiness is well merited, but the desirability of using existing reading-readiness tests almost exclusively to measure extent of readiness should be re-examined.[8]

Concept development needs to be reinforced at every step of the way in helping boys and girls to mature in their communication skills. Recognizing that the communication skills develop in young children in the established order of listening with understanding first, speaking second, reading third, and writing last, the need to keep concept development expanding can be explored in all the child's avenues to communication. Reflection, appraisal, and problem-solving need to be practiced

---

[8]Robert Karlin, "The Prediction of Reading Success and Reading Readiness Tests," *Elementary English*, 35: 320-322, 1957.

in oral discussion, in teacher-led but not teacher-dominated open-ended discussions, as well as in reading and writing lessons.

Horn defines reading in this way:[9]

> . . . reading includes those processes that are involved in approaching, perfecting, and maintaining meaning through the use of the printed page. Since there are many such processes, and since each one varies in degree, the term must be elastic enough to apply to all the varieties and gradations of reading involved in the use of books.

Horn further reminds us:[10]

> The author does not really convey ideas to the reader; he merely stimulates him to construct them out of his own experience. If the concept is already in the reader's mind, the task is relatively easy, but if, as is usually the case in school, it is new to the reader, its construction more nearly approaches problem-solving than simple association.

Then he concludes:[11]

> . . . it is clear that very little improvement may be expected from formal drill in reading unless at the same time provision is made for the enrichment of experience, the development of language abilities, and the improvement of thinking.

Gates describes the nature of the reading process in this way:[12]

> Reading is not a simple mechanical skill; nor is it a narrow scholastic tool. Properly cultivated, it is essentially a thoughtful process. However, to say that reading is a "thought-getting" process is to give it too restricted a description. It should be developed as a complex organization of patterns of higher mental processes. It can and should embrace all types of thinking, evaluating, judging, imagining, reasoning, and problem-solving. Indeed, it is believed that reading is one of the best media for cultivating many techniques of thinking and imagining. The reading program should, therefore, make careful provision for contributing as fully as possible to the cultivation of a whole array of techniques involved in understanding, thinking, reflecting, imagining, judging, evaluating, analyzing, and reasoning.

Gates explains further that reading is more than a mental activity; that emotional responses are also required:[13]

> . . . the child does more than understand and contemplate; his emotions are stirred; his attitudes and purposes are modified; indeed, his innermost being is involved. . . . The reading program should, there-

---

9Ernest Horn, *Methods of Instruction in the Social Studies,* (New York: Charles Scribner's Sons, 1937), p. 152.

10*Ibid.,* p. 154.

11*Ibid.,* p. 156.

12Arthur I. Gates, "Character and Purposes of the Yearbook," *Reading in the Elementary School,* (Nelson B. Henry, Editor, 48th Yearbook of the National Society for the Study of Education, (Chicago: University of Chicago Press, 1949), p. 3.

13*Ibid.,* p. 4.

fore, make provision for exerting an influence upon the development of the most wholesome dynamic and emotional adjustments.

One considers the process of reading as a developmental, thinking process which puts words to work solving problems. Gray's definition of the act of reading as a four-step process is re-stated: perception of the word, comprehension of its meaning, reaction to the meaning in terms of what one knows and integration of the idea into one's background of experience.[14] So reading is perceiving, comprehending, reacting, and integrating.

The four major jobs to be done in teaching beginning reading are (1) to begin with a very limited number of words and very gradually, with sufficient meaningful practice, to develop a basic sight vocabulary; (2) to teach a complete course of study in phonetic and structural analysis; (3) to teach, always, that reading, far from being a word-calling process, is the interpretation of the ideas behind printed symbols; and (4) to give every child a great deal of meaningful practice so he will achieve fluency, facility, and a love for reading as an avenue to learning.

The more recent work of curriculum experts in elementary education have further emphasized the job of the classroom teacher in developing understandings, concepts and generalizations. Taba states that the content of learning for the child consists of various levels of thinking: "One level is that of specific facts, descriptive ideas at a low level of abstraction, and specific processes and skills."[15]

> Basic ideas and principles represent another level of knowledge. The ideas about causal relationships between human culture and natural environment are of this sort. So are scientific laws and mathematics principles, the ideas stating relationships between nutrition and metabolisms of the human body, or ideas about how such factors as climate, soil, and natural resources produce unique constellations of a geographic environment.[16]
>
> A third level of content is composed of what one might call concepts, such as the concept of democracy, of interdependence, of social change, or of the 'set' in mathematics.[17]

Taba's levels of thinking are basic theoretical material for the reading teacher if he is going to help boys and girls develop reading skills commensurate with the full definition of reading as comprehending, reacting, and integrating. Levels of questioning as outlined below and the refining of conceptual thinking for critical reading ability are positively related. If the teachers' questions are now largely cognitive recall

---

[14]William S. Gray, *op. cit.*, pp. 35-37.
[15]Hilda Taba, *Curriculum Development: Theory and Practice* (New York: Harcourt, Brace and World, Inc., 1962), p. 175.
[16]*Ibid.*, p. 176.
[17]*Ibid.*, p. 178.

types of specific facts on a "low" level of abstraction, then reading teachers need to give attention to Sanders' levels of questioning.

Sanders, in *Classroom Questions, What kinds?*[18] has translated Bloom's *Taxonomy of Educational Objectives*[19] into seven levels of thinking and problem solving. These represent a hierarchy of levels of abstraction:[20]

1. Memory: The student recalls or recognizes information.
2. Translation: The student changes information into a different symbolic form of language.
3. Interpretation: The student discovers relationships among facts, generalizations, definitions, values, and skills.
4. Application: The student solves a lifelike problem that requires the identification of the issue and the selection and use of appropriate generalizations and skills.
5. Analysis: The student solves a problem in the light of conscious knowledge of the parts and forms of thinking.
6. Synthesis: The student solves a problem that requires original, creative thinking.
7. Evaluation: The student makes a judgment of good or bad, right or wrong, according to the standards he designates.

Fowlkes, in the introduction to Sander's text, writes:[21]

> . . . the teachers most talented in questioning are usually deep and continuing scholars. Good questions recognize the wide possibilities of thought and are built around varying forms of thinking. Good questions are directed toward learning and evaluative thinking, rather than determining what has been *learned* in a narrow sense.

So, with reference to the process of teaching reading to primary school children, one may conclude that they must be prepared to use the language of the school adeptly enough that they will be able to attack the process of reading at all levels of thinking and problem-solving as described by Taba and Sanders.

As suggested by Horn, Gates, and Gray, concept development is the greatest problem in the teaching of reading to all children. Readiness for reading necessitates the development of vocabulary concepts, use of language to discuss and solve problems, and even, for the six year old child, some appreciation of the fact that

> . . . The ability to communicate has permitted each generation to rise on the shoulders of the thinkers and achievers who have gone before, to profit from their gains, to avoid their mistakes, and to pursue their dreams and aspirations and make some of them realities.[22]

---

[18]Norris M. Sanders, *Classroom Questions, What Kinds?* (New York: Harper & Row, 1966).

[19]Benjamin S. Bloom (ed.), *Taxonomy of Educational Objectives* (New York: Longmans, Green, 1956).

[20]Sanders, *op. cit.*, p. 3.

[21]Sanders, *op. cit.*, Editor's Introduction, p. ix.

[22]Ruth G. Strickland, *The Language Arts in the Elementary School* (Boston: D. C. Heath and Co., 1951), p. 3.

The Questions Teachers Ask

Guszak visited second, fourth, and sixth grade classrooms and recorded the reading lessons for all the groups. The tapes were analyzed to evaluate the types of questions teachers asked in the reading groups. He found that 56.9 percent of the questions were simple recall (How many cats did Katy have? What color were they?); 13.5 percent were recognition questions (Which sentence tells the names of all the seven cats?). This total of 70.4 percent of all questions suggests the heavy emphasis on literal comprehension. Higher levels of thinking required for making inferences or evaluating were too infrequently asked for. Guszak found 13.7 percent inferential and 15.3 percent evaluative questions. He concluded that teachers lack understanding of the reading-thinking-questioning hierarchy and suggests that textbooks need to present a model for reading-thinking skills and a methodology for developing such skills.[23]

IV. TEACHING READING TO YOUNG CHILDREN

Such expressions as "all children are different" and "no two are alike" have become trite through verbalization but not through teacher performance day-by-day in the classroom. Children vary greatly in physical, mental, emotional, and social characteristics. Teachers are admonished at every turn to recognize that children grow at different rates in all these characteristics. Greater attention to putting these known principles into practice is indicated.

Since "No two children can learn the same thing in the same amount of time with the same amount of practice," there are no arbitrary standards for what constitutes first grade or fifth grade in the elementary school.

As children progress through the grades in the public schools, the extent of individual differences on various traits will become greater and greater, not less and less. It follows that twelve-year-olds vary more within their age group than six-year-olds. Consider only one characteristic: that of intelligence. If one assumes a valid measure of intelligence quotients, and that the range of I. Q.'s in a given class is 75 to 125, the six-year-olds have mental ages varying from four and one-half to seven and one-half. By the same criterion, the twelve-year-olds have mental ages varying from nine years to fifteen years and the fifteen-year-olds from eleven years three months to eighteen years, nine months.

The real problems in trying to teach six-, seven-, and eight-year-olds arise from the specific strengths and weaknesses inherent in the children

---

[23]Frank J. Guszak, "Teachers' Questions and Levels of Reading Comprehenson," Perspectives in Rdg.: *The Evaluation of Children's Reading Achievement* (Newark, New Jersey: International Reading Association, 1967), pp. 97-109.

when they are confronted with the complicated process of learning how to read the printed word. The four facets in learning how to read: (1) mastering a basic sight vocabulary, (2) learning phonetic and structural analysis skills, (3) developing comprehension skills, and (4) getting lots of easy practice, are sufficiently understood by most teachers so that a great majority of their children learn to read with encouraging degrees of success.

The child who has a vision or hearing impairment, a neurological handicap, poor general health, insufficient sleep or rest, a sub-standard living environment, a speech impediment, emotional upsets, inadequate language readiness for reading, or long absences from school, is apt to have difficulty beyond that experienced by other children in learning to read.

V. THE SKILLS OF READING

Reading in the School Day

It has been estimated that nearly 90 percent of the child's school day will be spent on reading and writing activities. While this is certainly not necessary and probably not desirable, observation indicates that this is the way classrooms are operating. This emphasizes that reading is not taught or practiced only in a scheduled "reading class." It is taught all day long in some form. Further observation indicates that it is often not taught at all, but more accurately "assigned" and "tested." The established fact that 10 to 15 percent of the boys and girls have problems with reading in school may be due in greater measure to "inadequate teaching" than it is to "failure to learn." No teacher can ignore this charge until he has competently examined both sides of the issue.

One classroom was observed where the sixth grade had been divided into three sub-groups for reading: high second grade level, easy fourth level, and easy fifth level. Yet, all the sixth graders were assigned the same spelling word list of sixth grade words for "regular" spelling and each member of the class was issued a sixth grade geography book adjudged to be too difficult for more than half of a class where the achievement normally fits sixth grade achievement level. Can even the "top" reading group, reading at easy fifth grade level, read with any degree of understanding a sixth grade geography book which is likely to be written at a more difficult reader level than a sixth grade reader?

"Learning to Read" and "Reading to Learn"

It has been said that the teachers in the primary grades teach children how to read and then all their other teachers assign reading for them to "learn" the content of the course of study. The idea is not true and teachers must be very careful to discredit it. Of course, in the first year and perhaps most of the second, children have to master a great deal of "decoding" ability so that they can pronounce or recognize words for the reading process. They must learn how to phrase, punctuate, and make proper uses of inflection. However, students all the way through the secondary school will still be improving these very same skills in a comprehensive reading program. On the other hand, children in the very first reading lessons are going to find the primary emphasis given to "getting the idea" or "finding the meaning in the story." Even while the decoding process is being learned (and no reading can happen unless the child can pronounce the words) the primary emphasis will be in teaching that reading is a process of deriving meaning through the interpretation of printed symbols. Just as reading for meaning is important in the initial reading program, it remains the primary reason for reading all of one's life. Consequently, one learns to read and reads to learn as two concurrent processes all the way through school.

Kinds of Reading Skills

A. Developmental: The how-to-read skills
   1. Word identification skills
   2. Comprehension skills
   3. Study skills
B. Functional reading
   1. Location activities
   2. Specific skills for study/comprehension
   3. Selection and organization
   4. Summarizing
   5. Providing for remembering
C. Recreational reading
   1. Reading as a "free-time" activity
   2. Locating books of interest in the library
   3. Developing tastes for a variety of reading material
   4. Giving pleasure to others through oral reading
   5. Fixing permanent habits of reading every day.

VI. OBJECTIVES OF THE READING PROGRAM

In its broadest sense, the objective of the teaching of reading is to make each person as literate as it is possible for him to become. This includes (1) mastering the necessary skills in decoding the written word so that it is immediately pronounceable and meaningful; (2) mastering the necessary skills of comprehension so that as one reads he demands meaning from the passage he is reading; (3) developing the abilities necessary to think about and react to what one reads to decide if it is useful to him; and (4) developing the life long habit of relying on reading as documented evidence to substantiate one's thinking, to solve new problems, or to corroborate new solutions. All teachers, undoubtedly, have some general purposes similar to the four above, as global purposes of teaching.

To determine successfully whether children learn what is taught, however, objectives must be much more clearly defined. For the administrator, Whipple has characterized the philosophy behind a good total-school reading program. She says

1. The goals of the reading program for the entire school must be agreed upon by the entire staff—for all grade levels, kindergarten through senior high school.
2. Success in reading is dependent upon the total process of child growth and development if learning, thinking, and problem-solving are to take place constructively.
3. Reading is only one of the communication arts. Listening, speaking, and writing are just as important . . . and are inter-related.
4. If each child is permitted to grow at his own rate, which is all any child can do, he must follow a well-worked out program from kindergarten through his entire school life.
5. Instruction must be planned for optimum individualization. Teaching reading skills and abilities in groups requires continuous evaluation, and ability to be flexible in adjusting to immediate needs.
6. A balanced reading program includes group instruction in developmental skills, programmed activities for individual growth, wide ranges of levels of reading in the content fields about given topics, and much opportunity for free and recreational reading. The balanced program also provides for all those needing corrective reading to learn 'missing' skills in the sequence in developmental reading. It provides, finally, for that small per cent (perhaps three to five per cent) who have serious disabilities which may result from psychological, physical, neurological or second language problems.
7. Evaluation of the success of the reading program must be on-going, with critical attention to providing for weaknesses and strengths.[24]

While this is an excellent set of criteria for providing a good total school program, it does not provide the classroom teacher any concrete basis for day-to-day work. It would be possible for teachers to analyze teachers' manuals for readers at various levels and find, for example, the skills and abilities developed at the first semester, third grade level. Some general objectives could be stated by the teachers that they intend to teach these skills and abilities while the student is reading this book.

[24]Gertrude Whipple, "Characteristics of a Sound Reading Program," Chapter III, *Reading in the Elementary School*, 48th Yearbook of the National Society for the Study of Education, Part II (Chicago: University of Chicago Press, 1949), pp. 34-38.

There is yet one more very important step, however, in determining the teacher's objectives for each day's lesson. Such objectives should be *specific* and describe concisely and clearly the intent of the teacher to teach a skill, an attitude, a work-type reading ability, or new concepts. A specific objective, then, is a statement of the teacher's intention to teach a specific thing in that day's lesson.

Behavioral Objectives

Objectives that convey most clearly what the intention is are those that tell how a student can demonstrate concretely that he has achieved the objective. Thus, the objective is measurable in terms of the student's behavior. These are called *behavioral objectives*.

For example, after the third grade story about "Snakebite"[25] has been read, the teacher's objective could be to expect each member of the group to be able to recall seven of the nine suggestions given in the story about what to do.

Or, after reading the pioneer story in the third reader about "Making Soap in Pioneer Days,"[26] the teacher's objective could be that each member of the group will be able to recall all the ingredients needed by the pioneer woman to make her own soap.

Or, if the sixth grade story contains such words as "momentary," "magical" and "suitable," the teacher's objective may be to teach the group that the suffix "ary" usually means "belonging to, or connected with," the suffix "al" usually means "having to do with something" and the suffix "able" usually means "telling what kind." The objective also states the minimum acceptable level of performance. The teacher might plan to give a five-point quiz and set as a minimum acceptable performance, four right choices.

A satisfactory behavioral objective meets the following criteria: (1) it indicates what the learner will do; (2) it states how the determination of achieving the objective will be measured; and (3) it establishes the minimum level of acceptable performance.

Contrast the following:

Non-behavioral objectives	*Behavioral objectives*
To find and give the meanings of idiomatic expressions.	To give the common meaning of five idiomatic expressions used in ten illustrative sentences on a ditto master.

---

[25]Ernest Horn, et al., *Progress in Reading Series* (Ginn and Co., 1940), Third Reader.
[26]*Ibid.*

To develop the ability to arrange ideas in a story in proper sequence.	After the story has been read, the eight ideas presented in the teacher's guide will be given to the students in the reading group in a mixed up order and they will number all eight of them in the correct order in which they appeared in the story.
To understand picturesque language.	Each member of the group will select and read aloud to the group a sentence containing picturesque language.

Should teachers learn to state their objectives behaviorally? Ojemann[27] answers the question "Yes, definitely," but he adds one caution for separating children's behaviors when in the classroom and when satisfying their own intrinsic interests:

overt behavior in the classroom is not the same as the overt behavior when the learner is on his own;
both kinds of children's behavior should be included in teaching and testing;
behavior in "controlled motivation" situations must not interfere with the child's feelings that what he is studying has personal significance for him.

VII. SUMMARY

In this chapter, the scope of the reading program has been discussed. Reading is defined as a four-step process: perception, comprehension, reaction, and integration. The importance of reading in the political and economic world must be understood by teachers. Learning to read is a complicated developmental process not yet taught to huge numbers of children around the world.

Objectives for teaching reading lessons should be stated behaviorally so that the teacher has a concrete method of determining the success of the learning immediately after teaching the lesson.

SUGGESTED ACTIVITIES

1. Demonstrate ability to write objectives for daily lessons in behavioral terms.
2. Use a teacher's manual for a basal reader and write objectives for a reading lesson that you would be able to teach.

---

[27]Ralph Ojemann, "Should Educational Objectives be Stated in Behavioral Terms?" *The Elementary School Journal,* 68: 231, February, 1968.

3. Select a story from a basal reader and write questions for it which elicit thinking at levels above that of recall.
4. Think about your own public school education and try to evaluate the degree to which your school followed Whipple's characteristics of a good school program. Which of the seven were fairly well met and which were not met at all.
5. Observe a teacher teaching a reading lesson and evaluate his "levels of questioning" used in a class discussion.
6. Take a standardized reading test and compare your results with norms provided. Do you read "better" than the average college student?

REFERENCES FOR FURTHER READING

GUSZAK, FRANK J., "Teachers' Questions and Levels of Reading Comprehension," Thomas C. Barrett, Ed., *Perspectives in Reading No. 8, The Evaluation of Children's Reading Achievement* (Newark, Delaware: International Reading Association, 1967), pp. 97-109.

HEILMAN, ARTHUR, *Principles and Practices of Teaching Reading* (Columbus, Ohio: Charles E. Merrill, 1967), Chapter I: "Principles of Teaching Reading."

MAGER, ROBERT F., *Preparing Instructional Objectives* (Palo Alto, California: Fearon Publishers, 1962), 62 pages.

SANDERS, NORRIS M., *Classroom Questions, What Kinds?* (New York: Harper and Row, 1966), 173 pages.

SMITH, NILA BANTON, *Reading Instruction for Today's Children* (Englewood Cliffs, New Jersey: Prentice-Hall, Inc., 1963), Part I: "The Changing Scene," pp. 3-161.

STAUFFER, RUSSELL G., *Directing Reading Maturity as a Cognitive Process,* (New York: Harper and Row, 1969), Chapter I: "Reading, a Thinking Process," pp. 3-31.

————, *Teaching Reading as a Thinking Process,* (New York: Harper and Row, 1969), Chapter I: "Reading: A Thinking Process," pp. 3-16.

TINKER, MILES A. and CONSTANCE M. McCULLOUGH, *Teaching Elementary Reading,* Third Edition (New York: Appleton-Century-Crofts, Inc., 1968), Chapter I: "Reading: Nature, Goals, Teaching Methods."

ZINTZ, MILES V., *Corrective Reading* (Dubuque, Iowa: Wm. C. Brown, 1966), Appendix A, "Teaching Reading: an Overview," pp. 323-356.

2

Psychological Foundations
for Reading Instruction

Each classroom teacher is confronted with problems of classroom management, of motivation of learning, and of articulating this year's work with last year and next year. Within the class, the teacher must expect to find the normal range of abilities in intellectual, physical, emotional, and social development.

There are a number of principles of learning that the teacher needs to understand, accept, and use in interpreting the school success of individual children.

> When the teacher and child meet, a major part of the teacher's armament must be a knowledge of the principles of learning. Many normal children learn readily in spite of the repeated violations of learning principles. By sharpening our awareness of some of these principles, as applied to teaching children, we can anticipate better adherence to them.
>
> Some of these major principles of learning include *overlearning, ordering,* and *sizing* (programming) of new material, *rewarding* only *desired responses, frequent review,* and avoidance of interference and negative transfer.[1]

Gagné discusses eight types of learning and defines them briefly.[2]

1. Signal learning: learning to make a general, diffuse response to a signal.

2. Stimulus response: a precise response to a discriminated stimulus.

3. Chaining: a chain of two or more Stimulus-Response connections.

---

[1]Barbara Bateman, "Learning Disabilities—Yesterday, Today, and Tomorrow," *Exceptional Children,* 31: 167-177, December, 1964.
[2]Robert M. Gagné, *The Conditions of Learning* (New York: Holt, Rinehart and Winston, Inc., 1965), pp. 58-59.

4. Verbal association: Learning of verbal chains.

5. Multiple discrimination: Even with "n" different responses to "x" different stimuli, the learner does discriminate.

6. Concept learning: Acquiring ability to respond to entire classes of objects or events with proper identification.

7. Principle learning: Chaining of two or more concepts.

8. Problem-solving: Using thinking to combine principles to obtain new solutions.

According to Hilgard, learning theory might be expected to answer questions one might ask about learning in everyday life. Any theory, then, may be appraised in terms of its attention to measuring:[3]

1. Capacity.   What are the limits of learning? How is learning measured? The range of individual differences.

2. Practice.   What is the role of practice in learning? Practice causes improvement in efficiency in performance only when the conditions of learning are suited to the one who is practicing.

3. Motivation.   How important are drives and incentives? What about rewards and punishments? Or Intrinsic vs. Extrinsic motives?

4. Understanding.   What is the place of insight? Or a hierarchy of steps leading to generalizations?

5. Transfer.   Does learning one thing help you in learning something else?

6. Forgetting.   What happens when we remember and when we forget?

This chapter reflects principles related to capacity, practice, motivation, understanding, transfer, and forgetting. These observations lead to principles underlying programmed learning, helping children learn to generalize, and recognizing the affective, the cognitive, and the psychomotor domains in the education of children.

I. PRINCIPLES BASED ON LEARNING THEORY

1. Capacity

The normal curve of distribution has now become a "household" word in describing range, the extent of, or the distribution of a skill or trait.

---

[3]Ernest Hilgard, *Theories of Learning*, Third Edition (New York: Appleton-Century-Crofts, Inc., 1966), pp. 7-8.

The concept of the distribution of any given attribute or skill or ability as falling normally around a central or average value is an important one.

For example, if one were to stop the first 100 men passing by a given street corner and measure their height, he would find out something about their sameness and their difference. Since the average American man is about 5′ 9″, most of the men measured would be about this height. Some would be shorter; some would be taller. If one were to graph the results, he would obtain something similar to Figure 2.1.

If one were to generalize from the graph to a curved line, one would see the cluster around the center and the tapering off. From such a tendency, the "normal curve" emerges.

Intelligence, problem-solving abilities, length of time required to memorize nonsense syllables, or scores on a vocabulary test are all skills and abilities that also fall in a "normal distribution" when a large unselected group is measured.

Statistically, the area under a normal curve can be divided into three equal deviations from the median or center. The standard deviation represents a given distance (in points) on the base line, and there are arbitrarily allocated pre-determined "*areas*" for each standard deviation. One standard deviation incorporates 34 percent just below or above the median; the second standard deviation is 14 percent on either side; and third, 2 percent. This tells a teacher that if there is a random distribution, 68 cases in 100 lie within one deviation above and below the median: 28 cases are in the second standard deviation; 14 above and 14 below the median; 4, in the third, two above and two below the median. (See Figure 2.2.)

Teachers have occasionally been told that class grades *must* follow this normal curve of distribution. This is not true. If teachers explain adequately what examination questions will be included in an examination, it should be *possible* for everyone to do a satisfactory job writing the answers.

When the median is defined, the result is that half of the class will perform better than, or above the median, and half the class will perform less well than, or below, the median. To try to get a class to perform in such a way that everyone is average or better, is to deny the existence of this spread of abilities.

This interpretation becomes meaningful when an arithmetic average (mean) or the location of the middle child in a distribution (median) gives a value for the "typical" or "average" level of performance. This state of affairs leaves half below and half above this typical level of performance.

For each teacher this means that the children he teaches should become more different in achievement, *not more alike*, during a year of

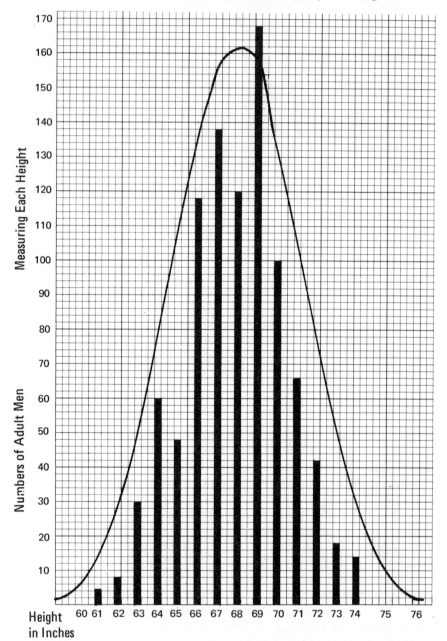

Figure 2.1. A Graph showing the distribution of measures of height of men selected at random. The measured height of 928 adults. (From Galton's measures of children and their parents illustrating the law of filial regression. Cited in Henry Garrett, **Great Experiments in Psychology**, (New York: Appleton-Century-Crofts, Inc., 1941, p. 67).

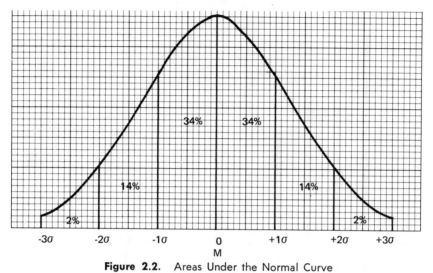

Figure 2.2.   Areas Under the Normal Curve

*The Greek letter, σ, is the statistical representation for standard deviation.

instruction. The range of differences in achievement in reading and arithmetic will get wider with good teaching.

Bright children grow faster academically; average children make average growth; and dull children grow slower academically. Figure 2.3 shows the increasing spread of intellectual abilities in the chronological age spread from four to fifteen years.

The Wechsler Intelligence Scale for Children is a common individually administered intelligence test in the schools and in children's clinics. It has been standardized so that a score of 100 is "normal" for any given chronological age. In other words, if a child of ten earns a full scale I. Q. score of 100, this represents "normal" or "average" intelligence and ranks him at the median or the 50th percentile in the distribution. Since the standard deviation for this test is 15, two standard deviations (a range from 70 I. Q. to 130 I.Q.) include 96 percent of the total sample tested as indicated in table 2.1. This corresponds to the normal curve of distribution already discussed. About 50 percent of all the people of a given age test between 90 and 110. This is called the normal intelligence range. (See Table 2.1, p. 25.)

The Spread of Differences

The longer children the same age attend school, the *more different* they become.

Teachers may expect to find in classes of unselected children (heterogeneous groups), that the range of reading achievement measured by a standardized test will be, on the average, three years at the end of grade

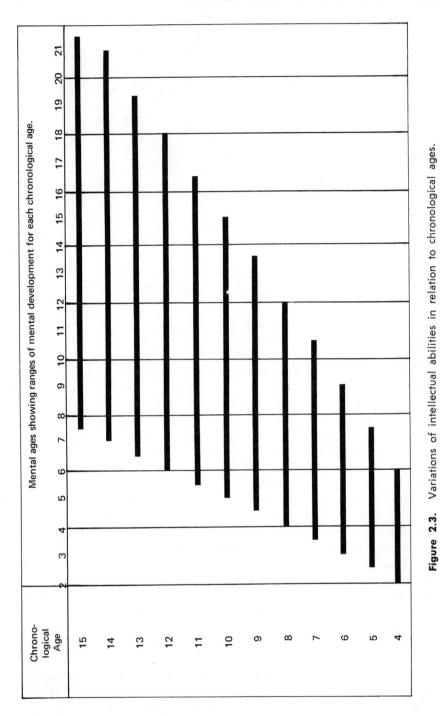

Figure 2.3.   Variations of intellectual abilities in relation to chronological ages.

TABLE 2.1. *Intelligence Classification for WISC I Q's*

IQ RANGES	CASSIFICATION	PERCENT IN EACH GROUP
130-	very superior	2
120-129	superior	7
110-119	bright normal	16
90-109	average	50
80- 89	dull normal	16
70- 79	borderline	7
68 below	mental defective	2
		100

From Garrett, Henry E., *Testing for Teachers, Second Edition,* (New York: American Book Co., 1965), p. 75.

two; four years at the end of grade three; five years at the end of grade four; six years at the end of grade five; and seven years at the end of grade six.

Many factors in the child's total growth and development contribute to these differences in achievement. Figure 2.4 details differences in school learning attributable to constitutional factors, intellectual factors, environmental factors, educational factors, and emotional factors.

2. Practice

Practice provides the circumstance for conditions of learning to operate.[4]

For effective practice, essential conditions include
(1) Motivation
(2) Immediate knowledge of results
(3) Distributed practice as an economical condition
(4) Elimination of error.
   Drill should be
(1) At the point of error;
(2) Spirited;
(3) Of short duration; and
(4) Meaningful and purposeful.

What the student practices must be meaningful *to him.* To stay motivated, the child must have some expectations of success. He cannot compete logically if he feels he cannot win. Marks that signify merit rather than failure should be assigned to the lowest achievers in class.

Immediate knowledge of results shows the child whether or not he is successful; such knowledge is a strong motivational factor.

---

[4]J. B. Stroud, *Psychology in Education* (New York: Longman's Green, 1946), pp. 372-382.

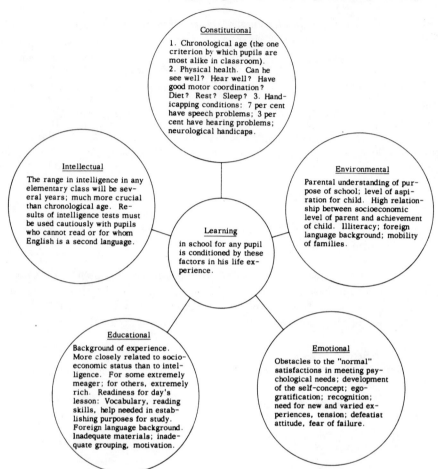

Figure 2.4.   Factors in the Range of Individual Differences

From Miles V. Zintz, *Corrective Reading*, (Dubuque: William C. Brown Company, Publishers, 1966), p. 230.

Distributed vs. Massed Practice

Ebbinghaus demonstrated that with any considerable number of repetitions of an act, a planned distribution of repetitions over a period of time is decidedly more advantageous than the massing of them at a single time.[5] More short practice periods return greater dividends than fewer long ones.

Teachers need to be aware of the importance of *distribution of exposure* to concepts and generalizations to be taught. Summarizing at the

[5]Stroud, *op. cit.*, p. 488, citing Ebbinghaus.

end of the class period, reviewing each lesson on succeeding days, and helping students write summarizing statements are important in this exposure of learning. This evidence should be used by teachers to reduce the amount of cramming and procrastinating students do for tests.

For the drill included in any subject, such as spelling, handwriting, and overlearning arithmetic algorisms, the principles from distributed practice in shorter periods apply. Short, lively, motivated drills on basic sight words, consonant blend sounds, commonest prefixes, or responding with synonyms or antonyms will be very profitable in the reading program.

3. Motivation

No learning takes place without a motive. Motives are conditions within the organism that cause it to seek satisfaction of need. The basis for the condition is obscure, generally speaking, since the real motivation a given student has for a specific learning objective may not be the same as the teacher suspects his motivation to be. An intrinsic motive to learn something may not be as strong as the extrinsic motive the student established at home, or as strong as his many psychological needs apart from his intellectual growth.

Motivating students is a complex, involved process for teachers and often leaves them baffled when their plans go awry. Since there will be no one way to motivate every child, the teacher must seek ways to cause each student to set his own goals, both immediate and mediate.

The effective teacher understands that there are many bases for motivation: (1) mastery motives—the desire to excel, desire to succeed, the desire to overcome difficulties; (2) social approval motives—desire for approval, desire for self-esteem, desire for attention; (3) conformity motives—desire to conform, desire to avoid censure.

Motivation should

1. include success experiences so the student has feelings of personal worth and security.
2. be greater in school if the school curriculum emphasizes social utility in what it teaches, with considerable emphasis on the usefulness, here and now, of what it teaches. In addition to school being preparation for future life, it is accepted that it is more importantly preparation for life here and now; and the result of learning to live here and now prepares one to live in an undefinable future.
3. include methodology to reinforce self-expression and self-esteem in *all* boys and girls.
4. maximize competition with one's own past record and minimize competition among all members of a class.

Intrinsic vs. Extrinsic Motivation

When young children enter school, much of their motivation may be teacher or adult generated. Elementary teachers take advantage of this extrinsic motivation and one occasionally hears, "You'd like to do that for Miss Brown, wouldn't you?" or "Miss Brown would like for you to finish that before you go out to play."

One of the goals of education in a free society is that the value of learning becomes its own reward. The extent to which the school achieves this goal will determine how successfully students are intrinsically motivated to achieve their personal "self-realization." The motivation for learning may be diagrammed as Figure 2.5, largely extrinsic in first grade and largely intrinsic in twelfth.

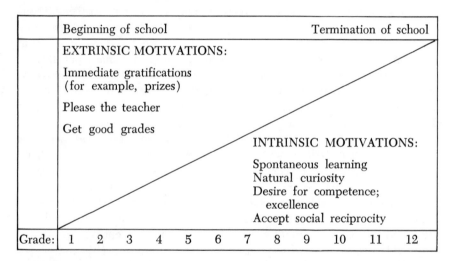

Figure 2.5. Growth in intrinsic motivations: Acquiring the desire to learn.

A hierarchy of needs described by Maslow leads to the conclusion that the well-integrated personality on the top-step in the hierarchy has a curiosity about life, the future, and the unknown that is satisfied through a need to know and to understand.

The physiological needs, safety, love and belonging, esteem, and self-actualization needs must be met to some degree before man explores his need to know and understand. When a more basic need is fairly well satisfied, the next higher order need emerges and serves as an active motivator of behavior. See Figure 2.6.[6]

---

[6]Herbert J. Klausmeier, and William Goodwin, *Learning and Human Abilities: Educational Psychology.* (Harper & Row, Second Edition, 1966), p. 427.

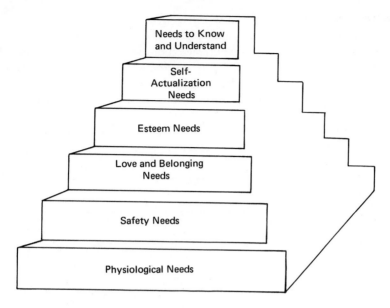

Figure 2.6. Hierarchy and Prepotency of needs.

From *Learning and Human Abilities* by Herbert J. Klausmeier and William Goodwin. Drawing based on esteem needs in *Motivation and Personality*, Maslow (Harper, 1954).

Maslow concludes:

These basic goals are related to each other, being arranged in a hierarchy of prepotency. This means that the most prepotent goal will monopolize consciousness and will tend of itself to organize the recruitment of the various capacities of the organism. The less prepotent needs are minimized, even forgotten or denied. But when a need is fairly well satisfied, the next prepotent (higher) need emerges, in turn, to dominate the conscious life and to serve as the center of organization of behavior, since gratified needs are not active motivators.

Thus man is a perpetually wanting animal. Ordinarily the satisfaction of these wants is not altogether mutually exclusive, but only tends to be. The average member of our society is most often partially satisfied and partially unsatisfied in all of his wants. The hierarchy principle is usually empirically observed in terms of increasing percentages of non-satisfaction as we go up the hierarchy. Reversals of the average order of the hierarchy are sometimes observed. Also it has been observed that an individual may permanently lose the higher wants in the hierarchy under special conditions. There are not only ordinary multiple motivations for usual behavior, but in addition many determinants other than motives.[7]

---

[7]A. H. Maslow, "A Theory of Human Motivation," *Psychological Review*, **50**: 394-395.

Rewards and Punishments

Praise works better than blame; rewards work better than punishments; and children need to experience more successes than failures.

Fear of failure can be sufficiently traumatic in children that they are unable to function in a given learning situation.

Jucknat[8] has graphed the effect on level of aspiration of experiences of success and failure. (Figure 2.7)

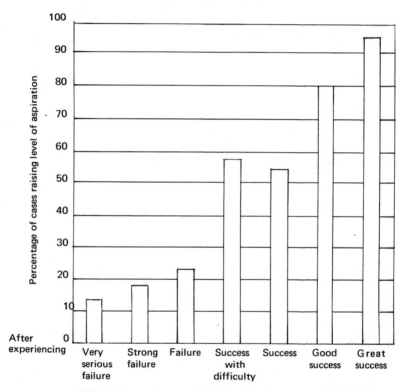

Figure 2.7.   Effects of Failure and Success on Level of Aspiration

From James M. Sawrey and Charles W. Telford, *Educational Psychology*, (Boston: Allyn and Bacon, Inc., 1958), p. 356. After M. Jucknat, *Psychol. Forsh.*, 1937, 22, 89.

4. Transfer of Training

Transfer of training is exhibited when the learner is able to make use of his learning in circumstances that are different from the situation in which the learning took place. Transfer is a necessary factor in all growth in learning. Transfer is absolutely necessary in the extension of any generalized skill taught in the elementary school, such as reading,

[8]Reported by James M. Sawrey and Charles W. Telford, *Educational Psychology*, (Boston: Allyn and Bacon, Inc., 1958), p. 356.

writing, and arithmetic. Thorndike explained the concept of transfer in this way: ". . . a change in one function alters any other only in so far as the two functions have as factors identical elements.[9]

The theory of identical elements explains an important condition in the probability of transfer. Judd advanced the theory of generalized training to explain the likelihood of transfer. His position was that the ability to generalize, understand or abstract, enhanced transfer.[10]

Ellis lists principles of transfer that include[11]

1. Over-all task similarity. Transfer of training is greatest when the training conditions are highly similar to those of the ultimate testing conditions.
2. Stimulus similarity. When a task requires the learner to make the same response to new but similar stimuli, positive transfer increases with increasing stimulus similarity.
3. Learning-to-learn. Cumulative practice in learning a series of related tasks or problems leads to increased facility in learning how to learn.
4. Insight. Insight, defined behaviorally as the rapid solution of problems, appears to develop as a result of extensive practice in solving similar or related classes of problems.
5. Amount of practice on the original task. The greater the amount of practice on the original task, the greater the likelihood of positive transfer.
6. Understanding and transfer. Transfer is greater if the learner understands the general rules or principles which are appropriate in solving the problems.

5. Understanding

Learning progresses from the concrete to the abstract. Dale's cone of experience presents the importance of concrete, direct experiences, and the difficulty of conceptualizing from only abstract, written verbal symbols.

Dale divides the cone of experience into those activities of "doing"; those of "observing" someone else do something; and those of interpreting abstract visual or verbal symbols.

I. Activities of action: The child is a participant in the learning process.
   1. Direct experience with a purpose. Experiences that involve the senses: touch, smell, see, hear, taste. For example, preparation of a meal in the class, construction of a piece of furniture, etc.

---

[9]E. L. Thorndike, *Educational Psychology* (New York: Lemcke and Buechner, 1903), p. 80.

[10]C. H. Judd, *Psychology of Secondary Education* (Boston: Ginn and Co., 1927), p. 441.

[11]Henry A. Ellis, *The Transfer of Learning* (New York: The Macmillan Co., 1965), pp. 72-74.

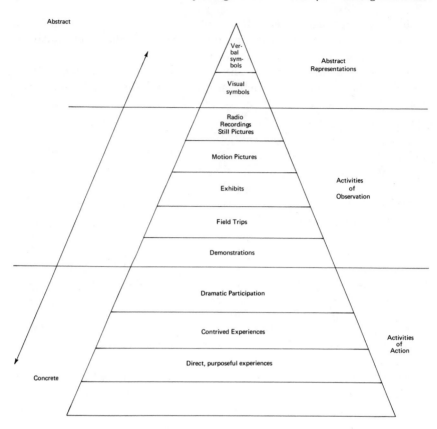

Figure 2.8.   Cone of Experience

From Edgar Dale, *Audio-visual Methods in Teaching*, Revised Edition, Copyright 1946, 1954 by Holt, Rinehart and Winston, Inc. Reprinted by permission of Holt, Rinehart and Winston, Inc.

     2. Contrived experiences: a method that simplifies the details. For example, a model or a small reproduction.
     3. Dramatization: Participating in a drama.
II. Activities of observation: The child only observes someone else doing the action.
     4. Demonstration. Performed by the teacher.
     5. Excursions away from the school. For example, to the dairy or to the store.
     6. Exhibitions: Collections of things in the experiences of children: stamps, coins, dolls, etc.
     7. Educational motion pictures.
     8. Vertical picture files, photos, the radio, records.

III. Abstract representations.
      9. Visual symbols: charts, graphs, maps, diagrams, etc. Each is only a representation of an idea.
    10. Verbal symbols: A word, an idea, a concept, a scientific principle, a formula. In each case, completely abstract.

The intellectual life functions on a very high level of abstraction or symbolization almost all the time. The point is that children need much experience at concrete levels before they can solve abstract questions and problems with good comprehension.

To enhance understanding in the school life of the child, the curriculum of the school should be based more on *process* than on *content*. When teachers are aware of the development of the cognitive processes of children and the necessity of putting new learning to work in order to be remembered, they are apt to see much that is objectionable in the traditional classroom of factual recall, parroting back explanations to the teacher, and performing on tests that require much regurgitation of factual information at the simple recall level. For emphasis, this methodology based on "process" of learning is contrasted with methodology based on the content learned.

Process Methodology	*Content Methodology*
1. Learning to think clearly to solve problems.	1. Careful memorizing of teacher's lecture notes.
2. Learning to categorize the *relevant* and the *irrelevant* in a problem situation.	2. Depending on the teacher to decide what is important.
3. Learning by discovery—learning by inductive methods is more valuable than learning what the teacher tells him.	3. Relying on information learned from teachers, books, and parents.
4. Experimenting with, testing, and integrating subject matter information.	4. Studying each subject as a small isolated body of necessary information.
5. Evaluating—using the evidence —and accepting or rejecting the results.	5. Accepting the judgment of teachers and textbooks as unquestioned authority.
6. Emphasizing *how* to read, study, think, and learn.	6. Emphasizing *what* to read, study, think and learn.
7. Free discussion and small group work to search for answers to the "larger" questions.	7. Recitation in class.

Children must learn a great deal of factual information *to use* in "how-to-think" situations. One should not make a dichotomy of "Do we teach children *what* to think or *how* to think?" since without the *what* it will not be possible to do the *how*.

6. Forgetting

The most widely cited historical study of forgetting is that of Ebbinghaus, first published in 1885. He reported that 66.3 percent of what one learns is forgotten within twenty-four hours. The conditions surrounding this fact are important. He was his own subject, his materials were nonsense syllables and his criterion was two errorless repetitions. The Ebbinghaus curve of forgetting is reproduced in Figure 2.9.

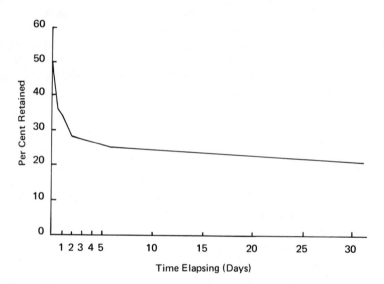

Figure 2.9. Curve of retention (Ebbinghaus) for nonsense syllables after various time intervals

From Henry E. Garrett, *Great Experiments in Psychology,* (New York: Appleton, Century-Crofts, Inc., 1941), p. 273.

The importance of review to reduce the very high rate of forgetting has been recognized for a long time. Reviewing very soon after learning and then reviewing several times at spaced intervals will help to minimize forgetting.

The practical bearing of the results obtained on education in general is that when associations have once been formed they should be recalled before an interval so long has elapsed that the original associations have lost their 'color' and cannot be recalled in the same 'shape', time, and order. In general it was found that the most economical method for keeping material once memorized from disappearing, was to review the material whenever it started to 'fade.' Here also the intervals were found to be, roughly speaking, in arithmetical proportion. For similar reasons the student is advised to review his 'lecture notes' shortly after taking them, and if possible, to review them again the evening of the same day. Then the lapse of a week or two does not make so much difference. When once he has forgotten so much that the various associations originally made have vanished, a considerable portion of the material is irretrievably lost.[12]

Spitzer's study of retention shows the importance of immediate recall and spaced review in helping sixth graders' scores on tests administered after different time intervals.[13] (See Figure 2.10.)

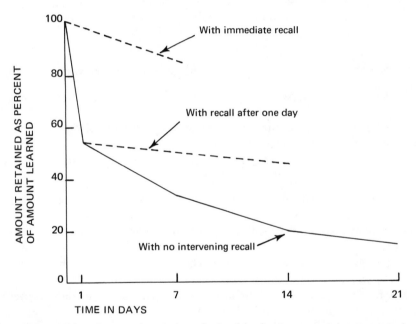

Figure 2.10. Curves of retention obtained by having equated groups read a selection and take tests at different time intervals. The solid line shows how forgetting takes place when there is no review before the test. The broken lines show the effect on retention when review follows either immediately after or one day after reading.

From Sidney L. Pressey, Francis P. Robinson, and John E. Horrocks, *Psychology in Education,* (New York: Harper & Brothers, 1959), p. 572, after H. F. Spitzer, "Studies in Retention," *Journal of Educational Psychology,* 30: 641-656, 1939.

---

[12]D. O. Lyon, "The Relation of Length of Material to Time Taken for Learning, and the Optimum Distribution of Time," *Journal of Educational Psychology,* 1914, 5: 155-163, cited in J. B. Stroud, *Psychology in Education* (New York: Longmans, Green and Company, 1946), p. 521.

[13]H. F. Spitzer, "Studies in Retention," *Journal of Educational Psychology,* 30: 641-656, 1939.

Rules for remembering:[14]

   a. Material is easy to remember in proportion as it is meaningful.
   b. Material is easier to remember if it gets well organized in the indi-·vidual's mind.
   c. Outlining, summarizing, or taking good notes are aids to remembering.
   d. An active intention to recall is an aid in trying to remember.
   e. A single reading is rarely enough. Reviewing and re-reading are necessary for remembering any length of time.
   f. Recall must be selective. One must sift out the main points.
   g. Immediately after reading, one should reflect on what is read and recite important points to oneself.
   h. What we learn and never review is gradually forgotten. What we want to remember must be refreshed from time to time by review.

II. PROGRAMMED LEARNING

Programmed learning is planned to utilize the following learning principles

1. The principle of easy steps.
2. The principle of continuous response at each step of the way.
3. The principle of immediate knowledge of results.
4. The principle of progressing at completely individual rates.
5. The principle of elimination of error and repetitive practice.

The principles are some of the most fundamental in promoting learning. Individualized lessons, paced to the tempo and the maturity of the individual student, and providing immediate feedback about correct and incorrect responses are the type of lessons conscientious teachers have been dreaming about for a long time. The greatest difficulties have arisen in the *qualities* of program; it has been easier to produce *programs* than it has to produce *high quality* programs which have adequate content that still conforms to the principles.

Three sets of materials based on the principles that have been successfully used are:

1. Wayne Rosenoff, Project Director, *Lessons in Self-Instruction in Basic Skills* (Del Monte Research Park, Monterrey, California: California Test Bureau, 1965), Reading: Reference Skills, Following Directions, Reading Interpretations, Levels A-B; C-D; E-F; and G.

2. Cynthia Buchanan, *Programmed Reading*, (St. Louis: McGraw-Hill Publishing Co., 1963), a series of 21 workbooks beginning with readiness and teaching vocabulary to approximately fourth grade reading level.

---

[14]Albert J. Harris, *How to Increase Reading Ability*, Fourth Edition (New York: Longmans, Green and Co., 1961), pp. 445-446.

3. Behavioral Research Laboratories, *Programmed Texts*: *Remedial Reading* (Box 577: Palo Alto, California: Behavioral Research Laboratories, 1966). A series of booklets designed for developing reading skills from the beginning in a format acceptable for adults.

Other materials of a traditional nature with comparable objectives are:

1. Science Research Associates, *Junior Reading for Understanding Laboratory* (259 East Erie Street, Chicago 11, Illinois: Science Research Associates, Inc., 1963).

2. Clarence R. Stone, *et al.*, *New Practice Readers*, Books A through F (St. Louis: Webster Division, McGraw-Hill Book Company, 1960-1962).

3. William A. McCall and Lelah Mae Crabbs, *Standard Test Lessons in Reading* (Bureau of Publications, Teachers College, Columbia University, 1961).

III. LEARNING TO GENERALIZE

A generalization is a statement or principle that encompasses the common characteristics of a cluster of ideas or individual statements. Teachers should use generalizations in helping students to generalize their knowledge in a given subject. Sanders points out that in a fourth grade geography book, the generalization "Life in the desert is difficult" is not stated directly but is clearly implied in such subordinate statements as: (1) the home is crude and the family moves frequently; (2) medical help is not available; (3) life is close to nature and welfare often dependent on the caprice of nature; (4) transportation is by foot or animal.[15]

This development of generalizations from the students in the class is an inductive method of teaching. Through the analysis of their own experiences and ability to form concepts that are meaningful and useful to them, children can accumulate descriptive information to allow them to arrive at a generalized statement.

Woodruff shows in the figure below how this process works in developing the extended understanding of the concept "tree." This process utilizes perception, conceptualization, thinking, evaluating, and selecting the contributing components to the generalization. (See Figure 2.11)

The most immediate perceptions about "tree" include its parts, its color, and its purpose for shade. Some of the abstract ideas learned later are the ways branches rustle in the wind, trees conserve moisture, and

---

[15]Norris M. Sanders, *Classroom Questions, What Kinds?* (New York: Harper & Row, 1966), p. 23.

they may be either evergreen or deciduous. Accumulating all of these perceptual experiences leads to concept formation and generalizing.

In understanding many elementary concepts about weather and its components, children grow toward the ability to draw generalizations about weather and climate. This is illustrated by Woodruff in Figure 2.12 showing a major concept developed from many supporting concepts.[16]

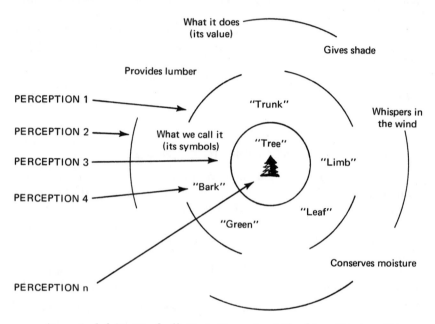

From Asahel D. Woodruff, *Basic Concepts of Teaching,* Concise edition (San Francisco, California: Chandler Publishing Co., 1961), p. 71.

Figure 2.11.   Accumulating Perceptual Experiences Grow into Concepts

Finally, one can construct a conceptual model of arriving at generalizations based on many individual, miscellaneous experiences, grouped into simple general concepts, leading to broader generalizations, and finally arriving at a generalized concept or generalization.

The concept of a culture is the comprehensive, generalized concept based on sorting and classifying myriad specific behaviors* that generalize to the social expectations of a given society and to the establish-

---

[16]Woodruff, *op. cit.,* p. 184.
    *Specific behaviors include the way we eat and sleep, wash and dress, go to work, goods and services we buy, use barter or money, live in families, satisfy sex needs, define our personal religion, rear children, greet strangers, travel, plan recreation, and value and believe.

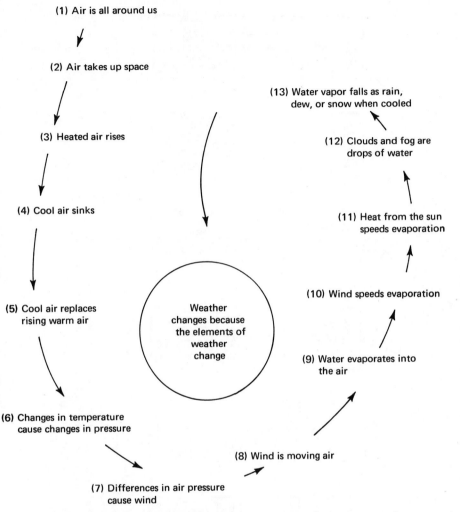

(1) Air is all around us

(2) Air takes up space

(3) Heated air rises

(4) Cool air sinks

(5) Cool air replaces
rising warm air

(6) Changes in temperature
cause changes in pressure

(7) Differences in air pressure
cause wind

(8) Wind is moving air

(9) Water evaporates into
the air

(10) Wind speeds evaporation

(11) Heat from the sun
speeds evaporation

(12) Clouds and fog are
drops of water

(13) Water vapor falls as rain,
dew, or snow when cooled

Weather
changes because
the elements of
weather
change

From Asahel D. Woodruff. *Basic Concepts of Teaching.* Concise edition
(San Francisco, California: Chandler Publishing Co., 1961), p. 184.

Figure 2.12. A Major Concept and Some Supporting Concepts

ment of basic social institutions that perpetuate a given value system.
Ulibarri and Condie have depicted a model for the concept of a culture.
(See Table 2.2)

Mitchell and Brown illustrate the development of generalizations at
the primary level in their book *Animals, Plants, and Machines.*[17] After

[17]Lucy Sprague Mitchell and Margaret Wise Brown, *Animals, Plants, and Machines,* (Boston: D. C. Heath and Co., 1944).

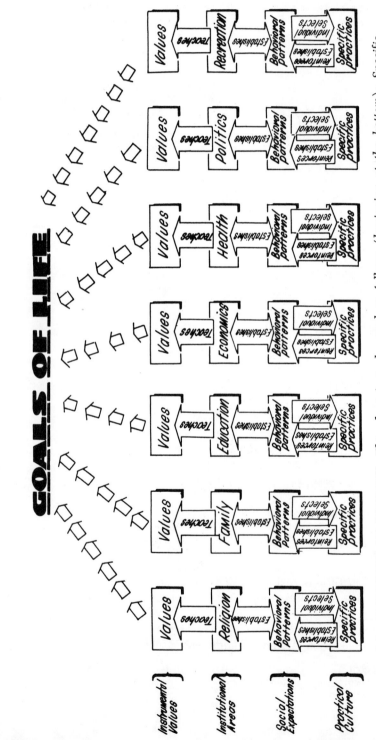

TABLE 2.2. BEHAVIOR IN SOCIETY. This chart is to be read as follows (beginning at the bottom): Specific practices refers to individual behavior. When many individuals adopt a specific practice, a group behavior pattern emerges. It will be noted that there is a reciprocal relationship between specific practices and behavior patterns. While specific practices combine to create behavior patterns, the behavior patterns, in turn, are followed selectively by the individual. He may choose to practice some kinds of behavior, reject others. In time behavior patterns assume a permanent quality. They then become institutions. Institutions reflect the group's values. The values . . . what is valued . . . orient the group, and the individual, toward the goals of life.

Chart developed by Horacio Ulibarri. Drawn by Le Roy Condie. From Miles V. Zintz, *Education Across Cultures* (Dubuque: Kendall/Hunt Publishing Co., 1969), p. 109.

Silly Will learned many answers to the questions "Who needs animals?" and "Who needs plants?", he was able to arrive at the generalizations shown in Figure 2.13 and 2.14: Cows provide people with meat, milk, butter, leather, and many other things they need; wheat provides people with many of the different foods they eat.

IV. THE COGNITIVE DOMAIN

Bloom's categories of thinking include
1. Memory—the student recalls or recognizes information.
2. Translation—the student changes information into a different symbolic form or language. He paraphrases.
3. Interpretation—the student discovers relationships among facts, generalizations, definitions, values, and skills.
4. Application—the student solves a life-like problem that requires the identification of the issue and the selection and use of appropriate generalizations and skills.

Figure 2.13. Cows provide people with meat, milk, butter, leather and many other things they need.

From Lucy Sprague Mitchell and Margaret Wise Brown, *Animals, Plants, and Machines,* (Boston: D. C. Heath and Co., 1944).

Figure 2.14. Wheat provides people many of the different foods they eat.

From Lucy Sprague Mitchell and Margaret Wise Brown, *Animals, Plants, and Machines*, (Boston: D. C. Heath and Co., 1944).

5. Analysis—the student solves a problem in the light of conscious knowledge of the parts and forms of thinking.
6. Synthesis—the student solves a problem that requires original, creative thinking.
7. Evaluation—the student makes a judgment of good or bad, right or wrong, according to standards he designates.[18]

Cognition is knowing. Knowing utilizes a hierarchy of abilities: the ability to recall facts, the ability to use factual information for solving problems, and the application of problem-solving abilities in new situations. Concrete knowledge, abstract thinking, reflection, application, deriving generalizations are all processes in cognition.

Knowledge may be specific bits of information, it may be terminology, it may be methods of dealing with specific information, it may be aware-

[18]Sanders, *op. cit.,* p. 3.

ness of the arbitrary conventions of social behavior, it may be classifying or categorizing, it may be stating principles and generalizations.

Intellectual skills and abilities are utilized in putting knowledge to work. These are skills and abilities in comprehension, translation (paraphrasing, interpreting figures of speech), interpretation, application, analysis, synthesis, and evaluation.

In this frame of reference, comprehension is the ability to understand the idea being communicated by the speaker or the writer. Translation is the listener's paraphrasing the ideas into his own thought patterns so they become his. Figures of speech have to be understood, story problems have to convey a message and ask for the calculation of a response. Translation includes the ability to summarize the important points or interpret data reported in a study.

Application requires the ability to use a rule, a method, or a generalization in a new situation. Critical analysis includes ability to separate fact from opinion, to evaluate supporting evidence, to understand the relationships among ideas, or to "see through" persuasion, advertising, or propaganda.

Synthesis is the ability to assemble ideas into an integrated unit.

Evaluation requires the ability to establish or accept criteria for judgment and to use them objectively.

V.   THE AFFECTIVE DOMAIN[19]

Krathwohl outlines categories of valuing in the affective domain as follows:

1. Receiving
   a. Awareness
   b. Willingness to receive
   c. Selective attention.
2. Responding
   a. Acquiesence in responding
   b. Willingness to respond
   c. Satisfaction in response
3. Valuing
   a. Acceptance of a value
   b. Preference for a value
   c. Commitment to a value

---

[19]David W. Darling, "Why a Taxonomy of Affective Learning?" pp. 221-226; D. R. Krathwohl, *et. al.*, "How and Why to Classify Affective Educational Objectives," pp. 183-201 in John T. Flynn and Herbert Garber, *Assessing Behavior: Readings in Educational and Psychological Measurement* (Reading, Mass.: Addison-Wesley Publishing Co., 1967).

4. Organization
    a. Conceptualization of a value
    b. Organization of a value system
5. Characterization by a value
    a. Generalized set
    b. Characterization

The top three levels, valuing, organization, and characterization, are the residue from the accumulation of many experiences over a long period of time. The total accumulation of experience produces many values which the individual must organize in a value hierarchy *for him* and this end result becomes his character as a person.

In the primary grades, most children may develop the attitude toward reading that it is something to be valued; some may develop a preference for reading over some other school activity; and a few, far too few, develop a real commitment to reading for what it can do for the individual.

Values and Teaching

The critical test of a person's insights is whether they provide him with a set of beliefs about himself in relation to his social and physical environment which are extensive in scope, dependable in action, and compatible with one another.[20]

Raths, *et al.*, define values as those elements that show how a person has decided to use his life.

Teachers recognize children's behavior as fitting a long continuum: those at one end seem to know clearly what they value while the others are apathetic, flighty, uncertain, inconsistent, or they may be drifters, overconformers, overdissenters, or role players. Those labeled unclear may be said to lack a clarity of relationship to society.[21]

Values are based on three processes: Choosing, prizing, and acting. One chooses freely from alternatives after thoughtful consideration of the consequences of each alternative. One prizes and cherishes his choices, is happy with them, and is willing to affirm the choices publicly. One does something with the choice, does it repeatedly, in some pattern in his life. These criteria of valuing about one's beliefs, attitudes, activities, and feelings are based on self-directed behavior.[22]

Teachers need to know and use a number of neutral clarifying responses to help children strengthen their choices and deepen their commitment to values.[23]

---

[20]Maurice F. Hunt and Lawrence Metcalf, *Teaching High School Social Studies* (New York: Harper & Row, Publishers, 1955), p. 52.
[21]Louis E. Raths, Merrill Harmin, and Sidney B. Simon, *Values and Teaching: Working with Values in the Classroom* (Columbus, Ohio: Charles E. Merrill Books, Inc., 1966), pp. 4-6.
[22]Raths, *et. al.*, *ibid.*, p. 30
[23]Raths, *op. cit.*, pp. 51-62.

Neutral statements that help to clarify responses include:[24]

Is this something that you prize?
Are you *glad* about that?
How did you feel when that happened?
Have you felt this way for a long time?
Did you *have* to choose that; was it a *free* choice?
Do you *do* anything about that idea?
Would you really *do* that or are you just talking?
What are some good things about that notion?
What other possibilities are there?
Is that very important to you?
Would you do the same thing over again?
Would you like to tell others about your idea?

The Affective Response to Reading

One of the surest ways to build in the child a permanent attachment for reading is to ensure *an effective response* to the reading world. The child who lives the experience of the mongoose in its struggle to kill the cobra in Kipling's *Jungle Book;* the boy or girl who reads Laura Ingall Wilder's *Little House on the Prairie, On the Banks of Plum Creek* or *The Long Winter,* is sure to develop strong empathy for Laura, her sisters and her father and mother in their pioneer struggles as farmers in the middlewest. Several examples from children's literature that emphasize this affective value can be cited.

Booker T. Washington's autobiography, *Up From Slavery,* has one recurring central theme—the struggle for education. First, his own, then his brother's, then the Indian's, and finally for more and more education for his own people. Interest, attitude, value, commitment, an organized value system, and a complete philosophy of life is exemplified.[25]

Elizabeth Yates, in her Newbery Medal Book, *Amos Fortune, Free Man,* shows how throughout his life he learned to treasure most freedom and education. All he earned as a free man helped others buy freedom. Freedom became the characterization of Amos as an *ultimate value.*[26]

In Doris Gates' *Blue Willow,* Janie never wanted to have to move again. She wanted to stay in one place and have a friend and go to school. Because her father was a migrant worker, she had no friends and did not go to school. If she could stay in one place she could have friends to play happily with as she had observed so many times when they drove through towns between jobs. When the story ends, Janie's father gets a regular job and they will not have to move.[27]

Boys and Girls find *Charlotte's Web* very sad when Charlotte explains to Wilbur, the pig, that she is going to die. Even though her babies do

[24]*Ibid.,* pp. 260-261.
[25]Booker T. Washington, *Up From Slavery* (Boston: Houghton Mifflin, 1917).
[26]Elizabeth Yates, *Amos Fortune, Free Man* (New York: E. P. Dutton, 1950).
[27]Doris Gates, *Blue Willow* (New York: The Viking Press, 1948).

hatch, and Fern, the little girl, realizes she is getting too old to come to
the barn to talk to the animals, it is very sad because Charlotte dies.[28]

When Travis must go out and shoot old yeller because he has rabies,
the reader is as emotionally involved as Travis is.[29]

By the time Billy has succeeded in training his pair of coon hounds
so they are the best hunting dogs around, the reader feels the same sadness Billy feels when the male of the pair is wounded and dies and the
female dies of a broken heart.[30]

Cavanah creates a strong affective response to the inherent drive for
learning held by young Abe when she tells how he learned *grammar*:

> One morning when Abe Lincoln was having breakfast at Graham
> Mentor's house, he said,
> "I have a notion to study English grammar."
> "If you expect to go before the public, I think it would be the best
> thing to do."
> "If I had a grammar I would commence now."
> Mentor thought for a moment. "There's no one in town who owns
> a grammar," he said finally, "but Mr. Vaner out in the country has one.
> He might lend you his copy."
> Abe got up from the table and walked six miles to the Vaner farm.
> When he returned, he carried an open book in his hands. He was study-
> ing grammar as he walked.[31]

Other books that will have value in developing the attachment for
reading that is based on emotional response include Eleanor Estes', *The
Hundred Dresses;* Esther Forbes', *Johnny Tremain;* Marguerite de Angeli's *Yonie Wondernose;* Joseph Krumbold's *And Now Miguel;* and Jade
Snow Wong's, *Fifth Chinese Daughter.*[32]

Dora V. Smith,[33] in her Kappa Delta Pi Lecture, *Communication: The
Miracle of Shared Living,* emphasizes the importance of reading (1) in
sharing experiences in living in the United States through greater understanding, insight, and awareness of oneself and others, (2) in sharing
experiences in living with people around the world, and (3) in sharing
experiences in living through history. At the end of the section of the
paper about shared living around the world, Smith writes:

---

[28]E. B. White, *Charlotte's Web* (New York: Harper & Row, 1952).
[29]Fred Gipson, *Old Yeller* (New York: Harper & Bros., 1956).
[30]Wilson Rawls, *Where the Red Fern Grows* (Garden City, New York: Doubleday & Co., 1961).
[31]Frances Cavanah, *Abe Lincoln Gets His Chance* (Chicago: Rand McNally and
Company, 1959), p. 78.
[32]Eleanor Ester, *The Hundred Dresses* (New York: Harcourt, Brace and World,
Inc., 1944); Esther Forbes, *Johnny Tremain* (Boston: Houghton Mifflin, 1943);
Marguerite de Angeli, *Yonie Wondernose* (New York: Doubleday and Co., 1944);
Joseph Krumbold, *And Now Miguel* (New York: Thomas Y. Crowell, 1953); Jade
Snow Wong, *Fifth Chinese Daughter* (New York: Scholastic Book Services, 1963).
[33]Dora V. Smith, *Communication: The Miracle of Shared Living* (New York:
The Macmillan Company, 1955).

Books such as these help young people the world over to share their experiences one with the other—to discover the ways in which they are very much alike and the ways in which they are different and therefore capable of making a unique contribution to the world's life. Truly the arts of communication are making possible the miracle of shared living.[34]

VI. THE PSYCHOMOTOR DOMAIN

The psychomotor domain encompasses such activities as muscular or motor skill, manipulation of materials and/or objects, or any act which requires a neuromuscular coordination. The following types of activities would be most common in elementary school physical education programs.

Dances and rhythms: fundamental movements and traditional creative dances.

Activities on equipment: jungle gym, ladder, rings, bars, swings, slides, seesaws.

Games: dodge ball, circle tag, endball, ring toss.

Classroom games: dodge ball, Simon says.

Team sports: softball, soccer, touch football, volley ball.

Stunts and tumbling.

Calisthenics.

Psychomotor objectives are those which emphasize some muscular or motor skill, some manipulation of material and objects, or some act which requires a neuromuscular coordination. Few such objectives are stated in education except in handwriting, physical education, and perhaps in speech education, trades skills, and technical courses.

With respect to six-year-olds entering the formal reading program, there are some areas of psychomotor abilities that could easily be tested by the classroom teacher to locate areas of potential difficulty before the child fails in academic skills.

The way in which certain skills develop as children master motor and perceptual components is illustrated in Figure 2.15.

These include the ability to

a. do directional skills; to know laterality, that is, his right from his left hand; to be able to copy letters, numbers, and designs correctly.

b. to sense (understand) the position of one's body in space.

c. to perceive figure-ground relationships, finding outline birds or squirrels in large pictures, recognizing what an object must be in terms of the things around it easily identified.

---

[34]*Ibid.*, p. 57.

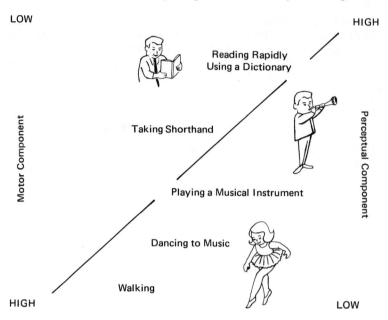

Figure 2.15.   Relative use of motor and perceptual components for different skills.

From Herbert J. Klausmeier and William Goodwin, Harper & Row, Publ., *op. cit.*, 1966, p. 321. Copyright 1966 by Herbert J. Klausmeier and William Goodwin. By permission of the publisher.

The efforts of de Hirsch, *et. al.*, in *Predicting Reading Failure*,[35] Frostig in *A Test of Visual Motor Perception*,[36] and Kephart in *A Perceptual Survey Rating Scale*,[37] are directed toward ways of screening children with psychomotor needs so they may have early rehabilitation before successive failures pile up in school.

VII.   SUMMARY

Educational psychologists have evolved many valuable generalizations about children and how they learn. The principles of programming are based on some of the most important generalizations.

1. The principle of easy steps
2. The principle of continuous response at each step

[35]Katrina de Hirsch, Jeannette Jansky, and Wm. S. Langford, *Predicting Reading Failure* (New York: Harper & Row, Publishers, 1966).

[36]Marianne Frostig, *Developmental Test of Visal Perception* (Palo Alto, California: Consulting Psychologist Press, 1966).

[37]Newell C. Kephart and Eugene C. Roach, *The Purdue Perceptual Motor Survey* (Columbus, Ohio: Charles E. Merrill, Books, 1966).

3. The principle of immediate knowledge of results
4. The principle of progressing at completely individual rates
5. The principle of elimination of error and repetitive practice.

Structuring learning situations so children learn to think inductively and arrive at generalizations is also developmental.

Behavioral objectives can be established in the cognitive, affective, and psychomotor domains.

Krathwohl, *et. al.*, indicate ways in which the cognitive and affective domains interact, overlap, or follow parallel steps in the following description:

1. The cognitive continuum begins with the student's recall and recognition of *Knowledge* (1.0),

2. it extends through his *Comprehension* (2.0) of the knowledge,

3. his skill in *Application* (3.0) of the knowledge that he comprehends,

4. his skill in *Analysis* (4.0) of situations involving this knowledge, his skill in *Synthesis* (5.0) of this knowledge into new organizations,

5. his skill in *Evaluation* (6.0) in that area of knowledge to judge the value of material and methods for given purposes.

1. The affective continuum begins with the student's merely *receiving* (1.0) stimuli and passively attending to it. It extends through his more actively attending to it,

2. his *Responding* (2.0) to stimuli on request, willingly responding to these stimuli, and taking satisfaction in this responding,

3. his *Valuing* (3.0) the phenomenon or activity so that he voluntarily responds and seeks out ways to respond,

4. his *Conceptualizations* (4.1) of each value responded to,

5. his *Organization* (4.2) of these values into systems and finally organizing the value complex into a single whole, a *Characterization* (5.0) of the individual.[38]

When the USOE completed a three year study about methods of teaching reading in the first grade where thousands of teachers used dozens of varying approaches, the one big generalization to be drawn was that *the good teacher*, not the special twist in methodology, was the variable that exercised most control over the teaching success.

---

[38]David R. Krathwohl, Benjamin S. Bloom, and Bertram B. Masia, *Taxonomy of Educational Objectives: The Classification of Educational Goals, Handbook II: Affective Domain* (New York: David McKay Company, Inc., 1964), pp. 49-50.

Students respect the teacher who "levels" with them, the teacher who works for them. Sitting in on class projects as an advisor, helping find jobs and scholarships, listening to problems and keeping them confidential. . . .

Teachers of the highest achieving groups are positive in their approach to teaching. They encourage responses even when they aren't exactly what the teacher had in mind. They explore content with the students at many thinking levels. (See Sanders' *Classroom Questions: What Kinds?* and Guszak's "Teachers' Questions and Levels of Reading Comprehension.")[39]

Good teachers try different approaches, they allow the child to demonstrate why he thinks he is right, and they praise him for his effort. Good teachers ask open ended questions so that there is no pat answer in reciting "a fact."

The kinds of questions teachers ask affect the classroom climate in other ways beside providing occasions for praising a student.

The relation of education to the level of motivation in the society is more direct than most people recognize. The goals the young person sets for himself are very heavily affected by the framework of expectations with which adults surround him. The educational system provides the young person with a sense of what society expects of him in the way of performance. If it is lax in its demands, then he will believe that such are the expectations of his society. If much is expected of him, the chances are that he will expect much of himself.

In summary, some general principles based on learning theory follow:

1. No learning takes place without a motive. Hopefully, motivation from childhood to maturity moves from greater to lesser *extrinsic* motivation and from lesser to greater *intrinsic* motivation.
2. Active participation in learning is better than passive reception of learning.
3. Material is more easily learned and remembered accordingly as it is more meaningfully understood by the learner.
4. Praise works better than blame; reward works better than punishment.
5. Generally, brighter people learn some things less bright ones don't.
6. Once crucial facts have been understood, they must be over-learned to reduce loss by forgetting. Memorization is important after understanding is established.
7. Immediate knowledge of results aids learning.
8. Distributed practice is better than massed practice.
9. Nothing succeeds like success.
10. Provision is needed for each one to grow at his own rate.

[39]*Op. cit.*, p. 11.

SUGGESTED ACTIVITIES

1. Be able to explain clearly how each of the following relate directly to teaching reading: (a) capacity, (b) practice, (c) motivation, (d) understanding, (e) transfer, and (f) forgetting.

2. Be able to list the principles on which programmed learning is based.

3. Be able to explain Krathwohl, Bloom, and Masia's statement of interaction, overlapping, and parallel progression of the cognitive and affective domains.

REFERENCES FOR FURTHER READING

AUSUBEL, DAVID P., *Educational Psychology: A Cognitive View* (New York: Holt, Rinehart and Winston, 1968), Chapter I, "The Role and Scope of Educational Psychology," pp. 3-34.

BRUNER, J. S., *The Process of Education* (Cambridge, Massachusetts: Harvard University Press, 1960).

GAGNÉ, ROBERT M., *The Conditions of Learning* (New York: Holt, Rinehart and Winston, 1965), Chapter II, "Varieties of Learning," pp. 31-61.

HILGARD, ERNEST R., "A Perspective on the Relationship Between Learning Theory and Educational Practices," in *Theories of Learning and Instruction*, 63rd Yearbook, National Society for the Study of Education, Part I (Chicago: University of Chicago Press, 1964), pp. 402-415.

POWELL, WILLIAM, "The Nature of Individual Differences," in Wallace Ramsey, editor, *Organizing for Individual Differences* (Newark, Dela.: 19711: International Reading Association, 1968), pp. 1-17.

STROUD, JAMES BART, *Psychology in Education* (New York: Longmans, Green, 1946), Chapter XII, "Conditions of Learning: Individual Differences," pp. 393-441.

3

The Informal
Reading Inventory

One of the most serious problems in elementary school classrooms today is the very large percentage of children who are kept reading at their *frustration* level. If a book is too difficult, if too many new concepts appear and are not repeated several times, and if the decoding process of unlocking new words has not been learned, boys and girls spend much time in school trying to gain information which is beyond their grasp. At the same time, when teachers look at standardized tests results and arbitrarily assign all the children in their rooms to three reading groups, they may be asking some children to stay frustrated all day long. Learning does not progress when children work at the frustration level.

While standardized reading achievement tests have a very important place in assessing the total school reading program, and they provide each teacher a distribution of his students from best to poorest performer, they do not provide the teacher an adequate measure of what book is the appropriate one for a child to read at his *instructional* level.

> The standardized test, if it is a timed test, is a power test, and may more nearly measure a child's frustration level of reading for a short period of time.[1]

Sheldon reports that teachers have found that standardized test scores may yield grade placement equivalents one or even two years higher than children can actually read with understanding.[2]

Wheeler and Smith found that the grade placement scores on standardized reading tests in the primary grades often have little relationship to the child's actual instructional reading level.[3]

---

[1] Emmett A. Betts, *Foundations of Reading Instruction* (New York: American Book Company, 1946), p. 449.

[2] William D. Sheldon, "Specific Principles Essential to Classroom Diagnosis," *The Reading Teacher*, 14: 8, September, 1960.

[3] Lester R. Wheeler and Edwin H. Smith, "A Modification of the Informal Reading Inventory," *Elementary English*, 34: 224, April, 1967.

The teacher cannot meet each child at his level of functioning and provide instruction from which he can profit unless he can somehow determine with a fair degree of accuracy what that functioning level is. An informal reading inventory will provide the classroom teacher with this fundamental information.

Betts has pointed out the advantages of the informal reading inventory as the teacher's primary tool in teaching developmental reading skills:[4]

1. The teacher uses the materials she has at hand; there is little cost.
2. With direct and rapid administration, the teacher gets some needed answers quickly.
3. In terms of textbook reading the child will do, it is more valid than other tests.
4. Informal reading inventories can be either group or individual for appropriate purposes.
5. The student can be made aware of how well he reads.
6. The student can be made aware of progress as he achieves it.
7. As achievement is appraised, specific needs are revealed.
8. Interesting materials can be selected to use in the inventory.
9. Readability of materials can be checked in series of texts.
10. The test situation can be a valuable instructional situation also.

I. WHAT IS THE INFORMAL READING INVENTORY?

The informal reading inventory (IRI) is an individual test in which the child reads orally and silently from increasingly difficult material until the material becomes frustrating either in terms of accuracy of pronunciation or understanding of ideas in the content. IRI's are referred to as informal tests for reader level, or "trying on a book for size." The informal reading test is diagnostic in that it reveals many specific areas of difficulty in reading for the observant teacher. Clearly, the values derived from administering the IRI depend entirely upon the competence of the teacher to make judgments as the child reads. An informal reading inventory should provide a passage of reading at each level from pre-primer through the sixth grade for each oral and silent reading. Comprehension questions must be provided to obtain a measure of the child's understanding of what is read.

The child should read from the book while the teacher has a reproduced copy for marking errors, making notes, and evaluating. At the level at which the child makes too many errors for his instructional level, either in comprehension or pronunciation, the teacher begins reading one passage orally at each reading level and asking the prepared questions to measure the child's capacity for understanding ideas when he listens

---

[4]Emmett A. Betts, *Foundations of Reading Instruction,* (New York: American Book Company, 1950), pp. 478-479.

to someone else read the material. This is referred to as his capacity level, or listening level, or hearing comprehension level.

II.   THE FOUR READING LEVELS TO BE DEFINED

The IRI will provide the teacher with information about levels of reading appropriate for his instructional work in the class, the level at which he might most enjoy free reading, and a level of understanding of ideas in written context even when it is too difficult for him to read for himself. These levels are called: (1) independent; (2) instructional; (3) frustration; and (4) capacity levels.

The independent level of reading is the *highest* level at which the child can read fluently and with personal satisfaction without help. In independent reading, the child encounters practically no mechanical difficulties with the words and no problems with understanding the concepts in the context. The level is generally defined as that level where the child makes no more than one error in 100 words in the mechanics of reading and where he has no difficulties in comprehension. Much of the material the child selects for free reading from the library should be at this level as well as some of the collateral reading he does for unit work in social studies and science.

The instructional level of reading is the teaching level. This is defined as the *highest* level at which the child makes no more than five uncorrected errors in reading 100 running words with at least 75 percent comprehension of the ideas in the text. Such materials are difficult enough to be challenging but sufficiently easy that the student can do independent seatwork with only the usual readiness help from the teacher when assignments are made. The most important task of the elementary teacher in all of his work is to establish for each child his instructional level of functioning in reading and provide him work to do at the level. Instructional reading material should be prepared silently before it is read orally. Then there should be no difficulties with phrasing, punctuation, finger-pointing or tension. Studies reported here indicate that many children are not given the opportunity to read at this level at all at school. The instructional level is reached when the child uses a conversational tone, without noticeable tension, with satisfactory rhythm, and with suitable phrasing. He also makes proper use of word recognition clues and techniques.[5]

The frustration level is the *lowest* level at which obvious difficulties cause confusion, frustration, and tension in the reading situation. Betts lists inability to anticipate meanings, head movements, finger pointing,

---

[5]Miles A. Tinker, *Bases for Effective Reading* (Minneapolis: University of Minnesota Press, 1965), p. 274.

tension, slow word-by-word reading vocalization, and too many substitutions, omissions, repetitions, and insertions as evidences of frustration.[6]

The teacher understands that there is not a clear line of separation between what is instructional level and what is frustration. The teacher's purpose is to keep the child on the growing edge of learning without pushing him along too fast. The teacher will do well to choose the lower of two possible reader levels when there is a question about which is appropriate for a given individual. It is preferable to let him have more practice at an easier level and strengthen his abilities and skills than to move him into material too difficult and stop his progress.

The capacity level for reading is the *highest* level at which the child can understand the ideas and concepts in informational material that is read to him. The teacher begins reading to the student at the level of difficulty at which he stops oral or silent reading because of reaching his frustration level. The questions prepared to ask if he read the material are now also appropriate to ask him after the teacher reads the material. The standard expected for instructional level, 75 percent comprehension, is an adequate measure of establishing capacity for understanding reading.

The importance of determining the capacity level for the student is that if his instructional level is only second level, second grade (2^2) and his capacity level for reading is fourth grade, his amount of reading retardation is one and one-half years. This is one indication that he has the innate ability to read much better than he is now reading.

III. LIMITATIONS OF THE INFORMAL READING INVENTORY

The severest limitation of the informal reading inventory is the competence of the teacher in its use. However, a minimum amount of practice by any classroom teacher will provide a great deal of confidence in its use and demonstrate its absolute necessity. It is the most accurate test measure that can be provided to evaluate the child's ability to use textbooks for instructional purposes.

Some classroom teachers who have never administered the IRI anticipate that it is a technical and complicated instrument. For this reason they avoid it. But the act of being a teacher places oneself in the position of having to responsibly meet this requirement. The reading inventory should be the very core of the teacher's whole reading work-program for the year. So, the teacher dare not believe it is too technical, since, if he does, he can no longer function as a teacher.

Any teacher can learn to prepare that part of a complete reading inventory that meets his present need, and with study and practice, learn

---

[6]Betts, *op. cit.*, p. 448.

a great deal about the abilities and disabilities of the boys and girls in his classroom with respect to developmental reading.

Since the child is reading only brief passages and the test situation represents only one small sample of the child's total behavior, it is easily possible that there are facets of reading not adequately assessed and it is possible that on another day or at another time, the same individual might perform somewhat differently.

Spache feels that the individual texts in the reading series are not accurately graded and that a readability formula needs to be applied to determine the level of difficulty. He also suggests that a passage needs to be sufficiently long to represent four minutes of reading time in order to adequately check comprehension of ideas.[7] Further, Spache reports that classroom teachers have been found to be very inaccurate in recording errors in the informal reading inventory.[8]

While these limitations described by Spache are valid criticisms, they in no way change the fact that it is the classroom teacher who, in the final analysis, *must make all the decisions* about the child's reading ability in day-to-day work. The teacher must *unavoidably* select his reading materials in language arts, social studies, arithmetic, science and literature. Hopefully, he will be able to provide shelves of books of many levels of difficulty for students to choose from, but the scope of the selections will be the teacher's responsibility.

Improvement in the accuracy of the interpretation of the IRI develops with practice—if this practice is guided, or based on further reading and study. An excellent way for a beginning teacher to get initial skill in administering an informal reading inventory is to record the child's oral reading on the tape recorder so that it can be played back a number of times. Most clinicians are apt to hear some few errors the second time that they missed completely the first time. Without a specific plan of what to listen for, the listener is probably not able to make any kind of objective summary of the results of the oral reading.

IV. CONSTRUCTION OF THE INFORMAL READING INVENTORY

The first step in preparing the inventory is the selection of a series of books, probably a series of readers. Preferably a series of readers not already familiar to the children being tested would be used. While there are many words *not common* to two series of readers, the controlled vocabularies, the picture clues, and the context clues all help the child anticipate meanings and most of the words are already in the "average" child's speaking vocabulary.

---

[7]George D. Spache, *Reading in the Elementary School* (Boston: Allyn and Bacon, Inc., 1964), p. 245.
    [8]*Ibid.*, pp. 248-49.

Selections from pre-primers, primers, and first and second readers, need to contain about 60 to 125 words and to be sufficiently informational in nature that questions can be made to measure understanding of the ideas in what is read. For grades three to six, passages need to be somewhat longer, perhaps 100 to 200 words in length.

One selection must be identified to be read orally and one to be read silently. The selection from each book should be taken out at the end of about the first one-third of the book. This follows the first few stories containing mostly review words from previous books in the series, but near the front of the book which is likely to get progressively more difficult at the child reads through it.

When the child reads, even if he begins at the beginning of the story, he must be given a synopsis of the story, or be otherwise "clued in" to the place where he begins reading. It is wise to select the silent reading selection immediately following the oral reading selection so the child can continue reading without teacher explanation and, thus, save time.

The comprehension questions should be carefully thought out so that they measure understanding as completely as possible. Levels of questioning are pertinent: factual or memory items; inferential items requiring reading between the lines; vocabulary items to test concepts; and items to test ability to use context clues. Authors need to provide meaningful concepts for new or difficult vocabulary items: "Erosion, which is the washing or blowing away of the soil, is therefore a serious problem."[9] The careful reader can now answer the question: "What is erosion?" "The stumpage, or timber in standing trees, is sold to lumbermen, who come in and cut the timber which is marked by the rangers for cutting."[10] The careful reader can answer the question: "What is stumpage?"

When choosing selections for the informal reading inventory, teachers should consider the nature of the context material. Can good comprehension questions be derived from the story? Vocabulary, sentence structure, human interest, and the number and complexity of the ideas dealt with influence the comprehension level of the material. Complexity of the ideas, idea density, is estimated by the number of prepositional phrases.[11] In preparing the questions, the teacher should use questions that can be answered from the reading material, not from what the child already knows. Also, one should ask questions requiring recall, rather than those requiring only yes or no. For example, ask "What color was the hound?" *not*, "Was the hound in the story red?"

---

[9]Ernest Horn, *et al.*, Progress in Reading Series, *Reaching Our Goals* (Boston: Ginn and Company, 1940), p. 138.

[10]*Ibid.*, p. 145.

[11]Jeanne Chall, "Ask Him to Try the Book for Fit," *The Reading Teacher*, 7:83, December, 1953.

Patty, in the fourth grade, was referred for a reading evaluation because she was unable to do her work in her content subjects. When she
was reading the Gilmore Oral Reading Test,[12] paragraph 2, she had little
difficulty with the words. She read, "The cat is looking at the girl. He
wants to play ball, too." But when she was asked, "What does the cat
want?" she replied, "Cat food." In paragraph 3, she read, "After father
has gone to work, the children will leave for school." To the question,
"When will the children leave for school?" she responded, "When they're
ready." This child apparently needs much help to develop powers of
concentration on what she is reading. But if she had been asked *yes—no*
questions, her inattention to the content of the story might have been
much less evident.

Depending upon the content of the material read there should be
five to seven questions to measure comprehension. If the questions are
of different types as suggested, this will provide some measure of the
individual's understanding. *New Practice Readers*[13] provide six exercises
over each short story read and these exercises have several types of
questions. Teachers might wish to check those if they are not familiar
with them.

The child should read from the book itself. This gives him the book
format, the appropriate size print, and picture clues. The selections need
to be reproduced in order that the examiner has a prepared copy for
marking reading errors, making notes in margins, checking comprehension, and observing the child's behavior in the reading situation. Smith
has prepared Graded Selections for Informal Reading Diagnosis, for
Grades 1-3, and for Grades 4-6,[14] which teachers can use with children
or which they can study for developing their own inventory. Also, each
teacher's manual in the *Sheldon Basic Reading Series*[15] has selections.
Spache has published the *Diagnostic Reading Scales*[16] to serve this purpose, also.

V. ADMINISTERING THE INFORMAL READING INVENTORY

Before the teacher can decide what selection to give the child to read
first, he must have some idea of the child's functioning level. There are
several ways to get information for making this decision:

---

[12]John V. Gilmore, *Gilmore Oral Reading Test* (New York: Harcourt, Brace &
World, 1952).

[13]Clarence Stone, *et. al.*, *New Practice Readers* (New York: Webster Division,
McGraw-Hill, 1960), Levels A, B, C, D, E, F, G.

[14]Nila B. Smith, *Graded Selections for Informal Reading Diagnosis*, Grades 1-3
(1959), and Grades 4-6 (1963) (New York: New York University Press).

[15]William B. Sheldon, *et. al.*, *The Sheldon Basic Reading Series* (Boston: Allyn
and Bacon, Inc.).

[16]George D. Spache, *Diagnostic Reading Scales* (Monterey, California Test
Bureau, 1963).

(1) In September, the teacher can check the cumulative record from the previous year and see in which book the child was reading when the last school year ended. Of course, there will be errors in such a listing, but if the selection is too difficult, the teacher will move to easier material;

(2) The teacher may be able to assemble sub-groups of children in a reading circle very early in the year, and ask them to "read around the circle" sampling a story which the teacher has developed readiness for. For those who have difficulty, only one sentence is sufficient. For those who read well, a much longer passage is fine.[17]

(3) If the teacher estimates that a book at second level, first grade is appropriate, a sampling of words can be made from the list in the back of the book to make a word recognition test of twenty words. The sample will be obtained by dividing the total number of words in the list by twenty and selecting words from the list at intervals of that quotient. For example, if there are 200 words in the list 200 divided by twenty is ten, so the teacher will select every tenth word through the list. If the child knows at least 80 percent of these words at sight, he will likely be able to read from the book.

The following list of 25 words have been selected from the word list in the back of the book, *Fields and Fences, Readiness Second Reader*,[18] by selecting every eighth word in the total list of 207 new words.

uncle	sister	people	brought	already
easy	nuts	threw	hopped	loud
getting	hide	shark	broke	send
past	Teddy	paw	bumpity-bump	held
it's	both	branch	drum	whole

If the child can pronounce twenty or more of these words at sight, this would be an appropriate book to sample for his instructional level of reading.

(4) The Dolch Basic Sight Word List can be administered as a recall test. This is done by asking the child to pronounce all the words, line by line, on the Dolch Sight Word Test.[19] Generally, the teacher has one copy of the test and writes comments and marks errors as the child works. (See page 437.) The child needs a three by five card to mark the line being pronounced and to move the card down the page as he pronounces all the words. The teacher strikes a line

---

[17]E. W. Dolch, "How to Diagnose Children's Reading Difficulties by Informal Classroom Techniques," *The Reading Teacher*, 6:10-14, January, 1953.

[18]William D. Sheldon, Mary C. Austin, and Richard E. Drdek, *Fields and Fences, Readiness Second Reader* (Boston: Allyn and Bacon, Inc., 1957), pp. 188-191.

[19]E. W. Dolch, *Dolch Basic Sight Word Test* (Champaign: Garrard Press).

through each word he recognizes *at sight*. The McBroom-Sparrow-Eckstein scale of known sight words indicates approximately which book in the reading series the child may be able to read. If he knows fewer than 75, he needs to read from a paper back pre-primer; if he recognizes 76-120, he can read from the first hard back book in the series, a primer or first level, first reader. If he recognizes 121-170, he can likely read the first reader (or, second level, first reader). If he knows more than 170 but fewer than 210, he may be able to read a second reader. If he knows more than 211, he may be able to read a third reader or a book of greater difficulty.[20]

Suggestions (3) and (4) above will give some diagnostic information about the kinds of word recognition errors the child makes in his reading, too.[*]

If the child makes more than five uncorrected errors in reading the first selection which he attempts, the teacher may select an easier one and continue reading until a satisfactory instruction level is found. It is occasionally true, that the child makes more errors on the first passage than he does on the next more difficult one so the teacher has to be alert for any psychological factors that may cause this to happen and be sure that she finds the highest level at which he meets the criterion for instructional level.

While the pupil is reading, the teacher will record all word substitutions, hesitations and words he fails to pronounce, repetitions, omissions, and insertions. The method of marking and scoring will be discussed in the next section of the chapter. If it is possible, it will be most helpful to the busy teacher to record the pupil's reading on the tape recorder so that the teacher can re-play it when the children are gone and he can give more concentrated attention to the reading. It is possible that the teacher can arrange the work of the rest of the class in independent activities, so that he is free for fifteen or twenty minutes in one corner of the room where the child can complete the inventory. The relatively uninterrupted environment is necessary. Some teachers arrange to test one child each day during a recess period or during the special music or physical education period. A properly conducted informal reading inventory is the best instrument the classroom teacher has to most adequately determine what the child can and cannot do in formal reading.

Once the child begins reading selections, he continues to read until the teacher is certain that he has reached the frustration level. Then she reads one selection at each level beyond that to the child as long as he can answer the comprehension questions.

---

[20]Maude McBroom, Julia Sparrow, and Catherine Eckstein, *Scale for Determining a Child's Reader Level* (Iowa City: Bureau of Publications, Extension Division, State University of Iowa, 1944).

[*]The use of the Dolch Basic Sight Word Test as a diagnostic instrument will be discussed in Chapter 18, "Corrective Reading."

Approximate Reader Levels Based on the Dolch Basic
Sight Word Recall Test[21]

Dolch Words Known	*Equivalent Reader Levels*
0– 75	Pre-Primer
76–120	Primer
121–170	First Reader
171–210	Second Reader or above
Above–210	Third Reader or above

The Basic Sight Word Test. Part 1[22]

Name_____ Date_____

1.	~~by~~	~~at~~	~~a~~	~~it~~
2.	~~in~~	~~I~~	~~be~~	~~big~~
3.	~~did~~	~~good~~	~~do~~	*good* / go
4.	~~all~~	~~are~~	*many* any	~~an~~
5.	*has* had	*had* have	~~him~~	~~drink~~
6.	~~its~~	~~is~~	~~into~~	~~if~~
7.	*as* ℯ ask	~~may~~	~~as~~	~~am~~
8.	~~many~~	~~cut~~	~~keep~~	~~know~~
9.	*do* does	*good* goes	*doing* going	~~and~~
10.	~~has~~	~~he~~	~~his~~	*for* far

The easiest way to establish rapport with the child is explain to him exactly what it is that you are doing and why determining his instructional level of reading is so important. If the child is interested, discuss with him the changing sizes of print in more difficult books, the amount of reading on a page, and the decrease in the use of pictures. The child must not be made to feel that the test is a "threat" to his status, and if he is the type of child who continually asks for reassurance (Am I doin' good?), the teacher needs to be completely reassuring.

VI. MARKING AND SCORING THE IRI

Method of Recording Errors

The system of marking errors in oral reading provided by Gilmore will meet the needs of most teachers for scoring the IRI. The errors to

---

[21]McBroom, Sparrow and Eckstein, *op. cit.,* p. 11.
[22]E. W. Dolch, *The Basic Sight Word Test, op. cit.*

be noted include substitutions, omissions, insertions, hesitations, words pronounced by the examiner, and repetitions. The important point for any teacher is to have a definite, well-learned system of marking that will be meaningful. By such a method, a child may read a passage of 300 words, for example, on which he makes twenty errors in the mechanics of reading. If three months later, he can read the same passage with only five errors in mechanics, the teacher has a very favorable measure of his growth. However, the use of the system of recording errors must be consistent if the pre- post-test record is to have value. Durrell and Gray have provided detailed systems for marking errors.[23] Each teacher must know one system well.

With only a minimum amount of practice, groups of experienced teachers find they mark children's oral reading with a very high per cent of agreement. So, even though the administration of the IRI has subjective qualities, and many judgments must be made informally by the teacher very quickly, with some practice the results become quite objective for the competent teacher.

Analyzing the oral reading.[24] The following types of oral reading errors constitute the most of children's difficulties:

1. Hesitation: Mark after two seconds of hesitation with a(✔). Proper nouns are given to the child as needed and are not scored as errors unless the proper noun is a word that most children would know. Example: Big, Brown.
2. Word pronounced for the child: If a pupil hesitates for approximately five seconds on a difficult word, pronounce it for him and make a second check mark (✔✔) above it.
3. Mispronunciation: This results in a nonsense word which may be produced by: (1) false accentuation, (2) wrong pronunciation of vowels or consonants, or (3) the omission, addition or insertion of one or more letters, without creating a real or new word. Example: *crēt'ĭk* for *critic*. Write the child's pronunciation above phonetically. Notice word attack methods and enunciation. If errors come too rapidly for recording, draw a line through mispronounced words. Do not count foreign accent or regional speech mannerisms.
4. Omissions: Encircle the omitted word, syllable, letter sound or endings that are omitted. "Count as one error the omission of more than one word of consecutive print."
5. Substitutions: This occurs when one sensible or real word is put in the place of the word in print. Write the substituted word directly above the word presented in print. Note if it makes sense or if it is irrelevant to the context.

---

[23]D. D. Durrell, *Manual of Directions, Analysis of Reading Difficulty* (Yonkers-on-Hudson: World Book Co., 1955); A. I. Gates, *Manual of Directions: Gates Reading Diagnostic Test* (New York: Teachers College Press, 1953).

[24]Dianne Brown, "The Preparation, Use and Analysis of the Results of the Informal Reading Inventory," unpublished Masters Thesis, Graduate School, University of New Mexico, Albuquerque, New Mexico, 1968.

6. Insertions: These are words that do not appear in the printed material. Place a caret (∧), and write the added word or words. Count as one error the insertion of two or more words consecutively.
7. Repetitions: A word, part of a word, or groups of words that are repeated; this may indicate that the child is having trouble understanding what he reads. Draw a wavy line under the repeated words.

Recording Errors in Oral Reading[25]

Type of error	Rule for marking	Examples
Substitutions	Write in substituted word.	*black* The boy is back of the girl.
Mispronunciations (Nonsense words)	Write in the word phonetically or draw a line through word.	*sim'-bol-ik* symbolic or symbolic
Words pronounced by Examiner (Hesitation: 5 sec. or more)	Make two checks above the word pronounced.	It is a fascinating story.
Disregard of Punctuation	Mark punctuation disregarded with an "X".	Jack, my brother, is in the navy.
Insertions (including additions)	Write in inserted word or words.	*the* The dog and ∧cat are fighting.
Hesitations (pause of two or more seconds)	Make a check above the word on which hesitation occurs.	It is a fascinating story.
Repetitions (a word, part of a word, or group of words repeated)	Draw a wavy line beneath the word or words repeated.	He thought he saw a whale
Omissions (one or more words omitted)	Encircle the word or words omitted.	Mother does all (of) her work with great care.

25John V. Gilmore and Eunice C. Gilmore, *Gilmore Oral Reading Test. Manual of Directions,* (New York: Harcourt, Brace and World, Inc., 1968), pp. 6-7. General directions modified by the writer. With permission.

The examiner must record these reading behaviors:

1. Corrections: Write a "C" by the mistake when the child corrects the error.
2. Phrasing: Use a diagonal mark to indicate undue pauses or incorrect phrasing.
3. Punctuation: Put an "X" on punctuation marks that the child ignores or passes over.
4. Rate: As difficulty increases, the child may read "slowly" and/or "haltingly." Indicate this. One must record reading time in seconds for each selection in order to determine words per minute.

In scoring the oral reading inventory, it seems logical to

1. Count only one error at any place in the reading. If the child repeats a phrase to correct a word substitution, the important error is that of sight word substitution.
2. If he omits a phrase of two or three words, count as only one error.
3. If he inserts a phrase of two or three words, count as only one error.
4. If the child makes one substitution error and then in the same sentence makes a second error to get proper grammatical structure with verbs or pronouns, count this as only one error.
5. If the proper names are unusual or difficult, do not include them in the error count. If they are common names like *Brown, Green,* or *Smith,* they should be counted as errors. If the proper names are miscalled several times in one passage, the teacher must decide whether to count this as only one error. For example, the child may have read regularly about Tom and Betty in the IRI consistently pronouncing Fred as Tom. This should be counted as only one error.
6. In basic sight word substitutions, the error should be counted each time it occurs. If the reader says "then" for "when" three times, this is three errors.

McCracken has appropriate recommendations for the teacher in making the evaluation of the reading.[26]

Method of Recording Comprehension

The teacher must record the child's responses to the comprehension questions as they are given so an accurate measure will result after the test is finished. When the child's comprehension falls below 70-75 percent, there is no need to continue the child's reading even if he has few mechanical difficulties.

---

[26]Robert A. McCracken, "The Informal Reading Inventory as a Means of Improving Instruction," in Perspectives No. 8, *The Evaluation of Children's Reading Achievement* (Newark, Delaware: International Reading Association, 1967), pp. 79-95.

General Reading Habits

Nervous mannerisms such as fidgeting, twisting hair, picking nose, drawing a heavy sigh, or undue restlessness indicate discomfort and frustration. These should be noted on the child's test. Also, such difficulties as losing the place in the story, holding the book close to the face, finger pointing, or head movements.

In silent reading, the child may vocalize everything he reads, read very slowly, or need encouragement to keep on reading.

Passage Marked Showing Oral Reading Errors

The page following contains a story passage with oral reading errors recorded using the system for marking provided in the Gilmore Oral Reading Test.

This exercise does not adequately represent instructional level of reading. However before making a firm decision, a classroom teacher would try other sample selections.

VII.   INTERPRETING THE RESULTS OF THE IRI

The teacher will be able to summarize the results of the reading of the IRI in a chart such as the following:

ORAL

Level of book	Total words	Total errors	Percent of error	Percent accuracy	Suitability of level of difficulty
———	———	———	———	———	———
———	———	———	———	———	———
———	———	———	———	———	———
———	———	———	———	———	———
———	———	———	———	———	———

When Mr. Zabriski decided to go to Los Angeles, Oscar wanted to ~~went~~

go with him. But Mr. Zabriski only shook his head. "I'm sorry," he

said, "but I can't be bothered with a seal on this trip, not even a

famous seal. You must stay here in New York. I have secret work to do."

Poor, neglected Oscar! He just couldn't stay in New York all

alone! "We always go everywhere together," he said to himself. "I know

Mr. Zabriski doesn't mean to be selfish. ~~He~~ The first thing tomorrow I'll

~~think~~ ~~talking~~
talk him into taking me along. I need a vacation."

~~When~~
Then Oscar got into his bath tub and slept until morning.

The next morning, when the seal climbed from his bathtub, he

~~he~~
found that his trainer was gone. In a few minutes, he ~~was~~ saw a letter

~~the~~
leaning against a large fish - Oscar's favorite food. The letter

said:

Dear Oscar:

    I can't bear to say good-by. I am ~~going~~ too unhappy about leaving

you. Take good care of yourself until I come back.

          Your Trainer,

          Zabriski

What did Mr. Zabriski tell Oscar? _+_	Substitutions _9/5_ *
What did Oscar think about this? _O_	Hesitations _2_
Where did Oscar sleep? _+_	Words pronounced by examiner _9/7_ **
What is Oscar's favorite food? _+_	Repetitions _2_
What did the letter tell Oscar? _+_	Omissions _1_
comprehension adequate	Insertions _0_
	TOTAL UNCORRECTED ERRORS _17_
Level of difficulty: 3^2	Percentage of error: _11_ %
Number of words: 160	Percentage of accuracy _89_ %

---

[27]Hildreth, Gertrude, *et. al.*, *Enchanting Stories*, (Philadelphia: Winston, 1952), pp. 181-182.
   *Four substitutions were self-corrected.
   **Proper names—Zabriski and Oscar—are not counted.

SILENT

Level of book	Total words	Time in seconds	Rate per minute	Percent of comprehension	Suitability of level of difficulty
————	————	————	————	————	————————
————	————	————	————	————	————————
————	————	————	————	————	————————

Gipe administered informal reading inventories to each of the thirty-one fifth grade children in a class and found that only *seven* were assigned to the instructional level which she found appropriate using the IRI. Ten were reading in books easier than their instructional level and fourteen were reading in books at their frustration level. Gipe concluded that 77 percent of the children were inaccurately placed in their present reading group.[28]

Brown found that of sixty children, fourteen or 23 percent were reading below their instructional level as determined using the IRI. Twenty-seven, or 45 percent were reading above their instructional level. Nineteen, or 32 percent were reading at their instructional level. Brown's study suggests, then, that 68 percent of the children were inaccurately placed in their classroom reading text by their teacher.[29] The spread of grade levels for these children in grades two through six are shown in Table 3.1.

TABLE 3.1. *Instructional Reading Level Determined by an Informal Reading Inventory (Brown, p. 52)*

Grade	PP	P	1^1	1^2	2^1	2^2	3^1	3^2	4^1	4^2	5^1	5^2	6^1	6^2	7	8	Total
No. in second	2	4	2	0	1	2	1										12
No. in third			1	0	3	2	3	1	1	0	0	0	0	1			12
No. in fourth					1	3	1	1	3	0	1	0	1	1			12
No. in fifth	1	0	0	0	0	1	0	1	1	1	1	1	4	1			12
No. in sixth													2	7	0	3	12
TOTAL	3	4	3	0	5	8	5	3	5	1	2	1	7	10	0	3	60

[28]Joyce Gipe, "Teacher Group Placement Compared to Informal Reading Inventory Placement," unpublished paper, College of Education, University of New Mexico, 1967.

[29]Brown, *op. cit.*

VIII. SUMMARY

The regular classroom teacher has the inescapable responsibility for the accurate assessment of the child's oral and silent reading abilities. He can attempt to do this using the informal reading inventory.

The informal reading inventory is a measure of each individual child's ability to read graded material at independent, instruction, and frustration levels of difficulty and his ability to understand what has been read as a measure of his capacity for reading. The difference between his instructional level of reading and his capacity level for reading represents the extent of his reading retardation.

The limitations, the construction and administration, the marking and scoring, and interpreting the results of the informal reading inventory in terms of specific difficulty levels of books for children to read have been presented.

SUGGESTED ACTIVITIES

Administer the informal reading inventory to five boys and girls with different levels of reading ability, interpret the results, and make recommendations for their reading program.

REFERENCES FOR FURTHER READING

IRA E. AARON, "An Informal Reading Inventory," *Elementary English,* 37: 457-460, November, 1960.

MORTON BOTEL, *Botel Reading Inventory* (Chicago: Follett Publishing Co., 1961).

DIANNE B. BROWN, "The Preparation, Use and Analysis of Results of the Informal Reading Inventory," Masters Thesis, Graduate School, University of New Mexico, Albuquerque, 1968.

JEANNE, CHALL, "Ask Him To Try the Book for Fit," *The Reading Teacher,* 7:83-88, December, 1953.

JOYCE GIPE, "Teacher Group-Placement Compared to Informal Reading Inventory Placement," paper prepared for Seminar in Reading, College of Education, University of New Mexico, Albuquerque, 1967.

ALBERT J. HARRIS, *How to Increase Reading Ability,* Fourth Edition (New York: David MacKay, 1961), Chapters VII and VIII, "Evaluating Performance in Reading I and II."

MARJORIE JOHNSON and ROY KRESS, *Informal Reading Inventories* (Newark, Del.: International Reading Association, 1965).

ROBERT A. McCRACKEN, "The Informal Reading Inventory as a Means of Improving Instruction," *Perspectives in Reading: The Evaluation of Children's Reading Achievement,* 8: 79-95, 1967.

————, "The Development and Validation of the Standard Reading Inventory for the Individual Appraisal of Reading Performance in Grades One

Through Six," in *Improvement of Reading Through Classroom Practice,* J. Allen Figurel, Editor, IRA Conference Proceedings, 9: 310-313, 1964.

W. R. POWELL, "The Informal Reading Inventory," University of Illinois, 1966 (mimeographed).

LAURA LEE SHARP, "An Evaluation of an Informal Reading Inventory in a Fifth Grade Classroom," Masters Thesis, Graduate School, University of New Mexico, 1968.

LESTER R. WHEELER and EDWIN H. SMITH, "A Modification of the Informal Reading Inventory," *Elementary English,* 34: 224-226, 1967.

MILES V. ZINTZ, *Corrective Reading* (Dubuque, Iowa: Wm. C. Brown Co. Pub., 1966), Chapter II, "Evaluating Oral and Silent Reading."

4

Organizing the
Classroom Reading Program

As demonstrated with the IRI in Chapter 3, the teacher can expect to find in his classroom of unselected boys and girls, a very wide range of differences in reading performance. Since differences in mental, physical, emotional, and social development are completely normal in children, the teacher *must accept* as normal the great variability in school achievement. With good teaching the *differences get greater, not less* as the year progresses.

The primary goal for the teacher becomes one of organizing the classroom to permit each child to learn, to administer to each child's need. He must possess methodology and materials to help each child progress in the acquistion of sequenced, developmental reading skills.

The teacher needs a completed informal reading inventory for each child in order to know best how to assign him to a working group. As is indicated in the previous chapter, finding an oral instructional reading level, a silent reading level with adequate comprehension, and an estimated capacity level for understanding, is a comprehensive task for the teacher. By the end of the first month of school, the teacher will have determined, as a minimum, the oral instructional reading level for each student, and have completed as much additional informal testing as time permits.

It becomes necessary for the teacher to use less exact group methods for finding out approximate reading abilities for most of the boys and girls. During the first week of school, when much teacher-pupil planning should be taking place, the teacher can ask groups of children to read a selected story orally. The teacher should give a synopsis of the story and then ask the members of the group to read "around the circle," taking turns and passing the book along to each succeeding person to read. If the child reads well, he can read a longer passage; if he has difficulty, he can read a much shorter one; if the level is obviously frustrating for him, he need read only one sentence. If one child does not wish to read or says he can't, the teacher *should not require him to do so* and then give him priority for a personal kind of conference when they can try the informal reading inventory. By this method, it will be possible for the teacher to find temporarily what level of difficulty is adequate for most of the members of the class. The few who read fluently at no level can be given work sheet types of assignments until further testing is completed.

Cumulative records, standardized test results, and conversation with children's previous teachers and principals are also sources of evidence, both cognitive and affective, for grouping children at the beginning of the year. These supplement, but do not substitute for, the teacher's listening to children read individually or in small groups.

I. READING IN THE TEACHER'S DAILY SCHEDULE

Most state courses of study recommend that teachers spend a minimum given amount of time teaching developmental reading in the elementary classroom. The amount of time is usually longer for the primary grades and somewhat less for the intermediate grades. Many teachers in the primary grades spend more than the minimum recommended time teaching reading and may, in fact, spend more than half of their teaching day in the teaching of reading. Upper grade teachers are apt to feel pressured to teach a great deal of content material in various subjects and often, to the detriment of the children, concentrate more on the teaching of the subject than upon the learning of the student. The individual teacher needs to adapt the quantity of work to be done to the amount of time that he has; and unless he adapts the teaching of content to the particular children he teaches, confusion rather than learning results.

This discussion centers on the management of the classroom for efficient teaching since it will not be possible to teach small groups in the room effectively if the teacher has not provided for relatively quiet, constructive work for all those not responding directly to the teacher.

Probably the most difficult task for new teachers to master is that of keeping two-thirds or more of the group actively working and personally motivated at their seats while he teaches or carries on a worthwhile discussion with a small group in the class. If the teacher plans to spend one hour teaching reading to the class, this hour must be broken down into the kinds of activities the children will be doing. From the teacher's point of view, his lesson plan will be sufficient to keep *him* busy teaching, checking other groups, and managing the room. From each child's point of view, the problem is very different. If the teacher works directly with one group for twenty minutes, what will that group do the other forty? They will not be busy very long doing the two or three pages provided in the workbook if they know how to do it when they begin it. If they do not know how to do it when they begin it, they will either need to interrupt the teacher to ask questions, talk to their neighbor, or do the work incorrectly.

How do teachers develop independence in children so they keep working when there are, of necessity, long periods when the teacher cannot directly supervise their work?

First of all, they should not be given *busywork* that only keeps their hands occupied. Coloring, cutting, and pasting are not instructive after the child knows how to do them.

On the other hand, constructive seatwork must be planned and have a purpose. The child must understand what he is doing and see sense in the assignment.

Such routine directions as "Draw a picture about some part of the story that you liked" soon gets tiresome for even young children and will require less and less time to complete as the child sees less value in such a task.

If the teacher plans with the boys and girls, there are many activities which they can do while he is busy teaching a reading group. If children are carrying on activities worthwhile to them, they need to have freedom to move about, and they need to talk quietly to one another occasionally, so *there will be noise* in the classroom. If it is work noise, and the teacher's level of frustration tolerance is sufficiently high, this is no problem. Each teacher must establish the room climate in which he can function efficiently.

Some of these activities are more appropriate at one grade level than another, but are types of exercises suitable for the period of independent study:

1. After appropriate readiness before leaving the reading group, they many complete the exercises in the reading workbook.
2. If the group wishes to prepare a series of pictures to tell a story, they may each draw a designated scene from the story in the day's lesson.
3. Some children like to be encouraged to write their own stories. They may or may not relate to the day's lesson. All need to be urged to do some writing of original paragraphs. In writing original paragraphs, the primary consideration should be having ideas to write about. However, it provides a teacher an excellent diagnostic instrument to determine which children lack sentence sense, which omit all mechanics of writing, which cannot spell common words, and which ones have special difficulties with the order of letters in words. At any grade level, a teacher will occasionally have a student who

has extremely poor phoneme-grapheme relationship and needs intensive training in auditory discrimination.

4. The reading table should contain sufficiently appealing books that any child who finishes his work could read, browse, or study pictures, charts, graphs, and maps. Hopefully, each child can always have a library book checked out and kept in his desk.

5. There are many word games that can be kept in one corner where small groups of children can utilize them. Such games as *Go-Fish*, first and second series, and *Vowel Dominoes* from Remedial Education Center, Washington, D. C., *Take*, from Garrard Press, Champaign, Ill., and *Old Itch*, *Bingobang*, *Full House* and *Syllable Count*, from Lyons and Carnahan, Chicago, are excellent for this purpose.

6. Each may choose a partner to study with, for example, writing regular spelling words, or at the point of mastery, the multiplication facts or division facts.

7. If some unit construction work, murals, models, or dioramas, are in progress in the room, it may be desirable for those with individual assignments there to work on them in their free time.

Teachers should have available many exercises that teach developmental reading and study skills. The *SRA reading laboratories*,[1] *the EDL laboratories*,[2] *New Practice Readers*,[3] *McCall-Crabb Test Lessons in Reading*[4] are some of these.

It is apparent that the teacher can be very busy teaching during the hour allotted to teaching reading, but *unless careful planning is done with the entire class, many boys and girls may not use much of this time profitably.* Some of the cautions that might be stated then, in summary, are

1. With respect to improving reading ability, the teacher must be concerned with what *each child needs* and that he is provided with exercises that help to meet these needs.

2. The teacher's biggest job is one of managing the total reading program, and while doing so, selecting an appropriate method of teaching. Keeping the individuals in the group busy and interested is the best assurance that discipline does not become a problem.

3. No child is going to profit from trying to handle material at his frustration level; the child cannot work quietly at his seat without asking questions if he either does not understand the instructions or cannot read the material required for completion of a given task.

---

[1]Chicago: Science Research Associates, Inc.
[2]Huntington, New York: Educational Development Laboratories, Inc.
[3]Stone, *et al.*, St. Louis: Webster Division, McGraw-Hill.
[4]New York: Bureau of Publications, Teachers College, Columbia University.

4. If each child understands his assignment, he is able to use his time wisely and can continue the next day completing the same job if he needs to.

Discipline

The word discipline suggests that there has to be a response to negative behavior. All teachers know, of course, that when thirty or more youngsters are working, living, and playing together in one room for a school year, negative behavior is sure to make its appearance occasionally. The danger is, though, that the teacher has in mind a specific standard of behavior that is acceptable to him and he wishes to "demand" this standard of behavior from everyone. A mature, confident teacher who feels secure in his work, does not *fear* the impudence of *an anxious child* or the aggresive, impulsive response of *an angry one.* Rather he accepts these behaviors as normal and maintains a room climate in which they can be tolerated by the group.

Mental hygienists have taught us the dangers of impulsive, punitive behavior on the part of the adult. Far too many adults judge the ability to discipline a class by just what they see on the surface.

"He used a naughty word so I washed his mouth out with soap. That worked!"

"He was impudent and sassed me so I slapped him. That worked!"

These responses to overt behavior treat *symptoms* and do not reveal *causes.* They push the pain, the hurt, the madness (the cause of this behavior) deeper down inside the offender and practically guarantee that it will *reassert itself* in some form again.

In helping children to grow in positive directions, in giving positive emphasis to expected behavior, teachers must look for the kinds of *influence techniques*[5] that will help the child to help himself in exercising self-control.

Teachers need a repertoire of techniques "on call" so they can anticipate difficulty and avoid it, so they can give a child assistance or support when he is apt to get into trouble, or in a crisis, they will know how to work the situation through without threatening, nagging, or becoming demanding. Some of these influence techniques are described below:

1. Getting the child's attention if he is about to commit an anti-social act. If the teacher catches his eye, and can convey a message by frowning, shaking the head, raising a finger, or clearing the throat. This may be *the warning* that the child needs to help him exercise self-control. Many children "forget" and trouble is avoided by merely helping them remember to conform.

---

[5]Fritz Redl and W. W. Wattenberg, *Mental Hygiene in Teaching* (New York: Harcourt, Brace and Company, 1951), Chapter XII, "Influence Techniques."

2. Place yourself in close proximity with the child. If the teacher places himself cautiously in the position to be tripped by a pair of legs extended across the aisle, they are likely to be retracted and placed under the seat. A pat on the shoulder, a friendly reminder spoken in an undertone, are not used to make the child fearful, but rather to help him find the strength to control himself.

3. Make sure the assignment the child is attempting to do is one which he has the ability to do. Much classroom disorder results from children not being able to cope with the problem in front of them at the moment. If a child can't read, he needs to be taught how, not punished for squirming, making noise, or leaving his seat too much.

4. Encourage the child to talk about his feelings. Then accept the feelings and evaluate them. Such frankness from a confident teacher can reduce tension.

5. Humor is a good way to change a tense situation into a face-saving, tension-reduced atmosphere. Boys and girls consider humor evidence of poise and self-confidence based on security.

6. A certain amount of routine so that children have some idea of *how* the day is going to be spent, is a steadying influence. The younger the class, the more important is knowing "what are we going to do next?" Everyone needs a certain amount of routine in his life.

7. Isolating a child is occasionally a necessity. This can happen for many reasons. It is important that teachers not evince anger, hostility, or rejection in doing the isolating. A hyperactive child often needs to be encouraged to work in a quiet, sheltered corner—not as a punishment but because he will be able to concentrate better, he will be able to attend to his learning task, and he will be able to regain his own self-control.

    An occasional temper tantrum, kicking, name-calling, or just getting "uncontrollable giggles" are all reasons for isolating a child. The important thing is the teacher's behavior in doing the isolation: it is not a punishment; it is the child's opportunity to regain his self-control. If occasionally, an industrious child wishes to get a task finished when considerable activity is going on and the teacher can *permit* this one to remove himself from the group, this is not only a good reason for isolation but it also demonstrates that isolation is not punishment but a constructive way to help. Continuous isolation of one child from a class to sit in the corridor for long periods of time is a crass misuse of this technique. Isolation without constructive help for such a child is only avoiding his real problem and encouraging more negative attitudes.

8. The teacher should try to help the class members anticipate, as much as possible, changes in their routine. New situations create some anxiety and tensions. The first time the group goes to the auditorium

to practice, to the dark room to see a movie, or on a field trip, getting set in advance will pay dividends.

9. Changing activity when everyone is beginning to get tired is a good way to avoid trouble ahead. With younger children, if the job needs to be done that day, it may be well to say something like this: "Let's leave everything just where it is and line up by the door." or "Let's move the papers over to the library table so we are free to march up and down the aisles here." Then five minutes of brisk walking, singing favorite tunes, formal arm and leg exercises, and time for drinks and toilet, may revive most everyone so that finishing the job doesn't look as forbidding. With older students, it may be necessary only to say, "We have this much more to get done before lunch. If you need to stand up and stretch or get a drink, do it quietly and let's give it a hard try." If most of the group want to finish (are allied with the teacher), this may be all the encouragement they need.

10. Having a fairly well understood way of operating without getting bogged down with too many rules to quibble about will help children define their own limits. Because the teacher has to be at different times a judge, a referee, a detective, a helper, an ego-supporter, or a leader of a group, children need a mature adult whose reactions to behavioral situations is reasonably consistent, fair, supportive and not punitive. Adults who basically do not like children have no business in the classroom.

Specific Suggestions to Help New Teachers with Discipline

When teachers talk about behavior of boys and girls in their classes, they reveal a great deal about their philosophy of classroom discipline. Teachers, in this respect, place themselves on a long continuum from strictly enforced discipline to constructively guided discipline. This writer is deeply committed to the philosophy of constructively guided discipline. Children are encouraged to express their attitudes, feelings, and ideas and are then guided in directing them in socially acceptable ways according to the standards of conduct understood by their local environment. Industry, cooperation, and acceptance of a plurality of ideas are desirable ends. The desirable goals may be contrasted with such undesirable ones as *passive* children in very quiet, orderly rooms dominated by an authoritarian teacher.

The discipline recommended here is more difficult to maintain since it is based on a friendly, cooperative spirit prevailing and working toward compatible concensus in matters of behavior, knowledge, and values. In this atmosphere, good, effective teaching generates good discipline in most of the boys and girls. Well planned lessons, careful attention to individual differences in both achievement and behavior, and a constructive, optimistic, work-like atmosphere will eliminate emphasis on behavior *per se* most of the time.

The new teacher may profit from a careful perusal of the following suggestions in preparation for the very complex job of guiding the learning of a roomful of boys and girls for the first time.

1. Learn to call the boys and girls by name as quickly as possible. Study their names on the class roll before they arrive and connect name to child as quickly as you can.

2. Take charge of the room by talking in a strong, confident voice; by presenting definite plans of working through each hour the first day; by conducting business in an impartial, confident way; and by providing a variety of tasks and keeping everybody busy *all the time* the first day.

3. Accept the standard of conduct for the group according to the neighborhood in which you teach. While you *must not permit* children to continually tell you "Miss Smith let us do that last year," or "We never did it that way last year," so you, too, *must not admonish* your group to behave the way you did when you were a child—or the way children do out in a city suburb.

4. Use every opportunity to make friendly comments throughout the day. These interchanges will cause the boys and girls to feel that you have a personal interest in them. Tell Mary she has a pretty ribbon in her hair, tell John that you appreciate the way he came in very quietly for a change, or write a one sentence note to Jack's mother and tell her the first time Jack gets all his spelling words right.

5. Begin every class promptly and enthusiastically. Being businesslike, however, does not change the fact that a good sense of humor and a friendly smile are two of your greatest assets. Knowing the lesson well will win respect for the teacher. A courteous use of enthusiasm, businesslike behavior, knowledge of the subject matter, and a good sense of humor are sure to win the confidence of the group in the long run.

6. Don't talk too much. Many a sixth grade boy has explained to his mother about his teacher who talks much too much, "We just turn off our hearing aids!" The lecture method has *no* place in the elementary school. This arbitrary point of view is intended to mitigate the far too prevalent situation in which teachers spend long periods of time "telling" students what is important and about what content they will be examined. The less response teachers accept or evolve from the group, the more they are apt to carry on an interminable monologue.

7. Sometimes teachers use words and sentence patterns that the children do not even understand. One third grade teacher teaching

language-handicapped children in the Southwest asked the boys and girls to be quiet while she talked to the visitor. They were soon talking with each other instead of working. The teacher turned to them, and said in a firm voice, "It seems that I cannot relax my vigilance for one minute!" They became quiet for a second so she turned back to talk to the visitor. Then they continued their conversations in an undertone.

8. When a situation arises that must be handled by the teacher, be sure to keep calm, dignified, and select something to do to resolve the problem that you can really carry out. The child may be asked to take his chair and sit outside the room *once* until the child and the teacher can have a private conference. *But* no child gets his education sitting out in the hall every day.

9. From the first hour of the day, your eyes must be skilled at catching each child's variant behavior no matter where you are standing in the classroom. The first few days, *do not* plan to turn your back on the class for such activities as writing extensively on the blackboard. If material needs to be written on the board, it can be done before the group comes in. Later in the year, you may be able to select a mature student to put things on the board for you. Little elementary school teaching is done in a sitting down position. The first week, you probably shouldn't sit down at all.

10. When you are having a large group discussion, or when you are teaching sub-groups, develop the easy practice of bringing the daydreamer or the mischievous one back to his work by asking him a question, by speaking his name, or by making a casual comment about whether or not "———" is going to get his work done today. When his attention is beginning to waver, all he may need is a reminder.

11. When a fracas has taken place, either between two students or between a student and teacher, don't insist on apologies. An insincere apology teaches hypocrisy.

12. Do not punish the whole class for a mistake committed by one or a few.

13. As a class proceeds, the teacher should note the number of *indifferent* pupils. In a class of twenty-nine fifth graders studying topic sentences for paragraphs, only five girls near the front were paying attention. The teacher needed to re-evaluate his own goals.

14. Do *not* end the lesson on a sarcastic note. "Nobody had his lesson well prepared today." "Most of you didn't get it—but then I didn't think you would!" Under such conditions, each succeeding lesson will likely get *worse*.

II. METHODS FOR THE READING CLASS PERIOD

Teachers often share their experiences about procedures in teaching reading. One may indicate that the problem centers on learning how to handle three reading groups. This gets things compartmentalized pretty well and once the organization is taken care of, the operation runs pretty smoothly. They *manage* three groups. Others talk about having four or five groups and occasionally a teacher refers to his room as a "regular three-ring circus." Many listeners to such a conversation might wonder what a teacher does to adequately *manage* a room with many things going on.

More and more teachers are talking about individualized reading in their rooms. Different problems are sure to arise if the teacher organizes his room for individual teacher-pupil conferences.

Finally, there are those teachers who are committed to the language-experience approach to reading. How do they operate?

Knowing that all children are so very different from each other, and that the longer the children attend school the greater become the range of differences in all types of skills, abilities, interests, and ambitions, teachers cannot rely on teaching *any one thing* to all members of a given class. Consequently, any teacher who *accepts the facts* about the way children grow, develop, learn, and satisfy their curiosities, must be searching for adequately innovative ways to manage his classroom so that each child does have opportunity to stretch himself outward on the growing edge of learning.

The following graph shows why it is impossible for the classroom teacher today to think of her group of boys and girls in the traditional sense as "doing fourth grade work" or "doing second grade work." The small block at the bottom of the graph shows the narrow limit of what may be thought of as "just one grade" while the long bars show the *range* of achievement in general knowledge to be *expected* in any single grade by the end of the year. The appalling dilemma of the sixth grade teacher who tries to teach only the content of "the sixth grade textbooks" is completely obvious if her group has an achievement range of over eleven years of knowledges, skills, and abilities. (See page 81.)

The novice in teaching needs a place to begin learning and developing security. This requires some tangible supports to which to anchor lesson plans. It may well be that dividing the class into three reading groups using the previous teacher's recommendation *and* the informal reading inventory is the most practical way to get a good year underway. Teacher's manuals contain storehouses of worthwhile information that many beginning teachers do not know. There can be nothing wrong in first acquiring that information.

After developing many techniques that work well, some confidence and security in successfully teaching developmental reading skills, a teacher has many, many avenues open to him to better direct the enthusiasm, interests, and aptitudes of all the boys and girls in his charge. Some of these avenues are sure to utilize abilities in individualizing work, in using language-experience assignments, and in having many small groups for specific teaching purposes during the year.

Beyond these challenges lie those more complicated tasks of (1) offering a planned program in corrective reading for the one who has missed many needed skills, (2) providing the adjusted reading program for the educable mentally retarded child who is not provided for in the special education program, (3) providing an environment in which the emotionally disturbed child can spend at least a part of his day in regular classroom, and (4) providing for the child of normal intelligence who has some physical handicap such as minimal brain dysfunction, limited vision, or defective hearing.

As an integral part of the functioning reading groups the teacher is responsible for all the special activities that are related to the reading lessons themselves. These include such activities as (1) preparing a TV program in which parts of stories are dramatized; (2) promoting reading of interesting books through oral book reports or panel discussions of books read; (3) reports compiled by committees about authors of favorite children's books, about books awarded the Newbery Medal or the Caldecott Medal; and (4) recording each child's voice on the tape recorder reading a passage at his instructional level of reading.*

The primary consideration is that the teacher decide what he can do and how he can best function within his limits. Teachers have individual differences just as the children whom they teach. They vary considerably in the amount of noise they can tolerate in the classroom; they vary considerably in the amount of freedom they can allow various committees or many small groups talking among themselves across the room; their levels of frustration tolerance are also different as evidenced in such statements as "Nothing *shakes* him," and "She's *so* conscientious."

In the sections of this chapter which follow, a few specific ideas outlined for the various types of lessons discussed above include (1) the directed reading lesson in the graded reader, (2) the language-experience lesson, (3) the individualized reading period, and (4) the monitored programmed reading-study period.

A directed reading lesson requires more time than many new teachers realize. Such a lesson may be introduced during one period and guided silent reading completed. It can be recalled and finished in a second

---

*The tape-recorder will be mentioned many times throughout the text. It is an excellent self-teaching device. Upper elementary children can operate it themselves and practice oral reading in any quiet corner or empty closet space.

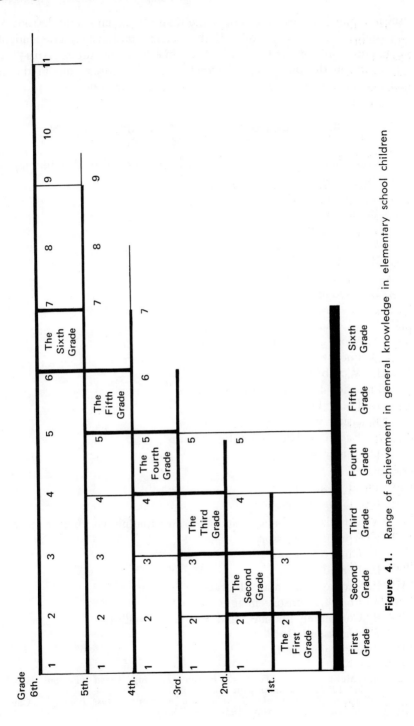

Figure 4.1. Range of achievement in general knowledge in elementary school children

session. Some stories need more time than others, and some lessons may be guided during one period with the teacher and finished independently. It is important for the teacher to take time to make sure of skills—learnings both in the phonetic and structural analysis areas and in the cognitive and affective areas relating to the thinking processes.

III. TEACHING THE DIRECTED READING LESSON FROM A GRADED READER

If one looks in the teacher's manual for a graded reader, he may find an outline like this:

The Lesson Plan[6]
  I. Preparation
    A. Setting the scene
    B. Introducing the new words
 II. Reading and discussion
    A. Silent reading
    B. Talking it over
    C. Oral reading
III. Word Analysis and Reading Skills
    A. Word recognition exercise
    B. Phonetic analysis exercise
    C. Workbook exercise
 IV. Provision for individual differences
    A. Using beginning sounds
    B. Using vowel sounds
    C. Exercise planned for fast groups
    D. Wider reading

or this:

The Lesson Plan[7]
  I. Preparing for reading
    A. Establishing background and anticipating vocabulary needs
 II. Interpreting the story
    A. Guided reading
    B. Rereading
III. Extending Skills and Abilities
    A. Forming sensory images
    B. Combining phonetic and structural analysis
    C. *Think-and-Do Book*
 IV. Extending interests

---

[6]Paul McKee, *et. al., Teacher's Edition, Looking Ahead* (Boston: Houghton Mifflin Co., 1957), Teaching Unit 23, pp. 255-263.
[7]William S. Gray, *et. al., Guidebook to Accompany Just Imagine!* (Chicago: Scott, Foresman and Company, 1953), pp. 133-140.

One can generalize that most of the reading lesson plans follow similar outlines. The teacher will attempt to motivate an interest in reading the story, teach the new vocabulary and review difficult words, guide the silent reading of the story and discuss the content, interpret the story through questioning or re-reading parts, and provide related activities as a follow-through for the lesson.

Motivating an Interest

The story may contain colored illustrations that reveal incidents in the story that can be discussed by thumbing through the pages. The teacher may have related pictures from the materials center vertical file. He may talk about new or unusual words in the story or raise questions to guide children's thinking about them. The incident around which the story is built needs to be related to the background of experience of the class. Only as it is meaningful, can children decide whether it is fact or fiction; real or imaginary. Finally, the teacher must establish a purpose for reading. The child starts reading to "find out something."

Making Sure of Vocabulary

New words should be presented in context and discussed so that they are meaningful to the boys and girls. They can then be practiced with flash card drills or games that give practice in matching, comparing, or using in sentences. Children should be led to discover new words for themselves if they have sufficient word analysis skills to do so. If they use their skills to unlock new words, there will be fewer and fewer strange words to present as they gain in reading independence.

Guiding the Silent Reading

In the first books, very young children need to be guided sentence by sentence or section by section to make sure that they are learning that the words on the page are telling them something just as the oral conversation using these words would. Guide questions should be specific enough to cause children to look carefully for specific information. As children gain in reading power, they can read longer and longer parts of stories without detailed teacher guidance. In the intermediate grades, those students reading at grade level should be able to read the entire story after adequate readiness and establishing purposes.

Interpreting the Story

While it is important that the teacher ask questions to make sure that the reader understood the story, that is only a minor part in evaluation. Understanding the sequence of events, and understanding what the author said is a prerequisite to using the story information for evaluation of ideas requiring use of judgment, reasoning, and looking at values.

As was pointed out in Chapter 2, most teachers' questions have tended to fall in the memory and translation (paraphrase) levels according to Bloom's taxonomy.

While memory and translation questions are necessary to establish common understandings and sequence of story events, it is at the higher levels of thinking that interpretation, reflection, application, and evaluation can be developed. As teachers require application, analysis and evaluation of ideas read, they more closely approach the affective life of the child and require him to reflect on his acceptance of, preference for, and commitment to *values*. There is opportunity for the teacher to use the story as a basis for interpreting happenings in light of the children's values, in analyzing at the children's level why the author may have ended the story as he did, or in making analogies from the story to actual happenings in their lives or in their community. Original thinking can be evoked with such questions as "What would you have done if you had been in Bob's shoes?" or "What would have been a more realistic ending for this story?"

Providing Related Activities

Related activities of the cognitive sort include comprehension exercises, further work on vocabulary, or studying phonetic or structural analysis skills. Related activities in the affective area require the child to relate story incidents to his own experiences in the areas of feelings or emotional response. He learns, affectively, how to evaluate ideas not as "all right" or "all wrong;" "all good" or "all bad;" or "all true" or "all false." Rather these ideas have all shades of meaning on a long continuum according to personal attitudes and relativity in time and space.

The lesson may be extended through the search for additional information in general references, free reading at the book table, or shared oral reading.

IV.   INDIVIDUALIZED READING

The recognition that reading is an active, thinking process; that reading is a developmental, complex process; and that reading is an individual and personal experience has led to changing concepts in the teaching of the reading program in the schools. One response that has evolved in this change is commonly called *individualized reading*. Individualized reading programs show an obvious effort, at least, to let each child proceed at his own rate of learning, and to allow him to select for himself reading material he desires to read. Individualized reading is a broad approach, not entirely new to many competent teachers, and not limiting or restricting in so far as other reading activities are concerned. Individualized reading promotes the principles of self-selection, self-seeking, self-pacing, and self-evaluation. To the degree that the teacher achieves her objective in this program, the child is learning independence in purposeful reading and building lasting reading interests.

In order to initiate a system of self-selection, self-seeking, and self-pacing of reading for each member of the class, it is necessary that the following criteria be met.

1. The classroom provides a variety of all types of reading to meet the needs, interests and abilities of all the members of the group. Administering and evaluating informal reading inventories for each one is the best way to obtain this information.
2. Types of reading materials include (1) trade books (library books) of adventure, animals, family life, humor, mystery, history, travel, science, folk tales, myths and legends, biography, and poetry; (2) basal and supplementary readers; (3) standard reference books; and (4) newspapers and magazines.
3. The teacher either takes sufficient time with the total group to work out purposes, methods of operating, and ways of reporting, or arranges for part of the group to continue with traditional ways of working and starts one sub-group at a time with the process of self-selection and independent study.
4. A system of assigning or checking out books needs to be devised so that it is monitored entirely by selected members of the group. This process must continue while the teacher works with other aspects of the program.
5. The reading program should be planned with the weeks of time as the basic unit. For example, perhaps each child is assured of at least one individual conference each week and Monday, Tuesday, and Wednesday are individual conference days. If there are thirty children in one room, this requires an average of ten conferences each day. If the conferences average from three to ten minutes each, it may be possible to hold ten conferences in one reading hour. Some teachers would prefer to have only six conferences each of five days and utilize some time each day in having a group discussion, or special reports given to the whole class.* Teachers will be able to note certain skills for which more than one child shows needs and a group can be formed to teach these particular weaknesses during the week.

Some attention needs to be given to specific work on skills and the teacher may wish to draw upon programmed materials other than basal reading workbooks for this work. How the teacher plans to keep large

---

*Scheduling must be sufficiently flexible that any child with a special problem can have a conference the day he needs it.

numbers of children busy while she gives her attention to one at a time will be discussed later in this chapter.

While some teachers plan one specific day in the week for skills enrichment, others plan for students to have work on skills in progress on two or three days during the week although the teacher may discuss it with the group on only one day.

A Sample Weekly Schedule for Individual Reading Conferences

Group	Monday	Tuesday	Wednesday	Thursday	Friday
I	Conferences 45 Min.	Silent Reading	Skills Exercises	Silent Reading and Reporting	Weekly Reader 30 Min. and Reporting 30 Min.
II	Silent Reading	Conferences 45 min.	Silent Reading and Reporting	Skills Exercises	Weekly Reader 30 Min. and Reporting 30 Min.
III	Skills Exercises	Silent Reading and Reporting	Conferences 45 min.	Silent Reading	Weekly Reader 30 Min. and Reporting 30 Min.
IV	Silent Reading and Reporting	Skills Exercises	Silent Reading	Conferences 45 Min.	Weekly Reader 30 Min. and Reporting 30 Min.

One method of record keeping for the teacher may be to have a five by eight inch card for each child on which the record is kept in brief, diary form, as in the following example.

A Diary Record for Individualized Reading

Std. Tst.
Name: _____ Score: _____ Date: _____ Grade: ____

September 25: Is reading *Little House in the Big Woods*. Visited the Laura Ingall Wilder home in Missouri in the summer, 1967. Thoroughly enjoys the story. Will plan a report on Friday recommending it to others. Is beginning SRA: RFU with card No. 26 (Gr. Pl. 5.7).

October 2: Is working with Betty on a special display and report about the Wilder books and the Wilder Home Museum.

October 9:

The teacher will try to keep such observations as: "misses many basic sight words in reading," "cannot divide words into syllables," "had a book that was a bit too difficult this morning," "gets implied meanings well."

Individualized reading implies that children are not in a reading circle in front of the teacher. They are at their desks or at tables. Each child has a different book that he selected himself. He receives help from the teacher or a helper—the help he needs when he asks for it. There will be a sharing time to share with the others what he has read. But, there will be some skills needed to grow in reading independence that will be taught to sub-groups as the need arises.

Knowing that the range of ability within any group of thirty children may be five to seven grade levels, the teacher uses interest and specified routine to allow children to conduct their own free reading practice. Each one can read what he feels it is that he *wants* to read. He learns how to choose books, how to handle the books, how to come and go in the room, how to get help when it is needed—that is, he learns to function independently. The individualized conferences provide opportunity for the teacher to keep a check on sight vocabulary in the primary grades. If the book is "at his instructional level" he will not meet too many *hard* words. The teacher will tell him words he doesn't know and he will have opportunity to read these same words in many situations. If children are selected to be helping teachers, they will tell words to those who need more assistance.

The social interaction in the room with sub-groups can teach children that one group is "average", one group is "inferior", and one group is "superior." It is argued that this problem does not exist with individualized reading. This is only partially valid. It would *not* be a serious problem in regularly assigned groups *if* the child understood why he was reading far below grade level, *knew* that he was making good growth at that level, and *felt* he would be rehabilitated. Recreational reading is not individualized reading. Recreational reading is easy reading practice to develop greater fluency, to learn that reading is fun and that there are lots and lots of interesting books.

To have children become acquainted with a wide variety of books, the teacher might encourage her class to share them with and advertise them to one another in interesting ways, thus stimulating them to read more books of good quality and, incidentally, give them opportunities to show their ingenuity and creative ability in art, writing, dramatic arts, and other fields. Veatch has suggested many ways teachers may do this.[8] *A Practical Guide to Individualized Reading* is also an excellent

---

[8]Jeannette Veatch, *Individualizing Your Reading Program* (New York: G. P. Putnam's Sons, 1959).

source book for teachers.[9] Carlton and Moore[10] raise a list of pertinent questions for the classroom teacher to consider:

1. What is individualized reading?
2. What is the teacher's responsibility?
3. What is the best time to begin an individualized program?
4. Are there any special materials needed for an individualized reading program?
5. How does a teacher acquire enough materials for an individualized reading program?
6. How does a teacher know which books to give a pupil?
7. How can a teacher be sure a child is reading at the level where he should be?
8. Can children be expected to select their own reading material wisely?
9. How do pupils develop a basic vocabulary in an individualized reading program?
10. How are word recognition skills incorporated into individualized reading programs?
11. What is the advantage of using individualized reading instead of the basal reader approach?
12. How does the teacher evaluate pupil progress in an individualized reading program?
13. Why do some studies show little difference in results between individualized reading programs and the more traditional approach of using basal reading with the groups?
14. What are some of the advantages of the individualized reading approach?

V. LANGUAGE EXPERIENCE APPROACH

In the language experience approach, the children will dictate stories based upon their activities in the school or outside of school hours. Experience stories may be individual, small group, or planned and dictated by the class as a whole.

Early in the first grade year, a kitten may be brought to school for sharing time. If the group shows enthusiasm, the teacher may catch some of their sentences and make a story on the chalkboard.

---

[9]Board of Education of the City of New York, *A Practical Guide to Individualized Reading* (Board of Education, Bureau of Educational Research, 110 Livingston St., Room 732, Brooklyn 1, New York, 1960).

[10]Lessie Carlton and Robert H. Moore, "Individualized Reading," *NEA Journal,* 63:11-12, November, 1964.

A Kitten

Tim has a kitten.
It is all black.
It came to school.
Tim likes his cat.

Or one child may tell the teacher:

My Toys

I have a ball.
I have a wagon.
I have a tractor.
I have a car.
I like to play with them.

The language experience approach is the most promising method of all to meet the reading objectives to help the child relate the written form of language to the spoken form. Experience charts written in the language of the child will make reading useful for remembering things; will make reading rewarding in preserving the child's ideas, and give him good practice for all the skills he needs later for more formal reading.

Allen, author of language-experience materials published by Britannica, says "Children who write, read! They have to read!" He continues:[11]

> To children who have experienced authorship many times, reading is not lessons, worksheets, practice exercises, or a time each day in a time schedule (perhaps to dread). It is the continuous discovery of stepping-stones to a lifetime of enjoyment of books. It results in the conceptualizations:
> What I can think about I can say.
> What I can say, I can write.
> What I can write, I can read.
> I can read what I can write and what other people have written for me to read.

Twenty elements that constitute the Language Experience Approach to reading are:[12]

    I. Converting experiences to words:
        1. Sharing experiences.
        2. Discussing experiences.

---

[11]Roach Van Allen and Claryce Allen, *An Introduction to a Language Experience Program, Level I* (425 North Michigan Avenue, Chicago: Encyclopedia Britannica Press, 1966), p. 21.

[12]Wilhelmina Nielsen, "Twenty Language Experiences which Form the Framework of the Experience Approach to the Language Arts," *Claremont Reading Conference: On Becoming a Reader* (Claremont, California: Claremont Graduate School, 1965), pp. 168-174.

        3. Listening to stories read.
        4. Telling stories.
        5. Dictating.
        6. Summarizing.
        7. Making and reading books.
        8. Writing independently.

II. Studying the words themselves:
        9. Developing word recognition skills.
     10. Developing basic sight vocabulary.
     11. Expanding English vocabulary concepts.
     12. Studying words.

III. Recognizing words and relating them to experience:
     13. Improving style and form.
     14. Using a variety of resources.
     15. Reading a variety of symbols: Facial expressions, Pictures, Calendar, Clock, Map, Road Signs.
     16. Reading whole books.
     17. Improving comprehension.
     18. Outlining.
     19. Integrating and assimilating of ideas.
     20. Reading critically.

VI. THE CLASSROOM TEACHER PLANS HIS READING PROGRAM

The teacher will surely have flexibility in planning his reading program. The best program will incorporate a variety of activities to best develop a whole range of abilities within the class. The teacher will rely on basal readers, and utilize an individualized reading program, a language-experience approach, and a writing way to reading as they provide activities to keep each child profitably working.

1. The basal reader program is not sufficient to provide for all the children in a given classroom.
2. The time spent with each child need not be the same amount spent with every other child. Length of time is not to be equated with providing equal opportunity.
3. The notion that there is a *basic book* for any given grade that all the children must finish is absurd . . . and must be discarded.
4. The superficial process of all children in a group reading and then answering memory questions over the story must be changed to reading followed by higher levels of questioning to evaluate the story read.
5. A whole set of study skills must be developed in the process of teaching developmental reading.

The suggestions for adapting basal readers made by DeBoer and Dallmann are appropriate here:

> Certain general cautions should be observed in the planning of a basal reading program. For example, reliance should not be placed upon

	Group A	Group B	Group C
Five Minutes.	For the teacher: Answering questions and reminding individuals and groups about work to be done in independent work periods. For the students: Asking questions and getting ready to complete independent seatwork.		
Period I 20 Minutes	Directed teaching of a reading lesson. Probably the least able readers will be first since they will be least able to plan independently. The teacher may plan to develop only some of the steps in a directed reading lesson.		
Three Minutes.	Attention to progress of individual and group work. Answering questions.		
Period II 20 Minutes		Directed teaching of a reading lesson. Hopefully, less attention to formal teaching in how to read the lesson and more free discussion of ideas in the story, and making value judgments about the reading.	
Three Minutes.	Attention to progress of work throughout the room. Answering questions.		
Period III 20 Minutes			If this group is the highest achieving group, greater attention can be given to vocabulary development, evaluating, and making critical judgments.

Figure 4.2. Planning work for the reading period. What independent seatwork will each child do?

a single basal reader for the whole class; indeed it should not be placed upon an entire single series. In any given class, basal readers designed for many levels of reading ability and containing many different kinds of materials should be provided. Basal readers should not be labeled according to grade level or difficulty, although the publisher's estimate of difficulty level may be indicated by some code device. All basal readers should be amply supplemented with general reading materials on many subjects and representing many levels of reading ability.[13]

The new teacher may have planned carefully how to teach three reading lessons for the reading groups in her room but finds herself in great difficulty with the majority of the boys and girls whose time (forty minutes of empty space in Figure 4.2) has not been planned. As every teacher can testify, "idle hands do often get into mischief." Knowing how to plan specifically for each child for his forty-minute work period without direct supervision of the teacher may be more crucial than careful study of the teacher's manual for teaching one subgroup.

The beginning teacher will likely plan his reading program around the use of the basal reading series as a starting point. With supervisory help, he may concentrate on developing a good three-group teaching plan using only the basal reader program for the first months of school. If he is sensitive to needs, he will soon begin to borrow from other reading approaches and his plan will become more flexible. (Figure 4.3.)

The experienced teacher will likely plan his reading program in such a way that more emphasis is given to individualized reading and language-experience reading. However, he needs to rely, at times, on the stories in basal readers for group reading practice, or when library books are returned and not re-issued on time, or when language-experience writing is not serving a purpose. He needs many techniques to maximally develop all those children requiring individual programs. (Figure 4.4.)

An experienced teacher who feels confident about the skills and work habits children need may wish to develop these skills and work habits through work produced by the children themselves. Of course such a program is supplemented with a great deal of reading, including basal readers, but the primary objective is for the group to produce stories, articles, and small illustrated books worth reading. (Figure 4.5.)

VII. SUMMARY

This chapter contains a discussion of the reading period in the teacher's daily teaching schedule. Using the recognized principles of child growth and development, the teacher remembers that the longer children go to school, *the more different* they become. Because these things are

[13]John J. DeBoer and Martha Dallmann, *The Teaching of Reading* (New York: Holt, Rinehart, and Winston, Inc., 1960), pp. 340-341.

BASAL READERS

A basal reader approach, with three reading groups, provides the new teacher with direction, well-planned lessons, and source materials.

This well-planned framework will give the teacher security and as he learns through experience what constitutes an adequate program he will gain self-confidence.

Through the year, as varying levels of ability and different kinds of reading problems become apparent, the teacher will move toward more individualizing of children's work.

SPECIAL READING ACTIVITIES

Dramatizing parts of stories;
Collecting information about books, making book week displays, studying favorite authors;
Using reading games and puzzles;
Using standard references.

INDIVIDUALIZED READING

Seeking, self-selection, and pacing are the key words in helping children develop individual reading habits. Each child reads what he enjoys; what he wants to learn about; what is useful to him.

Lots of trade books and some kind of reading record is important.

LANGUAGE-EXPERIENCE READING

Utilizing learning experiences in reading helps the beginner understand that reading is talk written down and once written down it is preserved and can be read back.

Older boys and girls can utilize and extend writing skills by well-illustrated booklets about the units of work they are doing in school.

CORRECTIVE AND REMEDIAL READING

Corrective reading is the remedial work done by the regular class teacher to help each child develop sequentially his reading skills—to fill in what has been missed and to re-teach what has been forgotten.

Figure 4.3. A reading program based primarily on the use of basal readers and teachers' guides.

INDIVIDUALIZED READING

Requires accessibility to the resources of a well-stocked school library. Minimum of 100 selected books in the classroom at one time—to be changed each month—range of difficulty to fit the entire class.

Most books will be trade books but good stories in readers are fine too. Minimum of one individual conference weekly; both child and teacher keep records. Must provide opportunity for class reporting, discussing, and evaluating.

PROGRAMMED TEXTS

Sequenced skill development is well-worked out in: *Programmed Reading and Programmed Remedial Reading* (McGraw-Hill); *SRA Reading for Understanding and SRA Elementary Labs; EDL Study Skills; Standard Test Lessons in Reading and Practice Exercises in Reading*. (Teachers College Press.)

LANGUAGE-EXPERIENCE

Writing original stories; Writing illustrated content lessons; Reporting.

BASAL READERS

The teacher must utilize small groups in basal readers at the instructional level to teach skills. This is especially necessary for all students in any grade whose instructional level of reading is third grade or below.

Interesting stories in readers should be shared as oral reading practice.

CORRECTIVE AND REMEDIAL READING

Corrective reading is the remedial work done by the regular class teacher helping each child develop sequentially the reading skills—to fill in what has been missed and to re-teach what has been forgotten.

Figure 4.4. A reading program based primarily on the individualized reading approach.

THE RESEARCH AND WRITING WAY TO READING

Through a series of planned lessons in keeping written records of their work, for example, of the fifth grade year, the primary reading job, could be the production of stories and well-illustrated books related to the fifth grade course of study for the school year.

PROGRAMMING TO TEACH THE SKILLS

Sequenced skill development is well-worked out in: *Programmed Reading and Programmed Remedial Reading* (McGraw-Hill); *SRA Reading for Understanding* and SRA Elementary Labs; EDL *Study Skills; Standard Test Lessons in Reading* and *Practice Exercises in Reading,* (Teachers College Press.)

CORRECTIVE AND REMEDIAL READING

Corrective reading is the remedial work done by the regular class teacher to help each child develop sequentially his reading skills—to fill in what has been missed and to re-teach what has been forgotten.

INDIVIDUALIZED READING

Seeking, self-selection, and pacing are the key words in helping children develop individual reading habits. Each child reads what he enjoys; what he wants to learn about; what is useful to him.

Lots of trade books and some kind of reading record is important.

For the beginning readers, this is a language-experience approach to reading; talking about interesting or common experiences and then writing about them; building sequences of such stories into interesting little booklets.

BASAL READERS

The teacher must utilize small groups in basal readers at the instructional level to teach skills. This is especially necessary for all students in any grade whose instructional level of reading is third grade or below.

Interesting stories in readers should be shared as oral reading practice.

Figure 4.5. A reading program emphasizing students writing text material

true, the teacher must plan for a wider and wider span of reading abilities as the children progress through the school. New teachers are apt to rely more heavily on basal readers and well-planned teachers' manuals, but many teachers base challenging, motivated developmental reading instruction on individualized reading programs, language-experience reading and writing, combinations of these approaches, and use of programmed study materials to teach skills. Every child should learn to read better during the school year than he *could read* when he enrolled in the beginning of the year. In order for him to achieve this, he must have materials to read that he can read successfully and he must be rewarded for successful work. The next chapter contains a discussion of the problems of interaction in the classroom.

QUESTIONS FOR DISCUSSION

1. In an essay of 250 words, explain why, on the basis of the principles of normal growth and development in children, the differences in achievement in a given group are sure to get greater as they progress through the elementary school.

2. Do you believe the basal reader approach is the best approach to teaching reading for inexperienced teachers? Why or why not?

3. How can the teacher make sure that he is planning adequately for the students performing above grade level, those at grade level, and those below grade level so that each group is receiving its fair share of the teacher's time and attention?

REFERENCES FOR FURTHER READING

GUY L. BOND and EVA BOND WAGNER, *Teaching the Child to Read* (New York: Macmillan Co., 1966), Chapter 5, "Current Approaches to Reading Instruction," pp. 81-92.

Bureau of Educational Research, Board of Education, City of New York, Publication No. 40, October, 1960, *A Practical Guide to Individualized Reading*, 158 pages.

ROMA GANS, *Common Sense in Teaching Reading* (New York: The Bobbs-Merrill Co., Inc., 1963), Chapter 6, "Differing Attitudes Toward First Grade Reading," pp. 95-117.

LYMAN C. HUNT, JR., *et al.*, *The Individualized Reading Program: A Guide for Classroom Teaching*, Vol. II, Part 3, Proceedings (Newark: International Reading Association, 1967).

DORRIS M. LEE and ROACH VAN ALLEN, *Learning to Read Through Experience* (New York: Appleton-Century-Crofts, 1963).

GEORGE MANOLAKES, "Instructional Practices in Reading: An Assessment for the Future," in Albert Mazurkiewicz, editor, *New Perspectives in Reading*

Instruction (New York: Pitman Publishing Corporation, 1964), pp. 96-111. Reprinted from *Frontiers of Elementary Education VI* (Syracuse, New York: Syracuse University Press, 1960).

WALLACE RAMSEY, editor, *Organizing for Individual Differences* (Newark, Del.: International Reading Association, 1968).

HARRY W. SARTAIN, *The Place of Individualized Reading in a Well-Planned Program*, Ginn and Co. Contributions in Reading No. 28 (Boston: Ginn and Co., 1965).

NILA BANTON SMITH, *Reading Instruction for Today's Children* (Englewood Cliffs, New Jersey: Prentice-Hall, Inc., 1963), pp. 78-161. Chapters 5, "Approaches Differ," 6, "Grouping Plans Take on New Forms," 7, "Individualized Instruction Receives Attention."

RUSSELL STAUFFER, "Language Experience Approach," in James Kerfoot, editor, Perspectives No. 5, *First Grade Reading Programs* (Newark, Del., International Reading Association, 1965), pp. 86-118.

ROACH VAN ALLEN and GLADYS C. HALVERSEN, *The Language-Experience Approach to Reading Instruction* (Boston: Ginn and Co., 1961).

JEANNETTE VEATCH, *Individualizing Your Reading Program* (New York: G. P. Putnam and Sons, 1959).

ELAINE C. VILSCEK, editor, *A Decade of Innovations: Approaches to Beginning Reading* (Newark, Del., 19711: International Reading Association, 1968).

5

Group Interaction
in the Classroom

An *effective teacher* needs to be aware of the interpersonal relations among the class members. He is continually assessing the emotional and social climate in the room.

Many young teachers working in a departmentalized program with older children, have experienced frustration with groups of sixth or seventh graders who are noisy, somewhat tense, and brusk when they storm into the classroom to start a new class period.

Mr. Jones noted such behavior early in the year when his seventh grade groups came to reading-language class. He responded by listening long enough to pick up some thread of the conversation. Then, instead of moving directly to the day's lesson, he chaired a discussion with the boys and girls about their behavior. After perhaps ten minutes and several gripes later, the class settled down to work.

In a casual conversation with Miss Quiet, a colleague who taught these groups the previous period and who had taught in the school system more than twenty years, Mr. Jones related the episode about the very restless behavior.

Miss Quiet assured him they were *not* restless in her room, that they worked very quietly, and that she tolerated no impudence from youngsters who tried to "talk back."

Mr. Jones soon learned from colleagues of the "pin-drop" silence in Miss Quiet's room and the rules about "no pencil-sharpening," "no whispering," and the introduction of *no* topic except the day's lesson.

It was not difficult to understand that after a twenty minute home room study period and a fifty-five minute recitation and study period with Miss Quiet just prior to reading-language with Mr. Jones that many of the twelve-year-olds had been "still and quiet" about as long as was physically possible.

Mr. Jones accepted the problem of a sudden transition from a highly authoritarian teacher for one long "quiet" period to a period which he hoped would be a free, interacting, group-planning, group conversation atmosphere. With this in mind, he closed his classroom door when the bell rang after classes passed, and planned a controlled conversation period that could last ten minutes if necessary to reduce tensions, let the held-in exuberance escape for a while, and then get the group back to the assignments of the hour.

It is hoped that most new teachers will not face such extreme teacher-behavior environments. However, just as teachers are admonished to accept children *as they are,* so faculties must accept teachers as *they* are. All teachers, naturally, represent the complete range of behavior from extremely authoritarian to extremely democratic. Some, confused between the two ends of the continuum, invite chaos because they fail to teach such discriminations as differences between freedom and license; privilege and responsibility; decision making based on logical reasoning or fact and decision making based on personal whim.

Yet these kinds of intelligent decisions are the primary purpose of education as a socializing institution. Therefore, finding ways for teachers to become sensitive to people's feelings, attitudes, and needs is basic to providing for social and intellectual needs in all human interaction.

Teachers probably tend to feel that they have a great deal of information (facts) which they must convey to a group of students in a short period of time. For this reason, they are inclined to use oral language as their means of *telling* boys and girls what they *need* to know. They overlook the need for students to communicate with each other and with the teacher. The learner must have the chance to think through, exchange ideas, talk to his peers and crystallize his thoughts, and correct some of his fallacious thinking. Teachers sometimes forget that communication has to be a a two-way process if it is to be effective.

When the curriculum is based more upon process and less upon content, the teacher operates as a group-centered person. This may be contrasted with classroom climate that is teacher-dominated. The former may be thought of as a leader who relies more on indirect teacher influences; the latter on direct teacher influences.

Lindgren has illustrated the various types of teacher-student language interaction in the sequenced, four steps in figure 5.1.[1]

Free and open discussion provides each member of the group the opportunity to participate, to answer any other member of the group, and to perpetuate the discussion indefinitely without domination by the teacher. Figure 5.2 illustrates this.

---

[1]Henry Clay Lindgren, *Educational Psychology in the Classroom,* (New York: John Wiley and Sons, 1956), p. 266.

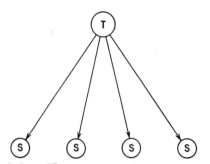

1. *Least Effective.* The teacher attempts to maintain one-way communication with individual students.

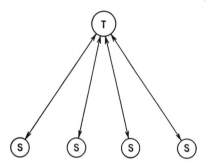

2. *More Effective.* The teacher tries to develop two-way communication with individual students.

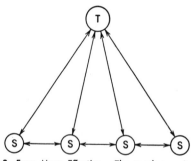

3. *Even More Effective.* The teacher maintains two-way communication with individual students and also permits some communication among students on a rather formal basis.

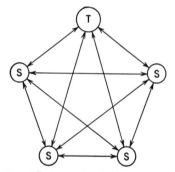

4. *Most Effective.* The teacher becomes a member of the group and permits two-way communication among all members of the group, including himself.

Figure 5.1. Various types of communicative relationships between teachers and students, in order of their effectiveness.

From Henry C. Lindgren. *Educational Psychology in the Classroom*, (New York; John Wiley and Sons, 1956), p. 266.

The kind of language communication within the group should be determined by the objectives to be met during a specific period of time. Certainly, there are a few periods of time when the teacher should be imparting needed information to the class with every member of the group giving the teacher his undivided attention. However, the statement sometimes made by junior high school teachers that they lecture to their classes for a forty-minute class period suggest that the teachers do not recognize the limitations of groups of boys and girls of that chronological age either to concentrate on an abstract academic lecture, or their ability to take adequate notes to have any record of the material covered. For the great majority of elementary and junior high students, "lecturing" by the teacher is a sheer waste of effort. Elementary teachers, too, have

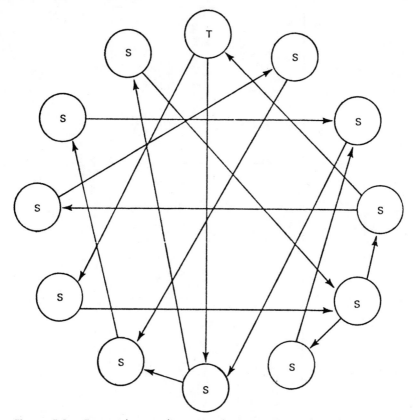

Figure 5.2. Free and open discussion does not permit domination by any one member of the group.

within their group, many who talk much too much. One sixth grade boy explained to his mother late in the fall that they knew how to handle their teacher who talked on and on. "When he just keeps talking, we just tune him out and go on thinking about something else."

In unit teaching, there is need in the beginning to arouse interest based on what everybody already knows and what everybody would like to learn. This requires free discussion. Then there is need for organized, fairly formal planning so that everyone can go to work efficiently to find information. Next, the unit plan requires sharing in committees, writing about information gained, discussing in small groups, and talking together quietly to crystallize thinking. Then, the entire group is ready to share, question, agree or disagree, and summarize. Finally they need some method to demonstrate that the original objectives for the unit of study have been met. These five steps in the development of a unit of work

I.	II.	III.	IV.	V.
Orientation to the unit of work	Teacher-pupil planning of assignments	Information gathering time	Information sharing time	Culmination
Problem identification.	Problem selection.	Planning and organizing.	Synthesis of ideas.	Evaluation.
Problem exploration.	Goal setting.	Coordinating and communicating.	End product.	Demonstration that objectives have been met.
Informal class interaction.	Teacher-directed discussion.	Committees, small groups, and some individuals doing research and writing activities.	Informal class interaction. Sharing information. Correcting some erroneous ideas. Summarizing. Selecting important ideas to remember.	Student performance: Making and explaining a mural; Preparing and performing a play; Giving a panel discussion; Performing a unit test.

Figure 5.3. The formal steps in the development of a unit of work suggesting different kinds of teacher-pupil interaction that would be the most significant in each of the steps.

with types of interaction of teacher and students, are presented graphically in Figure 5.3.

Simon and Sarkotich have suggested a list of nine skills that need to be strengthened if the teachers are to be more sensitive to individual student's verbal needs and are to be more cognizant of positive group interaction in the class. The list of skills is[2]

growing accustomed to being nonjudgmental with one another's ideas;
allowing the other person to have attitudes and feelings different from one's own;
growing in the skill of asking and answering questions—without being defensive;
to learn to listen for clues in responses;
to use neutral questions to expand the responses or to turn attention in new directions;
to learn how to report, diagnose, and evaluate classroom problems in group interaction;
to use open-ended questions: "How do you feel about this? Is there something else important?"
to learn that observation, participation and feedback have real meaning in problem-solving situations.
to learn to use "acceptance" and "silence" when useful in getting both participation and interaction.

The development of a sensitivity to children's needs with all the intellectual, physical, emotional and social differences which they bring to school, and a systematic way to analyze teacher behavior during the teaching act, may make it possible for teachers to study their personal behavior and teaching strategy to overcome weaknesses and emphasize strengths. Basically, this is the purpose of interaction analysis.

I. INTERACTION ANALYSIS

Classroom verbal interaction is a complex process and determines many important aspects of teacher-pupil interaction. Observers can categorize behaviors as arising in the affective domain or in the cognitive domain.

The affective domain includes the facets of the emotional climate: how the teacher reacts to feeling, ideas, work efforts, and pupil overt behavior.

The cognitive system deals with the thinking process. Different kinds of teacher information, teacher questions, pupil responses are differentiated.

The four dimensions of affective behavior are

1. teacher reaction to pupils' ideas or cognitive output;
2. teacher reactions to pupils' feelings or emotional output;

---

[2]Dan Simon and Diane Sarkotich, "Sensitivity Training in the Classroom," *NEA Journal*, 56:12-13, January, 1967.

3. teacher reactions to pupils' attempts to manage classroom procedure and set standards;
4. teacher reactions to pupils' nonverbal behaviors.

Affective behavior can be rated on a continuum from *accepting, praising, encouraging, neutrally accepting, ignoring,* to *rejecting.*

The first affective dimension is acceptance or rejection of pupil ideas; the second is acceptance or rejection of pupil feelings; the third includes classroom management and setting standards and work procedures; and the fourth is control over pupil behavior.

In the affective domain, Marie Hughes provided six categories for the analysis of teaching:[3]

1. Functions that control:
   a. structuring
   b. regulating
   c. informing
   d. setting standards
   e. judging
2. Functions that facilitate
   a. checking
   b. demonstrating
   c. clarifying
3. Functions that develop content by response
   a. serving as a resource person
   b. stimulating
   c. clarifying content
   d. evaluating
   e. turning questions back to the class
4. Functions that serve as personal response
   a. meeting requests
   b. clarifying problems
   c. interpreting
5. Functions of positive affectivity
6. Functions of negative affectivity

In the cognitive domain,

1. Cognitive dimensions
   a. data recall
   b. data processing
      enumerate, list, collect, read or report data
      group, classify, synthesize
      label, define
      analyze, compare, contrast
      infer, generalize, hypothesize
   c. evaluation
      no criteria specified
      private criteria specified
      public criteria specified
      pragmatic criteria specified

---

[3]Anita Simon and Gil Boyer, *Mirrors for Behavior,* (Philadelphia: Research for Better Schools, Inc., Temple University, 1968) pp. 4-5, System 10.

2. Categories of verbal behavior used to describe teacher and pupil talk about subject matter
    a. stating
    b. explaining
    c. quoting
    d. interpreting
    e. elaborating
    f. inferring
    g. opining
    h. etc.

The term "classroom climate" refers to generalized attitudes toward the teacher and the class that the pupils share in common despite individual differences. The development of these attitudes is an outgrowth of classroom social interaction. As a result of participating in classroom activities, pupils soon develop common attitudes about how they like their class, the kind of person the teacher is, and how he will act in certain typical situations. These common attitudes color all aspects of classroom behavior, creating a social atmosphere, or climate, that appears to be fairly stable, once established. Thus, the word "climate" is merely a shorthand reference to those qualities that consistently predominate in most teacher-pupil contacts and in contacts among the pupils in the presence or absence of the teacher.[4]

Interaction analysis can be used to study the spontaneous verbal communication of the teacher in a classroom. The purpose of such study is to analyze the role of the teacher in classroom management. One kind of teacher influence in classroom management is that which promotes integrative social forces through stimulating, clarifying, encouraging, and reflecting feelings and attitudes expressed by students either verbally or behaviorally. Another kind of teacher exercises those skills that control or manage the class much more in a superior-subordinate kind of relationship. This is expressed in the two categories below:[5]

The integrative pattern:
a. Accepts, clarifies, and supports the ideas and feelings of pupils.
b. Praises and encourages.
c. Asks questions to stimulate pupil participation in decision-making.
d. Asks questions to orient pupils to school work.

The Dominative pattern:
a. Expresses or lectures about own ideas or knowledge.
b. Gives directions or orders.
c. Criticizes or deprecates pupil-behavior with intent to change it.
d. Justifies own position or authority.

The classroom in the elementary school must become a learning laboratory where children can carry on a wide variety of learning activities

[4]Ned A. Flanders, "Teacher Influence, Pupil Attitudes, and Achievement," in James Raths, John R. Pancella, and James S. Van Ness, *Studying Teaching*, (Englewood Cliffs, New Jersey: Prentice-Hall, Inc., 1967), p. 44.
[5]Raths, Pancella, and Van Ness, *op. cit.*, p. 46.

simultaneously if teachers are going to take seriously the principle that great differences in intellectual, social, emotional, and physical maturity exist in every group. In a challenging learning laboratory, children can experiment with a wide variety of avenues to learning. A variety of equipment and materials and a well-stocked library must be provided if the classroom is to be a learning laboratory.

In a learning laboratory, there are jobs to do for which children see real purpose; jobs that will satisfy those who need immediate goals and those who can work toward long range goals; jobs that are easy and jobs that are difficult; jobs that can be performed by individuals and jobs that will be performed by groups. Planning time will be most crucial if the teacher is to feel sure that each child has definite goals in mind for his work period. Planning time needs to be an unhurried but structured period, in which questions are asked freely and arrangements are made to help those who will need either student or teacher help in finishing tasks.

The learning laboratory has another basic criterion: there are no minimum or maximum levels of performance set as a standard for any class group for any given year. Learning is an active, participating process; problem solving, creative thinking, memory work and drill are all engaged in—at all levels of difficulty from readiness (if indicated) to mature levels of reading, evaluating, reporting and discussing.

Operating this kind of classroom requires a maximum of group interaction, yet leaves the teacher free to work with small groups within the class during the greater part of the school day. In this kind of a classroom, a clear understanding of interaction analysis and how it works is very important.

Flander's system of interaction analysis provides a method for the teacher to study his own teaching behavior in terms of the behavioral objectives he has established for himself. His actual performance is fed back to him so that he has an opportunity to change his own behavior based on data about what he is doing in the classroom.

Classrooms are planned to help children continue to grow—this inherently implies helping them to change their behaviors. Change should be based on realistic information. If the teacher teaches a curriculum geared to memorizing facts, or controls behavior by keeping students afraid of being scolded, sent out of class, failed, or even expelled, or uses direct influence behaviors, clearly, a new approach is needed.

The Flanders system of interaction analysis involves learning ten categories that contain the verbal behaviors of the classroom. The observer judges the strategy of verbal behavior in the class. Pupils, content, teacher's objective, and length of time are evaluated to determine whether learning is taking place to accomplish the behavioral change anticipated in the lesson objective.

Teacher-pupil interaction can be changed by changing the climate of the classroom. Likewise, through improving the teacher's ability to ask meaningful questions, conduct in-depth discussions, and prepare better lectures, the classroom climate may be improved.

Verbal behaviors may be sub-divided as direct or indirect. Indirect influences include accepting feelings, praising or encouraging, accepting ideas, and asking questions. Direct influences include lecturing, giving directions, criticizing or justifying authority. Student talk in class is either initiating new conversation or responding to the teacher. See the summary of categories on the following page.

Direct influence—through lecturing, giving directions, criticizing, and justifying one's own use of authority—restricts freedom of action by focusing attention on the problem or on the teacher's authority.

Indirect influence—asking questions, accepting and clarifying ideas and feelings, and encouraging student responses—consists of the verbal statements of the teacher that expand a student's freedom of action by encouraging his verbal participation and initiative.

One might hypothesize that indirect teacher influence increases pupil learning when the student's perception of his objective is clear and acceptable.

Higher classroom behavior standards can be achieved by asking questions and then using student ideas, perceptions, and reactions to build toward greater student self-direction, responsibility, and understanding.[6]

Variability in teacher influence, flexibility, is associated with teachers whose students learned the most.[7]

If teaching behavior is to be changed, teachers must have opportunity to study their own teaching and evaluate what they did and why they did it. The teaching act itself must be brought into focus so it can be evaluated.

Systems for evaluating teacher behavior provide two dimensions for growth: (1) the teacher gets feedback on his own classroom interaction with students so he can "take stock" and look for new directions to move. (2) Also, the system of analysis presupposes some theoretical justification; the constructed system of analysis is designed so that teacher behavior that is in agreement with it will promote pupil growth in a positive direction. His present behavior is being compared to a standard which may provide specific new behaviors to be learned so that the use of the system may be giving developmental direction to the teacher.

The Flanders techniques, widely used in teacher-training situations, contains ten categories. The matrix technique provides a sequential ordering of data such that the behaviors are linked, and the reader can tell what preceded and what followed in teacher behavior.

---

[6]Raths, Pancella and Van Ness, *op. cit.*, p. 64.
[7]*Ibid.*

SUMMARY OF CATEGORIES FOR INTERACTION ANALYSIS[8]

TEACHER

TALK

INDIRECT

INFLUENCE

1. *Accepts feeling*: Accepts and clarifies the feeling tone of students in non-threatening manner. Negative or positive feelings; predicting and recalling feelings.

2. *Praises or encourages*: Praises or encourages student behavior. Accepts jokes that release tension, says "yes" or "Go on."

3. *Accepts or uses ideas of student*: Clarifies, builds, or accepts ideas given by students. (If teacher shifts to his own idea, shift to category five.)

4. *Asks questions*: Asking a question about content or procedure with intent that a student will answer.

DIRECT

INFLUENCE

5. *Lecture*: Lecturing about content of course; expressing personal ideas, asking rhetorical questions.

6. *Gives directions*: directions, commands, or assignments with which a student is expected to comply.

7. *Criticizes or justifies teacher authority*: Trying to change student behavior to an acceptable pattern; bawling someone out; rationalizing teacher's behavior.

STUDENT

TALK

8. *Student-talk: Response*: Talk by students in response to teacher. Teacher initiates contact and solicits response.

9. *Student-talk: Initiation*: Talk initiated by students. When called upon, if student "wanted to talk," use this category.

10. *Silence or confusion*: Pauses, short periods of silence. Periods of confusion which prevents understanding communication in the room.

---

[8]Flanders, N. A. *Teaching Influences, Pupil Attitudes, and Achievement,* Cooperative Research Monograph, No. 12, O. E.-25040 U. S. Dept. of Health, Education and Welfare, 1965.

A matrix is a table with the ten categories arranged in rows on the x-axis and in columns on the y-axis (page 110). The linking together of each two succeeding number ratings gives a "plotting" and as the total observation is plotted, the numbers make a pattern which can then be interpreted.

When the observer is observing the interaction in the classroom, he writes down a number every three seconds. After some practice, he finds himself able to record so that he writes about twenty numbers a minute. The numbers from one to ten are the categories of direct and indirect influence of the teacher and student talk.

10	If, as shown in the column to the left, the first recorded
6	numbers are 10, 6, 1, 3, 3, 4, 8, 8, 8, 7, 5, 5, 3, 3, 8, 8,
1	8, the linkages for plotting are 10-6, 6-1, 1-3, 3-3, 3-4, 4-8,
3	8-8, 8-8, 8-7, 7-5, 5-5, 5-3, 3-3, 3-8, 8-8, 8-8. These are
3	plotted below.
4	
8	
8	
8	
7	
5	
3	
8	
8	
8	

If 400 tallies are plotted for a twenty minute observation, one can quickly determine how many of the numbers are in the 1 through 7 categories of teacher talk, how many in 8 and 9 categories of student talk. For example, if 260 tallies are columns one through seven, teacher talk, this shows that 65 percent of the numbers represent teacher talk. If 120 tallies are in columns 8 and 9, then 30 percent of the numbers represent student talk.

A matrix should have at least 400 tallies, a minimum of twenty minutes of observation, before attempting to interpret teacher and student behavior.

The matrix may be divided into many areas that describe for the observer kinds of teacher influence. The following list represents visually specific areas differentiating types of teacher response.

AREAS DIFFERENTIATING TYPES OF TEACHER RESPONSE

Area A: Indirect teacher talk.
Area B: Direct teacher talk.
Area C: Student talk.

Columns

Rows	1	2	3	4	5	6	7	8	9	10
1										
2										
3													
4										
5										
6										
7										
8														
9										
10										

A worksheet for plotting classroom interaction.

Area D: Silence or confusion.

Area E: Acceptance of feelings, offering praise, using student ideas.

Area F: Giving criticism or offering self-justification. May suggest problems in classroom discipline or resistance on the part of the students.

Area G: Teacher responding to termination of student talk with indirect influence.

Area H: Teacher responding to termination of student talk with direct influence.

Area I: Pictures the types of teacher's statements that stimulate student participation. High tallies in 8-4; 4-8 cells, indicate question-answer emphasis by teacher.

Area J: Area J indicated (1) lengthy student responses or (2) student-to-student conversation. (See the following page.)

High frequencies in Area C, but not in Area J, indicate that short answers, usually in response to teacher stimulation, have occurred. One would normally expect to find high frequencies in Area C closely related to high frequencies in Area J.

There is no single standard of what is "best in assessing interaction." The "best" lesson is the one that fits the objectives of a particular lesson.

TABLE 5.1. Areas of Matrix Analysis[9]

Category	Classification	Category	1	2	3	4	5	6	7	8	9	10	Total
ACCEPTS FEELINGS	Indirect Influence	1		Area E							Area I			
PRAISE	Indirect Influence	2												
STUDENT IDEA	Indirect Influence	3												
ASKS QUESTIONS		4					Area F							
LECTURES	Direct Influence	5												
GIVES DIRECTIONS	Direct Influence	6												
CRITICISM	Direct Influence	7												
STUDENT RESPONSE	Student Talk	8		Area G			Area H				Area J			
STUDENT INITIATION	Student Talk	9												
SILENCE		10												
Total			Area A			Area B			Area C			Area D		
			Indirect teacher Talk			Direct teacher Talk			Student Talk			Silence		

An Interaction Matrix:

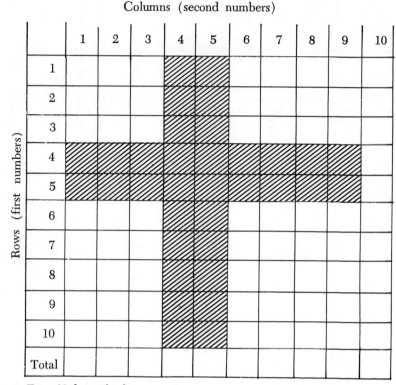

From Ned A. Flanders, *op. cit.*

Figure 5.4.   The Content Cross. The numbers 4 and 5 represent teacher talk consisting primarily of lecture; statements of personal opinion, ideas and information; and teacher originated questions about textbook content that has been presented.

Can it best be taught with a high per cent of teacher talk; or would it be better taught with a low per cent of teacher talk?

II.   SUMMARY

After the behaviors have been plotted and the area of concentration is evident, one can determine a predominance of teacher talk, indirect teacher influence, direct teacher influence, student talk in response to teacher questions, or student talk in which students are discussing points with each other. The only person who can really decide whether the plotted behavior is desirable or undesirable is the teacher himself, interpreting the behavior in terms of the purpose which he had set for himself in planning the lesson.

An Interaction Matrix:

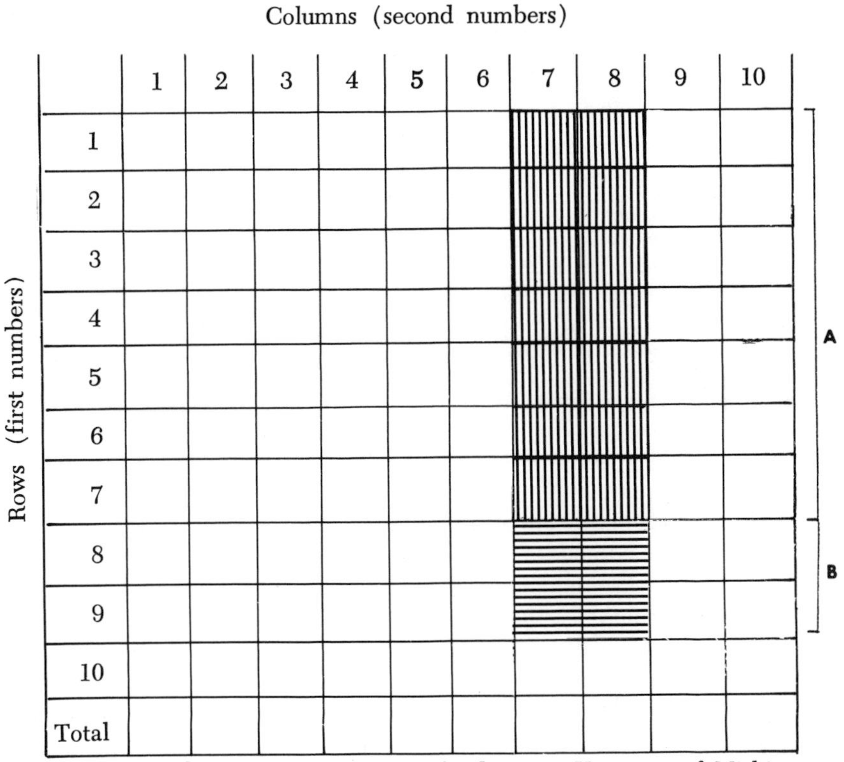
Columns (second numbers)
1
2
3
4
5
6
7
8
9
10
Rows (first numbers)
1
2
3
4
5
6
7
8
9
10
Total
A
B

From Dr. Ned A. Flanders, Professor of Education, University of Michigan, Ann Arbor, Michigan. *Op. cit.*

Figure 5.5. Student Talk Following Teacher Talk. Area A, Rows 1-7, indicate the teacher's statements tend to stimulate student talk. This suggests students are getting involved in classroom interaction. Area B, Rows 8-9, represent student talk which may be prolonged discourse by one student or conversation sustained by several students.

However, average percentages from recording many teachers' behaviors are available to reflect current practices in classrooms. Current pactice may not be the best or the practice desired in a specific instance.

Category 1—average: Direct teacher .1 of one percent; indirect teachers .5 of one percent.
Category 2—average: Both direct and indirect teachers, 2%.
Category 3—average: Direct teachers, 2%; indirect, 9%.
Category 4—average: Direct teachers, 8%, indirect, 11%.
Category 5—average: Both direct and indirect teachers, 25–50%.
Category 6—average: Direct teachers, 8%; indirect, 4%.
Category 7—average: Direct teachers, 5%; indirect, less than 1%.

Category 8—average: Direct teachers have most in 4-8 cell; indirect
                      teachers have most in 8-8 cell.
Category 9—average: Much greater use made by indirect teacher.
Category 10—average: More heavily loaded for the direct teacher.*

Gathering and interpreting verbal interaction data in the classroom
can provide very useful feedback for teachers who wish to improve
teaching performance.

> This instrument for measuring classroom interaction is not a finished
> product. However, one can see the possibilities of using the model to
> obtain quantitative measures of classroom interaction, including differ-
> ences among teachers. Interestingly, this system could be used as a
> basis for determining merit pay, inasmuch as Amidon and Flanders
> suggest that teachers of greater flexibility made the better pedagogues;
> that is, teachers equally at ease using indirect teacher influence, in
> addition to the usual direct teacher influence, were considered more
> effective. Some minor modifications of the Flanders' system have been
> recommended in connection with studying interaction in team-teaching
> classrooms.[10]

If the classroom teacher is going to be able to plan the kind of reading program recommended in Chapter 4, he must be able to exercise
effective control and management of the room with many children working independently while the teacher works either with small sub-groups
or with individual members of the class. For example, if the teacher is
to teach a directed reading lesson to one-third of the group for about
twenty minutes without interruptions from the majority of the class doing
independent seatwork, criteria for establishing group behavior will be
useful. Criteria that are recognized as generally accepted conventions
in behavior can be exercised without the individual feeling any personal
concern about being unfairly discriminated against. When there is a rule
that no more than three people can be at the reading table choosing a
book at one time, the teacher can say to Jack as he approaches the book
table, "There are already three people choosing now, Jack, you must
wait your turn." This will not have the same connotation as "Go to your
seat, Jack, you don't belong at the book table now."

The teacher can accomplish his own objectives for the reading program only if he can assess both cognitive and affective processes. In the
affective domain, children must express interest and satisfaction in reading; children must reveal values concerning what they read, how they
select and care for books, and what they read at home; and children show

---

[10]Herbert J. Klausmeier and William Goodwin (New York: Harper & Row,
Publishers, Second Edition, 1966), p. 172.
    *Edmund Amidon and Ned Flanders, "Interaction Analysis As a Feedback
System," in Edmund Amidon and John Hough, editors, *Interaction Analysis: Theory,
Research and Application,* (Reading, Massachusetts: Addison Wesley Pub. Co.,
1967), pp. 137-139.

their organizational level of developing values, attitudes and tastes through teacher-pupil conferences and class discussions.

The interaction of teacher and the entire class determines the extent to which the teacher can plan individualized conferences during the school day.

It is the aim of the teacher to change the response pattern of the students from mere compliance to independent action. A student who cannot recognize his own learning problem is much more dependent upon the teacher and enlists more help and direction from the teacher but the student who is hard at work on a problem in which he is interested, concentrates on its solution and frees the teacher for other tasks. Matching reading interests with appropriate books meets the teacher's classroom management problem at the same time that it meets the student's need. When the student satisfies a reading interest, he is constructively occupied in the classroom, and the teacher is free to work with the problems of others.

The ultimate objective of the teacher in the use of interaction analysis is that he will be able to *predict* the kind of verbal behavior he wishes to achieve. Then, by analyzing his own performance, he will be able to find out if he did what he predicted he would do. That is to say, the teacher can carefully consider what he thinks his verbal behavior should be in a given teaching situation; then he can use a tape recorder and record a sample of his teaching behavior for at least twenty minutes in that type of situation. He analyzes his own behavior by replaying the tape and tallying the verbal activity at three second intervals. This provides the evidence about whether he was able to predict the kind of behavior which he did, in fact, produce. Thus, it is clear that, while the use of interaction analysis technique has much value as an assessment of teachers' behaviors, it can have a greater ultimate value to the teacher in developing his ability to judge the kind of behavior that is most useful or effective, and then achieving the behavior he predicts for himself.

Suggested Activities

1. Study the ten categories for interaction analysis, then observe a teacher who is teaching for four five-minute periods, marking a category every *three* seconds (twenty numbers are to be recorded each minute). Tabulate the twenty-minute observation (400 numbers) and plot the teacher's verbal behavior on the Matrix.

2. Ask another teacher to observe your teaching for four five-minute periods. Then plot your own verbal behavior on the Matrix.

3. Tape record your teaching in several subjects and analyze the results using the Flanders system.

REFERENCES FOR FURTHER READING

EDMUND J. AMIDON and NED A. FLANDERS, *The Role of the Teacher in the Classroom* (1040 Plymouth Bldg., Minneapolis 55402: Association for Productive Teaching, Inc., 1967).

EDMUND J. AMIDON and JOHN B. HOUGH, *Interaction Analysis: Theory, Research, and Application* (Reading, Massachusetts: Addison Wesley Publishing Co., 1967).

EDMUND J. AMIDON and ELIZABETH HUNTER, *Improving Teaching: Analyzing Verbal Interaction in the Classroom* (New York: Holt, Rinehart and Winston, 1966).

MILDRED S. FENNER, "Editor's Notebook," *NEA Journal*, 57: 14-18, April, 1968.

NED A. FLANDERS, "Intent, Action and Feedback, A Preparation for Teaching," *Journal of Teacher Education*, 14: 251-260, 1963, reprinted in Amidon and Hough, *Interaction Analysis: Theory, Research, and Application* (Reading, Mass.: Addison Wesley Publishing Co., 1967), pp. 283-294.

NORMA FURST and MARCIENE S. MATTLEMAN, "Classroom Climate," *NEA Journal*, 57: 22-24, April 1968.

MARIE HUGHES, *Helping Students Understand Teaching* (Salt Lake City: University of Utah, 1959).

ANITA SIMON and E. GIL BOYER, *Mirrors for Behavior: An Anthology of Classroom Observation Instruments* (Philadelphia, Pennsylvania: Research for Better Schools, Inc., 1968).

DAN SIMON and DIANE SARKOTICH, "Sensitivity Training in the Classroom," *NEA Journal*, 56: 12-13, January, 1967.

HILDA TABA, *Thinking in Elementary School Children* (San Francisco: San Francisco State College, 1964).

6

Parent-Teacher Cooperation

The title of this chapter, by design, is meant to emphasize the working together aspects of a cooperative venture. Rather than suggesting "working *with* parents" or "counseling parents," teachers should recognize that parents have both information and concerns that can be most helpful in careful planning for a child.

As the school has come to take a more and more important place in the education of children, the parents' roles have become, perhaps, less well defined. Sometimes parents are criticized by teachers and, at times, teachers are criticized by parents. Stereotyped and prejudiced attitudes can develop on both sides. Sometimes parents are indifferent to school; sometimes they misunderstand the policies of the school.

The following episode reveals the need for teachers to exercise caution in carrying out their responsibility when having parent conferences about the academic progress of their children.

> One teacher recently said to half a dozen parents in her classroom prior to the regular PTA meeting, when someone asked about the school testing program, "Oh, our testing program. We've been giving some I.Q. tests." Then after a slightly embarrassed laugh, she continued, "But none of you folks have anything to worry about."

This seems like a very feeble explanation for parents. She might have been more constructive by saying:

> The tests are being given to obtain more information about the children's general abilities and to help us in future planning both *for* and *with* the children.

Hunt[1] has written facetiously about one teacher's appraisal of a boy's class work. He is raising the question about how meaningful the teacher's

---

[1]Herald C. Hunt, Professor of School Administration, Harvard University.

language is and how much the parents understand of what the teacher says if she tries to confer in educational jargon:

> He's adjusting well to his peer group and achieving to expectancy in skill subjects. But I'm afraid his growth in content subjects is blocked by reluctance to get on with his developmental tasks.

It has been suggested that there is an imperative fourth "R" to be added to *Readin', 'Ritin', and 'Rithmetic.* It is *Relationships,* focusing on a clearer relationship between teacher and child, teacher and parent, and the child's school life.

The conflicts pointed out by Redl and Wattenberg[2] are very real conflicts—parents who fear trouble for their children in school are apt to be the parents who feared trouble for themselves when they were children in school—and teachers who hope to maintain "safe" distances between themselves and parents may remember unpleasant experiences from their past in dealing with adults. Many teachers and principals have, in the past, harbored the prejudice that parents who come to the school are in trouble, apt to expose trouble, or predisposed to make trouble.

Merrill suggests:[3]

> Some of the negative undercurrents in parent-teacher relationships come from feelings most of us have about authority. We normally respond to those in authority in various ways, mixing hostility and submissiveness, the anxiety to please, awe, respect, and perhaps fear. . . . Parents and teachers tend to see each other as authority figures. . . . Many teachers and parents feel ambivalent about being cast in an authority role. They enjoy the prestige but do not wish to cope with negative feelings directed toward those in authority.

Insights into these ways of feeling may be helpful in accepting and dealing with them.

While these comments may seem negative to the beginning teacher, they reflect situations as they exist in some schools. However, parents are more and more finding their ways into the classrooms and offering their services in constructive ways to further the educational experiences of their children. They want cooperative sharing and planning to best structure the total environment of their children.

I. SCHOOL-HOME COOPERATION

Schools need to join forces with parents in order to: (1) extend the parents' knowledge of growth and development of children. Some parents need to learn that children are not miniature adults, but that their

---

[2]Fritz Redl and William W. Wattenberg, *Mental Hygiene in Teaching,* second edition, (New York: Harcourt, Brace and World, 1959), Chapter 17, "Working with Parents," pp. 452-476.

[3]Barbara W. Merrill, "Under the Surface of Parent-Teacher Relationships," *The Instructor,* 75: 35, No. 3, November, 1965.

total growth process starts at birth (it began long before birth but perhaps for the teacher's purposes this will be an adequate place to start). Growing is a continuous process during all the waking hours of the child, wherever he is. Being ready for school requires that from infancy he be taught the meaning of things in his environment, taught what his environment is, and taught how to use his environment. Language—not words, but cognitive growth of concepts—is of first importance in the pre-school years. (2) extend the parents' knowledge of availability of services of many community agencies which serve families, adults, or children. This includes making parents aware of their need for services which they have sometimes felt other people needed but they did not. It may also include such services as encouraging children to have library cards in the community library, visits to the city museum, or subscribing to, and reading, the P.T.A. magazine. (3) cement mutual understanding and acceptance of teachers and parents. When teachers and parents meet and talk, the face-to-face acquaintance permits building the kind of partnership that works for positive results. Negative reactions and feelings are more apt to be engendered when teachers say, "I sent a note asking the mother to come in but she never did." or when mothers say, " I couldn't write her a note; I couldn't spell the words."

Teachers could "make use of" many parents of the children in their rooms. Some father could help the third grade boys make bird houses easier than the teacher could; some mothers could teach sixth grade girls how to knit; many mothers would be glad to drive a car load of children to the airport, to the museum, or to the public library.

When parents have opportunities to meet and talk with other parents, they often find that they have many common interests and aspirations for their children.

It is much better to establish friendly relations on a face-to-face basis early in the year so that parent and teacher feel they know each other *before* there is any need to meet to thresh out a difficult problem that neither adult understands and for which each might like to blame the other.

Because written reports and report cards are, at best, limited in helping parents understand their child's progress in school, parents should have an opportunity to talk directly with the child's teacher about his academic progress. Recommendation No. 30 of the Harvard Report on Reading in Elementary Schools, was

> . . . that, in reporting school progress, parent-teacher conferences should be obligatory in conjunction with written reports.[4]

---

[4] Mary C. Austin and Coleman Morrison, *The First R, the Harvard Report on Reading in Elementary Schools* (New York: The Macmillan Company, 1963), p. 234.

Recommendation No. 31 was

. . . that school systems make concerted efforts to keep the public apprized of the system's reading policies and procedures, and to inform parents through newsletters, discussion groups, and informal conferences of their unique role in developing reading competency and interest.[5]

II. PARENT-TEACHER CONFERENCES

There are a few important points for the teacher to have in mind when the conference with a parent or both parents is to be held. It is hoped that the conference will begin and end on a pleasant and constructive note and that it will be held in a comfortable place that makes constructive conversation feasible. Both parent and teacher must feel at ease in the conversation and the teacher must be a good listener. The teacher must keep himself alert to comments that may have hidden meanings, "other" meanings than the specific references the parents intend in an anecdote being related. The teacher must be able to ask appropriate questions, make tactful answers, and extend the parent's conversation, or just listen. He should be constructive if the parent asks direct questions; although he should be careful to convey to the parent that in the area of serious learning problems, he, too, may need help from specialists. The teacher should follow-up constructively on questions, information, or further testing, referrals, or any other result of the conference.[6]

The following are a few general suggestions that may be helpful in planning initial contacts with parents or in working out informal ways of keeping them involved in the school program of their child.

1. Plan an opportunity to meet the parents of the children in your room as early in the school year as is convenient. Explain in general terms to the parents in a total group about the work for the year. Emphasize the extent of individual differences and the increasing range of achievement within a class as boys and girls progress through the school.

2. Invite parents to bring personal questions individually to be discussed in more private conferences. If personal kinds of questions are raised in group discussions, the teacher should make a constructive statement but arrange for an individual conference later to discuss a specific problem. Sending short informal notes home with the child whenever there is an occasion—to report a good performance some day, to offer encouragement, or to suggest a way for mother to help with a special assignment—will help to keep channels of communication open.

3. Encourage parents to visit the classroom to observe the children at work. Do not permit parents to carry on a conversation with you about the children in front of them. But, do plan to meet the parent in a suit-

[5]*Ibid.*, p. 234.
[6]Nila B. Smith, *Reading Instruction for Today's Children*, (Englewood Cliffs, New Jersey: Prentice-Hall, Inc., 1963), pp. 513-514.

able conference-environment after the observation so he will have sufficient time for questions and discussion.

4. Discuss freely with the parent the meaningful records that the school has in the child's cumulative folder. If the child is reading below grade level in reading, for example, make sure that parents understand that in unselected groups, the class average, or median, represents that level below which half of the class achieves. A sample performance on the informal reading inventory would provide a concrete illustration of how well the child reads context and what kinds of errors he makes. When parents ask about intelligence tests, teachers must understand their limitations. Group intelligence tests are dependent upon reading ability and sample a child's performance for only a short period of time in a special situation. At best it can only predict whether a child is a rapid learner, above average, average, below average, or a possible slow learner. Neither the teacher nor the parent should accept a group test result as a diagnosis of the limit of intellectual ability of a child. An individual intelligence test provides a much more reliable estimate of one's general learning ability. Parents are entitled to the best information the school can provide if they are to plan realistically for the future education of their children.

5. Encourage parents to give their children enriching kinds of learning experiences that are available to them. Studying the TV guides to seek out the worthwhile educational programs will improve the quality of the viewing of many school children. Traveling with parents and learning about places first hand will make reading about them later more meaningful. A library card at the local public library can be an enriching opportunity for any child.

A few other specific suggestions that teachers may recommend to parents are

1. Be sure your child is in an optimum state of physical health. See that he gets adequate sleep and rest, and adequate attention to hearing, vision, and neurological problems or symptoms.

2. Be sure the child feels secure and confident in his home and school environment.

3. Provide the child a reading environment and a positive attitude toward reading at home. This means a place to study, and evidence that adults in his home also read. Parents should read aloud to their children; and children should be encouraged to read aloud to their parents. Children will likely favor this if they are successful. Encourage parents to always tell children unknown words when they are reading. If the child misses too many, the material is too difficult and he should seek out easier stories to read.

4. Encourage the child to purchase paperbacks in book clubs and exchange them with others to provide wider reading.

There are also ways in which parents should *not* help. The emotional involvement of being the parent of a child who has problems in learning how to read often causes the parent to be anxious or frustrated himself. In such a situation, he may overtly express the idea that the child is stupid or convey it in ways other than language. These are a few behaviors parents must *not* exercise

1. Parents should not compare the child with siblings who are more successful in school.
2. Parents should not punish the child for making poor marks in school.
3. Parents should try to avoid losing their patience, raising their voices, or otherwise causing the child anxiety.
4. Parents should not try to teach phonic elements, new words, or other reading skills without fairly clear instructions from the teacher as to suitable methods.
5. Parents should not try to work with the child when he is upset, anxious, or feeling pressured about school.

Teachers Should Be Able to Explain Why They Teach as They Do

One of the needs of parents, both individually or in groups, is for teachers to explain the rationale for much of what they do. With respect to the reading program, Heilman[7] suggests that teachers should be able to explain

1. Why words are taught as whole units before children are asked to deal with letter components.
2. Why consonant sounds are taught before vowels.
3. Why memorizing phonics rules is often less valuable than having children deduce generalizations from words they already know.
4. Why too much emphasis on phonics in beginning reading interferes with seeing reading as a meaning-getting process.
5. Why the "controlled vocabulary" of basal series is not any more insipid than the vocabulary taught in any "phonetic method."
6. Why readiness instruction is not an educational waste, and that there are sound logical objectives in a readiness program.

The key word in these six suggestions is the word "why." Teachers need to be able to explain why they are doing what they do. If the parents could hear sound explanations that convinced them that teachers do know something about the nature of the reading process and the nature of the individual child who is learning the process, they would be more accepting of the program the school is offering.

Round and Hawkins state that collecting information about children with data processing and computer techniques is now big business. Then

---

[7]Arthur Heilman, "Theoretical Design for Teaching Reading," *Challenge and Experiment in Reading, J. Allen Figurel,* Editor, International Reading Association Conference Proceedings, 1962, Volume 7, p. 244.

they raise some concerns about the use of the information after intelligence tests and achievement tests have been administered. They ask, "Who should know that John's intelligence quotient is 98, or that Susan has a percentile score of 80 on the Stanford Achievement Battery?" Intelligence test scores have created considerable misunderstanding in the past. Not only parents and students, but also teachers and principals have looked upon intelligence test scores as fixed entities rather than useful general information that may be helpful in guidance and future planning.

School personnel would do well to use, wherever possible, the percentile score as the most informative method of explaining student performance to parents. To do this, teachers must emphasize repeatedly that the percentile refers to the per cent of the students whose performance a given pupil has equaled or surpassed, and that it is *not* the per cent of questions answered correctly.[8]

III. PARENTS AS AUXILIARY TEACHERS

Wilson and Pfau have suggested that since there are so many more children with reading problems than there are clinicians to help them, that perhaps teachers should take another look at ways parents might be able to help.

They suggest:[9]

1. There are types of instruction in remedial reading that are reinforcing practice, and these might be done by parents if they were helped to distinguish these from other types of instruction to be done only by teachers. Such things as mother helping seven-year-old Billy list all the things in the kitchen that start with "p" or "c", or playing *Go-Fish* or *Vowel Domino* are examples.

2. The teacher must teach the parent how to do correctly the activity he is to enjoy with the child. If the parent is going to listen to the child read, he must be a good listener, give his undivided attention, and be interested in discussing the story after it is read. He should tell the child the word he doesn't know, not make him "sound it out."

3. Parent should have a chance to try the activity, if a game, to play it with the clinician and child; if an exercise in the workbook, to ask the clinician any question that may arise.

4. Let the parent decide whether he can establish a good working relationship with his own child. If frustration mounts or the parent is too emotionally involved—still too concerned about possible mental re-

---

[8]Rounds, Haskins R., and Michael L. Hawkins, "How Much Should You Tell Parents?" *The Instructor,* 78: 55, 77, August-September, 1968.

[9]Robert M. Wilson and Donald W. Pfau, "Parents Can Help," *The Reading Teacher,* 21: 758-761, May, 1968.

tardation—still burdened with some guilt about the child's failure—then he should understand that it is better to discontinue parent help.

IV. REPORTS FROM TEACHERS OF HOME-SCHOOL COOPERATION

Parents can be a most valuable resource, collectively, for all the teachers in a building. One elementary school made a brief survey of the special skills, abilities, travel experiences, hobbies, and other interests which the parents in the district possesed. A surprising number of parents had traveled to Europe and returned with boxes of excellent colored slides which they were happy to show and talk about to the class; others had traveled many other interesting places and returned with artifacts, costumes, furniture, books, pictures, and musical instruments of endless variety. One man was a glassblower; one could demonstrate and teach elementary judo; several women could knit, crochet, tat, weave, braid, do textile painting, and one had learned flower-arranging skills in Japan. The more parents come to the school so that they actually see the school program in operation and participate in some activity, the more apt the total community is to think the school does the best it can under the circumstances.

> In helping children to succeed in school, parents and teachers play similar roles. Both need to offer the child a warm, supportive climate; opportunities for success; a variety of experiences; and above all, a chance to become actively involved in his own learning.[10]
>
> Much of Froebel's work was intended to cause mothers to take a positive part in their children's planned education. His *Mother's Songs, Games and Stories,* was meant to help the mother to train her child through play. Each rhyme had a definite educational purpose: for example, some were concerned with the infant's physical education ("Come! You little kicking toes!"), others with moral training ("It's all gone, Baby, all!"—intended to teach contentment), others again with the child's affection for the mother or with religious upbringing. An explanatory verse for the mother and additional notes, setting forth Froebel's educational intention, accompany each set of rhymes.[11]

In a community with a wide range of cultural systems, a somewhat transient population, disparity in family incomes, and a widespread lack of interest in school, a staff of teachers found by identifying basic behavior problems that inconsistency in rules and expectations within the school staff as well as inconsistency between home and school created many of the problems.

---

[10]Glennys G. Unruh, "Parents Can Help Their Children Succeed in School," *NEA Journal,* 55:14-16, December, 1966.

[11]H. H. Stern, *Parent Education, An International Survey,* (173 Cottingham Road, Hull, England: Institute of Education, University of Hull, 1960), p. 12, citing F. Froebel, *Mutter-und Koselieder,* 1843, translated by Frances and Emily Lord, *Mother's Songs, Games and Stories,* London, 1885).

The student council in the school, a committee of parents chosen to represent all socio-economic areas of the district, and a teacher committee worked out ways of working on the problem:

1. Teachers and children should work together to establish realistic goals and standards;
2. Conflict areas should be analyzed for causes and reasons;
3. Role-playing procedures should be used to analyze discipline and behavior problems;
4. School behavior units should be developed at each grade level;
5. Pupil interests and special abilities should be utilized;
6. Children, teachers, and parents need to understand all discipline regulations;
7. A conference and home visitation program should be developed;
8. Existing teaching methods and the curriculum should be evaluated.

When report cards were distributed through parent-teacher conferences, 96 percent of the parents responded to the invitation for such a conference. Observable changes in attitudes and behaviors were evident in not only the boys and girls, but also in both teachers and parents![12]

To provide for a personal communication with parents of her fifth grade class, Miss Hamblet provided each child a folder in which day-to-day exercises, homework exercises, study sheets, tests, quizzes, are filed throughout the month. At the end of each month, each child writes his parents a letter describing interesting happenings at school, the program in physical education, music, art, and other special subjects, as well as explaining the papers in the folders. The teacher also includes a note to the parents in the folder.[13]

Miss Hamblet feels that this effort, which is time consuming for her, pays big dividends in promoting the desirable team effort of parent-child-teacher in encouraging child growth in academic skills. Typical parent comments returned to the school reinforce the teacher's evaluation:[14]

> About all we can say for the spelling is that it's original. At least 'Duey Desmal Sistom' surpasses them all!
>
> I was disappointed that he hadn't shown much improvement over last month.
>
> For the first time since my son started school, I finally know what is going on.

---

[12]Jack L. Roach, "We Found Better Ways to Improve Pupil Behavior," *The Instructor*, 76: 29, February, 1967.

[13]Martha J. Hamblet, "Keeping in Touch with Parents," *The Instructor*, 77: 34, January, 1968.

[14]*Ibid.*, p. 34.

Just before report cards were due, one primary teacher invited parents to come to school to observe their children throughout one complete day. She gave those who came a list of things to look for:[15]

How well does he seem to know what to do?
Does he work steadily at a given task?
What distracts him?
What response does he make to his teachers?
What troubles does he have and how does he solve them?
Who does he play with?
Does he seem to have special friends?
Does he play alone or with older children?
Is his work the best he's capable of?
Are you satisfied with his progress?

Such visitations were sufficiently encouraging to cause the teacher to plan for other all day visits before succeeding report card days.

One school has a parents' waiting room with comfortable arm chairs, tables, exhibits of children's work, announcements, and magazines for parents. In one nursery school, mothers are encouraged to visit with the child and both stay only a short time during the first visits. In some schools, parents are encouraged to visit often in their child's classroom. They see their own child in contact with and in comparison with other children. The teacher helps them increase their perceptions of their child.[16]

In some schools, parents are often called on to give minor assistance, helping to make or repair something, taking school excursions, teaching skills the teacher lacks. One school arranged parent-teacher conferences during the school day and asked mothers to come to school to monitor classroom activities while the teacher conferred with other parents.

The child should not be lost sight of in the consideration of parent-teacher conferences. There are needs too for three-way conferences: child-parent-teacher. Teachers are occasionally able to enjoy such a conference with both parents and their child when they are invited into the home either during dinner or visiting in the living room when the child feels free to participate in the conversation. Many of the conferences with parents about boys and girls in the intermediate grades might be more profitable if the student, parents, and teacher all met together.

Economic changes in family life have transferred much of the traditional work of the home to outside agencies. Industrial technology has not only decreased the tasks of running the household and providing the food for the family, but also permitted millions of mothers to work outside the home. In this kind of a home, children have become an economic

15Magdalen Eichert, "Parents Come to School," *The Instructor,* 75: 50, No. 2, October, 1965.

16H. H. Stern, *Parent Education, An International Survey,* (173 Cottingham Road, Hull, England: Institute for Education, University of Hull, 1960), p. 41.

burden where once they were an economic asset. Child labor laws, compulsory education, and social and humanitarian motives of society have "freed" the child from accepting "work" responsibilities—but may also have created some anxieties for children about loss of independence, concern about personal security in the family, and many other problems.

V. SUMMARY

Parents are doing their part when they make sure that their child:
is in optimum state of physical health;
feels secure and confident in his family circle;
lives in a reading environment;
has a rich background of first-hand experiences;
gets undivided attention when he reads aloud to either parent.
Parents must be counseled by teachers to modify their behavior toward their child if they

1. take a punitive attitude toward the child who fails;
2. think he's lazy or unwilling to try;
3. force him to study when it is playtime;
4. nag, scold, or punish because he fails;
5. compare him with family siblings;
6. feel guilty and defensive about the child's lack of success.
   In conducting a teacher-parent conference, the teacher should
1. try to meet the parents early in the school year to get acquainted;
2. put them at ease during each conference;
3. assure them of his concern for their child;
4. open the conference by giving the parent the opportunity to talk first;
5. give an honest evaluation of the child's reading status:
   a. does he know basic sight words?
   b. does he know phonics and structural analysis?
   c. does he know how to write and spell (in manuscript or cursive) and at what level?
6. discuss with parents anecdotal records you have kept;
7. assure the parents that it takes a long time to learn how to read;
8. if other services, either in the school or privately, are indicated, discuss these candidly with the parent (psychological, medical, speech and hearing, remedial reading or other).

Suggested Activities

1. In your acquaintance find a mother of an elementary school age child whom you can interview briefly to find out the extent to which she feels the school is meeting the educational needs of her child. Make

a brief check list including his reading ability, study habits, interaction in play and games, and general satisfaction with school. Try to obtain some information related to all these areas.

2. If you have a student teaching assignment, or if you have any current assignment where you work directly with children, try to arrange an interview with one of the mothers to discuss her child's status in your group.

3. If you are working in an elementary school, try to arrange with your principal to sit as an observer when parents are in his office to discuss some academic or disciplinary problem of their child.

4. How can teachers best prepare themselves to meet the possible conflicts in parent-teacher relationships discussed by Redl and Wattenberg and Merrill in this chapter?

References for Further Reading

Mary C. Austin, "Report Cards and Parents," *The Reading Teacher*, 18: 660-663, May, 1965.

Althea Berry, "Schools Report to Parents," *The Reading Teacher*, 18: 639-644, May, 1965.

G. M. Della-Piana, R. F. Stahmann, and J. E. Allen, "Parents and Reading Achievement: Review of Research," *Elementary English*, 1968.

Nila Banton Smith, "Parents Are People," *The Reading Teacher*, 18: 624-628, May, 1965.

Nila B. Smith, *Reading Instruction for Today's Children* (Englewood Cliffs, New Jersey: Prentice-Hall, Inc., 1963).

Glennys G. Unruh, "Parents Can Help Their Children Succeed in School," *NEA Journal*, 55: 14-16, December, 1966.

Robert Wilson and Donald W. Pfau, "Parents Can Help," *The Reading Teacher*, 21: 758-761, May, 1968.

Miles V. Zintz, *Corrective Reading* (Dubuque, Iowa: William C. Brown Co., 1966), Chapter 8: "Working Cooperatively with Parents," pp. 198-211.

PART II

The Skills of Reading

Part II contains the chapters that discuss the various developmental skills necessary in order for children to become independent readers. It begins with teaching word-identification skills, comprehension skills, and the study skills. These three chapters give the teacher guidelines for developing in reading groups: (1) a stock of sight words; (2) phonetic and structural analysis skills; (3) comprehension of the ideas contained in material read; and (4) the provision of a great deal of easy reading material.

Learning to exercise critical judgment while reading, using oral reading judiciously, and cultivating permanent habits of reading are essential aspects of a developmental reading program.

7

Word Recognition Skills

I. METHODS OF TEACHING WORD IDENTIFICATION

Growth in the ability to recognize words in print is the most basic skill in learning how to read. None of the other necessary abilities can develop until the child has a stock of words in his reading vocabulary to read with.

In beginning reading the child needs to know the meaning of the word when he pronounces it if he is to grasp the principle of demanding meaning from whatever he reads. This presupposes an adequate listening and speaking vocabulary so that all the concepts he tries to read will be understood.

The typical middle-class first grade child comes to school with a relatively large vocabulary in terms of number of words known. Actually the child has not one but several vocabularies. At age six, his *listening* vocabulary is likely the largest, since he has understanding of many words spoken to him in context that he would not use in his own *speaking* vocabulary. Typically his *reading* vocabulary will be limited to a very few words if it exists at all. And most six year olds do not have a *writing* vocabulary. It has been estimated that a typical middle-class six-year-old child may have as many as 8,000 to 10,000 words in his listening vocabulary; 5,000 to 7,000 in his speaking vocabulary; and at the beginning of school no reading or writing vocabulary of significance. As he progresses through the elementary school, these vocabularies change greatly. Most people have a much larger reading vocabulary than writing vocabulary because they understand many more words than they use in their own writing. While the sizes of reading vocabularies vary greatly with children after they have learned word attack skills for discovering new words for themselves, perhaps grade five or after, the reading vocabulary will become larger than the speaking vocabulary for the able reader. Eventually, too, the reading vocabulary is greater than the listening vocabulary and the child must develop the dictionary habit in order to find quickly meanings of new words or meanings of old words in new contexts.

Historically, teachers have used several different methods in trying to help children learn word identification skills. When Bible reading was the main purpose for learning to read and the Bible was the source used, learners probably resorted mostly to memory of words from configuration clues and repetition. If they mastered this, they could learn to recognize syllables and sound words by syllables. While it is recognized that this was the method, there are few statistics to show how many boys and girls *did not learn* to read by it.

The synthetic methods of alphabet-spelling and phonics were based on putting the letters together to make words. The synthetic methods may be defined as those building larger elements (the word) from the simpler elements (the letters), or "going from the parts to the whole."

The Alphabet Method

The alphabet method is one in which the letters in the word are named in sequence and then the word pronounced. One sees the difficulty in English with this method since the names and the sounds of the letters have little similarity. (*Bat* would have been spelled as *bee aye tea* and then pronounced *bat*.) In those languages where the letter names are essentially the same as their sounds, this is much more effective, as, for example, in Spanish.

The Phonics Method

The phonics methods introduced many of the sounds of the letters and of letter combinations to the child so he could put them together to make words. *The Beacon Primer* (1912 copyright) introduced the child to some 150 phonetic elements on large charts which he could practice sounding. After he mastered the charts he was ready to begin reading context. For example, if the child learned the sounds *ra, ha, ma, ta,* and *sa,* he could use consonant "t" and form the words *ra-t, ha-t, ma-t, ta-t,* and *sa-t* which he could then pronounce more rapidly as *rat, hat, mat, tat,* and *sat.* See page 1 of the *Beacon Primer* following.

In the *Gordon Primer,* one learned initial consonant sounds and joined them to "families" to make long lists of words. This is somewhat different from the *Beacon Primer* method. With the "at" family, for example, he learned the sound of "m" and combined it with "at" and pronounced "mat." Then, with "r" he could build "rat" and with "h," "hat."

A sample lesson from the *Gordon Primer* appears below.

There has continued to be some controversy about which of the two approaches to sounding is better. Should one read "ra-t" or "r-at" as the word *rat*? Does it make a great deal of difference if the child knows what he is doing? There is one problem in sounding consonants separately at word beginnings. If the child says "bu-at" for "bat" he is making the sound of "b" as if it were *bŭ* as in *but*, which is "*b*" + *short* "*u*." The child's need is met when he can distinguish the sounds and be

BEACON PRIMER

PHONETIC TABLES

This book is planned to be used in connection with the Phonetic Chart. The following tables and exercises should not be taught until the Phonetic Chart is completed.[1]

After finishing the tables found in the chart, the child should come to this work with considerable phonetic power. The following words should be recognized silently and given as wholes at the rate of thirty to forty per minute.

had	map	rag	cat	had
ham	mat	ran	fan	lap
hat	pad	rat	fat	man
lad	pan	tag	bad	sat
lag	sad	tan	bag	rap
lap	sap	tap	nag	bag
man	sat	can	nap	fan

[1] If it is impossible to use the Phonetic Chart, teach the sounds of the following letters: *s, f, h, t, b, r, n, m, c, k, g, d, l, p,* and the short sound of *a;* also *ba, ha, la, ma, na, pa, sa, ra, ta, ca, ga, fa.* When the child has mastered these, build groups upon the blackboard as follows:

ra-n	ha-d	la-d	ma-d	ta-g
ra-p	ha-m	la-g	ma-n	ta-n
ra-t	ha-t	la-p	ma-t	ta-p

1

Page 1, *Beacon Primer*, Copyright 1912. Reprinted with permission of Ginn and Company, owner of the copyright.

Figure 7.1. The Beacon system developed as the basis for sounding words, the initial blends **ra, ha, ma, ta.** This may be contrasted with the final blends used in the **Gordon Primer.**

PHONIC LESSONS 25–26   **63**

I will make a picture of what each word says after you
sound it."

Children sound : Teacher draws with simple outlines :

First method				*Second method*	
1 2	3			1	2
m-at	mat			at	mat
r -at	rat			at	rat
h -at	hat			at	hat
c -at	cat			at	cat
s -at	sat			at	sat

Require each child to sound one of these illustrated words
before passing to his seat.   Those who have gained perception
of the blend will do this with little difficulty, as the picture
helps in getting the word.

Lesson 26.—Blending of Initial Consonant

Write family names upon the blackboard : *an, at, ash, op,*
eet, ilk. By means of the letter squares, present a succession
of initials to be used with them as in the previous exercises, or
prefix the same initial to each family name ; as,

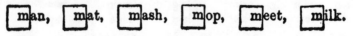
☐man, ☐mat, ☐mash, ☐mop, ☐meet, ☐milk.

Figure 7.2. Lessons 25 and 26 in the Teacher's Manual for the
Gordon Readers. Blending of initial consonant with the final phono-
gram or "family" is the procedure taught in this reader.

From the *Gordon Reader*, Book I by Emma K. Gordon, copyright
1918, Boston. D. C. Heath and Co., p. 63.

able to synthesize them so that he joins the correct vowel sound to the initial consonant or blend sound in identifying words.

Phonics methods were discarded as methods of teaching reading in the primary grades. There are several reasons. The most important is undoubtedly the unphonetic character of the English language. The irregularities in spelling and the exceptions to the rules provide much room for error. It is also generally agreed that this approach does not fit the learning style of the young child. His motivations, his attention span, and his persistence at tasks are better when the tasks are less abstract and relate much more to his level of growth and development. Further, many children, not highly motivated with abstract phonics drills, became word-callers, exhibiting slow, labored attempts at reading.

The Word and Sentence Method

The word and sentence method may be illustrated from a page taken from the Aldine Reader (Figure 7.3). When the child read such sentences as "Rain, rain, go away/Boys and girls want to play," he learned the few new words he needed as sight words. Then, the sentences on the remainder of the page gave some practice with the same vocabulary. One shortcoming with this attempt to put words in context was that it provided insufficient practice on the new sight vocabulary. Also, the pages provided isolated practice on a few words and did not tell a "story" so that reading did not have a meaningful purpose.

The word method was based on the point of view that the word was the smallest thought unit that the child needed to read for meaning. Proponents of the word method believed that one need not already know the letters of the alphabet in order to read the whole word. He could learn to recognize the word "look" as well as he could learn the letter "k," for example. With the severely controlled vocabularies in present-day pre-primers, the child learns in a relatively short time enough words to read the entire book. He relies on memory of visual configurations for this beginning.

Horace Mann, as early as 1838, recognized the advantage of the whole word method over the phonics or the spelling approaches. He wrote:

> Presenting the children with the alphabet is giving them what they never saw, heard, or thought before. . . . But the printed names of known things (dog, cat, doll) are the signs of sounds which their ears have been accustomed to hear, and their organs of speech to utter. Therefore, a child can learn to name 26 familiar *words* sooner than the unknown, unheard of and unthought of letters of the alphabet.[1]

---

[1]Lillian Gray, *Teaching Children to Read,* Third Edition (New York: The Ronald Press Company, 1963), p. 47, citing Horace Mann's *Report to the Board of Education in Massachusetts in 1838.*

The Story Method

The story method of teaching beginning reading was based on the belief that, from the beginning, children should be exposed to good literature. The authors of these series believed that such material could be written within the vocabulary reach of beginning readers. Free and Treadwell rewrote nine old folk tales, including "The Little Red Hen," "The Gingerbread Boy," and "The Old Woman and Her Pig," so they became the beginning reading lessons. The story method was essentially one in which the teacher read a complete story from the reader while the children followed along or listened. The children learned the story

Rain, go away.
Boys and girls want to play.
Boys want to jump.
Girls want to run.

The girls want to come with me.
The boys want to go away.

The girls want to play with me.
The boys want to run away.

Go away, boys.
Run away to the tree.

Come with me, girls.
Come and play with me.

Figure 7.3. The Aldine Primer taught a "word-and-sentence" method that flourished for several years.

Catherine I. Bryce and Frank E. Spalding, *Aldine Primer,* Copyright 1907, 1915, 1916. (New York City: Newsom and Company, 1916), p. 23.

sequence as it was reread so they were able to retell it in detail. Also, as the teacher read, they joined her in chorus on the many repetitions in the story. The story was then dissected into episodes, sentences, phrases, and finally words. After a few weeks, the child was expected to be able to read the story and recognize the individual words. If the study of one story had continued for many days, it is questionable whether many children still found it interesting.

Such folk tales as "The Little Red Hen," "The Billy Goats Gruff," or "The Gingerbread Boy" do provide much repetition of sight words as the sequences in the stories unfold; they are stories that provide conversation parts for dramatization or dialog reading, and children can illustrate idea sequence in pictures to retell the story.

The story of the gingerbread boy is a classic example of the vocabulary practice provided in repetitive episodes as the gingerbread boy runs away. Examine the section of the story as the gingerbread boy came to the fox:

> The gingerbread boy
> came to a fox.
> The gingerbread boy said,
> "Good morning, Fox.
> I am a gingerbread boy,
> I am, I am, I am.
> I ran away
> from the little old woman.
>
> I ran away
> from the little old man.
> I ran away from the hen.
> I ran away from the duck.
> I ran away from the goat.
> I ran away from the dog.
> I can run away from you.
> Here I go."[2]

Basal Readers

Basal readers utilize what might be called an *eclectic* approach to reading. Such a method utilizes desirable attributes of any of the other methods. Basically, the child masters a sight vocabulary *first* so he can read stories written with a severely limited number of words. Second, he begins learning a great deal about auditory discrimination of sound which is the beginning of word attack skills. The effective teacher achieves an appropriate emphasis in each of these jobs. To keep interest

---

[2]Miriam Blanton Huber, Frank Seely Salisbury, and Mabel O'Donnell, *I Know A Story* (New York: Harper and Row, 1962), pp. 20-21.

in reading at a high level so that children find it exciting to move on to new stories requires the acquisition of sufficient phonetic and structural analysis skills so that they increase their independence in attacking new words and reading harder material independently. Unless there is attention to getting meaning, reading may degenerate into a word-calling process. However, without word attack skills, reading can be a word guessing game.

While the child is learning his first basic sight vocabulary of about fifty words, he is beginning his phonics training in hearing words that begin the same, hearing rhyming words, and finding pictures of things that begin with the same sound. As soon as the words the child is learning have characteristics in common, the teacher begins pointing these out. Even in kindergarten, the teacher will help children to see that Mary, Mike, and Michele all have names that begin alike. When three of four words that begin with "d"—*dog, down, doll, duck*—have been learned, the child is ready to see that they have the same beginning letter and to hear the same sound at the beginning of each.

In summary, the eclectic method attempts to:

1. Emphasize the meaningful nature of reading as the most important factor in reading.
2. Teach an initial vocabulary of sight words as "sight" words learned (memorized) as visual configurations. This is achieved through chart reading, experience stories, labels in the room, blackboard work, workbook lessons, and direct teaching of the words in the first pre-primer.
3. Simultaneously with the reading of the pre-primers of a reading series, begin teaching a systematic course of study in phonetic and structural analysis skills.
4. Supplement the child's reading from the time he begins reading basal pre-primers with experience stories, chart reading, reading labels, and following directions.
5. Encourage children to "write books" of their own that can be bound by the teacher and kept on the reading table.
6. Emphasize the developmental, the functional, and the recreational nature of a balanced reading program.

II. SKILLS USEFUL IN WORD IDENTIFICATION

Word recognition skills are all those skills and abilities the student must acquire in order to be able to unlock words independently and rapidly as he reads. Memorizing a small stock of sight words may work very well for many children in order to read the first pre-primers in a reading series, but extending independent reading will require additional skills. Picture clues are also useful in the beginning and may be effectively used by a child as long as he is reading well-illustrated materials. However, the reader must be prepared to continue his reading when there are no illustrations to convey the story theme. There are some other skills, then, that the teacher must be prepared to develop with boys and girls to give them the independence in word recognition that is imperative for reading success. While memorizing visual configurations of a small stock of sight words and studying picture clues are helpful in initiating reading from the experience reading provided by the teacher in the classroom and in the pre-primers in basal readers, these are only temporary aids in developing permanent reading abilities.

The major helps the child needs for unlocking new words include techniques for overlearning a large sight vocabulary; using meaning clues contained in the reading; using phonetic clues; using structural analysis; and using the dictionary. Techniques for mastering a sight vocabulary may or may not include extensive study of word patterns or word structure based on a linguistic approach to reading. Linguistic methodology emphasizes patterns of speech, systems of phoneme-grapheme relationships, and the arrangement of word order in sentences.

The teacher will understand, then, that this discussion includes seven word identification skills, the first two of which are of considerable initial value but of little value in the fixing of permanent reading habits:

1. Memorizing visual configuration of a small number of words.
2. Using picture clues to story meaning and word identification.
3. Building a large stock of common words recognized at sight.
4. Identifying new words by using meaning clues in the rest of the sentence.
5. Using a sequence of phonetic analysis skills.
6. Using structural analysis skills.
7. Learning to use the dictionary for both pronunciation helps and meaning difficulties.

There are many phonics generalizations that have been taught in an effort to give boys and girls help in anticipating pronunciation in new situations. Some word-count studies have pointed to less than complete effectiveness in selected generalizations to teach. Section six in this chapter will present those considered most useful.

If one hopes that phonics will be the child's answer to word recognition, the poem, "Our Queer Language," shows some of the difficulties and inconsistencies in grapheme-phoneme relationships in the vocabulary to be mastered.

OUR QUEER LANGUAGE

When the English Tongue we speak
Why is "break" not rhymed with "freak"?
Will you tell me why it's true
We say "sew" and likewise "few"?
And the maker of the verse
Cannot cap his "horse" with "worse"
"Bread" sounds not the same as "heard"
"Cord" is different from "word"
Cow is "cow" but low is "low"
"Shoe" is never rhymed with "foe"
Think of "hose" and "dose" and "lose"
And think of "goose" and not of "choose"
"Doll" and "roll," "home" and "some"
And since "pay" is rhymed with "say"
Why not "paid" with "said" I pray?
"Mould" is not pronounced like "could"
Wherefore "done" but "gone" and "lone"
Is there any reason known?
And in short it seems to me
Sounds and letters disagree.

Source Unknown.

1. Visual Configuration

Young children are more motivated to "read a story" in the process of learning to read than they are in learning all the language, word analysis, and word identification that are involved in independent reading. If the teacher can help boys and girls to successfully read a story containing twenty words, and they can then successfully read that story to their mothers, they have reached one of their primary objectives in really reading. The first pre-primer in most basal reading series is prepared with a severely controlled vocabulary so that no more than fifteen to thirty words are used in the entire little book. By combining the picture clues that convey the story element and the noun words, visual configuration makes easily possible the early "reading" of such a book. The child will rely on word-form or the "look-and-say" method for recognizing these few words at this time.

As indicated in the preceding section, it is as easy for the child to learn "look" as a sight word as it is to remember the letter "k" as the last letter in the word "look." For a young child, learning the whole word is likely easier since the word is a concept while the letter "k" is not. From a typical first pre-primer, one can see that the child can learn these words by their differing configurations without too much confusion:[3]

---

[3]Odille Ousley and David H. Russell, *My Little Red Story Book,* First Pre-primer, the Ginn Basic Readers (Boston: Ginn and Company, 1948).

come see and here can the get fast ride

The colored illustrations throughout the book will help in the recognition of:

father	Father	Tom	Betty	Susan	apples
Mother	mother	bunny	Pony	balls	airplane

Printed in lower case letters, the letters provide some cues with "stems" above the line and "stems" below the line so that for some children there is value in helping him see that "come" and "ride" or "come" and "can" have different configurations.

come ride can

More important for beginners may be the more gross differentiations, however, "tomorrow" or "grandmother" may be much easier to remember because of the length of the word compared to "come" or "can." Also, long words with many letters that extend above or below the line (with ascenders and descenders) may be easy to differentiate visually.

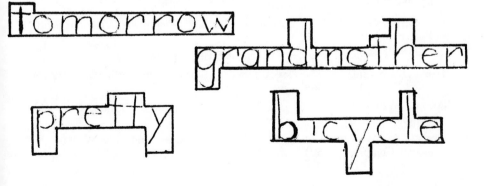

This ability may be of some value to readers if it teaches the habit of observing visual characteristics of new words that need unlocking. It must be pointed out, however, that visual configuration is not helpful to young children with pairs of words like "house" and "horse," "these" and "those," "tired" and "tried."

2. Picture Clues

Picture context can be as helpful to the beginning reader as sentence context is helpful to him later on. If the picture portrays the action, it is helpful in identifying verbs in sentence structure. Teachers should utilize pictures more maximally than they now generally do. In the intermediate grades, for example, social studies material will be understood if teachers discuss the pictures contained in the reading as a readiness activity. Through the questions which the teacher can raise by study of the pictures, students may acquire better motivation for study. In the page from the reader in figure 7.4 following, it is apparent that the sign in the picture will help the child anticipate meaning in the reading material if the teacher will ask the appropriate questions before the child reads. A question by the teacher, "Will father tell Andy he can have a dog?" can be answered by reading the sign, "No Dogs. No Cats." Then, "How does father explain this to Andy?" can be answered by reading the page.

Picture dictionaries can be useful in helping to recognize words through the use of picture clues. Associating the printed word with the picture that the word represents, developing the idea of finding information for himself, and teaching the idea of going to the dictionary to look for the information are lessons to be cultivated with young children using picture dictionaries. Some picture dictionaries available are the following:

Selma Lola Chambers, *The Little Golden Books of Words* (New York: Golden Press, 1948).

Alta McIntire, *Follett Beginning-to-Read Picture Dictionary* (Chicago: Follett Publishing Company, 1959).

Marion Monroe and W. Cabell Greet, *My Little Pictionary* (Chicago: Scott, Foresman, 1962).

—————, *My Second Pictionary* (Chicago: Scott, Foresman, 1964).

Mabel O'Donnell and Willmina Townes, *Words I Like to Read and Write* (New York: Harper and Row, 1961).

Hale C. Reid and Helen Crane, *My Picture Dictionary* (Boston: Ginn and Company, 1963).

Wendell W. Wright, *The Rainbow Dictionary* (Cleveland: The World Publishing Company, 1959).

"Father, I want a pet," said Andy.
"I would like to have a dog.
I would like to have a cat."
"No, Andy, you can not have a dog
where we live," said Father.
"You can not have a cat.
Come and look at something."
This is what Andy saw.

Figure 7.4. With teacher guidance, picture clues can be helpful to the child in his guided silent reading or his recreational reading.

Nila B. Smith, Hazel C. Hart, and Clara Belle Baker, Compilers and Editors, *Sunny and Gay*, (Indianapolis: The Bobbs-Merrill Company, 1960), p. 18.

3. Developing Sight Vocabulary

The child's first problem in learning to read is that he must *know some words*. This was exemplified in the definition of reading in Chapter 1, in the figure on page 6, where word perception is shown as the first of the four hierarchical steps in the reading process.

There are advocates of several methods of getting the child started. The learner might be taught by (1) a phonetic approach with intensive work on learning isolated phonetic sounds and joining them together to build words; (2) a "word family" or "word pattern" approach in which his first book contains no vowel sounds except short "a"; (3) a relatively quick introduction to book reading with a severely controlled vocabulary as is done in the basal reading program; (4) a language experience approach in which his class, as a group, and he, as an individual, dictate many stories based on both group and personal experience and the children read and re-read these stories; or (5) reading following primarily an individualized reading schedule.

Early in the school year in first grade, children generally become "word conscious" by various techniques used by the teacher. One of these techniques is that of labeling many things in the classroom. Each child's name written in manuscript and taped to his desk is useful in classroom management, but it is also one way to help children fix the idea that everything can be labeled to identify it. The words *door, window, desk, toy box, teacher, reading table,* further confirm the idea that abstract words correspond to real objects.

The best way for children to learn a small stock of sight words is by using them to read for meaningul purposes. As soon as they have a small stock of words there are many interesting little stories and books which they can enjoy. *Using* reading is basic to developing the habit of reading.

Through the use of the commonest service words in group and individual experience stories and books, labels in the classroom, and the anticipated vocabularies in the first books to be read, the teacher begins to build a small stock of words that boys and girls will encounter most frequently in their reading.

One of the teacher's most difficult tasks is fitting this phase of beginning to learn a sight vocabulary to the wide range of differences in the reactions of first graders to the learning of the vocabulary. Children who lack oral language skills and spontaneous oral language abilities should certainly have an extended oral language program before attempting to read. Children who lack visual motor coordination skills required in writing and in following consecutive lines of print may profit from special readiness to promote these abilities. Children who lack auditory discrimination skills need these skills to be developed. Those children who have these readiness skills will still provide the classroom teacher with a group who find little interest in learning to read just because the teacher finds it important. Other children have problems in the affective domain in their adjustment to school. Some are fearful, others anxious, others hostile. These need understanding and attention to their emotional adjustment before they will successfully retain what the teacher teaches.

Among the children who possess none of the limitations discussed above, the teacher will find fast learners, adequate learners, and slow learners in different kinds of tasks in the school curriculum. A few of the first graders may already possess a sizeable sight vocabulary and the teacher must identify these and encourage their continued growth in reading skills.

The Service Words of Reading

Stone has prepared a list of 100 words of high frequency in children's beginning reading. These have value to the teacher in identifying which of the words used in children's stories are the ones they most need to master for general reading. This list of words is given in Table 7.1.

It is apparent that several words in the story below are the service words of highest frequency.

> Tom said, "May I go with you?"
> George said, "Where are we going?"
> Tom said, "Let's go to the park.
> We can play ball in the park."
> "OK," said George, "I'd like to go."

The following sixteen words are on Stone's list of high frequency words:

said	go	where	to	play	like
may	with	are	the	ball	
I	you	we	can	in	

Below is another story that might be dictated by first grade boys and girls:

> Kee is a Navajo boy.
> He lives in a hogan in the canyon.
> He lives with his mother and father.
> Kee has a pony.
> It is a red pony.
> He likes to ride his pony.
> His pony can run fast.

TABLE *7.1.* *One Hundred Important Words for Pre-Book, Pre-Primer, and Early Primer Reading*

a	dog	I	not	the
after	doll	in	now	then
am	down	into	oh	they
and	father	is	on	this
are	find	it	one	three
at	for	jump	out	to
away	fun	kitten	play	too
baby	funny	laughed	rabbit	two
ball	get	like	ran	up
big	girl	little	red	want
blue	go	look	ride	was
bow-wow	good	make	run	we
boy	good-by	may	said	went
came	had	me	saw	what
can	have	new	school	where
car	he	milk	see	who
cat	help	morning	she	will
color	here	mother	some	with
come	home	my	something	yes
did	house	no	stop	you

From Clarence R. Stone, *Progress in Primary Reading*. Copyright McGraw-Hill, Inc., 1950.

The following seventeen words are on Stone's list.

is	he	with	and	red	ride
a	in	mother	father	like	can
boy	the		it	to	run

All of the high frequency words from the Stone word list except the nouns are also found in in the Dolch list of service words.

The 220 words in the Dolch Basic Sight Vocabulary constitute another abbreviated list of service words every child must know as sight words in order to read well. Dolch also selected ninety-five commonest nouns as a useful list for teachers.

Below is a child's story about dinosaurs.

This is a dinosaur.
It is an animal of *long, long*
ago.
Dinosaurs grew *very* large.
Dinosaurs laid eggs.
Dinosaurs *ate and ate.*
Some dinosaurs *ate only*
plants.
Some dinosaurs *ate only*
animals.
Maybe *little* animals *ate the*
dinosaur eggs.
Maybe *the* land dried *up.*
Maybe *there was not* enough
food.
Maybe *the* climate changed
to very cold winters.
All the dinosaurs died.

In this story about dinosaurs, there are sixty-three running words of text; thirty-three, or 52 per cent, are words from the Dolch Basic Sight Word List. The service words are italicized.

Pre-primers, with teacher's manuals, provide teachers with a sequenced introduction of vocabulary to be learned preparatory to reading a first book with twenty or fewer different words.

The Dolch Basic Sight Word List contains 220 service words that are used over and over in all the reading elementary school children do. No nouns are included since nouns change with subject matter and can be illustrated. The service words were those found to be common to three word lists containing the words used or understood by primary grade children.[4]

Based on 1,000 word samplings from elementary school texts, Dolch found that in grade one readers, 70 percent of the "running words" were on the Dolch List; 66 percent of the second grade readers; 65 percent of the third grade readers; 61 percent of the fourth; 59 percent of the fifth and sixth. See Table 7.2, p. 148.

Fry's Instant Words

Fry selected a list of most frequently used words that could be mastered in remedial reading situations to give the child maximum flexibility

[4]Gates, A. I., *A Reading Vocabulary for the Primary Grades* (New York: Teachers College, Columbia University, 1926); The Child Study Committee of the International Kindergarten Union, *A Study of the Vocabulary of Children Before Entering First Grade* (1201 Sixteenth St., N.W., Washington, D.C.: The International Kindergarten Union, 1928); and H. E. Wheeler and Emma A. Howell, "A First Grade Vocabulary Study," *Elementary School Journal,* 31:52-60, September, 1930.

Table 7.2. *Percentage of the Basic Sight Vocabulary in Running Words in School Textbooks.*

Textbook	No. of Series Used	Grade I	II	III	IV	V	VI
Reading	4	70	66	65	61	59	59
Arithmetic	2			62	63	57	57
Geography	2				60	59	54
History	2				57	53	52

From E. W. Dolch, *Teaching Primary Reading* (Champaign: The Garrard Press, 1941), p. 208.

in reading.[5] By combining and selecting from several word lists, Fry arbitrarily prepared a list of 600 words which he then divided into twenty-four groups of twenty-five words each. He attempted to provide for graduation in difficulty from easier to harder to learn. The lists from which Fry selected included the Thorndike-Lorge, Rinsland, and the Dolch Service Words. His first three hundred words will be very useful to all clasroom teachers.

The first hundred words of the Fry list contain ninety-five of the Dolch Service Words; the second hundred contains fifty-five of the Dolch Words; and the third hundred contains fifty-six of them. Thus, 206 of the total 220 Dolch Service Words are contained in the first 300 Instant Words. The first three hundred of the Instant Words can serve the same purposes as the comparable list prepared by Dolch.

The lists of words reproduced below are the first hundred of Fry's Instant Words, the second hundred, and the third, each group arranged in aphabetical order:

First Hundred

a	did	if	on	this
about	do	in	one	three
after	down	is	or	to
again	eat	it	other	two
all	for	just	our	up
an	from	know	out	us
and	get	like	put	very
any	give	little	said	was
are	go	long	see	we
as	good	make	she	were
at	had	man	so	what
be	has	many	some	when
been	have	me	take	which
before	he	much	that	who

[5]Edward Fry, "Developing a Word List for Remedial Reading," *Elementary English*, November, 1957, pp. 456-458.

boy	her	my	the	will
but	here	new	their	with
by	him	no	them	work
can	his	not	then	would
come	how	of	there	you
day	I	old	they	your

Second Hundred

also	each	left	own	sure
am	ear	let	people	tell
another	end	live	play	than
away	far	look	please	these
back	find	made	present	thing
ball	first	may	pretty	think
because	five	men	ran	too
best	found	more	read	tree
better	four	morning	red	under
big	friend	most	right	until
black	girl	mother	run	upon
book	got	must	saw	use
both	hand	name	say	want
box	high	near	school	way
bring	home	never	seem	where
call	house	next	shall	while
came	into	night	should	white
color	kind	only	soon	wish
could	last	open	stand	why
dear	leave	over	such	year

Third Hundred

along	don't	grow	off	stop
always	door	hat	once	ten
anything	dress	happy	order	thank
around	early	hard	pair	third
ask	eight	head	part	those
ate	every	hear	ride	though
bed	eyes	help	round	today
brown	face	hold	same	took
buy	fall	hope	sat	town
car	fast	hot	second	try
carry	fat	jump	set	turn
clean	fine	keep	seven	walk
close	fire	letter	show	warm
clothes	fly	longer	sing	wash
coat	food	love	sister	water
cold	full	might	sit	woman
cut	funny	money	six	write
didn't	gave	myself	sleep	yellow
does	goes	now	small	yes
dog	green	o'clock	start	yesterday

Techniques for Teaching Sight Words

Most reading series provide children the opportunity to discover new words for themselves if they have already learned the necessary skills to do so.

For example: using sight words the child already knows,

(1) from the "T" in Tom and the "oy" in boy, he can discover the new word "toy"
(2) from the "fl" in fly and the "ing" in sing, he can discover "fling"
(3) from the "sh" in show and the "ore" in tore he can discover "shore"
(4) from the "tr" in tree and the "end" in send he can discover "trend"
(5) from the "ch" in children and the "ance" in dance he can discover "chance."

The teacher can use the language which follows to give children practice:

Take "b" away from *boy*
Put in "t" and you have *toy*
Take "s" away from *sing*
Put in "fl" and you have *fling*
Take "t" away from *tore*
Put in "sh" and you have *shore*

The Reading for Meaning Series[6] of basal readers provides the teacher with a number of model exercises for reference in planning word recognition exercises:

1. Recognizing capital and small letters.
   Are "print" and "Print" the same?
2. Recognizing long vowel sounds.
   Does "idea" begin with the same sound as "island" or "idle"?
3. Discriminating between beginning sounds.
   Do "ice," "iris," "make," and "isle" all begin with the same sound?
4. Hearing consonant blends at the beginnings of words.
   Put "br" and the word *bridge* on the board. Say a list of words—brown, brook, could, letter, brave—and ask the class to identify the "br" words.
5. Discovering new words.
   From the word "say" take away "s."
   Put in "pr" and make *pray*.
6. Substituting final sounds.
   Take "d" away from *bud*.
   Put in "t" and make *but*.
   Put in "n" and make *bun*.
   Put in "s" and make *bus*.

---

[6]Paul McKee, M. Lucile Harrison, Annie McCowen, and Elizabeth Lehr, Teacher's edition for *Come Along, revised* (Boston: Houghton Mifflin Company, 1957), pp. 478-483.

Some Problems That May Be Encountered

Some boys and girls have much difficulty with the more abstract service words or with those often confused in pairs. Since many of these words that are abstract to teach and very difficult to illustrate visually are the structure words in sentence building, it is imperative that children have them early in reading if they are to read meaningfully. Later, in the chapter on linguistics and reading, emphasis is given to the learning of such words as *of, the, on, since, because* that do not fit word-patterns in linguistic approaches.

Words Often Confused

Teachers should use whatever devices they have found successful in helping children distinguish *then* and *when, where* and *there*, or *what* and *that* as they appear over and over in reading at the second grade level. The question words, *which, what, where, when,* and *why,* cause some children difficulty.

Exercises can be prepared by the teacher to give the child practice in reading the unknown word in context in sentences in which he is told that the word will be used, in sentences in which he must supply the word when it is appropriate, and later in sentences in which this word appears randomly with those with which it is often confused.

If the child has much difficulty confusing *then* and *when,* he might first complete exercises that use only one of these words; then he might complete exercises that use only the other one; and finally complete exercises in which he must choose between these two words. Teachers can prepare sentence exercises like the following:

---

(1) Write *then* on the blank and read the sentence.
  1. Put the book on the table, _____ bring me your paper.
  2. What will you do _____ ?
  3. _____ the teacher told us a story.

(2) Write *when* in the blank and read the sentence.
  1. _____ is Bill coming home?
  2. _____ will it be time to go?
  3. Tell me _____ you are ready to go.

(3) Read the sentence. Decide whether *when* or *then* belongs in the blank. Write in the correct word:
  1. I don't know _____ he is coming.
  2. He did his work; _____ he went home.
  3. The flowers will be blooming _____ .
  4. Apples are ripe _____ they are red.

Figure 7.5. Practice for Overcoming "When-Then" Confusion

Minimal Pairs

Hearing differences in words that sound almost alike is another difficulty with which teachers must help some boys and girls. Failing to hear the proper vowel sound in the word or consonant sound at the end of the word may cause the child to misunderstand or to be misunderstood. Discriminating minimal pairs is discussed in Chapter 12: Linguistics and Reading. Minimal pairs are word pairs that sound exactly alike except for one phoneme that differs. For example, *look* and *book* constitute a minimal pair because they differ only in initial consonant sound. However, the minimal pairs that present difficulty are likely to be those vowel sounds not discriminated or the final consonant sound or consonant sound cluster not heard or enunciated. While these sound difficulties are very common with children learning English as a second language, they are by no means limited to them. Common errors are final "g" and "k" confusion as in *pig* and *pick;* "th" and "f" as in *death* and *deaf;* "s" and "z" as in *rice* and *rise;* "f" and "v" as in *leaf* and *leave.* Vowels such as "ee" and "i" as in *sheep* and *ship;* and "a" and "e" as in *age* and *edge* also cause difficulty. A brief list of minimal pairs follows:

pi*g*—pi*ck*	du*g*—du*ck*	dea*th*—dea*f*
ba*k*e—beg	haw*k*—ho*g*	wrea*th*—ree*f*
be*t*—be*d*	*c*old—*g*old	buz*z*—bu*s*
*p*each—*b*each	a*ch*e—e*gg*	pla*ys*—pla*ce*
cu*p*—cu*b*	ro*p*e—ro*b*e	ri*s*e—ri*c*e
ca*p*—ca*b*	*p*ool—*p*ull	boat—bo*th*
lea*f*—lea*v*e	li*f*e—li*v*e	*th*ick—*t*ick
toe*s*—toa*st*	sh*ee*p—sh*i*p	p*ai*n—p*e*n
*a*ge—*e*dge	b*i*t—b*ea*t	

In the teaching of phonetic analysis skills, teachers will provide practice in the auditory discrimination of such word pairs.

4. Meaning Clues

Word perception or pronunciation is the first step in the reading process. If the process stops with word calling, then the act of reading as defined in Chapter 1 does not take place.

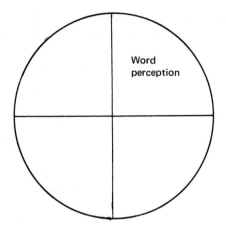

The next step is that of using meaning or conceptual skills to relate what is being read to what is already known. This may be thought of as comprehension of the idea. It is depicted in the four-step process of reading as the second step.

So,

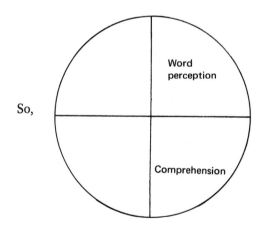

The reader constructs a concept or a meaning when he perceives what a word is.

In the sentence:

                                    bank
John played the drums in the band.
                                    bang
                                    bond

The reader first perceives that the four-letter word *is* ban*d* and not ban*k* or ban*g;* neither is it bo*nd.* Step one requires the proper *pronunciation* to match the graphic form of "band."

At the *comprehension* level, the reader must, in this case, know what a "band" is. However, this is a polysemantic word with more than one meaning. Before the reader can move to step three in the reading process to *react* to the sentence as a unit, he must understand the use of the word *band* in the sentence and the use of all the words in the sentence as they relate to the meaning stored in the concept "band."

This comprehension of words in any context necessitates a great storehouse of word meanings readily available to the reader. These meanings will be explored in greater depth in later chapters, but at the elementary level they include multiple meanings of common words, synonyms, homonyms, antonyms, perceiving word relationships in the sentence, and choosing the best dictionary definition.

Children must be taught many ways of arriving at adequate meanings:

A. Multiple meanings of common words:

The printed form of the word *run* represents many different words in our language. Horn illustrates:[7]

1. The disease has *run* its course.
2. The fence *runs* east and west.
3. To *run* to seed.
4. To *run* a garage.
5. To *run* a splinter in a finger.
6. To *run* out of money.
7. To *run* to ruin.
8. To *run* a risk.
9. To *run* up a bill.
10. To *run* across a friend.
11. To knock a home *run.*
12. A *run* on a bank.
13. The common *run* of persons.

Note the elementary uses of *down:*

1. I will walk *down* the stairs.
2. Jack likes to sleep under a *down* comforter.
3. The boy went *down* town.
4. The struggling swimmer went *down* for the third time.
5. The boxer was *down* for the count.
6. Jack fell *down.*
7. Elevators go up and *down.*

---

[7]Ernest Horn, "Language and Meaning," *NSSE Yearbook. The Psychology of Learning* (Chicago: University of Chicago Press, 1942), pp. 398-399.

Teachers' guides and preparatory books provide many exercises to help children understand the variant meanings of common words by asking them to match meanings as indicated in the following exercise:

Directions: Read the sentences in group 1, then put the letter above on each blank that is in front of a sentence in group 2 that has the same meaning:

Group I
    a. Did you pay the gas *bill?*
    b. Uncle *Bill* came to see us today.
    c. Did you *bill* them for the medicine?
    d. The bird's *bill* was broken.

Group II
_____ The boy paid the grocery *bill* today.
_____ The chicken pulled the worm out with his *bill.*
_____ Will *Bill* go to school tomorrow?
_____ He *billed* us for the things we bought today.

B. Comparing and contrasting word meanings:

The teacher can provide exercises to develop children's abilities in giving synonyms, antonyms, or deciding whether words given in pairs are alike or opposite in meaning.

    1. Exercises giving synonyms:
        a. We followed a winding _____. (path, trail, road)
        b. We brought water in a _____. (bucket, pail, container)
        c. Snow sometimes _____ the trail. (hid, covered, concealed)
    2. Exercises identifying antonyms:
        a. John went *up* the hill. I wanted to go _____ .
        b. That rose was *rare* around here. It is getting more_____ .
        c. The light was *red;* it changed to_____ .
        d. He was *tired* last night but this morning he seemed_____ .
    3. Exercises deciding whether words are synonyms or antonyms. For the child the instructions will read: "Write 's' on the line of two words meaning the same; write 'o' if the meaning is the opposite."

large	small	o
huge	gigantic	s
conceal	hide	s
common	rare	o
try	attempt	s

4. Homonyms:

scent	to	their	pear	Sew
cent	two	there	pair	sow
sent	too	they're	pare	so
sight	right	rowed	vane	rain
site	rite	road	vein	reign
cite	write	rode	vain	rein

Work sheet exercises to choose correct spelling to fit context are indicated.

5. Perceiving relationships between/among words:
Use the three words in *one* sentence.

    harvest, sale, cotton
    teacher, student, principal
    seed, irrigation ditches, planting

6. Choosing the best meaning in a given context. The child is asked to read the definitions and match the appropriate one with each example below:

Scale: (1) Instrument for weighting; (2) covering of the fish; (3) size represented on a map.

_____ a. The *scale* used was "1" = 1'.

_____ b. They removed the *scales* with sharp knives.

_____ c. They weighed the fish on the *scales*.

5. Phonetic Analysis

Smith[8] describes the way in which phonics instruction has been emphasized and de-emphasized in cycles through the past two centuries. The heavy emphasis on phonics as a *method* of learning to read has already been discussed.

With the new emphasis on reading for meaning in the mid-thirties and its concomitant attention to silent reading exercises to emphasize understanding, the teaching of phonics was de-emphasized to the point of neglect. Of course, the pendulum has swung back now so that *phonics is being taught today.* The great majority of teachers are teaching phonetic and structural analysis skills. Today teachers reinforce the phonetic skills taught with a number of other methods: context clues, analyzing word structure, checking for meaning, and using the dictionary.

Phonics is now taught to children with a different emphasis and with skills sequenced through the reading program with spaced reviews.

---

[8]Nila B. Smith, *American Reading Instruction* (Newark, Delaware 19711: International Reading Association, 1965). Also, Nila B. Smith, *Reading Instruction for Today's Children* (Prentice-Hall, Inc., Englewood Cliffs, New Jersey, 1963), pp. 187-195.

Phonics skills are introduced gradually in reading series as an integral part of the complete set of techniques in the eclectic approach. This approach was identified and developed by Gates as the intrinsic approach to phonics teaching.

Teaching phonics functionally in relation to the reading children are doing, with help in attacking difficulties as they arise, is defensible learning practice.

Instruction in phonetic analysis is sequenced to develop all the necessary abilities to unlock new words. Beginning in the kindergarten, children have a great deal of informal practice in auditory discrimination by: (1) hearing how each other's first names begin, as in Carl, Carolyn, Kate, and Karen; (2) hearing rhymes in Mother Goose, as in "Jack and *Jill,* Went up the *hill;* and (3) taking advantage of comments of individual children in conversation, as when one child says, "*home, house,* and *hospital*"—they all begin alike (or with "h")—or saying rhyming *sounds,* as in *at, bat, cat, dat, gat, lat.*

The phonetic elements to be taught include:
1. The sounds of the single consonant letters. (Q, X, Y, and Z will not be needed early in the program.)
2. The consonant blend sounds in both initial and final positions in words:
    Initial position: *sm*art, *sk*ill, *st*ick, *tr*ain, *sw*eep, *str*ing.
    Final position: cha*sm*, whi*sk*, ta*sk*, moun*ds*, fore*sts*, mea*sles*.
3. The consonant digraphs: *ch, sh, wh, th* in intial and final positions in words:
    Initial position: *ch*eck, *sh*all, *wh*en, *th*ink.
    Final position: mou*th*, ba*th*, wa*sh*, bun*ch*.
4. The short and the long sounds of the vowels:
    Short vowel words: b*a*g, b*e*g, b*i*g, b*o*g, b*u*g.
    Long vowel words: m*a*te, m*e*te, m*i*te, m*u*te, bone.
5. The "consonant-vowel consonant" (CVC) generalization:
    The vowel in a closed syllable usually has its short sound, as in f*i*n ish, c*a*n dor, l*o*t tery, b*u*t ter, g*e*t ting.
6. The vowel diagraphs: *ay, ai, au, ee, ea, ei, eu, ew, ie, oa, oo, ow.*
7. The vowel diphthongs: *oi, oy, ou, ow.*
8. In a syllable ending in a vowel, the vowel is usually long, *he, she.* (This is the consonant-vowel (CV) generalization.)
9. In a short word with a middle vowel and ending with "e"; usually the "e" is silent and the middle vowel is long. (This is the CVCV generalization.)
10. The schwa sound: (ə), as in *a*bout, penc*i*l.

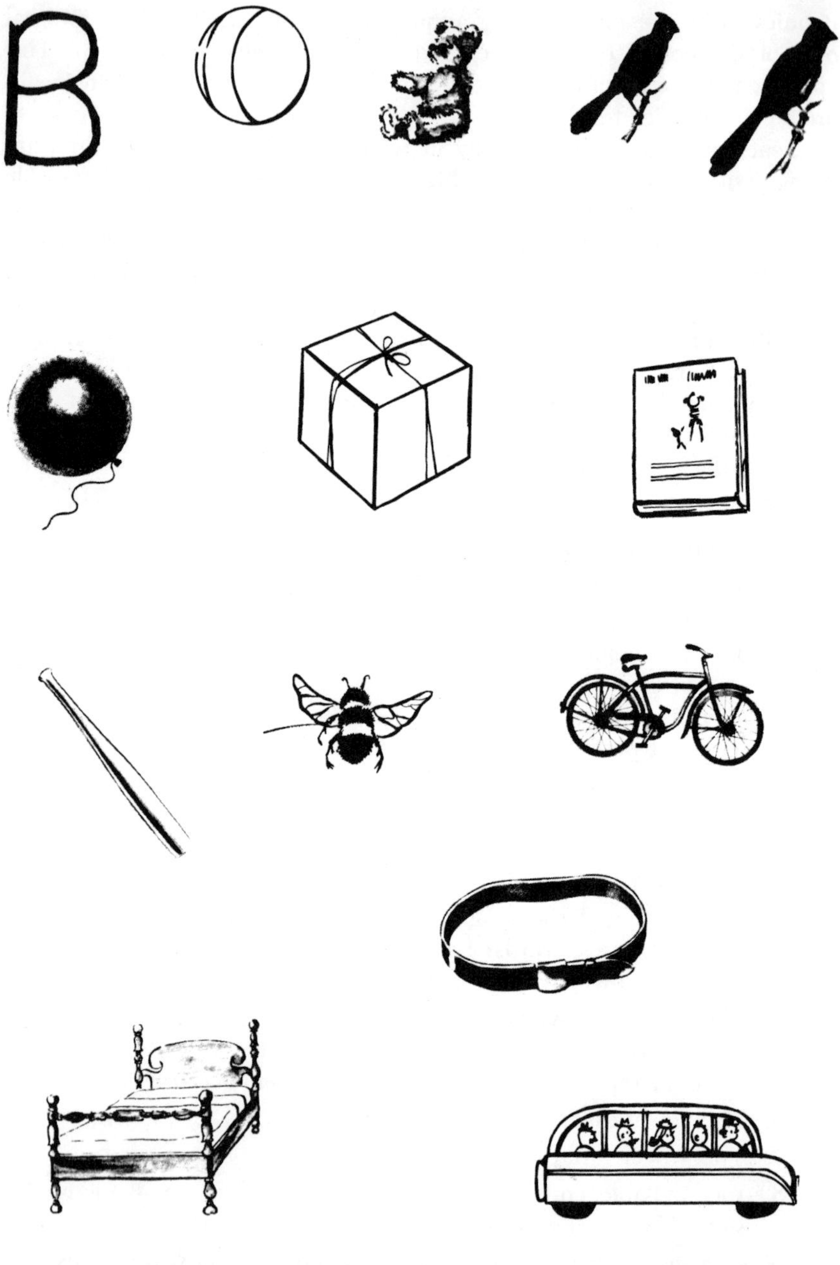

Figure 7.6. Many teachers help boys and girls learn the initial consonant sounds by collecting pictures of things that begin with each of the most used consonant letters. The pictures above were used for the "B" page in a first grade book of sounds.

The following list of words containing the schwa are taken from Cordts:[9]

ə̲bout	fath ə̲ r	Sat ə̲ rn	cupb ə̲ rd
at ə̲ m	doct ə̲ r	tap ə̲ r	surg ə̲ n
circ ə̲ s	doll ə̲ r	fash ə̲ n	ir ə̲ n
mart ə̲ r	tort ə̲ s	ac ə̲ rs	

11. The clues to silent letters in words. "Silent" consonants designate those letters in syllables that are not sounded when the syllable is spoken. Cordts gives the following generalizations:[10]
    (1) The letter *b* is silent after "m" and before "t": debt, doubt, climb, comb
    (2) The letter *g* is silent before "m" and "n": gnat, gnu, sign, diaphragm
    (3) The letter *h* may be silent before any vowel or when preceded by "r": rhyme, rhinoceros, honest, herb
    (4) The letters *gh* are silent after "a," "i," or "o": high, eight, bought, caught
    (5) The letter *k* is silent before "n": knock, know, knife, knee
    (6) The letter *l* is silent before "k," "d," or "m": talk, would, calm, salmon
    (7) The letter *p* is silent before "s," "t," or "n": psalm, pneumonia, ptomaine
    (8) The letter *t* following "s" or "f": listen, often, thistle, soften
    (9) The letter *w* before "r": wrist, write, wren, wrong
12. Several consonant sounds have more than one sound:
    a. The hard sound of *G*, when *g* is followed by *a, o,* or *u.*
    b. The soft sound of *G*, when *g* is followed by *e, i,* or *y.*
    c. The hard sound of *C*, when *c* is followed by *a, o,* or *u.*
    d. The soft sound of *C*, when *c* is followed by *e, i,* or *y.*
    e. The "s" sound as "s" in *fuse;* "sh" in *sugar;* and "zh" in *treasure.*
    f. The "x" sound as "ks" in *box;* "gs" in *exact;* and "z" in *xylophone, Xerxes.*
13. Syllabic consonants. There are many words in which there is no vowel letter for the sound in the unaccented syllable in the word. The consonants "l," "n," and "m" sometimes function as syllables by themselves. In the word *little,* "lit" forms one sounded syl-

---

[9]Anna D. Cordts, *Phonics for the Reading Teacher* (New York: Holt, Rinehart and Winston, Inc., 1965), p. 162.
[10]*Ibid.,* pp. 134-135.

lable and the letter "l" forms the other. In the word *garden,* "gard" forms one sounded syllable and the letter "n" forms the other. In the word *rhythm,* "rhyth" forms the first sounded syllable and the letter "m" forms the other. Because "l," "m," and "n" are capable of forming a syllable by themselves, they are known as syllabic consonants.

There are many examples in English words where the phoneme-grapheme relationships do not correspond but when there are few examples in children's work, it seems best to teach the element, or its exception, at the time when it is needed. Examples include, "ph" as "f"; "qu" always sounds like "kw"; the "s" is silent in *isle, aisle,* and *island*; and the "b" is silent when it follows "m" as in *comb* and *thumb.*

The pronunciation of suffixes beginning with "t," as in "tion," "tious," "tial," must also be taught as a special sound of "sh" for the letter "t."

6. Structural Analysis

Structural analysis is the means by which the parts of a word which form meaning units or pronunciation units within the word are identified. Structural analysis includes recognizing the root word as a meaning unit, identification of compound words, prefixes and suffixes, and generalizations about syllabication. Very important in this task is appreciating the influence of stress or accent on syllables in spoken language.

The dictionary attempts to retain the base word or the root as nearly as possible in its original form in showing how words can be divided, for example, at the end of a line of print. In other words, dictionaries show primarily how the word is divided when it is written. The spoken word may be divided differently to form meaningful pronunciation units. Cordts says:[11]

> The syllabication of the spoken word may or may not coincide with the way the word is divided when the word is written. The simple word *selfish* offers an example. When writing the word, it is correctly divided as *self'ish,* but the spoken word is *sel'fish.*

A. Inflectional variants:
1. Possessive forms: John's, the man's.
2. Plural nouns with *s* or *es*: apples, cups, boxes, bananas.
3. Verbs changed by:
   s or *es*: walks, finishes, takes, jumps;
   d or *ed*: walked, finished, hoped, filed;
   ing: walking, finishing, hoping, filing;
   n or *en*: taken, given, loosen, tighten.
4. Comparison using *er* and *est*:
   faster, fastest, taller, tallest.

---

[11]*Ibid.,* p. 172.

5. Dropping final *e*:   Doubling final consonant:

hope—hoping	hop—hopping
file—filing	bar—barring
bare—baring	can—canning
cane—caning	mat—matting
mate—mating	tap—tapping
tape—taping	mop—mopping
mope—moping	star—starring
stare—staring	pin—pinning
pine—pining	

6. Changing *y* to *i*:
   happy—happiest, crazy—craziest, pretty—prettiest.
7. Changing *f* to *v*:
   half—halving, shelf—shelving, calf—calving.

B. Recognizing independent parts of compound words:

something	became	broadcloth
grandmother	lifelike	newcomers
airplane	outlaw	wanderlust

C. Roots, prefixes, and suffixes:
   Each underlined root has both a prefix and a suffix:

   en *camp* ment   dis *approv* ing   in *adequate* ly

   Fifteen common prefixes constitute the majority of prefixes used in writing for elementary school children.[12] It is important that they be taught meaningfully to boys and girls in the fifth and sixth grades. Boys and girls need to learn that just because these letters appear at the beginning of a word is not a definite indication that they represent a prefix. Learning the meanings and selecting examples is a suitable exercise for sixth graders who perform at grade level. In the list below, the commonest meaning of the prefix and examples are given:

	Prefix	*Meaning*	*Examples*
1.	ab	from	abnormal
2.	ad	to	admit, adhere
3.	be	by	bedecked

---

[12]Russell C. Stauffer, "A Study of Prefixes in the Thorndike List to Establish a List of Prefixes that Should be Taught in the Elementary School," *Journal of Educational Research* (1942), 35:453-458.

	Prefix	Meaning	Examples
4.	com	with, together	compact, commiserate
5.	de	from	deduct, depose
6.	dis	apart	disappear, disengage
7.	en	in	enjoy
8.	ex	out	exhale, export
9.	in	in	inhabit, inhibit
10.	in	not	incorrect, inadequate
11.	pre	before	preview, prediction
12.	pro	for, forward	propel, pronoun
13.	re	back	renovate, reconsider
14.	sub	under	submarine, subjugate
15.	un	not	unhappy, uncommon

Some of the commonest suffixes with their meanings are given below:

	Suffix	Meaning	Examples
1.	able	tells what kind	suitable
2.	al	having to do with something	magical, national
3.	ance	act, process, or fact of being, quality, state of	disappearance
4.	ant	having the quality, manner, or condition of a person or thing	assistant, observant
5.	ary	belonging to, or connected with	legendary, momentary
6.	en	may mean "made of"	wooden
7.	ful	full of or characterized by	sorrowful, healthful
8.	hood	a state of being	manhood, falsehood
9.	ion	"the act of"	expression, perfection
10.	less	unable, without	needless, regardless
11.	ly	in what way or manner	gladly

Children will be expected to complete exercises like the following:
   Choose *less, like, ful, ness,* or *ly*:
1. In a cruel manner   *cruelly*
2. Without hope   *hopeless*
3. Full of/being good   *goodness*

    4. Like a bird   *birdlike*
    5. Full of peace   *peaceful*

D. Greek and Latin combining forms:

Combining Forms			*Literal Meanings*		
1. bio	+	logy	life	+	science of
2. geo	+	graphy	earth	+	to write about
3. thermo	+	meter	heat	+	to measure
4. tele	+	scope	far away	+	to view

E. Exercises to develop understanding of structural analysis include:
Copy the word that is underlined. Write down what it means:
1. Everyone needs a *friend*.
2. I lost my *friend's* address.
3. He is a *friendly* person.
4. Jim acts *friendlier* than Ted.
5. Ed is sometimes *unfriendly*.
6. I hope I never am *friendless*.
7. I admire his *friendliness*.
8. I need your *friendship*.
9. The Red Cross will *befriend* the flood stricken people.[13]

Building inflected and derived forms with root words:

	come			cross	
	come	s	a	cross	
	com	ing		cross	es
be	come			cross	ed
be	com	ing		cross	ing
	come	ly	un	cross	
in	come			cross	section
wel	come			cross	country
	come	back	double	cross	
over	come		hot	cross	buns
				cross	wise
				cross	eye
				cross	roads
			criss	cross	

---

[13]*100 Good Ways to Strengthen Reading Skills* (Chicago: Scott, Foresman and Company, 1956), p. 16.

Syllables are classified as open or closed and as accented or un-accented. Open syllables are those that end with a vowel sound; closed syllables are those that end with a consonant sound.

Open syllables	*Closed syllables*
se´ cret	sun´ set
po´ nies	mon´ key
ti´ ger	but´ ter
sto´ ries	rain´ bow
pota´ to	dif´ ferent
fa´ mous	cir´ cle

F. Rules for syllabication

1. When there are two consonants between two vowels in a poly-syllabic word, the syllables will divide between the two consonants unless the first vowel has its long sound. VCCV indicates letter order: vowel, consonant, consonant, vowel in words.

VCCV words	*VCCV words with the first vowel sound long*
mon key	se cret
ob ligate	mi crobe
cir cum ference	
per fect	
mis take	

2. When there are twin consonants between the separated vowel sounds, the word is divided between the consonants:

but ter	lad der	skim ming
cab bage	cop per	com mon
sum mer	cot tage	bal loon

3. When a word is composed of two complete words—that is, a compound word—it is first divided between the two words that make up the compound word. For example, no one, some where, any thing, who ever, grand mother, sun set, pop overs, cow boy, bird house, school yard, air plane, milk man, tooth brush.

4. Syllables usually do not break between consonant blend letters or special two-letter combinations:

chil *dr*en, an *gr*y, lea *th*er, bro *th*er.

5. When there is one consonant between two vowels, the consonant usually goes with the next syllable if the preceding vowel has its long sound, and with the preceding syllable if the vowel has its short sound or some other sound. VCV indicates letter order: vowel, consonant, vowel in words.

VCV words in which the consonant begins the second syllable			*VCV words in which the consonant remains with the preceding syllable*			
fa tal	be gin	to tal	shiv er	tax i	rad i cal	
pa per	sa ble	a muse	nov el	ex ert	pop u lar	
de lay	ti ger	a corn	trav el	mim ic	per il	
o ver	gro cer	po lite	fev er	ban ish	rock ets	
			sol id	rob in	mon ey	
			grav ity	cour age	fath er	
			cov er	com et	sec ond	
			rap id			

It follows from these examples that if the first syllable retains the long vowel sound, the consonant begins the second syllable. Also, if the consonant between the two vowels is either "x" or "v," this letter often remains with the preceding vowel to form a syllable.

6. When each of two vowels in a word forms a separate syllable, the word is divided between the two vowels. For example, *ru in, gi ant.* Other words in which each of the two vowels is joined to separate syllables, are *fu el, Su ez, cre ate, li ons, po etry.*

It is not expected that boys and girls will attempt to learn rules of syllabication until they have derived the generalization based on seeing a large number of words syllabicated in each of the various ways provided by these rules. Moreover, it is more important for children to be able to apply the rule in pronouncing the word than it is for them to be able to "recite" the rules.

Little words in big ones

Children cannot generalize about finding little words in big words:
At is not *at* in attack, dated, eat, fatal, fathom, material, patriot, path, patrol, station, water, watch.[14]
Up is not *up* in pupil, pupa, rupee, supervisor, superman, cupid, cupola, duplicate, duplex.

---

[14]William S. Gray, *On Their Own in Reading* (Chicago: Scott, Foresman and Company, 1948), p. 80.

Accent

Teachers need to give some consideration to accent in pronunciation. Some general statements are possible about the use of accent even though there are few rules that can be taught as widely applicable.

Accent is the amount of stress given a syllable in a word. In a two-syllable word, one syllable is usually accented and the other unaccented. In many polysyllabic words, one syllable gets a primary emphasis or stress and another gets a secondary accent. Boys and girls will best learn about accent through the deductive process of generalizing from the examples in which they apply stress to make the intonation and rhythm of their spoken language communicate properly. A vowel usually has one of its phonic sounds (long, short, controlled by *r*) when in an accented syllable, but is likely to have the schwa sound (ə) when in an unaccented syllable.

In a two-syllable word, in which the first syllable is *not a prefix*, the accent usually falls on the first syllable. For example, *res'cue, stu'pid, fun'ny.*

In a multisyllabic word with a root and prefixes and suffixes, the root of the word is often accented: for example, en *camp* ment, im *prove* ment, sur *round* ing.

In a polysyllabic word ending in *tion, cion, sion, tious, cious,* the accent falls on the next to the last syllable. For example, pre ven' tion, grav i ta' tion, lo co mo' tion, el e va' tion.

Cordts recommends three generalizations about placing accent in polysyllabic words but emphasizes that all such generalizations will have exceptions:[15]

1. Words that are used as both nouns and verbs will likely be accented on the first syllable as nouns and on the last syllable as verbs: per' fume is a noun; per fume' is a verb.

Nouns	*Verbs*
rec' ord	re cord'
prog' ress	pro gress'
pro' test	pro test'
sur' vey	sur vey'
per' mit	per mit'
in' sult	in sult'
con' flict	con flict'

2. Words having three or more syllables are apt to have both a primary accent and a secondary accent: as in con' sti *tu'* tion, mul' ti pli *ca'* tion.

---

[15]Anna D. Cordts, *op. cit.,* p. 178.

3. In counting, the first syllable of a number name is accented, but in saying the numbers both syllables are accented. One counts fif′ teen, six′ teen, sev′ en teen, eight′ teen; but one says fif′ teen′, six′ teen′, sev′ en teen′.

There are many words which have an accented syllable in which the vowel sound changes to an unaccented sound, that is, the schwa, when another form of the word is used:

Accented vowel sound	*Schwa sound*
at′ om	ətom′ ic
cor′ al	c ə r ral′
up′ per	ə p on′
par′ ti cle	p ə r tik′ yə l ə r

Winkley attempted to find out whether accent generalizations should be taught.[16] Using the eighteen accent generalizations listed by Gray,[17] Winkley prepared an Accent Test requiring students in the intermediate grades to underline the accented syllables, select the correct vowel sound for the accented syllable, and choose the correct meaning of the word. As a result of her testing, she concluded that the following generalizations should be taught in grades four to six:

1. When there is no other clue in a two-syllable word, the accent is usually on the first syllable. Examples: ba′sic, pro′gram.
2. In inflected or derived forms of words, the primary accent usually falls on or within the root word. Examples: box′es, untie′.
3. If de-, re-, be-, ex-, in-, or a- is the first syllable of a word, it is usually unaccented. Examples: delay′, explore′.
4. Two vowel letters together in the last syllable of a word may be a clue to an accented final syllable. Examples: complain′, conceal′.
5. When there are two like consonant letters within a word, the syllable before the double consonants is usually accented. Examples: begin′ner, let′ter.
6. The primary accent usually occurs on the syllable before the suffixes -ion, -ity, -ic, -ian, -ial, or -ious, and on the second syllable before the suffix -ate. Examples: affecta′tion, differen′tiate.
7. In words of three or more syllables, one of the first two syllables is usually accented. Examples: ac′cident, deter′mine.

Data concerning phonics generalizations judged by Burmeister to have high utility value, using data provided by Clymer, Emans, and Bailey, are summarized in the final section of this chapter.

---

[16]Carol K. Winkley, "Which Accent Generalizations are Worth Teaching?" *The Reading Teacher*, 20:219-224, December, 1966.
[17]William S. Gray, *On Their Own in Reading* (Chicago: Scott, Foresman and Company, 1960), pp. 66-199.

7. Use of the Dictionary

For purposes of finding words needed, determining proper pronunciation of words being used, and establishing meanings appropriate to the context in which the word is being used, every child must achieve proficiency in the effective use of the dictionary. Third grade boys and girls who read at or above grade level should be developing some of the dictionary skills outlined in this section. Much time will be devoted to teaching dictionary skills in both fourth and fifth grade because children will not all acquire the skills when they are taught and the teacher must provide for much re-teaching and review.

The skills needed for dictionary usage have been classified as location, pronunciation, and meaning skills and are outlined below.

In order to find words quickly in the dictionary, children need to know how entries are made and how many forms of a word are included in the dictionary. If the child is looking for *reporting* and there is no entry for this word, he must know that *reporting* is derived from *report* and that he must look for the *report* entry.

A number of dictionaries are available for boys and girls in the elementary school and it is recommended that classrooms be provided with sufficient copies of a good one so that each child can have easy access to it. This is necessary in order to develop the dictionary habit.

A few of the elementary school dictionaries of recent copyright are

Thorndike-Barnhart Beginning Dictionary. Clarence L. Barnhart, editor. Chicago: Scott, Foresman and Company.

Thorndike-Barnhart Junior Dictionary. Clarence L. Barnhart, editor. Chicago: Scott Foresman and Company.

Webster's A Dictionary for Boys and Girls. New York: American Book Company.

The Winston Dictionary for Schools. Thomas Brown and William Lewis, editors. New York: Holt, Rinehart and Winston, Inc.

The World Book Dictionary, 2 vols. Clarence L. Barnhart, editor-in-chief. Chicago: Field Enterprises Educational Corporation, 1969.

The skills outlined on the following page have been adapted from the *Thorndike-Barnhart Beginning Dictionary* and the reading textbooks of Heilman and de Boer and Dallmann.[18] The Thorndike-Barnhart dictionaries contain lesson plans for teaching boys and girls how to use the dictionary. The *Beginning Dictionary* contains seventy lessons for use in grades four and five.

III. USEFUL GENERALIZATIONS

Generalizations about sound and about syllabification are most productive when the word in question is unknown only in its written form.

---

[18]E. L. Thorndike and Clarence L. Barnhart, *Beginning Dictionary* (Chicago: Scott, Foresman and Co., 1952), pp. 13-85. See also Arthur W. Heilman, *Principles and Practices of Teaching Reading,* second edition (Columbus: Charles E. Merrill, 1967), pp. 385-387; and J. J. DeBoer and Martha Dallmann, *The Teaching of Reading,* revised edition (New York: Holt, Rinehart and Winston, 1964), pp. 200-204.

TABLE 7.3. Location, pronunciation, and meaning skills needed by boys and girls in the elementary school in the use of the dictionary.

Location skills:

1. Ability to arrange words in alphabetical order; by initial letter, by second letter, and by third or fourth letters.
2. Ability to find words quickly in an alphabetical list.
3. Ability to open the dictionary quickly to the section in which the word is to be found; to the proper fourth of the book.
4. Ability to use the two guide words at the top of the page.
5. Ability to think of the names of letters immediately preceding and immediately following the letter being located.
6. Ability to use special pronunciation-meaning sections of the dictionary, for example, medical terms, slang expressions, musical terms, and foreign words and phrases.

Pronunciation skills:

1. Ability to use the pronunciation key at the bottom of each page.
2. Ability to use the full pronunciation key in the front of the dictionary.
3. Ability to use and interpret accent marks, both primary and secondary.
4. Ability to select the proper heteronyms, for example rec′ord or re cord′; ob′ject or ob ject′.
5. Ability to identify silent letters in words pronounced.
6. Ability to recognize differences between spellings and pronunciations (lack of phoneme-grapheme relationship).
7. Ability to use phonetic spelling for pronunciation.
8. Abiuty to discriminate vowel sounds.
9. Ability to use diacritical marks as an aid in pronunciation.
10. Understanding of the way syllables are marked in dictionaries.
11. Ability to identify unstressed syllables in words.
12. Arriving at pronunciation and recognizing it as correct.

Meaning skills:

1. Learning meanings of new words by reading simple definitions.
2. Using pictures and meanings in the dictionary to arrive at meanings.
3. Using an illustrative sentence to arrive at meanings.
4. Using two different meanings for the same word.
5. Ability to approximate real life sizes by using dictionary pictures and explanatory clues.
6. Ability to select the specific meaning for a given context.
7. Understanding special meanings: idioms, slang expressions and other figures of speech.
8. Use of the concept of *root word.*
9. Interpreting multiple meanings of words.
10. Ability to know when meaning has been satisfied through dictionary usage.

For example, if the child . . . had previously heard the word *hypothesis*, or perhaps even knew it well enough to use it in his own conversation, then his skill in phonics, combined with his knowing the word in its spoken form, would probably be sufficient to help him identify the word the first time he encountered it in written form.[19]

Horn raised the question forty years ago whether the English language is so unphonetic as to make impractical teaching phonics generalizations in the primary grades.[20]

By second grade, the child has met at least six spellings for long *a* (a):

p*a*per	pl*a*y
*a*te	pr*a*ise
f*ai*l	gr*ea*t

and eight spellings for *ea*:

long a	gr*ea*t	ä	h*ea*rt
short e	br*ea*d	û	s*ea*rch
â	w*ea*r	ū	b*ea*uty
ē	*ea*t	ō	bur*ea*u

Cordts found 47 different sound-letter associations for the letter *a* in words actually occurring in First, Second, and Third readers.[21] ". . . the unphonetic character of the English Language constitutes a real obstacle to successful rationalization."[22]

The value of teaching "rules" in phonetic and structural analysis is open to serious question if some of the first words the child reads where he applies the "rule" happen to be "exceptions" to that rule. For example, the child may learn that "when two vowels go walking," the first one has its long sound, but he must learn to cope with "bread" and "break" about as soon as he does with "team" and "cream."

Oaks,[23] in 1952, found that vowel situations that need to be explained appear as early as the primer in basal readers.

Clymer,[24] in 1963, found that many generalizations being taught had limited value and that teachers must teach that there are many excep-

---

[19]Dolores Durkin, *Phonics and the Teaching of Reading* (New York: Bureau of Publications, Teachers College, Columbia, 1962), pp. 47-48.

[20]Ernest Horn, "The Child's Early Experience with the Letter A," *Journal of Educational Psychology*, 20:161-168, March, 1929.

[21]Cordts, *op. cit.*, p. 164.

[22]*Ibid.*, p. 168.

[23]Ruth E. Oaks, "A Study of the Vowel Situations in A Primary Vocabulary," *Education*, 71:604-617, 1952.

[24]Theodore L. Clymer, "The Utility of Phonics Generalizations in the Primary Grades," *The Reading Teacher*, 16:252-258, 1963.

tions to most generalizations being taught. Of forty-five generalizations which he found in primary grade teachers' manuals for basal readers, when checked against all the words in a composite word list, the per cent of utility was too low for many of them to justify teaching. Using 75 percent as an arbitrary criterion value of usefulness, he found only eighteen generalizations worth teaching.

Burrows and Lourie[25] found that teachers might look for other ways to pronounce double vowels than to try to use the "when two vowels go walking" generalizations.

Winkley[26] studied eighteen accent generalizations found in methodology, and concluded that twelve of these had sufficient applicability to justify their teaching. By combining and rewording these, she reduced the number to seven which she proposed as worth teaching to children.

Emans[27] studied the applicability of Clymer's generalizations in grades four and above and found that a few of Clymer's generalizations had less applicability above fourth grade and that there were a few not included by Clymer that had more applicability.

Bailey[28] evaluated the utility of Clymer's 45 generalizations and found some of them clearly stated and especially useful, while she found some less useful and others difficult to interpret.

Burmeisiter[29] sifted results from the studies of Oaks, Clymer, Fry,[30] Bailey, Emans, and Winkley which she combined with her own data and developed a list of especially useful generalizations.

The following selected, useful generalizations are based on these studies:

Generalizations about the behavior of consonants:

1. When *c* and *h* are next to each other, they make only one sound.
2. *Ch* is usually pronounced as it is in mu*ch*, *ch*eck, and not like *sh*.
3. When *c* or *g* is followed by *e, i,* or *y,* the soft sound is likely to be heard; otherwise they will have a hard sound.
4. When *ght* is seen in a word, *gh* is silent.
5. When a word begins *kn,* the *k* is silent.
6. When a word begins with *wr,* the *w* is silent.

---

[25]A. T. Burrows and Z. Lourie, "When 'Two Vowels Go Walking,'" *The Reading Teacher,* 17: 79-82, November, 1963.

[26]Winkley, *op. cit.,* pp. 218-224 ff.

[27]Robert Emans, "The Usefulness of Phonic Generalizations Above the Primary Grades," *The Reading Teacher,* 20:419-425, February, 1967; "When Two Vowels Go Walking and Other Such Things," *The Reading Teacher,* 21:262-269, December, 1967.

[28]Mildred Hart Bailey, "The Utility of Phonic Generalizations in Grades One Through Six," *The Reading Teacher,* 20:413-418, February, 1967.

[29]Lou Burmeister, "Usefulness of Phonic Generalizations," *The Reading Teacher,* 21:349-356, January, 1968; "Vowel Pairs," *The Reading Teacher,* 21:445-452, February, 1968.

[30]E. A. Fry, "A Frequency Approach to Phonics," *Elementary English,* 41:759-765ff, 1964.

7. When two of the same consonants are side by side, only one is heard.
8. When a word ends in *ck*, it has the same last sound as in *look*.

Generalizations about the behavior of vowels:

9. If the only vowel is at the end of a one-syllable word, the letter usually has its long sound.
10. the "r" gives the preceding vowel a sound that is neither long nor short.
11. When the letters *oa* are together in a word, *o* gives its long sound and *a* is silent.
12. Words having double *e* usually have the long *e* sound.
13. When *y* is the final letter in a word, it usually has a vowel sound.
14. When *a* is followed by *r* and final *e*, we expect to hear the sound heard in *care*.

Generalizations about syllabication and accent:

15. In most two-syllable words, the first syllable is accented (unless it is a prefix).
16. If *a, in, re, ex, de,* or *be* is the first syllable in a word, it is usually unaccented.
17. In most two-syllable words that end in a consonant followed by *y*, the first syllable is accented and the last is unaccented.
18. When *ture* is the final syllable in a word, it is unaccented.
19. When *tion* is the final syllable in a word, it is unaccented.
20. If the last syllable of a word ends in *le*, the consonant preceding the *le* usually begins the last syllable.
21. When the first vowel element in a word is followed by *th, ch, sh,* or *ph,* these symbols are not broken when the word is broken into syllables and may go with either the first or second syllable.

Rationale for Vowel Spellings

It is not possible to think of a very helpful rationale for the "spelling-to-sound" correspondence for the five English vowels. Generally considered, the spelling-sound relationships of the vowels show little regularity. Venezky states that "o" corresponds to seventeen different sounds, "a" to ten, "e" to nine, and the total five vowels to forty-eight.[31]

Nevertheless, there are some patterns that teachers of reading, especially in the early elementary grades, will find helpful.

1. The single syllable word ending in a consonant or the closed syllable, CVC, will contain a vowel that usually uses its short sound,

---

[31]Richard L. Venezky, "English Orthography, Its Graphical Structure and Its Relation to Sound," *Reading Research Quarterly*, 2:95, Number 3, Spring, 1967.

for example, can, men, fin, cot, but, candle, mention, finishing, cottage, butterfly.

The number of three-letter words fitting the patterns below suggest that this is a very important generalization for boys and girls to learn early in the reading program:

big	pat	not
beg	pet	nut
bag	pit	net
bug	put	nat
bog	pot	nit

A tachistoscope, as illustrated below, can be used to provide rapid drill practice for small groups of children in substituting short vowel sounds.

hit	pen	bid
hot	pin	bud
hat	pan	bed
hut	pun	bad

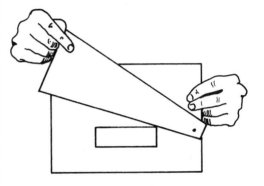

him	bit	den
ham	bat	din
hem	but	Dan
hum	bet	don

ten	fun	red
tan	fan	rod
tin	fin	rid

mat	sit	led
met	sat	lid
mit	set	lad

mid	top	dig
mad	tap	dog
mud	tip	dug

2. The vowel followed by a consonant followed by final "e" (V + C + e) usually has its long sound, cane, mete, fine, rote, mute.

The teacher may teach many short sounds of the vowels first. However, children do learn from contrasting too. It may be helpful for some children to contrast *not* and *note*; *hat* and *hate*, by listening to the separate sounds of the vowels as he looks at both words together. A short list of common pairs in this pattern are given below:

tap	tape	plan	plane	mop	mope	rid	ride
can	cane	bad	bade			dim	dime
pan	pane	fat	fate	pin	pine	fin	fine
man	mane			slid	slide	rip	ripe
hat	hate	not	note	win	wine	kit	kite
mad	made	hop	hope	bit	bite	hid	hide

3. The vowel may retain its long sound if the vowel is followed by another consonant followed by another vowel within the word:

canine   ladle   pilot   meter   potent   music

The vowel sound is short if the vowel is followed by a compound consonant unit (dg, x, ck) or by geminate consonants (dd, gh, nn). Geminate means to double, being doubled or paired, or occurring in pairs, as twin consonants, in cabbage, rubbed, and setting. The vowel preceding geminate consonant pattern is usually short:

badge   exit   taxi   pocket

saddle   antenna   cognate

4. The long vowel sound in V + C + e changes to a short sound in words that add syllables like *ic* or *ity* or when geminate consonants (twin consonants) appear:

sane	sanity	later	latter
mete	netting	caning	canning
cone	conic	hoping	hopping
rose	roster	motel	mottle
site	sitting	super	supper
induce	induction	biting	bitter
		tubing	tubbing

5. The final "e" pattern of V + C + e may also produce long vowel sounds in polysyllabic words that also end with V + C + e.

file	domicile
fume	resume
size	nationalize
robe	microbe
late	matriculate
gene	gangrene

6. Boys and girls need direct teaching of sounds for specific application for much of their beginning work with double vowels in one-syllable words. Double *e* producing long *e* and *oa* producing long *o* will be consistent in the words in the elementary school.* But *ea* may be long *e* in *lean* and *beat*, short *e* in *bread*, and long *a* in *break*. The double vowel *oo* uses one of its sounds in *book* and the other in *moon*. *Ou* and *aw* sound alike in a few words but have variant sounds in others.

---

*The child's few exceptions to this valid *oa* generalization are *boa*, when he learns about boa constrictors; *goa*, if he learns about the gazelle of Tibet; or, *Goa* a small land area in India.

IV. GAMES AND DEVICES

Games and devices can provide necessary drill or repetitive practice if the games are carefully evaluated. The use of carefully selected games and devices that give the child an opportunity to win may provide needed extrinsic motivation. Winning the game will be its own reward and at the same time the child will experience success in learning a reading-related skill.

The basic requirements for games and devices are:

1. The primary emphasis should be on learning the skill needed in reading:
   a. In the "Group-Sounding Game," the child has practice in self-help sounding at different levels;
   b. In *vowel domino,* each time a child plays a domino in the game he makes a decision about a short vowel sound.
2. The mechanics of the game should *not* be such that little time is spent on the learning of the skill needed in reading.
3. The "fun part" should center around reading skill rather than enjoying a physical skill not related at all to the reading act.

Available commercial games, a few selected games that teachers can devise, and a brief list of sources of good games and devices are given below:

A. Commercial Games:

1. *Go-Fish,* a card game for practicing and reinforcing auditory discrimination of initial consonant sounds (First series) and consonant blend sounds (Second series) (Kingsburg Center, 2138 Bancroft Place, N.W., Washington, D. C. 20008: The Remedial Education Press).

2. *Vowel Dominoes,* a card game played like dominoes practicing and reinforcing the short sounds of the vowels (Kingsburg Center, 2138 Bancroft Place, N.W., Washington, D. C. 20008: The Remedial Education Press).

3. *Take,* a card game designed to practice hearing the sounds at the beginning, in the middle or at the end of the word (Champaign, Illinois: The Garrard Press).

4. *Quizmo,* a bingo game designed to practice hearing initial consonant, consonant blend, and initial short vowel sounds. The box contains directions, a list of words for the teacher to "call," and thirty-eight bingo cards (Springfield, Massachusetts: Milton Bradley).

5. *The Syllable Game,* a card game in which words from the intermediate grade vocabulary are divided into syllables. Designed to help the student recognize and remember the commonest syllables in words. Like syllables become matched pairs. It may be played as a form of *solitaire* or as a group game (Champaign, Illinois: The Garrard Press).

6. *Word Wheels.* A word wheel is usually two circles fastened together, with the smaller one fastened so that it rotates in such a way that initial consonants and consonant blends can be matched to family words or that prefixes or suffixes can be matched to root words. *Phono Word Wheels* are available from the Steck Company, Box 16, Austin 61, Texas. *Webster Word Wheels* are available from the Webster Division, McGraw-Hill Publishing Company, Manchester, Missouri.

7. *Phonic Rummy,* a game played by matching vowel sounds. There are four sets of cards with sixty cards in each set. One set is for grades 1 and 2; one set is for grades 2 and 3; one set is for grades 2, 3, and 4; and one for grades 3, 4, and 5 (Buffalo, New York: Kenworthy Educational Service, Inc.).

8. *Phonics We Use Learning Games Kit.* Ten separate games for two or more players, reinforcing primary phonics skills. Games: *Old Itch* —for initial consonant sounds; *Spin-a-Sound*—initial consonant sounds, symbols; *Blends Race*—initial consonant blends, symbols; *Digraph Whirl* —initial consonant digraphs, symbols; *Digraph Hopscotch*—initial and final consonant digraphs, symbols; *Vowel Dominoes*—long and short vowels, symbols; *Spin hard, Spin soft*—hard and soft "c" and "g" sounds; *Full House*—vowels, vowel digraphs, diphthongs; *Syllable Count*—syllabication and accent (407 East 25th St., Chicago Illinois 60616: Lyons and Carnahan, Educational Publishers, 1967).

B. Games for the Teacher to Make:

1. *This to That.* Starting with one word, one of the letters in the word is changed each time, making a series such as: *his, him, ham, ram, ran, run.* The game can also be played with changing two-letter combinations, as: *sheep, sheet, shoot, shook, spook, spoke, broke.* This may be a better form of review than the monotony of word families.

2. *Fishing.* One word, a phrase, or a short sentence is printed on each of a number of small cardboard cutouts in shape of fish, to which paper clips are attached. The child picks up a fish by means of a tiny horseshoe magnet on a string (his fishing pole). He may keep his card if he can read it correctly. The one with the most fish wins the game. Similar games can be devised doing such things as pulling leaves off trees, etc.

4. I'm thinking of a word that begins like:

a. Use sight words learned and put them in the chart holder. One child says, "I'm thinking of a word that begins like *run*." The second child says, "Is it ride?" When a child guesses the right word, he gives the next clue.

b. This game can be only auditory discrimination practice without using word cards. The child says, "I'm thinking of a word that begins like dog." This child then whispers his choice of words to a score keeper. Children then may respond with any word that begins with "d."

C. Books of Good Suggestions:

1. DAVID RUSSELL and ETTA KARP. *Reading Aids Through the Grades* (New York: Bureau of Publications, Teachers College, Columbia University, 1951.)

2. DAVID RUSSELL. *Listening Aids Through the Grades* (New York: Bureau of Publications, Teachers College, Columbia University, 1959.)

3. MARY E. PLATTS, SISTER ROSE MARGUERITE, S.G.C., and ESTHER SHUMAKER. *Spice. Suggested Activities to Motivate the Teaching of the Language Arts in the Elementary School.* Benton Harbor, Michigan: Educational Service, Inc., 1960.

4. GUY WAGNER and MAX HOSIER. *Reading Games. Strengthening Reading Skills with Instructional Games.* Darien, Connecticut: Educational Publishing Corporation, 1961.

5. GUY WAGNER, *et al. Listening Games: Strengthening Language Skills with Instructional Games.* Darien, Conecticut: Educational Publishing Corporation, 196—.

V. SUMMARY

This chapter has contained a discussion of the skills in word recognition. Techniques for teaching a basic sight vocabulary, recognizing that meaning is essential to develop reading as a thinking process, using phonetic and structural analysis clues, and learning to use the dictionary were considered. Also, studies that reviewed the usefulness of phonic generalizations now presented in teachers' manuals that accompany basal readers were summarized. Games and devices for strengthening word recognition abilities were discussed and a brief list of resources for teachers were presented.

SUGGESTED ACTIVITIES

1. Administer the McKee Phonics Inventory, Level 3, to a child in third grade or above in the elementary school.

2. Take:

a. Durkin's Phonics Test for Teachers* and interpret the results.

b. Triggs Diagnostic Reading Survey: Word Attack, Silent.**

3. Using a teacher's manual for one grade level in the elementary school, outline the phonics skills being taught and reinforced in that textbook, or

4. Using the form on the following page, study a teacher's manual and summarize specific word recognition and word analysis skills for one reading group you teach.

---

*Durkin, Dolores, *Phonics Test for Teachers,* (New York: Teachers College Press, Columbia University, 1964).

**Triggs, Francis O., chairman, *Diagnostic Reading Test: Survey Section,* (Mountain Home, North Carolina: Committee on Diagnostic Reading Tests, Inc., 1952).

Your name _____ Date _____ Title of reading textbook _____ Grade level of text

Examples from the teacher's manual of lessons teaching word analysis skills. For all examples, give the page in the Teacher's Manual where it is found.

Type of skill	Example	Example
(For examples: Using context clues, strengthening memory of word forms, applying phonetic understandings, etc.)		

References for Further Reading

Bagford, Jack. *Phonics: Its Role in Teaching Reading.* Iowa City, Iowa: Sernoll, Inc., 1967.

Bailey, Mildred Hart. "The Utility of Phonic Generalizations in Grades One Through Six," *The Reading Teacher,* 20:413-418, February, 1967.

Burmeister, Lou. "Usefulness of Phonic Generalizations," *The Reading Teacher,* 21:349-356, January, 1968.

————. "Vowel Pairs," *The Reading Teacher,* 21:445-452, February, 1968.

Clymer, Theodore L. "The Utility of Phonic Generalizations in the Primary Grades," *The Reading Teacher,* 16:252-258, 1963.

Cordts, Anna D. *Phonics for the Reading Teacher.* New York: Holt, Rinehart, and Winston, Inc., 1965.

Durkin, Dolores. *Phonics and the Teaching of Reading.* Bureau of Publications, Teachers College, Columbia University, 1965.

Emans, Robert. "The Usefulness of Phonic Generalizations Above the Primary Grades," *The Reading Teacher,* 20:419-425, February, 1967.

————. "When Two Vowels Go Walking and Other Such Things," *The Reading Teacher,* 21:262-269, December, 1967.

Fuld, Paula. "Vowel Sounds in VCC Words," *The Reading Teacher,* 21: 442-444, February, 1968.

Gray, William S. *On Their Own in Reading,* Revised Edition. Chicago: Scott, Foresman and Co., 1960.

Harris, A. *How to Increase Reading Ability,* Fourth Edition. New York: David McKay, 1961. Chapter XII and Chapter XIII: "Developing Word Recognition Skills," pp. 315-360.

————. *Effective Reading Instruction.* New York: David McKay, 1963.

Heilman, Arthur W. *Phonics in Proper Perspective.* Columbus, Ohio: Charles E. Merrill Books, Inc., 1965.

————. *Principles and Practices in Teaching Reading,* Second Edition. Columbus, Ohio: Charles E. Merrill Books, Inc., 1967.

Horrocks, Edna M. and Norwick, Terese D. Word Study Charts (to accompany the sequence of phonetic and structural analysis skills on the Ginn Readers). Boston: Ginn and Company, 1958. A set of 20 charts, 22" by 28" in color, with plans for teaching.

Oaks, Ruth. "A Study of the Vowel Situation in a Primary Vocabulary," *Education,* LXXI:604-617, May, 1952.

Otto, Wayne, and McMenemy, Richard. *Corrective and Remedial Teaching.* Boston: Houghton Mifflin Co., 1966. Chapter 6: "Work Attack Skills in Reading," pp. 141-173.

Schell, Leo M. "Teaching Structural Analysis," *The Reading Teacher,* 21:133-137, November, 1967.

Smith, Nila B. *Reading Instruction for Today's Children.* Englewood Cliffs, New Jersey: Prentice-Hall, Inc., 1963. Chapter VIII: "Word Identification," pp. 167-253.

Spache, George D. *Reading in the Elementary School.* Boston: Allyn and Bacon, Inc., 1964. Chapter XII: "Word Recognition Techniques and Skills," pp. 280-317.

Winkley, Carol K. "Which Accent Generalizations Are Worth Teaching?" *The Reading Teacher,* 19:219-224, December, 1966.

8

Comprehension Skills

Developing meaningful concepts is the primary concern of the class-room teacher. Harrison illustrates clearly why the teacher must be sure that children are developing understanding when they become absorbed in interesting classroom activities:

> The children in a second grade had elaborately and painstakingly set up an Eskimo village on the floor of their schoolroom. The teacher had explained the igloo to the children and then proceeded to show them how they might make a satisfactory representation of an igloo from cornstarch and salt. The children molded the mixture on the inside of a bowl, cut out a low door, and turned it out upside down for the igloo. They were delighted with the result and showed it to visitors with pride. One visitor said, "And of what is an Eskimo igloo made?" to which an interested and enthusiastic pupil replied, "Cornstarch and salt." The teacher, very much chagrined, attempted to right the concept formed.[1]

Most teachers agree that pronouncing words correctly without getting meanings from the context read is *not* reading. Boys and girls must learn to synthesize meanings as they read through the passages in their text-books; otherwise, they have wasted their time. At the same time, teach-ers know that some children may pronounce words well and comprehend little or they may comprehend much but have great difficulty reading the words. For the majority, naturally, there is a positive relationship between the ability to handle the mechanics of the reading process and the ability to interpret the ideas in the passage read. Making sure that skills in comprehending what is read are developed in all elementary classrooms is one of the most basic jobs of the classroom teacher. What good can possibly result from accurate application of the necessary pho-netic or structural skills in pronouncing words, if one cannot understand

---

[1]M. Lucile Harrison, *Reading Readiness*. (Boston: Houghton Mifflin Co., 1936), p. 37.

or interpret the ideas contained in a paragraph after one has "read" it? Techniques for arriving at adequate meanings constitute the comprehension skills in reading.

I. AN OUTLINE OF COMPREHENSION SKILLS

To comprehend, or to understand what the author has written, takes place at different levels of difficulty according to the nature of the material and the purposes for which the reading is intended. Horn has written that boys and girls "understand at different levels" the content they attempt to read with understanding. He classifies readers deficient in comprehension abilities as of four types: the one who comprehends only a small portion of the ideas that a selection contains; the one who can answer comprehension questions only by answering with the words of the textbook, verbatim or in slightly paraphrased form, with little or no understanding of their significance; the one who makes no overt response or says "I don't know;" and the one who makes interpretive responses that are partially or wholly erroneous.[2]

Stauffer places students on a long continuum, with respect to comprehension abilities, all the way from one extreme of reproducing the exact idea of the textbook, or "parroting back what the book says", to producing mental constructs creatively and with originality. These are the thinkers. The ability of boys and girls to comprehend is then distributed along this long continuum.[3]

Taba's hierarchy of cognitive tasks in the development of thinking in children is applicable to levels of understanding in reading. Taba says that concept formation requires at the primary level three sequential mental operations of differentiation, abstraction, and ordering items in subordinate-superordinate positions. The next level of abstraction in this process requires arriving at inferences and generalizations. Generalizing requires separating relevant and irrelevant information, establishing cause and effect relationships, and perceiving implications beyond what is explicitly stated.[4]

In this text, comprehension skills are classified as those of literal comprehension, or the pre-interpretive skills, and interpretive skills. Critical reading ability is the application of these skills in reading and applying judgmental, evaluative, and selective skills while reading. These

[2]Ernest Horn, "Language and Meaning," *The Psychology of Learning,* Forty-First Yearbook of the National Society for the Study of Education, Part II, Nelson B. Henry, Editor, (Chicago: University of Chicago Press, 1942), p. 402.

[3]Russell G. Stauffer, *Directing Reading Maturity as a Cognitive Process,* (New York: Harper and Row, 1969), p. 59.

[4]Hilda Taba, *Teaching Strategies and Cognitive Functioning in Elementary School Children.* U. Office of Education, Cooperative Research Project No. 2404), San Francisco: San Francisco State College, 1966, pp. 36-43.

complex skills are discussed in a separate chapter. Literal comprehension requires basic skills in understanding vocabulary, remembering and using what one has read, finding details, following directions, and understanding paragraph organization. Literal comprehension also requires getting meanings from the context through such abilities as finding the main idea, putting ideas in proper sequence to tell a story, or finding pertinent information in paragraphs to answer questions.

The interpretive skills include learning to anticipate meanings, drawing inferences, drawing generalizations, and selecting and evaluating. The comprehension skills are outlined below:

The Skills of Comprehension

I. Literal Comprehension
  A. Foundation Skills
    1. Expanding vocabulary concepts
      a. Using the rest of the sentence to determine meaning
      b. Matching word meanings
      c. Putting words in categories
      d. Choosing synonyms
      e. Recognizing sequence of ideas within a sentence
      f. Determining if sentence explains *why, when, where*
      g. Understanding antecedents or pronoun referents
    2. Finding and remembering details
    3. Understanding and following directions
    4. Understanding paragraph organization
  B. Getting meaning from the context
    1. Reading to find answers
    2. Finding the main idea in a paragraph or in a story
    3. Putting ideas in proper sequence in a story
II. Interpretive skills
  A. Learning to anticipate meanings
    1. The cloze procedure
    2. Predicting what will happen next
  B. Drawing inferences
  C. Drawing generalizations
  D. Selecting and Evaluating
    1. Fact vs. fancy
    2. Selecting material pertinent to a given topic
    3. Overstatement or unfounded claims
    4. Judging emotional response to what is read

Distinguishing Comprehension Skills from Study Skills

Reading, comprehending, and making use of context constitutes the range of skills described above. In order to *study* successfully in the content areas, there are other skills necessary to be effective. Skills not included above include: (1) learning to locate information (2) learning to read graphs, charts, maps, and tables, and (3) learning organization skills for outlining, summarizing, and notetaking.

These latter skills are classified as the skills for study reading and are reviewed in greater detail in Chapter 9.

Part III of this chapter will provide illustrative exercises for all of the items listed in the outline of comprehension skills above.

II. HELPING CHILDREN WITH MEANING IN READING

Writing Techniques Aid Comprehension

Writers for children need to make use of techniques that will help children pick out meanings of new words within the context of what they are reading. Such techniques have been prescribed by Artley and McCullough.[5] They include:

1. A brief explanation of the word can be given in parentheses or in a footnote: The *cacique* ordered an inquisition of the intruders who came into the village. (The *cacique* is the chief, or person of the highest authority in the village.)
2. A clause or phrase which explains the meaning of the word can be inserted in the sentence:
   a. At certain times during the year in the northern skies one can see the *aurora borealis,* a colorful display of flickering, shifting lights.
   b. Moss, grass, and flowers grow in the *tundra,* the treeless plains found in Arctic regions.
3. A synonym or substitute phrase is used to indicate the meaning:
   a. "*shrimp,* a small shellfish"
   b. "*the lobby,* a small waiting room"
   c. "*the cacique,* the chief of the tribe"
4. A new word is *emphasized* by using italics, quotation marks, or bold-face type to call attention to it:
   a. The farmer uses a machine called a *combine* to harvest the wheat.
   b. Pioneer farmers used a "cradle," a scythe with a wooden frame attached, to harvest the grain.
   c. Farmers who shared their crops with the landowner were called **sharecroppers.**
5. A direct explanation of the word can be presented in a full sentence:
   a. "In the hot desert, the man makes his garden in an oasis. An oasis is a green spot where there is a water supply."

---

[5]A. S. Artley, "Teaching Word Meaning Through Context," *Elementary English Review,* 20:68-74, 1943. Constance M. McCullough, "The Recognition of Context Clues in Reading," *Elementary English Review,* 22:1-5, 1945.

    b. "The nomads of the desert are coming to the trading center. Nomads are people who constantly move about and who have no settled home."

    c. The farmer could guide his oxen by shouting "Gee!" or "Haw!" The oxen had learned that "Gee" meant to turn to the right and "Haw" meant to turn to the left.

The following suggestions will help children develop the ability to anticipate meanings while reading:

1. Sometimes a new word is set off by boldface type, italics, or quotation marks to call attention to it.
2. Sometimes the new word is followed by a parenthetical expression explaining its meaning.
3. Sometimes the new word is followed by a less technical or more generally known synonym or substitute phrase.
4. Sometimes the new word will be defined in the sentence following.
5. Sometimes the new word is one with several meanings, but in its current context it can possibly have only one intended meaning.
6. A pictorial illustration may help clarify a new concept.

Boys and girls will profit from directed practice in arriving at meanings through exercises suggested below:

1. Study the context to look for clues to the meanings.
2. Relate the word to previous content in the subject.
3. Study the word structure. If it has a prefix, root, or suffix that is already known, combine context and word structure to arrive at specific meaning.
4. Read the dictionary meanings; find the one that fits.
5. Once the word is understood, think of synonyms or antonyms.
6. Once the word is understood, use it purposefully in several situations.

Vocabulary Development

Extending children's vocabularies should be a continuing objective of every teacher. There are many ways in which teachers can motivate growth in vocabulary skills.

The development of good vocabularies is encouraged by:

1. Wide reading.
2. Association with people who have a wide vocabulary.
3. Travel.
4. Varied experiences such as excursions, activities, industrial arts projects, laboratory experiments.
5. Talking over what one has read.

6. Giving conscious attention to new words when one encounters them.
7. Asking for the meaning of non-understood words.

Suggestions to teachers for improving children's vocabularies:[6]

1. Teach children to ask about any new or unusual or non-understood words as they encounter them.
2. Put such words on the board, and encourage their frequent use.
3. Enrich the curriculum generally, so that children have much material to talk about and think about. Encourage the reading of other books and magazines. Nothing can take the place of varied experience and of wide reading in building up meanings.
4. Have frequent oral tests covering new words, using them in sentences and discussing their meanings.
5. As any unit of subject matter is finished, children may, alone or with the teacher, make lists of words or phrases which have been learned by the study of the unit.
6. Work on word meanings in specific contexts, not in isolation.
7. Keep the emphasis upon meaning rather than upon mere recognition or mechanical pronunciation of words.
8. Make definite provision for word study in the upper grades, that is, study of roots, prefixes, and suffixes.
9. Make specific attempts to break the habit of passing by unknown words in reading without looking them up. Develop the "dictionary habit."
10. Drill pupils in giving synonyms and antonyms, both for words and for phrases.
11. Give considerable practice in deriving meanings from the context.

Deighton outlines the following procedure in teaching for vocabulary development in the classroom:[7]

1. Students must understand what word meanings are and how they are determined. Dictionary definitions are only points of departure and do not circumscribe the word.
   What must be explained is the interaction of the reader's experience, the context, and the dictionary entry in deriving the meaning of a particular word in a particular context.
2. Students must be prepared to get the meaning out of unfamiliar words as they meet them. This includes prefixes, suffixes, and com-

---

[6]*Manual for Interpretation of Iowa Every-Pupil Tests of Basic Skills,* College of Education, State University of Iowa, Iowa City, Iowa, 1947, pp. 42-43.
[7]Lee C. Deighton, *Vocabulary Development in the Clasroom* (Bureau of Publications, Teachers College, Columbia University, New York, 1959), pp. 56-59.

bining forms with specific meanings. Establishing meanings of root words from context or the dictionary is also important.

3. Students need instruction in ways meanings can be derived from the context: by definition, by example, by restatement, by qualifiers, and by inference.

4. Understanding figures of speech will require some special attention. They appear frequently and are a source of confusion to young readers.

5. Students need their attention called to ways some words operate in the language: judgment words, relationships in time and space, words of indefinite quantity, and words of an absolute nature.

Questions Teachers Ask

Asking appropriate questions can be a way of motivating boys and girls to acquire better vocabularies. Fitzpatrick has suggested the following types:[8]

1. The Definition Question. Example: "What does *school* mean in this sentence: As he glided through the water, he met a *school* of small, flat fish."

2. The Semantic Question. Example: "What other meanings do you know for the word *school*?"

3. The Synonym Question. Example: "Look at the *italicized* word in the sentence: Jefferson began a policy of *strict* economy. What other word(s) could be substituted for *strict* without changing the meaning of the sentence?"

4. The Antonym Question. Example: "What word(s) could you use for *strict* in the above sentence to make it have an opposite meaning?"

5. The Homonym Question. Example: "Look at the *italicized* word in the sentence: The *seams* of the boat were leaking. What other word(s) sounds the same but is spelled differently and has a different meaning?"

6. The Key Word Question. Example: "What is the meaning of the italicized word in this sentence: The Russians have placed the first man-made planet in *orbit*?"

In short, one way to develop vocabulary is to ask questions about words appearing in written material being studied in every subject area. The advantage of this integrated approach is obvious. Not only is the teacher improving vocabulary, but he is also improving general comprehension of the material.

---

[8]Dr. Mildred Fitzpatrick, Director, New Mexico Title I Program, State Department of Education, Santa Fe, 1967.

In summary, then, children are helped to improve their vocabularies by all of the following:

1. Provision of a wide background of first-hand experiences.
2. Use of visual aids.
3. Provision of many opportunities for oral language expression and listening.
4. Careful explanation of concepts by the teacher.
5. Use of oral reading and story telling by the teacher.
6. Use of pupil-made materials.
7. Emphasis upon concept-building in the content fields.
8. Provision for wide reading experiences.
9. Use of the dictionary: picture dictionaries and standard elementary dictionaries.
10. Informal word study: thinking of many multiple meanings, compound words, word opposites, synonyms, classifying words, using descriptive words, knowing plurals or words where spelling changes.

III. ILLUSTRATIVE EXERCISES FOR TEACHING THE SKILLS OF COMPREHENSION

I. Literal Comprehension
  A. Foundation Skills
    1. Expanding vocabulary concepts
      a. Using the rest of the sentence to determine the meaning.[9]
        (1) Mrs. James was *puzzled* by Joyce's idea and even more *bewildered* by her actions.
        (2) Mrs. Collins *praised* her daughter, *saying that her idea was very good.*
        (3) Mr. Warren kept a plow, a hayrake, and other *implements* in the barn.
        (4) George *looked over* the cleaning job, and when he had completed his *survey*, he said, "I think this basement looks fine."
        (5) "See how *sleek* Danny looks after he's curried," said Art as he eyed the pony's *smooth, glossy* coat.
      b. Matching word meanings: What does each worker do?
        (1) Read carefully through the list of workers:

minister	shoemaker	surveyor	audience	author
farmer	swimmer	sculptor	general	actress
fireman	magician	doctor	artist	grocer
teacher	miner	clown	king	conductor

---

[9]Gray, Horseman, Monroe, *Basic Reading Skills for Junior High School Use.* (Chicago: Scott Foresman), p. 13.

(2) In the list below find the matching word for each word
above. On your paper, write the words that go together, for example, "1. minister preaches."

digs	preaches	sells	commands	paints
dives	reigns	juggles	listens	cultivates
measures	collects	acts	rescues	heals
writes	carves	jokes	mends	instructs

c. Putting words in categories.

All of the words below can be classified as four types:
flowers, foods, animals, and ways of describing behavior.
Rule your paper as shown below, and put each of the words
in its proper category.

Flowers	Foods	Animals	Describing behavior

The words are: primrose, kangaroo, prunes, happy, beets,
peony, healthy, butter, helpful, tulip, tortoise, buffalo,
kind, pansy, donkey, dahlia, zebra, salad, giraffe, cocoa,
busy, mule, polite, cheese, chimpanzee, generous, cheerful,
brave, thrifty, lilac, interesting, careful, soup, punctual,
dandelion, industrious, cauliflower, sandwiches.

d. Choosing synonyms.

(1) Read the list of words below:

finally	entrust	gradually	comment
declared	resented	despair	surveyed
grumbled	difficult	ridicule	compliment

(2) Now read the list of words or expressions below and
find one that means the same or nearly the same as

each of the words in (1). On your paper, match the word in (1) with its synonym below:

complained	was angry at	at last	hopelessness
remark	give	said	hard
make fun of	term of praise	looked at	little by little

e. Recognizing sequence of ideas within a sentence.[10]
Each group of words here is a part of a sentence—a beginning, a middle, or a last part. When you put them in the right order, they make a sentence. In each box you are to put 1 in front of the first part, 2 in front of the middle part, and 3 in front of the last part of the sentence.

(1) _____ Friday was the day

_____ on her vacation

_____ that Miss Spruce started

(2) _____ clear the table

_____ Patty helped

_____ and wash the dishes

(3) _____ and disappeared

_____ the starving beast

_____ leaped from the cage

(4) _____ these new books in the right order

_____ on the new bookshelf"

_____ Ruth said, "I'm going to put

(5) _____ so that the bee would fly out

_____ the window of the bus

_____ Mr. Hunter was going to raise

f. Deciding whether the sentence explains when, where, why, how or who: Read the sentence on the left and then write in the blank space on the right whether it tells when, where, why, how or who.

(1) The man sat *in the shade of the house.* _____

(2) Mary cried *because she could not go.*   _____

(3) Tell me *when you have finished.*   _____

(4) They lived *happily* ever after.   _____

(5) The boys won the ball game *easily.*   _____

(6) Do you always work so *rapidly*?   _____

McKee introduces this type of exercise at the second grade level: In each sentence the part that is underlined tells where or when or how. Read each sentence. After the sen-

---

[10]Gray, Monroe, and Artley, *Think-And-Do Book* to accompany *Just Imagine!* (Teacher's Edition), (Chicago: Scott, Foresman and Company, 1953), p. 24, and Guidebook to accompany *Basic Reading Skills for Junior High School Use,* (Teacher's Edition), (Chicago: Scott, Foresman and Company, 1957), p. 19.

tence you will see three words. Draw a line under the one word that shows what the underlined part of the sentence tells:[11]

(1) A golden coach came *down the street.*

                               When   Where   How

(2) Our cat likes to stay out *at night.*

                               When   Where   How

(3) I went to the store *in a hurry.*

                               When   Where   How

(4) Bob ran *as fast as he could go.*

                               When   Where   How

(5) *Last summer* I drank some
goat's milk.   When   Where   How

(6) Would a goat ride *in a golden coach?*

                               When   Where   How

g. Understanding antecedents or pronoun referents in the sentence. Directions: In each sentence below two or three pronouns are *italicized.* These pronouns refer to a person or thing in the sentence. Read each sentence. Write in the blank the name of the person or thing to which the pronoun refers.[12]

A stranger asked the policeman, "Can *you* tell *me* where Pennsylvania Street is from here?"

       you _____

       me _____

George saw at a glance that *his* boat had broken away from the dock and that *it* was stuck on a sand bar.

       his _____

       it _____

Jane carefully put *her* scrapbook on the highest bookshelf so that *it* would not be lost.

       her _____

       it _____

The girls *who* belonged to the drama club asked the principal for permission to have *their* cake sale.

       who _____

       their _____

2. Finding and remembering details.

This is probably the kind of questioning teachers emphasize too much: recalling all the details in a short passage.

---

[11]Paul McKee, *et al., Workbook for On We Go,* (Boston: Houghton Mifflin, 1963), p. 25.

[12]W. S. Gray and Gwen Horseman, *Basic Reading Skills for Junior High School Use),* (Chicago: Scott, Foresman and Company, 1957), p. 21.

Example 1[13]

Henry plowed his way through the snow to the barn. There he got a hammer, some nails, and a wide box, and filled a small sack with cracked grain. He then went to an open shed which was built near the woods and used as a shelter for cows in the summer. When he reached the shed, he saw that a flock of snowbirds had already come to live there for the winter. He nailed the box under the shed and then filled it with the cracked grain. As he hurried back through the snow, he heard the birds chirping their thanks.

1. The shed was built near the (a) barn (b) house (c) woods (d) box
2. The grain was to feed the (a) cows (b) pigs (c) birds (d) chickens
3. Henry put the grain (a) in the barn (b) in the box (c) on the ground (d) on the snow
4. The birds that came to the shed were (a) snowbirds (b) bluejays (c) sparrows (d) robins
5. The birds chirped because they were (a) cold (b) warm (c) happy (d) sad
6. Henry carried the hammer and nails to the (a) house (b) barn (c) woods (d) shed
7. The box was (a) deep (b) wide (c) narrow (d) long
8. The birds came to the shed to spend the (a) spring (b) summer (c) fall (d) winter
9. To get to the barn Henry had to (a) shovel a path through the snow (b) wade through the snow (c) go through the woods (d) go through the shed
10. Henry nailed the box (a) under the shed (b) to a tree (c) to the roof (d) outside the barn
11. What kind of person was Henry? (a) considerate (b) skillful (c) hardy (d) devoted
12. Which sentence isn't true? (a) Henry made use of nails and box. (b) The snowbirds were accustomed to winter. (c) The closed shed was warm. (d) The snow lay thick on the ground.

Example 2[14]

1. People used to think that night air was bad for them. They thought it was full of sickness and they kept their win-

---

[13]William A. McCall and Lelah Mae Crabbs, *Standard Test Lessons in Reading,* Book B, (New York: Bureau of Publications, Teachers College, Columbia University, 1961), p. 9.

[14]Arthur I. Gates, *Gates Silent Reading Test, Type D: Reading to Note Details,* Form 1, Grades 3-8 (New York City: Bureau of Publications, Teachers College, Columbia University, 1926).

dows shut at night. We know that night air is good and that we should keep our windows open. We should keep our windows open even in winter. If our bodies are warmly covered, no cold air we breathe can hurt us.

People thought that night air was full of—

  health stars sickness airplanes

At night we should keep our windows—

  closed shut broken open

Even on cold nights we should keep open our—

  mouths windows gates doors

Example 3[15]

Reading to Appreciate the General Significance of a Paragraph.

 Ben was a city boy who had never been to the country. He had lived all of his short life in city streets. One summer some friends took him to the country. He was shown the animals, the meadows, and the woods. He looked at them all in silence. Suddenly he looked up with tears in his eyes and asked, "But where are the streets to play in?"

Draw a line under the word that best tells how Ben felt.

  excited homesick happy joyful weary

 The little country boy had been brought to the city. He had been shown the high buildings. He had ridden in the subways and had seen bright electric signs at night. But after three days he began to grow weary of the sights of the city. He longed to go back to the country. "Oh, how I wish I could see a little running brook!" he sighed.

Draw a line under the word that best tells how the country boy felt.

  angry afraid homesick happy playful

3. Understanding and following directions.[16]

 a. A long time ago people used weather cocks to tell about the weather. When the wind blew from the north and it was to be cold, the weather cock faced the north. Draw a line around the letter that shows the way the weather cock should face when a cold wind is blowing.

---

[15]Arthur I. Gates, *Gates Silent Reading Test, Type A Reading to Appreciate General Significance*, Form 2, Grades 3-8, (New York City: Bureau of Publications, Teachers College, Columbia University, 1926).

[16]Ibid., Type C, *Reading to Understand Precise Directions*, Form 1, Grades 3-8 (New York: Teacher's College Press, Columbia U., 1926).

b. James and Mary go to a funny school. Instead of Saturday or Monday being their holiday, they have Wednesday and Sunday. They have to go to school on Saturday. Draw lines around the days of the week that James and Mary do not go to school.

c. Jane has scarlet fever. The health officer came and put this sign on the front door. He also placed a yellow flag close to the left side of the sign. This was to tell people that they were not to come into the house. Make a cross where the yellow flag was placed.

4. Understanding paragraph organization.

Boys and girls need to learn that paragraphs need to have topic sentences. It is to be hoped that most of the paragraphs they study will have topic sentences around which the details of the paragraphs will cluster. However, children must also learn that all writers are not so efficient in their writing and many paragraphs in the textbooks they read will not have any topic sentence at all. Further, they will have to accept paragraphs that contain details (extra sentences) that do not amplify the topic sentence for the paragraph.

Generally, in the elementary school, children will find that paragraphs contain a topic sentence which may be the first sentence in the paragraph. It will generally circumscribe the ideas to be discussed related to the topic sentence. Sometimes, the topic sentence is a kind of summarizing sentence placed at the end of the paragraph. Boys and girls need practice identifying topic sentences found at either the beginning or the end of the paragraph. Read the following paragraph.

The Banana

Growing and exporting bananas is the most important industry in Ecuador. These plants grow in the lowlands near the Pacific Coast. The farmers take care of the plants and select the largest bunches of fruit to cut and send to market. In the lowlands where the temperature is always hot and there is always abundant rainfall, the banana plants grow very well. When the bunch of fruit is cut from the stalk, the stalk is also cut off near the ground. The plant grows a new stalk from the same roots and it produces a new bunch of bananas. It takes about a year for the plant to grow and produce fruit. New stalks can grow from the roots four or five times. Trucks carry large shipments of bananas to the docks in Guayaquil where they are exported by boat to all parts of the world. Large steamships anchor in Guayaquil to be loaded with great quantities of green bananas. Some weeks later, the bananas are ready to be sold in fruit markets and supermarkets. By this time the fruit is ripe and yellow and tastes very delicious.

As an initial step in helping children learn to outline, the teacher can guide the discussion about the content of the paragraph to help children list, perhaps on the blackboard, the details that "attach to" the five key words in the paragraph:

Growing and Exporting the Banana

Farmers	*Climate*	*Trucking*	*Shipping*	*Selling*
Planting	Lowland	Loading in	Steamers	Fruit markets
Cultivating	Rainfall	fields	Banana	Supermarkets
Harvesting	Heat	Hauling to	boats	Condition
Marketing		wharves		of fruit

This list can be re-arranged into a topical outline:
The topical outline.

Growing and Exporting the Banana

    I. The Farmer
      A. Plants
      B. Cultivates
      C. Harvests
      D. Markets
    II. Climate
      A. Lowlands
      B. Rainfall
      C. Hot
    III. Trucking
      A. Loading in the fields
      B. Hauling to the docks
    IV. Shipping
      A. On steamships
      B. On banana boats

    V. Selling
        A. In fruit markets
        B. In Supermarkets
        C. Condition of the fruit.
B. Getting Meaning from the Context
  1. Reading to find answers.
    a. Reporting the content of the lesson.
    The following factual exercise lends itself to questioning to reconstruct the story content.

"Dingdong Bell"[17]

Dingdong, dingdong! Sunday morning bells ring out, calling people to church. These bells are heard in both city and country.

Fire engines still carry a bell. Firemen pull a rope to ring the bell when they go racing off to a fire. They also sound their sirens.

On board ship, bells ring every hour and half-hour to tell sailors the time.

In the old days children came into their schoolroom when the teacher rang a bell. Sometimes this was a big handbell. Sometimes the bell was on the roof of the school house.

The most musical bells were the old sleigh bells. You heard them when the horse trotted over the snow, pulling the sleigh. Their merry tinkling, jingling sound in the frosty air is almost forgotten now.

Depending upon the maturity of the student who read the story, there are many questions possible. For example: "What is the story about?" The story tells about five kinds of bells. The question, "What kinds of bells are told about?" could lead to making a simple outline:

Different kinds of bells

1. Church bells
2. Fire engine bells
3. Ship bells
4. School bells
5. Sleigh bells

Or,

1. The church bell calls _____ .
2. The fire bell tells _____ .
3. The bell on the ship tells_____ .
4. The school bell told the children_____ .
5. Sleigh bells made music when _____ .

---

[17]Arthur I. Gates and Celeste C. Peardon, *Reading Exercises, Preparatory, Level A,* (New York: Bureau of Publications, Teachers College, Columbia University, 1963), story no. 5.

2. Finding the main idea in a paragraph or a story

   a. Selecting the best title for a paragraph

Asking boys and girls to read paragraphs and (1) select the best title from a number of suggested titles, (2) decide whether or not the title given tells what all the paragraph is about, or (3) think of a good title, will help to develop understanding of paragraph meaning and organization. The exercise below provides the student practice in selecting the best title after reading the paragraph:[18]

Fresh vegetables for a salad should be washed and dried carefully. Then they should be placed in a refrigerator for a time. Just before the salad is to be served, the greens should be broken into pieces and put into a salad bowl. Then strips of carrot, rings of onions, or other vegetables may be added. Next, a small amount of French dressing should be poured over the contents of the bowl. The salad should be tossed lightly until each part of it has become coated with dressing.

Put a check (✔) before the title that tells the main idea of the paragraph.

_____ 1. Preparing a Salad

_____ 2. How to Toss a Salad

   b. Identifying the topic sentence

A good paragraph deals with only one topic. It should contain a topic sentence. All the details of a good paragraph develop the topic sentence. The topic sentence tells what the paragraph is about. Being able to identify the topic sentence will help the reader understand and organize the ideas he is reading. In the paragraph below, the first sentence tells what the whole paragraph is about. Since it states the topic of the paragraph, it is called the topic sentence.

The separate bones are held together by joints in ways that help make movement of the body possible. The joints in the neck make it possible for a person to move his head up or down as well as from side to side. The joint at the shoulder makes it possible for him to move his arm in a round-the-circle manner. It is because of joints that we are able to bend the back, pick up articles with our fingers, and perform other actions.[19]

The topic sentence is not always the first sentence. In the following example, the topic sentence is at the end of the paragraph.

Each person was in his proper place. Flags were flying. The band had begun to play a lively march. Suddenly there

[18]Guy L. Bond, Marie C. Cuddy, and Leo C. Fay, *Fun to Do Book to accompany Stories to Remember*, (Chicago: Lyons and Carnahan, 1962), p. 22.

[19]Guy L. Bond, Marie C. Cuddy, and Leo C. Fay, *Fun to Do Book accompany Stories to Remember*, (Chicago: Lyons and Carnahan, 1962), p. 34.

was a burst of applause as the marching began. The Fourth of July celebration was starting off with a big parade.[20]

In the following paragraph all the sentences relate to the general topic of roasting corn. The whole paragraph tells two ways to roast corn. The first sentence is the topic sentence because it indicates that the paragraph will tell about two ways to roast corn over an open fire.

I know two different ways to roast corn on an open fire. One way is to dip the ears, husks and all, in water. Then you put the ears on a grill over the fire to steam. These are good, but I like the second way even better. You take off the husks and put butter and salt on the ears. Then you wrap them in aluminum foil and roast them in the coals.[21]

Boys and girls in the intermediate grades should be able to underline the topic sentences in paragraphs like the following:

(1) When Marco Polo was seventeen years old, he went to China with his father and uncle. While there, he traveled through many little-known parts of the country in the service of the ruler. Many places he visited were very wild, and Marco had some exciting times. Then, three years after he returned to his homeland, he was called on to serve in a war. He was captured and was imprisoned for nearly a year. Marco Polo had many interesting adventures during his life—both in foreign lands and in his homeland.[22]

(2) By following a few simple directions, anyone should be able to raise lettuce. Light, well-fertilized soil should be used. The lettuce seeds should not be dropped too close together. If they are dropped close together, some of the young plants should be thinned out. There should be frequent stirring of the soil to encourage growth of the plants. Large amounts of water are not necessary for growing lettuce.[23]

(3) One of the oldest and most common of the human qualities is that of wanting animals as pets. Children at an early age learn to love pets. A small child will hug his toy dog and love it, but he will gladly exchange it for a live pet. Although we think of children as the persons who most desire and need pets, most older persons also love pets. Those who lose a pet are often very sad until they get another, or until they become accustomed to being without a pet.[24]

---

[20]*Ibid.*

[21]Harold Shane, *et al.*, *Using Good English, Book Five*, (River Forest, Illinois: Laidlaw Brothers, Publishers, 1961), p. 84.

[22]Guy L. Bond, Marie C. Cuddy, and Leo C. Fay, *Fun to Do Book to accompany Stories to Remember*, (Chicago: Lyons and Carnahan, 1962), p. 35.

[23]*Ibid.*

[24]Harold Shane, *et al.*, *Using Good English, Book Six*, (River Forest, Illinois: Laidlaw Brothers, Publishers, 1961), p. 81.

3. Putting ideas in proper sequence in a story.

   Boys and girls need practice in reading exercises to remember significant details and place them in sequential order after reading. It will be helpful to establish as a part of the purpose in reading to give special attention to the order of events in the story. The exercise which follows, about the twelve labors of Hercules, is well-adapted to help sixth-graders acquire this skill.

C. Punctuation.

   Punctuation marks in written material give meaning to connected written discourse. Reading the punctuation accurately, quickly, and meaningfully significantly enhances comprehension of material read.

   Failure to give proper attention to punctuation is certain to weaken meaningful understanding of sentences and longer reading units. Underachievers in reading often fail to read smoothly and fluently and need help in establishing the practice of watching for and using punctuation. Children need to learn precise uses of periods, question marks, commas, colons, semicolons, and exclamation marks. McKee suggests teaching seven uses of the comma:[25] (1) to separate words or groups of words written as a series; (2) after the words *Yes* or *No* when either of these words answers a question and the words following *yes* or *no* merely give additional information; (3) to set off an appositive; (4) to set off a parenthetical expression in a sentence; (5) to set off an expression of address; (6) to separate a dependent clause which precedes its principal clause; and (7) to set off an adverbial clause when it contains a form of a verb.

   The words "You want to go to the football game" may be merely a statement in a conversation acknowledging someone's desire to see the game. The same words may be asking if one does, in fact, want to go. Or, they may be voiced in considerable surprise that this individual does wish to see the football game.

   > You want to go to the football game.
   > You want to go to the football game?
   > You want to go to the football game!

   Clearly the use of commas and quotation marks changes the meaning in the following sentence:

   > Mary said Grace failed the test.
   > "Mary," said Grace, "failed the test."

---

[25]Paul McKee, *The Teaching of Reading in the Elementary School*, (Boston: Houghton, Mifflin Company, 1948), p. 87.

Which Is the Right Order?

Read the story about the twelve labors of Hercules carefully,
so you will know the order in which he accomplished the feats.

A woman who was jealous of the mother of Hercules was the person who sent the serpents to the cradle of the infant. This jealous woman intended that the gigantic serpents should strangle the infant, but instead the unusual child strangled them.

In his youth, Hercules got into some trouble, and for punishment he was made a servant to the king. The king required the young man to perform twelve feats.

First, Hercules had to kill a lion that was particularly fierce. His second feat was to kill a curious and very dangerous creature called the hydra. After he had killed the hydra, his next two tasks called for the killing of an exceedingly wild deer and an unusually dangerous wild pig.

Then came the fifth task—the cleaning of certain famous stables. This task took several years. It was finally completed after Hercules changed the course of a river so a stream would run through the stables.

The sixth, seventh, and eighth tasks were concerned with the killing of birds and the capturing of bulls and of horses. When these feats had been accomplished, the young man was sent on an even more dangerous errand.

The reason this errand was dangerous was that it required Hercules to go to the land of the Amazons. This country was a nation of women warriors. Any man who dared even to approach the country was in grave danger. But Hercules and a brave companion managed to carry out their mission.

For his next feat, Hercules was to seize a large herd of red cattle from their owner. This owner was a monster with three heads and three bodies from which grew enormous wings. In addition to fighting the owner of the cattle, Hercules also had to fight the gigantic herder and a fierce herd dog that had two heads.

Then came the task which required that Hercules go to the Hesperides in search of the three golden apples. From the Hesperides, the hero was sent to seize the dog that guarded the entrance to the Underworld. The dog not only had fifty heads, but also had the tail of a huge snake. It would have been a difficult task to kill this monster, but it was an even more difficult one to bring the dog back alive.

Number the tasks performed by Hercules to show the order in which they were done.

___1___ Kill a fierce lion
___4___ Kill a dangerous wild pig
_____ Kill some unusual birds
___2___ Kill the hydra
_____ Kill a wild deer
___5___ Clean the stables
___7___ Capture some bulls
_____ Obtain clothing from the Amazon Queen
___8___ Capture some horses
___11___ Capture the guard of the Underworld
___10___ Get three apples from the Hesperides
___9___ Seize cattle

From Guy L. Bond, Marie C. Cuddy, and Leo C. Fay, *Fun to Do Book to accompany Stories to Remember,* (Chicago: Lyons and Carnahan, 1962, p. 108.

Without the comma, the sentence below may be momentarily confusing:

When the hailstorm hit the large picture window was broken.
When the hailstorm hit, the large picture window was broken.

Heilman[26] suggests giving boys and girls material to read in which the punctuation has been put in the wrong places or omitted entirely. This will emphasize for them how easily the meaning is diminished. Below, the reader will find a paragraph in which the commas have been deleted and periods appear in the wrong places. If the first paragraph is meaningless, perhaps the one following it will be more easily read.

In the American Southwest there is much talk. About cultural diffusion it has been suggested. That traditional cultures of the Indian and the Spanish-American. Have much to offer the truth of this statement. Is not contested nevertheless. It is difficult to imagine. The typical middle-class Anglo internalizing values. Of life based on the economy education religion or health practices. Of the traditional minority group the diffusion usually talked about is the more obvious. Observable and superficial type. Eating green chili-mutton stew on feast days. In a pueblo with a friend wearing a fiesta dress with ostentatious jewelry. Owning a ring with a large turquoise set or an attractive squash blossom. Necklace or decorating a room in one's house. With Navaho rugs and an assortment of Pueblo Indian pottery it is highly questionable. Whether many people would change basic thinking patterns. Or would be willing to give up their two-bathroom houses. And their thermostat-controlled central heat!

In the American Southwest, there is much talk about cultural diffusion. It has been suggested that the traditional cultures of the Indian and the Spanish-American have much to offer. The truth of this statement is not contested. Nevertheless, it is difficult to imagine the typical middle-class Anglo internalizing values of life based on the economy, education, religion, or health practices of a traditional minority group. The diffusion usually talked about is the more obvious, observable, and superficial type: eating green chili-mutton step on feast days in a pueblo with a friend, wearing fiesta dresses with ostentatious jewelry, owning a ring with a large turquoise set or an attractive squash blossom necklace, or decorating a room in one's house with Navaho rugs and an assortment of Pueblo Indian pottery. It is highly questionable whether many people would change basic thinking patterns or would be willing to give up their two-bathroom houses and thermostat-controlled central heat![27]

---

[26]Arthur Heilman, *Principles and Practices of Teaching Reading,* (Columbus, Ohio: Charles E. Merrill Books, Inc., 1961), p. 185.
[27]Miles V. Zintz, *Education Across Cultures,* (135 South Locust Street, Dubuque, Iowa: William C. Brown Book Company, 1963), p. 25.

II. Interpretive Skills

A. Learning to Anticipate Meanings

1. Use of the cloze procedure.

Cloze is a procedure in which the reader attempts to anticipate meaning from context and to accurately supply the deleted words from a message. Taylor defines the cloze procedure as:

> A method of intercepting a message from a "transmitter" (writer or speaker), mutilating its language patterns by deleting parts, and so administering it to "receivers" (readers and listeners) that their attempts to make the patterns whole again potentially yield a considerable number of cloze units.[28]

The cloze test is constructed by selecting a passage of approximately 250 words and mutilating it by (1) omitting every *nth* word throughout and leaving in their places blanks of some standard length, or (2) omitting every *nth* noun or every *nth* verb. The first correlates highly with vocabulary and reading comprehension; the latter with story comprehension.[29] Schneyer found that cloze tests have sufficient validity in measuring reading comprehension to be useful evaluating devices.[30]

An individual's performance on a cloze test is a measure of his ability to understand the meaning of the material being read . . . meaning based upon general language facility, vocabulary relevant to the material, native learning ability, and motivation.[31]

In evaluating the cloze test results, the percentage of correctly completed cloze units is used to assign reading levels of comprehension. For example, if the per cent of correct answers is forty or below, this is equated with the frustration level of reading comprehension; if the per cent of correct answers is between forty and fifty, the score is appropriate for the instructional level of reading comprehension; if the per cent correct is above fifty, the score is appropriate for the independent level of reading comprehension.

---

[28]Wilson L. Taylor, "Cloze Procedure: A New Tool for Measuring Readability," *Journalism Quarterly,* 30: 416, Fall, 1953.

[29]W. W. Weaver and A. J. Kingston, "A Factor Analysis of the Cloze Procedure and Other Measures of Reading and Language Ability," *Journal of Communications,* 13: 253, 1963.

[30]Wesley J. Schneyer, "Use of the Cloze Procedure for Improving Reading Comprehension," *The Reading Teacher,* 19: 174, December, 1965.

[31]Wilson L. Taylor, "Cloze Procedure: A New Tool for Measuring Readability," *Journalism Quarterly,* 30: 416, Fall, 1953.

A Cloze Exercise[32]

Directions: In this exercise you will use context clues to think accurately and to supply the missing word to give the meaning. Read the selection all the way through before filling in the blanks. You will need only *one* word for each blank.

LIFE IN THE DESERT

In the northern part of Africa is a great amount of hot, dry 1._____ called desert. This desert is larger than our 2._____. The driest parts of the desert have hills and 3._____ of sand. No one tries to live there. In some other parts, most of them where the 4._____ is higher, there is enough rain for some plants to grow.

In these desert 5._____, there are hundreds of places where water 6._____ from springs or wells throughout the year. Such a place 7._____called an oasis. At an oasis we find palm trees and 8._____. Sometimes several hundred or even several thousand people live near a place with water.

Many of the 9._____ of the desert lands move about from one place to another. They do so to 10._____ more water and grass for their animals. These traveling people 11._____ called nomads.

Most of the land in desert country 12._____not owned by anyone.

Cloze Scoring Key. (Grade level = 4.5)
1. *land,* country, area, region, sand
2. *United States,* country, land, nation, deserts, state
3. *drifts,* dunes, abundance
4. *land,* altitude
5. *lands,* wastelands, areas, regions, parts, places
6. *comes,* spurts, collects, splashes, flows, pours
7. *is*
8. *gardens,* plants, shade, water, spring
9. *people,* nomads, occupants, natives, tribes
10. *find,* supply, get, gather, have, locate, provide, fetch
11. *are*
12. *is*

---

[32]Marian Tonjes, "Evaluation of Comprehension and Vocabulary Gains of Tenth Grade Students Enrolled in a Developmental Reading Program," Unpublished Masters Thesis, The Graduate School, The University of New Mexico, Albuquerque, 1969, pp. 66-67.

2. Predicting what will happen next.

Read the paragraph and two sentences in each column below. Then draw a line under the sentence that answers the question correctly.

a. The red fox was clever and full of tricks, and never had trouble finding something to eat. In summer he caught small animals and birds. In winter he caught fish through a hole in the ice.

The white fox did very little. He sunned himself in front of the den in summer. He slept in his warm bed during the cold, dark winter. Every day he waited for the red fox to come home.

How will the red fox get along without the white fox?
He will go hungry.
He will have all that he needs.

How will the white fox get along without the red fox?
He will go hungry.
He will have all that he needs.

1. What the white fox did_____ .

2. What the red fox did_____ .[33]

Read each of the next two paragraphs and the statements which accompany them. Underline the statement that best predicts the outcome for each paragraph.[34]

b. One winter day a country boy was driving a team of horses. It began to snow, and the wind blew the snow in his face. All around him the falling snow was like a thick curtain. He drove the horses where he thought the road was. Soon he knew he was lost. Then he remembered that horses always know the way home, even in a bad storm.

The horses ate the grass by the road.
He let the horses find the way home.
He made the horses stand still.
He took his sister in out of the storm.

A boy who had never seen snow was taken to a place where snow fell every winter. He could hardly wait to see the snow for he had heard how fluffy and white it was. He had been told that it made fences, roads, and even trash heaps beautiful. One morning when he opened his eyes he saw a strange white world through the window. It had snowed.

[33]William Burton, G. K. Kemp, Isabel Craig, and Vardine Moore, *Flying High, Developmental Reading Text Workbook, Grade Five,* (Indianapolis, Indiana: Bobbs Merrill Co., 1964), p. 98.

[34]Arthur I. Gates, Gates Silent Reading Test, Type B: *Reading to Predict the Outcome of Given Events,* Form 1, Grades 3-8, (New York: Teachers College Press, Columbia University, 1926).

He turned over and went back to sleep.

He pulled down the window shade at once.

He ran to the window and looked out.

He waited until the winter came.

B. Drawing inferences

    1. Based on factual information.

        In order to draw inference based on factual information, it is necessary for the reader to retain, select and evaluate the information he reads and then follow the directions to draw conclusions based on the evidence. The exercise below is based on a story read in a sixth grade reader.

Read Carefully

    Science reading must be done carefully. To show that you can read carefully, do what each paragraph tells you to do. You may wish to refer to *Stories to Remember.*

    Uranium is used in the production of atomic energy. If both *pitchblende* and *uranite* are rich sources of uranium, draw a line around those words at the right. If uranium is sometimes found in petrified wood, draw a line around the word *petrified.* If it is not found in all three, put a line around *dynamite.*

carnotite	dynamite
uranite	petrified
pitchblende	bauxite
cryolite	probe

    A Geiger counter detector is a box with earphones, dials, and other gadgets on it. It is used to detect uranium. If it does this by making a red light show when the probe is near uranium, draw a line around the picture of the Geiger counter at the right. If by making a clicking sound it shows that uranium is near, write the word *demonstrated* under the picture.

    From Guy L. Bond, Marie C. Cuddy, and Leo C. Fay, *Fun to Do Book to accompany Stories to Recember,* (Chicago: Lyons and Carnahan, 1962), p. 95.

    2. Ideas implied but not stated.

        If the student is able to evaluate as he reads—if he is able to read critically, he will be able to draw inferences and arrive at conclusions. Such an ability must be arrived at through practice. This skill is necessary in evaluating the characters in a story from the description given and from their behaviors described. In the story that follows, sixth graders are asked to infer appropriate meanings or to draw conclusions based on the reading.

Read and Think

Read the story and be ready to answer some questions about it.

Part I

Obed Swain was an old sailor, or, as he would have put it, "an old sea dog." He had once been captain of the good ship *Catawba* and had sailed the seven seas. Now that he was old, he had settled down to life in a village. The only difficulty which he had not been able to surmount was that of monotony. The captain had been accustomed to monotony at sea, but had always found diversion in regaling his shipmates with tales of his adventures. People in the village, which Obed Swain called a "landlocked town," did not seem to understand his seafaring language. At first they found it a diversion just to listen to the old captain talk, but soon they lost interest in his tales.

Mark your answer with a check (✓).

What is an "old sea dog"?

_____ 1. A dog that goes to sea

_____ 2. A worn-out ship

_____ 3. An old sailor

What do you think Obed Swain meant by a "landlocked town"?

_____ 1. A town with no land to sell

_____ 2. An inland town away from the sea

_____ 3. A town far away from other towns

Part II

Shortly after the captain settled down in his new home, a railroad was built through the village. Almost everyone was excited about it, but Obed Swain had paid no attention to the event until the day the first train came in. The sight had an electrifying effect on the captain.

"What kind of contrivance is that?" he asked. Then, seeing the smoke pour from the smokestack, he exclaimed, "See that black smoke! That contrivance must burn sperm oil!"

When the train stopped, the captain went over to look at the locomotive. As he approached it, a jet of vapor issued from the side of the engine.

"Thar she blows!" shouted the captain. "Thar she blows on the larboard side!"

When the vapor had disappeared, Captain Swain talked to the engineer.

"Ho, there! Are you the captain of this craft?" inquired Obed. "Where's your ratlines? I want to come aboard."

The engineer did not know what ratlines were, but he helped the old gentleman get up into the locomotive. Obed Swain asked questions about different devices he saw. He understood engines, so he and the engineer had an enjoyable time.

From that day on, the captain looked forward to train time.

Mark your answer with a check (✓).

Which of the following show that the story probably did not take place in recent times?

_____ 1. A railroad was just being built into the town.

_____ 2. The old man did not know a locomotive when he saw it.

_____ 3. Black smoke was coming out of the smokestack.

From Guy L. Bond, Marie C. Cuddy, and Leo C. Fay, *Fun to Do Book to accompany Stories to Remember*, (Chicago: Lyons and Carnahan, 1962), p. 60.

C. Drawing Generalizations

One lesson in generalizing is being able to read an episode like a fable and decide what proverb it illustrates:

___ One sunny day two ducks went out for a walk. "Child," said the mother duck, "you're not walking very prettily. You should try to walk straight without waddling so."

___ "Dear Mother," said the young duck, "if you'll walk the way you want me to walk, I'll follow you."

___ After fishing for a whole day, a fisherman caught only a single small fish. "Please let me go," begged the fish. "I'm too small to eat now. If you put me back into the pond, I'll grow. Then you can make a meal of me."

___ "Oh, no!" said the fisherman. "I have you now. I may not catch you again."

___ A lamb on a rooftop saw a wolf pass by on the ground below. The lamb shouted, "Get away from here, you terrible creature! How dare you show your face here!"

___ "You talk very boldly," replied the wolf. "Would you be as bold if you were down on the ground?"

___ One warm day a hungry fox spied a delicious-looking bunch of fruit. It was hanging on a vine that was tied to a high fence. The fox jumped and jumped, trying to reach the fruit. But each time he just missed it. When he was too tired to jump again, he gave up.

___ "I'm sure that fruit is spoiled," grumbled the fox as he went away.[35]

1. A bird in the hand is worth two in the bush.
2. It is easy to dislike what you cannot get.
3. Setting a good model is the best way to teach.
4. It is easy to be brave from a safe distance.

D. Selecting and Evaluating

1. Separating fact from fancy

Telling Which Could Happen[36]

Read the paragraph and accompanying sentence in each section below based on the article about Johnny Appleseed. Then draw a ring around the word *Yes* if the sentence is true according to the article and around the word *No* if the sentence is not true.

One day Johnny Appleseed came to a clearing in which a family had built a cabin. He stopped to

Johnny stopped beside a stream one day to eat some lunch. As he was sitting under a tree, a squirrel came up and sat on his knee.

---

[35]Think and Do Book to accompany *Just Imagine*, (Chicago: Scott Foresman, 1953), p. 42.

[36]William Burton, G. K. Kemp, Isabel Craig, and Vardine Moore, *Flying High*, Developmental Reading Text Workbook, Grade Five, (Indianapolis, Indiana: Bobbs Merrill, Inc., 1964), p. 95.

plant some apple seeds, and the family asked him to stay for the night. The next morning after breakfast he continued on his way.

"May I have something to eat, too?" asked the squirrel. I'm hungry."

This little story could be true.

Yes   No

This little story could be true.

Yes   No

2. Selecting material pertinent to a given topic
Determining whether all the sentences relate to a topic sentence in a paragraph is a skill children may develop from exercises like the following:
Directions: Read each of the following paragraphs and find one sentence that does not belong in each one.

1

As we shot up in the elevator to the top of the Empire State building in New York, I began to realize how high one hundred two stories are. We walked out upon the balcony from which we could look in all directions over the great city below. I caught my breath because of the distance I could see, and because the air seemed thin away up so high. I marveled at the huge tower of steel and concrete under me. We went aboard an ocean liner while we were in New York.

2

The Indians were friendly toward the earliest settlers in America. They taught the Pilgrims how to plant corn and how to hunt the deer for food. If the Indians had been hostile, they could have destroyed the tiny settlement, but they allowed the pioneers to build their homes and plant crops on the land that had been their hunting ground. King Philip later became the enemy of the whites.

3

A simple test will tell you whether or not silk has been woven with lead or other metals to make it seem of better quality than it really is. Flowered silks are pretty. Burn a sample of the material. If the silk burns up completely as if it were paper, it is probably pure silk. If a hard substance is left in the ashes, the material is not pure silk.

4

On our way home from the picnic Oliver stumbled and sprained his ankle. He could not walk, and we had to get to the nearest farmhouse to telephone for a doctor. We had taken bacon and eggs for our lunch. We made a chair for Oliver by crossing our hands and taking hold of each other's waists.

Our progress was slow, but we were able to reach the farmhouse and secure a doctor's services before the painful ankle had swollen badly.[37]

3. Overstatement or unfounded claims

"The good teacher of beginning reading, where she is not bound by an imposed methodology, operates on the theory that *beginning* reading is not a "thought getting" process but is based on translating letters into sounds." No evidence was cited as to the source of this data.[38]

Since the first sentence is a direct quote from another source, and the sentence following it is not, one may conclude that the writer of the second statement is pointing out that this is really an unfounded claim. He is also inferring that there is no evidence to substantiate this claim.

4. Judging emotional response to what is read
   1. If you were sitting on the roof of a house floating down toward the sea in a terrible storm, how would you feel?

      shy   terrified   sleepy

   2. If you knew that a policeman was coming to take your pet away, how would you feel?

      smart   alarmed   thirsty

   3. If you thought you were very beautiful but no one talked to you or wanted to be around you, how would you feel?

      happy   limp   lonely

   4. If a green-and-silver airplane popped out of a blackberry pie that you had bought at the bakery, how would you feel?

      stupid   surprised   chilly

   5. If you were the manager of a bus company and people called you all day about a queer-acting bus, how would you feel?

      puzzled   cunning   gay[39]

---

[37]R. W. Bardwell, Ethel Mabie, and J. C. Tressler, *Elementary English in Action,* Grade V, (Boston: D. C. Heath, 1935), p. 286.

[38]Arthur W. Heilman, *Principles and Practices of Teaching Reading,* Second Edition, (Columbus, Ohio: Charles E. Merrill Books, Inc., 1967), p. 260.

[39]Gray, W. S., *et al., Think and Do Book to Accompany Just Imagine,* (Chicago: Scott, Foresman & Co., 1953) p. 55.

IV. SUMMARY

The comprehension skills have been defined and illustrated as those that include getting literal meanings and formulating interpretive meanings. Literal comprehension was defined as basic understanding as illustrated in vocabulary concepts, sensing integrated ideas in sentences, and understanding paragraph organization. Literal meanings are also involved in getting ideas from the context and iccludes exercises such as reading to find answers to questions, finding main ideas, and arranging ideas in proper sequence to tell a story.

Interpretive skills include anticipating meanings, drawing inferences, drawing generalizations, and selecting and evaluating skills.

Suggested Activities

1. From the outline of comprehension skills, prepare a list of skills to be taught, then find in a teacher's manual for a graded reader, two examples of this skill being developed in a lesson plan. You may wish to head your paper like this:

Skill:	Example 1:	Example 2:
1. Predicting what will happen next. 2. Reading to appreciate the general significance.		

References for Further Reading

BOND, GUY and MILES TINKER, *Reading Difficulties: Their Diagnosis and Correction.* (New York: Appleton-Century-Crofts, Inc., 1967), Chapter 11, "Development of the Basic Comprehension Abilities."

BORMUTH, JOHN, "Cloze as a Measure of Readability," *Reading as an Intellectual Activity,* J. Allen Figurel, Editor, IRA Conference Proceedings, 8: 131-134, 1963.

DEBOER, JOHN J. and MARTHA DALLMANN, *The Teaching of Reading* (New York: Hold, Rinehart, and Winston, Inc., 1964), Chapter 7A, "Reading with Comprehension," pp. 130-145; Chapter 7B, "Developing Comprehension in Reading," pp. 146-169.

GALLANT, RUTH, "Use of Cloze Tests as a Measure of Readability in the Primary Grades," Reading and Inquiry, J. Allen Figurel, Editor, IRA Conference Proceedings, 10: 286-287, 1965.

GLOCK, MARVIN D., "Developing Clear Recognition of Pupil Purposes for Reading," *The Reading Teacher*, 11: 165-170, February, 1958.

HARRIS, ALBERT J., *Effective Teaching of Reading*, (New York: David McKay, 1962), Chapter 11, "Building Comprehension in Reading," pp. 233-258.

MCKEE, PAUL, Reading: *A Program of Instruction for the Elementary School*, (Boston: Houghton Mifflin, 1966), Chapter 8, "Coping with Meaning Difficulties," pp. 255-315.

RANKIN, EARL F., "The Cloze Procedure—A Survey of Research," *Yearbook of the National Reading Conference*, 14: 133-150, 1965.

SCHNEYER, J. WESLEY, "Use of the Cloze Procedure for Improving Reading Comprehension," *The Reading Teacher*, 19: 174-180, December, 1965.

SMITH, NILA B., *Reading Instruction for Today's Children*, (Englewood Cliffs, New Jersey: Prentice-Hall, Inc., 1963), Chapter 9, "Getting Meanings from Reading," pp. 255-303.

TAYLOR, WILSON L., "Cloze Procedure: A New Tool for Measuring Readability," *Journalism Quarterly*, 30: 415-433, Fall, 1953.

TINKER, MILES A. and CONSTANCE MCCULLOUGH, *Teaching Elementary Reading*, Third Edition, (New York: Appleton-Century-Crofts, Inc., 1968), Chapter 9, "Comprehension and Interpretation," pp. 185-203.

WEAVER, W. W. and A. J. KINGSTON, "A Factor Analysis of the Cloze Procedure and Other Measures of Reading and Language Ability," *Journal of Communications*, 13: 252-261, 1963.

9

Study Skills

The study skills, sometimes identified as the "functional skills of reading," deserve greater emphasis in the developmental reading program. The level of mastery of these skills will determine how efficient the learner is going to be in studying in all the content areas of the curriculum.

Some elementary teachers have failed to accept the responsibility for the planned, sequential development of specific abilities like making outlines, locating information, or learning to read maps efficiently. In this chapter, Van Dongen has provided the teacher with a detailed list of the specific skills in developing abilities in locating information, reading maps, graphs and charts, and organization. Carpenter, in the yearbook of the National Council for the Social Studies, has provided an excellent list of fifty-three skills to be taught in learning to use maps and globes. Teachers must be mindful, not only of the need to teach the skill, but also to provide the spaced review and reinforcement later in the school program to insure retention and efficient practice.

Van Dongen has incorporated the types of study skills with which this chapter is concerned in Figure 9.1.

I. READING IN SUBJECT-MATTER AREAS

Reading in subject matter areas is generally more difficult than the reading done in organized reading classes. Such reading requires special vocabulary, comprehension of concepts, ability to locate and read maps, graphs, and charts and utilize their content in further reading in the text, and organization and evaluation of the reading. Fay lists the following difficulties with reading in the content areas:[1]

---

[1]L. C. Fay, "What Research Has to Say About Reading in the Content Areas," *The Reading Teacher*, 8:68–72, 1954.

1. There is an unduly heavy load of facts and concepts;
2. The variations in typographical arrangement from one area to another may confuse the pupil;
3. All too frequently the materials are uninteresting to the pupils;
4. The readability of materials is often harder than basic readers;
5. Many writers tend to assume greater background than children possess; and
6. All this emphasizes the need for carefully fitting materials to children and for carefully organizing instruction in reading such materials.

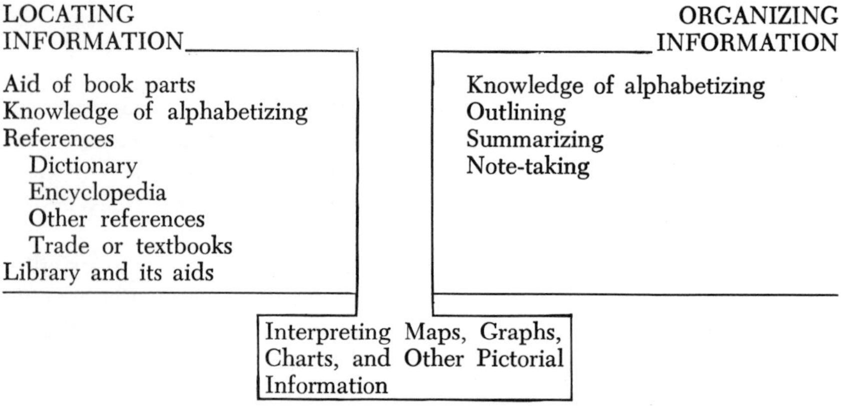

LOCATING   ORGANIZING
INFORMATION_____   _____ INFORMATION

Aid of book parts   Knowledge of alphabetizing
Knowledge of alphabetizing   Outlining
References   Summarizing
  Dictionary   Note-taking
  Encyclopedia
  Other references
  Trade or textbooks
Library and its aids

Interpreting Maps, Graphs, Charts, and Other Pictorial Information

Figure 9.1.   Basic Study Skills

From Richard D. Van Dongen, An Analysis of Study Skills Taught by Intermediate Grade Basal Readers. Masters thesis, University of New Mexico, August, 1967, p. 46.

The Teachers Handbook of Technical Vocabulary provides concise lists of important words in the various subjects in junior and senior high schools. Teachers, especially for any language-handicapped students, should find these lists very helpful.[2]

Are there specific steps that might help one to get more out of his reading?

Robinson suggests an easy-to-remember formula for students that has proved very useful. He calls it the SQ3R method of study. SQ3R is *survey, question, read, recite,* and *review.* He explains the steps in the SQ3R method in this way:[3]

[2]Louella Cole, *The Teachers Handbook of Technical Vocabulary,* (Bloomington, Ill.: Public School Publishing Company, 1940).

[3]Francis P. Robinson, *Effective Reading,* (New York: Harper and Brothers, 1962), p. 31.

Survey: Glance over the headings in the chapter to see the main points that will be developed. Also read the final summary paragraph if the chapter has one. This survey should not take more than a minute and will show the three to half a dozen core ideas around which the discussion will center. This orientation will help to organize the ideas as you read them later.

Question: Now begin to work. Turn the first heading into a question. This will arouse your curiosity and so increase your comprehension. It will bring to mind information already known, thus helping you to understand that section more quickly. And the question you have raised in your mind will make important points stand out while explanatory detail is recognized as such. Turning a heading into a question can be done upon reading the heading, but it demands a conscious effect on the part of the reader to make this query for which he must read to find the answer.

Read: Read to answer that question, that is, to the end of the first section. This is not a passive plodding along each line, but an active search for an answer.

Recite: Having read the section, look away from the book and try to recite briefly the answer to your question. Use your own words and include an example. If you can do this, you know what you have read; if you can't, glance over it again. An excellent way to do this reciting from memory is to jot down cue phrases in outline form on a sheet of paper.

Review: When the lesson has been completely read, look over your notes to get a bird's eye view of the points and their relationship and check your memory as to the content by reciting on the major subpoints under each heading.

Teachers can use newspapers as an aid to teaching skills in reading.[4]

The newspaper can be a fresh approach, a novel presentation of exercises such as the following:

Practices to strengthen comprehension skills, critical reading, study skills, vocabulary and creative writing.

Extracting main ideas: . . . news stories are tailormade to give the important facts in the first one or two paragraphs.

In the opening paragraphs of a news story, called the lead, are there answers to who, what, where, why and how?

Finding supporting details: after a couple of paragraphs covering the main facts, are the details supporting them unfolded in an organized way?

By-lined columns on the editorial page offer good debate material for critical readers.

The other study skills: locating materials, using maps, charts, and tables.

---

[4]Dorothy Piercey, "Teachers Use Newspapers as Aid to Reading," *The Arizona Republic*, Sunday, March 6, 1966.

II. AN OUTLINE OF BASIC STUDY SKILLS

Van Dongen has synthesized the following outline from his search to find what study skills are taught in commonly used graded series of readers.[5]

I. Ability to locate information

   A. Ability to locate information by using the aid of book parts

      1. cover, title page, title, author, publisher, location of publisher, editor's name, name of series, and edition

      2. copyright page and date of publication

      3. preface, introduction, foreword

      4. table of contents and locating topics by pages

      5. table of contents to locate topical organization of book or determine importance of topic by number of pages it gets

      6. locating specific pages rapidly

      7. lists of illustrations, maps, figures

      8. chapter headings, main headings, section titles, subtitles

      9. footnotes and references at end of chapters

    10. glossary

    11. indexes, select and use key word, cross-references

    12. locate and use the appendix

    13. locate and use the bibliography

   B. Ability to locate information by using knowledge of alphabetizing

      1. ability to locate any given letter quickly

      2. knowing sections: beginning, middle, end

      3. arranging words by initial letter

      4. arranging words by second letter

      5. arranging words by third or more letters

      6. alphabetizing any given list of words

      7. locating words or titles with *Mc* or *Mac*

      8. use of articles *a, an* and *the* in locating words or titles

      9. alphabetizing people names when first and last names are given

   C. Ability to locate information by using references

      1. locate information by using the dictionary

         a. finding words quickly

           opening the dictionary close to the desired word

           using the guide words

           using a thumb index

         b. locate the pronunciation key

         c. use of special sections of dictionary—geographical terms, biographical dictionary, foreign words and phrases

---

[5]Richard Van Dongen, *op. cit.,* pages 47-54.

  d. ability to use the dictionary as an aid in pronunciation
   ability to interpret phonetic spelling and diacritical marks
   determining pronunciation of words spelled alike
   determining preferred pronunciation
  e. use of dictionary to determine meanings
   select meaning from context
   pictorial or verbal illustrations
   determine what part of speech a word is
  f. use of dictionary as an aid in checking spelling
  g. locate base word as an entry
  h. derivations of the base word
  i. noting syllabic divisions of a word
  j. origin of words
  k. synonyms or antonyms
 2. locating information in the encyclopedia
  a. locating volume from information on the spine of the book
  b. using initial letters and guide words
  c. using the last volume index
  d. using specialized encyclopedias
 3. Ability to use and locate other references:
  selecting appropriate references for locating information
  locate and use various guides and sources:
    (1) Almanac
    (2) Atlas
    (3) City directory
    (4) Government publications
    (5) Junior Book of Authors
    (6) Newspapers and periodicals
    (7) Posters
    (8) Radio or television schedules
    (9) Telephone directory
    (10) Time schedules
    (11) Yearbooks
 4. Ability to use textbooks and trade books for locating information
D. Ability to use the library and its aids for locating information
 1. card catalog
  a. desired topic, author, or title
  b. alphabetical arrangement in card catalog
 2. organization of the library for locating material
  a. shelf plans, labels, and floor plans
  b. Dewey-decimal system or other methods
  c. locate reference books
  d. locate and use the magazine file

   e. locate and use appropriate indexes
    (1) *Readers' guide to periodical literature*
    (2) *Who's Who*
    (3) Biographical dictionaries
    (4) Thesaurus
    (5) Unabridged dictionary
    (6) *Subject index to Poetry*
  E. Locate information by using maps, graphs, charts, pictorial material

II. Ability to organize information
  A. use knowledge of alphabetizing or organizing information
  B. construct an outline
   1. ability to put material in sequence
    a. arrange steps of a process in order
    b. construct a time-line
   2. classify information on two-way charts, tables
   3. construct an outline
    a. main headings
    b. given main and subordinate topics
    c. provide subordinates when given main heading or provide main heading when given subordinates
    d. outline single paragraphs
    e. outline short selections
    f. outline more complex selections
    g. put ideas together from various sources in outline form
    h. outline what has been read and use outline in a presentation—either written or oral
  C. ability to summarize material
   1. summary statement for a paragraph
   2. write summary statements for a short selection
   3. write summary statements for more complex selections
   4. use a summary as data for oral or written reports
   5. bring together information from several sources
   6. write a summary using an outline
   7. construct maps, graphs, charts, or pictorial material as a summary of information
  D. ability to take notes
   1. take notes in brief, grammatically incorrect and abbreviated
   2. in outline form—formal or informal
   3. in precis writing (spaced intervals of listening or reading)
   4. take notes in fact-inferences charts
   5. note origin of information for footnotes and bibliography

III. Ability to use and interpret maps, graphs, charts and other pictorial material
    A. use and interpret maps and globes
        1. ability to locate desired information
            a. interpret key and map symbols
            b. use map scales
            c. interpret directions
        2. ability to demonstrate understanding of map distortions or type of projection
    B. Ability to use and interpret graphs, tables, diagrams, and other pictorial material
        1. interpret graphs
            a. bar graphs
            b. circle graphs
            c. line graphs
        2. interpret tables
        3. interpret diagrams
        4. interpret time lines
        5. interpret other pictorial material
    C. Ability to read and use charts.

III. SAMPLE LESSONS

1. Outlining

By studying children's workbooks and teachers' guides, teachers will find a graduated sequence of exercises similar to the types contained in the above outline. It is clear that authors intend for boys and girls to have a great deal of guidance before they are expected to make complete outlines independently.

A. Read the following essay:

HOW TO BECOME A GOOD ORAL READER[6]

Good readers select very carefully what they are to read. They try to choose an interesting story or a worthwhile article, one which their listeners will surely enjoy. If they are reading to prove a point, they read only the sentences that are necessary. If they are reading an interesting story or part of a story, they select one which is not too long to be interesting. Here is the first rule: If you want people to like to hear you read, select your story or article carefully.

Good readers know well the story or article which they are to read. In the first place, they know the exact meaning of what they are to read. It would be hard to give the meaning to other people if the readers

---

[6]Ernest Horn, Bess Goodykoontz, and Mabel I. Snedaker, *Progress in Reading Series: Reaching Our Goals*, Grade Six, (Boston: Ginn and Co., 1940), pp. 271-273.

themselves did not know the meaning. In the second place, they know the words in the selection so that they do not pronounce them incorrectly and spoil the meaning for the listeners. This all takes time and study, but it is necessary if people are to read aloud well. The second rule is: Know well the selection you are to read aloud.

Good readers keep their audience interested in what they are reading. They read loudly enough to be heard easily. They read clearly, so that the listeners do not have to guess what they are saying. They make the important points in the selection stand out plainly, and they read with expression so that the characters talk like real people. Good readers work and practice to do all these things well, in order to keep their audience interested. And so the last rule is: Keep your listeners interested to the very last of what you read.

Directions to the student:

In this article, you have read three rules for reading aloud well to others. Perhaps you noticed that the topic sentence at the beginning is the same as the rule stated at the end of each paragraph. The skeleton outline below tells you to find three details in paragraph one, two details in paragraph two, and four details in paragraph three. Complete the skeleton outline.

HOW TO BECOME A GOOD ORAL READER

    I.

        A.

        B.

        C.

   II.

        A.

        B.

  III.

        A.

        B.

        C.

        D.

B. *Sample Lesson: Outlining*

Read the following essay:

THE MONARCH BUTTERFLY

General description

The male monarch is one of the most beautiful of all the butterflies. He is not only neat looking and pretty, but on each hind wing he carries a little pocket of perfume to help get the attention of the female monarch. She is as brilliant as he but lacks the perfume pockets. Birds do not like to eat monarchs either as adults or as larva, probably because the monarch feeds on the milkweed which is a very distasteful plant.

Migration in winter
Evidence of traveling
long distances

The monarchs are great travelers. They travel north during our growing season but must go back south when we have winter. In the early spring, the mother butterfly flies north as far as she can find milkweeds growing and lays her eggs on the milkweed plant. These eggs hatch and the larva soon become adults and fly farther north because later in the summer the milkweed will be growing still farther north. Sometimes monarchs are found as far north as the Hudson Bay. When cold weather comes, these butterflies gather in great flocks and move back south. It is impossible for us to know how flocks of butterflies are guided in their migration. The monarch is the strongest flyer of all the butterflies. He has been seen flying out over the ocean five hundred miles from land.

Body parts and
how they
function

The monarch butterfly, like other insects, breathes by means of a system of air tubes through the sides of his body. The body is divided into three parts: the head, the thorax, and the abdomen. He has one pair of antennae, three pairs of legs, and two pairs of wings. He has two large compound eyes but no single eyes. The monarch has sucking mouth parts to draw the honey out of the flower, for example, but he cannot bite.

Metamorphosis;
life stages

There are four stages in the monarch's life: egg, larva, or caterpillar, chrysalis or pupa, and adult. When the egg hatches into a larva, the larva is very small. This larva molts, just as grasshoppers do, before it becomes as large as it will get. After molting out of its skin four or five times, the larva spins itself a cocoon and in about two weeks hatches out of the cocoon as an adult monarch. The adult monarch is a beautiful brown with the border and veins black and with two rows of white spots on the outer borders. If the adult does not meet with an accident, it will likely live for from four to six years.

Directions to the student:

The four major headings have been selected for you.

Using the outline form provided, complete the following topical outline:

A topical outline

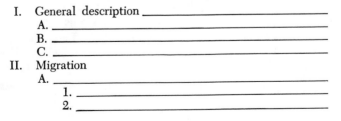

THE MONARCH BUTTERFLY

  I. General description _____

      A. _____

      B. _____

      C. _____

  II. Migration

      A. _____

          1. _____

          2. _____

B. _____
C. _____
    1. _____
    2. _____
D.
III. Structure and function
    A. _____
        1. _____
        2. _____
        3. _____
    B. _____
    C. _____
        1. _____
        2. _____
        3. _____
        4. _____
        5. _____
IV. Life stages (Metamorphosis)
    A. _____
    B. _____
    C. _____
    D. _____
        1. _____
        2. _____

C. *A scientist's method of classifying animals is an outline.*

The scientist has found it necessary to establish a rigid classification system to adequately identify each strain of living things in the plant or animal kingdom. The outline in the figure below presents the outline through which the dog known as a greyhound is identified in the animal kingdom.

THE CLASSIFICATION OF LIVING THINGS

The outline by which zoologists classify the greyhound dog:

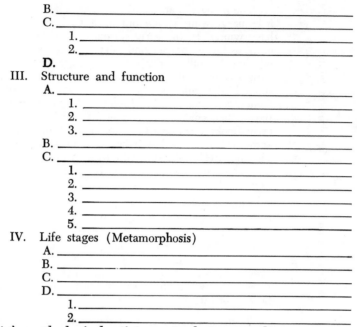

I. Kingdom   Animalia
  I. Phylum   Chordata
    I. Subphylum Vertebrata
      I. Class   Mammalia
        I. Subclass   Placentalia
          I. Order   Carnivora
            I. Suborder   Fissipedia (separated toes)
              I. Family   Canidae
                I. Genus   Canis
                  I. Trivia   Familiaris
                    I. Specie   Canis Familiaris
                               (Domestic)
                    I. Breed   Hound
                      I. Strain   Greyhound

2. A Time Line

A time line is a graphic presentation of a chronological outline showing important facts in outline form. If, in the fourth grade, the child has the concept of time introduced to him in terms of his own experience, the passing of a day as the earth rotates once, and in terms of his own lifetime, he will be ready for historical time lines in fifth and sixth grade. The suggested time line on the next page suggests many of the "events" presented in the fifth grade social studies program.

Greer suggests, concerning the use of analogies in teaching concepts at the sixth grade level, that the child can make the analogy between the chronology of mankind's history and the chronology of the child's personal history. She suggests that the child understands:[7]

> Before you were born, your parents were children and lived with their parents; later your parents had a home of their own; then you were born; you learned to walk, to talk, and started to school. In your life time there have been special events you remember most vividly.
> Mankind's history is divided into two parts: B. C. and A. D. In history, man lived in caves. He learned to make tools and use them in hunting. He began to live in groups called tribes. After Christ was born many events occurred in man's history. America was discovered; people came to live here; cars and planes were invented.

$$5 \qquad 4 \qquad 3 \qquad 2 \qquad 1 \qquad 0 \qquad 1 \qquad 2 \qquad 3 \qquad 4 \qquad 5$$

your birth
Christ's birth

3. Using Climatic Charts in the Study of Geography

The climatic chart is an excellent aid to guide intermediate grade students in generalizing about a geographic location. The students need to study first the climatic chart representative of the area where they live so they can use it as a reference point in later work. By knowing the length of months in the frost-free, or growing season, the extent of cold, cool, warm, and hot weather throughout the year and during which months, and the amount of rainfall and the distribution of rain throughout the year, the student can learn to generalize:

1. Is the growing season long enough to grow different cereal crops?
2. Is there sufficient annual rainfall to grow different cereal crops?
3. Is there sufficient hot weather at one time to ripen crops?
4. Would you expect to find four distinct seasons in this place?
5. Is this place north or south of the equator?
6. Will tropical fruits grow in this place?

---

[7]Margaret Smith Greer, "The Efficiency of the Use of Analogy in Teaching Selected Concepts at the Sixth Grade Level," (Unpublished M. A. Thesis, The Graduate School, University of New Mexico, 1966), p. 40.

7. What kind of vegetation would you expect to find here? Desert, mountain, tropical, or "temperate zone"?
8. Might there be snow here to add to the annual precipitation?
9. Since there is sufficient moisture, could two crops be produced annually on the same soil?

Conceal the station information at the top of the climate chart in Figure 9.2 and see if you can answer the above questions by studying only the rainfall, temperature, and growing season.

USING CLIMATIC CHARTS

A climatic chart is a visual aid that can successfully be introduced in the fifth grade. Geography texts at fifth and sixth grade, junior high, and senior high levels frequently include some type of climatic chart. When a climate chart is used in a comparative way, especially if one compares a chart of an area known to the pupils with a chart representing another area of the U.S.A. or a foreign country, similarities and differences become easily evident and a new area being studied becomes more meaningful climatically.[8]

The example of a climatic chart for Chicago, Illinois illustrates how the basic climate elements appear when graphed.

IV. INTERPRETING MAPS AND GLOBES

Maps are very common in the everyday experiences of boys and girls in the elementary school. Maps at every gasoline station help the family make the vacation trip by the most efficient route. Maps on the news casts on television show where major current events are happening. Newspapers, magazines, and advertising material present outline maps pin-pointing happenings, events, and commercial products. Even restaurants are apt to have placemats presenting an outline map to locate the place where you are now eating and the one where you should eat next!

Yet many boys and girls learn to pay little attention to these maps because they do not understand the legend, or the vocabulary, and they do not understand the representation contained in the map. If the adult does not take the necessary few minutes to orient the child then the child is missing a very useful lesson that could make the use of maps and diagrams meaningful to him. The nines, tens, and elevens in the intermediate grades are apt to be very interested in the symbols, signs, and codes in the legends that make maps meaningful if they are guided in their understanding.

---

[8]H. L. Nelson, *Climate Data for Representative Stations of the World,* (Lincoln: University of Nebraska Press, 1968), p. 69.

1000 1100 1200 1300 1400 1500 1600 1700 1800 1900

(1000) Leif Ericson discovers America

(1260) Marco Polo's Journey to China

(1492) Columbus discovers America

(1519) Magellan circumnavigates globe

(1609) Hudson discovers River and Bay

Make a time line (A.D. 1000-1875) like the one above and add the following events:

1420	Prince Henry establishes a school for sailors	
1486	Dias sailed to Cape of Good Hope	
1497	Cabot explored North America	
1498	Columbus made third voyage	
1500	Cabral claimed Brazil	
1513	Balboa discovered the Pacific	
1513	Ponce de Leon explored Florida	
1534	Cartier explored Gulf of St. Lawrence	
1541	DeSoto discovered Mississippi	
1577	Drake began world voyage	
1608	Champlain founded Quebec	
1620	Mayflower Compact signed	
1623	New Netherland settled	
1630	Massachusetts Bay Colony settled	
1636	Williams founded Rhode Island	
1647	First public school in America	
1664	New Netherland seized by English	
1682	Pennsylvania settled by Penn	
1814	First Power Loom built	
1825	Erie Canal opened	
1831	Steam locomotive pulled train	
1859	First oil well drilled in U.S.	

Prudence Cutright, A.Y. King, Ida Dennis, and F. Potter, *Living Together in the Americas*, (New York: Macmillan Co., 1960), Teacher's Guide, pp. 59, 61, Textbook, p. 63.

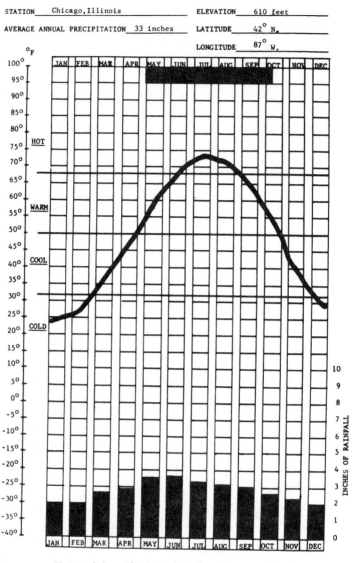

Figure 9.2. Climatic Chart for Chicago, Illinois

Children need to understand projections so that the difference between a Mercator and a polar projection is clear to them. It has been
suggested that cutting an orange peel in sections so it can be flattened
will show the polar projection when the world is produced on a flat
map. A hollow rubber ball could also be used and could be preserved
indefinitely.

SOCIAL STUDIES SKILLS: A GUIDE TO ANALYSIS AND GRADE PLACEMENT—*Continued*
(Code: EP, early primary; LP, late primary; EI, early intermediate; LI, late intermediate; J, junior high school; S, senior high school)

PART TWO: Skills which are a major responsibility of the social studies—*Continued*

Skill	Introduce, through planned readiness experiences	Develop systematically	Reteach, maintain, and extend
Interpreting maps and globes			
A. Orient the map and note directions			
1. Use cardinal directions in classroom and neighborhood	LP	EI-J	
2. Use intermediate directions, as southeast, northwest	EI	LI-J	S
3. Use cardinal directions and intermediate directions in working with maps	EI	LI-J	S
4. Use relative terms of location and direction, as near, far, above, below, up, down	EP	LP-J	S
5. Understand that north is toward the North Pole and south toward the South Pole on any map projection	LP-EI	LI-J	S
6. Understand the use of the compass for direction	EI	LI-J	S
7. Use the north arrow on the map	EI	LI-J	S
8. Orient desk outline, textbook, and atlas maps correctly to the north	EI	LI-J	S
9. Use parallels and meridians in determining direction	EI	LI-J	S
10. Use different map projections to learn how the pattern of meridians and that of parallels differ	EI	LI-J	S
11. Construct simple maps which are properly oriented as to direction	EI	LI-J	S

B. **Locate places on maps and globes**

1. Recognize the home city and state on a map of the United States and on a globe	EI	LI–J	S
2. Recognize land and water masses on a globe and on a variety of maps—physical-political, chalkboard, weather, etc.	LP	EI–J	S
3. Identify on a globe and on a map of the world, the equator, tropics, circles, continents, oceans, large islands	EI	LI–J	S
4. Use a highway map for locating places by number-and-key system; plan a trip using distance, direction, and locations	EI	LI–J	S
5. Relate low latitudes to the equator and high latitudes to the polar areas	EI	LI–J	S
6. Interpret abbreviations commonly found on maps	EI	LI–J	S
7. Use map vocabulary and key accurately	EI	LI–J	S
8. Use longitude and latitude in locating places on wall maps	LI	J	S
9. Use an atlas to locate places	LI	J	S
10. Identify the time zones of the United States and relate them to longitude	EI	LI–J	S
11. Understand the reason for the International Date Line, and compute time problems of international travel	J	S	S
12. Consult two or more maps to gather information about the same area	EI	LI–J	S
13. Recognize location of major cities of the world with respect to their physical setting	EI	LI–J	S
14. Trace routes of travel by different means of transportation	EI	LI–J	S
15. Develop a visual image of major countries, land forms, and other map patterns studied	EI	LI–J	S
16. Read maps of various types which show elevation	EI	LI–J	S
17. Understand the significance of relative location as it has affected national policies	LI	J–S	S
18. Learn to make simple sketch maps to show location	LP	EI–J	S

C. **Use scale and compute distances**

1. Use small objects to represent large ones, as a photograph compared to actual size	EP	LP–J	S

Skill			
2. Make simple large-scale maps of a familiar area, such as classroom, neighborhood	EP	LP-J	S
3. Compare actual length of a block or a mile with that shown on a large-scale map	EI	LI-J	S
4. Determine distance on a map by using a scale of miles	EI	LI-J	S
5. Compare maps of different size of the same area	EI	LI-J	S
6. Compare maps of different areas to note that a smaller scale must be used to map larger areas	EI	LI-J	S
7. Compute distance between two points on maps of different scale	EI	LI-J	S
8. Estimate distances on a globe, using latitude; estimate air distances by using a tape or a string to measure great circle routes	LI	J	S
9. Understand and use map scale expressed as representative fraction, statement of scale, or bar scale	LI	J	S
10. Develop the habit of checking the scale on all maps used	EI	LI-J	S
D. Interpret map symbols and visualize what they represent			
1. Understand that real objects can be represented by pictures or symbols on a map	EP	LP-J	S
2. Learn to use legends on different kinds of maps	EI	LI-J	S
3. Identify the symbols used for water features to learn the source, mouth, direction of flow, depths, and ocean currents	EI	LI-J	S
4. Study color contour and visual relief maps and visualize the nature of the areas shown	LI	J	S
5. Interpret the elevation of the land from the flow of rivers	LI	J	S
6. Interpret dots, lines, colors, and other symbols used in addition to pictorial symbols	EI	LI-J	S
7. Use all parts of a world atlas	J	S	S
E. Compare maps and draw inferences			
1. Read into a map the relationships suggested by the data shown, as the factors which determine the location of cities	EI	LI-J	S

2. Compare two maps of the same area, combine the data shown on them, and draw conclusions based on the data	EI	LI–J	S
3. Recognize that there are many kinds of maps for many uses, and learn to choose the best map for the purpose at hand	EI	LI–J	S
4. Understand the differences in different map projections and recognize the distortions involved in any representation of the earth other than the globe	LI	J	S
5. Use maps and the globe to explain the geographic setting of historical and current events	LI	J	S
6. Read a variety of special-purpose maps and draw inferences on the basis of data obtained from them and from other sources	J	J	S
7. Infer man's activities or way of living from physical detail and from latitude	EI	LI–J	S

From Helen McCracken Carpenter, Editor, *Skill Development in Social Studies*, National Council for the Social Studies, 33rd Yearbook, (1201 Sixteenth St., N.W., Washington, D.C.: National Education Association, 1963), pp. 322-325.

The need for a variety of maps, for an understanding of the legends that tell the story of the map, and for an understanding of the scales used in representing sizes in maps is made clear in the list of skills beginning on page 225. Boys and girls need these concepts if they are to study social studies in a competent manner.

From a careful look at the maps below, boys and girls can raise questions about which they can do their own research:

1. In which states are both corn and wheat important crops?
2. In which states are both corn and cotton important crops?

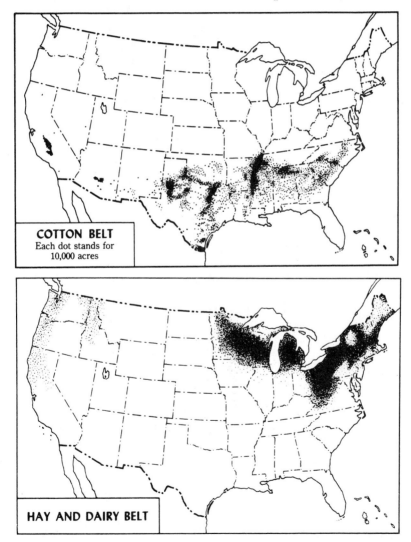

COTTON BELT
Each dot stands for
10,000 acres

HAY AND DAIRY BELT

3. Which states produce large quantities of corn, wheat, hay, and dairy products?
4. Why are *hay* and *dairy* together on one map?
5. Can you state that there is no corn grown anywhere in the dairy belt? Why, or why not?

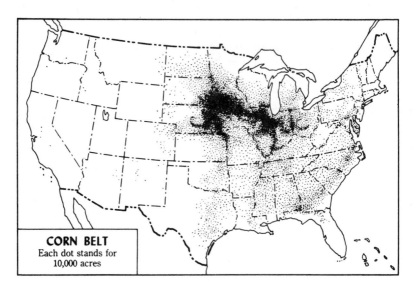

CORN BELT
Each dot stands for
10,000 acres

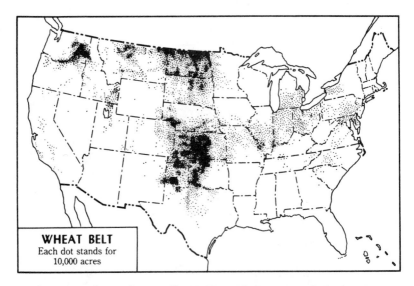

WHEAT BELT
Each dot stands for
10,000 acres

From Cutright, Prudence, Allen Y. King, Ida Dennis, and Florence Potter, *Living Together in the Americas,* (New York: The Macmillan Company, 1958), "The Corn Belt," p. 243; "The Wheat Belt," p. 251; "The Hay and Dairy Belt," p. 257; and "The Cotton Belt," p. 199.

From the location of the iron ore and the bituminous coal deposits, why might Pittsburgh, Pennsylvania have become one of the greatest steel producing centers in the United States? (consider the location of the ore, the Great Lakes as inexpensive transportation, and the dense population of the Metropolitan Cities.)

Locate the state in which you live. Which ores are mined there? How significant is mining in the economic life of your state?

Study the ore maps on page 232.

V. HOW TO TEACH A UNIT OF WORK

The teacher may think of the unit as having five rather distinct steps. They are explained below:

I. *Orientation*
   A. Create interest on the part of the class.
   B. Give the class some notion of the scope of the problem involved.
   C. Discuss with the group the possibilities of the unit in order for them to see the kind of problem this unit will help them to solve.
   D. An orientation period may require varying lengths of time, from a day to a week.

II. *Teacher-pupil Planning*
   A. Set down in writing the questions or problems to be answered by completing this unit of work.
   B. Many of the questions will be raised by the members of the class.
   C. The teacher is also a participating member and should raise those questions not raised by the class.
   D. A teacher-pupil planning period may evolve a number of experiments to be performed, a list of questions to be answered through reading or a study guide to give purpose to the phase of the unit *gathering information.*

III. *Gathering Information*
   A. Once the purposes of the unit have been designed, the class is ready to go to work collecting data. In the lower grades, these will be a short period with frequent questioning and evaluation. In the higher elementary grades, a class may work for several class periods gathering information from a variety of sources in a variety of ways.

IV. *Sharing Information*
   The sharing period makes it possible for the students to share the information which they have obtained from different sources, so that all members of the class need not read the same thing. The sharing period is especially important, too, to correct erroneous ideas which children may have gotten in their reading.

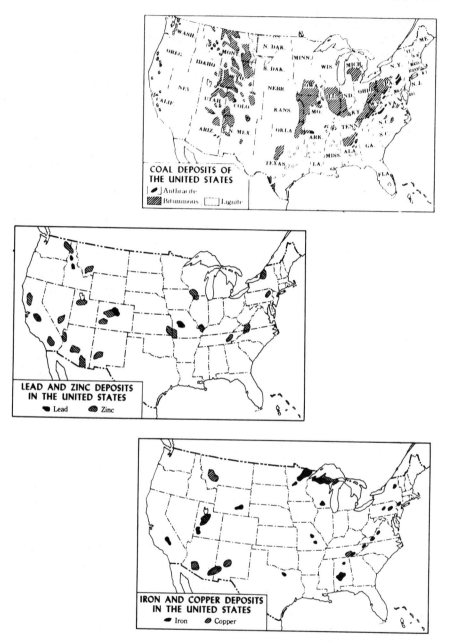

From Cutright, Prudence, Allen Y. King, Ida Dennis, and Florence Potter, *Living Together in the Americas*, (New York: The Macmillan Company, 1958), "The Iron and Copper Deposits in the United States," p. 114; "The Coal Deposits in the United States," p. 110; and "The Lead and Zinc Deposits in the United States," p. 261.

V. *Culminating Activity*

There needs to be some way to summarize what the group has learned with the completion of each unit of work. This may be done in any one of several ways:

A. Prepare a program of reports for another group of children, for the class, or for the parents.

B. Make notebooks in which they compile summary statements about work done in the unit.

C. Take a unit test covering the details that have been taught in the class.

D. Draw a mural that tells the story of the unit.
The discussion of what the class has learned is very important, since they need to handle the concepts of the unit through oral discussion.

The teacher-pupil planning period can be the most important both in setting up the objectives to be met, and in guiding the students in planning what they think is important, how they can carry out the activities of the unit, and which of them can exercise leadership in working with the teacher.

This method of teaching affords the teacher excellent opportunity for students to work in small groups or committees where they can work together and help each other. Organizing committees in the intermediate grades can be frustrating for a teacher if the boys and girls have never worked in this manner before. Yet, once they have learned to study together efficiently, many very important social interaction skills and social values are learned that are just as important as the subject matter being studied. If the group work is new, the teacher must guide the process skillfully. For example, groups can be set up for just one short period with no indication of their continuing after this first meeting. Then if they have a very clear purpose for meeting and the teacher has planned ahead with the chairmen of groups, the teacher can move from group to group and lend assistance as indicated. The boys and girls themselves must evaluate the technique afterward as a total group and reveal their own weaknesses and decide how to move ahead.

The tasks to be outlined in the study guide will be determined by the planning done by the group with the teacher. The detailed suggestions given here about the making and using of study guides as an aid in studying the material are presented as general suggestions or ideas that may be useful to a teacher who must plan many types of job-sheets, study guides, or test-exercises to help boys and girls better understand what they are studying.

The Study Guide

Graded study guides can help to give groups of children specific direction for doing silent-study exercises.

The study guide is one of the best ways of teaching children to study their content subjects such as science, history, geography, or hygiene. The chief purpose of the study guide is to help children read understandingly in the content subject-matter fields.

Study guides are called by such names as job-sheets, study-sheets, study-exercises, or study-test exercises. It should be just what its name implies, a *guide* to help the child to understand, to organize, and to remember what he is reading.

The study guide should help the child to understand what he reads.

Five main factors are involved here:

1. If the child cannot pronounce the words, he needs word recognition exercises over the material before he tries reading it silently.

2. If the child does not know the meanings of words, he needs vocabulary building exercises before he reads silently to try to understand.

3. In most textbooks, the new hard words are introduced too fast, and not repeated often enough for children to get them. Study guides will require intensive reading of small amounts of material and also require re-reading for different purposes.

4. Textbook sentences may be stated in unusual and difficult ways. Study guide exercises will require some re-stating or paraphrasing ideas from the text.

5. Often, children have not had enough experience with the ideas in the reading material. For example, children may have difficulty with the sentence, "Joe's father is working on the ditches that carry the water to irrigate the vegetable fields." If they have had no experience with ditches, nor irrigation, nor vegetables raised in large areas, they need experience, either first-hand or vicarious, to remove this difficulty. Pictures, either film or filmstrip, or from a flat-picture collection, going to see the thing described, or by reading easy material which describes it in terms of what the child already knows are ways of removing the difficulty.

The study guide should help the child to think about and use the material he has read.

Some of the reasons why a child cannot, or does not, think about and use material after he has read it are these:

1. The child may have had no clear-cut purpose in reading the material. He is just reading to get through the lesson.

2. A child may be so engrossed with the details of every sentence, pronouncing hard words, and so on, that he does not see the larger purposes of the material he is reading.

3. The child may consider all of the sentences of equal value. He needs to be taught that some ideas are more important than others, some are subordinate to others.

Study sheets are needed which require a child to choose the main ideas, or to choose minor ideas, to outline, summarize, or evaluate a selection. Durrell, in his book Improving Reading Instruction,[9] suggests that the teacher needs to plan *levels* and *types* of study tasks in social science and science. These suggestions will help in planning.

1. A series of short tasks is easier than a single long task.
2. Multiple-choice answers or short oral answers are easier than unaided summaries.
3. Questions prior to reading provide more help than questions after reading.
4. Evaluation at the end of a reading period (that is, immediately following the reading) helps more than evaluation at a later time.

A study guide for a unit of work needs to be prepared at two or three levels. It can be used in several ways, depending upon the group and their needs.

The easiest level may be presented in the form of a list of questions where children read to find specific answers in the text—or to read the text and then select the right choice in multiple choice questions. This task is easier when the answers are given orally than when they are written.

A more difficult level of functioning is when the children are asked to write a summary paragraph about a lesson that has been read and discussed.

Since study guides require time to prepare, they should be saved for future use.

Until study guides are provided with textbooks, teachers, or teachers in groups, will have to prepare them. A few have been prepared and are provided commercially but there is the problem of fitting the guide to the specific activities you wish to complete in your room.

The study guide should concentrate primarily upon thought processes, understanding, relating reading to children's experiences, seeing relationships, and paraphrasing ideas to insure retention.

---

[9]D. D. Durrell, *Improving Reading Instruction.* (New York: Harcourt, Brace, and World, 1956), pp. 285-308.

VI. RATE OF READING

While rate of reading has no value unless the student has comprehension of what he is reading, it is certain that most people could read
much more efficiently than they do and obtain just as much from their
reading. It is safe to generalize that fast readers get more from their
reading.

In the elementary school, however, it is necessary to establish mastery over the mechanics of reading before giving attention to the rate
of reading. Until the child has mastered the words to use in reading,
he cannot hurry up the process of assimilating the ideas expressed in
those words.

Many adults, unsophisticated in the complexities of the reading process, think about reading speed when they talk about reading problems.
If a child is already tense in the reading situation because he does not
know how to break words in syllables, or because parts of words reverse
themselves in the line of print (quiet-quite; form-from; angel-angle), or
if he occasionally reads a word from the line above and then one from
the line below the one he is really reading, to challenge him at that
point with "Now, read faster!" the teacher is creating emotional problems that may be difficult to overcome.

Average rates of reading at each grade level in the elementary school
have been provided by Harris and McCracken. These are given in the
table that follows:

TABLE. 9.1.   *Rate of Reading With Comprehension*

Grade	McCracken* Words per minute		Harris**
	Oral	Silent	Silent
1	60	60	80
2	70	70	115
3	90	120	138
4	120	150	158
5	120	170	173
6	150	245	185

By November, Tom was well into his senior year in high school. He
was being pressured to get ready to go to the university the next year
in spite of serious reading difficulties. His parents were college gradu-
ates and were expecting Tom and his brother to graduate, also. In his

---

*Robert A. McCracken, "The Informal Reading Inventory As a Means
of Improving Instruction," *Perspectives in Reading, The Evaluation of Children's Reading Achievement,* 8: 85, 1967.
**Albert J. Harris, *How to Increase Reading Ability,* Fourth Edition,
(New York: Longmans, Green and Company, 1961), p. 509.

first interview, he discussed his difficulties with reading, writing, and spelling. In his second session in a reading clinic, he read at a speed of 111 words per minute with 65 percent comprehension in material of approximately sixth grade level of difficulty.

During the six months that followed, Tom worked on:

1. Word forms. He faced problems of reversals of word parts by comparing, pronouncing, writing and spelling many paired words commonly confused.
2. Word meanings. He learned about roots, prefixes, suffixes, and Greek and Latin combining forms.
3. Writing original paragraphs. He selected philosophical or esoteric topics according to his ephemeral interests, and wrote short paragraphs which he and the tutor analyzed and corrected.
4. Rate of Reading. He kept graphs of his speed and comprehension in reading Simpson's *Reading Exercises*, Books I and II.[10]

Only part four of the work outlined above is reported here. Through twenty-seven reading exercises, Tom was able to increase his speed and maintain good comprehension. From a speed of 111 words on the first story, he read one exercise at the rate of 328 words per minute. By graduation time, he was maintaining a speed of about 290 words per minute which, other study conditions satisfactory, is adequate for college success. The graphs of his speed and comprehension are shown on the following pages.

VII. USE OF WORKBOOKS

If the classroom teacher is to find time to individualize instruction in the classroom, he will need to have seatwork exercises that can be done by children independently while the teacher is busy with subgroups in the room. Workbooks that accompany basic reading series provide some of the necessary practice children need in order to acquire the word analysis and comprehension skills of reading. Wisely used, they have a definite place in the reading program. The quality of exercises they contain, and the quality printing and format provided by publishers are undoubtedly both superior to the majority of teacher made exercises quickly prepared and reproduced.

Criteria for the Selection of Workbooks or Other Seatwork:

1. The workbook exercises the child does are usually related to the reading lesson of the day. In primary reading, this gives the child needed repetition in a new context of vocabulary being taught. With emphasis

[10]Elizabeth A. Simpson, *SRA Better Reading Books I and II*, (Chicago: Science Research Associates, 1951).

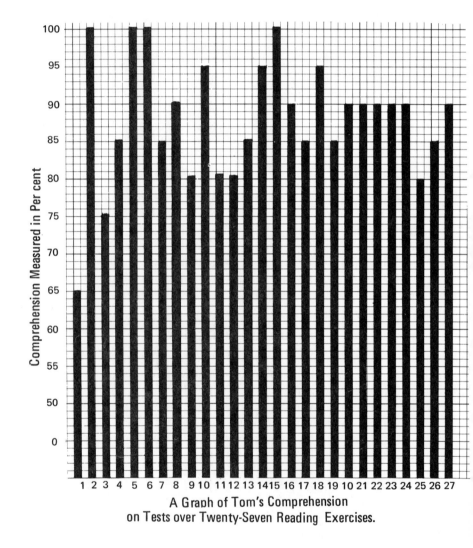

A Graph of Tom's Comprehension
on Tests over Twenty-Seven Reading Exercises.

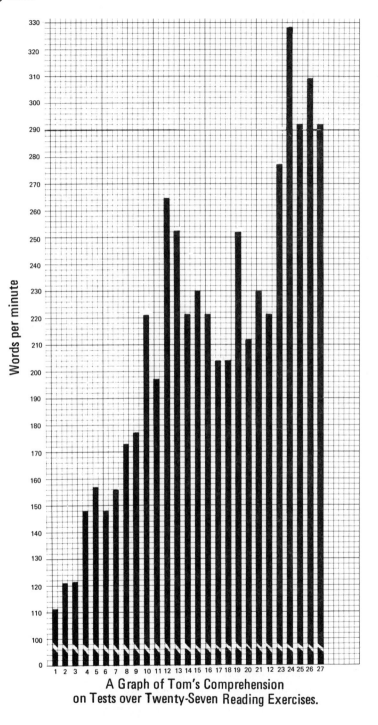

A Graph of Tom's Comprehension
on Tests over Twenty-Seven Reading Exercises.

on context reading situations, this further practice helps to fix vocabulary for the child.

2. The workbooks for a class must be procured in terms of the reading levels to be found in that class. Thirty identical workbooks for thirty third grade children who already have a reading range of at least five years is completely unjustifiable. The workbooks will have no value unless they are of the varying reading ability levels of the boys and girls using them.

3. Workbook exercises should be used by the groups that need them, can profit by them, and can complete them successfully. Exercises that are not needed and do not teach needed skills should not be used. The workbook itself does not take care of individual differences in the class, but the judicious use of the exercises in selected workbooks may make it possible for the teacher to accommodate for differences.

4. Workbooks must not be given an undue amount of time in a child's working day. The workbooks tend to be mechanical and stereotyped and are apt to crowd out more active and fruitful, enriching experiences the child should have. Workbooks leave little opportunity for a child to express initiative and to be creative in communication skills. If the teacher recognizes these limitations of the workbooks, and is providing these other experiences for the child, the workbook falls into a proper perspective.

5. Workbooks, generally, provide good practice with developmental reading skills. The gradual introduction of skills in a specifically planned sequence make it possible for the child to learn to read by reading. Study skills, selecting titles for paragraphs, judging whether the anecdote is fact or fancy, and giving definitions for new words are all skills introduced early.

6. It it is necessary for the child to be able to accomplish the work he is assigned to do in the workbook. He must *feel* that he can do it. If he has had unfortunate failure experiences, if his reading power is too limited, if he just marks answers without reading the exercises, the work may really be too difficult for him. A child cannot work independently for any length of time until he has achieved sufficient reading power to keep him motivated.

A workbook that accompanies a basic reader can have many advantages for the student if it is well taught. Presented in good format, with clearly stated instructions, the exercises are likely superior to those prepared by the classroom teacher. Boys and girls can learn work habits and personal responsibility with attention to duty for extended periods of time while the teacher is busy with other individuals or sub-groups in the class.

Workbooks can teach such study skills as following directions and using general reference materials, improve organizational ability, and develop and expand vocabulary through many kinds of exercises.

In the primary grades, workbooks have an added value of re-teaching and giving added repetitive practice on the sight vocabulary being taught in the stories in the child's reader.[11]

According to Smith some of the misuses of basal readers are

Using workbooks indiscriminately with all children; failing to check workbook activities; failing to develop workbook pages with children who are not able to work independently with them without preceding explanations.[12]

As specific suggestions for teachers in making *desirable* uses of workbooks, Smith writes:[13]

Use workbooks as they are needed as a whole or in parts, the latter being more desirable. With slower children develop new workbook activities before leaving children to work by themselves. By all means *check* the workbook results carefully after each use. Study these results to ascertain skills needed. Follow up with additional help for children whose workbook activities reveal special needs.

Recommendation No. 13 of the Harvard Report asks that teachers either make workbooks purposeful to students or discontinue their use:

13. Workbooks which accompany basal reading series are fairly standard items in most school systems throughout the country. These workbooks can be properly used in a variety of ways, but at present they are more apt to be misused or abused. Primarily they are meant to aid in the differentiation of instruction or as followup lessons of the reading instruction which is given on a more formal basis. Thus, in theory, workbooks are intended to reinforce skills already taught, to give extra practice to those children who may require it, and to be utilized in such a way that errors are pointed out immediately and corrected. Unless teachers use workbooks in appropriate ways, these tools will not perform their functions. Therefore, it is recommended:

that those persons responsible for the direction of the reading program re-evaluate the ways in which workbooks are used, and where such materials are not being used to advantage that they be discontinued or that teachers be given specific instruction in the utilization of the workbooks accompanying basal readers in order to ensure that these materials are in fact doing their proper jobs.[14]

If the skills to be taught in workbooks were programmed in individual worksheets, flexibility in their use would be greatly enhanced and the cost of buying large numbers of workbooks so every child in a class is issued one would be greatly reduced. Individual worksheets

---

[11]Hildreth, *NSSE Yearbook, op. cit.,* p. 110.

[12]Nila Banton Smith, *Reading Instruction for Today's Children,* (Prentice-Hall, Inc., Englewood Cliffs, New Jersey, 1963), p. 100.

[13]*Ibid.,* p. 102.

[14]Mary C. Austin and Coleman Morrison, *The First R, The Harvard Report on Reading in Elementary Schools,* (New York: The Macmillan Company, 1963), pp. 224-225. Recommendation No. 13 from the forty-five recommendations of Chapter IX: "Will Tomorrow Be Another Day?"

classified by skill to be developed and sequenced in order of difficulty of exercise could provide much ready made material for any teacher who knows the study skills needed and the sequence in programming by level of difficulty. Such worksheets need to be so programmed that the child can check his own work as soon as he finishes it. Individual teachers have built such files of materials by removing pages from many workbooks, mounting them, sequencing them into a skills program, and placing each one in a plastic envelope so that the child writes on the plastic with a grease pencil.

Materials for Independent Seat Work

1. SRA, Junior Reading for Understanding. (259 E. Erie St., Chicago, Ill.: Science Research Associates).

2. STONE, *et. al.*, New Practice Readers, (St. Louis: Webster Division, McGraw-Hill, 1962) Levels A, *2.5*; B, *3.2*; C, *4.5*; D, *5.1*; E, *5.7*; F, *6.2*; and G, *6.8*.

3. Reading Skill Texts (workbooks) Eleanor Johnson, Editor, Charles E. Merrill, 400 S. Front St., Columbus 15, Ohio, grade 1 through grade 6.

4. *Gates-Peardon-Reading Exercises*, A. I. Gates and Celeste Peardon, (New York: Bureau of Publishers, Teachers College, Columbia University, 1963).

> Introductory, Levels A and B
> Preparatory, Levels A and B
> Elementary, SA: What is the Story About?
> Elementary, RD: Can you Remember Details?
> Elementary, FD: Follow Precise Directions
> Elementary, PO: Predict Outcomes of Given Events.

5. Standard Test Lessons in Reading. William A. McCall and Lelah Mae Crabbs, (New York: Bureau of Publishers, Teachers College, Columbia University, 1961) Levels A, 3rd; B, 4th; C, 5th; D, 6th; E, 7th.

VIII.   SUMMARY

The abilities needed to put reading to work identifying and solving problems are called the study skills. The study skills have been discussed under the three general headings (1) location, (2) graphs, maps, and charts, and (3) organization. An excellent detailed outline of study skills, mentioned in the teachers' guides for basal readers, prepared by Van Dongen has been included in this chapter.

Study skills utilize all the abilities of the student in vocabulary and concept development and are dependent upon mastering comprehension skills of reading.

Teachers may consider the following statements in judging the value of workbooks:

1. Workbooks give more practice on the same vocabulary being mastered.

2. Workbooks teach word attack skills in sequence to give the child greater independence in reading.
3. The systematic approach to reading skills is more expertly done than a classroom teacher will likely be able to do.
4. The teacher must rely on seatwork to keep many children working independently while he gives his direct attention to sub-groups in the room.
5. Workbooks provide *some* exercises to teach skills and concepts; children may need much more practice with some types of skills than are provided in the workbook.
6. The teacher needs a greater *variety* of approaches to learning than mere daily use of workbook exercises.
7. If an exercise is not appropriate, or for any reason it serves no purpose for a given child, it need not be used.

Suggested Activities

1. Study the materials in the curriculum center either in your campus library or in an elementary school and select an annotated list of sources which will be useful to you in planning the long seatwork periods for children during the language arts periods in the grade which you teach.

2. Select one skill that is of major importance at the grade level you teach. Prepare a sequence of exercises graduated in difficulty which you could use as seat work during the independent work periods.

3. Teachers refer to exercises that can be used over and over as *permanent* seatwork. Prepare a set of materials for permanent seatwork in your room. You may use separate answer sheets for recording answers; you may provide grease pencils for writing on plastic covered exercises, or you may devise some other means for the child to complete and check his work.

References for Further Reading

BOND, GUY L. and EVA B. WAGNER, *Teaching the Child to Read,* Fourth Edition, (New York: Macmillan Company, 1966), Chapter 11: "Basic Study Skills," pp. 225-239.

CARPENTER, HELEN McCRACKEN, editor, *Skill Development in Social Studies,* National Council for the Social Studies, 33rd Yearbook, (1201 Sixteenth St., N.W., Washington, 36, D. C.: National Education Association, 1963).

COLEMAN, MARY E., "How to Teach Dictionary and Index Skills," in Albert J. Mazurkiewicz, *New Perspectives in Reading Instruction,* (New York: Pitman Publishing Corporation, 1964), pp. 425-436.

HARRIS, ALBERT J., *How to Increase Reading Ability*, Fourth Edition, (New York: Longmans, Green and Co., 1961), "The Development of Study Skills," pp. 446-465.

HEILMAN, ARTHUR W., *Principles and Practices of Teaching Reading*, (Columbus, Ohio: Charles E. Merrill, Inc., 1967), Chapter 12: "Teaching Reading-Study Skills," pp. 371-396.

HEILMAN, ARTHUR W., "Teaching the Reading-Study Skills," in Albert J. Mazurkiewicz, *New Perspectives in Reading Instruction*, (New York: Pitman Publishing Corporation, 1964), pp. 418-424.

McKEE, PAUL, *Reading: A Program of Instruction for the Elementary School*, (Boston: Houghton Mifflin Co., 1966), Chapter 9: "Studying Informative Material," pp. 316-376.

SMITH, NILA B., *Reading Instruction for Today's Children*, (Englewood Cliffs, New Jersey: Prentice-Hall, Inc., 1963), Chapter 10: "Study Skills Needed in Reading Content Subjects," pp. 305-352.

TINKER, MILES A. and CONSTANCE M. McCULLOUGH, *Teaching Elementary Reading, Third Edition*, (New York: Appleton-Century-Crofts, Inc., 1968), Chapter 10: "Comprehension and Study Skills," pp. 204-223.

10

Developing Critical
Reading Abilities

One does not believe everything he reads. If he tried to, he would become hopelessly confused. One relates new ideas that he hears, sees, or reads with his previous knowledge, or prejudice, and accepts or rejects the new idea.

Politicians try to say to their public what they think their public wants to hear. This requires many compromises with the "whole truth" and promises made which can only be partially fulfilled.

Re-read some of the lines from the "Ballad of Davy Crockett."

> Born on a mountaintop in Tennessee
> Greenest state in the land of the free
> Killed him a b'ar when he was only three.
> Raised in the woods so he knew every tree.
>
> Fought single-handed through the Injun war
> 'Till the Creeks was whipped and peace was in store.
>
> He went off to congress and served a spell
> Fixing up the government and laws as well
> Took over Washington so we heard tell
> 'N patched up the crack in the liberty bell.[1]

Was he born on a mountaintop? Is Tennessee the greenest state? Can anyone kill a bear when he is only three years old? Does one know the names of all the trees in a forest just because he lives there and sees them? Could anyone fight a war single-handed? Does any *one* man do much to stabilize or improve the government of the country? And the crack in the Liberty Bell is not patched!

People do honor the legendary hero, of course, without the statements having any accuracy. Teachers might explain that the author was not trying to relate facts, but rather portray a heroic, gallant spirit

---

[1]Words by Tom Blackburn. Copyright 1954 by Walt Disney Music Company, 800 Sonora Ave., Glendale, Calif. Used by permission.

to whom all good citizens can respond emotionally, with warmth and affection.

In educational literature, the primary concerns are with the aims of education, problem-solving approaches, the decision-making process, thinking critically, weighing and evaluating, and making logical use of knowledge.

> . . . while a good education can be a great good, a bad education can be a very great evil; it can be infinitely worse than no education at all. With a good education a child learns to think clearly and to draw sound conclusions from evidence; with a bad education he will learn to accept plausible falsehoods, to confuse propaganda with truth. With a good education he will come to cherish what is most worthwhile; with bad education he will learn to value the trivial. With a good education he will learn to make ethical judgments even when they are unpopular; with a bad education he will learn to follow the crowd wherever it may lead him and to be convinced that he is right in so doing.[2]

The Socratic Method taught the demand for accurate definition, clear thinking, and exact analysis.[3]

> Socrates collected opinions, asked questions, clarified terms and ideas, and indicated commitments. That is all he did. All that was required of those who took part with him was that they should try to think and to understand one another. They did not have to agree among themselves. If they came to conviction, they did so by their own free will. The only constraint upon them was the law of contradiction. They could not answer "Yes" and "No" to the same question at the same time.[4]

The teacher must himself posses those virtues of attention, curiosity, courage to be himself, and adherence to the same quality of standards he nourishes in his students. He must know how to accept and evaluate opposing points of view or dissenting opinion. The teacher must have knowledge. He can guide discussion properly only if his own information and skill in thinking is adequate.

The student who is not taught the habit of critical attention is apt to arrive at adulthood with superficial knowledge and, in turn, base poor judgment on inadequate knowledge.

Critical reading cannot be done without *knowledge*. Through knowledge, the reader is able to make the comparisons and judge the relevance. If the knowledge on which judgments are made is not valid, the conclusions will not be either.

---

[2]Paul Woodring, *A Fourth of a Nation*, (New York: McGraw-Hill Book Co., 1957), p. 4.

[3]Will Durant, *The Story of Philosophy*, (New York: Pocket Books, Inc., 1953), p. 6.

[4]Robert M. Hutchins, *The Conflict in Education*, (New York: Harper and Brothers, 1953), p. 96.

Much stress must be placed on the need to organize information. Organizing clearly will help in eliminating misuse of information and in rejecting irrelevant information. Practice in developing skeleton outlines should be the *modus operandi* by the time boys and girls finish the elementary school.

Social studies programs offer teachers excellent chances to develop critical reading skills. In one elementary school classroom, the watchword committee was set up for the purpose of looking for "loaded" words used in reporting research. Building informational background and eliminating prejudices, comparing different authors' conclusions on controversial issues, recognizing authenticity and authors' specialization, and detecting emotionally charged words that tend to bias the reader are all tasks of the critical reader. Teaching critical reading skills is possible only with adequate library resources.

I. EXTENDING LANGUAGE FOR CRITICAL READING ABILITY

Figures of speech, foreign words in English language context, and prefixes, suffixes, and combining forms all require precise understanding on the part of the critical reader.

1. Figures of Speech

Many adults use common expressions every day without knowing their origin. Yet, mad as a hatter, my man Friday, the camel in the tent, sour grapes, or a Pandora's box would all be more meaningful to the user if he were familiar with the source of the expression.

There are many of these expressions that are derived from the Bible. They assume greater importance when teachers remind themselves that there are many boys and girls who may have grown up without hearing references to the Bible or to the New Testament. Some of these expressions commonly used in figures of speech are given below:

as old as Methusalah
as patient as Job
"Whither thou goest I will go"
"There entered into the garden a snake"
another Daniel in the Lion's den
the golden rule
Jezebel led him on
Doubting Thomas
Don't be a Lot's wife
The land of milk and honey
The faith of Abraham
It was a David and Johnathan friendship
A voice crying in the wilderness
Greedy as Judas

the wailing wall
the tree of knowledge
they crucified her
Vanity, vanity all is vanity, saith the preacher
It's a whited sepulchre
like the seven plagues
though your sins be as scarlet
the wisdom of Solomon
back to Eve's fig leaf
and the walls came tumbling down

Expressions in which words are used in a way other than their literal meaning or out of their ordinary use to add beauty or force are called *figures of speech.*

One of the causes of misinterpretations in reading is that of taking figures of speech literally. This may cause the reader to take seriously something that the author intended to be taken humorously.

Strang and Bracken point out difficulties students may have with literary allusions:

> Unless the student knows the history of certain literary allusions, he will miss the meaning of the passage. For example, "He's a Jonah" would not be understood by a person who did not know the Bible story of Jonah and the whale. When selections from the Bible, mythology, and other frequently quoted literary sources are included in the English course of study, they have double value—the value inherent in the selections themselves and their future usefulness in helping the reader to interpret allusions in other books.[5]

In *Miracle on 34th Street,* after Fred had promised Kris Kringle his freedom and gone to unlimited detail to prove him competent, he found that Mr. Kringle had deliberately failed the test he has been given. Fred "had *talked himself way out on a long, long limb,* and now he felt it cracking." Later, before Mr. Kringle's trial, Mr. Sawyer "*placed himself in a frying pan and . . . was squirming and wriggling to get out.*" Later when Fred is talking with his girl friend, he says, "Well, *it all boils down to this*: You don't have faith in me."[6]

Literal meaning of words used in the italicized expressions will be of no help in understanding the meaning intended. Such idiomatic expressions have a special meaning for those familiar with the use of the language.

> A figure of speech is a departure from the direct method of saying a thing in order to make it more beautiful or more effective.[7]

[5]Ruth Strang and Dorothy Kendall Bracken, *Making Better Readers,* (Boston: D. C. Heath and Company, 1957), p. 216.

[6]Valentine Davies, *Miracle on 34th Street,* A Special Scholastic Book Services Edition, (New York: Pocket Books, 1962), pp. 77, 82, 90.

[7]Wilhelmina G. Hedde and William N. Brigance, *The New American Speech,* (Chicago: J. B. Lippincott Co., 1957), p. 295.

Types to Be Considered

A. *Simile*: A simile expresses a likeness between two things that in most respects are totally unlike.

> Examples: After one day on his new job, Jack said the next morning, "I'm *stiff as a board* today."
>
> In making his choices, he was *as sly as a fox.*

B. *Metaphor*: A metaphor is an implied comparison but omits the words "like" or "as."

> Examples: He has *a heart of stone.*
>
> Tom stood *rooted* to the spot.

C. *Irony*: Irony is a method of expression in which the ordinary meaning of the words is the opposite of the thought in the speaker's mind. (Subtle sarcasm.)

> Examples: Thanks for forgetting to show up to help with all this work!
>
> You are setting a *fine* example for the rest of the class!

D. *Hyperbole*: Hyperbole is a figure of speech in which exaggeration is used for effect.

> Examples: Waves *mountain high* broke over the reef.
>
> The horses sped *like the wind* over the prairie.

E. *Personification*: Personification is endowing animals, plants, and inanimate objects with personal traits and human attributes.

> Examples: Death won in the traffic race.
>
> Duty calls us.

There are other types of figures of speech, such as idea contrasts (antithesis), repetition of sound (alliteration), adaptation of sound (onomatopoeia). Figures of association are those where one word is used for a related word which it suggests or calls to mind, as in synecdoche or metonymy.

2. Use of Foreign Words in Context Reading

Some words in common use are borrowed directly from other languages. The selected list below contains those that are sure to appear occasionally in the reading done by critical readers:

Words or Phrases	Language	Dictionary meaning
1. a la mode	French	in the fashion
2. a priori	Latin	from the cause to the effect
3. ad infinitum	Latin	to infinity
4. ad valorem	Latin	according to the value

5.	alma mater	Latin	a fostering mother
6.	coup d'etat	French	a stroke of policy in public affairs
7.	e pluribus unum	Latin	one out of many; one composed of many
8.	espirit de corps	French	the animating spirit of a collective body
9.	ex cathedra	Latin	with high authority
10.	ex officio	Latin	by virtue of his office
11.	ex post facto	Latin	after the deed is done
12.	in loco parentis	Latin	in the place of a parent
13.	in memoriam	Latin	in memory
14.	ipso facto	Latin	in the fact itself
15.	laissez faire	French	let alone
16.	modus operandi	Latin	manner of operation
17.	noblesse oblige	French	much is rightly expected of one of high birth or station
18.	nom de plume	French	a pen name. An assumed title
19.	non sequitur	Latin	it does not follow; unwarranted conclusion
20.	papier mache	French	chewed or mashed paper
21.	par excellence	French	by way of eminence
22.	per diem	Latin	by the day
23.	poco a poco	Spanish	little by little
24.	pro rata	Latin	in proportion
25.	sine qua non	Latin	an indispensable condition
26.	status quo	Latin	the state in which
27.	sub rosa	Latin	under the rose; privately
28.	tabula rasa	Latin	a smooth or blank tablet
29.	tempus fugit	Latin	time flies
30.	terra firma	Latin	solid earth; a safe footing
31.	vice versa	Latin	the terms being exchanged
32.	vis-a-vis	French	opposite; facing

3. Knowledge of Prefixes, Suffixes, and Combining Forms
COMMON PREFIXES

Word	Prefix	Meaning of Prefix	Literal Meaning
inhabit	in	in	to live in
collaborate	com, con, col	together with	to labor together
disapprove	dis	not	not approve
prejudice	pre	before	to judge before
submarine	sub	under	under the water

COMMON SUFFIXES

Word	Suffix	Meaning of Suffix	Literal meaning
decorative	ive	relating to	relating to decoration
helpful	ful	full of	full of help
needless	less	without	without need
friendship	ship	state of being	having friends
conjunction	tion	act, state of being	act of joining with

COMBINING FORMS

Word	Word Parts	Meaning	Literal Meaning
biology	bio logy	life study of	study of living things
geography	geo graph	earth write	write about the earth
thermometer	therm meter	heat measure	measure the heat
polygon	poly gon	many angle	having many sides
telephone	tele phone	far sound	sound from far away

If learning is to be an active, exchanging process, it is necessary to provide environments for children other than straight rows of "screwed down" desks. Being able to provide flexible seating arrangements so the students face each other, to permit maximum pupil-to-pupil communication without teacher judgment interfering, and to encourage students to have and to express well-founded opinions puts to work the critical thinking skills recommended here.

II. JUDGING AUTHORITIES

Blough raises the question for the elementary teacher about what to do when the community disagrees with the principle he wishes to teach. Teachers should remember that young children are not, generally, ready to be asked to choose between "what father says" and a scientific principle in the textbook. Blough suggests that teachers may point out that scientists *search for answers.* Scientists themselves do not purport to know all the answers. Many of the statements in textbooks are tempered with "It is generally believed that," "Evidence seems to show," "Some scientists think," or "Probably." Teachers can keep the conversation "open" with comments such as, "Everyone has a right to believe what he really thinks. As time goes on, most of us keep on thinking and can change our ways of thinking about particular things if we see fit to do so."[8]

It is the ultimate goal of the school to help the student find his own defensible position between the conformist on the one hand and the non-conformist on the other. He will conform to the standards he accepts based on the careful evaluation of the situation in terms of what he has learned.

Conformity to the group without *basis in reason* implies lack of creative thinking and is the result of too much dependence on the teacher as a voice of authority or the textbook as the source of fact.

Critical reading requires all the steps in problem-solving: (1) knowing where to go to find information; (2) knowing how to select the specific information needed from various sources; and (3) knowing how to evaluate the information in terms of adequacy, validity, and relevance. It also requires separating fact from opinion even when opinion is subtly disguised as fact, determining the author's authority and his biases, and recognizing propaganda.

Criticism, to be valid and consistent, must be done on the basis of specified criteria. Teachers and children should set up their criteria for judging good oral reporting, for good story telling, for evaluating units of work, and many other activities throughout the year.

To develop critical reading abilities, one must learn: (1) to establish standards of judgment; (2) to develop the ability to make comparisons; (3) to judge the authority and background of the source; (4) to recognize relevance and irrelevance, fact and opinion; and (5) to make inferences and draw conclusions.

To make *judging* a participating experience for elementary school children, they must also have opportunity to judge. This technique has been used in asking children to rate each other on some performance, giving an oral report, for example. Probably, children should be asked to evaluate each other's work periodically. If work has been done by committees so that each group is being evaluated it may be easier to keep the discussion on relative merits of the project itself rather than personalities.

Social studies projects lend themselves to such evaluation. Children may be severely critical of each other at first, and always forget to mention desirable qualities of work, but this is the method by which they eventually learn to evaluate on more objective bases. When the peer group evaluates, the values accrue both to the judges and the judged.

Time spent in class discussion about value judgments—the problems of one student monopolizing the conversation, the basing of decisions

---

[8]Glenn O. Blough, Julius Schwartz, and Albert J. Huggett, *Elementary School Science and How to Teach It*, Revised Edition, (New York: Holt, Rinehart and Winston, 1958), pp. 77-78.

on personal feelings for individuals, and the arguing without facts—these are all part of the behavior of many adults and it is possible they might have developed better ways of solving problems if time had been given to these types of discussion in school rooms. Teachers are apt to feel that quiet time with each one performing in writing at his desk is more profitable learning time than an unstructured guided discussion. The values of the oral interaction should not be overlooked.

Much too much time is spent in traditional schools making children's minds act like sponges that will accept authority of parents, teachers, and textbooks without question.

The mythical "Cherry Tree Story" can be put in proper perspective by a more mature evaluation of the character and leadership qualities of the first president.

Is the story of Lincoln's undying love for Ann Rutledge another myth? Was the story started by Lincoln's law partner, William Herndon, because this partner had such an active hatred for Mary Todd Lincoln and wanted to discredit her? Do the historians agree?[9]

Statements students might find and evaluate as to which has the most evidence:

One opinion	A differing opinion
John Brown was insane.	John Brown was a great abolitionist.
The South had superior leadership.	The South was led by unrealistic cavaliers.
The North was fighting a moral battle to free the U. S. from slavery.	The North did not know what it was fighting for—therefore there were many desertions and disinterest.
The Merrimac was victorious!	The Monitor was victorious in the famous sea battle of the iron clads.
The North won the Civil War.	The South did not lose, she simply stopped fighting.

The period of the Civil War can be used to sample differing viewpoints and evaluate the reasons of both sides for plunging the nation into her bloodiest war. *Which is right?*

Pro-South	or	Pro-North
James Street, *The Civil War*, Dial Press, 1953, p. 64.		Bruce Catton, *U. S. Grant and the American Military Tradition,* Little Brown, 1954, p. 120.
The world had given U. S. Grant a hard time, partly due to tough luck and partly to liquor, but mostly because he was a long ways this side of brilliant. In fact in many things, he was sort of dumb.		Grant was a part of a unique team. He was a realist, seeing clearly how the country could get what the country professed to want.

---

[9]William Herndon, *Life of Lincoln*, (Fine Editions Press, 1949), p. 106; Ruth P. Randall, *Lincoln's Sons*, (Little, Brown and Co., 1955), p. 242; Benjamin P. Thomas, *Abraham Lincoln*, (A. A. Knopf, 1952), p. 51.

In summary, all of these activities represent uses of critical thinking in relation to reading.[10]

1. Identifying and selecting material directly relevant to a given topic.
2. Selecting material appropriate for a particular assignment, audience, or occasion.
3. Distinguishing fact from opinion; sense from nonsense.
4. Comparing the ideas in different sources of information; finding contradictions to a given point of view.
5. Considering, and accepting or rejecting, new ideas or information in light of previous knowledge.
6. Sensing biases in an author's point of view.
7. Identifying and rejecting gross overstatements and dogmatic statements with unfounded claims. (Many advertisements discussed in the following section of this chapter illustrate this point.)

III. DETECTING AND RESISTING PROPAGANDA INFLUENCES

Are most people able to make critical evaluations of what they read?

The success of full-page advertisements in color in all of the popular magazines and the extensive purchase of spots on radio and TV to advertise demonstrate that this high cost is readily paid for by gullibility of the audiences. This poses the question of people's ability to "see through" the propaganda techniques in constant use all about us. The reader may doubt that millions of people will respond to such phases as "Be the first in your block to own a Volkswagen!" or "And nothing but Nylon makes you feel so female!" or "Remember how great cigarettes *used* to taste? Luckies still do!"

But the advertiser, who paid for it, must have found it profitable!

Reading is probably becoming increasingly more important in our society and its ultimate end is to make the reader ably critical. Any thinking, participating citizen in our free society must read critically and make value judgments all the time. Resisting propaganda, discarding irrelevant information, choosing between two opinions when both are strongly supported, and being able to change one's thinking patterns when new evidence proves an old idea wrong or obsolete—are all examples of critical thinking while one reads.

Critical thinking involves considering new ideas or information in light of one's previous knowledge or beliefs. Too many adults have closed minds to new ideas and automatically reject the unfamiliar or challenging conclusion—like the legendary farmer whose comment about the giraffe he saw in the circus was, "There ain't no sich animal!"[11]

---

[10]The reader may also wish to read: Donald D. Durrell, *Improving Reading Instruction*, (New York: Harcourt, Brace and World, Inc., 1956), pp. 305ff; Albert J. Harris, *How to Increase Reading Ability*, (New York: Longmans, Green and Co., Fourth Edition, 1961), p. 443ff.

[11]Albert J. Harris, *How to Increase Reading Ability*, 4th Edition, (New York: Longmans, Green and Co., 1961), p. 443.

He never had any idea there was such an animal before, and even after seeing it, he was unwilling to admit it.

One may recognize the existence of the giraffe, but in terms of some of the ideas of other people that they would like to convey to him, he may be, in a figurative sense, denying the existence in his own thinking.

Rokeach has written about the nature of people's attitudes, beliefs, prejudices, and tolerances. He dichotomizes the open mind versus the closed mind: authoritarianism versus broad tolerance. Teachers concerned with developing critical reading and thinking skills will find this book worthwhile reading.[12]

Most children have been victims of "rumors" in the course of their school life. "The teacher said . . .", "The coach is going to . . .", "Anybody who can't work these problems in arithmetic . . .", and many other expressions that bear threat, anxiety, or fear are often passed around. The one who has little to fear from the threat may be the one who most enjoys spreading it among the less fortunate. Most boys and girls, by the time they pass to the sixth grade, have had the personal experience of being a victim of rumor that was, for them, an agonizing experience for a short time.

Propaganda devices that can mislead, have been described by the Institute for Propaganda Analysis, New York City. Propaganda is defined as "any plan or method for spreading opinions or beliefs." Frequently it is sincere or at least harmless; sometimes, however, it deliberately skirts or conceals the truth. One needs to be alert to the devices and able to evaluate them.

1. *Name calling*: using labels instead of discussing the facts. This technique consists primarily of attaching a negative symbol to someone —for example, calling a politician a crook or a person whose ideas are unpopular a fascist. By branding a person with these negative symbols it is often possible to avoid citing facts. Names, rather than facts, can be used to get a desired reaction from you.

2. *Glittering generalities*: vague phrases that promise much. The glittering generality usually consists of associating positive symbols, slogans, and unsupported generalization with an idea or person; for example, saying in a political campaign that "this act will benefit all Americans and will enhance our position abroad." Only a careful weighing of the facts will determine whether such a glittering generality has much truth in it.

3. *Transfer*: applying a set of symbols to a purpose for which they are not intended. This method of convincing people consists primarily of transferring the attraction of strong positive symbols or the repul-

---

[12]Milton Rokeach, *The Open and Closed Mind,* (New York: Basic Books, Inc., Publishers, 1960).

sion of strong negative symbols to some person, group, or idea. For example, a subversive group might display the American flag and pictures of Washington and Lincoln at their meetings. These positive symbols help gain public support. Only careful thinking on the listener's part can determine whether such uses of these symbols are supported by the facts.

4. *Testimonials*:   getting some prominent person to endorse the idea or product. The endorsement of some prominent person or group is often used to elicit a favorable reaction from you. Motion picture stars and outstanding athletes are often used for this purpose.

5. *Plain folks device*:   pretending to be "one of the folks." People are sometimes convinced of the worth of a candidate for office because he takes a "folksy" approach to problems. In other words, he uses simple idiomatic English and repeats old proverbs. Sometimes the plain folks approach includes kissing babies, wearing Indian feathers, or posing with a fishing rod in hand. Although very common in American politics, it proves little, if anything, about the qualifications of a candidate for office.

6. *Bandwagon*:   claiming that "everyone is doing it." The bandwagon method of persuading people is effective because many people don't make up their own minds and instead follow the lead of the majority. The bandwagon approach consists of giving the impression that everyone is doing it, or everyone is voting this way, or buying this product, and so it's best to get on the bandwagon if one wants to keep up with the crowd. It's an appeal to the desire to conform. To resist this approach, one must stand firmly on his right to make up his own mind. Appealing to the desire to "keep up with the Joneses" is one of the most common methods used to persuade people to do certain things, and is one of the *most difficult to withstand.*

Boys and girls in the intermediate grades have already learned to use the "getting on the bandwagon" technique. How many mothers have wondered anxiously if their little girls in fifth grade should do a given activity, only to be coaxed and wheedled into saying "*yes*" to the child when, if they had telephoned other mothers, they would have found more than enough agreement to have unanimously said "No" with no ill effects. Boys and girls in school, with a teacher whom they trust and in whom they have confidence, will testify that it is very necessary to know how to "play the game." They can cite examples of specific situations where they and their friends achieved their goal by convincing their separate parents that everyone else highly approved of something. Occasionally the child has felt "pressure" on the one hand that he must do what the rest of the group wants to do, but felt considerable anxiety on the other hand because he didn't really want to be a participant at that time.

7. *Cardstacking:* presenting only the parts of the facts that favor one side. Examples of this can be found in using quotations out of context, omitting key words from a quotation, or using favorable statistics while suppressing unfavorable ones. The important thing to keep in mind is that a series of half-truths usually add up to a complete lie. And, since cardstacking usually claims to cite some reliable facts, one must be quite astute to see the basic falseness of this approach. In other words, cardstacking is one of the most effective propaganda devices and it will require the use of ones intelligence to see through it.

Henry writes of the psychological undertones and unconscious motivations in advertising.[13] He raises the questions: "What individual child is more important than the gross national product?" and "Is it not true that TV is an anesthetic?"[14]

Through television, advertisers whet children's appetites for certain toys . . . Children let their parents know that nothing else will do for Christmas . . . Desperate parents comb stores only to find that the supply has been sold out . . . parents *do want* to buy what *their* children want![15]

Henry goes on to say:[16]

> Deprive business of its capacity to appeal to children *over the heads of their parents* and what would happen to most cereals, some of the drugs, and many toys?

With advertising expenditures running currently at twelve billion dollars annually and increasing at a rate that may soon double that figure, advertising firms and their clients bend the mass media almost exclusively to pecuniary ends.[17]

Attitudes, beliefs, and biases interfere more with critical reading than they do with literal comprehension. The cognitive process is colored by the affective process.[18]

According to Robinson, critical reading requires

> . . . judgment of the veracity, validity or worth of what is read, based on sound criteria or standards developed through previous experience.[19]

---

[13]Jules Henry, *Culture Against Man* (New York: Random House, 1963), Chapter 3.

[14]*Iibid.*, p. 71.

[15]*Ibid.*, p. 74.

[16]*Ibid.*, pp. 75-76.

[17]*Ibid.*, p. 98.

[18]Anne S. McKillop, *The Relationship Between the Reader's Attitude and Certain Types of Reading Responses*, (Teachers College Press, Teachers College, Columbia University, New York, 1952).

[19]Helen M. Robinson, "Developing Critical Readers," in Russell G. Stauffer, editor, *Dimensions of Critical Reading,* Eleventh Annual Reading Conference, (Newark, Deleware: University of Delaware, 1964), p. 3.

IV. TEACHING CRITICAL READING

Boys and girls in the elementary school can learn to read carefully for the following:

unwarranted generalizations;
making everything a dichotomous—either-or—situation;
half-truths;
quoting words, or sentences, out of context;
emotionally charged words; and
sensing biases in writer's accounts.

If critical reading abilities are important in the developmental reading program, they must be taught. Learning how to investigate sources; comparing and contrasting different reports; searching for the author's purpose; separating fact from opinion; forming judgments; and detecting propaganda are types of skills that will eventuate in better critical reading.

> Critical readers are those who, in addition to identifying facts and ideas accurately as they read, engage in interpretive and evaluative thinking. They project the literal meanings of what they read against their own background of experience, information, and knowledge, *reasoning with and reacting to the stated facts and implied ideas.* Noncritical readers, on the other hand, are those who restrict their thinking to the identification of the clearly stated facts and accept these facts literally and unquestioningly. . . . critical reading is the most difficult of all reading skills to teach.[20]

Piekarz reports asking teachers in graduate classes in reading to read a passage and construct five questions that they might ask pupils. The result: about 97% of all questions are of a literal nature; 2.7% are of an interpretive nature, and .3% are of an evaluative nature. She concludes:

> Students who spend 97% of the time answering literal questions during the twelve years of elementary and high school should expect to experience difficulty with critical reading and thinking when they reach college. Expecting otherwise is unrealistic.[21]

Skills needed to develop critical reading ability:

1. Determining the relevance of the material
2. Evaluating the reliability of authors
3. Differentiating fact and opinion
4. Examining assumptions
5. Checking data
6. Detecting inconsistencies

[20]Josephine Piekarz Ives, "The Improvement of Critical Reading Skills," *Problem Areas in Reading—Some Observations and Recommendations,* (Coleman Morrison, Editor, Oxford Press, Inc., Providence, Rhode Island, 1966), p. 5.
[21]*Ibid.,* p. 56.

7. Drawing conclusions, based upon
   a. gathering of adequate information
   b. testing possible conclusions in light of the data
   c. reaching tentative conclusions subject to revision if new information is discovered.[22]

Again, levels of questioning and questioning strategies assumes primary importance as pointed out by Taba:[23]

> The role of questions becomes crucial and the way of asking is by far the most influential single teaching act. A focus set by the teacher's questions circumscribes the mental operations which students can perform, determines what points they explore, which modes of thought they learn. A question such as "What are the important cities in the Balkans?" provides poor focus in several respects. Because no criterion of importance is available, such questions develop an unproductive mode of thinking, in addition to training in arbitrary judgment. Such questions (1) suggest that one can judge the importance of cities without a criterion. For example, does one look for large cities, capitols, ancient ones or what? Most students faced with such questions have only two alternatives: guessing what the teacher wants, or trying to recollect what the book said, both cognitive not productive. Asking "right" answer questions also (2) builds a "convergent" mind—one that looks for simple right answers, and which assumes that "right" answers depend on authority rather than on rational judgment.

Flamond delineates the meaning of the term "critical reading":

> . . . merely getting the facts is not critical reading. The reader must first determine whether he is reading facts or merely opinions and/or assumptions. Sensing the relationships among the facts, comparing the facts with experience, knowing when the facts are relevant, evaluating these facts against other facts to arrive at some conclusion, and going beyond the facts to get the inferred, but explicitly stated, meaning are aspects of critical reading.[24]

> To really think while reading, to evaluate, to judge what is important and unimportant, what is relevant or irrelevant, what is in harmony with an idea read in another book or acquired through experience, constitutes critical reading.[25]
> In intellectual development, the child is increasingly able to understand cause-effect relationships, to form generalizations, and to think logically. He makes amazingly clear distinctions between fact and fancy.

---

[22]Dorothy Fraser and Edith West, *Social Studies in Secondary Schools,* (New York: The Ronald Press Company, 1961), pp. 222-227.

[23]Hilda Taba, S. Levine, and F. F. Elzey, *Thinking in Elementary School Children,* (San Francisco: San Francisco State College, U. S. Office of Education, Cooperative Research Project No. 1574, 1964), pp. 53-54.

[24]Ruth K. Plamond, "Critical Reading," in Albert J. Mazurkiewicz (ed.), *New Perspectives in Reading Instruction,* (New York: Pitman Publishing Corporation, 1964), p. 256. Reprinted from *Explorations in Reading,* 1962.

[25]Walter T. Petty, "Critical Reading in the Primary Grades," *Education Digest,* 22: 42-43, October, 1956.

When problems are within his experience, his thinking appears to be like that of an adult.[26]

Providing proper environment that enhances learning is one of the teachers' primary goals. As has already been stated, the attitude of the teacher in the class circumscribes to a very great extent the functioning of the children. How this attitude sets the climate for the thinking boys and girls: whether the child sees authority as domineering, accepting, guiding, or questioning, has been concisely described by Shapiro:

> The teacher introduces the children to the world of thought through the kinds of rules and rituals with which she surrounds the thinking process; the kinds of content she introduces, accepts, and rejects from the children; the kinds of approaches to problem solution she encourages and sustains; the amount of freedom she allows for independent and explanatory thinking; the speed with which she closes down inquiry; the respect she shows for their fumbling, their confusion—all create for them an image of that world and a set of expectations about their own potency as learners and thinkers.[27]

V. SUMMARY

Developing the ability to read critically requires (1) extending language concepts in figures of speech, knowing commonly used words borrowed from other languages, and understanding prefixes, suffixes, and combining forms; (2) evaluating the primacy or superiority of authorities; and (3) detecting and resisting propaganda influences.

These critical reading abilities must be developed by classroom teachers. Harris has aptly stated:[28]

> Children whose education is centered around the investigation of vital problems, who learn to investigate, to experiment, and to reason for themselves should grow up to be more able than the typical adult of today to resist propaganda influences.

Suggested Activities

1. Take the Watson-Glazer *Test of Critical Thinking*[29] and compare your results to the National Norms. According to this test and its interpretation, are you able to read critically?

---

[26]Nelson B. Henry (ed.), *Development in and Through Reading*, 60th Yearbook, National Society for the Study of Education, Part I, (Chicago: University of Chicago Press, 1961), p. 288.

[27]Edna Shapiro, "Study of Children Through Observation of Classroom Behavior *Theory and Research in Teaching*. (Arno A. Bellack (ed). Bureau of Publications, Teachers College, Columbia University, New York: 1963), p. 101.

[28]Albert J. Harris, *How to Increase Reading Ability*, Fourth Edition, (New York: David McKay, 1961), p. 444.

[29]Watson, Goodwin and Edward M. Glaser, *Watson-Glaser Critical Thinking Appraisal*, Forms Ym and Zm, (757 Third Avenue, New York, New York 10017: Harcourt, Brace and World, 1964).

2. Observe in a classroom during a class discussion. In 30 minutes, determine per cents for categories of questions: memory of facts, interpreting facts, evaluation of the written statements, and application of principles.

REFERENCES FOR FURTHER READING

ARTLEY, A. STERL, "Critical Reading in the Content Areas," *Elementary English*, 41: 122-130, February, 1959.

ELLER, WILLIAM, "Essentials of Critical Reading," *Education Digest*, 21: 35-37, March, 1956.

————, "Critical Thinking: More on Its Motivation," *Progressive Education*, Vol. 33, No. 2, March, 1956.

————, "Essentials of Critical Reading," *The High School Journal*, 39: 66-40, November, 1955.

FRANK, ROBERT, "Learning to Read Critically," *Junior College Journal*, 26: 371-372, March, 1956.

HEILMAN, ARTHUR, *Principles and Practices of Teaching Reading*, Second Edition, (Columbus, Ohio: Charles E. Merrill Books, Inc., 1967).

HENRY, JULES, *Culture Against Man*, (New York: Random House, 1963).

HILL, JERALDINE, "Teaching Critical Reading in the Middle Grades," *Elementary English*, 39: 239-243, March, 1962.

HILLS, R. JEAN, "Reading and the Art of Thinking," *Elementary School Journal*, 59: 215, January, 1959.

KARLIN, ROBERT, "Critical Reading is Critical Thinking, *Education*, 84: 8-11, September, 1963.

DREBS, STEPHEN O., "Teaching Critical Thinking," *Education*, November, 1960.

MANEY, E. S., "Literal and Critical Reading in Science," *Journal of Experimental Education*, September, 1958, pp. 57-64.

ORR, CATHERINE E. and HAZEL SCHROBENHAUSER, "First Graders Do Research Too," *Elementary English*, 34: 19-21, January, 1957.

PETTY, WALTER T., "Critical Reading in the Primary Grades," *Education Digest*, October, 1956, pp. 42-43.

————, "Critical Reading in the Primary Grades," *Elementary English*, 33: 298-302, No. 5.

ROBINSON, "He Reads But Does He Understand?" *Grade Teacher*, November, 1955.

RUSSELL, DAVID, *Children's Thinking*, Boston, Ginn and Co., 1956.

SHAPIRO, EDNA, "Study of Children Through Observation of Classroom Behavior," in Arno A. Bellack, editor, *Theory and Research in Teaching*, (New York: Bureau of Publications, Teachers College, Columbia University, 1963).

SOCHOR, ELONA, "Nature of Critical Reading," *Elementary English*, 36: 42-56, January, 1959.

SMITH, NILA B., "Levels of Discussion in Reading," *Education Digest*, 26:42-44, September, 1960.

STAUFFER, RUSSELL G., "Children Can Read and Think Critically," *Education*, May, 1960, pp. 522-525.

TABA, HILDA, "The Teaching of Thinking," *Elementary English*, 42: 534-542, May, 1965.

TABA, HILDA, S. LEVINE, and F. ELZEY, *Thinking in Elementary School Children*, (San Francisco: San Francisco State College, U.S.O.E. Cooperative Research Project No. 1574, 1964).

THOMAS, ELLEN LAMAR, "A Critical Reading Laboratory," *Education Digest*, May, 1960.

TRIGGS, FRANCES O., "Promoting Growth in Critical Reading," *Education Digest*, September, 1959.

————, "Promoting Growth in Critical Reading," *The Reading Teacher*, 12: 158-164, February, 1959.

WILLIAMS, G., "Provisions for Critical Reading," *Elementary English*, 36:323-331, May, 1959.

11

Oral Reading

While some teachers may utilize too much oral reading under quite ineffective conditions,[1] many teachers could do more effective *teaching* of oral reading. The element of cruciality must not be overlooked. Once in a while, it is very important to be able to read the minutes for a meeting, read to substantiate a point of view, read a report of consequence in one's work, read to one's children, or to participate in group reading in church or social gatherings.

On the other hand, oral reading can be one of the most abused aspects of the reading program. When teachers ask children to read by turns just so everyone in the group has to read one page without the reading serving any other purpose, the result is disastrous for everyone. Children should have an opportunity to read silently any material they are expected to later read orally and should not be asked to sit and listen quietly while one child reads something they have all already read and discussed. Taking turns around the group is sure to frustrate the fast readers who are "sneaking" ahead and to embarrass the slow readers that cannot read fluently or pronounce all the words. An authoritarian teacher that demands that all the class listen quietly while one person struggles through a paragraph is teaching many negative values and few, if any, positive ones.

Prior to 1930, when the emphasis in teaching children to read changed to silent reading practice and learning comprehension and study skills, the emphasis was largely on "good oral reading." Correctness of enunciation and pronunciation and practicing proper inflection, emphasis, and feeling tone were primary goals.

---

[1]Sarah W. Wildebush, "Oral Reading Today,"*The Reading Teacher*, 18: 139, November, 1964. Wildebush states that many precious hours are being "consumed in the round robin of continuous oral reading."

McCutchen emphasizes this oral reading skill in the preface of his fourth reader published in 1883:

> A critic of the day has observed that "in the great Republic of North America reading aloud is justly considered to be one of the most important elements of a child's education."
>
> • • • • •
>
> Reading aloud, if properly directed, serves a double purpose: it tends to correct errors in articulation and pronunciation, and to break up certain careless habits of speech; and it also enables the teacher to see whether the pupil *comprehends* what he is reading.
>
> • • • • •
>
> It is the business of the teacher to insure exactness in articulation and pronunciation purely by the force of example; the class thus become mere imitators of a good model . . . It is only when the meaning is too abstruse for the pupil, or when it is desirable to give examples of modulation or style for those pupils who rarely hear good reading, that the teacher may read for the class and let them imitate his emphasis, his pauses, his inflections, as well as his articulation and pronunciation.[2]

And Baldwin and Bender still give this same emphasis in 1911:

> The design of this series of School Readers is to help children to acquire the art and the habit of reading so well as to give pleasure not only to themselves, but also to those who listen to them. The selections have been chosen and arranged with strict reference to the capabilities and tastes of the pupils who are to read them, thus making every exercise in oral reading both easy and enjoyable as well as instructive.
>
> • • • • •
>
> The notes under the head of "Expression," which follow many of the lessons, are intended to assist in securing correctness of pronunciation and enunciation, a clear understanding of what is being read, and the intelligible and pleasing oral rendering of the printed page. These notes should be carefully studied by both teacher and pupils.[3]

In this chapter, the separate topics are (1) the place of oral reading; (2) the task of oral reading; (3) improving oral reading; (4) rate of oral reading, and (5) using oral reading as a diagnostic tool.

I. THE PLACE OF ORAL READING

There seems to have been for the past few years, and to continue to be today, considerable controversy about the place of oral reading in the reading program. Part of this controversy stems from the fact that some people feel that if the child is put in an oral reading situation in which he doesn't do well, this will do very damaging things to his per-

---

[2]Samuel Mecutchen, (ed.), *The Fourth Reader*, (Philadelphia: E. H. Butler and Co., 1883), pp. 7, 8, 10.

[3]James Baldwin and Ida C. Bender, *Reading with Expression: Second Reader*, (New York: American Book Company, 1911), pp. 5-6.

sonality. And, of course, if he is expected to read at his frustration level all the time, it will do such damage. Another argument in the controversy is that people do no oral reading outside the school, that is, all of their reading outside the school is going to be silent reading. Therefore, they should do only silent reading in the school. These two arguments have some validity.

Valid criticisms can be leveled against oral reading in situations that are *not oral reading situations.* (1) if the child does not have a purpose for reading, or if he does not understand the purpose, if he is given too little help on technical difficulties prior to oral reading, if the selection is not suitable either in type of reading material or in level of difficulty for the child for audience reading, then the oral reading that he does will be neither helpful for him nor interesting to his listeners. (2) Those situations in which all the people in the audience have copies of the material which the child is reading are *not* audience situations. (3) Many teachers now evidence little interest in oral reading. Teachers themselves may be deficient in oral reading ability. Oral reading that the child does under such adverse conditions as those presented here will not constitute a worthwhile experience for him.

These criticisms can be overcome by teachers who acknowledge a legitimate place for oral reading in the total reading program for all children. A considerable place for oral reading is justified for the student of whatever grade placement who is reading at a *primary reading level.* First of all, oral reading is more like talking, more like the use of oral language that the child enjoys all day long in and out of school. When the child begins his formal reading program in first grade, he may feel that he has more in common with it if it continues to be a talking kind of language. In grade one, the teacher can expect to commit about 50 percent of the time to oral reading, and 50 percent to silent reading. From the beginning of formal reading through the first grade, the teacher will have reading groups first read silently whatever story they are learning how to read. They will also re-read most of these stories during the first year orally. The teacher will set up new purposes for reading, but one of *the teacher's purposes* for a second reading is to provide the child reading practice on the basic sight vocabulary.

In second grade, but not for all the children in second grade, those children reading at second grade reader level should have a little more time for silent reading and less time for oral. Perhaps, for those now able to do independent reading, two-thirds of the time will be silent reading time and one-third oral. This provides time for all children to have opportunity to read aloud. After children establish an independent third grade reader level, the amount of time spent on oral reading is sure to decrease. Probably not more than 20 percent of the time in working with developmental reading classes above third grade level will be given to oral reading. This should include the teacher's evaluation of reading in all subjects, not just the reading class itself. The Iowa Elementary Teachers Handbook lists four purposes:[4] (1) the child will have an opportunity to entertain others by his reading, (2) the child will get satisfaction and security in oral expression when he reads to others, (3) this reading will give him satisfaction in group participation, and (4) the reading will give the child effective speech practice. A fifth purpose is the diagnostic teaching one; it gives the teacher a check on the child, noting how well he reads or what specific errors he makes in reading a passage.

The child should have an opportunity to entertain others by his reading, but when are they entertained? Not if the reading is not the right kind of material, and not if the child cannot read it well. When does the child get satisfaction and security in oral expression? Does he not get this satisfaction and security only when he expresses himself reasonably well? He can get satisfaction through group participation only if he gives something to the group that they antcipate or understand. He gets effective speech practice only if he has poise, self-confidence, and a feeling that he is doing a good job, so that he uses adequate speech.

Horn and Curtis say that the child reads a poem or story to entertain his classmates, or he reads aloud softly to himself to aid in his appreciation of a literary selection.[5] The poems below can illustrate these objectives in oral reading for some children. Yet, as the questions following the poems suggest, they cannot meet these objectives for *all* the children in the group.

Mice
By Rose Fyleman

I think mice
Are rather nice

Their tails are long,
Their faces small,
They haven't any
Chins at all.
Their ears are pink,
Their teeth are white,
They run about
The house at night.

---

[4]Department of Public Instruction, *Iowa Elementary Teachers Handbook: Reading,* (Des Moines: The Department, 1943).

[5]Ernest Horn and James F. Curtis, "Improvement of Oral Reading," in Nelson B. Henry, Editor, *Reading in the Elementary School,* (Chicago: University of Chicago Press, 1949), 254-265.

They nibble things
They shouldn't touch
And no one seems
To like them much.

But *I* think mice
Are nice.[6]

Galoshes
by Rhoda Bacmeister

Susie's galoshes
Make splishes and sploshes
And splooshes and sploshes,
As Susie steps slowly
Along in the slush.
They stamp and they tramp
On the ice and concrete,
They get stuck in the muck in the mud;
But Susie likes much best to hear

The slippery slush
As it slooshes and sloshes,
And splishes and sploshes,
All around her galoshes.[7]

Eletelephony
By Laura Elizabeth Richards

Once there was an elephant,
Who tried to use the telephant—
No, No, I mean an elephone
Who tried to use the telephone—
(Dear me, I am not certain quite,
That even now I've got it right.)

Howe'er it was, he got his trunk
Entangled in the telephunk;
The more he tried to get it free,
The louder buzzed the telephee—
(I fear I'd better drop the song
Of elephop and telefong!)[8]

---

[6]"Mice" by Rose Fyleman, Copyright 1932 by Doubleday & Company, Inc. From the Book *Fifty-One New Nursery Rhymes* by Rose Fyleman. Reprinted by permission of Doubleday & Company, Inc.

[7]From the book *Stories To Begin On* by Rhoda W. Bacmeister. Copyright, 1940, by E. P. Dutton & Co., Inc. Renewal, ©, 1968 by Rhoda W. Bacmeister. Reprinted by permission of the publishers.

[8]From *Tirra Lirra* by Laura E. Richards, by permission of Little, Brown and Co. Copyright 1935 by Laura E. Richards.

Arbuthnot[9] suggests the next poem, *Where's Mary?* be called a study in irritability. The woman searching for Mary gets angrier with each succeeding line.

Where's Mary?
by Ivy O. Eastwick

Is Mary in the dairy?
Is Mary on the stair?
What? Mary's in the garden?
What is she doing there?
Has she made the butter yet?
Has she made the beds?
Has she topped the gooseberries
And taken off their heads?
Has she the potatoes peeled?
Has she done the grate?
Are the new green peas all shelled?
It is getting late!
What! She hasn't done a thing?
Here's a nice to-do!
Mary has a dozen jobs
And hasn't finished two.
Well, here IS a nice to-do!
Well, upon my word!
She's sitting on the garden bench
Listening to a bird![10]

Will the child entertain others by his reading if he does not read well? Will he get satisfaction and security in oral expression? Will he get satisfaction in group participation? Will this be effective speech practice? These are poems one teacher particularly likes to read, and perhaps when teachers make assignments they tend to give children what they would particularly like to do themselves.

Arbuthnot has done as much as any other teacher of children's literature to emphasize the effective use of oral reading to encourage boys and girls to read freely from the great storehouse of well-written children's books available to them today.

Certainly reading aloud is the way to introduce children to exceptional books that they might not choose for themselves or might not enjoy without this added lift of family enjoyment and the reader's enthusiasm. *The Wind in the Willows, The Children of Greene Knowe, The Gammage Cup, Rifles for Watie, Smoky* . . . just a sampling of the choice books . . . To hear *Penn* or *Johnny Tremain* beautifully

[9]May Hill Arbuthnot, *The Anthology of Children's Literature: Book I, Time for Poetry,* (Chicago: Scott, Foresman and Co., 1952), p. 8.
[10]From the book *Fairies and Suchlike by Ivy O. Eastwick.* Copyright, 1946, by E. P. Dutton & Co., Inc. Reprinted by permission of the publishers.

read is a literary treat; and to read *Winnie-the-Pooh* silently, in solitude, isn't half the fun as to read it aloud or to listen to it read aloud.[11]

In summary, the place of oral reading in the reading program can easily be justified. Teachers recognize that oral reading is more difficult than silent reading. In order to be effective, it not only presupposes the ability to understand and appreciate the selections that one reads, but also involves the attitudes and abilities for portraying these ideas to other people.

II. THE TASK OF ORAL READING

Horn and Curtis have described concisely the oral reading task:

> Oral reading is more difficult than silent reading since, to be effective, it not only presupposes the ability to understand and appreciate the selection to be read, but in addition, involves other attitudes and abilities. In the process of good oral reading, the eyes lead by a considerable distance the words being spoken. . . . The dominant influence in effective reading, whether oral or silent, is not the peripheral processes such as eye movements, but the central processes, including purpose and understanding. The best results are obtained when the material to be read orally is first read silently.[12]

The real purpose of reading aloud to others is to share information with them, to entertain them, or to enjoy a good story which they do not have. To meet this criterion, then, the audience being read to will not have copies of the material in their hands.

A second criterion for good oral reading is that the reader must be prepared beforehand. This means he has help with technical difficulties in the reading, he understands the content of the passage very well, and there are no words he cannot pronounce. He may practice reading orally before his own reading group.

A third criterion is that the selection needs to be one that lends itself to the oral reading situation. If it will not generate interest, if it will not easily appeal to the listeners, the teacher may suggest other content to be read.

It is also hoped that oral reading is used in the classroom where it serves as the best medium for achieving other purposes. Some of these might be:

1. Giving a report, either individual or committee.
2. Giving specific directions to be followed, reading announcements of interest to the group, sharing special items of interest.

---

[11]May Hill Arbuthnot, *Children and Books, Third Edition,* (Chicago: Scott, Foresman and Company, 1964), pp. 647-648.

[12]Ernest Horn and James F. Curtis, "Improvement of Oral Reading," in Nelson B. Henry, Editor, *Reading in the Elementary School,* (Chicago: University of Chicago Press, 1949), p. 258.

3. Reading to prove a point, to settle an argument, or to give evidence of a different point of view.
4. Sharing the many aspects of recreational reading.

In addition, too, of considerable importance, is the need for the teacher to "hear" each child read orally on occasion during the school year. The teacher should have some kind of a check list which can be kept up to date easily and record his evaluative impressions of each child's oral reading *at sight* (without first reading silently)as the teacher asks the child to do in the informal reading inventory and reading prepared selections that have been read silently first.

Until children have established an independent reading level of second grade or above, they need opportunity to do a great deal of oral reading. Oral reading reinforces for them that reading is a written down form of communication. The teacher has opportunity to continually evaluate the kinds of errors the child makes in his reading by keeping track of the word recognition errors, punctuation errors, omissions and insertions, use of context clues, and ability to attack new words unfamiliar to him. This kind of on-going evaluation has diagnostic value in appraising pupil growth throughout the year.

The reader will note that the above paragraph indicates that oral reading serves this purpose for all boys and girls who have not established an independent reading level at third grade or above. Of course, this includes the first grade, most of the children in the second grade, and many children in third grade. However, it also includes *some* in the *fourth, fifth,* and *sixth* grades.

Children enjoy sharing their reading when they have confidence in their ability to read well and they find the story interesting. This sharing an enjoyable experience has much affective value for boys and girls. Following are some of the major values accruing to the teacher from oral reading situations:

1. Oral reading makes it possible to enjoy with the reading group the most interesting parts of stories they have read.
2. Until children have established at least a fluent second grade level of reading, the teacher needs a careful check on how accurately they do read.
3. By listening to oral reading, he can note errors and confusions in the "mechanics" of reading and place teaching emphasis on these errors. Such reading done *at sight* helps the teacher continually evaluate children's instructional level of reading.
4. For the child in trouble, the teacher can interject questions, stop the reading to discuss or clarify a point, take turns reading pages or paragraphs, and generally lend encouragement.
5. The teacher can develop with the children a criterion for improvement in abilities to read well for others.

6. The teacher can build confidence, and keep the child at his growing edge of learning to promote his optimum growth.

III. IMPROVING ORAL READING

Children need guidance in becoming satisfactory oral readers. The first criterion is that they must be permitted to read material which seems comfortably easy *to them*. The following criteria are important:
1. Adequate phrasing;
2. Voice modulated to comfortable speech;
3. Opening the mouth so enunciation is clear;
4. Recognizing punctuation marks;
5. Eliminating distracting mannerisms;
6. Flexible use of stress, intonation and pitch appropriate to the content of the story being read;
7. Developing a comfortable composure, stance or sitting position; and,
8. Developing the ability to enjoy the story with the audience.

Extensive use of tape recorders in classrooms has made possible permitting children to record their oral reading, to practice the same passage under strong motivation, and to prepare tapes of "one's best reading" for the teacher to save. These reading samples are helpful to the teacher when holding parent-teacher conferences, as he can let the parent listen to a sample of the child's oral reading.

Greer recommends the following procedure:

> Ask the student to read a few paragraphs from the Gilmore Oral Reading Test and then analyze the tape with him. Together, compile a list of items which he should check in his oral reading. Paste this check list in the front of his notebook (so it will not be lost) and he can use the list to check subsequent recordings of oral reading.
>
> Save the original tape and let him listen when he likes. After a while he forgets about this tape but continues oral practice. Then near the end of the semester the teacher can bring out the first tape for comparison with his present reading.
>
> In sixth grade, I've had some really excellent results in oral reading improvement with this technique. An advantage is that the child can take care of much of the practice on his own because he knows how to operate the tape recorder.[13]

The contribution oral reading can make to personality development will evidence itself in clear speech, self-confidence, poise, and an in-group feeling of contributing to group pleasure. Audience reading requires: First, a real purpose for reading to others, a purpose that is meaningful to the child who is doing the reading. Second, a selection that is appropriate and interesting to read in an audience situation on

---

[13]Margaret Greer, Sixth Grade Teacher, Albuquerque Public Schools.

the level of difficulty that the child can handle as his independent or instructional level of reading. The third step is adequate preparation which usually includes preliminary silent reading with some attention to vocabulary difficulties followed by oral reading practice before reading to the entire class. And fourth, an audience which has a reason for listening and does not have a copy of whatever is being read to them. Hopefully, the reading shares information which they want but which they do not already have.

Oral reading can help the child who needs remedial reading. It will be helpful for poor readers to have some lessons read to them. Oral reading practice is very important for the poor reader in establishing a level of fluent reading. Sharing is important and the child is sharing his reading when he reads to the teacher or to another child. If his reading ability is limited, he may never have enjoyed silent reading as a means of acquiring new ideas. He can learn this eventually; and if his reading power is strengthened he can launch into an interesting book with a low level vocabulary load. The teacher makes reading enjoyable and rewarding by enjoying with the child the point of an interesting easy story that he does read. He must be convinced that reading can be fun and a revealing, informative way of learning.

If he has difficulty giving his attention to the job of reading, the teacher will be able to judge when to interject questions, when to stop to discuss points in the story and when to lend ego-support with encouraging remarks. As his skill in the mechanics of reading improve, he needs less support from the teacher. The poor reader may have developed poor speech habits because he cannot read. If so, he needs help in general speech improvement as he gains confidence, as he finds his level for optimum growth, and as he begins making reading progress. He may need help with accurate phrasing, modulating his voice to a comfortable level, opening his mouth sufficiently for clear enunciation, putting zest and confidence into his reading, recognizing punctuation marks, eliminating distracting mannerisms developed in his period of frustration about reading, and getting inflection into character parts.

In oral reading, one can follow the child's reading word by word, syllable by syllable, and can find out exactly what kind of errors he is most prone to make. Two common problems in oral reading are word-by-word reading and context reading. In word-by-word reading, the word-caller plods along slowly, tending to make a noticeable pause after each word. When he does attempt to phrase his reading, he may group the wrong words together or he may disregard or misinterpret the punctuation marks. Keeping the place with the finger is the common fault of word-by-word readers. If a child is a word-by-word reader, one may help him by giving him *easier material* so that he will have to think less about how he reads and more about what he reads. As he does this, he will improve his memory of the details in what he is reading and his understanding should be somewhat better.

The context reader, as contrasted to the word caller, may be quite fluent in what he is trying to read but rather inaccurate in the way he reads it. He may skip over words; he may add words; or he may substitute one word for another. He may be unable to attack any words not already in his sight vocabulary except as he guesses at them from context. These sentences illustrate the typical kind of reading the context reader does. The sentence may read, *"The little rabbit went down the road."* The context reader, studying the picture at the top of the page and then looking at the words in the sentence may say, *"The little bunny hopped down the lane."* He's gotten the idea, but he has changed four basic words in the sentence. Or the sentence may read, *"Behind the band came a man on a big elephant."* But the context reader reads, *"After the bandwagon went, a man came by on a elephant."* The child who is a context reader, probably needs easy reading material to read for practice, then needs his attention directed to word attack skills, phonetic and structural analysis, and while he is reading in context he should have his attention directed to reading with complete accuracy for part of the lesson. For example, "Now on the next page, I'm going to watch to see if you pronounce every word exactly as it is in the story."

A sixth grade boy who was reading an easy second grade reader was making several errors. At the end of a page, the teacher said to him, "Now you are getting the idea across to me and that is the thing that is important, but since we are reading an easy book this morning, let's just re-read these two pages now and be sure we read completely accurately." Without much difficulty, this boy was able to concentrate both on the story that was very elementary and on the mechanics of how he was reading. He was able to pay more attention to how he was reading and soon stopped making up the sentence the way he thought it probably ought to end or the way it would end according to the picture.

A good reader knows how to utilize context, how to blend, how to use visual clues. A poor reader is apt to have only one method of attack and he may often use it incorrectly. The classroom teacher will keep a record; as was suggested in using the Informal Reading Inventory, so he can help the child analyze specific faults more completely later.

IV.   RATE OF ORAL READING

One important consideration is that of rate of reading in contrasting silent and oral reading. By third or fourth grade, the child should begin to perform more rapidly in silent reading than oral. The average oral reader who enunciates clearly as he reads, is likely reading at a rate of between 150 and 170 words per minute. This is about as fast as oral reading will be done. However, by the time the child finishes sixth grade, he should have developed a silent reading rate about double his oral reading rate. McCracken has established comparative rates of silent and oral reading through the elementary school. (See Rate of Reading, p. 236, Chapter 9).

Price and Stroud reviewed investigations of children's oral reading, and concluded that there was little, if any, evidence to show that oral reading has much effect on silent reading.[14] Teachers have two distinct problems: the teaching of silent reading skills on the one hand, and the teaching of oral reading ability on the other. The way to get good oral readers is to have a person practice reading orally; the way to improve silent reading skills is to practice reading silently and work on the desired skills.

Easy, effective oral reading habits take time to develop. Their development should not conflict with developing competent silent reading abilities.

V.   USING ORAL READING AS A DIAGNOSTIC TOOL

Throughout this chapter, the reader has been reminded of the ways teachers may make use of oral reading to improve oral reading abilities through practice, to help the context reader, and the word-by-word reader, and to record on tape oral reading by each child.

Accumulating such data can be, in itself, diagnostic. If the word-by-word reader understands what his problem is, practices reading material sufficiently easy for his free reading level, and begins to read more fluently by phrases, he is overcoming his problem. If he is a context reader, but practices reading easy material accurately and records a story accurately read for his teacher, he is also overcoming his problem.

Teachers need to become skilled in using a marking technique such as is found in Chapter 3 in administering the IRI. Then any oral reading the student does can be quickly marked and scored to determine instructional and frustration levels of reading, not just in the reading class but in all subjects of the school curriculum.

VI.   SUMMARY

The major purposes of oral reading have been presented as (1) to entertain; (2) to give personal enjoyment and satisfaction; (3) to en-

---

[14]Helen Price and James B. Stroud, "Note on Oral Reading," *Quarterly Journal of Speech*, 31: 340-343, October, 1945.

courage effective group participation; (4) to provide effective practice for speech improvement; and (5) to provide for the teacher a diagnostic measure of the strengths and weaknesses in children's oral reading abilities.

Other important ideas discussed in the chapter included (1) Criteria of what constitutes an oral reading (audience) situation; (2) The need for teachers to be able to read well orally; (3) The use of oral reading practice to improve word recognition skills of poor readers; (4) The use of the tape recorder to allow children to practice oral reading independently; (5) The importance of the teacher understanding the *child's purpose* in oral reading as well as the teacher's purpose; and (6) The use of oral reading to open the doors to the great exciting world of children's literature for all boys and girls.

SUGGESTED ACTIVITIES

1. Practice and read a story on the tape recorder that you would read to a class in the elementary school.

2. Ask three children to read something they each think is easy. Record their oral reading on the tape recorder. Listen to each one as many times as necessary and judge the suitability of the material for instructional or independent reader levels.

3. Prepare and read an appropriate story to a class in the elementary school. Evaluate your success in helping them enjoy the story.

REFERENCES FOR FURTHER READING

BOND, GUY L. and EVA B. WAGNER, *Teaching the Child to Read,* Fourth Edition, (New York: The Macmillan Co., 1966), Chapter 12: "Oral Reading," pp. 240-249.

HORN, ERNEST and JAMES CURTIS, "Improvement of Oral Reading," in Nelson B. Henry, Editor, *Reading in the Elementary School,* (Chicago: University of Chicago Press, 1949), pp. 254-265.

TINKER, MILES A. and CONSTANCE M. McCULLOUGH, *Teaching Elementary Reading,* Third Edition, (New York: Appleton-Century-Crofts, 1968), Chapter 11: "Reading Aloud," pp. 224-236.

WILDEBUSH, SARAH, "Oral Reading Today," *The Reading Teacher,* 18: 139, November, 1964.

ZINTZ, MILES, *Corrective Reading,* (Dubuque, Iowa: William C. Brown, 1966), pp. 345-347.

12

Use of the Library in Developing Permanent Reading Habits

All teachers want children to develop permanent interests in reading. Attractive bulletin boards showing new book acquisitions, a free reading table, children's book reviews, and reinforcing understanding through reading are all ways teachers work to develop these permanent interests.

If teachers are to find suitable materials to accommodate the wide ranges of ability in any class, they must rely on the centralized library in the school. Adams expresses the possibility of the school library meeting this multi-level materials need in this way:[1]

> If each child is to reach his highest potential in every subject area at the elementary school level he must have access to vastly different materials and instruction than were offered to that grade level in previous years. A multi-level approach is required and multi-level materials must follow this thinking. Although the multi-level materials are maintained in part within the classroom, it has become evident that many supplementary materials must be utilized, and budgetary consideration make it advantageous to place them in some type of central repository. The obvious choice for this centralization is the elementary school library.

In order to develop the *habits* of permanent use of books, one must have developed, at least to some degree, all of the skills in word identification, comprehension, study skills, and oral reading. The development of permanent reading habits becomes, then, a kind of over-all goal of the school's reading program for boys and girls.

I. THE ELEMENTARY SCHOOL LIBRARY

The basic purpose of the library is to expose children to much good literature and to develop permanent interests in reading—and in read-

---

[1]Hazel Adams, "The Changing Role of the Elementary School Library," *The Reading Teacher*, 18: 563, April, 1965.

ing from a wide variety of materials. Hopefully, such experience will also have a desirable effect in devolping tastes for literature worth reading.

The attitude generally should be that to read is pleasant. Schools must provide for reading opportunities for all children; children must be guided in making wise choices about which reading materials best serve their purposes; and adequate provision must be made by each teacher to move children toward permanent interests and habits in reading.

Reading opportunties for *all* children require that:

1. Materials must have high interest appeal and be of appropriate difficulty so that children can read with relative ease.
2. Wide ranges of choices must be provided: both fact and fiction; travel, history, myth, science, legend, biography, poetry and plays.
3. They cannot enjoy vicarious experiences in reading unless they have the ability to live the incident meaningfully. They must learn to empathize, internalize the feelings, see the sights, smell the smells, hear the sounds.
4. Materials can be recommended, made available, and reported favorably, but each child will have interests that are unique and individual so that the teacher should not anticipate that all children will be equally interested in books, stories, or poems because the teacher feels that they have special merit.

Activities to promote growth in reading interests:

1. Individual card files: annotations about books read
2. Use of MY READING DESIGN[2]
3. Group discussion once a week or once every two weeks
4. Oral reporting
5. Recommending books to others
6. Oral reading by the teacher
7. Oral reading by individual children

USE OF MY READING DESIGN

My Reading Design is a structured plan to help boys and girls broaden and extend their reading interests. In the circle graph pictured on the next page, the child keeps a record of the reading he has done in all the different subject areas of the school curriculum. In the four-page folder designed by Simpson, there is one page provided for listing all the titles of books read, on another page is a long list of topics given

[2]G. O. Simpson, "My Reading Design," (Defiance, Ohio: The Hubbard Co., P.O. Drawer 100, 43512, 1962).

for each of the various categories to help the child decide the topics to which this book relates in the circle graph.

The number of the book on the child's list is then recorded in the small circles nearest the center of the design, under the different categories that tell what you enjoyed in the book. Some books relate to only one topic, others may relate to two or three. As children read a number of books and record each one on the graph, they will, no doubt, be pleased to see their patterns grow in the design.

Teachers sometimes use excellent bulletin board devices for this same motivation. The segmented book worm, bar graphs made by using tiny construction paper folders for each book read by each child, and other similar visual aids are often seen in elementary classrooms.

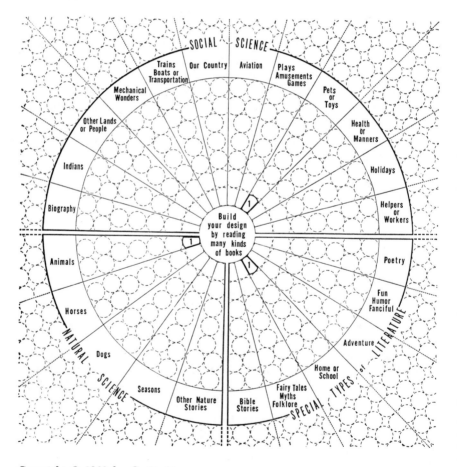

Library Skills to Be Learned

Boys and girls can begin learning early many of the location skills they need for using the card file, locating a book on the shelf, and being able to quickly recognize the ascending and descending numbers in the area where the book sought is shelved. Special designations can be learned if pointed out to the children. Certain behaviors will enhance both the child's confidence in using and his finding the time to use the library. He needs to be able to find easily the books and magazines he likes and wants. He should be able to withdraw and return on time all the books he can make effective use of. He must be able to use the card catalog and to recognize the order of Dewey Decimal or Library of Congress numbers on the shelves. He needs to know how to take care of books and to practice good "library behavior."

Greer has listed seven skills to be taught to elementary school boys and girls:[3]

1. How to locate books by author, title, and subject headings.
2. How to find information in alphabetical order to third or fourth letter.
3. Kind of information on a card in the file: full name of author or authors, complete title, publisher, copyright date, whether or not illustrations are included, and a call number, either Dewey Decimal or Library of Congress.
4. Books are filed by call numbers.
5. Every library book has an accession number, which indicates how many volumes have already been cataloged. If the accession number is 50,000, then the library has already cataloged 49,999 before it arrived.
6. The Library has a reference legend explaining which subject headings are assigned to which call numbers on the shelves.
7. Special designations need to be learned: "B" is biography; "F" is fiction; "R" is reference; and "Zi" or "Cla" represents first letters of author's last name.

Arbuthnot reminds us:

> One tremendous service a library can render both homes and schools is to supply quantities of those books which bridge the gap between reading ability and reading skill. That lag can, by third or fourth grade, assume discouraging proportions for some children. For instance, a child may be reading a first or second grade level but be capable of comprehending and enjoying books which he can't possibly read for himself at fifth, sixth, or even seventh grade level. Then the experts, among other recommendations, advise that the child be given a lot of practice

---

[3]Margaret Greer, "The Efficiency of the Use of Analogy In Teaching Selected Concepts at the Sixth Grade Level," Masters thesis, University of New Mexico, Albuquerque, 1966.

reading and that he be provided with easy-to-read books in order to acquire the confidence that comes from a sense of comfortable fluency.[4]

And Adams explains:

In the child's mind the library is no longer merely a place where he goes once a week to change a book (or, get a book for a book report he must write). It is still a place where a child may on any day take out and return books, but it is also a center of information, a place for leisure time activities, for story hours, for discussion of books and a place to listen to music or view filmstrips.

The teachers, the librarians, and the reading consultant see the library as the center of multi-level materials, the research center and training center for the advancing skills of the students.[5]

A good elementary school library has a wholesome balance between non-fiction books and books for recreational reading. It maintains this balance in various subject fields and fields of children's interests. Intelligent and effective use of available book selection aids will insure the variety of books to extend the experiences of every child. A report of the American Library Association has suggested the following analysis of juvenile library book collections.

ANALYSIS OF BOOK COLLECTION[6]

Subject	Percent of total
Reference Books	1.2
Religion and Mythology	1.2
Social Sciences and Folklore	9.1
Language	0.3
Science	23.0
Fine Arts	5.0
Literature	3.2
History and Biography	22.5
Fiction	21.5
Picture and Easy-to-read Books	13.0
	100.0%

If the weeding-out process is properly done, about 10 per cent of the books will be discarded annually. The most-used books and those with poor quality bindings will have to be replaced or renovated often.

The library program must include the teaching of library skills and the appreciation of good books.

The issue today is not whether or not to have good classroom libraries or to have a good, well-stocked central library in the elementary school. It is absolutely necessary to have a good central library to keep interesting, changing library shelves in a given classroom within the school.

---

[4]May Hill Arbuthnot, *Children and Books,* Third Edition, (Chicago: Scott, Foresman and Company, 1964), p. 654.

[5]Adams, *op. cit.*

[6]American Library Association, *A Basic Book Collection for Elementary Grades,* (Chicago: American Library Association, 1960), p. iv.

Librarians and teachers together select the shelf of books needed for each new social studies unit and make them readily available to the room teacher who returns the shelf of books that is no longer needed from the previous unit.

A good central library contains no less than 6,000 volumes. The collection of books is made available to all the students and teachers during the entire school day.

The library provides a "comfortable" learning situation where children are "learning how to learn." If this happens, they will move easily to the junior high and high school, and to public library situations the way "life" situations ought really to keep encouraging them to read.

The library is planned to meet the individual differences in the reading abilities of large groups of children. The fourth grade boy with third grade reading power can read on his level pursuing his interests; the fourth grade girl reading independently at the sixth grade level can pursue learning much higher on the scale of developmental skills.

Sources for the Teacher

A number of general reference books must be available to teachers in order for them to select books to meet the needs and interests of boys and girls and to supplement the units of work being taught in their classrooms.

All, or as many as possible, of the following general reference books will be useful to classroom teachers if they are available in the elementary school library:

1. *Children's Catalog* edited by West and Schor. A classified annotated guide to over 4,000 books for elementary school libraries. 11th edition, 1966. (There will be five annual supplements and then these will be incorporated into the next edition.) H. W. Wilson Company, 950 University Avenue, Bronx, New York 10452.
2. *Adventuring with Books: Reading List for Elementary Grades,* Elementary Reading List Committee, National Council of Teachers of English, Over 1,000 titles arranged in twelve categories. 1960 with 1963 supplement. NCTE, 508 S. Sixth Street, Champaign, Illinois.
3. *A Basic Book Collection for Elementary Grades,* Miriam Snow Mathes, et. al., More than 1,000 essential books for an elementary school library; includes list of children's magazines. 7th edition, 1960. American Library Association, 50 East Huron Street, Chicago 11, Illinois.
4. *Best Books for Children,* compiled by Patricia Allen, a list of 3,300 recommended books, grouped by age level and grade along with several subject groupings. 1964. R. R. Bowker Co., 1180 Avenue of the Americas, New York 10036.
5. *A Bibliography of Books for Children,* ACEI, a list of 1,700 books for supplementary reading by children in grades 4 through 12. Association for Childhood Education International, 3615 Wisconsin Avenue, N.W., Washington, D. C.

6. *Children's Books Too Good to Miss* compiled by May Hill Arbuthnot, helpful list for parents and teachers. 3rd edition, 1963. Western Reserve University, 2029 Adelbert Road, Cleveland, Ohio.
7. *Good Books for Children,* edited by Mary K. Eakin. Books published 1950-1965. Titles reviewed in Bulletin of the Center for Children's Books, 3rd edition, 1966. University of Chicago Press, 5750 Ellis Avenue, Chicago 37, Illinois.
8. *A Parent's Guide to Children's Reading,* by Nancy Larrick. Books and magazines for children. Revised, 1964. Pocket Books, Affiliated Publishers, Inc., 630 Fifth Avenue, New York 10020.
9. *Subject Index to Books for Intermediate Grades* compiled by Mary K. Eakin. Analyses contents of 1,800 books, under 4,000 headings of today's curriculum interest and needs for grades 4-6. 3rd edition, 1963. American Library Association, 50 East Huron St., Chicago 11, Illinois.
10. *A Subject Index to Books for Primary Grades,* compiled by Mary K. Eakin, and Eleanor Merritt. Indicates independent reading level and interest level of over 900 trade books and readers. 2nd edition, 1961. American Library Association, 50 East Huron Street, Chicago 11, Illinois.
11. *The Horn Book Magazine,* discriminating reviews of children's books and an annual list of outstanding books. The Horn Book, Inc., 585 Boylston Street, Boston, Mass.
12. *The AAAS Science Book List for Children,* compiled by Hilary J. Deason. Books in science and mathematics for grades 1-8. Annotations indicate content and grade level. First purchase items starred. 2nd edition, 1963. American Association for the Advancement of Science, 1515 Massachusetts Avenue, N.W., Washington, D. C. 20036.
13. *Books about Negro Life for Children,* by Augusta Baker. An annotated list of books arranged by subject and age level. 3rd edition, 1963. New York Public Library, Fifth Avenue and 42nd Street, New York, New York 10018.
14. *Children's Books to Enrich the Social Studies for the Elementary Grades,* by Helen Huus, an annotated list of books covering subjects usually covered in the social studies curriculum in K-6. 1961. National Council for the Social Studies, 1201 Sixteenth Street, Washington, D. C. 20036.
15. *Good Reading for Poor Readers,* compiled by George Spache. Revised edition, 1962. Garrard Press, 1607 North Market Street, Champaign, Illinois 61821.
16. *I Can Read It Myself,* compiled by Frieda Heller. Titles selected for the begining reader, grades one and two, and for the primary reader ready for longer books. 1960. Ohio State University, 242 West 18th Avenue, Columbus, Ohio.
17. *Resources for Teaching About the United Nations,* by Elizabeth Thompson, annotated bibliography of titles about various aspects of the U. N. 1962. National Education Association, 1201 Sixteenth Street, N.W., Washington, D. C. 20036.

Organizing Enriching Resources for Unit Teaching

The methodology for teaching a unit of work was discussed in the chapter on developing study skills. The purpose here is to point out that the well-stocked library is the teacher's enriching resource for any social studies units he may be teaching.

Once the students and the teacher have stated in behavioral terms the objectives for the study of the unit, the books and other materials of instruction must be made available if students are to achieve their objectives. The fifth grade unit, "The Westward Movement" has been used in this section to suggest some kinds of materials (folk lore and folk songs, student reading materials, teacher reading materials, sources of free materials, audio-visual aids, and because this unit includes the Southwest, a limited Spanish vocabulary). All of these resources might be used to develop the understandings in the unit. The knowledges rooted in geographical concepts and those rooted in economic concepts are presented graphically to help the students better understand the historical significance of the Westward Movement in our country. It is clear that librarian-teacher cooperation is necessary for the most effective teaching of these units.

Suggestions are provided for the enrichment necessary to make the fifth grade social studies unit on the Westward Movement challenging and interesting to the boys and girls. These suggestions for teaching a unit on *the Westward Movement* were supplied by Dr. Jean Legant, Lecturer in Education, University of New Mexico, teaching the methodology course, *Social Studies in the Elementary School.*

Behavioral objectives can be formulated in teacher-pupil planning sessions:

1. Each child learns about faith in our American Heritage by: _____

2. Class members learn greater awareness of and respect for ethnic groups, their beliefs and values, by: _____

3. The United States extended its boundaries to the West Coast through buying land, exploring new territory, importing the total economic life of the nation, and removing Indians to reservation lands. Children understand these happenings by: _____

4. Society is always changing: children sense this by observing:_____

5. Even in rough pioneer days, there was a social and recreational life for the people. Children will learn about this by:_____

6. Education moved with the families. Children can observe the extension of public education to the west by:_____

7. Communication between the East and the West was established by: _____

8. Extending law and order to the far west was a complex operation. Children can understand many of the problems by: _____

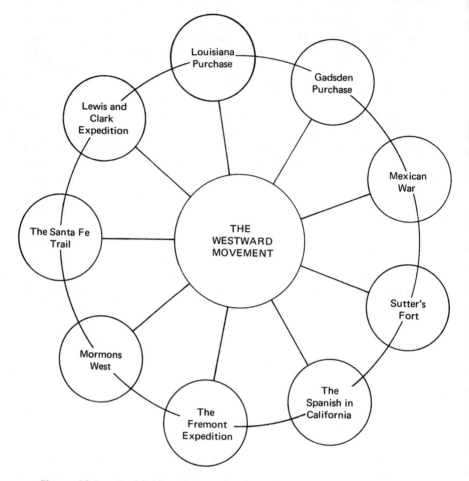

Figure 12.1. Establishing Geographical Understanding of the Westward Movement in the United States.

A. Folklore and Folk Songs
  1. How folklore, ballads and literature began
  2. What folklore, ballads, and literature used as their subject matter
  3. What is folklore and folk music?
    a. Folklore
        (1) It includes all the customs, beliefs, and stories that people themselves have handed down through the years.
        (2) When people didn't have printing or when printing wasn't used as widely as it is today, people passed down stories from generation to generation.

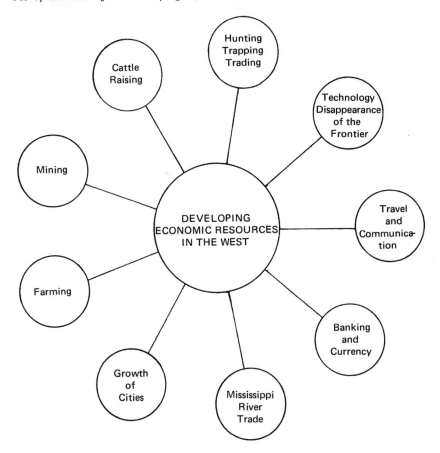

Figure 12.2. Establishing Economic Understandings of the Westward Movement in the United States.

    b. Folk Music
        (1) Music which has grown up among the people as an important part of their life.
        (2) It is very old and was never written or printed until recent years.
        (3) Usually it contains unusual rhythms and unusual scales, with frequent changes from major to minor.
        (4) The author is not known.
        (5) The language and customs of the people are reflected in this kind of music. The American folk song is generally narrative and tells the story of a person or an event.
  4. Examples of folklore and folk music.

B. Student Reading, Grades 3-4 (Five selected readings)
1. *I Am a Pueblo Indian Girl.* Abieta. Cadmus.
2. *Wild Bill Hickok.* A. M. Anderson. Wheeler.
3. *Portugee Phillips and the Fighting Sioux.* A. M. Anderson. Row Peterson.
4. *In My Mother's House.* Ann Nolan Clark. Viking.
5. *A Child's Story of New Mexico.* Clark. University Publishing Co., 1960.

C. Student Reading, Grades 5-6 (Five selected readings)
1. *Kit Carson, Mountain Man.* Margaret Bell. Morrow.
2. *Buffalo Horse.* Cardell D. Christenson. E. M. Hale and Company.
3. *Sam Houston, The Tallest Texan,* Wm. Hohnson. E. M. Hale and Company, 1953.
4. *The Santa Fe Trail: The Opening of the West.* Editors of *Look.* Random House, 1946.
5. *The Lewis and Clark Expedition.* Richard Newberger. Random House.

D. Teachers Background Reading
1. "Frontier Lawman." Wm. G. Bell. *The American West,* Summer, 1964, p. 5.
2. *Indian Legends from the Northern Rockies.* Ella E. Clark. University of Oklahoma Press.
3. *Of Men and Rivers.* Virginia Eifert. Dodd, Mead.
4. *New Mexico's Troubled Years.* Calvin Horn, Horn and Wallace.
5. *Tales of the Frontier: From Lewis and Clark to the Last Roundup.* E. Dick. University of Nebraska Press.

E. Free Materials
1. Map of U. S. (80 x 60) color map of Indian reservations, national parks.
2. Pioneer Life SA-082
3. Westward Across the Land No. 4451 (poster of U. S. purchases.)
4. Lewis and Clark Expedition map.
5. Routes of Principal Explorers 1700-1852 map.

F. Audio-visual Aids: Educational Motion Pictures
1. U. S. Expansion Series: Northwest Territory, the Louisiana Purchase, Texas and Far Southwest, The Oregon Country, Coronet Films.
2. Cultural Influence Series: English, French, Indian, Spanish Influences in the United States. Coronet Films.
3. Johnny Appleseed: A Legend of Frontier Life. 1955, Coronet.
4. Indians of the Southwest. Arts and crafts of the Southwest Indians, Ceremonial Dances of the Southwest Indians, Hopi Indians, Life of the Navajo Indians, Pueblo Indians.
5. How the West was Won. *Life,* color.

G. A Glossary of Western Words: Spanish
1. acequia . . . irrigation ditch
2. adobe . . . unburnt brick dried in sun: used for building
3. angoras . . . chaps made of goat hide with hair retained
4. broncho-busting . . . horse-breaking
5. bronco, broncho . . . unbroken Mexican, or Californian, horse
6. buckaroo, buccarro . . . cowboy (Northwest)
7. caballada . . . band of horses
8. caballero . . . Spanish knight or horseman; gay cowboy; expert horseman
9. caballo . . . horse
10. cabestro . . . rope; horsehair-rope halter
11. calabozo . . . Spanish name for jail
12. caracole . . . to make a half turn to the right or left on horseback
13. cataloes . . . cross-breed of cattle and buffaloes
14. cholla . . . type of large cactus with sharp spines
15. compadre . . . boon companion; pal
16. conchas . . . silver disks worn for decoration on chaps, hats, etc.
17. corral . . . pen for livestock
18. dinero . . . money
19. frijole, frijol . . . type of bean much cultivated in Mexico as a food
20. hacienda . . . in Spanish America, a large plantation on which the owner is resident; an establishment for raising stock
21. jacal . . . small hut or cabin
22. javalina . . . a wild boar
23. junta . . . the junction; sometimes refers to business meeting
24. latigo . . . leather strap attached to girth and used to fasten saddle on horse's back
25. lobo . . . wolf
26. loco . . . crazy, foolish
27. maguey . . . rope made of the fibers of the century plant
28. mañana . . . to morrow; late
29. mantas . . . type of blanket or wrap
30. mesa . . . elevated tableland
31. mestizo . . . half-breed
32. peso . . . Mexican dollar; hence, any dollar
33. pinto . . . piebald; small calico horse of the Western plains; Mexican Indian
34. pueblo . . . building or group of buildings constructed by Indians of the Southwest.
35. ranchero . . . rancher; especially Mexican rancher
36. reata . . . leather rope; lariat

37. remuda . . . band of saddle horses; extra mounts
38. romal . . . whip fashioned from leather thongs, and attached to bridle or saddle
39. serape . . . blanket worn as cloak by Mexicans
40. sudaderos . . . leather lining or underside of saddle
41. vaquero . . . cowpuncher, cowboy
42. vara . . . Spanish measure of length equal to about a yard

The Values of the People

Social studies textbooks designed to provide the overview of a full year of work for any given grade level, must, of necessity, be digests of much factual material. If teachers rely heavily on basic text material, boys and girls will be attempting to absorb many facts for which they may not always see relevance. Typical kinds of abbreviated facts include for most any geographical area: the important crops, the major cities, the chief industries, the latitude and longitude, the mountain ranges and the navigable rivers.

Relevant to the cultural, social, and economic values of the people about whom the social studies text is written, teachers need to seek out those fiction and non-fiction accounts that will teach something of the affective life of the people. What was daily living like for the pioneers? What was fun? What games did they play? What were the causes of happiness or unhappiness? What about the fears and anxieties of boys and girls. For historical fiction or biography, the questions need to be in the past tense. Of course, the questions also apply in the present tense for stories about boys and girls today.

There is a great deal of historical fiction that can help the reader understand the thinking and feeling of the people in their daily living. Cavanah has written such a book about Abraham Lincoln's boyhood that many boys and girls enjoy.

> Abe Lincoln was hired to work as a clerk in Denton Offut's general store. Customers could buy all kinds of things there—tools and nails, needles and thread, mittens and calico, and tallow for making candles. One day a woman bought several yards of calico. After she left, Abe discovered that he had charged her six cents too much. That evening he walked six miles to give her the money. He was always doing things like that, and people began to call him "Honest Abe."[7]

Laura Ingalls Wilder has made pioneer days in the middle west live for many boys and girls in the intermediate grades with her *Little House in the Big Woods, On The Banks of Plum Creek, The Long Winter,*

---

[7]Frances Cavanah, *Abe Lincoln Gets His Chance,* (Chicago: Rand McNally and Company, 1959), p. 78.

Farmer Boy, Little House on the Prairie, By the Shores of Silver Lake, Little Town on the Prairie, and *These Happy Golden Years.*[8]

Fifth Chinese Daughter provides the reader with many specific episodes that reveal the strong conflict between the parents and the children growing up as first generation immigrants in San Francisco:[9]

> Jade Snow was seventeen and had just arranged her first date without her mother's or father's permission. Her very traditional father chastised her in this way:
>
> "Where and when did you learn to be so daring as to leave this house without permission of your parents? You did not learn it under my roof."
>
> When Jade Snow tried to explain her behavior to her parents, her father became very angry and continued:
>
> "Do I have to justify my judgment to you? I do not want a daughter of mine to be known as one who walks the streets at night. Have you no thought of our reputations if not for your own? If you start going out with boys, no good man will want to ask you to be his wife. You just do not know as well as we do what is good for you."

Louise Stinetorf has written delightfully of the experiences of Abed, a Sudanese boy who lived in the Nubian Desert in North Africa, when he took his parents' ceramic pots to market to sell them. He had brought his donkey loaded with pots to the marketplace in Fadwa and found a little empty space and began calling out his wares:

> Presently a woman stopped in front of the pots and began looking them over. As she moved, Abed heard a little tinkling sound, and although her dress was so long he could not see her feet, he knew she was wearing iron anklets. He knew also, that this meant that God had given her many children, but that God had also taken them away from her.
>
> There was no choice among Abed's wares. Every pot was exactly the same size and shape and color. In Africa, a potter makes exactly one size and kind of pot. If the customer wants something different, he goes to another potter. Abed knew his pots were good ones. His father and mother were careful workmen. They chopped the straw they used until it was almost as fine as flour, and they used enough of it to make their wares good and strong. Their clay, too, was not half sand, but a good red product carried half way across the Sahara Desert on the backs of strong camels.
>
> In spite of all this, the woman lifted up one pot, then another, and examined them all carefully. One pot was too heavy and too shallow, and another made from the same mold was too thin and too deep. At last she chose a pot and offered a price.
>
> Abed took the pot away from the woman, dusted it off carefully, and put it back on the pile. To offer such a tiny price for so excellent

---

[8]Harper and Row, 1953.
[9]Wong, Jade Snow, *Fifth Chinese Daughter*, (New York: Scholastic Book Services, 1963), pp. 163-165.

a pot was an insult to his ancestors, he told her. The woman seized the pot and pointed out all the rough spots. Abed patted it lovingly as though it were a kitten. The woman thumped the pot with the flat of her hand. See, she cried, it sounded as though there were weak spots in it. It would probably crack wide open the first time she put it over the fire. But she was a charitable woman, and she would offer a little more money for it.

Abed plinked the pot with his thumb nail and cocked his head on one side. It had the ring of strength and purity, he answered. It was sweet toned like a metal camel bell. It had been in the glazing kiln over a fire of hot sheep's dung for two days. It would give hard service for years. Possibly this woman's children would cook in this same pot long after she was dust! But he, too, was charitable and he would take a little less money for the pot although, he assured his customer, it was a very jewel of a pot.

Abed and his customer haggled for some time. She found every possible fault with the pot—and finally every possible fault with Abed and his family, shrieking at him that he was a thief and the child of a family of thieves. But little by little she raised her price.

And the more fault the woman found with the pot, the more Abed praised it. Finally he, too, began to berate her, telling her she was surely blind to find fault with such an excellent pot and saying that if he sold his wares at her price his father and mother would without any doubt starve to death. But little by little he lowered his price.

Then, just when the woman was calling terrible curses down upon Abed's donkey's eyebrow, and it seemed as though they would come to blows, they agreed upon a price. The woman paid Abed, and just as softly as they had sounded loud and angry before, they asked God's blessing on each other and parted good friends. No one seemed disturbed at the shouting nor surprised at the sudden calm and friendship —that is just the way marketing is done in Fadwa![10]

Two recent books about Navaho children provide some insights into the thinking of the young Navaho in relatively recent times.

When Sad-Girl's grandmother decided that Sad-Girl must go away to the Off-Reservation boarding school to learn the white man's reading and writing, she arranged with the trader at the trading post to have her registered for school, then arranged for her to ride to the trading post at the appointed time with the neighbors, the Yuccas. Enroute to the trading post, the Yucca children explained that the Navaho name was not sufficient in the white man's school and after due deliberation, named her Rose Smith.

Later in the boarding school, she was awakened one night by the crying of her roommate in the lower bunk. She had been a bit frightened by the strange, muffled sound which the crying had made. Her first thought was that it might be the ghost of an earth person because she

---

[10]Louise A. Stinetorf, *Children of North Africa,* (Philadelphia: J. B. Lippincott Company, 1943), pp. 53-55.

knew that ghosts appear only after dark and only on moonless nights. Rose must help her friend, Isobel.

> If Isobel had contracted sickness or disease it was because she had violated a taboo or had been attacked by a ghost or a witch. If the latter was the case and the spectral attack was very recent it could be averted or lessened by certain precautions.
>
> She fumbled her way through the darkness to the dresser. Her fingers slipped down, counting, until they arrived at her own drawer. Inside, carefully laid away with her change of underwear and her sweater, was a tiny sack of gall medicine. Grandmother had made it for her just before she left home, so it was fresh and potent. It was composed of fried and pulverized galls of many animals and was a sure cure for anyone who had unknowingly absorbed a witch's poison.[11]

Mrs. Momaday's story of Haske, a book titled *Owl in the Cedar Tree,* presents Haske's conflict between the two cultures. Haske is a little boy who rides the bus each day to school from his mother's hogan. This delightful story tells how a painting Haske makes at school wins him a prize so that he can buy the horse that he had admired and wanted for a very long time. But, woven into the story is the cultural conflict between Old Grandfather, who tells Haske that he should become a medicine man when he grows up and that he should start now by going into the hills for four days to fast and pray, and his father, who is determined that Haske must go to school every day and learn the white man's language and culture.

One day when Haske asks his father to tell the bus driver that he will not be there that day, or the next three days, the father is indignant and tells him that he most certainly will go school as usual. He also says that the Old One has not given Haske good advice. When Haske returns from school, only his mother and sister are there. He knows that his father has gone to sing for a sick friend and will not return. But he also knows that since Old Grandfather is not there that his father has spoken to him and he has gone away feeling unwanted.

Then Mrs. Momaday explains how the mother resolves the situation:

> At supper Riding Woman saw that Haske was not eating his food. By the light of the center fire she saw that her son was troubled, and she understood how he felt.
>
> Finally she said, "Your father told me all about it, my son. This morning he spoke to the Old One and tried to explain that school is good. But Old Grandfather could not understand. He was hurt and offended. He left without saying goodbye."
>
> Haske did not try to hide his tears. He kept his eyes on his mother's face. For the first time in his life he saw the strength and courage in her face. Until now he had seen only the beauty and tenderness. Sud-

---

[11]Evelyn Lampman, *Navaho Sister,* (New York: Doubleday and Co., Inc., 1956), p. 93.

denly he was ashamed of his tears. He stopped crying and smiled at his mother.

Riding Woman said, "Now you feel better and must eat your supper."

She put hot food on his plate and warmed his coffee. While Haske ate hungrily, his mother explained all the things he needed to know.

She said, "My son, you have made an anthill look like a mountain. You have worried about which trail to follow. There is only one trail. You have come to believe that some things are all good and some things are all bad. This is not true. The Indian and the white man are not so different as you might think. Both have the same needs, and each must try to understand the other. This is why school is important. At school you learn the white man's language. You cannot understand another person until you can talk with him. By speaking with others you learn what they are thinking and how they feel. This brings understanding between people."

Riding Woman saw that Desbah had gone to sleep by the fire. She picked up the little girl and wrapped a blanket about her. Then she tucked Desbah into her sheepskin bed and sat down again beside Haske.

"So you see, my son, there is only one trail," she continued. "Follow it and keep the best of the old ways while learning the best of the new ways."

Haske felt very happy. His mother had made him understand, and he no longer felt that he was being pulled in two directions. She had set his feet upon the trail as surely as the Navaho gods could have done. And he would make it a trail of beauty.[12]

Reading Good Books to Children

Books that are especially "good books" may well be read in their entirety to children. Good books that supply background information for units of work but that are still too difficult for children to handle the mechanics of reading, should be read, in whole or in part, to the class.

> Books of story type that present such a vivid picture of life in other times and places that the reader is able to recreate them in imagination lend reality to social studies and help children to realize their drama and romance. The voyages of Columbus . . . told by Armstrong Sperry in *The Voyages of Columbus* . . . becomes a thrilling adventure.[13]

McKee provides a long list of books for teachers to read aloud to first grade boys and girls.[14]

---

[12]Natachee Scott Momaday, *Owl in the Cedar Tree*, (Boston: Ginn and Co., 1965), pp. 82-84.

[13]Mabel I. Snedaker, "The Social Studies Curriculum in the Elementary School," *Report of the 36th Annual Conference on Administration and Supervision*, (State University of Iowa: Epsilon Chapter of Phi Delta Kappa, College of Education, 1952), p. 6.

[14]Paul McKee, *Reading: A Program of Instruction for Elementary Schools*, (Boston: Houghton Mifflin, 1966), "Books to Read Aloud in the First Grade," pp. 91-98.

One fifth grade teacher reported reading the following books to her fifth grade class during the school year. All had a high interest level for the group.

1. ROBB WHITE, *The Lion's Paw*, (New York: Doubleday Co., Inc., 1946).
2. ESTHER FORBES, *Johnny Tremain*, (New York: Houghton Mifflin Co., 1943).
3. STERLING NORTH, *Rasal*, (New York: E. P. Dutton Co., Inc., 1963).
4. JAMES DAUGHERTY, *Daniel Boone*, (New York: Viking, 1939).
5. CAROL BRINK, *Caddie Woodlawn*, (New York: Macmillan, 1935).
6. JOSEPH KRUMGOLD, *And Now Miguel*, (New York: Crowell, 1953).
7. ELIZABETH G. SPEARE, *The Bronze Bow*, (New York: Houghton Mifflin, 1961).

The same fifth grade teacher reported that the first two or three chapters of the following books were read and considerable interest generated, and then the book was given to an individual student who asked if he might finish it.[15] These were some of the books introduced to the class during the school year.

1. LAURA INGALLS WILDER, *On the Banks of Plum Creek*, (New York: Harper, 1953).
2. LAURA INGALLS WILDER, *The Little House in the Big Woods*, (New York: Harper, 1951).
3. MAY McNEER, *Armed with Courage*, (Nashville: Abingdon, 1957).
4. ANNA SEWELL, *Black Beauty*, (New York: Grossett, 1877).
5. SCOTT O'DELL, *Island of the Blue Dolphins*, (New York: Houghton Mifflin, 1960).
6. JOSEPH KRUMGOLD, *Onion John*, (New York: Crowell, 1959).
7. LOIS LENSKI, *Strawberry Girl*, (New York: Crowell, 1945).
8. ALICE I. HAZELTINE, *Hero Tales from Many Lands*, (Nashville: Abingdon, 1961).

Julie is explaining about her life at school with her teacher-aunt Cordelia, with whom she also lived. Julie makes clear that Aunt Cordelia was "only" the teacher at school and pretended to know her no better than the other children.

> ". . . She read aloud to us on Friday afternoons, and she read beautifully; I came very close to loving Aunt Cordelia during those long afternoons when I rested my arms upon the desk in front of me and became acquainted with Jim Hawkins and Huck Finn, with little David and Goliath, with Robinson Crusoe on his island, and with the foolish gods and their kinfolk somewhere above the clouds of Mount Olympus."[16]

---

[15]Mildred Hillyer, "A Report of a Supervised Recreational Reading Program," unpublished Masters thesis, Graduate School, The University of New Mexico, 1968, p. 39.

[16]Irene Hunt, *Up A Road Slowly*, (Chicago: Follett Publishing Company, 1966), p. 20.

The Wind in the Willows is one of the children's classics that should be read aloud too, and enjoyed with children. The Mole, the Water Rat, the Badger, and the Toad are *gentlemen* of the woods and river. Children do enjoy the subtle humor in the behavior of the characters.

Green writes:

> The book for me is notable for its intimate sympathy with Nature and for its delicate expression of emotions. When all is said the boastful, unstable Toad, the hospitable Water Rat, the shy, wise, childlike Badger, and the Mole with his pleasant habit of brave boyish impulse, are neither animals nor men, but are types of that deeper humanity which sways us all. . . . And if I may venture to describe as an allegory a work which critics, who ought to have known better, have dismissed as a fairy-story, it is certain that *The Wind in the Willows* is a wise book.[17]

Fisher evaluates the book for children in this way:

> *The Wind in the Willows* is a wise book; it is a complicated book; yet it has given more pleasure to children than almost any other. Firm and strong it certainly is in its implications. Grahame's story will not push philosophy or satire at a child. It will arouse in him, at different times, pity and anger, enjoyment and laughter; it will satisfy the desire for these things as it satisfied Grahame when he wrote it; and it will leave the animal world where it was, untouched by human sentiment or speculation. The animals return to the river and the wood unchanged; but the reader, young or old, can never again feel blank or indifferent towards them.[18]

The Newbery Medal Books are selected annually by a committee of competent librarians for their literary qualities. A book has been selected each year since 1922 and the award is given for "the most distinguished juvenile book written by a citizen or a resident of the United States and published during the preceding year." The award is made at the annual meeting of the American Library Association.[19]

John Newbery (1713-1767) has come to be known as the father of children's literature. As a London bookseller, he worked diligently to promote the idea that children needed their own book shelves of books written for children. He printed in all about two hundred little books selling for about six pence each.[20]

The books that have won the Newbery award are, for the most part, excellent books of classic and enduring qualities. Teachers will do well

---

[17]Peter Green, Kenneth Grahame, (Murray, 1959), p. 259.

[18]Margery Fisher, *Intent upon Reading, A Critical Appraisal of Modern Fiction for Children*, (575 Lexington Avenue, New York City 22: Franklin Watts, Inc., 1962), p. 64.

[19]Lillian Hollowell, Editor, *A Book of Children's Literature*, (New York: Rinehart and Co., Inc., 1959), p. 649.

[20]*Ibid.*, p. 8.

to know these books and use each opportunity to recommend the appropriate book to individuals in their classes. The list of Newbery Award Books is presented below:

NEWBERY PRIZE BOOKS

1922   *The Story of Mankind,* Hendrick Van Loon. Liveright Publishing Corporation.
1923   *The Voyages of Dr. Doolittle,* Hugh Lofting. J. B. Lippincott Company.
1924   *The Dark Frigate,* Charles B.Hawes. Little, Brown and Company.
1925   *Tales from Silver Lands,* Charles J. Finger. Doubleday and Co.
1926   *Shen of the Sea,* Arthur B. Chrisman. E. P. Dutton and Co., Inc.
1927   *Smoky, the Cowhorse,* Will James. Charles Scribner's Sons.
1928   *Gayneck: The Story of a Pigeon.* Dhan Gopal Mukerji. E. P. Dutton and Co.
1929   *The Trumpeter of Krakow,* Eric P. Kelly. The Macmillan Company.
1930   *Hitty: Her First Hundred Years,* Rachel Field. The Macmillan Co.
1931   *The Cat Who Went to Heaven,* Elizabeth Coatsworth. The Macmillan Co.
1932   *Waterless Mountain,* Laura Adams Armer. David McKay Co., Inc.
1933   *Young Fu of the Upper Yangtze,* Elizabeth F. Lewis. Holt, Rinehart & Winston, Inc.
1934   *The Story of the Author of Little Women: Invincible Louisa,* Cornelia Meigs, Little, Brown and Company.
1935   *Dobry,* Monica Shannon. The Viking Press, Inc.
1936   *Caddie Woodlawn,* Carol Ryrie Brink. The Macmillan Company.
1937   *Roller Skates,* Ruth Sawyer. The Viking Press, Inc.
1938   *The White Stag,* Kate Seredy. The Viking Press, Inc.
1939   *Thimble Summer,* Elizabeth Enright. Holt, Rinehart & Winston, Inc.
1940   *Daniel Boone,* James Daugherty. The Viking Press, Inc.
1941   *Call It Courage,* Armstrong Sperry. The Macmillan Company.
1942   *The Matchlock Gun,* Walter D. Edmonds. Dodd, Mead and Company, Inc.
1943   *Adam of the Road,* Elizabeth Janet Gray. The Viking Press, Inc.
1944   *Johnny Tremain,* Esther Forbes. Houghton Mifflin Company.
1945   *Rabbit Hill,* Robert Lawson. The Viking Press, Inc.
1946   *Strawberry Girl,* Lois Lenski. J. B. Lippincott Company.
1947   *Miss Hickory,* Carolyn Sherwin Bailey. The Viking Press, Inc.
1948   *Twenty-one Balloons,* William Pene DuBois. The Viking Press, Inc.
1949   *King of the Wind,* Marguerite Henry. Rand McNally and Company.
1950   *Door in the Wall,* Marguerite de Angeli. Doubleday and Company, Inc.
1951   *Amos Fortune, Free Man,* Elizabeth Yates. Aladdin.
1952   *Ginger Pye,* Eleanor Estes. Harcourt, Brace and World, Inc.
1953   *Secret of the Andes,* Ann Nolan Clark. The Viking Press, Inc.
1954   *And Now Miguel,* Joseph Krumgold. Thomas Y. Crowell Company.
1955   *The Wheel on the School,* Meindert de Jong, Harper and Row, Publishers.
1956   *Carry On, Mr. Bowditch,* Jean Lee Latham. Houghton Mifflin Co.
1957   *Miracles on Maple Hill,* Virginia Sorenson. Illustrated by Beth and Joe Kruch. Harcourt, Brace and World, Inc.

1958   *Rifles for Watie,* Harold Keith. Thomas Y. Crowell Company.
1959   *The Witch of Blackbird Pond,* Elizabeth George Speare. Houghton Mifflin Company.
1960   *Onion John,* Joseph Krumgold. Thomas Y. Crowell Company.
1961   *Island of the Blue Dolphins,* Scott O'Dell. Houghton Mifflin Company.
1962   *The Bronze Bow,* Elizabeth George Speare. Houghton Mifflin Company.
1963   *A Wrinkle in Time,* Madeleine L'Engle. Farrar, Strauss and Co., Inc.
1964   *It's Like This Cat,* Emily Neville. Harper and Row.
1965   *Shadow of a Bull,* Maia Wojciecbowska. Antheneum.
1966   *I, Juan de Pareja,* Elizabeth B. deTrevino. Farrar, Strauss, and Giroux.
1967   *Up the Road Slowly,* Irene Hunt. Follett Publishing Co.
1968   *From the Mixed-up Files of Mrs. Basil E. Frankweiler,* Atheneum.

Bibliotherapy

Personal values can be cultivated through reading since children identify strongly with story characters they like and strongly reject those they dislike. Empathy for physically handicapped people may be developed through reading.

When the person who has a problem follows a planned course of reading about characters in stories who have analogous problems so that he will gain insights for a better understanding of himself, the process is termed bibliotherapy. The term means literally therapy through books.

Russell and Shrodes have described the term bibliotherapy in this way:

> (Bibliotherapy is) . . . a process of dynamic interaction between the personality of the reader and literature . . . interaction which may be utilized for personal assessment, adjustment and growth. This definition suggests that bibliotherapy is not a strange esoteric activity but one that lies within the province of every teacher of literature in working with every child in a group. It does not assume that the teacher must be a skilled therapist, nor the child a seriously maladjusted individual needing clinical treatment. Rather, it conveys the idea that all teachers must be aware of the effects of reading upon children and must realize that, through literature, most children can be helped to solve the developmental problems or adjustment which they face.[21]

A few books that many teachers use to develop affective values in all children are listed below with annotations.

The Hundred Dresses, by Eleanor Estes (Harcourt, Brace and World, 1944). Wanda, a little Polish girl who always wears the same faded blue dress, is ridiculed by the other children.

Blue Willow, by Doris Gates, (The Viking Press, 1948). With her father and step-mother, Janey moves from one crop to another, always hoping

---

[21]David Russell and Caroline Shrodes, "Contributions of Research in Bibliotherapy to the Language Arts Program, I," *The School Review,* 58: 335, September, 1950.

there will be work and shelter. The blue willow plate, which she carries as her one treasure, is all she has to remind her of better days.

Johnny Tremain, by Esther Forbes (Houghton Mifflin, 1943). The moving story of an apprentice silversmith of Paul Revere's day, whose maimed hand causes deep bitterness. Excellent details about the Colonists' fight for independence. Newbery Medal winner in 1944.

Crow Boy, by Taro Yashima (The Viking Press, 1955). Picture story of a shy Japanese boy who withdraws to a world of daydreams until his teacher makes him feel at home. Very distinctive drawings.

Door in the Wall, by Marguerite DeAngeli (Doubleday, 1949). A crippled boy in old England wins the right to Knighthood.

Two Is A Team, by Lorraine and Jerrold Beim (Harcourt, Brace, and World, 1945). A little Negro boy and a white boy learn that each can help the other and that they can have more fun together.

Old Rosie The Horse Nobody Understood, by Lilian Moore and Leone Adelson (Random House, 1952). Farmer Dilly thought he was doing Rosie a favor when he stopped working her and turned her out to sleep, eat, and rest. Rosie became very lonesome and really missed doing all the things she'd been used to. She made a great nuisance of herself until the day she happened in at just the right time to frighten away burglars.

Kintu, by Elizabeth Enright Gilham (Holt, Rinehart and Winston, 1935). Kuntu, who lives in the African Congo, overcomes his fear by making himself venture into the jungle and then finding that he knew what to do to keep himself safe.

Yonie Wondernose, by Marguerite DeAngeli (Doubleday, 1944). The story of a Pennsylvania Dutch boy whose curiosity was never satisfied.

The development of personal values in all children may be enhanced in reading about a lonely, crippled, or impoverished child. Such reading may help the nonhandicapped *more* than it does the handicapped. Empathy, understanding life experiences of others very different from ourselves, and acceptance of other people's values, attitudes and beliefs are all character traits desired in the whole generation of elementary school children.

Nancy Larrick expresses clearly and concisely how teachers help children grapple with the "personal touch" in their affective lives:[22]

> Personal problems are not solved by applying a lotion advertised over television. And a lifetime set of values is not established in a day. Countless factors exert influence. Probably the most effective are the personal ones.
> The way a word is spoken may decide the way it is heeded. And the way a book is introduced may make or break its influence on a child.

---

[22]Nancy Larrick, *A Teacher's Guide to Children's Books,* (Columbus, Ohio: Charles E. Merrill Books, Inc., 1969), p. 104.

This is particularly true of the books which might have special meaning for a child with problems. Certainly it will not help to say, "Here's a book about a boy who is shy, too." That simply hits where it hurts, and wounds are not healed that way.

But if you read *Crow Boy* in class and show your children those extraordinary pictures, the shy one will hear. The others, not so shy, may realize that their own Chibi yearns for friendship. No word need be said about a lesson in the story unless the children bring it up. If they do, let their discussion flow naturally. As they talk, they may be forming conclusions important to them.

Michael selected four character-building stories for fifth and sixth grade children to read so that she might study the children's reactions in relation to their own personal and social adjustment.

Less than half of the 245 cases participating were able to state the main idea of each of the four stories; only 13, about 5 1/2 percent, were able to state the main idea for all four stories. Michael concluded that the use of stories in the classrooms to effect positive changes in behavior presents many complex problems. The teacher must know the content of the story, and have a thorough knowledge of the personal and social needs of each child, and know the reading ability and interests of each, before she is ready to undertake such a challenge.[23]

Personal Ownership of Books

The child that grows up in a reading environment, where the adults around him *do read,* is much more apt to develop an early interest in reading. Becoming confident in ones ability to read makes it possible for children to use reading as a pleasant way of filling periods of "free" time.

Children imitate the adults around them that they love and respect. If mother or father often has something interesting, funny, or unusual to read aloud to the rest of the family, it is more likely that the child will sooner or later appear with something he would like to share.

Some of the books children read will be more appealing, seem more worthwhile, than others. Parents who see that children begin accumulating books as personal possessions are wise. Many girls have proudly collected *The Little House Books*[24] and read and reread them through their late childhood years.

With the availability of inexpensive paperback books, children have the opportunity to build their own libraries at no greater cost than can

---

[23]Arthura Michael, *An Exploratory Study of Children's Responses to Character-Building Stories,* Doctoral dissertation, Graduate College, University of Iowa, 1951, reviewed in Epsilon Bulletin, (Epsilon Chapter of Phi Delta Kappa, College of Education, University of Iowa, 1952), 27: 27-29.

[24]Laura Ingalls Wilder, *Little House in the Big Woods* (1951); *On the Banks of Plum Creek* (1953); *Little House on the Prairie* (1953); *The Long Winter* (1953), (New York: Harper and Row).

be a part of their regular weekly allowance. Scholastic Book Service has made many excellent book choices available to boys and girls—*Tab Books* at the junior high school level and *Arrow Books* at the elementary school level—with prices ranging from twenty-five cents up to one dollar.

Group orders in classrooms encourage children to obtain books which they would probably otherwise not get. Preparation of the group order is a good school exercise, and the boys and girls do enjoy the anticipation of receiving the order. Reading the books so that they can evaluate them for the group and recommend them to others is a motivating experience.

The child who has a book shelf of books of his own is more apt to have and use the public library card, and because he cares for his own books he may be more apt to exercise proper care of borrowed books.

The importance that parents attach to books will be learned very early by children. The home has an important responsibility in encouraging not only reading as a permanent habit, but also reading good books of lasting value. Ideally, the home library will contain a set of encyclopedias and a few other reference books which the child may use in pursuing his school assignments and personal interests.

SUMMARY

This chapter has emphasized the importance of all the facets of the child's experience that would build toward permanent interests in reading that will be well established by the time the child leaves the elementary school. The key person in this interest building will be the classroom teacher for most children. He must be sufficiently sophisticated in the broad field of children's literature so he can recommend "the right book for the right child." This requires more than a casual, "Why don't you read this one; it looks interesting." Most children will react entirely differently if the teacher can tell him why the book is very interesting by retelling a few episodes from the story or giving a brief synopsis of the whole story.

In order to build broad, permanent reading interests, the school must have a centralized, well-stocked library staffed by a competent librarian; standard references for teachers to use in seeking out the particular materials that fit their course of study; adequate reading materials so that teachers can draw shelves of books related to the social studies units being taught; and teachers and parents who read well to children and who encourage them to be curious about the great wide wonderful world of books.

SUGGESTED ACTIVITIES

1. Using the general references listed in the chapter as sources of books for children, find books related to a unit which you expect to

teach in the social studies in the elementary school. Make a bibliography of fifty books or stories related to this unit topic. Make sure you have selected reading material that covers a wide range of levels of difficulty. For example, if you teach fourth grade, you need materials that range from about easy second grade to sixth or seventh grade level. Write brief annotations of the books that will help you to distinguish the value of the book at a later time. If the book was rated by a committee of readers and especially recommended, note that, also, for your later use. A useful bibliography identifies books by author, exact title, publisher, and copyright date.

2. Make a list of topics about library books to be used for bulletin board displays: for example, "Animals," "Space Travel," or "Pioneer Days." Plan a variety of media in the displays—make use of book jackets, children's summaries of different books, felt cutouts, yarn, and/or any other materials often found in collages.

3. Have children plan a bulletin board or set up a table display illustrating a scene or depicting the characters from a particular book.

Reading References

Arbuthnot, May Hill, *The Arbuthnot Anthology of Children's Literature,* (Chicago: Scott, Foresman and Company, 1952).

Arbuthnot, May Hill, *Children and Books,* Third Edition, (Chicago: Scott, Foresman and Company, 1964).

Arnsdorf, Val, "Selecting and Using Collateral Materials in Social Studies," *The Reading Teacher,* 20: 621-625, April, 1967.

Dawson, Mildred A., editor, *Children, Books,* and *Reading.* Perspectives in Reading No. 3, (Newark, Delaware: International Reading Association, 1964), 150 pp.

DeBoer, John J. and Martha Dallmann, *The Teaching of Reading.* (New York: Holt, Rinehart and Winston, Inc., 1964), Chapters 11A, "Children's Interests in Reading," and 11B, "Developing Children's Interests in Reading," pp. 249-292.

Dietrich, Dorothy and Virginia Matthews, Editors, *Development of Lifetime Reading Habits,* (Newark, Delaware 19711: International Reading Association, 1968), 80 pages.

Harris, Albert J., *How to Increase Reading Ability,* (New York: David McKay, 1961), Chapter XVII: "Fostering Reading Interests and Tastes," pp. 466-502.

Huus, Helen, Editor, Perspectives No. 10: *Evaluating Books for Children and Young People,* (Newark, Delaware 19711: International Reading Association, 1968).

Larrick, Nancy, *A Teacher's Guide to Children's Books,* (Columbus: Charles E. Merrill, Inc., 1960).

Sebesta, Sam Leaton, Editor, *Ivory, Apes,* and *Peacocks: The Literature Point of View,* (Newark, Delaware: International Reading Association, 1968).

SMITH, DORA V., *Communication, The Miracle of Shared Living*, (New York: Macmillan and Co., 1955).

SMITH, DORA V., *Fifty Years of Children's Books*, (Champaign, Illinois: The National Council of Teachers of English, 1963).

SMITH, NILA B., *Reading Instruction for Today's Children*, (Englewood Cliffs, New Jersey: Prentice-Hall, Inc., 1963), Part III, "Developing Interest and Taste in Reading Literature," pp. 385-442.

STAUFFER, RUSSELL G., *Directing Reading Maturity As A Cognitive Process*, (New York: Harper and Row, 1969), Chapter 8: "Libraries and Reading Instruction," pp. 355-403.

TINKER, MILES A. and CONSTANCE McCULLOUGH, *Teaching Elementary Reading*, (New York: Appleton-Century-Crofts, 1968), Chapter 15, "Interests and Tastes," pp. 301-317.

TOOZE, RUTH, *Story Telling*, (Englewood Cliffs, New Jersey: Prentice-Hall, Inc., 1959).

Many adults have arrived at their station as classroom teachers without having acquired much understanding of the **one** language that is their only vehicle of communication. Language usage conforms to **definite** principles of which the teacher should be very much aware. With an appreciation of these principles, the phonology, morphology, syntax, and semantics of the language can be studied. In second language learning, contrastive analysis and phonemic differences provide clues to second language teaching.

At Present, most schools are wrestling with teaching **all** children **in only the English language medium.** Good techniques in teaching English to speakers of other languages will facilitate this process. However, in the relatively near future, it is hoped that bilingual schools will have a place in the public school system. Only in this way can children develop and extend their fluency in two or more languages through their use in the school curriculum.

Diagnostic teaching has been tragically neglected in working with children for whom English is a second language. The accepted communication skill hierarchy of listening-speaking-reading-writing has often been violated. Chapter 14 suggests some informal techniques by which teachers can measure English language fluency before planning the child's program. Chapter 15 contains a brief discussion of the problems of teaching reading to the children of the inner city poor.

13

Linguistics and the Elementary Teacher of Reading

Linguistics is the scientific study of languages. It encompasses the sounds of language (forty-four phonemes in English) which is called phonology; the meanings in words which is called semantics; and the order of words in sentences which is called syntax, or structure, or the grammar of the language.

The study of language as connected with human behavior is called psycholinguistics and is equally as important to the teacher as descriptive linguistics.

The scientific study of language is meaningful only in the context of the cultural values, practices, attitudes and ideals which are expressed through language. Some general principles about the nature of language and the methodology of teaching English as a second language are discussed briefly in this chapter.

I. CULTURAL DIFFERENCES AND ENGLISH LANGUAGE LEARNING

In the publication *Educating the Children of the Poor*,[1] it is pointed out in "the task ahead" that adequate theory requires an integration of the wisdom of sociologists and psychologists so that environmental factors and personality variables will each get proper attention. If applied anthropology is left out, a very important portion of the total appraisal of the child has been omitted. His cultural heritage includes all the values, ideals, aspirations, anxieties, taboos, and mores that structured his fundamental habits of behaving.

Some excerpts from the literature will make clear the anthropological contribution to understanding behavior. The inter-dependence of lan-

---

[1] Alexander Frazier, editor, *Educating the Children of the Poor* (1201 Sixteenth Street, N.W., Washington, D. C. 20036: ASCD, 1968).

guage and culture is discussed briefly in Chapter 14 in the section on developing bilingual schools.

Salisbury relates a rather sobering story of the Alaska Indian child's problem with the middle-class Anglo-oriented course of study:

> By the time the native child reaches the age of seven, his cultural and language patterns have been set and his parents are required by law to send him to school. Until this time he is likely to speak only his own local dialect of Indian, Aleut, or Eskimo, or if his parents have had some formal schooling he may speak a kind of halting English.
>
> He now enters a completely foreign setting—the western classroom situation. His teacher is likely to be a Caucasian who knows little or nothing about his cultural background. He is taught to read the Dick and Jane series. Many things confuse him: Dick and Jane are two gussuk[2] children who play together. Yet he knows that boys and girls do not play together and do not share toys. They have a dog named Spot who comes indoors and does not work. They have a father who leaves for some mysterious place called "office" each day and never brings any food home with him. He drives a machine called an automobile on a hard covered road called a street which has a policeman on each corner. These policemen always smile, wear funny clothing and spend their time helping children to cross the street. Why do these children need this help? Dick and Jane's mother spends a lot of time in the kitchen cooking a strange food called "cookies" on a stove which has no flame in it.
>
> But the most bewildering part is yet to come. One day they drive out to the country which is a place where Dick and Jane's grandparents are kept. They do not live with the family and they are so glad to see Dick and Jane that one is certain that they have been ostracized from the rest of the family for some terrible reason. The old people live on something called a "farm," which is a place where many strange animals are kept—a peculiar beast called a "cow," some odd looking birds called "chickens" and a "horse" which looks like a deformed moose. And so on. For the next twelve years the process goes on. The native child continues to learn this new language which is of no earthly use to him at home and which seems completely unrelated to the world of sky, birds, snow, ice, and tundra which he sees around him.[3]

Evvard and Mitchell have analyzed the concepts in the stories in the Scott-Foresman Basic Readers and found many conflicts with the young Navajo child's concepts of himself, his family, and his community. They have contrasted beliefs and values encountered in the Scott-Foresman Basic Readers for the primary grades with the beliefs and values of the traditional Navajo child:[4]

---

[2]Eskimo term for white person. Derived from Russian word, *cossack.*
[3]Lee H. Salisbury, "Teaching English to Alaska Natives," *Journal of American Indian Education,* 6:4-5, January, 1967.
[4]Evelyn Evvard and George C. Mitchell, "Sally, Dick and Jane at Lukachukai," *Journal of American Indian Education,* 5:5, May, 1966.

Middle-class, Urban Values:	*Navaho Values:*
Pets have human-like personalities	Pets are distinct from human personality
Life is pictured as child-centered	Life is adult-centered
Adults participate in children's activities	Children participate in adult activities
Germ-theory is implicitly expressed	Good health results from harmony with nature
Children and parents are masters of their environment.	Children accept their environment and live with it
Children are energetic, out-going, obviously happy	Children are passive and unexpressive
Many toys and much clothing is an accepted value	Children can only hope for much clothing and toys
Life is easy, safe, and bland	Life is hard and dangerous

The student internalizes much of his way of behaving by the demands placed upon him by his culture. The culture instills group goals, mores, taboos, values, and levels of aspiration.

The attitude of the teacher, of course, is vital in these circumstances. Unless the teacher is patient and understanding, the student who must learn English as a second language develops "insecurity instead of security, worry instead of certainty, fear instead of competence and makes enemies instead of friends for the English language."[5]

The following paragraph has *too* accurately and for *too* long expressed the viewpoint of too many Anglo-American teachers toward the Mexican-American students and their parents:

> They are good people. Their only handicap is the bag full of superstitions and silly notions they inherited from Mexico. When they get rid of these superstitions, they will be good Americans. The schools help more than anything else. In time, the Latins will think and act like Americans. A lot depends on whether or not we can get them to switch from Spanish to English. When they speak Spanish they think Mexican. When the day comes that they speak English at home like the rest of us, they will be part of the American way of life. I just don't understand why they are so insistent about using Spanish. They should realize that it's not the American tongue.[6]

Most teachers come from homes where middle-class values have been internalized or they adopt such values in the process of becoming teachers. Too often they are inadequately prepared to understand and accept

[5]Robert Hall, *Linguistics and Your Language* (Garden City, New York: Doubleday, 1960), p. 193.
[6]William Madsen, *The Mexican-American of South Texas* (New York: Holt, Rinehart and Winston, 1964), p. 106.

the dissimilar cultural values of the students they teach. Teachers must be continually alert to the differences in languages, values, customs—the whole cultural heritage—and seek to understand the students they teach as real people with all the feelings, attitudes, and emotional responses that make them behave the way they do. Most important is the realization that one way of life is not better, not superior, and not "more right" than another.

II. LINGUISTIC PRINCIPLES OF ENGLISH SENTENCE STRUCTURE

There are several linguistic principles that impinge directly on the work of the classroom teacher. Many teachers are undoubtedly aware of these; others may need to study them carefully and reflect upon their meanings.

1. Language is oral. It is *speech* before it is *reading* or *writing.* Spoken language is the "natural" expression commonly used by the native speaker with its contractions, idiomatic and slang expressions, and one word answers. "How are you?" may be spoken as if it were only one word and "It is a book" is sure to be spoken "Itza book."

2. Language is habit. It is learned behavior. Native speakers are not conscious of each sound or word they say nor of the sequence of the sounds of words. They are primarily conscious of the ideas or thoughts they are trying to convey. The stringing together of sounds in certain positions is an unconscious act. The language habit is automatic for children by the time they start to first grade. Because language is learned behavior, it is learned through the repetition of producing it. When children learn the first language in a free, relaxed, trial-and-error atmosphere, there is time for error, correction, and repetition without conscious effort. When any language is super-imposed as a second language, there is much interference between the two sound patterns and much guided repetition, correction, and drill are indicated.

3. Language is arbitrary. It has a specific, prescribed structure. There are only a few basic sentence patterns in the English language that are used frequently. The teacher *models, expands, amplifies, and reinforces,* always hoping that the language is related to concepts, to teach this arbitrary structure. In second language learning, the student should not be permitted to practice an incorrect pattern and reinforce it since it will have to later be unlearned.

Young children learning English in a classroom were heard composing sentences about "things" visible around them. One child said, "This is a book." Another said, "This is leaves." Another said, "This is children." The teacher accepted the contributions and went on to something else. *This was wrong.* She should, of course, accept the contribution of each child and encourage him. But, he must either learn the first time to always say, "These are leaves" and "These are children" or he will need later to try to unlearn something that he thought "his teacher taught him." Many other examples of the arbitrariness of the structure of English are detailed in the section on interferences between English and Spanish.

4. Language is personal. Language reflects the individual's self-image and is his only avenue to expressing all that he is, all that he has as a heritage, and all that he aspires to be.

In primary schools throughout the world, young children who must learn a second language have generally been taught the first years in school in the mother tongue. Usually, in the first two years, the child can learn to read and write the vernacular to some degree, then transfer to the language used for education, commerce, industry, and government. This cognizance of the importance of the vernacular is being felt currently in the new bilingual act of the United States Congress in 1967. A few research studies suggest there are psychological values, even for the "little-used" languages, for the child to know that his own language, and hence, his people, are respected and valued.

5. The language of a given group of people is neither "good" nor "bad"; it is communication. Dialects of English other than "standard" English are best referred to as "non-standard" rather than "sub-standard."

6. Language is more than words. This is evidenced by the fact that the spoken language can reveal more meanings than the written language. The suprasegmentals of pitch, stress, and juncture as well as facial expression, gesture, and bodily movement add a great deal to meaning and interpretation of language.

7. Language is culturally transmitted.

8. Language is always slowly changing.

III. DESCRIBING LANGUAGE IN TESOL

"Meaning bearing utterances" must be practiced in meaningful, functional, pleasant, and rewarding circumstances. Children work with all the changes in sentence patterns for developing fluency and establishing habits. Substitution drills, question-answer practice, deletions and combinations, and dialog practice provide ways both to habituate patterns and to teach intonation, stress, pitch, and juncture. Any sequenced program requires stimulating experiences, rewards for the use of language, audio-visual materials, field trips, and maximum exposure to "talk" in English.

Learning English as a Second Language vs. Learning It as a First

Teaching English as a second language is not at all like teaching English to English speakers although teacher preparation in most colleges for teachers ignore this very important fact. Most teachers find themselves totally unprepared when they go to teach in areas where large percentages of children enrolled in school are learners of English as a new language. On the other hand, the fact remains that no one can "help himself" in our English-speaking society anywhere until he can speak the language of his peers fluently and spontaneously. The audio-lingual approach to second language learning can prepare boys and girls for much more profitable formal school experiences. These specific methods of second language teaching have been getting efficient results in bi-national centers in foreign capital cities all over the world.

The learning of English by the native speaker may be contrasted with learning English as a second language in several ways:

When learning English as a native language:	*When learning English as a second language:*
1. *Time* is not a factor, the *child* has six pre-school years to master the sound system of the language of his mother.	1. *Time* is a crucial factor. One may have eight weeks in the summer; an intensive course; or one must continue an academic course of study in English while learning English.
2. Infants are usually richly rewarded for each *imitative effort.* Trial-and-error works very well—with much time—in a friendly, supportive, informal atmosphere.	2. The student must "*Listen, repeat, and memorize.*"
3. Parents and friends are very patient and expect to *repeat, reward, and reinforce.*	3. The student is "expected" to speak the language of the school. He must have a course of study that is organized, sequential, and efficient. Those who have the patterns internalized are often impatient with older students. *Teachers must* repeat, reward, and reinforce.
4. The child grows up in an environment where he enjoys a maximum opportunity to repeat and to remember everything he hears.	4. The classroom situation is conducive to much forgetting. What one learns during one hour, he has all day, all weekend, all vacation period to forget. One tends to forget almost all of what he studies in a "formal" manner.
5. What the child doesn't remember today, or whatever mistakes he keeps making today, he can unlearn or relearn in the weeks or months in the future.	5. Drills cannot be avoided. Students must have many repetitions, and carefully spaced reviews on all patterns they need to learn to use automatically.

Linguists have given us words to use to describe the language. *Phonology* is the study of the sounds of the language; *morphology* is the study of the structure of words; *syntax* is the grammar of the language, word order, kernel sentences, and modifiers which give variety to the sentences we use; and *semantics* is the study of meanings communicated through languages. The chart on the following page will help the reader to visualize elements of each of these four ways to describe the language.

Much is written about both the morphology and semantics in other parts of this text. Therefore, the remainder of this chapter will be devoted to illustrating two of the most important phonological problems in teaching the new language and the transformations which native speakers learn very easily to make in the mastery of spoken English. The nine basic transformations are taken from Robert's transformational grammar.

Phonologically, children must learn to hear all the phonemes that are used in English that were not used in their native language. For Spanish-speakers learning English, there are several substitutions likely to be made such as "thumb" as "sumb"; "path" as "pass." Variant vowel sounds need to be heard clearly as do the several consonant sounds often substituted. Related to this is the ability to discriminate minimal pairs with practice. Minimal pairs are two words that are sounded exactly the same except for one sound that changes the meaning. Ending consonant sounds are often troublesome, for example, "pick" is spoken as "pig"; "map" is spoken as "mat." Juncture is accent-discrimination in which the accent changes the meaning of an expression.

Minimal Pairs: (Two words that have only one phoneme sound that is not the same. This auditory discrimination practice is important in second language teaching.)

pick-pig	sheep-ship	map-mat
big-pig	force-fours	death-deaf
niece-knees	lacy-lazy	bus-buzz
price-prize	witch-which	bit-beat
age-edge	taste-test	boat-both
pain-pen	dip-deep	tuck-tug
ache-egg	bake-beg	

Juncture: (Inflection determines meaning.)

Mary was home sick.	Mary was sick at home.
Mary was homesick.	Mary wanted very much to go home.

TABLE 13.1. *Ways to describe language. Language has:*

1. Phonology	2. Morphology	3. Syntax	4. Semantics
Phonology is the study of the sounds of the language.	Morphology is the study of the structure of words. The important structures in elementary school communication are:	Syntax is the grammar of the language. Grammar is the set of rules governing the use of the language so that people can communicate meaningfully with each other.	Semantics is the study of the meanings communicated through language.
a. There are 44 phonemes in the English language. (Sources differ: 40, 44, 45, 47).	a. Compound words.	a. Basic sentence patterns: (1) Noun–transitive verb–object (2) Noun–linking verb–predicate noun or adjective (3) Noun–verb–prepositional phrase	a. English is a hybrid language containing much word borrowing from many languages.
b. Differences in sounds are how we know on given occasions what is being said.	b. Inflectional endings including er, est, ed, ing, s, es.	b. Variations: (1) Making negative answers (2) Choosing "or" (3) Expansions	b. The listener or the reader must rely on context clues; meanings depend upon context.
c. Minimal pairs are two words with only one phonemic difference. A phonemic difference is one that changes meaning. (Pick-pig; map-mat; big-pig.)	c. Prefixes and suffixes.	c. Transformations: (1) "There" changes (2) "Question" changes (3) Question words (4) Passive transforms (5) Changing verbs to nouns (6) Combining kernel sentences (7) Using *until, if, because* (8) Changing to past (9) Tag-on questions	c. The language contains many figures of speech, idiomatic expressions, and slang expressions.
d. Accent patterns also change meanings. (A blue bird is not necessarily a bluebird.)	d. The common Greek and Latin combining forms.		d. The vocabulary contains antonyms, heteronyms, homographs, homonyms, synonyms.
e. The phoneme-grapheme relationships are often confusing in English because five vowels have many variant spellings.	e. Reversible compound words: *A pocket watch is not a watch pocket.*		e. Suprasegmentals, which are phonemic because they change meanings, are also semantic in communicating meaning changes.
f. The suprasegmentals of stress, pitch, and juncture convey distinct phonemic differences.			

Was that the green house?	Was it a green color?
Was that the Green house?	Do the Greens live there?
Was that the greenhouse?	A place where plants are nurtured the year around.
I saw a blue bird.	The bird I saw was a blue color.
I saw a bluebird.	It was a bluebird.
Bob said he saw a horse fly.	The horse had wings.
Bob said he saw a horsefly.	A fly that bothers horses.

And in these:

I scream.	Send them aid.	night rate	lighthouse keeping
Ice cream.	Send the maid.	nitrate	light housekeeping

Structure Words: Words that have no referent are called "structure" words. It is estimated that there are no more than 300 such words in English but they comprise nearly half of all of the *running words* in elementary context. This underscores the need for mastering them as service words as early in the reading process as possible. They are termed "markers" for the type of structural element they precede:

Noun markers: a, the, some, any, three, this, my, few . . .

Verb markers: am, are, is, was, have, has, had . . .

Phrase markers: up, down, in, out, above, below . . .

Clause markers: if, until, because, that, how, when . . .

Question markers: who, why, how, when, what, where . . .

These little words have been called, in addition to "structure" words, "glue" words or "service" words. In and of themselves, they do not convey meaning and they do not fit any linguistic pattern for teaching. They must be taught early because they are the necessary connectors. They play a significant part in helping the reader to anticipate meanings which verbs or nouns following will carry in a given sentence structure.

Gesture—The Unspoken Language. With a quick twist of the wrist, a Lebanese taxi driver can convey utter contempt for a traffic policeman. A South American may show admiration for a beautiful woman by opening one eye wide with thumb and forefinger. An American Indian warrior could indicate sadness by making the sign for heart, then drawing his hand down and toward the ground. He signified "friend" by putting his two forefingers together, symbolizing brothers in each other's company.[7]

---

[7]*Read Magazine*, "Gesture—The Unspoken Language," 16:24, September, 1966.

Pronunciation Problems

Some Spanish-English pronunciation problems include:

For:	The child is apt to say:

Consonants:

"th" as in thumb, path	"s" as in sink, sin, and pass
"j" as in judge	"ch" as in church
"th" in though and this	"d" as in dough and dis
"sh" in she and shoe	"s" as in sea and sue
"s" in pleasure, treasure	simply as "s"
voiced "s" in zinc, zoo	"s" as in sing, rice, and sue
"b" in bar, rabbit, cab	"p" in par, rapid, cap
"v" in vote, sail, vest	"b" in boat, bail, best
"d" in din and den	"t" in ten and tin
"ch" in watch and chew	"sh" in wash, cash, and shoe
use and yellow	juice and jello
final "m" in comb, dime	as "n" in cone, dine
"g" in dug, goat, pig	as "c" in duck, coat, and pick
"w" as in way, wash	preceded by "g"—guay, guash

Vowels:

hat, cat, map	hot, cot, mop or het, ket, mep
don, sung, cut	dawn, song, caught
leave, feel, sheep	live, fill, ship
late, mate, gate	let, met, get
pool and fool	pull and full
coal, bowl, hole	call, ball, hall

IV. CONTRASTIVE ANALYSIS OF SPANISH AND ENGLISH

Most teachers of native Spanish speakers in classrooms where English is the medium of instruction have heard sentences like the following: "We went through the rooms bigs," "Mary is wear a dress red," "He no go to school," "Yesterday your brother I saw," "I am ready for to read," "I see you later," "Is Tuesday," and "This apple is more big than that one."

The following contrasts in structure are taken from *Teaching English as a New Language to Adults*:[8]

Native English speaker	*Spanish speaker learning English*
The use of not with the verb forms: "Mary is not here."	Usually replaced by "no": "Mary is no here."
The use of "s" in our simple present: "The boy eats."	Verbs are fully inflected. Learning our comparatively uninflected English, the student tends to drop even the inflections which persist, to say: "The boy eat."

---

[8]Board of Education of the City of New York, *Teaching English as a New Language to Adults*, Curriculum Bulletin No. 5, 1963-1964 series (Board of Education of the City of New York, Publications Sales Office, 110 Livingston Street, Brooklyn 1, New York), pp. 7-9.

Negatives with do, does, did: "He did not go to school."	No auxiliaries exist: The tendency is to say: "He no go/went to school."
English adjectives usually precede the noun: "The red dress."	Adjectives usually follow the noun: "The dress red."
Going to to express future time: "I am going to sing."	Tendency is to substitute the simple present: "I go to sing."
The auxiliary *will* in our future: "I will see you later."	Tendency is to carry over the inflection and to say: "I see you later."
The use of *it* to start a sentence: "It is Tuesday."	Tendency to make the omission of *it* and to say: "Is Tuesday."
Use of *to be* to express age: "I'm twenty years old."	*To have* is used: "I have twenty years."
Use of *to be* to express hunger, thirst, etc. "I am thirsty."	*To have* is the more common usage: "I have hunger." "I have thirst."
Our negative imperative: "Don't run!"	Replaced by *no*: "No run!"
Questions with do, does, and did: "Does this man work?"	No auxiliaries exist in Spanish. Tendency is to say: "This man works?" or "Works this man?"
Indefinite article in usual prenominal position with words identifying occupation: "She is a nurse."	Indefinite article not required in such usages; tendency is to say: "She is nurse."

English-Spanish language differences that distress teachers:

1. English uses the sound feature of voicing (as voiced vs. voiceless sounds) which distinguishes (s) from (z) as the sole contrasting item that separates meanings of words. Ex.: Race-raise; lacy-lazy; niece-knees; seal-zeal; price-prize. This is never the sole feature to separate meanings in Spanish.
2. English uses the sound difference between (n) and (ng) as a means of distinguishing meanings while the Spanish language does not. Ex.: Ran-rang; sin-sing; kin-king; thin-thing; fan-fang; ban-bang.
3. The Spanish speaker learning English must learn many new consonant blend sounds. "Sh" in *shine* and "wh" in *when.*
4. While Spanish uses only five vowel sounds, English uses many more *to distinguish meanings.* Practice must be given to develop auditory discrimination of these pairs of vowels. Heat-hit; met-mate; tap-tape; look-luck; pin-pine; hat-hot; sheep-ship; mit-meet; eat-it; late-let; bed-bad; fool-full; coat-caught; caught-cut.
5. Consonant sounds can cause trouble, too: Pig-big; pig-pick; thank-sank; then-den; place-plays. Also, clusters like "ts" in *hats*; "lpt" in *helped*; "lkt" in *talked.*
6. *Minimal pairs.* The phoneme is the minimum feature of the expression system of a spoken language by which one thing that may be said is distinguished from any other thing which might have been said. Thus, *bill* and *pill* differ only in one phoneme. They are, then, a *minimal pair.* All of the vowel contrasts in no. 4 above are minimal pairs.

7. Modifiers do *not* follow the noun in English:
   The blue sky, not *the sky blue.*
   The juicy apples, not *the apples juicy.*
   Also,
   The bus station is not the same as *the station bus.*
   The pocket watch is not the same as *the watch pocket.*
8. Word order in sentences has more flexibility in Spanish than in English.

For example:	Translates literally:
Ayer vine aquí	Yesterday I came here
Aquí vine ayer	Here I came yesterday
Vine ayer aquí	I came yesterday here
Ayer aquí vine	Yesterday here I came

While all are grammatically correct in Spanish, they are not all acceptable English.
9. The irregularity of some words causes difficulty after children learn to generalize from *regular* forms: I teared the paper. I throwed the ball. I dood it.
10. Intonation and stress are very important in conveying meanings:
    Which book did *you* buy?
    Which book *did* you buy?
    Which book did you *buy*?
    Are *you* going back to school this fall?
    Are you going back to school *this* fall?
    Are you going *back to school* this fall?

Programs of English as a second language in the United States have been based generally upon the contrastive analysis of Spanish and English. Weaver has suggested that this bias does not fit the needs of the Indian child if one tries to teach him English structure through the use of materials derived from the Spanish phonemic differences. Weaver suggests that the difficulties the Navajo children are most likely to encounter are:

1. Distinction of number.
2. Expression of possession.
3. Application of adjective to noun.
4. Distinction of gender.
5. Usage of subject and object.
6. Usage of definite and indefinite articles.
7. Usage of definite and indefinite pronouns.
8. Usage of correct verb inflections.
9. Usage of negative questions.[9]

---

[9]Yvonne Weaver, "A Closer Look at TESL on the Reservation," *Journal of American Indian Education,* 6:28, January, 1967.

Indian languages need the same contrastive study as European languages have had if educators are to adapt language instruction to meet the specific language needs of Indian people.

Loban[10] and Strickland[11] have helped teachers to understand the way in which English language is used by children. Establishing the fact of the arbitrary structure of language and knowing there are only a very few basic patterns in ordinary conversations gives teachers a basis for language practice that will help children who speak non-standard English or a second language. Word order in the sentence learned in oral usage probably needs to carry over into written usage; that is, the subject comes first and the reader takes clues from all the determiners and structure words. Reading comprehension should be greater in materials that utilize high frequency sentence patterns from oral language structure than in materials using unusual or unfamiliar types of sentence patterns. Goodman questions the artificially controlled sentences in primers and pre-primers.[12] He points out that the reading process requires, beyond word recognition, both the syntactic use of the word and the semantic meaning that it conjures up. In other words, beyond the recognized word as it comes into focus in the line of print, lie all the contextual clues which the child is anticipating before he reads it—he is projecting ideas ahead of the print as he reads. This point of view emphasizes a very important structural problem in writing pre-primers and primers for young children. Children with a fully developed *grammar* and a storehouse of semantic meanings, can much more easily anticipate meanings in a completely expressed sentence:

Betty said, "I am going with my mother to the store."

Pete said, "May I go along with you?"

than they can in the artificially controlled sentences which Goodman has called "Name the Word Game."

"Come here, Betty."

"Here I come," said Betty.

Even beginning readers must sample and draw on syntactically and semantically anticipated meanings if children are reading from "fully formed English language" sentence structures.

---

[10]Walter Loban, *The Language of Elementary School Children* (Champaign, Illinois: National Council of Teachers of English, NCTE Research Report, No. 1, 1963).

[11]Ruth Strickland, *The Language of Elementary School Children: Its Relationship to the Language of Reading Textbooks and the Quality of Reading of Selected Children* (Bloomington, Indiana: Indiana University Bulletin of the School of Education, Vol. 38, No. 4, 1962).

[12]Kenneth S. Goodman, "Reading: A Psycholinguistic Guessing Game," *Journal of the Reading Specialist*, 1967.

V. SOME METHODOLOGY IN TEACHING ENGLISH AS A SECOND LANGUAGE

Language has three basic relationships besides transformations:

(1) Function, i. e., objects, prepositional phrases, indirect objects
(2) Agreement of number and person
(3) Placement, clearly understood use of antecedents

The process of TESOL methodology includes:

(1) Substitutions
(2) Ordering
(3) Deletions
(4) Expansions

Substitution and expansion are illustrated below.

Substitutions for Oral Practice

1. The school is just around the corner.
   store The teacher models "The school is
   restaurant just around the corner." The class
   post office repeats. Small groups and then indi-
   department store viduals repeat. Then the teacher says
   house only the word "store" and the class
   apartment repeats, "The store is just around the
   corner." The teacher says "restaurant"
   and the class repeats "The restaurant
   is just around the corner," etc.

2. Please ask Jack to turn the light off.
   turn the light on.
   leave the light alone.
   turn on the light.
   put the light on the table.

3. How many chairs are there in that room?
   desks
   pictures
   boys
   girls
   people
   tables

Expansion Sentences

Basic sentence patterns are, of course, made to serve their purposes more clearly for speakers by being expanded. Boys and girls who are native speakers of the language get much practice in this in English lessons. Speakers of non-standard English will need a great deal of help with these exercises.

Ex. 1.

<pre>
                          dogs bark
                          dogs bark loudly
             The people's dogs bark loudly.
             The people's dogs bark loudly every night.
We could hear the people's dogs bark loudly every night.
We could hear the people's dogs bark loudly every night when we
                          were at grandmother's house.
</pre>

Ex. 2.

<pre>
                  The roses   are beautiful.
              The red roses   are beautiful.
The red roses by my window   are beautiful.
</pre>
I gave the red roses by my window to the elderly couple that lives next door.

Ex. 3.
<pre>
I can play.
I can play this afternoon.
I can play this afternoon for a while.
I can play until five o'clock this afternoon.
I can play in the park until five o'clock this afternoon.
</pre>

Transformations

Transformation in English grammar is the means by which basic sentence structures are changed, or modified, into other types of structures. So the sentence, "There are four chairs in the room" can be transformed into a question by changing the positions of "there" and "are" and asking "Are there four chairs in the room?"

Observe the many "variations" or transformations in the following sentence:

The girl knitted her sweater.
The girl did knit her sweater.
The girl was knitting her sweater.
The girl didn't knit her sweater.
The girl wasn't knitting her sweater.
Did the girl knit her sweater?
Didn't the girl knit her sweater?
Wasn't the girl knitting her sweater?
Was the sweater knitted by the girl?
The sweater was knitted by the girl?

Lenneberg defines *transformation* in this way:[13]

We have illustrated a universal principle of grammatical knowledge or understanding: there must be lawful ways in which certain types of structure may be related to other types of structure. The grammatical laws that control these relations have come to be called *transformations*.

Transformations are statements of grammatical as well as semantic and phonological connections.

[13]Eric H. Lenneberg, *Biological Foundations of Language* (New York: John Wiley and Sons, 1967), pp. 291-292.

Roberts' basic sentence patterns in transformational grammar are presented below. The primacy of practice in the basic types is that all English sentences are derived, by various changes and combinations, from a few basic sentence types:[14]

1. "There" transformations:

Statements	*Questions*
A man is at the door. There is a man at the door.	Is there a man at the door?
The day is warm. It is a warm day.	Is it a warm day?
The job is a tough one. It's a tough job.	Is it a tough job?
Four chairs are at the table. There are four chairs at the table.	Are there four chairs at the table?
Three boys are in the principal's office. There are three boys in the principal's office.	Are there three boys in the principal's office?

2. Question transformations:

He is at school.	Is he at school?

He reads fast. (He does read fast.) Does he read fast? (This sentence requires the intermediate step *to provide the verb* to change positions with the subject.)

He is going now.	Is he going now?

3. Question transformations supplying the question word:

Statement	*Asking the question the statement answers:*
John works here.	*Who* works here?
Robert lives in *Arizona*.	*Where* does Robert live?
The books should have cost *ten dollars*.	*How much* should the books have cost?
Bill is in his *office*.	*Where* is Bill?
He studies *geography*.	*What* does he study?
He *works* in an office.	*What* does he do?
He studies in the *afternoon*.	*When* does he study?
He writes letters *at night*.	*When* does he write letters?

4. Passive transformations:

---

[14]Paul Roberts, *English Sentences* (New York: Harcourt, Brace and World, 1962).

Active voice	Passive voice
They built a house.	The house was built by them.
John shot a deer.	A deer was shot by John.
Our country fought a civil war.	A civil war was fought by our country.
The third grade worked that problem.	That problem was worked by the third grade.
The old man planted the garden.	The garden was planted by the old man.

5. Transformations where the verb is changed to a noun:

John works.	John is a worker.
Julio gardens.	Julio is a gardener.
Mary teaches.	Mary is a teacher.
Ramon farms.	Ramon is a farmer.
Enrique drives a truck.	Enrique is a truck driver.
Mr. Jones practices law.	Mr. Jones is a lawyer.
Marianna cooks.	Marianna is a cook.
Mrs. Chacon makes dresses.	Mrs. Chacon is a dressmaker.
Mr. Acosta plays chess.	Mr. Acosta is a chess player.
Larry studies at the university.	Larry is a student.

6. Combining kernel sentences into one sentence:
   a. Coordination of simple sentences:
      1. It is the end of summer. School will begin soon. — to — It is the end of summer and school will begin soon.
      2. Girls work. Boys play. — to — Girls work and boys play.
   b. Coordination—omitting repeated words: The teacher was fair. The teacher was helpful. The teacher was completely honest. — to — The teacher was fair, helpful and completely honest.
   c. Subordination of a clause:
      1. The book was *The Wind in the Willows*. The book was lost. — to — The book which was lost was *The Wind in the Willows*.
      2. The man in the library reads most every evening. He knows a great deal about Mexico. — to — The man who reads in the library most every evening knows a great deal about Mexico.
      3. Some pupils know the story already. They should not tell the ending. — to — Some pupils who know the story already should not tell the ending.

7. Combining parts of sentences using *because, until, when,* etc.:

I came home early. The library was closed.	I came home early because the library was closed.
The farmer didn't plant potatoes. The ground was too wet.	The farmer didn't plant potatoes because the ground was too wet.
Mother complained. I didn't help get dinner.	Mother complained because I didn't help get dinner.

I didn't finish.
The bell rang.

I didn't finish because the bell rang.

I can't go with you.
My homework isn't finished.

I can't go with you until my homework is finished.

I have to wait.
I get paid on Friday.

I have to wait until I get paid on Friday.

I can't buy the groceries.
She didn't give me the list.

I can't buy the groceries until she gives me the list.

I'll stay here.
The library stays open.

I'll stay here if the library stays open.

Jose will work every day.
His brother can work too.

Jose will work every day if his brother can work too.

8. Changing to the past tense:

Present:

I go to work.
I need help.
I walk to class.
I bring my books.
I eat lunch at school.
I work.
He works.
She works.
You work.
We work.
They work.
I go.
He goes.
Did you tear your shirt?
Did you pay your bill?
Did you choose that tie?
Did you buy that car?
Did you find your room key?

Past:

I went to work.
I needed to help.
I walked to class.
I brought my books.
I ate my lunch at school.
I worked.
He worked.
She worked.
You worked.
We worked.
They worked.
I went.
He went.
Yes, I tore it.
Yes, I paid it.
Yes, I chose it.
Yes, I bought it.
Yes, I found it.

9. Tag-on questions:

You can go, can't you?
He has the book, hasn't he?
He is working today, isn't he?
He was in your office, wasn't he?
He will come back soon, won't he?
You wash it every day.
He cleans his room every day.

George takes it with him.

Mary practices her music.

They collect the papers.

You can't go, can you?
He doesn't have the book, does he?
He isn't working today, is he?
He wasn't in your office, was he?
He won't come back soon, will he?
You do wash it every day, don't you?
He does clean his room every day, doesn't he?

George does take it with him every day, doesn't he?

Mary does practice her music, doesn't she?

They do collect the papers, don't they?

TESOL Text Materials

A brief list of textbook series available to the teacher for teaching English as a second language includes:

1. National Council of Teachers of English. *English for Today,* William R. Slager, General editor (New York: McGraw-Hill Book Company, 1965-1967). Six textbooks in a series. A teacher's guide is available for each of the six books.
2. English Language Services, Inc., *English This Way* (New York: The Macmillan Company, 1964). Twelve textbooks in a series. One teacher's guide is available for books I-VI; one for Books VII-XII.
3. English Language Services, Inc. *English 900* (New York: The Macmillan Company, 1964). Six textbooks in a series. A teacher's guide is available for the series. Audio-tapes are also available for each unit of each text.
4. The Institute of Modern Languages, Inc., *Contemporary Sopken English.* A six-book series prepared by John Kane and Mary Kirkland (New York: Thomas Y. Crowell Co., 1967-8).
5. BUMPASS, FAYE L., *We Learn English.* Six volumes (New York: American Book Company, 1959).
6. BUMPASS, FAYE L., *We Speak English.* Two volumes (New York: American Book Company, 1967).
7. LANCASTER, LOUISE, *Introducing English: Oral Pre-Reading Program for Spanish-Speaking Primary Pupils* (Boston: Houghton Mifflin, 1966).
8. Miami Linguistc Readers. Fifty-three booklets (Boston: D. C. Heath, 1964-1966).
9. New York City, Board of Education, Puerto Rican Study. *Teaching English to Puerto Rican Pupils.* Four volumes. Language Guide Series (New York: Board of education of the City of New York, 1957).
10. Puerto Rico, Department of Education. *American English Series: English as a Second Language.* Four volumes (Boston: D. C. Heath, 1965-1967).
11. ROJAS, PAULINE M., Director, *Fries American English Series: For the Study of English as a Second Language.* Six volumes (Boston: D. C. Heath, 1952-1957).
12. WHELEER, GONZALES *Let's Speak English.* Six volumes (New York: McGraw-Hill, 1967).

VI. SUMMARY

This chapter has contained linguistic principles and basic transformations in English grammar that are important for teachers teaching any children to better understand the language they use every day. These principles and the understanding of structure become even more important when the teacher has in his class those students who speak non-standard English or those for whom English is a second rather than a first language.

The principles emphasized here:
1. Language is oral
2. Language is habit
3. Languags is arbitrary
4. Language is personal
5. Language is communication
6. Language is more than words. It uses pitch, stress, intonation, and juncture to change meanings
7. Language is culturally transmitted
8. Language is always slowly changing.

Roberts lists nine basic English sentence transformations:
1. There transformations
2. Question transformations
3. Questions; student supplying the question word

4. Passive transformations
5. Transformations where the verb is changed to a noun
6. Combining kernel sentences into one sentence
7. Combining parts of sentences using *because, when, if, until,* etc.
8. Changing to past tense
9. Tag-on questions

The basic principle for teaching English to speakers of other languages is: The learner acquires the ability to use the language communication skills of English in the order of listening, speaking, reading, and writing. First, he hears with understanding; second, he reproduces the language he has heard—trying to imitate a "good" model; third, he is then ready to learn to read that part of the language he has heard and spoken; and fourth, he can then learn to spell and write the language he needs to use, but only after he has heard, spoken, and read it.

READING REFERENCES

CARROLL, JOHN B. *Language and Thought* (Englewood Cliffs, New Jersey: Prentice-Hall, Inc., 1964).

DeCECCO, JOHN P., Editor, *The Psychology of Language, Thought, and Instruction* (New York: Holt, Rinehart and Winston, 1967).

FRIES, C. C. *Linguistics and Reading* (New York: Holt, Rinehart and Winston, Inc., 1963).

GLEASON, H. S., JR. *An Introduction to Descriptive Linguistics* (New York: Holt, Rinehart and Winston, Inc., 1961). Revised Edition.

GOODMAN, KENNETH S. "The Linguistics of Reading," *Elementary School Journal,* 64:355-361, April, 1964.

GOODMAN, KENNETH. "Reading: a Psycholinguistic Guessing Game," *Journal of the Reading Specialist,* 1967.

HALL, EDWARD T. *The Silent Language.* A Premier Book (Greenwich, Conn.: Fawcett Publications, Inc., 1966).

LAMB, POSE. *Linguistics in Proper Perspective* (Columbus, Ohio: Charles E. Merrill Publishing Company, 1967).

LEFEVRE, CARL A. *Linguistics and the Teaching of Reading* (New York: McGraw-Hill Book Company, 1964).

LOBAN, WALTER. *The Language of Elementary School Children* (Champaign, Illinois: National Council of Teachers of English, NCTE Research Report, No. 1, 1963).

SOFFIETTI, JAMES P. "Why Children Fail to Read: A Linguistic Analysis," *Harvard Educational Review,* Spring, 1955. Reprinted in Albert J. Mazurkiewicz, *New Perspectives in Reading Instruction: A Book of Readings* (New York: Pitman Publishing Corporation, 1964), pp. 49-72.

STRICKLAND, RUTH. *The Language of Elementary School Children: Its Relationship to the Language of Reading Textbooks and the Quality of Reading of Selected Children* (Bloomington, Indiana: Indiana University Bulletin of the School of Education, Vol. 38, No. 4, 1962).

WEAVER, WENDELL W. "The Word As the Unit of Language," *The Journal of Reading,* 10:262-268, January, 1967.

14

Teaching Reading
to the Bilingual Child

The failure to achieve academically and the negative attitudes so often manifested among many children who must learn English as a second language after they enroll in school are rooted in culture, language, and experience. The discussion that follows includes (1) cultural expectations of the school; (2) cognitive learning; (3) developing language arts skills in bilingual children; (4) linguistic reading programs and the reading teacher; (5) special aspects of vocabulary in the second language; and (6) bilingualism in the Southwest.

I. CULTURAL EXPECTATIONS OF THE SCHOOL

The child whose cultural heritage is different from that of the value system perpetuated by the school is in need of special educational services that will cross the cultural barriers and meet the language needs *before* the child can profit from the typical course of study with which he is apt to be confronted.

Each child coming to the school is expected to become oriented to certain values emphasized in the dominant culture. Some of these values are:

1. He must climb the ladder of success, and in order to do this he must place a high value on competitive achievement.
2. He must learn time orientation that will be precise to the hour and minute, and he must also learn to place a high value on looking to the future.
3. He must accept the teachers' reiteration that there is a scientific explanation for all natural phenomena.
4. He must become accustomed to change and must anticipate change. (The dominant culture teaches that "change," in and of itself, is good and desirable!)
5. He must trade his shy, quiet, reserved, and anonymous behavior for socially approved aggressive, competitive behavior.

6. He must somehow be brought to understand that he can, with some independence, shape his own destiny, as opposed to the tradition of remaining an anonymous member of his society.[1]

Too many teachers are inadequately prepared to understand or accept these dissimilar cultural values. Teachers come from homes where the drive for success and achievement has been internalized early, where "work for work's sake" is rewarded, and where time and energy are spent building for the future. Many children come to the classroom with a set of values and a background of experience radically different from that of the average American child. To teach these children successfully, the teacher must be cognizant of these differences and must above all else seek to understand, without disparagement, those ideas, values, and practices different from his own.

Robert Roessel, Director of the Experimental Educational Program for Navajo children, at Rough Rock, Arizona, attempted to give his staff an awareness of the peculiar texture of Navajo life. He hoped to avert just such episodes as the small-scale tragedy that resulted from a teacher's inexperience at a reservation school. The teacher was from the East.

> Her credentials were excellent, but she had never taught Navajo children before. She noticed one morning that the face and arms of one of the third grade boys were covered by something that looked like soot. In his hair was a substance that resembled grease. With a normal respect for cleanliness, the teacher asked the boy to wash himself. When he refused, she took him to the washroom and washed him.
>
> The boy never returned to school. It turned out that his family had conducted an important healing ceremony on his sick sister, the "soot" and "grease" being part of the ceremonial painting. With her soap and water, the teacher destroyed the healing powers of the ceremony. The girl died and the parents could not be shaken in their belief that it was the teacher's fault. No member of the family has set foot in a school since.[2]

Examples from teachers about the misuse of words by children showing lack of understanding of concepts follow:

1. One elementary school in the city enrolls children from both a very high socio-economic class and from a lower class, culturally deprived area. One child was relating a story about their butler serving at a recent dinner party in their home, and dropping a plate of food on the floor. The child described his mother's embarrassment and concern. A little boy from one of the poor homes listened intently during the story and then said, "What is a butler?" One of the boys near him explained the duties of their butler and when he was

---

[1]Miles Zintz, *Education Across Cultures* (Dubuque, Iowa: Kendall/Hunt, Publishing Co., 1969), p. 28.

[2]Paul Conklin, "A Good Day at Rough Rock," *American Education* (Reprint), February, 1967. Unnumbered pages.

finished, the boy who had asked the question said, "Oh, I thought it was a [sic] animal of some kind."

2. One afternoon the teacher sent a little girl from her room to the office to get a box of ditto masters, which she called stencils. The teacher repeated the word "stencil" several times and showed her one so she would know exactly what to get. Soon after that, the secretary in the office called on the inter-communication system and asked the teacher what she was planning to do with a box of tonsils.

3. One cold day in December, before the children were dismissed for recess, the teacher said that no one should leave the room until they had put on their *wraps*. Everyone got in line except five little Spanish-speaking children. She questioned why they were not in line, and they said, "But Mrs. Williams, we don't have any wraps." As soon as she said that she really meant to get their *caps* and *coats*, they *wrapped* up and got in line.

Kelley, in the ASCD Yearbook, *Perceiving, Behaving, Becoming,* describes the behavior of the fully-functioning self in present-day society:[3]

We live in a moving, changing, becoming-but-never-arriving world . . .
He needs to see process, the building and becoming nature of himself. Today has no meaning in the absence of yesterdays and tomorrows.
The growing self must feel that it is involved, that it is really a part of what is going on, that in some degree it is helping shape its own destiny.
The acceptance of change as a universal phenomenon brings about modifications of personality . . . one who accepts change and expects it, behaves differently . . .
He sees the evil of the static personality because it seeks to stop the process of creation . . . Life to him means discovery and adventure, flourishing because it is in tune with the universe.

But the Indian child has likely already learned that nature provides. Man's objective is to remain in harmony with nature. The dances, the rituals, the seasonal prayers, and the chants are learned perfectly and passed from one generation to another—hoping to maintain and restore harmony.

Indians believe that time is always with us. Life is concerned with the here and now. Accepting nature in its seasons, they will get through the years one at a time.

So, too, the Indian child is early made to feel that he *is involved* and personally responsible for doing his part so that all of life—in the village—in the natural order—all the cosmic forces—would be kept running smoothly and harmoniously. *But,* not with the goal of changing his des-

---

[3]Earl C. Kelley, "The Fully Functioning Self," in *Perceiving, Behaving, Becoming, A New Focus on Education,* ASCD, NEA (1201 Sixteenth Street, N.W., Washington, D. C., 1962), pp. 10-12.

tiny determined for him by the older and wiser ones. He best fulfills his destiny by remaining an anonymous member of his social group. He accepts group sanctions, placing primary emphasis on conformity.

The Indian child will be able to understand the values of his teacher much better if the teacher has some understanding and acceptance of the child's values.

Dora V. Smith, in her Kappa Delta Pi lecture, *Communication: The Miracle of Shared Living*, tells a story of a little Japanese girl who was spending a year in the United States attending an elementary school:

> At Christmas time her American classmates sent a package to her school in Tokyo. They decided to write a letter to accompany it. When Reiko was asked whether she wished to add a line, this is what she wrote: "The boys and girls in America sound funny when they talk. We have to read in English, too. But they laugh and cry and play in Japanese."[4]

Perhaps if all teachers made children feel that laughing, crying, and playing were universal languages, there would be less need to be concerned about the languages that create barriers to understanding. Perhaps Reiko is expressing the idea that time to laugh together and time to play together help to counteract the tensions that result from language differences in communication.

II. COGNITIVE LEARNING

Hildreth, in *The Reading Teacher*, makes some generalizations about teaching beginning reading in English and Arabic. This one generalization is most pertinent in teaching bilingual children:

> Oral language readiness appears to be the most important aspect of readiness and beginning reading, both because reading is a form of language and because a pupil's linguistic maturity reflects his thought level and his experiential background. Responses in beginning lessons should be primarily oral. If the reading deals with situations that are meaningful to the children there is nothing in daily oral practice to prevent the pupils from developing into good silent readers. Children the world around retain best the words in print that they can pronounce and commonly use in conversation.[5]

Stauffer discusses the problem of concept development:

> Concept development merits a first order rating in the teaching of reading as a thinking process. This is so because concepts are cognitive structures acquired through a complex and genuine act of thought, and

---

[4]Dora V. Smith, *Communication: The Miracle of Shared Living*, (New York: The Macmillan Co., 1955), p. 51.

[5]Gertrude Hildreth, "Lessons in Arabic," *The Reading Teacher*, 19:210 (No. 3), December, 1965.

they cannot be absorbed ready-made through memory or drill. A concept is symbolically embodied in a sign, usually a word, and, as such, a word represents an act of generalization.[6]

Stauffer continues:

> If children are to acquire concepts and words to represent them, they must make use in varying degrees of efficiency of such intellectual functions as deliberate attention, logical memory, abstraction, the ability to note likenesses and differences, and so on. To successfully instruct a school child, methods must be employed that will require pupils to be articulate about and put to deliberate use such intellectual functions.[7]

For example, the kindergarten children can eat and enjoy the apple. But they can also learn to describe it as *big, red,* and *shiny.* They can discuss other pertinent adjectives: *delicious, juicy,* or *Jonathan.* Or, the apple may be described as *little, shriveled,* or *soft.* It might even be identified as *rotten, spoiled,* or *bad. Apple* can first be identified as a concrete object, the apple itself, and then by a wax imitation of the real thing. Both are three-dimensional. Then it can be identified by a flat picture which is only semi-concrete. In the early years, this is the extent of the language phase for most children. Next year, they can learn that the combination of letters "a-p-p-l-e" stands for the object *apple.* The recognition that *the spelling of the word using the letters of the Roman alphabet is an extremely abstract process* is very important for teachers. The abstractness of this process for young children is very often missed completely by literate adults.

But, at any age—four, five, or six—there are many things children could learn orally about apples—classifying them as fruit, knowing they are good for boys and girls, that they grow on trees, that they may come from Uncle Jim's Apple Orchard, and that they sometimes produce a million dollar crop in the Rio Grande Valley in New Mexico. So, this developmental process utilizing concepts is a thinking process—in which children put words to work solving problems.

III. DEVELOPING LANGUAGE ARTS SKILLS IN BILINGUAL CHILDREN

1. Learning a language means forming new habits through intensive practice in hearing and speaking.
2. It is deemed advisable that the teacher use and repeat a limited number of sentence patterns and give the children intensive practice in those patterns only. The teacher should learn to pronounce

---

[6]Russell Stauffer, "Concept Development and Reading," *The Reading Teacher,* 19:101 (No. 2), November, 1965.

[7]*Ibid.,* p. 102.

these patterns as perfectly as possible. He should learn when to use them and with which other combinations they are normally used. He should learn how to develop and how to judge accurate pronunciation in his pupils. Too, he should learn how to give varied, interesting practice in the limited patterns being taught. Improvisation by teacher and pupils at this level is not recommended.

3. *Habitual use of the most frequently used patterns* and items of language should take precedence over the mere accumulation of words. The acquisition of vocabulary should be a secondary goal at the beginning stage. Vocabulary will increase rapidly when reading is begun. To reiterate the same principle—because it is of utmost importance—*learning a foreign language is not primarily acquiring vocabulary,* necessary as that is. It is much more important for the student to engage in practice which will most quickly form habits of articulation, of stress, of intonation, of word-order, and of word formation. The sooner these patterns become habit and not choice, the sooner he will achieve mastery of the language.

4. Vocabulary should be taught and practiced only in the context of real situations so that meaning will be clarified and reinforced.

5. Classroom activities should center about authentic speech situations —dialogues, interchanges (I'm six. How old are you?), descriptions, rejoinders ("Are you ready?" "Of course.")—where two or more children are involved.

6. Speech should not be slowed down nor the rhythm distorted because of the mistaken idea that it will increase understanding.

7. New patterns of language should be introduced and practiced with vocabulary that students already know. For example, if one were teaching the interrogative form, "Do you have ————?" the point of departure would be a sentence the children already know, e. g., "I have a dog at home."[8]

The aural-oral method of learning a language is a method of instruction that places emphasis, especially in the beginning, on *hearing and speaking* the new language rather than on learning grammatical structure, translation, reading or writing. The emphasis is entirely upon hearing and speaking the language first. When this method is correctly followed, the learner says only what he has heard (with understanding), reads what he has said, and writes what he has heard, said, and read.

How shall primary teachers develop the language arts in these bilingual boys and girls in the primary grades?

To answer this question on the basis of the previous discussion, the first task is to teach the child learning English as a second language

---

[8]Mary Finocchiaro, *Teaching Children Foreign Languages* (New York: McGraw-Hill, Inc., 1964), pp. 26-28.

the necessary oral language skills so that he can function more nearly the way the native speaker functions.

A year—or longer—much longer if necessary—may be required to teach the commonest sentence patterns with dialogue practice, substitution drills, and questions and answers. Lessons to accomplish this are now commercially available to all teachers, recognizing that each teacher will adapt any text to fit the needs and specific experiences of his group.

The "pressure" to move children into formal reading groups before they have learned listening and speaking habits in the language is one of the gravest errors which teachers continue to make with young non-English speaking children.

Tireman recommended that:[9]

1. The teacher know something of the language of the child's parents
2. The teacher know something of the cultural practices and cultural contribution of the foreign culture
3. The teacher have tact, common sense, and sympathetic understanding
4. The teacher visit the home, not once, but many times
5. The teacher explain the basic purposes of the school and clarify erroneous concepts brought home by the child
6. The teacher show genuine appreciation for the worthwhile values of the culture of the parents

Hildreth observed Cuban children in Florida schools and wrote:[10]

. . . few could express their ideas well in oral English. All were trying to read material that was too difficult and none were familiar with the life portrayed in the textbooks. The pupils could recognize few words at sight and none of them could use phonics to work out new words. To instruct these children in reading and written work before they speak English is sheer waste of teaching effort.

Recognizing the absence of language, and recognizing the failure of so many of these children, teachers need guidelines that will insure greater school success.

The following suggestions all center on the oral language emphasis to teach common language patterns, to provide experience units of work that can be carried out with the teacher doing what little writing needs to be done, and the children having much opportunity to talk about the experiences, to evaluate the problems involved, and to discuss freely what is going on in various situations.

Six-year-olds can learn orally why irrigation is necessary in much of the Rio Grande Valley for the cultivation of garden vegetables and

---

[9]Lloyd Tireman, "School Problems Created by the Homes of Foreign-Speaking Children," *California Journal of Elementary Education*, 8:234-238, May, 1940.

[10]Gertrude Hildreth, *Teaching Reading* (New York: Holt, Rinehart, and Winston, Inc., 1958), p. 564.

their harvest. One kindergarten class became interested in a new house that was being built near the school and on many successive days they visited the house and had continuous discussion on how water would get piped into the house, how the electricity would work, and who all the kinds of skilled laborers were who helped to build the house. In reference to the water pipes, because one child was especially interested, a trip was arranged to the city water works department to see a large wall map of exactly how the water lines were laid throughout the entire city.

Through meaningful experiences like these, with respect to formal reading, children learn that:

1. Reading is nothing more than talk written down.
2. Once written down, it can be read back exactly as it was said.
3. The printed word and the picture can mean the same thing.
4. The reading process is a left-to-right operation.
5. Punctuation changes meaning in language context.
6. Pets, places, people, toys provide stimuli for writing down their own experiences.
7. Letters that make up words are different from each other.[11]

A teacher can now develop a language-experience approach to reading.

Use of the Miami Linguistic Reading Series

The *Miami Linguistic Readers*[12] attempt to give the teacher specific materials for sequential language lessons out of which learning to read can be accomplished. In the linguistic readers, one primary emphasis is on teaching the child to pronounce the English language correctly. This is excellent. He is given a great deal of practice on discriminating minimal pairs and enunciation of all of the phonemes that exist in English that he has not already learned in Spanish. The *Miami Linguistic Readers* do, if the manual is followed, make sure that the child has aural-oral control of the material he is going to try to read.

Some teachers have progressed through only two or three books of the *Miami Linguistic Readers* in one year when working with children who knew little English at the beginning. This demonstrates excellent judgment on the part of the teacher. The language program for such children must include concentrated teaching of oral language all day long but withholding formal reading until the boys and girls can learn with understanding to read the books in the series.

---

[11]Russell Stauffer, "Language-Experience Approach," in James Kerfoot, Editor, *First Grade Reading Programs,* Perspectives in Reading (Newark, Delaware: IRA, 1965).

[12]*Miami Linguistic Readers* (Boston: D. C. Heath, 1965).

A linguistic approach to beginning reading for bilingual children (English and Spanish languages) and planned as a two-year program, the *Miami Linguistic Reader Series* follows linguistic, as well as pedagogical, premises:[13]

1. The referential content of beginning reading material must deal with those things which time has shown are interesting to children.
2. The materials must reflect the natural language forms of children's speech.
3. The child must have aural-oral control of the material he is expected to read.
4. The focus must be on the process of reading as a thinking process rather than on the uses of reading after decoding has been mastered.
5. Sound-symbol correspondences (Phoneme-grapheme relationships) in beginning reading should be in terms of spelling patterns rather than in terms of individual letter-sound correspondences.
6. Grammatical structure as well as vocabulary must be controlled.
7. Children must learn to read by structures if they are to master the skills involved in the act of reading.
8. The learning load in linguistically oriented materials must be determined in terms of the special nature of the materials.
9. Writing experiences reinforce listening, speaking, and reading.
10. Materials must be sequenced so that they enable the learner to achieve success as he progresses through the materials.

Teachers not familiar with the methodology of teaching English to speakers of other languages[14] will be able, by studying the teachers' guides, to help those children with limited English language power to repeat the sentences in the stories in the beginning readers by use of such techniques as *the backward buildup*. The pages in the big book, or in the guide book, will emphasize reading by structures. The teacher and the children will build the items into a statement with falling intonation at the end of the line. By familiarizing the child with the end of the line before he tries to say the complete sentence assures better vocalization of all the words to the end of the sentence when he does attempt to repeat it in its entirety. See below the pages taken from the *Big Book, Readiness Levels Two-Six*:[15]

---

[13]Ralph F. Robinett, "Linguistic Approach for the Bilingual," *Perspectives in Reading: First Grade Reading Programs* (Newark, Delaware 19/11: International Reading Association, 1965), pp. 132-149.

[14]TESOL, Teaching English to Speakers of Other Languages, is a national organization that holds a national annual conference and publishes a journal, The TESOL Quarterly. Its offices are in the Institute of Language and Linguistics, Georgetown University, Washington, D. C. 20007.

[15]*Miami Linguistic Readers, Readiness Levels Two—Six*, Ralph F. Robinett, Production Director, Revised Experimental Edition, (Boston: D. C. Heath, 1965), pp. 45 and 59.

45	59
fat and fat big and fat is big and fat Tug Duck is big and fat. a bug a fat bug a big fat bug Buzz Bug is a big fat bug.	his hand in his hand an ax in his hand Pop has an ax in his hand. a rock on a rock is slipping on a rock Ann is slipping on a rock. a rod with a rod is fishing with a rod Tom is fishing with a rod.

While the *Miami Linguistic Readers* provide the best approach available to teachers today for teaching beginning reading to second language learners, the series has two shortcomings: (1) An extremely vigorous attack on the English phonemes that are new to the Spanish speaker—short "i" in *Biff* and *Tiff,* ending sounds like "f" in *Biff,* "sh" in *fish,* "z", "g" and "k" in *Buzz Bug* and *Tug Duck*—creates difficult problems with pronunciation at the same time the teacher is beginning formal reading which is, in itself, a complicated process; and (2) The introduction of *formal* reading *early* in the program is not really necessary. While the manuals do emphasize aural-oral mastery of the material to be read, the child may lack sufficient knowledge of the English language to have any dynamic interest or motivation in *formal* reading.

IV. LINGUISTIC READING PROGRAMS AND THE READING TEACHER

Two types of reading materials have been published as "linguistic." It is clear from the advertising emanating from all the major publishing houses in 1968 that they have found some basis for saying that their series of reading books are now linguistically oriented or have taken carefully into account the theory of linguistics in their foundation. Probably no new series of language arts materials will appear in the ensuing years without the name of a linguist as co-author or consultant to the authors. This, sadly enough, is partially the publisher's response to the competitive market to be sure his salesman can keep his sales moving.

Nevertheless, to date, three or four "Sets of Linguistic Readers," based on the general principle that the spelling patterns of new words introduced initially must be rigidly controlled and the decoding process emphasized to the exclusion of teaching reading as a meaningful process, have been published. These books have nothing to offer the classroom teacher of reading. It is a violation of any first grade teacher's positive efforts to develop good oral language, promote expanding conversations, vocabulary, and lengthen attentions by reading good stories to children and then to tell them that they can read only uninteresting, artificial bits of context containing no vowels except short "a." Few teachers could motivate much interest in "day-after-day" reading of such passages as this:

> A cat sat.
> A fat cat sat.
> A cat had a hat.
> A man had a cat.
> A cat had a fat rat.

A remedial reading clinician who had occasion to put such books in the hands of boys and girls in individual tutoring situations and to encourage them to read either silently or orally, was invariably asked at the next succeeding session if they could please have a different book to read from.

On the other hand, the *Miami Linguistic Readers* have been specifically developed to help children learn to read in English when they must master the English sound system and the English spoken language as a second language. This series bears little or no relationship to those "Linguistic Readers" mentioned here. *The Miami Readers* have proved to be very effective in the hands of capable, creative teachers, especially those with competency in teaching English as a second language.

Craker[16] studied the personal pronoun occurrences in recommended instructional talk in three reading readiness programs. Craker's purpose was to investigate the extent to which authors of reading readiness programs assume listening comprehension using the personal pronouns of the English language. She counted the personal pronouns and their frequency of occurrence in the first twenty pages of reading readiness instruction in teacher's manuals. She selected the *Bank Street Readers*,[17] the *Scott, Foresman Readers*,[18] and the *Miami Linguistic Readers*.[19]

---

[16]Hazel Craker, "Personal Pronoun Occurrences in Recommended Instructional Talk in Three Reading Readiness Programs," unpublished paper, College of Education, University of New Mexico, 1968.
[17]Macmillan Company.
[18]Scott, Foresman and Company.
[19]D. C. Heath and Company.

The twenty-three personal pronouns were not all used in any series; *Scott, Foresman* used seventeen, *Bank Street Readers* used sixteen, and *Miami Linguistic Readers* used six.

The Scott, Foresman program designed for middle-class children provides much "teacher talk," and utilizes pronouns in a greater range of grammatical form, case, and number.

Bank Street Readers designed for inner city children with culturally disadvantaged backgrounds, reduces the listening load, and makes more limited use of pronouns in kernel sentence slots. However, it uses almost as many different pronouns as the Scott, Foresman.

Miami Linguistic Readers were designed for non-English speaking children with Spanish language background. This series has controlled the use of pronouns to use one pronoun in several sentences and to avoid ambiguities in pronoun use. This finding supports the principle that linguistically, the *Miami Readers* are sequenced to aid the child learning English as a second language by limiting the structures presented to him in early lessons.

V. SPECIAL ASPECTS OF VOCABULARY

Through several years of personal observation, it has been both rather amazing and frightening to see dozens of classrooms of mixed ethnic groups in elementary, junior high, and senior high classrooms utilizing traditional textbooks devised for unilingual, English-speaking, middle class students with the teacher carrying out a traditional lesson plan *as if all the students were profiting* from the lesson. Even casual friendly conversations with the boys and girls from minority ethnic groups whose first language was not English, or observing the teacher in the room carrying on an interminable monolgue, is convincing evidence that much of the English is very difficult to understand and the student has far too limited language-power to make use of the written text for study with comprehension.

Without first mastering the sound system of the language, the student gets hopelessly lost and, if he stays in school, his achievement level drops farther and farther below that of the English-speaking students.

To demonstrate in an empirical manner that the language was severely limited, a number of language tests were devised and administered to large groups of these boys and girls. Selected results are reported here.

An Idioms Test

On an idioms test of ninety multiple-choice items based on statements taken directly from readers used in the fourth, fifth, and sixth grades in 1959, Yandell[20] found that 164 unilingual Anglo sixth graders earned a median raw score of 68. Seventy-six Spanish-American children earned a median score of 49, which ranked at the fifth percentile in the total Anglo distribution. Fifty-two Pueblo Indian children earned a median score of 39, which ranked at the second percentile in the total Anglo distribution. Two hundred twenty-four Navajo children earned a median score of 30, which is little better than guessing.

Sample items from the idiom test follow:

1. In this story Betsy *turned the tables* on several people.
   a. made the people move over
   b. changed her mind
   c. surprised everyone
   d. turned the tables around
2. The black clouds let fall *sheets of rain.*
   a. squares of rain
   b. solid rain
   c. heavy downpour of rain
   d. white rain
3. Uncle started *in a beeline* for the river.
   a. following an imaginary line
   b. straight and fast
   c. busy like a bee
   d. with a bee after him
4. But Mother, who understood thoroughly how Lucy was feeling, tried *to turn the matter off lightly.*
   a. to turn away
   b. to turn off the lights
   c. to dismiss the matter without seriousness
   d. to turn the matter off quietly
5. The old lady was kindhearted, but a bit *sharp-tongued.*
   a. her tongue was too long
   b. she talked too much
   c. her tongue was too sharp
   d. she spoke harshly

In 1967,[21] 655 sixth graders in the same county school system completed the same test. In 1967, 209 unilingual English speakers earned a median score of 65; 104 students with Spanish surnames earned a median score of 55; 76 students from the Zuni Indian Pueblo earned a median

[20]Maurine Yandell, "Some Difficulties Which Indian Children Encounter with Idioms in Reading," M. A. thesis, University of New Mexico, Albuquerque, 1959.
[21]Appreciation is expressed to Dr. W. B. Fitzsimmons, Superintendent of the Gallup-McKinley County School System, and his staff for completing the testing program.

score of 53; and 266 Navajo Indian students earned a median score of 31. These median scores show that both Spanish surnamed children and the Zuni group made very encouraging progress in use of idiomatic expressions during these intervening eight years while the Navajo group demonstrated a one-point median increase. These results are tabulated in Table 14.1.

When the 1967 test results are compared with the 1959 results, generalizations can be drawn.

1. There is a noticeable "drop" in scores earned by the unilingual Anglo-American students. This may be an indication that the teachers work so hard to teach English to students in minority groups that they do not give attention to vocabulary development and work study to those who already know English. One of the inherent dangers in teaching heterogeneous groups, including other-language speakers and native speakers of English, is that the teacher does not effectively "teach" the complete range of differences all at the same time.

2. The Spanish-American and Zuni children have shown consistent growth at all decile levels since the first testing. The median score for the Zuni children moved from the second percentile to the ninth percentile on the norming group distribution; the median score for the Spanish-American children moved from the seventh percentile to the tenth percentile. The school system needs to evaluate whether or not the changes in teaching English as a second language account for this progress, and if so, to redouble its efforts. Percentile ranks *do not* show the real progress clearly, however. This is because the native speakers upon whose scores norms are based naturally "pile up" at the median in a normal distribution. The entire quartile range, from the 25th percentile to the 75th percentile, encompasses only ten raw score points. It is more revealing to point out that the Zuni median score increased from 39 to 53, or 14 raw score points; the Spanish-American from 49 to 55, or six raw score points.

3. The effect of any teaching of English as a second language program has not yet produced any measurable effect with the Navajo students. While a few Navajo students earned higher scores, the median raised only from 30 to 31. Administratively, this group constitutes a very serious problem because they are extremely deficient in English and are now entering the junior high school. They must be taught English as a second language on a systematically planned basis before they can profit from any other kind of academic education. One may conclude that this problem is equally severe in all grades from seventh through twelfth.

4. While primary teachers are continuing the emphasis on teaching English as a second language with all primary students entering school,

TABLE 14.1. *Comparison of Raw Scores Earned on an Idioms Test of 90 Items by Sixth Grade Students in 1959 and 1967 in the Gallup-McKinley County Public Schools**

Percentile Rank	Norming Group: 1959 N = 237	Anglo-American		Spanish-American		Pueblo Indian		Navajo Indian		Percentile Rank
		N=164 1959	N=209 1967	N=76 1959	N=104 1967	N=52 1959	N=76 1967	N=224 1959	N=266 1967	
99	84	82	83	78	76	74	80	64	73	99
90	78	77	76	66	67	58	66	48	59	90
80	76	75	73	62	63	52	63	43	48	80
75	75	74	71	60	62	46	60	40	46	75
70	74	73	70	58	61	43	58	38	41	70
60	72	70	68	52	58	41	56	33	35	60
50	71	68	65	49	55	39	53	30	31	50
40	69	65	60	44	51	34	48	26	27	40
30	66	62	56	38	46	28	40	23	24	30
25	65	61	53	34	44	26	33	22	23	25
20	62	57	50	32	42	24	29	21	22	20
10	55	45	42	25	34	17	22	17	19	10
05	45	31	34	21	30	14	20	16	16	05
02	39	25	22	20	25	12	16	13	15	02
01	38	20	17	18	24	10	13	12	14	01

*The 1959 testing is reported in Maurine Yandell, "Some Difficulties Which Indian Children Encounter with Idioms in Reading," M. A. Thesis, University of New Mexico, 1959.

there is a ten-year gap between this program and the students who are now seniors in high school. Every student who has not internalized the sound system of English as the language of the school, must be grouped at whatever grade level he now is, and taught English as a second language. Every teacher must learn the ways in which teaching English as a second language is not at all the same as teaching English to native speakers. Then, the only salvation for many of these students in junior and senior high school is to group them for special second language learning in all subject areas. Subject matter teachers with support from second language specialists can do this very well. There are excellent texts on the market to guide teachers in teaching English to speakers of other languages (see Chapter 13).

On tests prepared to measure responses to antonyms, simple analogies, and multiple meanings of words, fourth grade Anglo children who constituted norming groups, performed statistically significantly better than sixth grade students from the minority groups.

A Multiple Meanings Test

Cox[22] prepared a 100-item test of multiple meanings of common words and administered it to sixth grade students from all the minorities with the same results. Repeated administration of this test in unilingual, English-speaking, middle-class neighborhoods shows an average class median for middle-class Anglo children of 87 raw-score points while Spanish-American sixth graders with second language interference achieved a median score of 58. The mean scores for the three Indian groups were: Apache, 62; Navajo, after direct teaching, 58; and Pueblo, 44.

The following are sample items from the multiple meanings test developed by Cox:

Directions: Select the correct definition above the sentence to replace the word in the sentence which appears in italics:

1. a. place where liquor is sold   b. fasten   c. ale   d. barrier
   e. the court
   _____ 1. Don't *bar* the door.
   _____ 2. The men had a drink in the *bar*.
   _____ 3. The class constructed a sand *bar*.
   _____ 4. The lawyer pleaded the man's case at the *bar*.

2. a. snouts.   b. chests   c. axle   d. shorts   e. bases
   _____ 1. The athletes wore white *trunks*.
   _____ 2. They bore holes in the *trunks* of the trees.
   _____ 3. The elephants picked up the sugar with their *trunks*.
   _____ 4. *Trunks* of gold were found in the cave.

---

[22]Clara Jett Cox, "An Experimental Study in the Teaching of Certain Facets of the English Language to Navajo Pupils in the Sixth Grade," unpublished paper, College of Education, University of New Mexico, July, 1963.

3. a. square designs   b. figures   c. ticket showing price   d. mark
   e. control

   _____ 1. She placed a red *check* on the best paper.

   _____ 2. The matron had to keep *check* of the girls.

   _____ 3. She prefers *checks* to stripes.

   _____ 4. The man waited until the waitress gave him his dinner *check*.

4. a. lower   b. remove   c. weapon   d. knotted ribbon   e. front of
   a ship

   _____ 1. They have learned to use a *bow* and arrow.

   _____ 2. Janet always wears a *bow* in her hair.

   _____ 3. The minister asked them to *bow* their heads as he prayed.

   _____ 4. Water seeped into the *bow*.

5. a. church   b. festival or exhibition   c. just   d. average   e. light

   _____ 1. The judge asked the jurors to be *fair*.

   _____ 2. His mother is very *fair* and dainty.

   _____ 3. The children had fun at the *fair* in Window Rock.

   _____ 4. Timothy made *fair* grades in school.

TABLE 14.2.   *Comparison of Average Scores on the Multiple Meanings Test by Ethnic Groups of Sixth Grade Students.*

Ethnic Group	Average Score*	Number of Pupils
Anglo	87	84
Apache Indian	62	17
Navajo Indian	58	81
Spanish-American	58**	61
Pueblo Indian	44	31

*Mrs. Cox reported Mean Scores for the three Indian groups; the Anglo and Spanish-American are Median Scores.
**The score for the Navajo group was determined after Mrs. Cox had planned special units of work for teaching multiple meanings of words.

A seventh grade social studies teacher administered the multiple meanings test, a simple analogies test, and the idioms test to his multiethnic class and reported the following mean scores on Multiple Meanings: Eleven Anglo students earned a mean score of 82; sixteen Spanish-American students earned a mean score of 68; and nine Navajo students a mean score of 43. This teacher, who had had no orientation to the problem of teaching English to speakers of other languages, was very much surprised with these results. Although school had been in session about six weeks when he administered it, he was not anticipating such divergent scores by ethnic groups. The scores from the other tests are given in Table 14.3.

TABLE 14.3.   *A Seventh Grade Class Performance on Three Language Tests (1965-66 School Year)*

Ethnic Group	N	Mean Score
I. A Test of Simple Analogies* (Possible Score: 100)		
Anglo-American 12		62
Spanish-American 16		53
Navajo 9		35
II. A Multiple Meanings Test** (Possible Score: 100)		
Anglo-American 11		82
Spanish-American 16		68
Navajo 9		43
III. A Reading Test of Common Idioms*** (Possible Score: 100)		
Anglo-American 12		81
Spanish-American 15		54
Navajo 9		34

*Based on the test developed by Veta W. Mercer, "The Efficiency of Bilingual Children in Understanding Analogies in the English Language," M. A. thesis, University of New Mexico, Albuquerque, 1960.
**Cox, *op. cit.*
***Yandell, *op. cit.*

Candelaria[23] prepared a 75-item simple analogies test and sampled Anglo-American and Spanish surname students from a middle-class area of the city, Spanish surname students from the lower socio-economic area in the city, and Negro students from a downtown area. Mean scores of the four groups were most interesting: Anglo: 60.5; Spanish-American middle-class: 56.5; Negro: 46; and Spanish surname lower socio-economic status: 42.5. The Spanish surname student whose parents move into the middle-class areas and into Anglo neighborhoods are able to function significantly better in English than those in low socio-economic areas. Yet, the course of study recommended for the Spanish surname child in the low socio-economic areas is the same as that recommended for the Anglo-American child in the middle-class school. Candelaria's test results are given in Table 14.4.

TABLE 14.4.   *Results of Analogies Test Administered to Selected Middle-Class and Lower-Class Children in a School System.*

Ethnic Group	N	Mean	S. D.	Significance of Difference with all other groups
Anglo-American 142		60.6690	7.0948	.01
Span-American Middle-Class 60		56.5167	7.8901	.01
Negro 29		46.0345	10.6687	.01
Lower Socio-Economic Area 53		42.5660	10.2779	.01

23William A. Candelaria, "A Comparative Investigation of the Understanding Which Sixth-Grade Anglo, Spanish-American, and Negro Children Have of Analogies in the English Language," an unpublished study, College of Education, University of New Mexico, 1968, pp. 29, 31.

Lessons for Developing Aspects of Vocabulary

Teachers will be able to devise many lessons using various audio and visual aids to motivate language learning.

1. Using elementary stories and poems. The poem "What Is Black?" by Scott could reinforce many meanings for the word *black* if the teacher gathers some pictures from the vertical picture file and some three dimension toys from ten-cent stores, drug stores, and department stores.

What Is Black?[24]

Black is good earth where little seeds grow;
Black is the bird that we call a crow.
Black is a berry which grows on a vine;
Black is the night, unless moon and stars shine.
Black are the shoes that you wear on your feet;
Black is the pepper on food that you eat.
Black is sweet licorice—yum, yum, yum!
Black is the spot of ink on your thumb.
Black is the skunk with stripe down his back;
Black is the engine that runs on a track.
Black is a fierce old Halloween cat;
Black is a witch's steeple hat.
Black is the marker with which you write;
Black is the opposite of white!

—Louise Binder Scott

2. The picture illustrating helpful little words, Figure 14.1, can make common prepositions meaningful and provide for review. The teacher must be careful to present such abstract words *one at a time* and "fix" their meanings so as not to confuse the child.

3. Finding matched pairs. Cut pictures from magazines and catalogs and mount them on cards (3 by 5 or 4 by 6 size). Some possible pairs of pictures are:

cup — saucer	fork — knife	ball — bat
pen — pencil	boy — girl	shirt — tie
doll — doll buggy	chair — desk	comb — hair
broom — dust pan	light bulb — lamp	hammer — nail
pan — lid	ring — finger	foot ball player — football
mare — colt	baker — cake	fireman — fire truck
hog — pigs	nose — face	mailman — letter
leaf — tree	paint — brush	dog — bone

4. Association of opposites. Cut pictures from reading readiness books and picture dictionaries and mount them. Some possible pairs of pictures are:

empty — full	left — right
in — out	large — small
inside — outside	on — off
above — below	tall — short

---

[24]Louise Binder Scott and J. J. Thompson, *Talking Time*, Second Edition (New York: McGraw-Hill, Inc., 1966), p. 327.

5. Seasons of the year. Compile a stack of pictures that can be divided into summer, fall, winter, spring.

6. Action verbs. Swinging, sitting, reading, pasting, cutting, playing, falling down, getting off of, reaching, falling, kneeling, running, standing, painting, leaning over, setting, jumping, flying, sliding down.

7. Clothing we wear. Putting in categories, pictures of all the things for mother, father, brother, sister.

8. Tools we use. Catalogs, such as Sears or Montgomery Ward, are an excellent source.

9. Dogs, toys, furniture, time pieces, kinds of chairs, kinds of lamps, ways we travel, domestic animals, dishes, money, sharp objects, musical instruments. All these are categories of pictures that might be compiled in packets for different kinds of games or drills that might be planned with or without direct teacher supervision.

VI.   BILINGUALISM IN THE SOUTHWEST

Introduction

The word "bilingual" is used very loosely wherever children in school must use a second language as the language of instruction whether they know anything about the language or not. This includes all the boys and girls on a long continuum from those lower-class children who know only a non-standard dialect of English to those who come to the English-speaking school but, up to that time, have never used English as a means of communication at all.

Rather than the real meaning of "bilingual" as speaking in two tongues, the term is used to mean any person who is in a two-language environment, even if he can only say "hello," "thank you," and "good-by" in the second language in which he needs to communicate.

In the Southwest, children are spoken of as bilinguals if they speak an Indian tongue or Spanish until they enroll in school where English is the medium of instruction. Naturally, these children are not *bi*-lingual by any stretch of the imagination. In the past, they have *not* been given systematic instruction in the learning of a second language so they have had little opportunity to become bilingual.

Were the school to take advantage of the language that the child already knows as well as to make him efficient in the language of the school, he would then be truly bilingual. With the needs around the world so great as they are today for peoples to be able to communicate across the language barrier, it seems extremely foolish that in the United States the child who brought a language other than English to school has been asked to forget it.

Helpful Little Words

Figure 14.1. The common prepositions must be taught one at a time in meaningful situations and with sufficient review provided so that the child uses them confidently.

From Hale C. Reid, and Helen W. Crane, *My Picture Dictionary*, (Boston: Ginn and Company, 1965), p. 37.

The basic problem in the Southwest is *biculturalism*, not bilingualism. Language expresses the values of a culture; culture, by determining behavioral practices and goals, limits the connotations and denotations of the language. The scope of bilingualism is illustrated in the use of the word *father* in Anglo-America and in Zuni Indian culture. For the Zuni child, the word *father* represents his mother's husband—a man who enjoys his children as companions. He takes no part in disciplining his children, nor does he have any concern for their economic security. In his matrilineal society, the mother owns the property and her brothers assist in the rearing of and disciplining of the children. Further, it is said that she may divorce her husband by leaving his shoes and ceremonial garb outside the door while he is away and that this act will be his cue to gather up his few belongings and return to his mother's house. Family organization is of an extended nature, and the marriage does not decree that a man-wife love relationship is more important than the consanguinal mother-son or sister-brother relationship. In short, in a matrilineal, consanguinal, extended family, *father* may mean a specific set of behavior patterns such as described above.

Father, for the Anglo middle-class child, represents the legal head of a household who is held responsible for the rearing and disciplining of his children. His marriage to his wife is based, at least theoretically, on a conjugal, or love relationship; and even if dissolved in a court of law, he may still be held accountable for her full support. For this child, *father* is a full set of meanings derived from a patrilineal, conjugal, nuclear family relationship.[25]

The interdependence of language and culture for the young child has been well stated by Davies:[26]

> To change a child's medium of instruction is surely to change his culture; is not culture bound up with language? And if the language should disappear, can the culture remain? Everyone must have his own orientation to life, and language provides the most natural means of reacting to life. In the deepest things of the heart, a man or woman turns naturally to the mother tongue; and in a child's formative stages, his confidence in that tongue must never be impaired.

It is hoped that the child holds two psychological values about his language and his family who speak that language. First, he should feel that his language is a good one; that it expresses his ideas and wishes adequately; and that he may be justly proud to use it. Second, all of the people in his extended family use the language which he has learned as his first language and he derives his ego strength and sense of per-

---

[25]Miles V. Zintz, "Cultural Aspects of Bilingualism," in J. Allen Figurel, (ed.), *Vistas in Reading,* 11th Annual IRA Proceedings, p. 357.
[26]R. E. Davies, *Bilingualism in Wales* (Capetown, South Africa: Juta and Co., Ltd., 1954), p. 14.

sonal worth as a member of that particular ethnic group. If the school teaches, however, that English is the only acceptable language there, and that use of another language even during free play on the playground will be punished, the child can only conclude that his school feels that his language is inferior to the one that must be used *all the time* during the school day.

If the teacher reacts negatively to the child's first language, the child will further conclude that only people that speak English are adequate in his teacher's eyes. In the Southwest for many years, both of these things were done to children. They were denied the use of their own language and subtly taught that their language and their people were inferior. To cite one very bad example of this kind of teaching, a dormitory counselor in a bordertown dormitory for Indian students is reported to have met a bus load of boys and girls at his school in the fall of the year, and asked them to group themselves around him so that he might say a word to them. He then made the following announcement: "The first thing I want you to do here is to forget that you are an Indian, and the second thing I want to tell you is that we speak only English around here."

Bilingual schools taught in Spanish and English would be natural, workable solutions in many schools in the Southwest. Since Spanish is a major language of the world, books, newspapers, and periodicals are readily available in that language. Many nations in the Americas have some 200,000,000 speakers of the language with libraries, government, business, and schools functioning in Spanish.

The question of young Navajo children receiving instruction in school in the Navajo language is an entirely different question—though no less important. Although there are no libraries and there is no indicated future use, the two psychological values are just as valid for the Navajo as for the Spanish child.

Maybe even for him, at age five and at age six, the school should spend up to two-thirds of his day in the Navajo language with planned, sequenced, intensive teaching of English as a spoken means of communication. Learning concepts and reading readiness in Navajo would save the child some time later on. Hopefully, by age seven or eight, he would begin to learn to read in English and use it as his medium of reading and writing instruction. Yet, by the behavior of the adults at school during the first three years, he would know that the school valued his language, and in turn his cultural heritage, and he might well participate in a Navajo conversation class throughout his school life.

What Is a Bilingual School?

Few programs operate in public schools in the United States as bilingual, that is, putting two languages to work in the conduct of the school.

A bilingual school is one in which instruction during the school day is afforded in more than one language. This means that content subjects will be taught in both languages. One might study his mathematics in English and his history lesson in Spanish in a Spanish-English bilingual school. This is to be contrasted with studying Spanish for one period of the day as a foreign language with little attention given to that language except in the class period. Few students who study Spanish as a foreign language in the high school are able to master the sound system of that language so that they can understand native speakers of that language.

The only test results of educational achievement of the bilingual school in operation have been reported by Malherbe concerning Dutch-English bilingualism in South Africa.[27] In statistics released in 1946, he reported that students in the secondary school divided themselves into three groups: those who were educated in English-speaking schools; those who were educated in Afrikaans-speaking schools; and a relatively small number educated in Afrikaans-English bilingual schools.

Malherbe tested about 18,000 students in three types of South African schools: Unilingual Afrikaans, Unilingual English, and Bilingual Schools. Some of his conclusions are:

> The main point . . . is that the figures show a clear advantage in favour of the bilingual school as regards language attainment in both English and Afrikaans at all intelligence levels . . . the gains, though seemingly small, are all statistically significant.[28]

> . . . those children with a bilingual home background who attend the bilingual medium school top the list, while right at the bottom of the list come the children with a unilingual home environment who attend a unilingual medium school.[29]

> In geography the pupils in the bilingual school were, on an average, about *four-fifths* of a school year ahead of those in the unilingual school. In arithmetic they were *half a year* ahead.[30]

> Adverse sectional discrimination is from three to four times as great in unilingual as in bilingual schools. The children with bilingual home environment display the least adverse discrimination . . . The consistency of our data on the main issue leaves no doubt about the fact that in bilingual medium schools, where pupils of both sections mix and associate freely, the children display a comparatively low degree of intercultural antagonism.[31]

---

[27]E. G. Malherbe, *The Bilingual School* (Capetown: Juta and Co., Ltd., 1946).
[28]*Ibid.*, p. 62.
[29]*Ibid.*, p. 69.
[30]*Ibid.*, p. 73.
[31]*Ibid.* p. 84.

Davies writes about second language learning and describes one situation in Wales.

> The supplementing of second language teaching by the study of another subject through its medium, is the only way in which the second language will ever come to life in unilingual environments, in South Africa or anywhere else . . . The mastery of a language must become subconscious, and this can never be achieved merely by studying that language in the language lesson only . . . World Geography is a possibility.[32]

> A pleasing feature of parallel-medium of "two-stream" schools in Wales is their complete lack of separatism. The Primary School, Aberystwyth, reorganized in 1948, has 340 pupils, of whom 225 are English- and 115 Welsh-speaking. The staff is bilingual, and the spirit of the school on the whole is Welsh, with Welsh the language of the staff and staff meetings. English is used as the medium of instruction for the English-speaking section throughout, with Welsh introduced as a subject in the second year and taught in every subsequent year. For the Welsh-speaking section, English is introduced during the second half of the first year, the time devoted to it being increased during the second and subsequent years; by the third year, the medium of instruction has become 50% Welsh, 50% English, and by the fourth, equal facility in the use of both languages is aimed at.[33]

Peal and Lambert demonstrated that bilingual children are superior on both verbal and non-verbal intelligence tests when compared with monolinguals. They compared monolingual and bilingual groups of ten-year-old children who were students in six French schools in Montreal, Canada. Their groups were matched on age, sex, and socio-economic status. They concluded that their bilingual subjects had greater mental flexibility than did the monolingual children and in addition demonstrated a superiority in concept formation.[34]

Rojas reported at the end of the 1964-65 school year about a bilingual school in Miami:

> The bilingual school has two groups of Spanish-speaking pupils and two of English-speaking pupils in grades one through four with eight native Spanish-speaking teachers and eight native English-speaking teachers. English is the medium of instruction for all pupils for approximately half of each day; and Spanish, the medium of instruction for all pupils during the other half. Next year the fifth grade will be added

---

[32]R. E. Davies, *Bilingualism in Wales* (Capetown: Juta and Company, Ltd., 1954), p. 90.

[33]*Ibid.*, p. 17.

[34]Elizabeth Peal and Wallace Lambert, "The Relationship of Bilingualism to Intelligence," *Psychological Monographs: General and Applied*, No. 76:1-23 (Washington: American Psychological Association, 1962).

and the following year the sixth. The expectation is that at the end of the sixth grade both groups of pupils will know the two languages well enough to operate effectively in both.[35]

Modiano did a comparative study of two approaches to the teaching of reading in the national language.[36] She studied reading achievement of native Indians in the Chiapas highlands in southern Mexico, where some of the Indian children are taught to read first in their native Indian languages while others are immediately taught in Spanish. In each of three tribal areas studied, the researcher found significantly better reading ability among children who were first taught to read in their original language.

Modiano's findings are applicable to all schools, and to test this hypothesis she urges experimental programs to begin in regions in the United States having large linguistic minorities. She found no school system in the nation now employing the native-language-first approach.

Materials for Spanish-English Bilingual Schools

Schools interested in finding text materials for elementary school classes in Spanish will be able to find an adequate supply. The following brief bibliography suggests sources from which school administrators may select:

Textbooks:

(1) Laidlaw Brothers, Inc., River Forest, Illinois, Angeles Pastor, *et al.*, *Por el mundo del cuento y la aventura, Serie de textos básicos para Hispano-américa*, 1962.

Mis juegos y cuentos	Apresto
A jugar y a gozar	Precartilla
¡ A la escuela!	Cartilla
Amigos de aquí y de allí	Libro Primero
Pueblo y campo	Libro II, Nivel I
Sorpresas y maravillas	Libro II, Nivel II
Por esos caminos	Libro III
Nuestro mundo maravilloso	Libro IV
Aventuras por mundos desconocidos	Libro V
Una mirada al pasado	Libro VI

Puertas de la Luz, Angeles Pastor, *et al.*, Una serie de libros de lectura para los tres primeros grados, 1959-1962.
Campanillitas Folklóricas
Esta era una vez bajo las palmeras
Esta era una vez bajo los yagrumos

---

[35]Pauline Rojas, "The Miami Experience in Bilingual Education," Carol J. Kreidler, Editor, *On Teaching English to Speakers of Other Languages*, Series II (Champaign, Illinois 61820: National Council of Teachers of English, 1966), p. 45.

[36]Nancy Modiano, "A Comparative Study to Two Approaches to the Teaching of Reading in the National Language," New York University School of Education, 1966.

Personal del programa de salud, por Edwina Jones, Paul Landis, Edna Morgan, and Thelma Shaw, six book series for grades I-VI.
A series of arithmetic books with teacher's editions have also been published by Laidlaw.

(2) *La Serie Meso-América,* Regional Office for Central America and Panama, ODECA, El Salvador, San Salvador.
(a) A reading series finished through the fifth grade.
(b) An arithmetic series finished through fourth grade.
(c) A social studies series in preparation.
(d) A language series in preparation.
(e) A science series in preparation.

(3) *Serie Educativa de Ciencia Básica,* por Bertha Morris Parker (Evanston, Illinois: Row, Peterson and Company, 1958).
24 titles are available, for example:
La vida a través de las edades

(4) *Serie de libros de lectura* (San Jose, Costa Rica: Editorial Las Américas, 1959).

Flor nueva	I y II grados
Mi pequeño mundo	II grado
Leer y hacer	III grado
Patria grande	IV grado
Madre América	V grado
La tierra y el hombre	VI grado
Nuestro país	III o IV grado

(5) *Biblioteca Popular Latinoamericana,* Panamerican Union Building, Washington, D. C., 1962.
Serie de Civismo
Serie de Agricultura
Serie de salud
Serie de economía y asuntos sociales
Serie de conocimientos básicos
Serie de recreación
Serie de didáctica

Library Books and Magazines:

(1) *Pequeños Libros de Oro* (Donato Guerra, No. 9, Mexico 1, D. F.: Editorial Novaro, 1962).
Creaciones de Walt Disney, 21 titles
Producciones Diversas, 66 tiles

(2) Novelas (Tlacoquemecatl, 73, Mexico, D. F.: Editorial Diana, S. A.) Pearl S. Buck, *La buena tierra,* 1963. (Many such titles)

(3) *Classics of Spanish Literature* (200 Park Avenue, South, New York 3, New York: Latin America Institute Press, 1963).

(4) *Caminos,* Colegio Americana, Apartado Postal No. 83, Guatemala, Guatemala, C. A., magazine published September through May.

(5) Scholastic Magazines, Inc., 50 West 44th St., New York, N.Y. 10036.
¿Qué tal?
Hoy Día
El Sol

V. SUMMARY

. . . There is general agreement all over the educational world that the child should begin his education in his mother tongue or . . . the language he most easily understands.[37]

. . . we are not producing bilingual school children and we never shall, as long as the second language is *not* used as an instrument of expression and *not* merely as a subject to be learned for an examination. In other words, the second language must be used as a medium in the school.[38]

Thompson and Hamalainen state:[39]

In the ever shrinking world the attainment of goals of communication and understanding among its people is imperative if we are to live in peace and security. It is an obvious fact known to almost everyone that we are only one day's distance from every place in the world. Not only are we this close to each other in time, but in increasing numbers we are establishing contact with each other.

The United States government, aware of the importance of foreign languages to the national interest, enacted pertinent legislation to provide support for research and training. The National Defense Act (NDEA) of August 1958 in its Title VI promoted the study of foreign languages and the quality of instruction. NDEA has provided more schools and colleges with the opportunity to teach foreign languages more effectively than any other measure in recent years.

The focus on foreign language study has shown that learning a second language is most difficult. The learner must follow many of the same steps a child takes in learning his native language. However, the adult learner experiences much interference from previously learned speaking and reading and writing habits. Yet, he must learn to hear and to discriminate the significant sounds of that new language as used by its speakers. The learner must produce sound units that are new, and therefore, difficult because these sounds are not found in the structure of his native language. Since the learner is fluent and at ease in the use of his native tongue, there are additional barriers to overcome: feelings of awkwardness, of inhibition, and limitations in language expression.

The communication explosion presents promises and problems. While it makes the world one village, technology alone cannot bring about human understanding. Knowledge of one or more foreign languages has become a practical necessity.[40]

---

[37]T. J. Haarhoff, "Introduction," in E. G. Malherbe, *The Bilingual School* (Capetown: Juta and Company, Ltd., 1946), p. 8.

[38]*Ibid.*, p. 5.

[39]Elizabeth Thompson and Arthur Hamalainen, "Foreign Language Teaching in the Elementary Schools,". *An Examination of Current Practices* (Washington: ASCD, National Education Association, 1958), p. 9.

[40]Dolores Gonzales, "Auditory Discrimination of Spanish Phonemes," Ed.D. dissertation, University of Pennsylvania, 1967, pp. 4-5.

Teaching reading in English to the bilingual child will not differ as a process if the child has an opportunity to master the sound system of the English language before he is expected to learn to read and write it. Teachers need to understand and appreciate the cultural background of the child, the cognitive learning processes for all children, some of the phonemic and syntactical differences between their language and the child's, the present-day methods of teaching the reading and writing skills and the contribution of linguistics to this process, and the problems of vocabulary expansion for the language-handicapped student. In addition, where children already understand the sound system of another language, opportunity should be found for them to retain and develop it. If large numbers of children have a common "other" language, a successful bilingual school has deep significance to the community and to the larger society.

SUGGESTED ACTIVITIES

1. If you teach in a classroom where children are learning English as a new language, prepare test exercises to measure understanding of idioms, multiple meanings, antonyms appropriate to your grade level.

2. Ask three children to discuss something in the regular school work on the tape recorder. Allow a prescribed time period, for example, two minutes, then count the number of words in spontaneous speech of each of the three children and compare the results.

READING REFERENCES

DAVIES, R. E. *Bilingualism in Wales* (Capetown: Juta and Company, Ltd., 1954).

HILDRETH, GERTRUDE. *Teaching Reading* (New York: Holt, Rinehart, and Winston, 1958), Chapter 23: "Reading for Non-English-Speaking Children," pp. 560-579.

MALHERBE, E. G. *The Bilingual School* (Capetown: Juta and Company, Ltd., 1946).

MANUEL, HERSCHEL. *Teaching Spanish-Speaking Children of the Southwest* (Austin: University of Texas Press, 1965).

YANDELL, MAURINE, and MILES ZINTZ. "Some Difficulties Which Indian Children Encounter with Idioms in Reading," *The Reading Teacher*, 14:256-259, March, 1961.

ZINTZ, MILES V. "Developing a Communication Skills Program for Bilinguals," in Ruth Strang, *Understanding and Helping the Retarded Reader* (Tucson: University of Arizona Press, 1965), pp. 64-75.

ZINTZ, MILES. "Teaching Language-Handicapped Children," *Corrective Reading*, Chapter V (Dubuque, Iowa: Wm. C. Brown Co., 1966).

15

Teaching Reading to the Children of the Inner City Poor

A few years ago a kindergarten teacher in an inner city kindergarten wanted to develop some feeling about the importance of George Washington and Abraham Lincoln during the month of February. On Lincoln's birthday, the concept that Mr. Lincoln had been president of the United States was discussed and his picture was observed. The comment was made that Mr. Kennedy was now president of our country.

Mark asked, "Why Lincoln not president now?"

Teacher, "Mr. Lincoln is dead now."

Mark persisted: "Why he daid?"

The teacher realized that these children knew something of the reality of life and that shooting was not uncommon in the neighborhood, so she said, "A man shot him."

The kindergarteners looked big-eyed at the teacher and asked, "Who?" "Why?"

Mark said, unbelieving, "He shot him daid."

Mr. Booth was discussed briefly as a man who thought some of the things President Lincoln had done were not right and that he had become mentally ill and committed the act of violence.

Mark continued all day to go look at the picture of President Lincoln and repeat to himself, "He shot him daid." He took the teacher's hand and led her to the picture several times and said, "That good man. He shot him daid."

The teacher responded calmly, "Yes, Mark, he shot him dead."

Mark responded, "That good Mr. Lincoln. (Pause.) Bastard!"[1]

If any kindergarten teacher is distressed with the vivid way in which Mark characterizes John Wilkes Booth, she must first understand why "bastard" is the word that Mark brings easily to the conscious level.

---

[1]This episode was contributed by Dr. Catherine Loughlin, Associate Professor of Education, University of New Mexico.

If he has heard it often at home or near home, should she tell Mark it is "bad" language or "wrong" for him to say it? How soon should Mark learn there is one language spoken at school and another at home? If the teacher wishes to encourage Mark to use language, to expand language, and to evaluate through language, she must start where he is with the language he has.

This chapter presents briefly (1) the problems of people who live in poverty; (2) the problems of elementary school children who live in the homes of these poor; (3) some problems of language and concept development to improve literacy skills; and (4) adapting developmental reading instruction to meet the needs of students.

I. THE CULTURE OF POVERTY

Among the fifty million people in the United States who fit the classification of "poor," Lewis estimates that perhaps one-fifth, or ten million, live in a culture of poverty. The largest numbers of this group are made up of Negroes, Puerto Ricans, Mexicans, American Indians, and Southern Poor Whites.[2]

The "hard core" poor in the United States are said to live in a culture of poverty. The *culture of poverty*, in this sense, indicates that they are caught in a vicious circle—with no solution to meeting even minimum economic needs. The individual who grows up in the culture of poverty develops attitudes of fatalism, helplessness, and inferiority. Because his primary concerns are immediate, he exhibits a strong "present-time" orientation in his behavior. With a weak ego structure, he has little disposition to defer personal gratification or to think about his future.[3]

Miller defines the "hard-core" lower class in our country as being primarily "female-based" households as the basic child-rearing unit and as having "serial monogamy" mating as the primary marriage pattern.[4]

> The lower-class Negro family pattern commonly consists of a female dominated household, with either the mother or the grandmother acting as the mainstay of the family unit. The husband, if present, is often an ineffective family leader. The boy growing up in a Negro family frequently perceives his father as a person with a low-status job, who is regarded with indifference or varying degrees of hostility by members of the out-group. In short, the lower-class Negro adult male is seldom regarded as a worthwhile masculine model for the boy to emulate.[5]

---

[2]Oscar Lewis, "The Culture of Poverty," *Scientific American*, 215:25, October, 1966.

[3]*Ibid.*, pp. 19-25.

[4]Walter B. Miller, "Lower-Class Culture as a Generating Melieu of Gang Delinquency," *Journal of Social Issues*, 1958.

[5]Israel Woronoff, "Negro Male Identification Problems and the Education Process," *Journal of Education Sociology*, September, 1962.

Harrington details the insoluble economic problems that keep the poverty cycle operating:

> Here is one of the most familiar forms of the vicious circle of poverty. The poor get sick more than anyone else in the society. That is because they live in slums, jammed together under unhygienic conditions; they have inadequate diets, and cannot get decent medical care. When they become sick, they are sick longer than any other group in the society. Because they are sick more often and longer than anyone else, they lose wages and work, and find it difficult to hold a steady job. And because of this, they cannot pay for good housing, for a nutritious diet, for doctors. At any given point in the circle, particularly when there is a major illness, their prospect is to move to an even lower level and to begin the cycle, round and round, toward even more suffering.[6]

Harrington goes on to describe ways in which the family structure of the poor is different from that of the rest of society. Then, as a specific behavioral example, he contrasts the attitudes of the middle class and the urban poor toward the city policeman:

> . . . For the middle-class, the police protect property, give directions, and help old ladies. For the urban poor, the police are those who arrest you. In almost any slum there is a vast conspiracy against the forces of law and order. If someone approaches asking for a person, no one there will have heard of him, even if he lives next door. The outsider is a "cop," bill collector, investigator (and in the Negro ghetto, most dramatically, he is "the Man").[7]

People in the culture of poverty talk about the middle-class values as if they accepted them, but, in day-to-day living, they fail to live by most of them. Poverty forces them to buy small quantities of goods at high prices, to pawn personal goods often, and to pay usurious rates of interest on bits of borrowed money.

Very early in life, children learn, in the home, values about help from adults, security with adults, trust of others, and the extent to which life is a pleasant or a painful experience. Communication develops early, too. Words, intonation, gesture, inhibitions, listening with care, or withdrawing are all learned as the child learns how he is valued in the family and how he is to value others—both peers and adults.

> One mother, speaking of a previous Parents Association meeting, said, "In that there meeting the principal and all the teachers called us dopes—poor slobs that don't know what our kids are getting from school." To which the principal immediately countered: "Why, Mrs. ————, you know very well that no one said anything of the kind in that meeting," and the mother in question replied, "Maybe you didn't

---

[6]Michael Harrington, "The Invisible Land," reprinted in Staten W. Webster, editor, *The Disadvantaged Learner* (124 Spear Street, San Francisco, California 94105: Chandler Publishing Company, 1966), p. 17.

[7]*Ibid.,* p. 18.

say it, but that's what the atmosphere said." However correct or incorrect this parent was in her perception, it is clear that communication between her and the professional staff would be difficult.[8]

Since many of the parents are reluctant to come to school until they know and trust the people there, it is necessary for the school to go to the parents. Visiting in the homes gives each teacher an opportunity to see the child at home in the family. It usually convinces the parents that the teacher is interested in learning ways to work successfully with their child. Such visits need to be made when there are no pressing negative problems needing solutions. Schools should do everything possible to help parents help their children learn in school. . . . Even though these parents look to the school with hope, many of them are fearful and confused in relation to the school. . . . Principals in schools . . . who wish to bring about change are often baffled by what seems to them to be teacher indifference, if not opposition.

Many of the undesirable characteristics of the poor of Appalachia are common to the inner city poor. Scarnato reports from Appalachia:

> A few years ago, a public spirited group of doctors in Kanawha County, in which the state capitol is located, gave a physical and psychiatric examination to some 329 welfare clients listed as totally disabled, and they found no cases of conscious malingering and found that strong and conscious feelings of inferiority and guilt were resulting in depressive apathy and serious physical illness. The result of their findings was summed up in the graphic phrase, "Idleness is a disease."[9]

Negroes in Chicago ghettos have been relegated to a world incomprehensible to many beginning middle-class teachers who may be selected to teach them. Hilliard found that for millions of the "hardcore" poor, their ghetto was a segregated one, unemployment was very high, and many, many adults lacked adequate literacy skills for unskilled employment. Lost in a feeling of hopelessness, discriminated against in many subtle ways, and without resources to climb out of the deep rut that entombs them, these people have no way to become sufficiently urbanized to practice the mores and culture of the middle class. Yet, Hilliard found also that when these people were offered literacy education, their response as a group was enthusiastic, their attendance was excellent, their personal appearance indicated a strong desire to conform, and the adult education classes had few discipline problems.[10]

---

[8]John Niemeyer, "Some Guidelines to Desirable Elementary School Reorganization," in Staten W. Webster, editor, *The Disadvantaged Learner* (San Francisco: Chandler Publishing Company, 1966), p. 394.

[9]Samuel A. Scarnato, "The Disadvantaged of Appalachia," a presentation made at a meeting of a special language study committee of the National Council of Teachers of English, Champaign, Illinois, July, 1968.

[10]Raymond M. Hilliard, "Massive Attack on Illiteracy," *American Library Association Bulletin*, 57:1034-1038, 1963.

An excellent summary of the conflicts in values between the lower-class child and the middle-class teacher is provided in the table by Segalman. The concepts of authority, education, religion, goals, society, delinquency, time orientation, violence, sex, and money are viewed very differently by the middle-class teacher and the families of the inner city poor. (See page 359.)

THE CHILD IN THE LEARNING SITUATION IN THE INNER CITY SCHOOL

Ausubel considers the motivational aspects of learning as an integral part of the real life learning situation:

> Doing without being interested in what one is doing results in relatively little permanent learning, since it is reasonable to suppose that only those materials can be meaningfully incorporated on a long-term basis into an individual's structure of knowledge that are relevant to areas of concern in his psychological field. Learners who have little need to know and understand quite naturally expend little learning effort; manifest an insufficiently meaningful learning set; fail to develop precise meanings, to reconcile new ideas with existing concepts, and to formulate new propositions in their own words; and do not devote enough time and energy to practice and review. Material is therefore never sufficiently consolidated to form an adequate foundation for sequential learning.[11]

Intrinsic motivation to learn is derived generally from natural curiosity and its related predisposition to explore, to manipulate, and to cope with the environment. Theoretically, meaningful school learning, when successful, furnishes its own reward. Acquisition of knowledge is an end objective to be desired. Teachers should never completely give up the idea that with adequate success experience in the learning situation, intrinsic motivation can be developed. This is most apt to happen when a teacher is able to generate contagious excitement and enthusiasm about the subject he teaches, and when he is the type of person with whom the learner can identify.

Because it is true that lower-class students will, characteristically, assume a more anti-intellectual and pragmatic attitude toward the academic purposes of the school, motivation becomes a major problem. For the new teacher, it may indeed be much harder to establish motivations that are intrinsic in value, but intrinsic motivation is *more* necessary with the inner city child than with the typical middle class. Intrinsic motivations probably require more immediate rewards, more incentive to job acquisition, more concrete kinds of experiences to make learning meaningful.

---

[11]David P. Ausubel, "A Teaching Strategy for Culturally Deprived Pupils: Cognitive and Motivational Considerations," *The School Review*, 71:457, Winter, 1963.

THE CULTURAL CHASM RECONSIDERED

The Ideals Espoused, the Middle-class Realities and the View From Beneath*

By Ralph Segalman, ASCW, Ph.D.

The concept of	The ideal meaning	The Middle-class reality meaning.	The Lower-class reality meaning.
Authority (courts, police, school principal)	Someone we helped choose and whose activities we are responsible for.	Security—to be taken for granted, wooed and used for personal benefit.	Something to be hated and avoided.
Education	A means of learning more about the world God gave us.	The road to better things for one's children and one's self.	An obstacle course to be surmounted until children can go to work.
Joining a Church	To recharge our spiritual and ethical batteries and motivations.	Affiliation for social acceptance and activity.	An emotional release.
Ideal Goal	To be a better person.	Money, property, to be accepted by the successful.	"Coolness;" to make out without attracting the attention of the authority.
Society	Something we all are responsible for and from which we cannot stand idly by.	The pattern one conforms to in the interest of security and being "popular."	"The Man"—An enemy to be resisted and suspected.
Delinquency	An act of injustice to someone or one's self.	An evil originating outside the middleclass home.	One of life's inevitable events to be ignored unless the police get into the act.

*Portions of the above chart are reproduced from *Harpers* and the *Rocky Mountain Social Science Journal.* Reprinted with permission of the author, Ralph Segalman.

THE CULTURAL CHASM RECONSIDERED
(continued)

The concept of	The ideal meaning	The Middle-class reality meaning	The Lower-class reality meaning
The Future	Something which we make for ourselves (subject to supernatural cancellation).	A rosy horizon.	Non-existent. So live each moment fully.
"The Street"	A road for which we are responsible and which we need to use responsibly.	A path for the auto—somewhere to throw our used beer cans and cigarette wrappers.	A meeting place, an escape from a crowded home, the place where the "action" is.
Liquor	Something to be used with caution and for fulfillment.	Sociability; cocktail parties, etc.	A means to welcome oblivion.
Violence	Something to be abhorred, as destructive to humans.	A last resort of authorities for protecting the law-abiding; is acceptable when used.	A tool for living and getting on. A way of getting attention of those who won't listen.
Sex	Only a part of (but important part of) a deeper mutual intertwining of two lives.	An adventure and a binding force for the family-creating problems of birth control.	A tool for living and getting on —usually short in time and "body centered."
Money	Something to be used for personal growth and participation in further support and improvement of society.	A resource to be cautiously spent and saved for the future.	Something to be used quickly before it disappears.

McCreary finds:

> Early in the school careers of many socially disadvantaged youths, teachers notice an eagerness, a very great responsiveness to new experiences and especially to the kindness, personal attention, and assistance that some teachers give. Some children come to school very early in the morning, because they like the teacher and the warmth, physical and personal, that they find in the classroom. Some want to stay on after school to help the teacher or to talk with her. But for far too many, the early responsiveness to affection and to learning is destroyed by experiences of failure. Teachers need to find ways to strengthen and maintain the initial enthusiasm for school characteristic of many disadvantaged children by providing continuing opportunities for success and recognition.[12]

Levy studied elementary education at Harvard and did student teaching in a middle-class school in Lexington. Then she writes of her experience as a fourth grade teacher in Harlem:

> What impressed me most was the fact that my children (9-10 years old) are already cynical and disillusioned about school, themselves, and life-in-general. They are hostile, rebellious, and bitter. Some belong to gangs, some sniff glue, and some even have police records. They are hyperactive and are constantly in motion. . . .[13]
>
> Most teachers . . . grow up in and are trained to work in a middle-class environment. Working in a Negro slum school is in many ways like going to a foreign country. The values, interests, goals, experiences, and even language of the children are quite different and often in conflict with the middle-class oriented school and its teachers.[14]

Levy further emphasizes two points in teacher education:

> . . . need to train teachers to be able to deal with and attempt to overcome their own "culture shock" and "culture bias" . . . need to be prepared to deal with parents who may be illiterate or partly illiterate, concerned but helpless, or hostile and abusive.[15]

Deutsch, studying underprivileged Negro children in New York City, found that early in life Negro children develop a "negative self-image." His observers recorded derogatory remarks made by teachers toward individual children:

> The most frequent such remark was to call a child "stupid," and as a result, the teacher, and through the teacher, the school played a role

---

[12]Eugene McCreary, "Some Positive Characteristics of Disadvantaged Learners and Their Implications for Education," in S. W. Webster, editor, *The Disadvantaged Learner* (San Francisco: Chandler Publishing Company, 1966), pp. 51-52.

[13]Betty Levy, "An Urban Teacher Speaks Out," in Staten W. Webster, editor, *The Disadvantaged Learner* (San Francisco: Chandler Publishing Company, 1966), p. 430.

[14]*Ibid.*, p. 434.

[15]*Ibid.*, p. 435.

in reinforcing the negative self-image of the child, and contributed a negative reason for learning.[16]

Bettelheim indicates that occasionally teachers "mis-read" children's behavior and do not really understand the deep-seated feelings children have. He counsels teachers to take seriously the remarks of the hurt child:

> If a child says to you, "I hate your ugly white face," you are certainly going to be bothered unless you don't take the child seriously. . . . If we don't take a person's nasty remarks seriously, that means that we really don't take him seriously. It implies, "You're irresponsible, no good, of no account." Because if a person is of any account, then it seems to me that we must take seriously what he says.[17]

Henry, in an article called "White People's Time, Colored People's Time," says:

> Poor children often come to school unfed, after wretched nights torn by screaming, fighting, bed-wetting; often they cannot sleep because of cold and rats. They come to class hungry, sleepy, and emotionally upset. To start routine schoolwork effectively at once is impossible.[18]

To attempt, constructively, to meet this problem, Henry suggests:

> Their teachers should breakfast with them at school. The school should, of course, furnish the food, perhaps out of government surplus. School breakfast would accomplish two things: it would feed hungry children, otherwise unable to concentrate adequately on their work; and it would bring teacher and pupil together in an informal and friendly atmosphere, associated with satisfaction, before the strain of classroom constriction and peer-group pressures dictate that teacher become an enemy. It is essential, therefore, that the teacher be present.[19]

A program like this suggested by Dr. Henry in Kansas City brought about immediate and sharp improvement in attendance, behavior, and in schoolwork. The more the teachers know about the emotional management of these children, the better.

President Nixon's message to Congress on the Economic Opportunity Act emphasizes pointedly the current thinking about providing during the early years the intellectual stimulation needed to enable the child

---

[16]Martin Deutsch, *Minority Gorup and Class Status as Related to Social and Personality Factors in Scholastic Achievement*, Monograph No. 2 (Ithaca: The Society for Applied Anthropology, Cornell University, 1960), p. 26.

[17]Bruno Bettelheim, "Teaching the Disadvantaged," *NEA Journal*, September, 1965.

[18]Jules Henry, "White People's Time, Colored People's Time," in S. W. Webster, editor, *The Disadvantaged Learner* (San Francisco: Chandler Publishing Company, 1966), p. 190.

[19]*Ibid.*

of the inner city poor to be able to interact with the middle-class child when he enrolls in the public school:[20]

> We have learned . . . that environment has its greatest impact on the development of intelligence when that development is proceeding most rapidly—that is, in those earliest years. . . . So crucial is the matter of early growth that we must make a national commitment to providing all American children an opportunity for healthful and stimulating development during the first five years of life.

III. LANGUAGE AND CONCEPT DEVELOPMENT TO IMPROVE LITERACY SKILLS

The inner city child may have come to school at age six without ever having had his mother sing him the traditional lullabies, and with no knowledge of the nursery rhymes, neither may he know any of the fairy stories or the folklore of his country. He may have taken few trips—Deutsch found many children had not been farther than two miles from home even in downtown New York City. He may well be a child of a minority group, a product of inferior schools, taught by indifferent teachers. Even by age six, he has been isolated from many rich experiences others his age have enjoyed. His isolation may have been caused by poverty, meagerness of intellectual resources at home, or by the incapacity, illiteracy or indifference of the adults with whom he has lived.

Brooks recommends:

1. Standard English should and can be taught successfully as though it were a second language to children who speak non-standard English as a result of cultural differences or cultural deprivation, and
2. If standard English is taught as a second language it is not necessary to insist that the child reject entirely the other or "first" language.[21]

Language serves different purposes for the lower-class, inner city child. For him, language controls others more than it conveys information. The child learns to respond because the speaker is a figure of authority. Verbal interchange is apt to be orders, requests, or threats expressed in single words, idiomatic expressions, or short sentences.

The language of the disadvantaged child is considered substandard by the middle-class employer. His language might better be considered

---

[20]From the President's message to Congress on the Economic Opportunity Act, *A News Summary of the War on Poverty,* Office of Economic Opportunity, February 24, 1969.

[21]Charlotte K. Brooks, "Some Approaches to Teaching English as a Second Language," in William A. Stewart, editor, *Non-Standard Speech and the Teaching of English* (Washington, D. C.: Center for Applied Linguistics, 1964).

non-standard since it is an effective way for him to communicate at home and with his friends. Effective communication is the primary goal of language. However, if the disadvantaged child is to have a fair chance in our mobile society, he must learn standard English for use in school and on the job. He may retain his dialect for use with family and close friends.[22]

Della-Dora states three implications for the school if it hopes to move toward a solution of the problems of the culturally disadvantaged. There must be increased coordinated effort among schools, local government, and other social and civic agencies; school faculties must carry out academic studies of the impact of social-class differences on students and teachers and these studies need to be done school by school; and there must be direct teaching aimed at changing attitudes and self-concepts for both students and their parents.[23]

Planning teaching strategies for the culturally deprived child requires three basic considerations: gearing the initial teaching to the learner's existing state of readiness; providing the necessary foundation for successful sequential learning; and providing structured learning materials that will facilitate efficient sequenced learning.[24] Such planning demands rigid elimination of all subject matter that the learner cannot economically assimilate at his present level of academic functioning.

Shepard's program, in the St. Louis Schools, asked the parents:

> Manage the homework. See that your children have a time and a place to study. Give them a good light, and shut off the radio and TV. Above all, make sure they increase their skill in reading. That's the key that will give them a better life than yours.[25]

The child was given a homework assignment notebook to be signed each week by the parents. To expand their horizons, field trips were planned to radio and television studios, the St. Louis planetarium, the zoo, museums, parks, the Jefferson Memorial, the famous Shaw gardens, the city markets. In six years, the elementary schools in this program raised the general achievement for Negro pupils to the national norms for white children.

The San Francisco Program includes provision for small groups of disadvantaged elementary school pupils taught by techniques that allow

---

[22]Ellen Newman, "An Experiment in Oral Language," in Staten W. Webster, editor, *The Disadvantaged Learner* (San Francisco: Chandler Publishing Company, 1966), p. 570.

[23]Delmo Della-Dora, "The Culturally Disadvantaged: Educational Implications of Certain Social-Cultural Phenomena," in Everett T. Keach, editor, *et al.*, *Education and Social Crisis: Perspectives on Teaching Disadvantaged Youth* (New York: John Wiley and Sons, Inc., 1967), pp. 279-280.

[24]David P. Ausubel, "A Teaching Strategy for Culturally Deprived Pupils: Cognitive and Motivational Considerations," *The School Review*, 71: 454-455, Winter, 1963.

[25]Paul Friggens, "Sam Shepard's Faith," *Readers Digest*, March, 1964.

them to look, to listen, and to touch. They are also taken on field trips beyond the narrow six-block area in which many slum children live from day to day. Audio-visual devices—records, tape recorders, and filmstrips —are used. Specific plans are made for discussing or reading aloud in order to correct speech patterns, build vocabulary, broaden concepts, and elevate levels of aspiration.[26]

In the Hough Community Project in Cleveland, parent education in informal group meetings at schools and a strong reading improvement program are major concerns. Saturday morning recreation programs and one week of summer camp have also been very worthwhile aspects.[27]

> . . . a broad range of health services is offered, including physical examinations for newcomers, dental examinations and hearing tests, revaccination, tuberculin tests, and persistent follow-up in cases of referral for correction and treatment of physical defects.[28]

One of the Philadelphia programs provides for an on-school-time in-service training program for teachers. While the teachers are attending in-service sessions, their classes participate in a carefully planned program of story-telling, literature films, filmstrips, and recordings. Library books have been provided to support the special literature program. This program has been very effective in raising reading achievement levels.[29]

The Junior High School 43 Project in New York City, in a comprehensive approach to the effective education of culturally disadvantaged children, provided all of the following services: systematic guidance and counseling; clinical services when indicated; a cultural enrichment program which included trips to the theater, museums, opera, college campuses; a parent-education program; and a systematic supplementary remedial program in reading, mathematics, and languages.[30]

When teachers have a low expectation level for their children's learning, the children seldom exceed that expectation, which is a self-fulfilling prophecy.

> Acceptance of the child is of vital importance. It is based on a firm belief that the child is capable of self-determination. It seems to be a respect for the child's ability to be a thinking, independent, constructive human being.[31]

---

[26]Dorsey Baynham, "The Great Cities Projects," in Everett T. Keach, editor, *et al., Education and Social Crisis: Perspectives on Teaching Disadvantaged Youth* (New York: John Wiley and Sons, Inc., 1967), p. 328.

[27]*Ibid.*, p. 329.

[28]*Ibid.*

[29]*Ibid.*, pp. 329-330.

[30]Kenneth B. Clark, "Educational Stimulation of Racially Disadvantaged Children," in Everett T. Keach, editor, *et al., Education and Social Crisis: Perspectives on Teaching Disadvantaged Youth* (New York: John Wiley and Sons, Inc., 1967), p. 308.

[31]Virginia Mae Axline, *Play Therapy* (Boston: Houghton Mifflin, 1947), p. 21.

When a teacher respects the dignity of a child, whether or not he be six or sixteen, and treats the child with understanding, kindliness, and constructive help, she is developing in him an ability to look within himself for the answers to his problems, and to become responsible for himself as an independent individual in his own right.

Possibly the greatest contribution that educators can make to the younger generation is the type of guidance that places the emphasis on self-initiative and transmits to the young people by living example the fact that each individual is responsible for himself. In the final analysis, it is the ability to think constructively and independently that marks the educated man. Growth is a gradual process. It cannot be hurried. It comes from within the individual and cannot be imposed by force from without.

It is the relationship that exists between the teacher and her pupils that is the important thing. The teacher's responses must meet the real needs of the children and not just the material needs—reading, writing, arithmetic.[32]

Our culturally disadvantaged inner city schools contain thousands of boys and girls who are innately bright, intellectually speaking. The schools must identify those individuals and challenge and stimulate them so that they will be sure to overcome the shackles of poverty and keep alive their intellectual curiosity. Perhaps the highly intelligent student who is culturally disadvantaged is one of the most neglected in our system of mass education. Stimulation for him in enriched programs in language, social studies, and general science early in the elementary school may keep him motivated to succeed in the intellectual life.[33]

IV. ADAPT READING TO THE CHILD'S NEED

Reissman has written about discrimination of rather obvious and well-documented forms against the lower-lower-class child in the schools:

. . . the reading texts used in the classrooms which typically contain material far less attuned to the interests of the disadvantaged; the Parent-Teacher Associations which often patronize or ignore underprivileged parents; the intelligence tests, the applicability of which to lower socio-economic groups is increasingly being questioned; the school psychologists and guidance counselors, who frequently underestimate the possibility of the economically underprivileged child going to college; the friendship cliques and clubs which favor less the child from a poor neighborhood; the teacher's unfavorable images and expectations which militate against the respect and encouragement so needed by the child.[34]

---

[32]*Ibid.*, pp. 75-76.

[33]Staten W. Webster, editor, *The Disadvantaged Learner*, Part III, The Disadvantaged Learner (San Francisco: Chandler Publishing Company, 1966), pp. 580-581.

[34]Frank Reissman, *The Culturally Deprived Child* (New York: Harper and Row, 1962), pp. 17-18.

The children of the inner city poor:

1. Are not accustomed to listening to long speeches and cannot concentrate very long in a strictly verbal situation.
2. Have trouble expressing themselves, and typically do not verbalize well in response to words alone. (Role playing can be used in many ways: role-playing can be a way to stimulate discussion and thinking; role playing can help the teacher determine how clearly students understand concepts.)
3. Need teachers who can combine the traditional behaviors inherent in structure, order, discipline, and firm expectations for achievement on the one hand and practical methods of learning by doing on the other.
4. Do anticipate failure and have anxiety about failing.
5. "Sense" the teacher's attitude and know if it is one of acceptance or rejection.
6. May best be helped, not by junior and senior high school enrichment programs, but by reaching down into the pre-school years and building readiness experiences in the lives of the threes and the fours.

> Least effective are the readers set in middle-class or suburban environments with children who never cheat or steal, who do not have to fight for life, sustenance,. and recognition; who are never frustrated, thwarted or defeated; who never seemingly encounter parental tyranny, yellow, red, or black skins; who do not know poverty, squalor, hunger or fatigue. They do know these—only they know them outside of their books. Out of school they frequently have experienced these and even more impressive facts of life.[35]

The Language Experience Approach to Reading

The language experience approach to reading, competently developed, may offer the child of the inner city poor a better chance of success in learning to read than does the traditional "basal reader" approach to reading. These children have not learned to listen as well as more advantaged children; neither do they speak as well nor have as large vocabularies. If they have had the privilege of nursery school and kindergarten in an enriched, permissive environment where many, many language experiences were nurtured, they will be ready to progress to the language experience story early in first grade. However, if they have had no previous school experience, then the teacher must provide all the language development and concept development which children need *before* they are ready to read. If the words "reading program" were

---

[35]William Jenkins, "Reading Skills in Teaching Literature in the Elementary School," *Elementary English*, November, 1964, cited by Edith V. Walker, "In-Service Training of Teachers to Work with the Disadvantaged," *The Reading Teacher*, 18:497, March, 1965.

changed to "language program" the teacher might proceed in a more realistic manner. The reader is referred to the chapter on beginning reading for the concise statements about the weaknesses and strengths of basal and language experience programs. While basal reader programs provide an abundance of suggestions for teaching reading skills effectively to the middle-class children, there may be more effective ways of reaching the children of illiterate or semi-literate parents in inner city.

Teachers of the children of the inner city poor must, in the same spirit of all other teachers, teach diagnostically. Without first diagnosing learning difficulties, it will not be possible to provide for the conditions of effective teaching and learning. Effective diagnostic teaching will require:

1. Sophistication on the part of the teacher about what the developmental skills in reading are and how to teach them.
2. Competence in using remedial reading teaching techniques.
3. Ability to organize and routinize classroom procedures so that maximum effort can be directed toward teaching and learning.
4. Ability to effectively handle aggression and violence.
5. Understanding of the non-standard dialect of English that may be used by the majority and a gradual acceptance on the part of the group of learning "standard-English" as a second language.
6. Ability to decide when a child should be referred to specialized personnel for further diagnosis of problems.
7. Acceptance of the boys and girls as people and an ability to realize personal satisfaction in working with them.

Reading for the inner city child should:

1. Avoid the textbooks that emphasize and stereotype the middle-class life style. Black reports a study in an elementary school in the Los Angeles area in which a selected group of first grade children were taught reading through the language experience approach. The language experience approach was supplemented by the use of preprimers twice a week, a related activity book, and a multitude of trade books.[36]
2. Provide many other kinds of experiences than *just reading*. Activities that include acting out, role playing, dramatization, use of audio-visual aids.
3. Teach the boys and girls "school know-how." If the language of the school—the expressions teachers generally use—is not familiar, it should be taught directly. Knowing how to ask questions, knowing

---

[36]Millard H. Black, "Beginning Reading Programs for the Culturally Disadvantaged," in *Perspective in Reading: First Grade Reading Programs* (Newark, Delaware 18711: International Reading Association, 1965), p. 167.

how to take tests, knowing how to utilize guidance opportunities are very important and may make the difference between success and failure for the child.

4. Combat the anti-intellectual attitude apt to prevail. The teacher's first responsibility is to understand the nature of an anti-intellectual attitude and to accept it. Some of the reading experiences suggested in other activities here may be helpful in stimulating higher levels of aspiration and in developing intrinsic motivation.

5. Reading itself cannot masculinize the school but it might help boys identify with mature, stable, striving, successful male adult figures. In this way the boys might be encouraged to higher, yet realistic, aspirations and also to develop the necessary stable personalities to achieve their goals.

6. Help children choose reading material that shows people as they actually respond to the color, ethnic, or social-class bars in housing, education, employment; and then help them evaluate critically what they read.

7. Acquaint culturally deprived boys and girls with examples of successful professional people originating from their own racial, ethnic, and class backgrounds. The bulletin prepared by the National Council of Teachers of English, *We Build Together*, provides a teacher with an extensive annotated bibliography of books about Negro people.[37]

8. Parents should be encouraged, sympathetically, to accept and lend support to ambitions and aspirations expressed by their children. When parents can be enlisted either as volunteers in the school or as aides, their presence in the school atmosphere can be an asset in interpreting the school to the community.

SUMMARY

This chapter has contained a discussion of the culture of poverty, of the problems faced by the child who lives in poverty, and some of the language and concept needs of many of the inner city poor. Segalman has provided a concise contrast of the value systems of the middle-class teacher and the lower class child. A few great cities rehabilitation programs that have been successful have been identified.

Suggested Activities

1. Outline some specific adjustments you would expect to make in your reading program if you were an elementary teacher in inner city.

---

[37]Charlemae Rollins, editor, *We Build Together: A Reader's Guide to Negro Life and Literature for Elementary and High School Use* (Champaign, Illinois: National Council of Teachers of English, 1967).

Start first with the basal reader program and explain how you would modify it; then start with a language experience approach and explain how you would expect to modify it.

2. Review the strengths and weaknesses of different approaches to teaching beginning reading and select which elements you think would be most helpful from any of the methods in teaching inner city children.

3. Contrast "poverty" and middle-class cultures.

4. Enumerate the consequences of the poverty culture which have implications for educating the children of the poor.

5. List specific needs of the ghetto child that are related to reading.

6. Describe ways in which the reading program may be adapted to meet specific needs.

READING REFERENCES

ALLEN, VIRGINIA FRENCH. "Teaching Standard English as a Second Dialect," *Teachers College Record,* 68:355-370, February, 1967.

BETTELHEIM, BRUNO. "Teaching the Disadvantaged," *NEA Journal,* September, 1965.

BLACK, MILLARD H. "Programs for the Culturally Disadvantaged," *Perspectives in Reading: First Grade Reading Programs.* Newark, Delaware 19711: International Reading Association, 1965, pp. 150-172.

BLOOM, S. B., DAVIS, A., and HESS, R. *Compensatory Education for Cultural Deprivation.* New York: Holt, Rinehart and Winston, 1965.

Board of Education of the City of New York. *Non-Standard Dialect.* Champaign, Illinois: National Council of Teachers of English, 1968.

DAVIS, A. L., editor. *On the Dialects of Children.* Champaign, Illinois: National Council of Teachers of English, 1968.

DILLARD, J. L. "The English Teacher and the Language of the Newly Integrated Student," *Teachers College Record,* 68:115-120, February, 1967.

EVERTTS, ELDONNA, editor. *Dimensions of Dialect.* Champaign, Illinois: Naational Council of Teachers of English, 1967.

FRAZER, ALEXANDER, editor. *Educating the Children of the Poor.* Champaign, Illinois: National Council of Teachers of English, 1968.

GOTTLIEB, DAVID, and RAMSEY, CHARLES E. *Understanding Children of Poverty.* Chicago: Science Research Associates, Inc., 1967.

HENRY, JULES. "White People's Time, Colored People's Time," *Trans-Action,* 2:2, March-April, 1965.

HOLBROOK, DAVID. *English for the Rejected.* New York: Cambridge Press, 1964.

LEWIS, OSCAR. *The Children of Sanchez, Autobiography of a Mexican Family.* New York: Vintage Books, A Division of Random House, 1961.

PASSOW, HARRY A. *Education in Depressed Areas.* New York: Bureau of Publications, Teachers College, Columbia University, 1963.

REISSMAN, FRANK. *The Culturally Deprived Child.* New York: Harper and Row, 1962.

WALKER, EDITH V. "In-Service Training of Teachers to Work with the Disadvantaged," *The Reading Teacher,* 18:493-498, March, 1965.

WEBSTER, STATEN W., editor. *The Disadvantaged Learner.* San Francisco, California: Chandler Publishing Company, 1966.

A good beginning for boys and girls in the primary grades is based on an adequate screening and sorting process to determine which ones learn best verbally, which ones lack adequate motor coordination, and which ones enter school emotionally immature.

Diagnostic teaching requires that the teacher continually examine and re-examine teaching failure and insure that children are taught at levels at which they can succeed. Teaching diagnostically demands that causes of reading failure are carefully analyzed to permit rehabilitative teaching.

Lee has very wisely said:[1]

> Diagnostic teaching permits the child to deal with familiar concepts and procedures as he continues his growth in the unfamiliar school setting. When the school year opens with a plan of procedures, a set of materials, a topic on which to focus, many children are placed at a disadvantage; the teacher loses much valuable time and a variety of opportunities for enriching the learning that children already have.
>
> Some instructional programs are now swamping children with a multitude of experiences which their meager backgrounds ill prepare them to perceive or from which they can gain little meaning.

[1]Dorris M. Lee, *Diagnostic Teaching* (1201 Sixteenth St., N.W., Washington, D. C. 20036: Department of Elementary-Kindergarten-Nursery Education, National Education Association, 1966), p. 9.

16

The Concept of
Reading Readiness

Since our society is deeply entrenched in a traditional practice of starting all children to first grade at age six, chronological age has become the only criterion for deciding if children are "ready" for this new and exciting adventure. Of course, chronological age will be the only characteristic that many of these children have in common even though it is the least important in assessing whether or not each child has the psychological, intellectual, and neurological maturity to profit from this experience.

Because the school accepts children who are chronologically six, it needs to provide for a much better sorting and selecting process after the children arrive so that each one can be kept learning and developing *appropriate behaviors at his growing edge of learning.* Those who are already reading should be encouraged to continue reading, with proper precaution that reading isn't being emphasized to the exclusion of all the other areas of growth and development. For those children who are "ready" to read, there is no reason to insist that they complete "all the pages in a readiness workbook" just because the school has a copy for each child to use. They can begin reading if they are "ready" to read. However, many children, perhaps a sizeable minority of all the children, lack language skills, lack vocabulary concepts, lack experiences with the middle-class life pictured and assured in most of the textbooks children will read. Moreover, in perhaps one child in ten or twelve, English has not been the first language of the home. With our extremely mobile population today, it becomes necessary for every elementary teacher to know something about English as a second language.

There is an optimal time for learning. Those skills that build upon currently developing behavior are most easily learned. If a child does not have such developing behavior for learning to read, then he is apt not to learn to read. Reading readiness should be thought of as preparatory

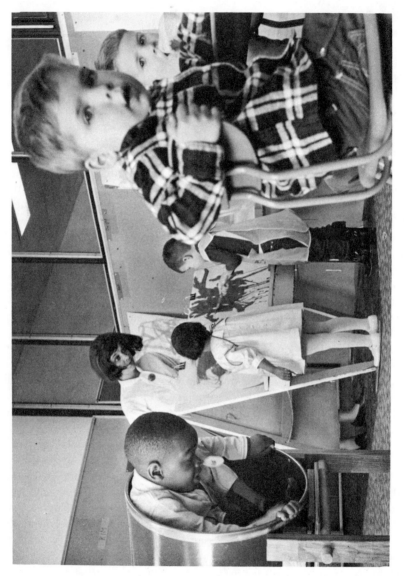

Will these boys and girls be ready to read? Photo courtesy University of New Mexico Photo Service.

adjustment to the reading situation. If skills are missing at any step of the way, they should be developed before confronting the child with the abstract process of reading.

The more mature the learner, the less adaptation is needed to attain a given level of proficiency in acquiring specific skills. This is clearly demonstrated in any large group of six year old children; some few have learned how to read, some are optimally ready for learning to read; and some will not exhibit this developing behavior for some time. Children who are permitted to learn to read *when they are ready* will generally learn easily and read a great deal.

Teaching "formal" readiness and beginning reading before the child has appropriate neurological, psychological, or intellectual maturation is almost sure to result in failure to achieve the standards set by the school. This "too early" attempt may cause the child to develop no natural curiosity about reading and may be the beginning of emotional problems that will later become stumbling blocks to learning.[1]

The child who is ready to read is one who has achieved a criterion level of intellectual development, possesses a body of relevant knowledge, and has control of the "grammar" of the language he will read. Obviously, this statement is a subjective one and has only a relative value. There is a minimum functioning level of use of concepts, verbalizing and general understanding before the child is greatly interested in such an abstract process as deciphering the printed word.

Two very important related areas which the teacher must also evaluate are the child's emotional stability and maturity and his physical and neurological development. The child will not learn to read well if he has problems in vision and hearing or if he lacks visual-perceptual skills required for reading.

The jobs of the first grade teacher then should be those of evaluating children's skills when they come to the first grade, determining their degree of readiness for the reading act, and making sure that those who give evidence of lack of readiness in any area have opportunity to develop needed skills *before* they are presented formal reading tasks.

Much of what has traditionally been done in readiness programs has been ineffective because whole groups of children have been asked to work through skills which many of them already knew well and a few understood neither before nor after the teaching.

The present point of view is that the teacher must, with whatever supplemental judgment she can generate from the principal, the school nurse, school social worker, school psychologist, and reading supervisor, determine the learning levels of children and keep them growing toward

---

[1]Based on Ernest R. Hilgard, *Theories of Learning* (New York: Appleton-Century-Crofts, Inc., 1957), pp. 60-63.

maturity without regard to their place on a learning continuum when they enroll.

The following section will indicate and discuss briefly several standardized measuring instruments that might be used in a school to provide the classroom teacher with the kinds of information that would make it possible for her to more confidently make judgments about the learning levels of children in her class. Section II contains a discussion of language and concept development in young children. Section III contains a discussion of the complexity of "being ready."

I. EVALUATING CHILDREN WHO MAY NOT BE READY FOR READING

Psychologists have now developed a number of different tests that afford investigation into many areas of the child's skills and abilities—a composite of many of the general abilities which are known to be necessary for successful performance in school. Among these tests are:
1. *The Illinois Test of Psycholinguistic Abilities* (ITPA).[2]

The Illinois Test of Psycholinguistic Abilities is designed to measure language development of young children. It was originally conceived as an instrument for assessing language in exceptional children of preschool age. Those children who lack sufficient depth of cognitive language for beginning reading in first grade need some kind of assessment to discover areas of weakness so that they can be developed. This test is a good measure to help determine these weaknesses. The test contains the following sub-tests:

1. Auditory-Vocal Automatic Test. This test samples the child's knowledge of standard sentence usage of inflected forms of words:
   "Here is an apple. Here are two_____."
   "This box is big. This box is even_____."
   "This man is painting. He is a _____."
   "Father is hanging a picture. Now the picture has been_____."
2. Visual Decoding Test. This test asks the child to locate, among several pictures, the stimulus picture previously presented. For example, on one page is a picture of a shoe. On the following page are many pictures, one of which is a shoe. The child must point to the shoe.
3. Motor Encoding Test. The child is shown a picture and he must gesture to demonstrate the use of the object. For example, for the picture of a cup, the child simulates drinking; for pencil, he simulates writing.

---

[2] By Samuel A. Kirk and James J. McCarthy (Champaign: University of Illinois Press, 1968).

PROFILE OF ABILITIES

DEVELOPMENTAL AGES

YEARS AND MONTHS	CA	MA	PLA	OTHER
10-0				
9-6				
9-0				
8-6				
8-0				
7-6				
7-0				
6-6				
6-0				
5-6				
5-0				
4-6				
4-0				
3-6				
3-0				
2-6				

ITPA SCORES

REPRESENTATIONAL LEVEL / AUTOMATIC LEVEL

SCALED SCORES	Reception (Auditory / Visual)		Association (Auditory / Visual)		Expression (Verbal / Manual)		Closure (Grammatic / Visual)		Sequential Memory (Auditory / Visual)		Supplementary Tests (Auditory Closure / Sound Blending)	
64												
60												
56												
52												
48												
44												
40												
36												
32												
28												
24												
20												
16												
12												
8												
4												

*Samuel A. Kirk, James J. McCarthy, and Winifred D. Kirk, *Illinois List of Psycholinguistic Abilities: Revised Edition* (Urbana: University of Illinois Press, 1968). Used by permission.

Summary Sheet

SUBTEST	REPRESENTATIONAL LEVEL								AUTOMATIC LEVEL								
	AUDITORY-VOCAL			VISUAL-MOTOR				AUDITORY-VOCAL				VISUAL-MOTOR				
	Raw Score	Age Score	Scaled Score	Raw Score	Age Score	Scaled Score		Raw Score	Age Score	Scaled Score		Raw Score	Age Score	Scaled Score		
AUDITORY RECEPTION																
VISUAL RECEPTION																
VISUAL MEMORY																
AUDITORY ASSOCIATION																
AUDITORY MEMORY																
VISUAL ASSOCIATION																
VISUAL CLOSURE																
VERBAL EXPRESSION																
GRAMMATIC CLOSURE																
MANUAL EXPRESSION																
(Supplementary tests) AUDITORY CLOSURE																
SOUND BLENDING																

SUMMARY SCORES: Sum of Raw Scores [ ]   Composite PLA [ ]   Sum of SS [ ]   Mean SS [ ]   Median SS [ ]

*Samuel A. Kirk, James J. McCarthy and Winifred D. Kirk, *Illinois List of Psycholinguistic Abilities: Revised Edition* (Urbana: University of Illinois Press, 1968). Used by permission.

4. Auditory-Vocal Association Test. This is a test relating verbal symbols by analogy. For example, "I sit on a chair. I sleep on a _____." "Cotton is soft; stones are _____." "A rabbit is swift; a turtle is____."
5. Visual-Motor Sequencing Test. This test measures the ability to reproduce a sequence of visual stimuli from memory. For example, the examiner places in the tray, in this order, pictures of dog, potato, cat. They are then removed and the child is to make one just like the examiner's. Geometric figures are used: triangles, squares, circles, hexagons, diamonds, pentagons, and trapezoids.
6. Vocal Encoding Test. The child is asked to "tell all he can" about a simple object such as a block or a ball. The examiner can help him get started by asking questions for the first object: what is it? what is it made of? what color is it? and what do you use it for?
7. The Auditory-Vocal Sequencing Test is a test of the child's ability to reproduce a sequence of digits from memory. Digits in sequences beginning with two numbers are pronounced at the uniform rate of two per second.
8. Visual-Motor Association Test. This test measures the ability to relate a pictured stimuli to one picture in a series. For example, the stimuli picture is *sock* to be related to *hammer* or *shoe*.
9. Auditory Decoding Test. This test measures the child's understanding of oral questions.

Do you eat?	Do cars cry?
Do you rain?	Do bananas telephone?
Do airplanes fly?	Do goats eat?

A profile of any child's abilities using these nine scores, prepared to test language ages between three and nine, can show the teacher diagnostically in which areas of language development the child is weak. Teaching can then be directed to these needs.

The ITPA results in a language-age for the individual child. The profile makes clear in which of the nine sub-tests the child is performing below his age level, at his age level, or above age level. Such information could be most useful to the classroom teacher in planning concept development, language experiences, or other growth areas for the child. The profile and summary sheets of the 1968 edition of the ITPA are shown on pages 377-8.

2. *The Valett Developmental Survey of Basic Learning Abilities.*[3]

Valett Developmental Survey of Basic Learning Abilities, by Robert E. Valett, is a survey of seven major categories of readiness abilities. It

---

[3]Robert E. Valett, *Valett Development Survey of Basic Learning Abilities* (577 College Avenue, Palo Alto, California: Consulting Psychologist Press, 1966).

is administered by the classroom teacher and can be profiled to show areas of strengths and weaknesses. The seven major categories are:

1. Motor Integration and Physical Development
2. Tactile Discrimination
3. Auditory Discrimination
4. Visual-Motor Coordination
5. Visual Discrimination
6. Language Development and Verbal Fluency
7. Conceptual Development.

If a survey of abilities can provide the teacher with an indication of those areas in which the child is not functioning normally, he can plan a program to meet these learning needs and build a more even profile in the child before introducing him to teaching levels where he is apt to experience failure.

3. *Pre-Reading Screening Procedures* and *Screening Tests for Identifying Children with Specific Language Disability* by Beth H. Slingerland.[4]

These tests support the rationale in the diagnostic teaching of reading. While no research has as yet appeared in the literature, first grade teachers, especially, should be aware of as many ways as possible to judge readiness for reading in beginning boys and girls. The purpose of the pre-reading screening procedures is to help teachers identify any children who make errors in perception or in recalling language symbols. Such errors alert teachers to possible specific language disabilities. Slingerland hopes that this screening device can help teachers divide children into those groups who are (1) all ready to learn to read by conventional methods; (2) alert and appear to be ready but need corrective instruction for perceptual difficulties; (3) not ready for formal instruction because of persistent reversals, language hesitation, and lack of fine muscle coordination; (4) lacking in readiness for reading in all areas; and (5) in need of individual testing and clinical referral. The readiness test measures discrimination of letter forms, discrimination of word forms, visual perception memory, visual-motor abilities in copying, visual-motor memory exercises, auditory discrimination and letter knowledge.

Three tests are available for screening to identify children with specific language disability: (1) Grade I and beginning Grade II; (2) Grade II and beginning Grade III; and (3) Grade III and Grade IV. The subtests include copying, visual perception memory, visual discrimination, auditory recall, auditory discrimination of sounds, and auditory association based on auditory-visual discrimination. Identifying weak-

---

[4]Beth H. Slingerland, *Screening Tests for Identifying Children with Specific Language Disability,* (Cambridge, Massachusetts 02138: Educators Publishing Service, 1969).

nesses in children's abilities makes possible the teaching of skills missing before the children experience failure and its concomitant psychological trauma. Children need minimal skills in all areas of growth and development if they are to succeed at the complicated task of learning to read.

4. *Predicting Reading Failure.* De Hirsch, Jansky, and Langford have selected ten tests that can be administered at the kindergarten level for determining the child's readiness for "formal school." These ten tests can be administered in about forty-five minutes after some familiarity has been established by the teacher. These authors have established critical score levels below which they expect the child will have difficulty.[5]

The following table[6] which resulted from scores of children who failed in beginning reading when contrasted with other children who did not fail is given by de Hirsch, *et al.*

TABLE 16.1. *Critical Score Levels on 10 Kindergarten Tests Included in the Predictive Index*

Test	*Score Range (best-poorest)*	*Critical Score Level*
1. Pencil Use	0 − 2	0 (Level expected for age)
2. Bender Visuo-Motor Gestalt (A, 1 , 2, 4, 6, 8)	0 − 6	(At least 5 designs copied correctly)
3. Auditory Discrimination (Wepman)	0 − 11	1 (X-error)
4. Number of words	594 − 54	226 words
5. Categories	0 − 3	(All series correctly categorized)
6. Reversals (Horst)	0 − 9	4 (at least 5 rows correctly matched)
7. Word matching (Gates)	0 − 12	3 (at least 9 words correctly paired)
8. Word Recognition I (Pack)	0 − 2	0 (both words identified)
9. Word Recognition II (Table)	0 − 2	0 (both words identified)
10. Word Reproduction	6 − 0	3 (No. of letters reproduced correctly)

Adaptation of table "Criitical Score Levels on 10 Kindergarten Tests Included in the Predictive Index," p. 114, from PREDICTING READING FAILURE by De Hirsch, Jansky and Langford. (Harper & Row, 1966).

De Hirsch and Jansky found that six tests which they administered —the Bender Gestalt, the drawing of human figure, auditory discrimination, classifying or putting things in categories, presence of reversals, and word recognition—distinguished the failing readers, the slow starters, and the high achievers with respect to school success at the end of the

[5]Katrina de Hirsch, Jeanette Jefferson Jansky, and William S. Langford, *Predicting Reading Failure* (New York: Harper and Row, 1966).
[6]*Ibid.,* p. 114.

second grade. With limited study and instruction, first grade teachers could evaluate beginning first grade boys and girls on all these abilities and rank them, after some experience, with considerable confidence. Such an endeavor could be a much needed step toward prevention of failure and set the stage for the diagnostic teaching needed to overcome weaknesses.[7]

De Hirsch and Jansky, concerning early identification of school failure in children, state:[8]

> Since development is by and large a consistent and lawful process, it seemed safe to assume that a kindergarten child's perceptuo-motor and oral language level would forecast his performance on such highly integrated tasks as reading, writing, and spelling. The tests covered several broad aspects of development: behavior and motility patterning; large and fine motor coordination; figure-ground discrimination; visuo-motor organization; auditory and visual perceptual competence; ability to comprehend and use language; and more specifically, reading-readiness.

5. *Individual Tests of General Intelligence*

A. *The Revised Stanford Binet Test of Intelligence.*[9] This test is also an individually administered test of general learning ability. It yields only one total score which is a mental age. It requires considerable manipulation at the three and four year old levels but becomes highly verbal at the older ages of childhood.

B. *The Weschler Intelligence Scale for Children.*[10] This test by David Weschler is an individually administered test of general learning ability. It obtains a verbal and a performance score separately and a total score from the combination of the two. The verbal section measures vocabulary, comprehension, information, similarities, and arithmetic. The performance section presents pictures to identify missing parts; one-inch cube blocks to reconstruct designs; a series of jigsaw puzzles, assembling pictures in sequence to tell a story; and mazes. An observant examiner may gain many worthwhile insights into a child's behavior during the administration of the test.

6. *Perceptual Survey Rating Scale*[11]

The Perceptual Survey Rating Scale, by Newell C. Kephart, evaluates children, typically between the ages of six and nine, in their abilities to

[7]Katrina de Hirsch and Jeannette J. Jansky, "Early Prediction of Reading, Writing, and Spelling Ability," in Marjorie Seddon Johnson and Roy A. Kress, editors, *Corrective Reading in the Elementary Classroom,* Perspectives in Reading No. 7 (Newark, Delaware 19711: International Reading Association, 1967), p. 50.
[8]*Ibid.,* p. 47.
[9]Published by Houghton Mifflin, Boston, Mass., 1960.
[10]Published by the Psychological Corporation, 304 East 45th Street, New York 17, New York.
[11]Newell C. Kephart and Eugene C. Roach, *The Purdue Perceptual Motor Survey* (Columbus, Ohio: Charles E. Merrill Books, Inc., 1966). See also, Newell C. Kephart, *The Slow Learner in the Classroom* (Columbus: Charles E. Merrill Books, Inc., 1960), pp. 120-155.

perform eleven motor or visual-motor or visual perception tasks: (1) The Walking board; (2) Jumping; (3) Identification of body parts; (4) Imitation of movements; (5) Obstacle course; (6) Angels-in-the-snow; (7) Stepping stones; (8) Chalkboard; (9) Ocular pursuits; (10) Visual achievement forms; and (11) the Kraus-Weber tests. Kephart is concerned with such factors in body image as laterality, directionality, control, and rhythm. Eye-foot coordination as well as eye-hand coordination help evaluate visual-motor abilities; ocular control, following the target easily, and figure-ground relationships are observed.

7. *The Vineland Social Maturity Scale*[12]

The Vineland Social Maturity Scale standardized by E. A. Doll, is a scale for measuring social development. The information for checking the scale is obtained by a skillful interview with the parent and may be supplemented by direct observation of the child. The items are equated with what would be expected normal development in children and evaluate self-help, locomotion, communication, self-direction, and socialization. A social age is determined by the total number of items passed. A social quotient is obtained by dividing the child's social age by his chronological age. As specific examples, a child at age two may be expected to ask to go to the toilet; a child at age four may be expected to wash his face unassisted; and a child at age six goes to bed unassisted.

8. *Developmental Test of Visual Perception*[13]

The Developmental Test of Visual Perception, by Frostig, has five parts. The perceptual skills measured are (1) Eye-Motor Coordination; (2) Figure-Ground; (3) Constancy of Shape; (4) Position in Space; and (5) Spatial Relationships. The test can be administered by the classroom teacher who has been well oriented to the test and has worked with another examiner. Administration time ranges from 30 to 45 minutes.

9. *The Visual Motor Gestalt Test*[14]

A sample, for orientation, and eight figures or designs are presented on individual cards with the instruction: "Here are some figures for you to copy; just copy them the way you see them." Evaluation depends upon not only the form of the reproduced figures, but also their relationship to each other, to the spatial background, to the time patterning, and to the clinical setting.

Primary teachers must develop competence in the use of some of these tests to use as screening devices. Diagnostic teaching requires that

[12]E. A. Doll, *The Measurement of Social Competence* (Philadelphia: Educational Test Bureau, 1953).

[13]Marianne Frostig, *Developmental Test of Visual Perception* and *Administration and Scoring Manual* (Palo Alto, California: Consulting Psychologist Press, 1966).

[14]Lauretta Bender, *A Visual Motor Gestalt Test and its Clinical Use*. Research Monograph No. 3, American Orthopsychiatric Association, 1938.

the teacher find out *first* what the child does not know and help him overcome his weaknesses.

II. LANGUAGE AND CONCEPT DEVELOPMENT

In order that the teacher may place sufficient emphasis on developing language concepts, provide for thinking in the language, and deliberately work for expanded vocabulary, *planned, sequential verbal bombardment* is called for. This is probably the only way the culturally deprived child can ever hope to catch up sufficiently to profit from the compulsory school classes of middle-class schools. A "supercharged" verbal environment[15] will keep the children on the growing edge of learning as much of their short school day as possible.

Since reading success correlates most highly with verbal behavior, it is recommended that teachers place their greatest emphasis on types of oral language lessons that will *develop concepts* in children if they lack readiness when they enter school. Exercises such as those suggested below should be helpful:

1. Using word "opposites" in meaningful ways:

big — little	winter — summer	clean — dirty
on — off	good — bad	above — below
in — out	before — after	left — right
long — short	open — close	stop — go
up — down	front — back	sick — well
over — under	first — last	push — pull
boy — girl	wide — narrow	noisy — quiet
man — woman	young — old	right — wrong
happy — sad	buy — sell	top —bottom
		friend — enemy

2. Classifying things:

red, blue, and yellow	colors
two, three, four	numbers
lion, tiger, giraffe	wild animals
cat, dog, goldfish	pets
Tom, Dick, Harry	boy's names
men, woman, boy, worker, nurse	people
sofa, chair, stove, table	furniture
pants, suit, hat, socks, shirt	clothes
houses, barns, stores, restaurants, hotels, bars ..	buildings
robin, wren, blackbird, sparrow, warbler	birds

---

[15]This term is borrowed from Carl Bereiter and Seigfried Engelmann, *Teaching Disadvantaged Children to Read* (Englewood Cliffs, New Jersey: Prentice-Hall, Inc., 1966), p. 51.

train, ball, doll, dishes, doll buggy, blocks ...... toys
a, b, c, d .... letters
round, oblong, square, triangle, cone .... shapes
bus, car, train, wagon, horse .... transportation
    (ways we travel)

hut, cabin, bungalow, apartment, motel,
duplex, flat, hogan .... kinds of houses
    people live in

3. Counting concrete objects and recognizing numbers of things to five.

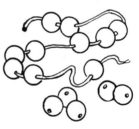

How many baby chickens?

How many cherries?

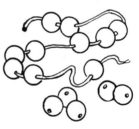

How many beads are
not on the string?

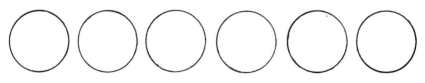

Which is the fifth circle?

4. Words associated in pairs:

cow — calf	ring — finger	mail — postman
knife — fork	hen — chicken	shirt — tie
cup — saucer	cat — kitten	doll — dress

mother — baby	frog — tadpole	sheep — lamb
ball — bat	milk — milkman	horse — colt
cream — sugar	pen — pencil	dog — pup
salt — pepper	comb — hair	fire — fireman
hammer — nails	dog — bone	pan — lid

5. Common prepositions:

The large chart prepared by Ginn to illustrate the nine commonest prepositions should be useful in first grade where the children are all speakers of English. In, out, on, off, beside, between, up, down, over, under are presented. (See the picture in Chapter 13). Special attention needs to be given to the presentation of such prepositions when teaching English to speakers of other languages. The list of common prepositions in children's speech is not long and the teacher can provide opportunity to make sure children have control of them:

about	before	from	on	until
across	beneath	in	out	up
after	beside	inside	outside	upon
against	by	into	over	with
along	beyond	like	since	without
among	but	near	through	
around	down	of	to	
at	for	off	under	

6. Homonyms

to — too — two	blew — blue	no — know	through — threw
knew — new	deer — dear	ate — eight	cheap — cheep
our — hour	sale — sail	son — sun	waist — waste
tale — tail	by — buy	week — weak	he'll — heel
rode — road	right — write	read — red	fair — fare

7. Words with several meanings:

We went to the state *fair* yesterday.

The weather will be *fair* today.

Boys should play *fair*.

The leaves *fall* from the trees in October.

We start to school in the *fall*.

Please *fall* in line! (Take your place)

There is a *fire* in the furnace.

The soldiers will *fire* at the enemy.

His boss will *fire* him.

Most of the girls wear *bangs*.
Bang! went the gun.
The baby was *banging* the pots
    and pans together.

(If children volunteer "Tom banged the door" or "Mother says not to bang the door," very good.)

He was cutting the *bark* from the tree.

The dog will be sure to *bark*.

We sat on the river *bank*.

John put his money in a savings *bank*.

(If one child knows "bank the fire" or "Don't bank on that," be sure to praise him.)

Put the pigs in the *pen*.

Dad writes with a *pen*.

My *pet* is a dog.

He wouldn't let me *pet* him.

I was asleep in *bed*.

He made a lettuce *bed*.

We had a pet *show*.

Please *show* me the picture.

Ted is a *show* off!

8. Word association exercises:

You sit on a chair; you sleep on a _____ .

A bird flies; a fish_____ .

Soup is hot; ice cream is_____ .

Feathers are light; stones are_____ .

You have fingers on your hand; you have toes on your_____ .

You can cut with scissors; with a pencil, you can_____ .

A rabbit goes fast; a turtle goes_____ .

A mile is long; an inch is_____ .

9. Automatic language structures:

I have one apple. There are two *apples*.

Here is a box. Now there are two *boxes*.

This one is long. This one is *longer*.

This one is big. This one is *bigger*.

This one is high. This one is *higher*.

This one is old. This one is *older*.

This one is pretty. This one is *prettier*.

Here is a mouse. There are two *mice*.

Here is a child. There are two *children*.

Here is a goose. There are two *geese*.

I do my work every day Yesterday I *did* it.

I go to work every day. Yesterday I *went* to work.

I throw the ball to jack. Yesterday I *threw* it.

10. Readiness Concepts for Quantitative Thinking:

Teachers may use the following list as a guide in informal conversations with beginners and identify those children who lack the concepts:

1. *up* and *down* and their relationship to each other
2. *in* and *out*
3. *on* and *off*

4. *big* and *little*
5. *front* and *back* (*forward* and *backward*)
6. *beginning* and *end*
7. *before* and *after*
8. *tall* and *short*
9. *high* and *low*
10. *near* and *far*
11. *long* and *short*
12. *early* and *late*
13. *fast* and *slow*
14. *hot* and *cold* (*warm* and *cool*)
15. *left* and *right*
16. *under* and *over*
17. *heavy* and *light*
18. *narrow* and *wide*
19. *thick* and *thin*
20. *empty* and *full*
21. *more* and *less*
22. *all* and *none*
23. *quickly* and *slowly*
24. *winter* and *summer*
25. *night* and *day*
26. *on time*
27 *late*
28. *round*
29. *square*
30. *oval-shaped*
31. *rectangle*
32. *triangle*
33. morning
34. afternoon
35. mid-day
36. curved
37. straight
38. mid-night
39. beneath
40. above
41. noon
42. boxful
43. cupful
44. spoonful
45. pailful (bucketful)
46. jarful

47. glassful
48. teaspoonful
49. pint
50. quart
51. gallon
52. bushel
53. foot (measure of length)
54. yard
55. rod
56. acre
57. many
58. some
59. any
60. each
61. next
62. pair
63. few
64. one-half of single objects
65. counting numbers: one, two, three, four, five, six, seven, eight, nine, and ten.
66. ordinal numbers: first, second, third, fourth, fifth, sixth, seventh, eighth, ninth, tenth.
67. *less than* and *more than*
68. Recognizing one-to-one correspondence: put one spoon in one cup; count one stick for one sheep.
69. close, closer, closest
70. *more* and *most*
71. associate time with important daily activities: "We eat lunch at twelve o'clock." "We go home at four o'clock."
72. concept of handful
73. concept of faster and slower, and their relationship to each other
74. concept of fast*est* and slow*est*
75. concept of time: a day ago; a week ago; a month ago; etc.

11. Some Comprehension Questions that help teachers evaluate understanding concepts
    1. Why do we have books?
    2. Why do we have stoves?
    3. How old are you?
    4. Where do we put the paper that is no good?
    5. Tell me two things that you wear on your head?
    6. What tells us what time it is?
    7. Does a house have doors?

   8. What color is the flag?
   9. Is a baby cat a puppy? What is it?
  10. What two things can you do with a pencil?
  11. What things fly?
  12. What animals have long ears?
  13. What do we call a baby dog? cat? goat? hen? cow? sheep?
  14. Where does the bird put her eggs?
  15. What do you see in the sky in the day time?
  16. When do you need an umbrella?
  17. Can you write with scissors? What can you do with them?
  18. How many days do you come to school in a week?
  19. What are all the things that you can do with a ball?
  20. What does a car have to have to make it go?

12. Bereiter and Engelman have experimented with the problem of concept development in young disadvantaged, lower-class children who will enter the middle-class school kindergarten program at age five. They have worked largely with four-year-olds from the lowest income urban Negro groups. They believe that retarded language development is a most urgent problem that can be generally combatted, if not overcome, by intensive teaching. Once the child has the command of oral language, he is then equipped for verbal learning and thinking. Some of the language goals of their program are:[16]
   1. The ability to use both affirmative and negative responses to simple questions: What's this? It's a ball. It's not a marble.
   2. The ability to handle opposites: If it's not little, it must be big. If it's not up, it must be down. If it's not long, it must be short.
   3. The ability to use the following prepositions correctly: on, in, under, over, and between.
   4. The ability to classify items in categories and then to respond affirmatively or negatively about suggested items for classification: a table is a piece of furniture; is a kitten a piece of furniture?
   5. The ability to perform simple "if-then" deductions.
   6. The ability to use "not" in deductions.
   7. Ability to use "or" in simple deductions. Is it red or green? Do you want the red book or the blue book?

13. Using interesting pictures to encourage conversation and discussion. Some of the major publishers of children's textbooks have sets of large pictures emphasizing elementary concepts in social studies, science and health that can be very useful in this respect. One of

---

[16]Carl E. Bereiter, "Academic Instruction and Preschool Children," in National Council for Teachers of English, *Language Programs for the Disadvantaged* (Champaign, Illinois: NCTE, 1965), pp. 199-200.

the learning aids provided by the Field Enterprises Educational Corporation is a 25″ by 38″ picture with city life depicted on one side and country life on the other. Suggestions for the teacher for use of these pictures are also provided.[17]

III. THE COMPLEXITY OF "BEING READY"

Durrell concluded after a study that involved hundreds of first grade children:

> . . . most reading difficulties can be prevented by an instructional program which provides early instruction in letter names and sounds, followed by applied phonics and accompanied by suitable practice in meaningful sight vocabulary and aids to attentive silent reading.[18]

And Ellingson and Cass reminded teachers:

> . . . Frequently the first grader with the neurological development of a four-year-old is forced into the same classroom mold as his classmates with the advanced perceptual skills of seven-year-olds. The large numbers of children troubled with specific language disability fall into this category.[19]

Physical Factors Affecting Reading
Vision

It is perfectly clear that good vision is an asset in becoming a good reader. Reading requires the ability to see clearly at close range for extended periods of time. Some children are sure to come to the school with some problems for which adjustments can be made. The teacher must be alert to the subjective behaviors that can be observed and if the child appears to have problems in the area of vision, make sure that the proper referrals are made. Reading clinicians, reading clinics in large school systems, and school nurses will be able to administer such tests as the SNELLEN CHART, the EAMES EYE TEST, or the KEYSTONE VISUAL TELEBINOCULAR SURVEY TEST.[20] When indicated, medical referrals will then be made.

Because of the great amount of color used in pictures and in all teaching media today, the child who is color-blind has a distinct disadvantage. These children need to be identified and given special help when identification, naming, and use of color is required. Possibly more

[17]*Farm Life* (1963) and *City Life* (1965), (Chicago: Field Enterprises Educational Corporation).

[18]Donald D. Durrell, ed., "Success in First Grade Reading," *Boston University Journal of Education*, CLX (February, 1958).

[19]Careth Ellingson and James Cass, "Teaching the Dyslexic Child: New Hope for Non-Readers," *Saturday Review*, April 16, 1966.

[20]The Snellen Chart, American Optical Company, Southbridge, Massachusetts; The Eames Eye Test, Harcourt, Brace, and World Publ. Co.; Keystone Visual Telebinocular Survey Test, Meadville, Pennsylvania: Keystone View Co.

emphasis on auditory methods can be emphasized with the color-blind child. About four per cent of the enrollment is likely to be color-blind and almost all are boys.[21]

Olson screened 275 first grade boys at the end of the school year with the AO H-R-R Pseudo-Isochromatic Plates and identified twelve color-blind boys. She matched these with twelve color-vision boys and compared their achievement on the California Reading Test, Lower Primary, Form W, given in May. The differences in achievement were significant at the .01 level of confidence in favor of the color-vision boys.[22]

Schiffman[23] identified 201 color-blind boys in first grade. Teachers of fifty-one of these boys were told that this particular child was color blind, but no other treatment was given. At the end of the year, the fifty-one whose teachers had been informed performed better than those whose teachers were not informed. The difference was statistically significant at the .05 level of confidence.

Children should be screened early in their school careers for color blindness. For those identified, adjustment should be made early in the course of study to prevent failure and the parents and teachers should plan to give support to the child in meeting his psychological and societal demands if adjustments are necessary.

Auditory Discrimination

In order to learn to read, it is necessary for children to have acquired skills in auditory discrimination, the identification of likenesses and differences in beginning and ending sounds that are alike or almost alike. The discrimination of minimal pairs is emphasized by Fries.[24]

Examples of minimal pairs:

pig	pig	man	fat	fun	shop
pin	big	pan	pat	fur	shot

Minimal pairs are two words containing all the same sounds except one phoneme which changes the meaning of each word. (See page 310).

Reading to Children

Teachers must find time to read a great deal to young children: stories, both fanciful and true, and poetry and Mother Goose. Of course,

---

[21]A. Chapanis, "Color Blindness," *Scientific American*, 1951, 184, 48-53; F. E. Kratter, "Color Blindness in Relation to Normal and Defective Intelligence," *American Journal of Mental Deficiency*, 62: 436-441, 1957.

[22]Arleen L. Olson, *An Experimental Study of the Relationship Between Color Blindness and Reading Achievement in the First Grade*, unpublished Master's thesis, The Graduate School, University of New Mexico, 1963.

[23]G. B. Schiffman, *The Effect of Color Blindness upon Achievement of Elementary School Males*, Experimental Research Series Report No. 106 (Towson, Maryland: Board of Education, 1963).

[24]C. C. Fries, *Linguistics and Reading* (Columbus: Charles E. Merrill, 1963).

the child's readiness for literature is predetermined by his stage of language cognition. All children in the group will not see, hear, and feel the same things when the teacher reads to them.

Especially for those lacking in all kinds of experiences, the teacher needs to be able to supply as much as she can to remove the deficit. *Jam* is a poem that can be enjoyed and hopefully "tasted" until it is a meaningful experience for all the boys and girls in the class.

JAM

Jam in the morning, jam at noon,
Bread and jam by the light of the moon.
Jam
is
very
nice.
Jam on biscuits, jam on toast,
Jam is the thing I like the most.
Jam is sticky, jam is sweet,
Jam is tasty, jam's a treat—
Raspberry
Strawberry
Gooseberry,
I'm very
FOND OF JAM!
                    —by Russell Hoban[25]

Sources of good materials for literature in grade one include: May Hill Arbuthnot,[26] Geismer and Suter,[27] and *The Real Mother Goose.*[28]

Facility with language may be one of the most important factors in reading readiness. Language facility will vary tremendously in any unselected group of six-year-old children, of course. The gamut includes the little girl of three and one-half years, who, after playing with paper boats in nursery school one morning, asked her mother to make her a paper boat to float in the dishpan of water in the afternoon. In a few minutes she brought a crumpled piece of wet paper to her mother in the living room and said, "My boat has *disintegrated* in the water." The other end of the continuum includes both the child who has very meager language and gives one word answers or says "Me go" when he means "I want to go," and the child whose native language is not the language of the school.

Language is being developed when parents, other adults and teachers encourage children in the use of the language. When they answer many

25Donald J. Bissett, Editor, *Poems and Verses to Begin On* (124 Spear Street, San Francisco, California 94105: Chandler Publishing Co., 1967), p. 31.
26May Hill Arbuthnot, Editor, *The Arbuthnot Anthology of Children's Literature* (Chicago: Scott, Foresman and Co., 1952).
27Geismer and Suter, *Very Young Verses,* (Boston: Houghton Mifflin, 1945).
28*The Real Mother Goose* (Chicago: Rand McNally, 1944).

of the child's questions, when they repeat for children so they can understand concepts in a conversation, and when they ask children to correctly repeat sentence patterns to form verb phrases correctly or to straighten out pronunciations. These are always done in an informal, encouraging way and the child learns, unlearns, and relearns the language which he has much time to assimilate through trial and error.

One of the great differences between language depth of culturally advantaged and culturally deprived children lies in the way in which they are "talked to" by the adults around them. If they are "talked to" in one word commands, or given instructions with minimum word usage, they respond in the same way and remain "language-less" to a much greater degree than other children who are answered, asked to amplify answers, given synonyms for many words they know, and so on.

Speaking and understanding spoken language involving concepts, asking questions or presenting problems; using language to formulate concepts; differentiating words that sound much the same but mean many different things; formulating meanings from context when one word has many meanings; and holding ideas in mind and organizing and classifying them in sequential order; all of these things are evidences of language power—and correlate highly with academic learning and success in developing reading skills.

Needlessly carrying on an extensive readiness program for children who are already ready is as foolish as ignoring readiness kinds of activities when they are needed.

Some five-year olds are more advanced intellectually, physically, socially, emotionally than some six-year olds.

It should be just as possible to put learning on a long continuum in a kindergarten or first grade class as in any other—recognizing that each child has an optimum readiness for learning at some point along the continuum.

Environmental experiences—trips and excursions—fact and fancy in stories and poems—skills and habits in visual-auditory-visuo-motor discrimination—creative expression through art, music, games, and rhythms are needed.

Telling the story, seeing it written down, hearing it read back, and listening to its contents and knowing that it is what was said before— this sequence helps the child understand what reading is.

A child can learn in many informal experiences to *extend* his vocabulary.

Not, it's a bird—but rather, it's a robin.

Not, it's a tree—but rather, it's a maple tree.

Not, it's a dog—but rather, it's a big collie dog.

Many activities in the first two years of the child's school life can contribute to his emotional and social growth. If the teacher is sensitive to such traits as timidity, aggression, fear, anxiety, and the need for success and approval, he creates opportunity to "help" each child in terms of his need. The children learn, through planned group work experiences, to work cooperatively to achieve group goals, to share with each other, and to exchange ideas through informal conversation. These comfortable emotional and socializing experiences contribute to greater maturity, stability and confidence when he is confronted with the formal learning-to-read process. In the informal atmosphere of a kindergarten or first grade classroom, the teacher can promote vocabulary enrichment, correct English usage, fluency in extemporaneous speaking, and the ability to give his attention in listening, all of which are essential skills demanded in the learning-to-read process.

Following is a list of activities leading to readiness for formal reading:[29]

1. Many, varied opportunities for oral expression.
2. Practice in listening to other people tell about things, for example, "show and tell" time.
3. Discussing experiences or things shared by others.
4. Opportunities to hear stories and poems read by the teacher or presented on records and tapes.
5. Field trips and other excursions, preceded by preparedness directions and followed by a discussion, experience charts, and critique.
6. Activities, such as choral speaking, dramatization, radio or television skits, and practice with a tape recorder, that will promote accurate pronunciation and enunciation.
7. Arranging pictures into a story sequence. This is carried out in a variety of situations, including flannel boards and pictures mounted on individual cards.
8. Picture interpretation.
9. Practice in recognizing the central ideas in stories read by the teacher.
10. Extensive practice in auditory discrimination and identification of familiar sounds. This work may involve not only words, but also sounds like wood on wood, spoons tapping together, paper crumbling, shoes scraping, and so on.
11. Practice in marking words or drawings that are alike or different.
12. Learning the names of letters in random order.

[29]From Warren G. Cutts, *Modern Reading Instruction* (Washington, D. C.: The Center for Applied Research in Education, Inc., 1964), p. 18. See also Roma Gans, "This Business of Reading," *Progressive Education,* 21:70, 72, 93, 94; and Lucille M. Harrison, "Getting Them Ready to Read," *NEA Journal,* 40:106-108.

13. Developing left-to-right sequence.
14. Learning to use context to supply missing ideas.
15. Developing visual discrimination.
16. Making children aware of reading in their daily lives by having them distinguish their own names, looking at and talking about stories, reading or seeing signs, bulletin boards, and messages.
17. Keeping records of words that have been of interest to the group.
18. Arranging the classroom for individual and group experience to encourage self-reliance.

Testing Readiness for Reading

When the teacher feels the child is ready for formal reading, he can supplement his judgment by the administration of a standardized reading readiness test. Three commonly used reading readiness tests are the following:

1. *The Metropolitan Readiness Test,* by Gertrude Hildreth and Nellie L. Griffiths (New York: Harcourt, Brace and World, Inc., 1964) is a school readiness test for end of the kindergarten year or beginning first grade. In addition to the reading readiness activities, there is a number readiness sub-test, and space for a child's drawing of a man. The subtests of the reading readiness include: (1) word meaning; (2) understanding sentences; (3) using information; and (4) visual discrimination of pictures, geometric forms, and letters. (See illustration).

2. *Harrison-Stroud Reading Readiness Tests,* by M. Lucille Harrison and J. B. Stroud (Boston: Houghton Mifflin Co., 1956), is a reading readiness test that may be used in the first grade when the teacher believes the child is ready for reading. It measures visual discrimination; using context clues; making auditory discriminations; using context and auditory clues; and identifying the letters of the alphabet.

3. *Murphy-Durrell Diagnostic Reading Readiness Tests,* by Helen Murphy and D. D. Durrell (New York: Harcourt, Brace and World, 1964), is a reading readiness test that measures visual discrimination, auditory discrimination, and learning rate. (See illustration next page.)

It is apparent that the areas of visual perception, visual motor and visual auditory coordination, and social and emotional maturity are not adequately tested in the usual group readiness test. For that reason, the preventive kinds of assistance to be rendered by the school psychologist become extremely important to insure the young child a successful start in school.

IV.   SUMMARY

This chapter has contained a discussion of the factors most important in the child's readiness for learning how to read. These may be sum-

FORM
A

Metropolitan Readiness Tests

by GERTRUDE H. HILDRETH, NELLIE L. GRIFFITHS, MARY E. McGAUVRAN

NAME _____ BOY___ GIRL ___ DATE OF TESTING _____
Year Month' Day

TEACHER _____ SCHOOL _____ DATE OF BIRTH _____
Year Month Day

CITY_____ COUNTY _____ STATE _____ PUPIL'S AGE Yrs_____ Mos. _____

GRADE _____ NUMBER OF MONTHS KINDERGARTEN TRAINING _____

TEST	RAW SCORE
1. WORD MEANING	
2. LISTENING	
3. MATCHING	
4. ALPHABET	
5. NUMBERS	
6. COPYING	
Total Score, Tests 1-6	
Percentile Rank	
Letter Rating	

Readiness status, recommendation, other scores, remarks:

HARCOURT, BRACE & WORLD, INC. NEW YORK

marized as: (1) *physical-neurological factors* including the ability to see and hear well, visual and auditory discriminatory abilities, length of attention span; willingness to attend; and the presence of specific disabilities that may be neurological dysfunctioning; (2) *emotional and social factors* such as ability to adjust to and cooperate in the group; adequate attention span; and the possible presence of behavioral disorders; and (3) *intellectual factors* including cognitive development in relevant knowledge, comprehension, quantitative thinking, word association, story sequence, and extension of vocabulary. It is in the intellectual area that the teacher hopes to develop curiosity about reading and a genuine interest in learning how to read.

Schonell lends support to the point of view throughout this chapter that concept building and thinking processes are basic to making reading a useful tool to the new reader:[30]

> Research shows that it is fatal to "push" young children along in the initial stages of learning to read, particularly if there have not been activities to create a functional language background beforehand. Many children fail in reading because they are plunged into formal reading with an over-analytic method employing abstract symbols before they really understand what words and sentences mean in spoken, let alone printed form. Young immature minds need opportunity and time to "sort things out," to understand what they are doing, and to see the purpose in the operations with which they are confronted. My strongest plea in the teaching of reading is, don't hurry children, don't expect too much in the early stages—do all you can to provide a language background. This slower, wider approach will repay doubly later on.

SUGGESTED ACTIVITIES

1. Observe a psychologist, counselor, or reading clinician administer one of the tests recommended in this chapter for children who need special evaluation for readiness for school.

2. Study the manual for the Illinois Test of Psycholinguistic Abilities and make a list of informal types of questions first grade teachers might use to help determine a child's readiness with language for formal reading instruction.

3. Examine several teachers' manuals for first grade reading programs in basal readers and study the informal check lists of reading readiness items. Prepare a check list appropriate for a first grade teacher that you think would be useful.

4. Administer a reading readiness test to a child of four, five, or six and try to evaluate the results in terms of his readiness for formal school.

---

[30]Sir Fred J. Schonell, *The Psychology and Teaching of Reading* (New York: Philosophical Library, 1961).

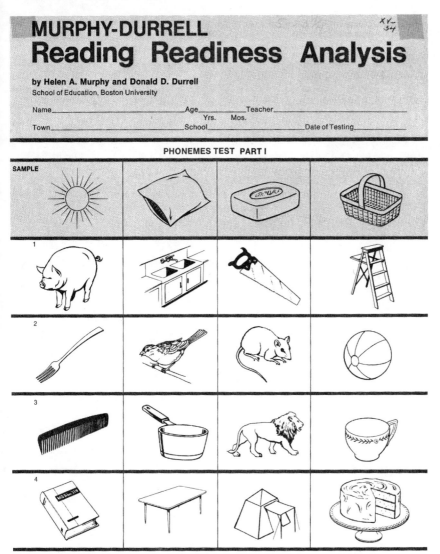

MURPHY-DURRELL
Reading Readiness Analysis

by Helen A. Murphy and Donald D. Durrell
School of Education, Boston University

Name_____Age_____Teacher_____
                                Yrs.   Mos.
Town_____School_____Date of Testing_____

PHONEMES TEST PART I

5. As a result of No. 4 above, select specific activities from the teacher's manual designed to meet the readiness needs of the individual as revealed by the test performance.

READING REFERENCES

ANDERSON, VERNA DIECKMAN. *Reading and Young Children* (New York: Macmillan, 1968). Chapter 4: "Getting Ready to Read, Part I," pp. 58-86; Chapter 5: "Getting Ready to Read, Part II," pp. 87-126.

BEREITER, CARL, and SEIGFRIED ENGELMANN. *Teaching Disadvantaged Children to Read* (Englewood Cliffs, New Jersey: Prentice-Hall, Inc., 1966).

DE HIRSCH, KATRINA, JEANNETTE JANSKY, and WILLIAM S. LANGFORD. *Predicting Reading Failure* (New York: Harper and Row, 1966). Chapter 9: "Recommendations," pp. 84-92.

DUNN, LLOYD. *Peabody Language Development Kits* (Circle Pines, Minnesota 55014: American Guidance Services, Inc.).

FROSTIG, MARIANNE. *Administration and Scoring Manual for the Developmental Test of Visual Perception* (Palo Alto, California: Consulting Psychologist Press, 1966).

HARRIS, ALBERT J. *Effective Teaching of Reading* (New York: David McKay, 1961). Chapter 2: "Getting Ready for Reading," pp. 22-42.

HEILMAN, ARTHUR W. *Principles and Practices in Teaching Reading*, Second Edition (Columbus, Ohio: Charles E. Merrill, Inc., 1967). Chapter 2: "Preparing for Reading," pp. 25-72.

KEPHART, NEWELL C. *The Slow Learner in the Classroom* (Columbus, Ohio: Charles E. Merrill Books, Inc., 1960). Part II: "Perceptual Survey Rating Scale," pp. 120-155.

LOBAN, WALTER. *Problems in Oral English* (Champaign, Illinois: National Council of Teachers of English, 1963).

NOAR, GERTRUDE. *Living With Difference* (New York: Anti-Defamation League, 1965).

STAUFFER, RUSSELL. *Language and the Higher Thought Processes* (Champaign, Illinois: National Council of Teachers of English, 1965).

TINKER, MILES A., and CONSTANCE McCULLOUGH. *Teaching Elementary Reading* (New York: Appleton-Century-Crofts, 1968). Chapter 4: "Getting Ready to Read," pp. 73-98.

17

Teaching Beginning Reading

Most reading specialists have always given priority to the notion that reading is first and foremost a thinking process and that without meaning there is no reading. Comprehension, interpretation and integration into one's thinking processes are all integral parts of the reading process from the start. Of course, the visual perception of words and the ability to call up the meanings they represent make word recognition a prerequisite to comprehending, interpreting, and integrating.

If one cannot "recognize" the word, it will be difficult to make meaning with the sentence containing it. For very young children beginning the reading process, it is safe to assume that if they cannot pronounce the word, they will not be able to get the full meaning of the sentence containing it.

Reading programs, generally, then, try to teach children to recognize a small stock of sight words so that they may read context and extract meaning in the very first books of a reading series. In some first pre-primers there will be no more than twenty different words. The significant point is, though, that the child will, with this limited stock of words, read meaningful sentences and little stories for which his teacher will ask guide questions and build story plots. Even from this beginning, the teacher will request the child to "read with his eyes and not with his lips" so that he will form the habit of recognizing all the words in a sentence and then practice saying it as he might speak it instead of reading word-by-word slowly and with observable difficulty.

While the child is mastering a sight vocabulary of some 50 words, he is already profiting from directed lessons in auditory discrimination of initial consonant sounds. From pictures, he is becoming aware of the beginning sound of "goat," "girl," "goose," and "gun" and labeling it as the "g" sound. He will learn to recognize the visual symbol as soon as he has learned to read a few "g" words in print. As soon as he associates the phoneme (sound as spoken) with the grapheme (letter as written), he can then make systematic use of his phonics. Most reading series will present a sequenced program in phonetic analysis through the six grades, with the heaviest dosage in grades two and three. He will learn structural analysis all the way through public school but have much familiarity with compound words, root words, prefixes, suffixes, and syllables by the end of grade three.

Beginning formal reading, then, is the transition from expanding language development, through the acquisition of an acuity in auditory discrimination of English phonemes, a basic sight vocabulary of from 50 to 100 words and some fluency in reading meaningfully.

Chall suggests in *Learning to Read: The Great Debate,* that there are only a few innovations in widely used reading programs through the past decade:

1. Somewhat more emphasis on learning the alphabet and its phoneme-grapheme relationship;
2. Adjusting the content of readers to make them more broadly interesting to all the children;
3. Accepting the reality of individual differences in children and providing for more individualization in teaching.[1]

I. CHARACTERISTICS OF PRIMARY READING PROGRAM

A reading program in the primary grades
1. Is part of a continuing growth from readiness to reading.
2. Emphasizes the phoneme-grapheme relationships between symbols and ideas.
3. Uses many opportunities to emphasize the principle that reading is "talk written down." Reading preserves talk.
4. Does not rely on only one "method" or "technique" for learning. Good methods are eclectic.
5. Has as its first objective the mastery of a sight vocabulary of words to read with. One can't read without words.
6. Teaches a variety of ways for working out new words since the independent reader must discover new words for himself.
   a. Configuration
   b. Similarity to known words: from *pail* to *mail,* or *pail* to *pain.*
   c. Context clues
   d. Picture clues
   e. Sounding out
   f. Analyzing the word structure
   g. Accent

---

[1]Jeanne S. Chall, *Learning to Read: The Great Debate* (New York: McGraw-Hill, 1967).

7. Emphasizes that reading is, above all else, a thinking process.
8. Teaches appreciations. Children begin early to learn to like to read; to anticipate enjoyment in good books.
9. Requires interesting, exciting, changing things in the room to read. Bulletin boards, displays, labels, questions, current events.

II. THE BASAL READER APPROACH

Basal reader materials generally are a series of books and auxiliary material adapted to systematic development of reading abilities. Basal reading series provide (1) carefully sequenced order in presentation of skills, (2) continuity of all skills through the grades, and (3) integration of materials and skills to facilitate independent learning. Organization of the series is coordinated horizontally in the gradual progression to more difficult steps; and coordinated vertically in broadening the children's conceptions of social organization, vocabulary, word analysis skills, and evaluative abilities.

Basal readers have been heavily criticized as shallow, repetitive, and uninteresting. For children not from the typical middle-class American culture, they have failed to present life realistically; they have not motivated the underprivileged; they have portrayed too much of the comfortable easy life of children not from the lower socio-economic classes.

Nevertheless, for the *beginning* teacher who must meet the demands of all the children in his classroom each day, through the gradual introduction of skills, the necessary repetition, the seatwork ready-made, and the tests provided by the publishers, basal texts make it possible for the inexperienced or the unknowing to provide a well-worked out program of reading skills to a class.

Usually there are readiness materials—often in the form of a workbook for the child, three pre-primers introducing the first sight vocabulary, a primer or two, and a first reader for the first grade reading program. Beyond first grade, there are usually two books for each grade, for example, *Second Grade, Semester One* and *Second Grade, Semester Two*. For all of these books, publishers provide workbooks of exercises, and teachers' editions of the readers, or separate manuals.

Under the impetus of ESEA, Title I, with federal money available to aid in purchase of materials, publishers have provided text films, film strips, recordings, word and phrase cards, and many supplementary reading materials. Many major publishers now provide reading series for schools:

1. THE ALICE AND JERRY READING PROGRAM, Revised. Mabel O'Donnell. Harper & Row.
2. THE BANK STREET READERS, Bank Street College of Education, Irma Simonton Black, Senior Editor. The Macmillan Company.

3. BEST OF CHILDREN'S LITERATURE, Nila B. Smith, Hazel C. Hart, and Clara Belle Baker. Bobbs-Merrill Co.
4. BETTS BASIC READERS, Second Edition. E. A. Betts. American Book.
5. THE CHALLENGE READERS, Lee Harrison Mountain and Walter M. Mason. McCormick Mathers Publishing Co.
6. DEVELOPMENTAL READING SERIES, Guy L. Bond. Lyons and Carnahan.
7. GATEWAYS TO READING TREASURES, Co-Basal Literary Readers, Harold G. Shane and Kathleen Hester. Laidlaw Brothers Publishers.
8. GINN BASIC READERS, David Russell. Ginn and Co.
9. THE MACMILLAN READING PROGRAM, Albert J. Harris and Mae Knight Clark. The Macmillan Co.
10. NEW BASIC READING PROGRAM, Curriculum Foundation Series, W. S. Gray. Scott, Foresman and Company.
11. READING CARAVAN, Paul A. Witty and Alma Moore Freeland, D. C. Heath and Co.
12. READING FOR MEANING SERIES, Paul McKee. Houghton Mifflin Co.
13. SHELDON BASIC READING SERIES, Wm. D. Sheldon. Allyn & Bacon Co.
14. THE TIME TO READ SERIES, Bernice E. Leary, Edwin C. Reichert, and Mary K. Reely, J. B. Lippincott Co.
15. THE WOODLAND FROLIC SERIES, Adda Mai Sharp and Epsie Young. Steck-Vaughn Co.

As is indicated by Salisbury cited in the chapter on bilingual education, Chapter 13, p. 305, the stories of middle-class children written directly about their interests in the United States may not have applicability in many areas of our country, in bi-national schools outside the United States, or on Guam. Nevertheless, major efforts have been made to write as interestingly as possible when the vocabulary is drastically limited.

Estimates of school systems using reading series as basal readers run as high as 90 per cent with many schools recommending a second and third series as co-basal or tri-basal. Basal readers also provide much material for supplementary reading.

After the young teacher has taught basal reading programs and learned the skills sequences, he needs to organize his own resources and venture more broadly into language-experience approaches or individualized reading programs. Needless to say, the confidence of the teacher in his ability to carry out a competent program is the first requisite, and until he himself feels confident of the many word recognition and comprehension skills that children need for reading in today's world, he must adhere to an organized program that will insure success for the children he teaches. His goal must be that of seeing children as individuals, and his approach to teaching must be diagnostic with respect to the learning needs of each one.

Stone has identified the one hundred most used words in early reading in first grade basal reading programs. Most of these words must be learned as sight words. They do provide a "core" of service words to be used in a great deal of easy reading practice. The words are found on page 146.

Dolch selected a list of *service* words most needed by children in all textbook reading in the elementary school. The list of 220 words contains no nouns and constitutes about *two-thirds* of all the running words read by children in first and second grades and *half* of all the running words read by boys and girls in fourth, fifth, and sixth grades. Since they appear over and over in all elementary reading, knowing them as sight words is crucial for all readers. Fry's 300 Instant Words List contains almost all of the Dolch Words and is found on page 148-9.

III. THE LANGUAGE EXPERIENCE APPROACH TO READING

Writing down the language contributions of the young child is one of the most natural ways of extending his learning in the communication arts. The kindergarten teacher stops by the child's desk and tells him he has made an interesting picture. When the teacher asks the child to tell about the picture, he says, "My dog has chased the cat up a tree." The teacher can say, "Billy, would you like for me to write that under your picture?" Of course he would because the teacher is preserving something personal and valuable to him. The result is the illustration on the following page.

The kindergarten class goes to the baby animals zoo for a field trip. When they have returned to the classroom and talk about their trip, the teacher encourages a great deal of discussion—verbalization about whatever topics of conversation are of most interest to the individual members of the group. By encouraging their responses, the teacher may be able to get each child to express one idea he best rememebered that he can now illustrate with crayon. As these pictures evolve, the teacher can write a sentence for each child about what his picture tells. If the teacher is lucky, he will be able to bind all the work of the children into a big book for the reading table which they may then peruse in their free time. Each one is apt to remember his sentence and, without knowing individual words at this time, be able to tell the class what his picture "says." Each child builds his vocabulary as he gains new ideas,

discusses with others, asks questions about things he sees, and as the teacher talks with the group.

The heightened effect produced by the teacher arranging to meet individually with each child, albeit for only very short periods, to write down what he would like to record, develops a sensitivity to oral and written language and encourages the child to be more observant of his environment, more observant of the language he hears, and more impressed with the recording of oral language as a means of preserving ideas.

Stauffer has described the language-experience method of operating with small groups or individuals in the classroom.[2] Nielsen's steps in developing the language-experience approach were given in Chapter 4.

How to Prepare Experience Charts

I. Getting ready to make an experience chart
   A. The teacher needs to select an experience that has been common to all the children. Many charts can be based on usual happenings in daily school routine. A common experience of the group, such as an excursion, provides a basis for several stories. (See the story *At the Zoo* dictated by the kindergarten class.)

[2]Russell Stauffer, "Language-Experience Approach," in *First Grade Reading Programs,* James Kerfoot, Editor (Newark, Delaware 19711: International Reading Association, 1965), pp. 86-118.

    B. After the experience has been selected, it is necessary to develop, through group discussion, the important concepts and to state them in complete sentences.

    C. The concepts need to be analyzed and organized so that different members of the group will present the concepts in proper chronology.

    D. The teacher writes the sentences in the story as they are dictated by the children. Other children in the group may edit sentences or extend the discussion to clarify concepts.

II. The content of the chart should contain:

    A. Sentences dictated by individual children.

    B. Complete sentences.

    C. All sentences "one-line" length in early charts.

    D. Ideas clearly and accurately stated.

III. Making the experience chart:

    A. Use large size chart paper, 22″ by 30″ or larger. The lines should be spaced three-fourths inch apart. Such lined paper is available commercially for primary teachers.

    B. Center the title three spaces from top of page.

    C. Capitalize only the first letters of words in the title.

    D. Leave a two-inch margin on the left and a neat margin on the right.

    E. Begin the first line three spaces below the title.

    F. Use three spaces for each line of manuscript writing. A middle space is the base line for writing, a space above is for the tall letters and a space below for the letters with stems below. (See *Zaner-Bloser* alphabet).

    G. Leave a fourth space for separation of lines of manuscript writing.

    H. Make lines fairly uniform in length if possible.

    I. When a sentence is too long for one line, be sure to break it between phrases without regard to length of written line. (See story *Uncle Jim's Apple Orchard*).

Experience charts provide the teacher several avenues to language development that are practical and useful in daily activities in the classroom. They can contain (1) short, written accounts of children's experiences that can be read and re-read for review; (2) announcements, directions, reminders or lists of duties; (3) summaries of subject matter discussed; (4) samples of children's creative writing; or (5) plans for the day or for special work periods.[3]

---

[3]Virgil E. Herrick and Marcella Nerbovig, *Using Experience Charts with Children*, (Columbus: Charles E. Merrill Books, Inc., 1964), pages iii-iv.

CURSIVE ALPHABET   **Grade three**

Cursive alphabet: Aa Bb Cc Dd Ee Ff Gg Hh Ii Jj Kk Ll Mm Nn Oo Pp Qq Rr Ss Tt Uu Vv Ww Xx Yy Zz 1 2 3 4 5 6 7 8 9 10

MANUSCRIPT ALPHABET

ABCDEFGHIJKLMNOPQR
STUVWXYZabcdefghijklm
nopqrstuvwxyz 12345678910

Used by permission of the Zaner-Blazer Co., Columbus, Ohio 43215.

At The Zoo

We went to the zoo.

We went on the bus.

We saw the animals.

We saw the monkeys.

We saw the giraffe.

We saw the elephant.

We like the zoo.

        The Kindergarten.

Uncle Jim's Apple Orchard

We went to visit
Uncle Jim's Apple Orchard.

Mr. Garcia drove the bus.

We rode for about an hour.

We saw Uncle Jim.

He gave us apples to eat.

He has more than
a thousand bushels.

He has twenty pickers.

He has cold rooms
in his packing shed.

He has many kinds of apples.

Apples are good for you.

We like Uncle Jim's Apple Orchard.
The First Grade.

Teachers should practice appropriate editorial skills so that charts will be finished with both good form and good content so they can be displayed in the room and reused at later times. Some of the editorial skills include organization on the page, line arrangement, spacing, the use of pictures, editing and expanding to include additional information when indicated. An excellent handbook outlining the range of uses for, the preparation of, and the rationale for experience charts is *Using Experince Charts with Children* by Herrick and Nerbovig.[4]

A chart, "Migration of the Arctic Tern," designed as a summary of subject matter content is found on the following page

MIGRATION OF THE ARCTIC TERN

The Arctic Tern is a great traveler.
He makes his summer nest near the North Pole.
He lives there only a few short weeks of summer.

[4]*Ibid.*

He flies south in the autumn.
He flies past the southern tip of South America.
He may spend the winter near there.
He may fly to Antarctica.
Bird migrations have been studied by bird
banders.
Records can be kept by finding the same bird in many places.

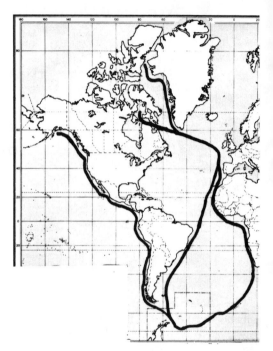

Why does the Arctic
Tern start north with the
first warm day of spring?

How does the young
tern know the route of his
migration when it is time
to go?

Why does he not get
lost traveling thousands of
miles a year?

How do birds get ready
for such long migration
flights?

In summary, Lamoreaux and Lee write:[5]

In general, then, certain principles can be drawn which distinguish
good charts. First, each chart must serve the purpose it is intended to
serve, and, over a period of time, charts should serve a variety of purposes. They should be simple and unified. They should be suited to
the ability of the children for whom they are intended. There should
be adequate word control. The mechanics should be good, the print
clear and large enough, and the lines well spaced. The sentences
should be correctly phrased in thought units and indented in regular
paragraph form.

---

[5]Lillian A. Lamoreaux and Dorris M. Lee, *Learning to Read Through Experience*
(New York: Appleton-Century-Croft, Inc., 1943), p. 180.

IV. OTHER METHODS

The Initial Teaching Alphabet

The Initial Teaching Alphabet has 44 symbols instead of the conventional 26; each of the 44 symbols represents one and only one sound. The alphabet is basically phonemic rather than strictly phonetic. Capital letters are not used in i/t/a. The capital is only a larger (in size) duplicate of the small letter. Thus instead of small letters in manuscript, capital letters in manuscript, small letters in cursive, and large letters in cursive, the child has only 44 symbols that always stay the *same* to learn.

While the vowel sound in the word "pie" is long "i," that same sound can be spelled many different ways in other words in traditional orthography. Not in i/t/a; this sound is the same when it appears in *buy, sigh, aisle, island, kite.*

Most children are ready to make the transition from i/t/a to traditional orthography by the end of the first grade year. The traditional basal readers rewritten into i/t/a would serve no purpose since i/t/a vocabulary is not as severely controlled. The traditional reading program is apt to introduce the child to only 350 words the first year but i/t/a may introduce him to that many in a few weeks. Once he has learned the sounds and realizes they remain constant, he can read much more widely much more quickly.[6] The alphabet in i/t/a and a few sentences written with the i/t/a alphabet are shown following.

Words in Color

Words-in-Color is a system of writing the language in a phonetic manner by having a distinct color for each phoneme. First developed by Caleb Gattegno, the system proved very successful in languages more phonetically structured or with fewer variant sounds. Having developed the system in other languages in Africa, Gattegno used the same color system for the English language. This required forty-seven shades of color to "fit" the forty-seven phonemes which he identifies in the English language. By this system, a vowel sound is always the same color regardless of how it is spelled. Long *a,* for example, may be:

ey in they	*ei* in vein
ay in day	*eigh* in sleigh
ai in wait	*aigh* in straight
ea in great	*a — e* in gate

However, in the words-in-color method, all these spellings will be the same color as long *a.*

---

[6]Albert J. Mazurkiewicz, *New Perspectives in Reading Instruction* (New York: Pitman Publishing Corporation, 1964), pp. 539-544. "The Initial Teaching Alphabet (Augmented Roman) for Teaching Reading."

girlz and boiz lern

tω reed with ita

Pitman's Initial Teaching Alphabet, with its 44
symbols and words illustrating the sounds these
symbols represent.

Reproduced by permission of Initial Teaching Alphabet Publications, Inc., New York, New York.

fill in the missing caracter.

| ɛɛ | h | u | h | h |

1. hœld it in yꙍr ___and.

2. ꝥe indianꙅ rœd ___orseꙅ.

3. ꝥæ ___unted buffalœꙅ.

4. ie cliemd ___p ꝥe ladder.

5. Cats dꙍ not n___d ladderꙅ.

fill in the missing caracter.

| a | ꝥ | æ | ꙍ | o |

1. Wɛɛ tell tiem bie ꝥe cl___ck.

2. nan feedꙅ cat f___d tꙍ her c___t.

3. ie ___t sꙍp for dinner.

4. ꝥe we___er iꙅ cœld.

From *Workbook to Accompany Houses*, pp. 53-54 (New York: Initial Teaching Alphabet Publications, 1965).

On the other hand, the sound of *a* in *ago, ran, rain, arm,* and *call* would be represented by a different color in each word. So, *s* in *sell* and *say* is the "s" sound; *s* in *his* and *turns* is the "z" sound; *s* in *sugar* and *sure* is the "sh" sound; and *s* in *pleasure* and *treasure* is the "zh" sound.

In the words-in-color system, eight charts present the forty-seven different phonemes in English in forty-seven different colors or color combinations. It is doubtful that such a complicated system of matching colors to sounds will prove very useful for the teaching of reading as a thinking process as expounded throughout this text. After making all the phoneme-grapheme associations, one will only be able to pronounce words. Perceiving what words are called is only the first step in the reading process.

Phonics Methods

Many phonics systems have been published through the years to provide children with methods of decoding printed words for reading. Fifty years ago, the Beacon Charts[7] were widely used to teach children many isolated sounds and then provide practice in integrating these sounds into family endings and sight words.

Usually the pages in the primers contained sentences unrelated to each other. They were prepared for the specific purpose of giving the child a number of repetitions in pronouncing the phonetic element being taught.

Today, phonics is not considered a *method* of teaching reading. Phonics is a very necessary skill in word analysis and word identification. As emphasized throughout this text, this is not *reading*. With respect to Gray's four-step definition: "Reading is perception, comprehension, reaction, and integration," phonics can possibly be of help only with the first step. Of course it is necessary to perceive words before reading can take place, but perceiving what words are is not reading. This is illustrated clearly by using the same circle presented in Chapter 1, p. 6, and seeing that phonics helps the child only with the first quarter of the circle:

Phonics is useful
only in word
perception

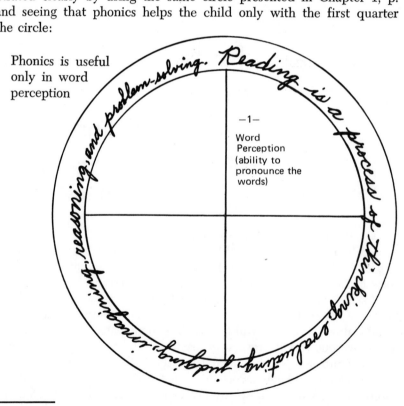

-1-

Word
Perception
(ability to
pronounce the
words)

---

[7]James H. Fassett, *The Beacon Primer* (Boston: Ginn and Company, 1912).

Any child who has low word recognition abilities after being taught developmental reading might profit greatly from some definite instruction in phonetic skills through the use of such workbooks as those provided by Lyons and Carnahan, (*Phonics We use*), Webster Publishing Co., (*Eye and Ear Fun*) and McCormick Mathers, (*Building Reading Skills*).

Some phonics systems should be available to all teachers in their classrooms. Some of these are

1. *Programmed Reading*, McGraw-Hill Publishing Co.
2. *The Phonovisual Method*, Phonovisual Products, Inc., 4708 Wisconsin Avenue, N.W., Washington, D. C. (See the Phonovisual Consonant and Vowel Charts).
3. *The SRA Basic Reading Series*, Workbooks Level A, B, C, D, E, Science Research Associates, Inc., Chicago, Illinois.

These systems are not intended to take the place of the regular reading program which expands sight vocabulary, develops meaning vocabulary, and provides a great deal of easy reading practice. These materials should be used as parallel teaching materials.

Use of the Rebus in Beginning Reading

The Peabody Rebus Reading Program, American Guidance Services, Inc., Circle Pines, Minnesota 55014, is a method of using pictographs to describe a picture so the child reads a sentence without the English words being presented in their written form. This is described in the chapter on special problems in reading.

Either the rebus or the structured phonics materials may be especially appropriate for emotionally disturbed or neurologically impaired children who need to work in tightly structured situations and sheltered from the confusion of many other children working near them.

V. RECOMMENDATIONS FROM THE HARVARD REPORT

Three of the forty-five recommendations in the Harvard Reading Report—*The First R*—are directly related to successful teaching of beginning reading. These three recommendations follow:

4. In all the furor over deciding which method of teaching children to read is the most valuable, certain facts have been lost sight of: that children can and do learn to read in a variety of ways; that what is beneficial instruction for one child may not do for another; and that there are many different kinds of experiences which will aid in the attainment of good reading habits, skills, and interests. Reading is an essential tool for all children and, in the introduction of this major component of a child's elementary school experience, great care should be

Phonovisual® Consonant Chart

By Lucille D. Schoolfield and Josephine B. Timberlake

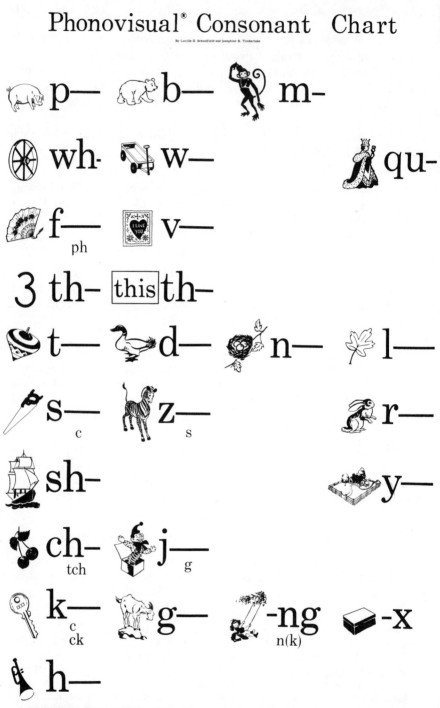

p– b– m–

wh- w– qu-

f– v–
ph

3 th– this th–

t– d– n– l–

s– z– r–
c   s

sh– y–

ch– j–
tch   g

k– g– -ng -x
c   n(k)
ck

h–

Phonovisual® Vowel Chart

By Lucille D. Schoolfield and Josephine B. Timberlake

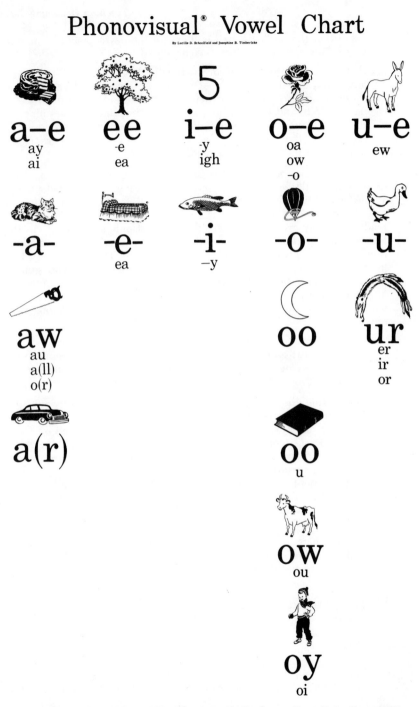

a–e
ay
ai

ee
-e
ea

5
i–e
-y
igh

o–e
oa
ow
-o

u–e
ew

-a-

-e-
ea

-i-
—y

-o-

-u-

aw
au
a(ll)
o(r)

oo

ur
er
ir
or

a(r)

oo
u

ow
ou

oy
oi

exercised that the methods used will ensure the development of mature reading habits. Therefore, it is recommended:

> that no single method of instruction in beginning reading be advocated but that a variety of approaches be utilized and that these be adjusted to the competencies and needs of the individual children, and that research studies be initiated to determine the interrelationship of personality, socio-economic backgrounds, ability, and the various approaches to teaching reading, particularly at the initial stages of reading instruction.[8]

7. One deficiency in the teaching of reading today is the absence of a sequentially organized program of reading skills development. While ample time is devoted in most schools to the identification of new words and to the beginning comprehension skills, higher level reading abilities are often neglected or treated only superficially in the intermediate grade curricula. If children are to become mature readers, they must become critical and creative readers. They must be challenged as to their understanding of what has been read and guided beyond the acquisition of mere factual information. Many pupils are intellectually capable of expanding their horizons over and above what is demanded of them in elementary school classrooms. Therefore, it is recommended:

> that a definite program be initiated in which all children are taught critical and creative reading skills at levels appropriate for their development, and that teachers find ways to stimulate thinking beyond the literal meaning of passages read.

10. During the course of the field study it became obvious that basal readers were often misused. Many teachers apparently were unaware of the real purposes of basal texts and frequently relied on these books as the sole tool of instruction. Furthermore, although the manuals for most basal series contain specific instructions regarding the use of a wide variety of other materials, few children are exposed to these supplementary materials on anything approaching a regularly sustained basis. The omission of such materials can have serious consequences in limiting the children's education. Therefore it is recommended:

> that teachers be instructed in the appropriate use of basal readers as one instructional tool and that basal readers be used in conjunction with other reading materials, such as trade books, reference books, newspapers, magazines, and audio-visual aids.[9]

Fitzpatrick reports that the different approaches used to teach beginning reading in 1966-1967 in New Mexico included:[10]

---

[8]Mary C. Austin and Coleman Morrison, *The First R, The Harvard Report on Reading in Elementary Schools* (New York: The Macmillan Company, 1963), pp. 220-221. From the forty-five recommendations of Chapter IX: "Will Tomorrow Be Another Day?"

[9]*Ibid.* Recommendations No. 7 and No. 10, pp. 222-223.

[10]Mildred Fitzpatrick, "Reading is Talk—Written Down," *New Mexico School Review*, 47:12-13ff., October, 1967.

1. an eclectic basal reading approach
2. "meaning" to "sound-symbol" approach
3. language-experience approach
4. teaching English as a second language approach
5. a multi-sensory approach
6. a thinking approach to learning
7. a phonetic approach
8. a programmed approach
9. the linguistic approach
10. an individualized instruction approach
11. machine approach

Observing research studies in progress, one sees that there are greater differences among classrooms than among the methods being used—and a prime factor in these findings is the differences in the teachers themselves and their individual abilities to relate to the children being taught.

In all teaching of reading, a primary consideration must be the development of concepts—the translation of concrete experiences into abstractions. In order to be a good reader, one must be able to do abstract and critical thinking.[11]

Based primarily on the IRA Perspective in Reading, *First Grade Reading Programs*, the strengths and weaknesses of various methodologies are pointed out in the following tables.[12]

TABLE 17.1. *Summary of Strengths and Weaknesses of the Basal Reader Approach to Teaching Reading*

Strengths	Weaknesses
1. Eclectic in nature with practices integrated from all systems	1. Too much vocabulary control—dull, repetitious
2. *Sequential* order in presentation of skills	2. Limited content in pre-primers: shallow, unrealistic, lack of literary style
3. *Continuity* of all skills through the grades	3. Lack of visibility in the way skills are developed
4. *Integration*—coordination of materials and skills	4. Stories are not related to boys' interests in general
5. Gradual introduction of vocabulary and word analysis skills	5. Sentence patterns appear haphazardly without repetition or mastery
6. Organization is horizontal (coordination of materials) and vertical (social organization, vocabulary, word analysis skills, comprehension)	6. Race and ethnic groups are stereotyped and stylized
	7. Tell only easy and comfortable life
	8. Attitudes: society not realistic
	9. Not enough done to stimulate curiosity
	10. Need to make important things *interesting*

[11]*Ibid.*, p. 46.
[12]Kerfoot, James F., Editor, *Girst Grade Reading Programs*, Perspectives in Reading, No. 5 (Newark, Del. 19711: International Reading Association, 1965)

TABLE 17.2.   *Summary of Strengths and Weaknesses of the Language Experience Approach to Teaching Reading*

Strengths	Weaknesses
1. Shows children that reading is just talk written down	1. Vocabulary may be too uncontrolled
2. Encourages communication—free and easy talk	2. May not provide continuity in teaching phonics skills
3. Makes reading a meaningful experience	3. May not learn thinking, problem-solving skills in comprehension
4. It is flexible	4. Important gains in child progress may not be measured on standardized test at end of school
5. Encourages greater creative experience in writing original stories	5. Classroom may seem disorganized during reading class
6. Provides a source of materials for the culturally deprived child	6. Charts used must seem to the children to have specific purposes
7. Gives opportunity for the teacher to emphasize the left-to-right direction in beginning sentence reading	7. Requires extra preparation: chart making, planning firsthand experiences on the part of the teacher
8. Children learn to share their own ideas—but, more importantly, they learn to listen to the ideas of others	
9. Children learn use of punctuation marks	
10. Pitch, intonation, and stress can be more meaningful using child's natural spoken language in his sentences	

TABLE 17.3.   *Summary of Strengths and Weaknesses of the Individualized Reading Approach to Teaching Reading*

Strengths	Weaknesses
1. Self-selected books are more likely to satisfy reading interests	1. Inadequate library materials in the schools
2. Greater opportunity for interaction among students in bringing togther ideas gained from independent reading	2. Danger of insufficient skill development
3. Child progresses at his own rate	3. Puts heavy clerical burden on the teacher
4. Individual teacher-pupil conferences develop rapport	4. Difficult to find time for enough individual conferences
5. Diminishes competition and comparison; avoids stigma of being in lowest group	5. Young children need much guidance in material selection
6. Each child experiences greater self-worth; takes more initiative	6. Hard to judge difficulty of books
7. Flexible—no ceiling on the learning	7. Is only one of possible ways to accommodate for differences in children
	8. Inordinate amount of time spent in preparing individual skills lessons

8. Some children can be introduced to a much greater variety of reading materials
9. Small groups are formed as needed for specific purposes
10. Through time, teachers should develop greater skill and flexibility in teaching
11. Some children can be guided in more oral and written expression and in critical thinking

9. Inefficient to teach a skill to an individual that half a dozen need at that time
10. May cultivate habits of carelessness in reading and lack of thoroughness
11. Difficult to administer written seatwork
12. Control (discipline) of room may be more difficult for teacher
13. Demands a teacher of unusual ability
14. Teacher must do a good job of interpreting program to the parents

---

TABLE 17.4. *Summary of Strengths and Weaknesses of the Miami Linguistic Readers in Teaching Reading to Children Learning English as a Second Language*

Strengths	Weaknesses
1. Designed for Spanish-speaking bilinguals	1. Teacher needs experience in second language teaching
2. Aural-oral approaches in TESL precede formal reading and develop sound contrasts between Spanish and English	2. Teachers and administrators are frightened by the title words "Linguistic" and "Miami"
3. Child has aural-oral control of material he is expected to read	3. The system looks deceptively simple
4. Sound-symbols are presented systematically in terms of spelling patterns	4. Teachers and administrators must both be receptive to the materials —and so must the parents
5. Has controlled vocabulary	5. Must be followed sequentially
6. Has controlled grammatical structures	6. Program must be carried through to completion for best results
7. Language experience precedes reading and is integrated with reading, providing reinforcement	7. Slow progress at first in terms of reading the first pre-primer. Parents may expect the child to read materials that are familiar to them —traditional basal readers
8. Listening, speaking, reading and writing and spelling are developed through the same material reinforcing each other	8. Not enough concern for beginning development of thinking skills
9. Learner achieves success at each level as he progresses	9. Long range effectiveness not yet known through research
10. Repetition of patterns and structures for review and relearning	
11. Uses good principles of both structural linguistics and developmental reading	
12. Reflects *natural* language forms of children's speech	

TABLE 17.5. *Summary of Strengths and Weaknesses of a Strong
Phonics Approach to Teaching Beginning Reading*

Strengths	Weaknesses
1. Aids in auditory perception	1. Inhibits other skills if overempha-
2. Aids in visual-auditory discrimi-	sized in the beginning
nation	2. Over-reliance narrows flexibility in
3. Aid to word recognition	reading
4. Aid to unlocking new, strange	3. Memorizing phonics rules *does*
words	*not* assure ability to use them
5. Systematic system of learning let-	4. Meaning is really much more im-
ter sounds	portant than sounding
6. Builds independent and confident	5. Too many sounds are spelled alike
reading	6. Too many rules—and most of them
7. Useful in spelling and composi-	have exceptions
tion	7. No good for children with hearing
8. Scientifically sound if taught in	defects
logical sequence, has universal ac-	8. Intensive drill can kill interest in
ceptance	reading

Cutts reminds teachers that:

> Six-year-olds who cannot talk coherently can scarcely be expected
> to begin reading as soon as they enter school. Teachers need to ap-
> proach English language instruction for underprivileged children as if
> they were teaching a foreign language. Children whose language is
> limited to grunts and crudities need extensive experiences before they
> are ready for any formalized reading instruction. Underprivileged chil-
> dren must have plenty of time to react to talk about the things they
> have seen and heard. Many culturally deprived children have extremely
> limited horizons; many have never traveled more than two blocks from
> home before entering school. [13]

For children with problems, Jastak and Jastak have some pertinent
advice for teachers:

> The literature on reading instruction contains various prescriptions
> as to what children should not be encouraged to do in learning to read.
> Sometimes such prescriptions are in the form of indirect allusions that
> children are slowed down when they use certain ways of learning.
> Among the Taboos are pointing with the finger, moving lips, oral
> reading, reading without comprehension, spelling aloud before reading,
> reading without inflection, phonic reading, breaking words up into syl-
> lables, etc. These interdictions are taught with complete confidence in
> their validity without evidence that they are bad habits except that
> they "slow children down." Furthermore, they are applied as absolute
> rules to persons of any age and at any point of the learning stage. We
> have heard of supervisors and reading specialists visiting classrooms for
> the sole purpose of checking whether any of the children move their
> lips or point with their fingers while reading. Teachers whose children

---

[13]Warren G. Cutts, "Reading *Unreadiness* in the Underprivileged," *NEA Journal*, 52:24-25, April, 1963.

move their lips are condemned as inferior and are given poor professional ratings. This strange behavior on the part of supervisors and reading experts causes more retardation in reading than any moving of the lips or pointing with the fingers has ever done. It can be demonstrated that some children who point with their fingers read faster and more accurately than when they do not. The fallacy of "being slowed down" stems from the observations that good readers do not point with their fingers but poor readers do. It is known however to students of statistics that correlation is not causation. The poor reader, finding that he loses his way or that his performance is not what it should be, hits upon the device of using his finger to help himself. Pointing with the finger becomes an important temporary aid in overcoming the coordination difficulties that exist in poor readers. Pointing with the finger is not a cause but an effect of reading disability. It is helpful in the early stages of learning to read and is spontaneously abandoned as the skill of reading gains in efficiency.[14]

VI. SEX DIFFERENCES IN FIRST GRADE

Expected behavior roles of children are different. It is not without reason that we have the Mother Goose Rhyme:

What are little girls made of?
Sugar and spice and all that's nice
That's what little girls are made out of.
What are little boys made of?
Snaps and snails and puppy dog tails
That's what little boys are made out of.

These behavior roles are sometimes evident in ways parents, especially fathers, expect little boys to be "little men" when they really feel like crying! Boys are "supposed" to learn to defend themselves, never act like "sissies," and display sufficient masculine aggression.

Little girls are expected to wear pretty little starched pinafores, sit quietly like little ladies and "be nice." A mother whose first little girl turns out to be a "regular tomboy" sometimes expresses disappointment.

Language development, on the average, is more favorable to girls. As a total group, they are likely to speak in sentences earlier, use longer sentences and more of them than boys, and achieve clear enunciation of all the phonemes of the language younger than boys.

This suggests that girls may enter first grade with two distinct advantages: (1) greater ability to sit still and do "sitting still" activities and (2) greater facility with language. Add to this the bland pre-primer reading one can do with eighteen or twenty basic sight words, and a

---

[14]Careth Ellingson, *The Shadow Children* (Five North Wabash Avenue, Chicago, Illinois 60602: Topaz Books, 1967), pp. 92-93, quoted from J. F. Jastak and S. R. Jastak, *Wide Range Achievement Test—Manual of Instructions* (Wilmington, Delaware: Guidance Associates).

woman teacher who may emphasize female values and the girls *do* have an advantage.

Durkin has suggested that if first grade teachers could liven up beginning reading with stories about jet planes and how they work, or rockets and the boosters they need to get into space, boys would probably fare much better.

Since boys outnumber girls about ten to one in need of remedial reading instruction, there is obviously need for schools to do everything possible to alleviate non-achievement problems of boys.

There is some evidence of greater difficulty of mothers in giving birth to baby boys. Statistically, about 53 births in 100 are boys and this may be nature's way of compensating for the "weaker" sex to insure equal numbers of males and females in the population. It has been theorized that the boy baby may be larger in size and the head subject to greater danger of injury during the birth process with resulting incidence of minimum brain dysfunction, neurological impairment, or brain lesions.

While all of these facts point up evidence that statistical averages favor school success for girls, one must immediately caution that this in no way admits of individual differences within each sex. In other words, boys fall along the whole continuum of readiness for reading in school, as do girls. Therefore, it is clear that *some* boys at age six are much more ready for formal school than *some* girls of the same chronological age. The suggestion, occasionally voiced, that girls might enter school a year younger than boys, cannot be generalized to *all* six year olds.

> The average girl of six is more advanced than the average boy of that age in general development, including skeletal structure, and she maintains this superiority throughout the usual span of ages of the primary grades. In both height and weight, as well as in other aspects of size, the average boy surpasses the average girl.[15]

Tests measuring success in school generally show girls superior in performance all the way through high school in English and courses heavily laden with language concepts. In high school, boys overtake girls in science and mathematics courses.

The attitude toward school is apt to favor girls all the way through. Boys are more apt to rebel, become belligerent, or fail to see reasons why school needs to be largely unrelated to life.

Deutsch[16] found important sex differences among Negro children in severely culturally deprived areas. Negro girls could aspire, with some

---

[15]Martha Dallman, *Teaching the Language Arts in the Elementary School* (Dubuque, Iowa: William C. Brown Company, Publishers, 1966), p. 13.

[16]Martin Deutsch, *Minority Group and Class Status as Related to Social and Personality Factors in Scholastic Achievement,* (Cornell University, Ithaca, New York: Society for Applied Anthropology, Monograph No. 2, 1960) pp. 8-13.

likelihood of achieving, to jobs as clerks, clerk typists, secretaries, while Negro boys were apt to see that Negro men were usually thwarted in job opportunities if "Whites" were available to fill them. Also, the Negro children more often saw the mother as the family authority figure and the man more often less able to contribute to the family's needs. With no economic value to the family, he has little ego strength and is a negative psychological force rather than a positive one.

Stanchfield reports a study designed to determine whether or not boys might experience greater success in reading if taught in classes of boys only.

> . . . Using 550 children in the first grades of the Los Angeles City Schools, reading was taught in sex-segregated groups. Care was taken to provide a wide range of socio-economic levels. Two reading periods were offered, one in the morning and one in the afternoon. The outcome of this study was that, after statistical analyses of reading achievement and reading growth, boys taught in the absence of girls did not show more significant gains in achievement or in growth than boys taught in mixed groupings. Again, the girls as a group achieved more significantly than boys and showed greater reading growth.[17]

Following are comments of teachers who taught "boys only" groups in Stanchfield's study.

> "Boys are so overwhelming active, so frighteningly energetic, so terribly vigorous, so utterly strenuous." "It's so hard for a six-year-old boy to keep himself occupied with reading a book." "Boys tend to wiggle, twist, push, turn, shove, and, in general, bother each other instead of reading."

> "Girls are so quiet and controlled—they can sit quietly and read a book." "Girls are easier to teach—so ladylike and easy to handle."

> . . . Generally, boys were less anxious to please the teacher, less motivated to develop good work habits, lacked desire to assume responsibility and were less self-motivated in learning to read. Gates . . . suggested that boys in the culture have had less goal-direction for the act of reading than the girls, while they have more motivation for physical involvement and activity.[18]

Betts makes these observations about sex differences and beginning reading:

> First, there is some evidence to the effect that girls are promoted on lower standards of achievement than boys are. Second, girls use read-

---

[17]Jo M. Stanchfield, "Do Girls Learn to Read Better Than Boys in the Primary Grades?" in Ralph Staiger and David Sohn, Editors, *New Directions in Reading* (271 Madison Avenue, New York, New York 10016: Bantam Books, Inc., 1967), p. 60; see also, Jo M. Stanchfield, "Boys' Achievement in Reading," in J. Allen Figurel, Editor, *Reading and Inquiry,* International Reading Association Conference Proceedings, 10:290-293, 1965.

[18]Jo. M. Stanchfield, *ibid.,* pp. 60-61; see also, Arthur I. Gates, "Sex Differences in Reading Ability," *Elementary School Journal,* 61:431-434, May, 1961.

ing activities for recreation more often than boys do. Third, there is a need for more reading materials to challenge the interests of boys.[19]

Yet, at the same time, Betts cautions:

Sex differences in readiness for reading may be over-emphasized. After all, there is considerable overlap between sexes. Girls as well as boys may be characterized by speech defects and delayed language development.[20]

VII. SUMMARY

Beginning reading should incorporate all the methodological skills the teacher can bring to bear. Teaching reading includes developing a basic sight vocabulary, learning phonetic and structural analysis skills, developing comprehension, and practicing reading in rewarding situations. Teachers' problems arise much more from the complexity of children than from the lack of method.

This chapter has evaluated basal reader approaches, language experience approaches, individualized reading, use of phonics in reading, and some of the less widely used methodology.

Suggested Activities

1. Compare and contrast the teaching of beginning reading with teaching reading at successively higher levels.

2. Enumerate the major strengths and weaknesses of the three main methods of teaching beginning reading.

3. Compare teaching for readiness to read with teaching beginning reading.

Reading References

Allen, R. V. and Allen, Clarice. *Language Experiences in Reading: Teacher's Resource Book*, Levels I through VI (Chicago: Encyclopedia Britannica Press, 1965-67).

Chall, Jeanne. *Learning to Read: The Great Debate* (New York: McGraw-Hill, 1967).

DeBoer, J. J. and Martha Dallmann. *The Teaching of Reading* (New York: Holt, Rinehart and Winston, Inc., 1964). Chapter 14: "The Reading Program in the Primary Grades," pp. 351-371.

Durkin, Dolores. "Early Readers—Reflections After Six Years of Research," *The Reading Teacher*, 18:3-7, October, 1964.

---

[19]Emmett Albert Betts, *Foundations of Reading Instruction* (New York: American Book Company, 1950), p. 137.
[20]*Ibid.*, p. 137.

First Grade Reading Studies. U. S. Office of Education, *The Reading Teacher,* Vol. 19, No. 8, May, 1966, and Vol. 20, No. 1, October, 1966.

HARRIS, ALBERT J. *Effective Teaching of Reading* (New York: David McKay Co., Inc., 1962). Chapter 3: "Beginning to Read," pp. 43-68.

HEILMAN, ARTHUR W. *Principles and Practices in Teaching Reading,* Second Edition (Columbus, Ohio: Charles E. Merrill Books, Inc., 1967). Chapter 3: "Beginning Readers," pp. 73-95; Chapter 4: "Beginning Reading," pp. 97-135; Chapter 5: "Beginning Reading—The Instructional Program," pp. 137-167.

KERFOOT, JAMES F., Editor. *First Grade Reading Programs,* Perspectives in Reading, No. 5 (Newark, Delaware 19711: International Reading Association, 1965).

KLINEBERG, OTTO. "Life Is Fun in a Smiling, Fair-Skinned World," *Saturday Review,* 46:75-77, 1963.

LAMOREAUX, LILLIAN and DORIS M. LEE. *Learning to Read Through Experience* (New York: Appleton-Century-Crofts, Inc., 1943).

LEE, DORRIS M. *Diagnostic Teaching* (1201 Sixteenth St., N.W., Washington, D. C. 20036: Department of Elementary-Kindergarten-Nursery Education, National Education Association, 1966).

LEE, DORIS M. and ROACH VAN ALLEN. *Learning to Read Through Experience* (New York: Appleton-Century-Crofts, Inc., 1963).

MACKINTOSH, HELEN K., Editor. *Current Approaches to Teaching Reading* (1201 Sixteenth St., N.W., Washington, D. C.: Department of Elementary-Kindergarten-Nursery Education, National Education Association, 1965).

McKEE, PAUL, *Reading: A Program of Instruction for the Elementary School* (Boston: Houghton Mifflin Co., 1966). Part II: "The First Major Phase of Instruction," pp. 45-220.

SMITH, NILA BANTON. *American Reading Instruction* (Newark, Delaware 19711: International Reading Association, 1965).

TINKER, M. A. and CONSTANCE McCULLOUGH. *Teaching Elementary Reading,* Third Edition (New York: Appleton-Century-Crofts, Inc., 1968). Chapter 21: "Recommended Practices in First Grade," pp. 439-472.

In the final section of the text, children with learning problems are described. The need for diagnosis is explicit in the many causes of reading disability.

Many children are not functioning as well in the reading process as their capacity for learning would suggest; many profit greatly from the teacher's use of corrective techniques in the classroom. Special programs must be provided for the intellectually gifted, the mentally retarded, and the few who have special learning disabilities rooted in neurological impairment or in emotional disturbance. Those with special learning disabilities, more often than not receiving no special help today, desperately need special methodologies. When no provision is made in the school system for their diagnosis and teaching in special clinics, classroom teachers must incorporate special reading programs for them. The teacher needs help, support, and encouragement from many professionals who can help the teacher better understand and work with the handicapped child.

Through continuous diagnosis and identification of children's abilities, disabilities, and possibilities, the teacher will be able to formulate measurable, behavioral objectives so that tangible results will reveal whether learning is taking place or whether there is need for further study.

Many of the children who become remedial reading cases—Bond and Tinker[1] estimate seventy-five per cent—could be helped successfully by the classroom teacher without extensive diagnosis, if

1. all the **pressure** from the teacher for every child to complete the same work in the same amount of time with the same amount of practice were **eliminated**;
2. each child were accepted as an **individual** and permitted to work at his **instructional** level of reading, and to move only as fast as he is able to learn;
3. the teacher's effort were bent toward providing many learning activities at many levels of difficulty so that each child would be challenged at his growing edge of learning;
4. the philosophy of the school were that there were other personnel also concerned about each child's learning so that no teacher need operate as an island unto himself.

---

[1]Guy L. Bond and Miles A. Tinker, *Reading Difficulties: Their Diagnosis and Correction* (New York: Appleton, Century, Crofts, Inc., 1967), p. 245.

18

Corrective Reading

Holt's comment suggests that the expectations of the school and the efforts of boys and girls are not directed toward the same goals:

> When I started, I thought that some people were just born smarter than others and that not much could be done about it. This seems to be the official line of most of the psychologists. It isn't hard to believe, if all your contacts are with students in the classroom or the psychological testing room. But, if you live at a small school, seeing students in class, in the dorms, in their private lives, at their recreations, sports, and manual work, you can't escape the conclusion that some people are much smarter part of the time than they are at other times. Why? Why should a boy or girl, who under some circumstances is willingly observant, imaginative, analytical, in a word, intelligent, come into the classroom and, as if by magic, turn into a complete dolt?[1]

When Carolyn came for instruction in remedial reading, she made it quite evident that as far as she could tell, neither the school's effort nor her evaluation of the school program were designed to help her.

> Carolyn's mother called and asked if her daughter, age fourteen and finishing the eighth grade, might have an evaluation of her reading skills. It was the final week of school late in May and an appointment was made for early June.
>
> Carolyn came for testing in an obviously belligerent mood. Her mother brought her and waited for her during the testing and this was an obvious irritation for Carolyn.
>
> Carolyn explained to the clinician that she was stupid. When the clinician raised some doubt about it, Carolyn said, "Just ask all the teachers over at Junior High, they'll all tell you I'm stupid." The clinician presented a brief list of polysyllabic words to be pronounced and divided in syllables, and Carolyn commented, "O. K., so you can see how stupid I really am."

---

[1] John Holt, *How Children Fail* (New York: Harper and Row, 1964), p. 5.

Part of the diagnosis of a reading disability is the taking of an individual intelligence test.

After diagnosis and recommendations, the teacher provides individualized instruction to meet the needs of the student. Photos courtesy of University of New Mexico Photo Service.

When she defined the vocabulary words in the Stanford-Binet test and earned an "average adult" score on that subtest, the clinician used this bit of evidence to say that she was apparently doing as well as the average on that particular test. At this, Carolyn said acidly, "So that's an intelligence test! I've had those at junior high, too, and the counselor there told me I was stupid."

Later the young lady revealed that, not only was she stupid, but she was also huge. She thought she was as big as a horse. She was a large-boned fourteen-year-old and taller and heavier than the average girl in her class.

On the reading survey test, she scored at beginning fifth grade on vocabulary, speed, and comprehension. This was no surprise to Carolyn and she let it be known that she understood that the clinician was collecting further evidence of her stupidity.

Carolyn's summer program included one lesson a week, during which she studied spelling, phonetic and structural analysis, and syllabication, and wrote paragraphs about topics of her choice. In addition, she came twice a week to complete, independently, exercises from the SRA Junior Reading for Understanding Laboratory. She began with card No. 17, at beginning fifth grade level. At this level, she was successful, and completed two cards at each level until she reached beginning sixth grade level in about two weeks. When she read the table of grade placement values in the teacher's guidebook, she began to appear much more confident. By the end of eight weeks, she was ready for cards at beginning ninth grade level and appeared confident that she would be able to do her reading work in the fall.

Her summer program had been well-planned apart from the reading lessons, too, and she had enjoyed short courses at the YWCA in cheerleading, drama, and charm. In addition, she was an excellent swimmer and participated as a member of a girls swimming team.

Corrective reading is the instruction provided by the regular classroom teacher during the school day to help individual children overcome whatever stumbling block besets them in the achieving of developmental skills in reading. Children who fail to master a basic sight vocabulary, who fail to develop auditory discrimination of phonemes in the English language, who fail to learn to read fluently so that they can read entertainingly to others are in need of remediation, re-teaching, special help, or tutoring to master the missing mechanical skills. Of course, the problem of adequate comprehension of material read must also be considered. Children who fail to comprehend may or may not have adequate word recognition skills. To distinguish these needs from remedial instruction is only to indicate that in these cases, the effort is made by the teacher within the framework of the regular teaching day, rather than by a remedial reading clinician who teaches the child during a period of time outside the classroom. While no clear-cut distinction can be made between what is remedial and what is corrective, it is convenient to think specifically about ways the classroom teacher will function "all day long" as a teacher of these children with special difficulties.

Hopefully, the corrective reading cases will not be severely complicated by emotional problems, neurological problems, or language deficits, but they may well be. Hopefully, if the philosophy of teaching throughout the elementary school has been a diagnostic one, many of these problems will have been identified early and deep-seated emotional problems may have been averted.

With early identification, teachers need to emphasize ways in which children learn best, try to strengthen ways of learning that are difficult, and provide a systematic program of sequenced instruction of skills over as long a period of time as is indicated.

Hildreth points out:

> One of the most baffling problems the primary teacher has to meet is that of the average boy in the third grade who cannot read. Usually these cases have been slow learners right along, but they are pushed ahead because they obviously do not belong with the younger children. Often these children have small talents of some sort but not the kinds of abilities the school values highly. Part of the solution to the problem these boys present lies in providing readiness activities and individualized procedures in the beginning stages of their schooling. Another attack on the problem lies in discovering their small talents, seeking out their interests and then providing reading and other activities that harmonize with these interests, making all their reading instruction functional and practical, and developing all their linguistic skills right along with the reading. Extreme cases of retardation and nonreaders with personality difficulties may need clinical help if no progress is shown during the second or third years.[2]

One of Hildreth's recommendations is:

> When a new supply of books is at hand, it is a good plan to start the books several grades above the indicated grade level. Let the third grade try out the new first readers for easy storyreading. As lower-grade pupils get ready for the more difficult books, pass them on down. In this way the older children are provided with plenty of interesting new material they can read fluently and younger children feel they are growing up in ability to use older children's books.[3]

I.   WHY DO CHILDREN FAIL?

It may be well to look at the negative approaches to the question first. These are some of the issues often cited that are *not* the reasons why so many children fail in reading.

---

[2]Gertrude Hildreth, "Programs in Grades II and III," *Reading in the Elementary School,* Forty-Eighth Yearbook of the National Society for the Study of Education, Part II, Nelson B. Henry, Editor (Chicago: University of Chicago Press, 1949), p. 124.

[3]*Ibid.,* p. 103.

1. It is *not* because teachers do *not* teach phonics in the elementary schools today. In the lessons on word attack skills, specific techniques are presented in all teacher's guides.
2. It is *not* because teachers do not know how to teach reading. If a teacher in a busy, crowded classroom teaches 85 per cent of her class to read successfully in terms of their potential ability to achieve, it is unfair to look at the small percentage who fail to progress and place all blame on the teacher. Might it not be much more logical to say that the overcrowded conditions of the classrooms may be a primary cause?
3. It is *not* because schools are progressive and permit anarchy in their classrooms. Sufficient standard test data is available today to prove convincingly that groups of children today read better than comparable groups did at any time in the past. Further, there is evidence to show that children who are taught in classrooms where "activity" work, teacher-pupil planning, and student responsibility are encouraged, read better, on the average, than those taught in more formally organized classrooms.
4. It is *not* because too little time is devoted to the 3 R's. If one visits many classrooms, he will soon see that teachers have never gotten away from devoting much time to the 3 R's . . . and really spend too much time working on routine, unmotivated, monotonous lessons trying to help children learn the 3 R's.
5. It is *not* because the parents won't cooperate with the schools. Although there are a few "incompatible" situations between teachers and parents, parent-teacher conferences help immeasurably to clarify problems of children in school.

While it is emphasized that none of these five causes should be used as a generalized vague reason for our problems, it is acknowledged that any one of these may be a primary contributing factor in individual cases.

The causes stem from the traditional organization of the school and the necessity of putting children in classes where "standards" have been defined arbitrarily in terms of grade placement, automatically leading to failure for all those who do not "measure up." All children may come to school when they are six and enroll in the first grade. All parents are strongly pressured by the mores of the community to see that their child fits a "normal" pattern.

The "organized school" works far too hard trying to make everybody alike—to conform to a preconceived stereotype—rather than really encouraging individuality. Even when schools give lip service to the idea of accepting individuality, they often work against it in practice. Teachers are habituated to a deeply entrenched practice of teaching *books* rather than teaching *children* to read books.

The continuing practice that every first grader must read first grade readers, every second grader, second grade readers, and every third grader, third grade readers, and so on, will never work.

Teachers should have children read for regular classes only books that are appropriate for their instructional level. (Instructional level is that level at which in reading 100 words running, the child fails to pronounce no more than five, and can answer questions to show that he understands 75 per cent of the ideas. See Chapter 3.)

Teachers who do not hold stringently to this standard and allow children to work in books that are too difficult, keep them "grinding away" at the frustration level. Children can do little more than "memorize statements and parrot facts" when they are kept reading at this level.

Teachers, generally, have not followed an application of our knowledge of the psychology of individual differences to its logical conclusion. One hears from teachers and administrators, "What are you going to do when they get to the fourth grade?" "What will they do when they get to seventh grade?" or "How about when they come to high school at ninth grade?"

One accepts the situation as he finds it. Two basic principles about learning apply here: (1) the spread of mental ability in any grade is going to increase as children go through school; and (2) no child can read a harder book until he can read an easier one. If these two principles are accepted, one has no alternative but to start where the child is. Not knowing or rejecting these principles, a few teachers have said, "But I'm a sixth grade teacher and I don't know anything about phonics," or "I'm an upper grade teacher and I don't know how to teach primary reading," or "I teach seventh grade and they're supposed to learn that in the lower grades."

Teachers need to remember that in their classes children exhibit different levels of understanding what they do understand. Level of understanding is determined by degree of intelligence and previous experiences either first hand or vicarious. Children may understand a concept very well; they may understand some things about the concept; or they may have only a rather vague idea of what the concept is about. It helps little to try to clarify concepts in children's thinking if their chief concern is remembering facts to give back to a teacher. Concepts are clarified best by seeing that the same concept is dealt with in many ways, using the concept in problems related to the child's life experience.

Finally, many schools do not have an overall school policy that gives teachers confidence in what they do in one calendar year. Over-all policy gives continuity to the school program from grade to grade. Present-day school programs must recognize the necessity of teaching reading all the way through the secondary school and having a cumulative record available for each child so that each teacher has access to all the helpful information compiled by the child's previous teachers.

Causes of reading failure will be met only by:

1. *Doing* something about individual differences. This means doing something about them *all day long*. If the child reads a fourth grade reader much of the year while he is in the sixth grade, then he should spell fourth grade spelling words and read factual information in all his content subjects no more difficult than fourth grade reader level. It means accepting careful measures of readiness for reading before putting all children into a formal reading program in first grade. It means that educators must stop expecting all children in a class to "learn the same thing, in the same amount of time, with the same amount of practice."

2. Knowing how to use information about children and where to get it:

   Cumulative records should contain:
   a. Intelligence test records
   b. Health records
   c. Reading record of books read previously
   d. Summaries of personal conferences with child, parent, or other professional
   e. Standardized tests of achievement

3. Having an accepted school policy that everybody is willing to put into effect. The school program should be well enough understand by each teacher to give her maximum security. Over-all school policies should accept these basic principles:
   a. The school exists solely to help children. This means that no child is a "misfit." They *all* belong.
   b. Since no two are alike, the teacher must start "where each child is" to help him. This means each teacher rests securely in the fact that each succeeding teacher will also accept the wide range of differences in a class when they are promoted.
   c. Every teacher is a reading teacher. Children must be taught how to read all the different kinds of material with which they are confronted: extensive reading, intensive reading, reading to evaluate critically, reading to remember details, and recreatory reading are some of the types.
   d. An accepting, analytical approach to existing problems. An open-mindedness and "pooling of ideas" when teacher, principal, and special services representatives discuss a child with a problem.

No one should feel insecure in asking for help with children who present difficult problems. (See below, the need for "staffing" case studies.)

4. Having a Special Services Department to analyze problems. This means personnel who are able to analyze problems in areas of:
   a. Remedial reading
   b. Behavior
   c. Mental retardation or acceleration
   d. Physical handicaps
   e. Speech correction and speech improvement

   When a child's problem has been studied and a case study has been prepared, a round table discussion where participants include teachers, parents, principal, school guidance counselor, school social worker, school nurse, school psychologist, school doctor, visiting teacher, and special therapists or as many of these people as are concerned with the case (or as are on the staff) should be of primary importance in implementing the findings.

5. Having adequate *materials of instruction*

   Probably the one greatest obstacle to improvement of classroom instruction today is the lack of adequate materials of all sorts (books, magazines, pamphlets, charts, maps, pictures, films, filmstrips, models, workbooks) for teacher use.

6. The best practice in reporting a child's progress to his parents must come by way of some kind of two-way communication. There must be some time and some way that the teacher can discuss in a "face-to-face" situation with the parents the progress in academic work and social development the child is making. The parents can say in the same "face-to-face" situation to the teacher what they are thinking, and then, in this same conversational atmosphere, they can work out any semantic differences. While they may not agree, at least they have a greater degree of understanding of each other's opinions. Sometimes, such a conversation gives them much mutual support.

In summary, six suggestions have been discussed for meeting the problems in reading failure:

1. Recognizing and meeting individual differences
2. Knowing how to obtain and use information about children
3. Accepting a school policy that is effective from the first year through senior high school
4. Utilizing special services and special personnel in studying about children
5. Providing adequate materials of instruction
6. Working cooperatively with parents

II. REMEDIAL TECHNIQUES

The reader will recall from the four reading levels defined in Chapter 3 about the Informal Reading Inventory, that the child can operate at one of three levels: the independent level at which he does his free reading; the instructional level at which he can function in the classroom with usual readiness for reading; and the frustration level at which he makes too many errors in mechanics of reading and/or comprehends too few of the ideas in the context to profit from the work. In corrective reading materials, the teacher should take every precaution that the reading the child may do outside the classroom is no more difficult than his independent reader level. The child may do easy oral reading practice for his parents if they will give him their interest and attention, but if it is *not* done at his independent reading level, his parents are apt not to understand his difficulties and may render him a great disservice.

It is generally not recommended that parents try to help their own children who have problems with their reading. This recommendation is sound for two reasons: first, without specialized training the parent is apt not to have the concept of fitting remedial teaching techniques to a specific child, and second, the mere situation of being the parent of a child who is *failing* in a task at which all children "*should*" succeed creates an emotionally stressful situation. With these two conditions present, when the child has difficulty, the result is apt to be an "emotional scene" of belligerence, aggression, crying, or some combination of these.

If a philosophy of diagnostic teaching has been followed, then corrective reading instruction is part of standard operating procedure. Difficulties are worked on as soon as they appear. Difficulties are uncovered, and reteaching is the next order of business. All children need spaced reviews and a great deal of reinforcement of important learnings.

Specific Difficulties

1. *Word recognition.* Many children finish the third grade without establishing automatic mastery of the 220 Dolch Basic Sight Words. Because this list is composed of the service words that constitute half of all the running words in elementary school textbooks, they must be mastered. Dolch also identified 95 commonest nouns in children's reading experience. No nouns were included in the basic sight words list since Dolch did not consider naming words to be "service" words. Any corrective reading program must provide for the teaching of these most used words. Suggestions for such teaching are included in Chapter 16.

Using The Dolch Basic Sight Word Test to Diagnose
Word Recognition Errors

Criteria for knowing a word as a *sight* word:

1. The child looks at the word and pronounces it correctly
2. He does not sound the word letter-by-letter
3. He does not need more than a few seconds to say the word.

If the child has difficulty and is missing as many words as he is recognizing as sight words, he should be allowed to stop the test. With older children making many errors, the teacher may decide to do only Part I or Part II of the *Basic Sight Word Test Sheet*.

A sample of the errors made by Pat on Part I are shown below. It is possible to make a more detailed analysis of the errors he has made. They may be grouped into the following categories: wrong beginnings, wrong middles, wrong endings, reversals, wrong several parts, and words he failed to pronounce. Pat's errors are analyzed in Table 18.1, page 439.

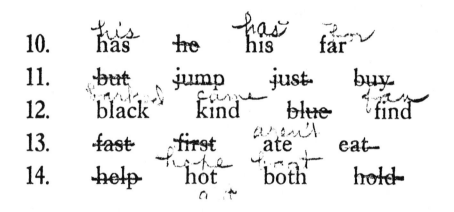

The analysis shows that Pat makes all types of errors. However, if *brown* for *down* is caused by reversing *b's* and *d's,* and *now* for *how* is caused by confusing *n's* and *h's,* Pat made fewer errors in beginnings. This is significant since, at the level at which he will be able to read context, attention to "How does the word begin?" seems most appropriate. Since Pat has pronounced about 55 of the words at sight, he might have known another 55 on the second part. By estimating a score of 110, the McBroom, Sparrow, Eckstein scale indicates a primer level of reading. (See table in Chapter 3.)

Wrong beginnings is probably the lowest "level" of error since first grade teachers work very hard on helping children perceive words from left to right. The teacher will probably want to give Pat some help with studying the word "all the way through" to be sure to get the endings

TABLE 18.1. *Analysis of Errors Made on Part I, Dolch Basic Sight Word Test*

Wrong beginnings	Wrong middles	Wrong endings	Reversals	Wrong several parts	Failed to pronounce
it for at	hid for had	his for him	me for am (?)	barked for black	drink
brown for down	here for have	bringing for bring	brown for down	came for kind	ask
now for how	my for may	boat for both	now for how	fan for find	as
gray for give	his for has	became for		aren't for ate	found
gray for gave	has for his	because		hope for hot	eight
	for for far	less for let		get for grow	better
(5)	a boat for about	go for got		a little for always	light
	fall for full	can for came		game for again	done
	bean for been			afraid for after	draw
	like for live	(7)	(3)	couldn't for clean	get
	din't for don't			four for five	
	came for come			bus for best	
				lake for laugh	
	(12)			hart for hurt	(10)
				could for carry	
				could for call	
				heard for here	
				had for here	
				(18)	

right. It becomes clear in the analysis that vowel sounds are giving Pat a great deal of difficulty in the middle of words. As his reading level increases to second grade, he will need complete instruction in all his vowel skills.

2. *Measuring abilities in phonetic and structural analysis.* The teacher can test informally the abilities of children in a reading group to identify the initial, medial, and final sounds in words by merely asking

a. What is the first sound you hear in: book, toy, forest, party, kitchen, candy (either *k* or *c*)?
b. What are the first two letters in these words: fright, snake, skate, scales (either *sk* or *sc*), praise, dwelling?
c. What is the middle sound you hear in: cabbage, forest, balloon, reading, practice?
d. What is the vowel that this word begins with: Indian, olives, elephant, umbrella, apple?

The teacher needs, however, a more standard measure of which phonetic elements a child knows and which ones he does not. There are some inventories available to the teacher for this purpose.

The McKee Inventory of Phonetic Skills[4] is one of these. The inventories are developed for end of grade one, end of grade two, and end. of grade three and are called Test One, Test Two, and Test Three. They sample those phonetic and structural elements that have been taught in the Houghton Mifflin Reading Program through the respective grade levels. Test two includes seven subtests: initial consonant sounds, final consonant sounds, structural elements, vowel elements, initial consonant sounds (more difficult), structural elements(more difficult), and vowel elements (more difficult). Test Two is reproduced on the following pages. A teacher's guide contains the rationale for the test, directions for administering and scoring and suggestions for reteaching items missed.

The California Phonics Survey,[5] designed for grades seven-twelve, tests vowel confusions, consonant confusions with blends and diagraphs, consonant vowel reversals, configuration, endings, negatives, opposites, and rigidity. There are two forms of this test and it may be done with machine-scored separate answer sheets.

McCullough Word-Analysis Tests,[6] Grades 4-6: initial blends and digraphs, phonetic discrimination, matching letters to vowel sounds,

---

[4]Paul McKee, *The McKee Inventory of Phonetic Skills,* Tests One, Two, and Three (Boston: Houghton Mifflin Company).

[5]Grace M. Brown and Alice B. Cottrell, *California Phonics Survey* (Monterrey, California: California Test Bureau, 1963).

[6]Constance M. McCullough, *McCullough Word Analysis Tests* (Boston: Ginn and Company, 1963).

sounding whole words, interpreting phonetic symbols, phonetic analysis, syllabication, and root words.

A fourth phonics survey is that provided by Science Research Associates.[7] A complete survey of phonetic and structural analysis skills, the test has twenty-one subtests including: initial consonants, final consonants, initial digraphs, final digraphs, initial blends, short vowels, long vowels, common phonograms and initial consonants, common phonograms and initial blends, easy endings, compound words, vowel digraphs, vowels followed by magic "r," special sounds, prefixes, and suffixes. This test serves very well for a teacher who wishes to use the first subtests and find how many subtests a child can do correctly, then to withhold the remainder of the test until more teaching has taken place, and afterwards to continue testing to measure progress.

Several of the subtests of the *Silent Reading Diagnostic Tests*[8] are also useful in analyzing phonetic and structural errors in children's reading test performance. They provide for analyzing initial, medial, and final errors in word recognition errors, in locating visual elements in words, syllabication, locating root words, hearing beginning sounds, hearing rhyming words, and identifying letter sounds.

3. *Directional sense on the page—left-to-right—orientation.* The arbitrary necessity for reading from left-to-right on the line of print is a learned behavior needed in our culture—although not in all cultures. A number of children have difficulties with this orientation when they come to school. The difficulty varies in intensity from one child to another, but teachers must have a few techniques for helping children overcome their confusion.

Children may reverse whole words: "was" for "saw"; "ten" for "net." They may reverse some of the letters inside words: "form" for "from"; "left" for "felt"; "tired" for "tried." Or, they may reverse only one letter: "pig" for "dig"; "put" for "but"; "way" for "may."

It is common, for instance, for the so-called dyslexic child to have imperfect directional sense—to confuse left and right and up and down. As a result, he is likely to reverse letters and words, or syllables within words: "b" becomes "d," "p" becomes "q"; "saw" may be written as "was," "left" as "felt," "on" as "no," and "sorrow" as "sowro"; and numbers may be similarly reversed with "42" substituted for "24." Up and down confusion leads him to write "M" for "W" and "d" for "p." All children, up to about age six, may have a few difficulties of this kind,

---

[7]Don H. Parker and Genevieve Scannell, *Phonics Survey*, to accompany Reading Laboratory I (259 East Erie Street, Chicago 11, Illinois: Science Research Associates, 1962).

[8]Guy L. Bond, Theodore Clymer, and Cyril J. Hoyt, *Silent Reading Diagnostic Tests* (Chicago: Lyons and Carnahan, 1970).

SECTION A

1. took	book	cook	nook	hook	24. saw	straw	claw	thaw	craw
2. hide	side	wide	bide	tide	25. must	rust	crust	thrust	trust
3. jar	par	bar	mar	tar	26. cap	clap	chap	flap	trap
4. just	bust	dust	gust	rust	27. made	trade	blade	glade	shade
5. more	tore	wore	bore	sore	28. trick	thick	brick	stick	chick
6. right	sight	fight	tight	wight	29. game	shame	frame	flame	blame
7. cent	dent	vent	bent	rent	30. than	bran	clan	scan	plan
8. round	pound	bound	hound	mound	31. well	cell	dell	jell	yell
9. hot	lot	pot	rot	cot	32. bag	drag	brag	flag	snag
10. mail	fail	wail	nail	hail	33. part	smart	chart	start	cart
11. bank	tank	sank	yank	rank	34. still	grill	drill	chill	thrill
12. send	lend	bend	tend	mend	35. top	drop	shop	crop	flop
13. black	track	shack	stack	whack	36. snow	blow	glow	slow	grow
14. lock	rock	sock	dock	mock	37. hand	grand	bland	brand	strand
15. match	hatch	batch	patch	latch	38. him	brim	whim	trim	slim
16. store	shore	snore	score	chore	39. dog	frog	smog	clog	flog
17. keep	weep	seep	peep	jeep	40. line	whine	twine	shine	brine
18. hit	sit	bit	kit	pit	41. tip	hip	lip	zip	dip
19. make	rake	fake	bake	lake	42. twin	skin	thin	chin	shin
20. bring	cling	fling	sting	sling	43. hide	slide	pride	bride	stride
21. truck	cluck	stuck	struck	pluck	44. will	gill	fill	hill	pill
22. knew	blew	grew	flew	chew	45. plow	brow	prow	chow	scow
23. line	dine	fine	pine	vine	46. take	stake	snake	shake	flake

SECTION B

47. stand	stamp	stab	stack	stag	61. fish	fit	fib	fix	fin
48. big	bid	bit	bib	bin	62. jack	jam	jag	jazz	jab
49. still	stick	sting	stiff	stitch	63. rope	rose	robe	rote	rode
50. ran	rag	rash	rat	rack	64. land	lash	latch	lass	lack
51. race	rate	rage	rake	rave	65. wink	wick	wing	wind	witch
52. ride	rife	rile	rice	ripe	66. cap	camp	cash	cab	cast
53. dot	doll	dock	doff	don	67. bank	bask	bash	bath	bang
54. bridge	brick	brisk	brink	brim	68. hand	hang	hash	hack	hank
55. tip	tick	tin	tiff	till	69. mine	mile	mind	mice	mild
56. hit	hilt	hip	hint	hitch	70. well	west	wend	web	weld
57. hide	hike	hive	hire	hind	71. lamb	lad	lax	lamp	lash
58. pal	pass	path	pack	past	72. wire	wild	wind	wise	wife
59. man	mad	map	mat	mast	73. pig	pink	pill	ping	pick
60. store	stoke	stone	stole	stove	74. milk	mint	mist	mink	mill

Inventory of Phonetic Skills, Test Two, Houghton Mifflin, 1966.

SECTION C

75. took   tick   tuck   (tack)   teak
76. wood   wide   (wade)   weed   wed
77. band   bound   bind   bond   (bend)
78. boat   (beet)   boot   bet   bait
79. put   pat   (pit)   pot   pet
80. tell   tool   tale   (tile)   till
81. road   raid   rude   (rod)   rid
82. pull   pale   pill   pile   (pole)
83. hat   hate   (hut)   heat   hoot
84. mail   (mule)   meal   mile   mole

85. men   (moan)   mean   moon   main
86. still   steal   (stool)   stole   stall
87. hide   hod   (hood)   heed   hid
88. full   feel   fool   fowl   (fail)
89. by   bee   bow   (bay)   boo
90. too   toe   (tie)   tee   tea
91. find   fond   fund   (fiend)   fend
92. show   (shy)   shoo   shay   shaw
93. tried   treed   trade   trod   (tread)
94. not   net   (neat)   nut   newt

SECTION D

95. (arms)   army   armed
96. (kinder)   kindly   kinds
97. stretching   stretcher   (stretched)
98. roomy   (roomed)   rooming
99. poster   posting   (posted)
100. (dresses)   dresser   dressing

101. (pushing)   pushed   pushy
102. sounded   (soundly)   sounding
103. (handy)   handed   handing
104. (piping)   piper   piped
105. hurried   (hurries)   hurrying
106. wins   winning   (winner)

SECTION E

107. black   (quack)   knack   crack   track
108. gray   stray   (spray)   slay   pray

109. bell   bent   best   (belt)   bench
110. puff   (punch)   puck   punt   pump

SECTION F

111. shaping   (reshape)   unshapely
112. (untie)   tied   tying
113. coming   (become)   comely
114. loudly   louder   (aloud)

115. widely   (widest)   widen
116. growing   (grown)   grower
117. deepest   deeply   (deepen)
118. minded   remind   (mindful)

SECTION G

119. cow   (coy)   caw   cay   coo
120. bell   bawl   (boil)   bowl   bull
121. hole   hull   (howl)   haul   heel
122. flew   (flow)   flaw   flay   flea
123. sell   seal   sail   (soul)   soil
124. feel   fail   fool   foal   (foul)
125. mail   mull   mill   meal   (maul)

126. line   (lawn)   lean   loan   loin
127. door   dour   (dare)   deer   dire
128. bear   burr   bier   (bar)   boar
129. park   pork   peak   (perk)   peck
130. store   (stir)   steer   star   stare
131. more   mare   mar   mere   (mire)
132. hill   hail   (hurl)   heal   hull

Inventory of Phonetic Skills, Test Two, Houghton Mifflin, 1966.

but the so-called dyslexic child's reversals are far more numerous and persist much longer.[9]

The teacher will utilize any device that will help a child to remember to always begin on the left until he has established the habit. Uncovering words from left to right; coloring the first letter of a word green and the last letter red; moving the hand over and over left-to-right under lines of print when reading with the boys and girls; comparing two words already confused, for example, "was" and "saw," to talk about how they are alike and how they are different . . . all these are ways of teaching directional sense. If the teacher learns that a child has such a problem, then he should not, at the same time, teach two words that are often confused. For example, if the word "left" is being used in reading, avoid using the word "felt" in writing until emphasis on remembering the word "left" has been made. The teacher will find lists of suggestions in both Harris[10] and Zintz.[11]

Ellingson reports in her book, *The Shadow Children*:[12]

> A favorite anecdote among the group I have worked with concerns a boy who, after painstaking care, finally learned the composite parts of the word "until," but still could not "pull" the word instantly from memory when he tried to read it. Finally, he said to his teacher, "If I could just *see* an 'until,' I know I could remember it." What was necessary to complete the boy's mastery of the word was an associative method. The boy was instructed to draw, from within himself, his idea of the word—to make a picture to go with a sentence using the word. The boy then carefully drew a picture of a herd of cows, pastureland, a fence with a gate, and a farmhouse in the distance, with the cows going through the gate toward the farmhouse. He then wrote his sentence, "I will wait until the cows come home." For this boy, with this word, "until the cows come home" provided the needed association and visual memory that firmly "set" it in his mind. From then on, whenever he came across the word, no matter how different or complicated the context, he could look at it and say, "Oh, yes, that's until—until the cows come home." This achievement is not inconsequential. The child had used all of his avenues of learning—then added association and was able to read, write, spell, and comprehend the word "until."

4. *Easy oral-reading practice.* While it is difficult for the teacher to find time, it is necessary for each child to have as much oral reading

---

[9]Careth Ellingson and James Cass, "Teaching the Dyslexic Child," *Saturday Review*, April 16, 1966.

[10]Albert Harris, *How to Increase Reading Ability*, Fourth Edition (New York: David McKay, 1961), pp. 371-372.

[11]Miles V. Zintz, *Corrective Reading* (Dubuque, Iowa: William C. Brown Company, Publishers, 1966), p. 60.

[12]Careth Ellingson, *The Shadow Children, A Book About Children's Learning Disorders* (Five North Wabash Avenue, Chicago, Illinois 60602: Topaz Books, 1967), pp. 89-90.

practice as is possible. Those who do not have mastery over the sight words must read them over and over and over in interesting stories until they do know them. Other children can be pupil-teachers if the teacher plans carefully with them how to read in pairs; older brothers and sisters who read well can also be very helpful in listening to a child read. Placing the tape recorder in a quiet corner and stationing one child with it who knows how to operate it makes it possible for children to go there for three-or five-minute intervals to record their oral reading and the teacher can evaluate the results after school or with the child at an appropriate time.

BOOKS OF HIGH INTEREST LEVEL AND LOW VOCABULARY LOAD FOR CORRECTIVE AND REMEDIAL READING

1. *Our Animal Story Books Series.* D. C. Heath. Pre-primer level vocabulary.
2. *Follett Beginning to Read Series.* Follett Publishing Company. Some pre-primer level, first grade level, second grade level, and third grade level.
3. *Beginner Books Series.* Random House. Dozens of titles of first and second grade levels of difficulty.
4. *Easy Reader Wonder Books.* Wonder Books. Inexpensive editions with vocabularies controlled to between 100 and 200 words.
5. *Cowboy Sam Series.* Benefic Press. Ten titles ranging in difficulty from pre-primer to third grade level.
6. *Button Family Adventure Series.* Benefic Press. Twelve titles ranging in difficulty from pre-primer to third grade level.
7. *Sailor Jack Series.* Benefic Press. Ten titles ranging in difficulty from pre-primer to third grade level.
8. *Dan Frontier Series.* Benefic Press. Ten titles ranging in difficulty from pre-primer to third grade level.
9. *Jim Forest Reading Series.* Field Educational Publications, Inc. Six books ranging in difficulty from first grade to third grade.
10. *Deep Sea Adventure Series.* Field Educational Publications, Inc. Eight books ranging in difficulty from high first to low fifth grade level.
11. *Morgan Bay Mysteries.* Field Educational Publications, Inc. Eight mystery stories written at about independent third grade reading level.
12. *Checkered Flag Series.* Field Educational Publications, Inc. Four books especially designed to appeal to older boys with severe reading handicap.
13. *Wild Life Adventure Series.* Field Educational Publications, Inc. Stories of wild animals written with about fourth or fifth grade reading level of difficulty.
14. *American Adventure Series.* D. C. Heath. About twenty titles ranging in difficulty from second through sixth grade.
15. *Pioneer Series.* Benefic Press. Many titles with vocabulary controlled to about third grade reading level.
16. *Childhood of Famous Americans Series.* Bobbs-Merrill. More than 100 titles with vocabulary controlled to about fourth grade level.

17. *Interesting Reading Series.* Penns Valley Publishers, Inc. Ten titles written for older boys and girls with vocabulary controlled to about third grade reading level.
18. *Simplified Classics.* Scott, Foresman and Co. Many children's classics rewritten at about fourth grade level of difficulty.
19. *Landmark Books.* Random House. More than 100 titles ranging in difficulty from fourth grade through ninth grade level.
20. *Signal Books.* Doubleday and Company. Ten titles in the series with reader level controlled to about fourth grade level.

5. *Helping children read in phrases.* To help children overcome word-by-word reading, practice of reading phrases may help them better to anticipate endings of prepositional phrases. Such phrases as the following might be used for motivated flash card drill:

On phrases	*In phrases*	*To phrases*
on the house	in a minute	to the river
on the hilltop	in a hurry	to the house
on the mountainside	in the basket	to the window
on the far side	in her pocketbook	to the candy store

6. *Helping children to expand their understanding of word meanings.* Multiple meanings of commonly used words, opposites, homonyms, synonyms, context clues, picture clues, word analysis, selecting appropriate dictionary definition, interpreting figures of speech, simple analogies, putting nouns in categories. (See also, Chapter 5.)

7. *Developing the comprehension skills.* Comprehending sentence meanings, evaluating emotional responses, comprehending paragraphs, generalizing, organizing, and summarizing. (See also, Chapter 6.)

III. DIAGNOSTIC INFORMATION AND RECORD KEEPING

When a teacher initiates a corrective reading program for a child, he must also try to find out why the child has failed to learn to read to expectancy. To obtain this information, the teacher will build a kind of case study about the child. Hopefully, there will be a school psychologist, a school social worker, and a reading specialist in the school system who can provide much needed information to the teacher. Case history information will relate to intelligence, physical problems, neurological difficulties, and social and emotional factors.

The diagnosis and planning needed is diagrammed in Table 18.2. Five types of information will go into the case history: (1) a parent interview concerning family background, significance of read-success in the family, and probable reasons for reading failure; (2) a medical examination which evaluates visual and hearing acuity and general health. The family doctor will make referrals to specialists when neurological problems, problems of basal metabolism, or convulsive disorders are present; (3) a psychological evaluation will include both tests of general intelligence and structured or unstructured personality tests; (4) a school history revealing grades, attendance, persistent problems, teachers' evaluations, and work habits; and (5) guidance information concerning motivation, aptitude, and level of aspiration.

This body of information gathered in the case history must be studied and analyzed by the school psychologist or the school social worker. In turn, it must be interpreted to the pupil, the parents, and the pupil's teacher and principal.

Basic to analyzing problems of specific learning disabilities are four areas of diagnosis:

1. Possible genetic findings. If the boy's father had serious learning problems in school, or if he has uncles or brothers or sisters who "never learned to read," the possibility that such a trait is inherited gains feasibility.

2. The diagnostician will eliminate other factors *not causing* the difficulty: the child is *not* emotionally disturbed, has *no* perceptual defects, does *not* have low intelligence, is *not* the victim of poor reading instruction, and does *not* appear to be poorly motivated. Since these usually understood causes are *not* related to this child's problem, then "specific learning disability" admits of genuine lack of success and keeps professionals searching for more adequate answers.

3. The diagnostician utilizes "clues" or "indications," sometimes referred to medically as "soft signs": low subtest scores on block design or object assembly on the Wechsler Intelligence Scale for Children, mild electroencephalogram abnormalities but not definitive, lack of cerebral dominance, or inefficient eye movements in reading.

4. Do specific teaching methods produce positive results? If techniques help these children, then the clinician categorizes the child's problem with greater confidence.

For those children needing corrective reading instruction, a teacher can provide himself with a progress report by completing a summary of an informal reading analysis every two months or nine weeks through the school year. A suggested form is presented in Table 18.2.

TABLE 18.2.   *Problems in Remedial Reading in the School:*
Diagnosing and Planning

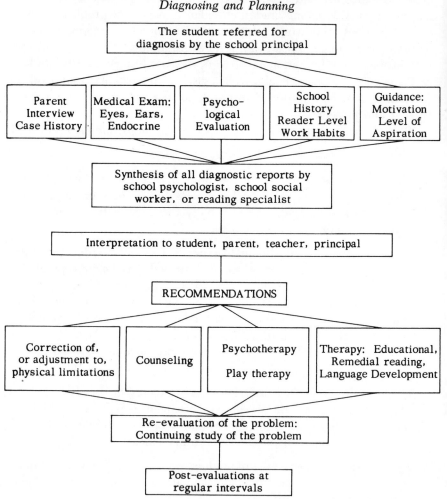

Zintz, Miles V., *Corrective Reading* (Dubuque: Wm. C. Brown Company, Publishers, 1966), p. 158.

TABLE 18.3. *Summary of Informal Reading Analysis*

Teacher (Clinician)_____ Date_____
      Student_____ C. A. _____Grade_____Date____

I. Reader level found in a series of readers

A. Oral Reading

Level of book	Total words	Total errors	Per cent of error	Per cent of accuracy	Suitability of level of difficulty

B. Silent Reading

Level of book	No. of words	Time in sec.	Rate of reading	Percent of comprehension	Suitability of level of difficulty

C. Capacity level for Reading:

_____

_____

_____

II. Dolch Basic Sight Word Test: Analysis of errors
    Initial errors   Middle errors   Final errors
(Commonest difficulties, grade level indicated, comments)

_____

_____

_____

III. Other word perception abilities
    Does he always recognize compound words:_____
    Errors in any area of McKee Phonics Survey:_____
    At what grade level can he spell? (60 per cent correct before study):__
    Does he have reversals and confusions:_____What kinds?_____

IV. Summary_____
    Inst. lvl. of rdg. _____
    Plans for rdg. prog. _____

Following are some suggested forms for record keeping which a teacher might wish to adapt and use on 5″ by 8″ cards, or in a loose-leaf notebook, to keep records of progress for individuals or small groups.

TABLE 18.4 *Initial Summary of Information about the Child Who Has a Reading Disability*

Name (last name first)	Date	Grade in school
Parent or guardian	School	Attended kindergarten
Home address	Home telephone number	Grades repeated
Estimated capacity level for reading	Intelligence level (individual or group test?)	Date of birth
Instructional level for reading	Knowledge of phonics	Grade level spelling
Vision	Hearing	Motor coordination
School absences last year	Socio-economic status	No. of siblings
Report from parents		Report from family doctor
Specific plans for beginning work		Report from previous teacher

TABLE 18.5. *Record of Progress in Working with a Child in Reading through the School Year*

Name (last name first)	Grade in school
Standardized reading test	Date given — Results (grade place-ment)
Standardized reading test	Date given — Results (grade place-ment)
(1) IRI (material used)	(1) Date of IRI — Instructional level
(2) IRI (material used)	(2) Date of IRI — Instructional level
(3) IRI (material used)	(3) Date of IRI — Instructional level
Notes:	Interest inventory findings
	Personality data

TABLE 18.6. *Books and Materials Used for the Reading Program*

Name	Date	Grade in school
Name of book or program:	Beginning date:	Finishing date:

IV. SUMMARY

One may generalize the following principles of corrective reading for the classroom teacher:

1. Corrective reading instruction must be based on a diagnosis of the reading problem and the instruction must be directed to supplying the missing skills in the developmental sequence.
2. Corrective reading instruction must begin at the level where the child will be successful in whatever he does. The maxim "Nothing succeeds like success" is still true.
3. The teacher and the child need to feel mutually, and to express this feeling, that it is "all right" for the child to begin "where he is" and progress from there.
4. Corrective reading instruction teaches the missing skills but takes care to see that all skills needed for successful reading are developed.
5. The key element in corrective reading, as in any teaching of reading, is meaningful practice. The learner must put all the reading skills to work in meaningful situations.
6. Corrective reading materials must be selected to meet both the teaching of skills and the cultivation of the student's interests and aptitudes.
7. In corrective reading, one should build on strengths. If one avenue to learning produces better results, use it.
8. In developmental reading, corrective or otherwise, there is a sequence in levels of difficulty, and the child moves from the simple to the complex.
9. The student must grow toward independence. Long range goals should include preparing the student for longer and longer periods of independent seatwork without direct supervision.
10. Records must be kept to indicate progress, regression, or change, in both the cognitive and the affective areas.

For each child with reading difficulties, the teacher must be prepared to measure his (1) instructional level of reading using the IRI; (2) knowledge of basic sight words using an instrument like the 220 Dolch Basic Sight Word Test or Fry's Instant Words as a recall test; and (3) ability to use the phonetic and structural skills commensurate with his instructional reader level: moving progressively from initial consonant sounds, consonant blend sounds, most elementary suffixes (s, ed, ing), short and long vowel sounds, variant vowel sounds, roots, prefixes, and suffixes.

These three measures will be sufficient to prevent assigning children work at their frustration level. Preventing this frustration will greatly reduce concomitant emotional problems in children.

454   *Corrective Reading*

READING REFERENCES

BOND, GUY L., and MILES A. TINKER. *Reading Difficulties: Their Diagnosis and Correction* (New York: Appleton-Century-Crofts, Inc., 1967).

BOTEL, MORTON. *Dyslexia: The State of the Art* (Newark, Delaware 19711: International Reading Association, 1968).

DELLA-PIANA, GABRIEL. *Reading Diagnosis and Prescription* (New York: Holt, Rinehart and Winston, Inc., 1968).

HARRIS, ALBERT J. *How to Increase Reading Ability* (New York: David McKay, 1961). Chapter VII: "Evaluating Performance in Reading, I," pp. 152-184; Chapter VIII: "Evaluating Performance in Reading, II," pp. 185-219.

HEILMAN, ARTHUR W. *Principles and Practices in Teaching Reading* (Columbus, Ohio: Charles E. Merrill Books, Inc., 1967). Chapter 15: "Remedial Reading," pp. 451-483; Chapter 16: "Working with Remedial Readers," pp. 485-523.

JOHNSON, MARJORIE S., and ROY A. KRESS. *Corrective Reading in the Elementary School*, Perspectives in Reading No. 7 (Newark, Delaware 19711: International Reading Association, 1967).

OTTO WAYNE, and RICHARD A. MCMENEMY. *Corrective and Remedial Teaching* (Boston: Houghton Mifflin Co., 1966).

SCHUBERT, DELWYN, and THEODORE L. TORGERSON. *Improving Reading Through Individualized Correction*, Second Edition (Dubuque, Iowa: Wm. C. Brown Co., Publishers, 1968).

SILVAROLI, NICHOLAS. *Classroom Reading Inventory* (Dubuque, Iowa: Wm. C. Brown Co., Publishers, 1969).

SMITH, HENRY P., and EMERALD V. DECHANT. *Psychology in Teaching Reading* (Englewood Cliffs, New Jersey: Prentice-Hall, Inc., 1961). Chapter 15: "Diagnosis and Remediation in the Development Program," pp. 407-435.

STRANG, RUTH. *Diagnostic Teaching of Reading* (New York: McGraw-Hill Book Company, 1964). Chapter 4: "Oral Reading as a Diagnostic Technique," pp. 67-73; and Chapter 10: "Reading Tests Administered Individually," pp. 187-209.

WILSON, ROBERT M. *Diagnostic and Remedial Reading, For Classroom and Clinic* (Columbus, Ohio: Charles E. Merrill, Books, 1967).

ZINTZ, MILES V. *Corrective Reading* (Dubuque, Iowa: William C. Brown, Co. Publishers, 1966).

19

Teaching the Gifted
and the Retarded

Any teacher who has spent a few years in elementary school classrooms is well aware from firsthand experience that there are in all heterogeneously grouped classes, a few rapid learners, a few more who are above average learners, a larger group of middle achievers, a smaller number of below average achievers, and a few slow learners. Occasionally, the teacher has one whom he considers a *very* rapid learner or a *very* slow learner. While the limitations of intelligence tests in current use are well known, one can accept without qualification the inevitable range of abilities (see Chapter 2) that must be dealt with in teaching in any self-contained classroom.

Bond and Brueckner have illustrated the variations in combinations of rate and accuracy among the students in a given class with the diagram on the following pages.[1]

Individuals in Groups I, IV, and VII are able to perform their work in a highly accurate manner while individuals in Groups I, II, and III are all reading at rapid rates but with very different degrees of accuracy. Group V pupils represent those at the middle of the distribution in both rate and accuracy while those in Group IX are both very slow and very inaccurate. It should be emphasized that the diagram is only theoretical, there is no class that really has these nine distinct categories, but it may help beginning teachers appreciate group variability.

If the teacher is going to respect the basic principle that the longer children attend the school the more different they become—the greater the spread of differences in almost any selected ability—then he must make some adaptations to his total program to fit the rapid learner and

---

[1]Leo J. Brueckner and Guy L. Bond, *The Diagnosis and Treatment of Learning Difficulties* (New York: Appleton-Century-Crofts, Inc., 1955), p. 18.

ACCURACY			
	High I	Average II	Low III
RATE High	High in both rate and accuracy	High in rate—average in accuracy	High in rate—low in accuracy
	IV	V	VI
Average	Average in rate—high in accuracy	Average in both rate and accuracy	Average in rate—low in accuracy
	VII	VIII	IX
Low	Low in rate—high in accuracy	Low in rate—Average in accuracy	Low in both rate and accuracy

From *The Diagnosis and Treatment of Learning Difficulties,* copyright 1955, Meredith Corp. Reproduced by permission of Appleton-Century-Crofts.

the slow learner. These are not differences *in kinds* of learning methods of teaching, but they are basically differences *in degree* in children's accomplishments.

Therefore, it is pointed out that the general suggestions offered in teaching a developmental program for the majority of the class will apply equally well for bright and dull students who are also in the class. These aspects of a good developmental reading program have been covered in Chapters 7 (Phonetic and Structural Analysis), 8 (Comprehension Skills), 9 (Critical Reading Abilities), 10 (The Study Skills), and 12 (Developing Interests and Tastes in Reading).

It is necessary in this chapter to present briefly some of the characteristics of gifted children, of slow children, and of gifted children with special problems, and some working principles for teachers who have these children in their classes. A great deal of literature is readily available in each of these areas and the teacher will greatly profit from specialized courses in professional schools learning about gifted children, enrichment programs for all children, and methods of teaching the retarded children.

I. EDUCATION OF THE INTELLECTUALLY GIFTED

The goals of education for the able learners, the gifted, are the same as for all children: self realization, human relationships, economic efficiency, and civic responsibility. For the gifted, greater emphasis may be given to creativity, use of abstract intelligence, critical reading and thinking, development of the values in socio-centrism—growth toward concerns of what is best for the group—and opportunities to experience leadership and to develop leadership qualities.

Teachers need desperately to help the general citizenry understand that equality of opportunity in education does not mean identical opportunities for all children of the same chronological age in a community. The bright and gifted may begin the year in September with most of the knowledges and skills another child in their same classroom will hopefully have acquired at the end of that school year. If his year is to be a constructive investment for him, he must be challenged to grow from the level where he is at the beginning of that year. He does not need to do the exercises that many other children do just to demonstrate that *he can do them.* Teachers have inventories, check lists, pre-tests, unit tests of skills and abilities to be taught which can be administered to find out which children already have the skills before they are taught. Then, those who do already know them can spend their time on enriching kinds of activities making use of those skills. It is imperative that classroom teachers have children in a class doing many different activities since there is no other way that each individual can "dig into" jobs that are challenging for him.

Most schools accept the recommendation that some combination of moderate acceleration and enrichment will produce the best results in the education of gifted children. Each child must have the enrichment types of activities that enrich for him. Acceleration, achieved by making it possible for a child to finish elementary school in five years instead of six; junior high school in two years, not three; and/or senior high in two years, not three, is a better recommendation for some children than for others; such acceleration can be extended to two years for a few more appropriately than it can be even one year for others.

Acceleration should evolve from "staffing conferences" at which principal, teacher, psychologist, and parent sit down together to review the case. Information should be available from the school social worker, the school nurse, and the school physician if it is contributory to the case.

It is completely logical that if the so-called normal child spends twelve years going through the public school with its present academic bent, the slow-learner should be privileged to spend thirteen or more, and the gifted ought to be permitted to spend eleven or less. Terman[2]

> This raises the issue of educational acceleration for the gifted. It seems that the schools are more opposed to acceleration now than they were thirty years ago. The lockstep seems to have become more and more

[2]Lewis M. Terman, "The Discovery and Encouragement of Exceptional Talent," *The American Psychologist,* Vol. 9, June, 1954.
wrote in 1954:

the fashion, notwithstanding the fact that practically everyone who has investigated the subject is against it.

In his follow-up studies of 1500 gifted students, Terman found that 29 per cent graduated from high school by age 16 1/2.[3] This group constituted his "accelerated" group who, compared to the remainder (ages 16 1/2-18 1/2 at graduation), made better grades in college, were more apt to graduate and were more apt to continue in graduate school.

The major concern in the school for the gifted child should be that of freeing the child to learn. If schools are able to provide adequate learning experiences, the gifted child will be challenged without respect to acceleration, enrichment, or segregation, per se. Children must be *free* to acquire learning outside the classroom, *free* to acquire information apart from formalized teacher-pupil efforts, and *free* to work in small groups with good teacher-pupil planning but little teacher supervision. Providing learning experiences for children does not mean necessarily that the child even comes to school to learn . . . the school may make it available somewhere else.

One of the greatest obstacles to better education of children is poor communication between parents and teachers. While parents may be poor communicators, it should behoove teachers to go more than half way since they are supposedly prepared, ready, and anxious to communicate. Teachers generally do not communicate nearly well enough with parents.

It is especially important that teachers watch their language and not allow the desire to help gifted children become beclouded by certain words about which some people have strong sentiments and negative notions. If teachers are to bog down in whether they will enrich, accelerate, *or* segregate, they will get nowhere. Maybe schools need to discard these words that have taken on varieties of compartmentalization, have been misused and misapplied, and begin to think clearly of *all the ways* by which they can bring adequate learning experiences to children. Probably they best meet the needs of gifted children in the elementary school by individual and unique combinations of accelerating, segregating, and *always* enriching.

Most of the country's gifted children are the direct responsibility of teachers in regular classrooms. In fact, almost every year, each teacher has enrolled in his class one or two gifted children.

Teachers' attitudes vary. Some ignore high-ability children and try to teach them as if they were average. Others do nothing "special" to help them and rationalize that in a large class one can't. Others do give extra time to slow-learners and rationalize that gifted ones will take care of themselves.

---

[3]Terman used the Stanford-Binet I. Q. Score of 140 as a criterion of giftedness.

Havighurst and De Haan[4] report a case study of a gifted boy[5] in junior high soical studies class. As his special report, he chose to work alone on a study of national highway construction because this was one of the current events in the news at that time.

An office of a large highway engineering company was located in the city. This company was working on projects in several states and had many books on materials, surveys, machinery, and cost estimates. As James began to develop his project of designing a system of highways, the teacher made appointments for him to go to the offices of the engineers and to laboratories. Soon he was making his own appointments. Sometimes he was gone from her class for as long as two weeks at a time, visiting these offices, making appointments with the engineers, consulting with them, and taking pictures of their models of highways. He learned how to make maps and drawings on sheets of clear plastic that would overlay each other. He compiled data from the maps, describing how various cities and regions would be affected by the highway plan.

When the time came to make his report, he had a table piled with material and notebooks filled with figures and charts. He used an opaque projector to present his material. The report was a masterpiece. Later he made a report to the regional meeting of the engineers of the company where he had obtained so much help.

The authors point out that the significant aspect of the boy's experience described above is that the office staff of engineers was an invaluable resource in that community to help this boy in his project in the social studies. In another community, it may not be engineers but rather other specialists who can, in their way, be as helpful to other gifted children.

Havighurst states:

Thinking, then, of the unusual child as the talented child, I suggest that we speak of four areas of talent. We have found this useful in our work: first, the area of intellectual talent—a child with high intelligence or high I. Q.; second, the area of artistic talent—talent in music, drawing or dramatics, and so on; third, the area of social leadership—this is something we sometimes do not think of as a talent, but certainly in our society a gift for social leadership is an important and precious thing; and, fourth, something which I cannot define so clearly but I like to call "creative intelligence" or the ability to find new ways of doing things and solving problems. . . .

The principal factor within the individual which affects the supply of talent is motivation. Motivation is necessary to the development of intellectual or artistic talent—the motivation being a desire to seek train-

[4]Robert F. De Haan and Robert J. Havighurst, *Educating Gifted Children* (Chicago: The University of Chicago Press, 1957), p. 151.
[5]De Haan and Havighurst recommended that qualities of leadership and special abilities also be evaluated and believed that the top 15 to 20 per cent of the population should be considered talented. A lower I. Q. score, perhaps 120, would be sufficient consideration in this group.

ing and willingness to sacrifice other desires while undergoing training. Lack of motivation appears to be more powerful than lack of money in reducing the supply of talent.[6]

Pintner reminds school personnel:

> Educators at all levels of instruction must divest themselves of the belief that gifted students can get along by themselves and that it is undemocratic to give them special education suited to their particular needs. And we must also dispel the fear sometimes expressed that the gifted may become selfish through too much consideration, for "it is precisely this group of individuals of great ability who, in the long run and as a group, will be the least selfish, the least likely to monopolize the good things in this world, and by their inventions and discoveries, by their creative work in the arts, by their contributions to government and social reform, by their activities in all fields, will in the future help humanity in its groping struggle upward toward a better civilization."[7]

The teacher is the most important factor in the classroom success of the gifted child.

> Teachers of gifted children should display unusual sensitivity in recognizing the potentialities of such pupils; they should maintain a balance between individual and group work in the classroom; they should help pupils solve problems and resolve conflicts; they should aid pupils in mastering the knowledge needed for understanding themselves and the world; and they should display a sincere interest which will inspire confidence.[8]

Leta Hollingworth tell us that she repeatedly met with resistance to the idea of providing any special opportunities for superior children, although she found that philanthropic agencies always gave large sums of money for the care of the dependents of society. The typical attitude of the successful businessman is that "bright children should take care of themselves."[9]

> The exigencies of providing a common-school education for all the children of all the people in this vast country have resulted in a school

---

[6]R. J. Havighurst, Virgil M. Rogers, and Paul Witty, *Are the Community and the School Failing the Unusual Child?* pp. 1, 28. University of Chicago Round Table, April 27, 1952. Chicago: University of Chicago Round Table, 1952, cited in Helen M. Robinson, *Promoting Maximal Reading Growth Among Able Learners* (Chicago: University of Chicago Press, 1954), pp. 29-30.

[7]Paul Witty, Editor, *The Gifted Child* (Boston: D. C. Heath and Company, 1951), p. 275, citing Rudolph Pintner, "Superior Ability," *Teachers College Record*, 42:419, February, 1941.

[8]Louise Krueger, W. Paul Allen, Elsa Ebeling, and Robert H. Roberts, "Administrative Problems in Educating Gifted Children," in Paul Witty, *The Gifted Child* (Boston: D. C. Heath and Company, 1951), p. 266.

[9]Leta S. Hollingworth, "What We Know about the Early Selection and Training of Leaders," *Teachers College Record*, XI (April, 1939), 590.

regimentation that masks individual powers. The resulting educational casualties among the gifted are our greatest extravagance—extravagance in the destructive effects of warped and misguided genius, extravagance in unborn contributions to the race heritage, but, worst of all, extravagance in lost personal fulfillment for the gifted individual.[10]

"Young children can be bored by the school work offered to them. One first grader spoke sharply to his teacher, 'Take that pusillanimous primer away!' One can imagine how that teacher warmed up to him!"[11]

The objectives of reading instruction for the gifted are:[12]
1. Gaining proficiency in the techniques of reading and refining these skills in each successive year.
2. Learning how to use books for study projects: outlining, summarizing, and reporting on information gained from reading.
3. Exploring the wide world of reading, discovering the best books for every possible purpose and the books of special interest to the individual reader.
4. Learning how to use the facilities of the school library.
5. Becoming acquainted with the best literature and learning to appreciate the value of reading great books.

II. THE BRIGHT LANGUAGE-HANDICAPPED CHILD

For many, many of our school children today, there is the dilemma in which the child is blessed with a bountiful amount of innate learning ability and on a test of learning ability which does not involve a considerable use of English, he is able to demonstrate a high degree of intelligence. Yet, in school, he is almost completely unable to function because the school uses some language other than his.

In many parts of Southwestern United States, schools have done untold damage to boys and girls in the psychological realm first, by devaluing their first language, and second, by causing the child to suspect that the school devalues him, and in turn, his family. If the school denies the child the right to speak his own language, he can only conclude that it must be inferior—or at least that his teachers think it is inferior. If his language is no good and it is the only language

---

[10]Grace Munson, "Nature of the Adjustments in Teaching to Meet the Needs of Bright and Dull Pupils: The Exceptionally Bright Child," *Adjusting Reading Programs to Individuals*, p. 278. Supplemtary Educational Monographs, No. 52 (Chicago: University of Chicago Press, 1941).

[11]Paul Witty, Editor, *The Gifted Child* (Boston: D. C. Heath and Company, 1951), p. 151.

[12]Gertrude H. Hildreth, *Introduction to the Gifted* (New York: McGraw-Hill Book Company, 1966), p. 217.

his parents and whole extended family can use, he can only conclude that they too must be inferior. Such ego-destruction can do serious harm to the child as he progresses through the school.

The major difficulties of Indian students in college occur in the area of the English language. One group of Indian students entering college expressed need for help in all the following areas: reading skills, vocabulary development, written and oral expression, spelling, taking notes, taking examinations, listening to lectures, and effective studying.

One student wrote about his reading problem in this way:

> Looking back to my high school days, I find that the *ACADEMIC* course that caused the *UTMOST* agony was English. It was my belief that English was an *insurmountable obstacle*; but after a lengthy discussion with my English tutor, Mr. Charles, who is also a philosopher, I was enlighten [sic] that my belief was false. He said that English can be mastered if a student is willing to persistently and diligently works [sic] at it . . . The principle cause of slow reading is lip reading of which I am guilty. To become an efficient reader, I must overcome this impediment. This I did by placing a pencil between my teeth.[13]

In a tutoring-counseling program on the university campus, a number of Indian students were given the Wechsler Adult Intelligence Scale. Almost invariably, large discrepancies existed between the functioning level on the verbal scale and on the performance scale. A performance I. Q. score of 120 and a verbal I.Q. score of 80 were not uncommon. The low verbal score was attributable to the language, culture, and experience barrier faced by the student.

An Eighth Grade Girl Learns English as a Foreign Language

Edna was a young Japanese girl transplanted overnight unexpectedly to an urban southwestern city. She had come to live with her uncle's family and attend school. While she was very bright, and spoke Japanese expertly, the school taught only in English. Having heard very little English as spoken by native speakers and studied only a few isolated words, this thirteen-year-old young lady found herself attending eighth grade classes in a junior high school where her peers studied mathematics, American history, English grammar and literature, and general science.

Edna's aunt, who really wanted to be her substitute mother, had difficulty herself using and understanding English and was most perplexed that the school had no provision for meeting this problem. Her

---

[13]Miles V. Zintz and Joyce Morris, "Tutoring Counseling Program for Indian Students" (Albuquerque: The College of Education, University of New Mexico, 1962), p. 13.

problem may be partly illustrated by an early telephone call with Edna's new language clinician when she was explaining trying to make the young lady feel at home. She said, she was "trying to break out the ice."

Edna was enrolled in the remedial reading clinic to study English as a second language. She reported daily at 8:30 A.M. and left at 10:00 to catch a city bus to her school. Using the principles of second language teaching developed in Chapter 12, and developing oral language ability to reproduce the language she heard, her teacher quickly taught all the commonest utterances used in casual conversation. Every day for several weeks she practiced all the previously studied questions and answers and substitution drills and added new ones. The commonest sentence structures were taught, modeled, repeated, drilled, and reviewed and because Edna was a very bright girl, and living in an environment where remembering them had such high reward value, she quickly mastered them.

Special attention was devoted to the common prepositions, the verb tenses, homonyms, antonyms, synonyms, the personal pronouns. Dictation of simple sentences was begun early using subject matter to be presented in her history and literature classes.

Her tutors were relatively unskilled in techniques for teaching English as a second language since they had formally prepared to teach developmental reading skills remedially. Edna attended her tutoring sessions from about December 10 until the following August when eight weeks of summer school ended.

Humorous moments did evolve to break the rather tense feelings that Edna had in the English class, wishing she could learn English much faster than was humanly possible. One day, early in the spring, when Edna was responding to elementary antonyms in English, her clinician gave the stimulus word "noisy." She looked puzzled and the clinician said, "The class is very noisy today." Edna's eyes lighted up, she smiled and said in a loud voice, "Shut up!"

This case is presented here to emphasize the importance of planned, sequenced lessons in learning a second language to prevent frustration and failure. For methodology in second language teaching, the reader is referred to Chapter 13, "Linguistics and the Reading Teacher," and Chapter 14, "Teaching Reading to the Bilingual Child."

III. MENTALLY RETARDED CHILDREN IN REGULAR CLASSES

Teaching Reading to the Educable Mentally Retarded Child in the Regular Classroom

John is nine years and six months old. He entered kindergarten at five and a half and after several weeks of observation of his intellectual and language immaturity, his kindergarten teacher had referred him to the school psychologist for an evaluation. There were no physical findings in his medical evaluation to indicate lack of development; his muscle tone, his vision, his hearing, his motor coordination, his reflexes, seemed to be within the normal limits for a five-year-old. However, the individual intelligence test was administered and yielded a mental age of three years and nine months although he was five years and nine months old at the time of testing. He was permitted to repeat kindergarten at age six and a half, and to spend two years in the first grade. At nine and a half, he has been placed in a second grade, and because of his physical growth and development he will be permitted only one year in each grade from now on—unless he should be able to attend classes for the educable mentally retarded at some future date.

John has recently been retested by the psychologist and even though his chronological age is now nine years and seven months, his mental age is only six years and three months. He comes from an "average" family with two girls ages seven and six who are doing well in school. Even though John is not quite as large as many boys nine and a half, he is one of the largest in his class of seven and eight-year-olds. His physical skills in active play approximate those of second and third grade children. John is reasonably well accepted in the group but he needs a great deal of help to adjust socially: not to laugh too much, not to pester the other children, and not to put his hands on the others.

Since John must spend the year in the regular class, there are a few cautions the teacher must remember. He will try never to think or say aloud: "He doesn't really belong here; he ought to be in a room for the retarded." He will realize that John is only one other different individual in a whole class of different individuals who needs plans made to meet specific objectives for him. The attitude about differences —the way teachers feel—are most contagious, and, for this reason, of primary importance.

The objectives for John's school year include both learning social behaviors and academic behaviors.

General objectives are

1. To help John adjust to other members of the group.
2. To extend reading readiness and develop beginning reading abilities.
3. To promote habits of good health and safety.
4. To develop personal habits of cleanliness, grooming, and neatness.
5. To develop a knowledge of his immediate environment.
6. To develop language and quantitative concepts.
7. To promote habits of punctuality, orderliness, and following directions.

In language arts:

1. more use of oral than written language
2. much instruction in following directions
3. extending ability to listen with understanding
4. skills in beginning reading
5. practice reading with another child for much repetition on basic sight words, at a level commensurate with his mental age and understanding
6. reading signs, labels, brief explanations.

With John's motor coordination, he will be able to write anything he can read. Motivating him to do very well with manuscript writing will be one possible place where John can excel in the class. In the unit work of the class, there will be activities associated with the content in which John should be able to participate with small groups. Generalizations in science, social studies, health and safety that are explained in class may be understood to some degree by all members of the class.

The appreciations, music, art, physical education and literature are all areas where John can participate to some degree with the others. The teacher will be able to accept different levels of performance in the same activity.

The most important thing is that John is *not the only one* in the group of thirty who is different. He may be different in some respects to a greater degree than others, but no two are anything alike.

The classroom teacher must be alert to the appearance of the *slow learner* in his class. If the child can be identified early, his program can be planned in terms of his functiong levels of ability so that his time in school will be used constructively even though he does not attain the statistical norms for the class median. It is likewise extremely important for the teacher to know who the slow learner *is not*. He *is not* the child who learned another language as his first language and enrolls in school as a so-called "bilingual" with a severe English language handicap. He *is not* the child who has speech, hearing or vision problems or is diagnosable as having neurological impairment or minimal brain dysfunction. He *is not* the child whose primary problems in school success stem from emotional, social, or other personality difficulties. However, any child who is a slow-learner may also have any of these problems concomitantly. Diagnosis should reveal the child's primary problem which should have the attention of the special educator before the secondary problems can be adequately habilitated.

The slow-learner is the student whose general learning ability, as best it can be measured by individual tests of intelligence, is below that of the average and above average boys and girls. The slow-learner has a degree of mental retardation which, to date, is believed to be a permanent handicap for which he must make the best possible adjustment. Regular classroom teachers will find, from time to time, mentally retarded boys and girls in their classrooms because there is no special class provision in the school system. Or, in individual cases, it may be recommended that the child remain with the *regular* class instead of being enrolled in a class for *slow learners* or a class for the *educably mentally retarded.*

Doll offers the following comprehensive definition of mental deficiency:

> Mental deficiency is a state of social incompetence obtaining at maturity, or likely to obtain at maturity, resulting from developmental mental arrest of constitutional (hereditary or acquired) origin; the condition is essentially incurable through treatment and unremediable through training except as treatment and training instill habits which superficially compensate for the limitations of the person so affected while under favorable circumstances and for more or less limited periods of time.[14]

The curriculum goals for the mentally handicapped child are theoretically the same as for any child: achievement of self-realization, learning proper human relationships, achieving economic efficiency, and assuming civic responsibility. Achieving behavioral goals of self-discipline, self-development, self-actualization is primary. A life experience curriculum will help the learner to achieve physical and mental health, useful knowledges and skills, appreciations and worthy use of leisure, and some sense of the interdependence of individuals in their social group. A life experience curriculum teaches these values, knowledges, skills, and abilities through units such as (1) home and family life; (2) the community, its helpers and its resources; (3) expanding concepts about the community to the city, the state, and the nation. Activities other than dependence upon reading from textbooks are utilized maximally to enrich these concepts for slow learners.

Functional learning for the slow-learner includes all the tasks in everyday living: filling out an application blank, being able to use efficiently telephone directories, road maps, travel schedules, street guides, restaurant menus, written directions of various sorts, radio and TV program schedules, want-ads, and various types of catalogues.

The life-experience approach to teaching retarded children is primarily concerned with helping children understand, put into practice, and extend their knowledge of those very practical problems of living that will persist all through life. Persistent life problems include under-

---

[14]Edgar A. Doll, "Essentials of an Inclusive Concept of Mental Deficiency," *American Journal of Mental Deficiency*, 46:217, October, 1941.

standing and using money, understanding and making efficient use of time, developing social competencies for all kinds of interaction with people, and learning, from as early an age as is profitable, prevocational skills.

Slow learners generally:

1. Are satisfied to continue doing work that is repetitive in nature.
2. Need more drill and practice and are more apt to enjoy it.
3. Need careful guidance in all assignments. Goals need to be fairly immediate and carefully explained.
4. Need more help with planning; both in specific directions to follow and in ego-support and close supervision to see that the directions are carried out.
5. Need success experiences. They should have opportunities to do things they can do well (e.g., handwriting).
6. Have trouble when assignments are abstract, when abstract reasoning is required, or when evaluation "beyond the book" is under discussion.

For slow learners in regular classes, teachers need to remember the following:

1. Formal reading and using reading as a thinking process must be developed in proportion to the extent of mental retardation. A child of six with an I.Q. of 85 is more like a five year old than a six. An eight year old with an I.Q. of 75 is more like a six year old than an eight. While children at all these ages profit from any language and concept development experiences which they can understand, moving to the complex, abstract process of reading should come much later chronologically. When children have sufficient language and understanding of concepts, and verbalize freely, they will be ready to move toward more formal reading and writing activities. However, when children are provided with this compensatory training, increases in M.A. sometimes are greater than one might expect if the I. Q. is used as the sole determinant of M.A.
2. The way reading is taught to slow-learning children is more like the way it is taught to normal children than different. However, there are differences. When the child is ready for reading, more repetition on basic sight vocabulary, more reading from simple books, more language experience reading, and a structured, systematic phonics and spelling program may be indicated. The Hegge-Kirk-Kirk RE-MEDIAL READING DRILLS[15] were first prepared for mentally

---

[15]T. Hegge, S. Kirk, and W. Kirk, *Remedial Reading Drills* (Ann Arbor, Michigan: George Wahr, 1955).

retarded boys. If a child growing at the normal rate needs one year at second grade level of difficulty, a retarded child growing two thirds of normal needs perhaps one-third year more of time to grow through the same quantity of learning. He is not so fundamentally different, he just grows slower.

3. Overlearning the core of basic sight words is basic to any further reading. Slow learners must have "all the time they need" to master them. This necessitates more books, more stories, more language experience reading, developed horizontally before progressing to more difficult levels.

4. He must give much help in making directions clear in preparation for independent seatwork before leaving slow learners to work on their own.

5. Concrete experiences are more valuable than abstract ones. The reader is referred to Dale's *Cone of Experience* in Chapter 2. Pictures, objects, drawings, cartoons, photographs all help to make "words" more meaningful.

6. The teacher can take advantage of his acceptance of repetition and monotony. Stories can be re-read for different purposes. He needs few purposes at one time under any circumstances. So he may re-read to learn something he missed the first time. Beyond reading to find out what happened in the story, he may practice reading aloud so he can record his "best" reading on the tape recorder. Every re-reading is providing additional practice on the basic sight words he needs to overlearn.

7. Teachers will probably encourage more oral reading with slow learners.

Slow learners, as a total group, may exhibit behavior characteristics that have resulted from continual failure experiences in the classroom, poor motivation, dislike for school, compensations for academic failure, and dropping out of school. Poor health and poor home conditions may be more prevalent among slow-learners because of socio-economic factors in their lives. It is logical that slow learners need a longer period of years of compulsory school attendance than normals if they learn at a slower pace. For too long schools have operated on an opposite principle, that because they are retarded, they can be terminated as soon as they pass the age for compulsory attendance.

Schools must anticipate and hasten the day when *all* children will be provided for according to their individual talents. Then there need be *no* forgotten children. Today, however, Rose's experience pointedly suggests she has been forgotten:

Rose was an *unfortunate* retarded child who was assigned to a special room half-days and to a regular class the other half. One day a university student appeared to administer a test to Rose. When he asked for Rose in the special class, he was told she was in another classroom near by. When he asked there for Rose, he was told there was no one there by that name. He returned to the school office and asked again. Upon returning to the same classroom and stating that the office records indicated that she should be there in the afternoon, the teacher thought a moment then said, "Oh, that must be her over there. She just sits in the corner."

IV. SUMMARY

Although Roger is eleven years old *chronologically* the teacher must not expect him to be eleven *behaviorally*—or *academically*. He may not even seem to be eleven *physically*, although he is most apt to approximate the norm in this respect. Roger may be *eight* behaviorally, or eight academically. What teachers must be able to do is to see through the eleven-year-old exterior and see the eight-year-old inside and work from there. This has been called "X-ray vision"—to look through the structure to see the *real* child inside.

For the bright child, the problem is comparable. An eleven-year-old exterior can harbor a fifteen-year-old problem-solver. The intellectually gifted child is apt to have a social age above but approximating his chronological age. As emphasized, a bright child who must function in a second language, or the weaker of his two languages, needs technical help if he is to succeed in school.

Suggested Activities

1. In the school where you teach, ask for permission to give an informal reading inventory to the child with the highest I.Q. score in a given grade, one child with an I.Q. score of about 100, and the one with the lowest I.Q. score. Evaluate the IRI results and contrast the performances.

2. Choose a child in the grade you teach who has a high I.Q. score or gives other indication of keen intelligence. Observe him with respect to his total growth. Evaluate his development in leadership, group interaction, aggression, and success in academic areas.

Suggestions for Further Reading

ABRAHAM, WILLARD. *The Slow Learner* (New York: Center for Applied Research in Education, 1964).

ADLER, MANFRED. "Reported Incidence of Giftedness Among Ethnic Groups," *Exceptional Children*, 34:101-106, October, 1967.

BENYON, SHEILA DORAN. *Intensive Programming for Slow Learners* (Columbus, Ohio: C. E. Merrill Publishing Company, 1968).

BERNSTEIN, BEBE. *Everyday Problems of the Child with Learning Difficulties* (New York: John Day Co., 1967).

GALLAGHER, JAMES JOHN. *Teaching the Gifted Child* (Boston: Allyn and Bacon, 1964).

GARDNER, WILLIAM I. "Social and Emotional Adjustment of Mildly Retarded Children and Adolescents: Critical Review," *Exceptional Children*, 33:97-106, October, 1966.

GETZELS, JACOB W., and PHILIP W. JACKSON. *Creativity and Intelligence* (New York: Wiley, 1962).

KEPHART, NEWELL C. *The Slow Learner in the Classroom* (Columbus: Charles E. Merrill Books, 1960).

KRIPPNER, STANLEY. "The Boy Who Read at Eighteen Months," *Exceptional Children*, 30:105-110, November, 1963.

LESSINGER, LEON M. "Enrichment for Gifted Pupils: Its Nature and Nurture," *Exceptional Children*, 30:119-123, November, 1963.

MARTINSON, RUTH A. "Issues in the Identification of the Gifted," *Exceptional Children*, 33:13-18, September, 1966.

National Society for the Study of Education, Committee on Education of the Gifted, Nelson B. Henry, Editor. *Education of the Gifted* (Chicago: University of Chicago Press, 1958).

RAINEY, DAN S., and FRANCIS J. KELLEY. "An Evaluation of a Programmed Textbook with Educable Mentally Retarded Children," *Exceptional Children*, 34:169-178, November, 1967.

REYNOLDS, MAYNARD C. "Some Research—Related Thoughts on Education of the Gifted," *Exceptional Children*, 30:6-13, September, 1963.

RICE, JOSEPH P., and GEORGE BANKS. "Opinions of Gifted Students Regarding Secondary School Programs," *Exceptional Children*, 34: 269-274, December, 1967.

ROWE, ERNEST RAS. "Creative Writing and the Gifted Child," *Exceptional Children*, 34:279-282, December, 1967.

SEAGOE, MARY V. "Verbal Development in a Mongoloid," *Exceptional Children*, 31:269-276, February, 1965.

SPICKER, HOWARD H., WALTER L. HODGES, and BOYD R. McCANDLESS. "A Diagnostically Based Curriculum for Psychosocially Deprived, Preschool, Mentally Retarded Children: Interim Report," *Exceptional Children*, 33:215-220, December, 1966.

STRANG, RUTH. "Out of the Classroom: Step by Step Instruction in Beginning Reading for Slow Learners," *Exceptional Children*, 32: 31-36, September, 1965.

TORRANCE, ELLIS PAUL. *Gifted Children in the Classroom* (New York: Macmillan Company, 1965).

WERBLO, DOROTHY, and E. PAUL TORRANCE. "Experiences in Historical Research and Changes in Self Evaluations of Gifted Children," *Exceptional Children*, 33:137-142, November, 1966.

WITTY, PAUL, ALMA MOORE FREELAND, and EDITH H. GROTEBERG. *The Teaching of Reading* (Boston: D. C. Heath and Company, 1966), "A Case Study of a Verbally Gifted Child," pp. 349-353.

WITTY, PAUL, and ROCHELLE BLUMENTHAL. "The Language Development of an Exceptionally Gifted Pupil," *Elementary English*, 34:214-217 (April, 1957).

20

Special Remedial
Reading Problems Among
Children in Regular Classrooms

This text has dealt at length with the problems of normal children in their attempts to acquire all the developmental skills of reading under the tutelage of the teacher in the self-contained elementary classroom. The preceding chapters have developed a framework for teaching corrective reading for those students who have failed to acquire developmental reading skills commensurate with their chronological age and usual corresponding grade placement.

In the present chapter, it is necessary to discuss that small percent of the student population who do not readily acquire the reading skills. Further, children in this group usually fail to make the expected progress even when the teacher uses the best individualized and corrective techniques at his command. The illustrative case studies at the beginning of each section will serve as an introduction to the major areas of concern for these special problems: the neurologically handicapped child and the emotionally disturbed child.

I. THE NEUROLOGICALLY HANDICAPPED CHILD

Jill, in the fifth grade, was one of the children who had not made adequate progress in developmental reading despite a great deal of special attention from her teachers and some additional tutoring with a competent clinician during the summer following third grade. Although she was a bright child, her instructional level of reading was only middle-third grade. While she had never repeated a grade, her classroom teachers had observed her carefully and forwarded their observations. From year to year, written anecdotes for her cumulative folder more strongly underscored teacher dissatisfaction with her progress. The teachers noted that after the tutoring following third grade, Jill had overcome many of her problems of reversals and confusions. Jill's teachers, in a shared decision, concluded that the basic problem was an emotional instability exhibited at school in a very short attention span, inability to concentrate, and general lack of efficient organization. They reasoned that the father's manner and discipline might be excessively rigid and authoritarian while the mother was too indecisive and *laissez faire*. Since the father traveled and was away from home at times, this could cause the child to be mixed up about which pattern of values and behaviors to follow. Fortunately, the teachers conveyed, as tactfully as possible, their thoughts to the parents, who insisted on further clinical study.

The Wechsler Intelligence Scale for Children confirmed an above-average I.Q. finding reported on a previous group test, the *California Test of Mental Maturity.*

However, an especially low score on the block-design test in the performance scale was judged to be clinically significant and a *Bender-Gestalt Visual Motor Test* was administered. This instrument revealed a tendency for the child to rotate her drawings by ninety degrees when she reproduced drawings from a set of dots on cards—sufficient evidence to recommend a complete neurological examination.

The neurologist did, in fact, discover an unusual neurological problem. While Jill had never demonstrated any overt symptom of epilepsy or other convulsive disorder, her electroencephalogram indicated the brain wave pattern of a person with some form of *petit mal* or *grand mal*. The neurologist counseled with the parents and the reading therapist that this positive finding might account for the short attention span, "flighty" behavior, and resultant poor progress in school. After a few weeks of establishing the appropriate anti-convulsant drug therapy, Jill's behavior did change noticeably. Her progress in the reading clinic was rapid, and she was more "conforming and competent" in the regular classroom.

Not only does this case study show the cruciality of competent diagnosis and treatment, but also the implications of not having such a thorough diagnosis. The ramifications of such dangerous, unfounded "blaming" assumptions are clear when parents says, "If teachers would only . . . ," or when teachers say, "The parents are inconsistent in their discipline, so. . . ." Jill's problem also emphasizes that the most competent classroom teacher, teaching all of the developmental skills of reading in the most commendable way, is apt to experience failure in a situation where organic disorders are primary causes of learning disability.

Steward synthesizes a sketch of a typical hyperactive child in this way:[1]

---

[1]Roger Signor, "Hyperactive Children," *News Bulletin Quarterly,* describes the work of Dr. Mark A. Stewart, Professor of Child Psychiatry, Washington University School of Medicine, St. Louis.

Charles was nine years old when first seen, and the chief complaint was that he was doing badly in school. He vomited a lot as a baby, banged his head and rocked in his bed for hours, and cried much more than his sister. He walked at eleven months, talked first at two-and-a-half years, did not talk in sentences until four. Always very active, he has broken a bed and a trampoline and wears out the double knees in his jeans before the second washing. At age five, he was constantly turning off the furnace and water heater. He does not learn from punishment, is afraid of nothing, wanders from home and gets lost, dashes into the street without looking. He never completes projects at home and never finishes work at school. Hard to get to bed at night, he takes two hours or more to go sleep and gets up at six A.M. Neighbors "live in quiet terror" because he has run water into their basements through the hose, ridden his bicycle over their gardens, and blocked their sewers. He fights all the time with the neighborhood children and has no friends. In school he is "creative" in avoiding work, he hides his books, eats crayons, tears papers, and pokes the other children. Every teacher reports that she has to stand over him to get him to do any work. Though bright, he has had to repeat second grade twice and is now in a special school.

Lehman and Hall have described the neurologically impaired child in this way:[2]

> Who is this child? He is not mentally retarded; yet in certain skills he is retarded. He is not emotionally disturbed; yet he may have developed emotional problems as a result of his difficulties. What he is not is often more obvious than what he is. Parents are perplexed and bewildered and, accordingly, take their child to a doctor, psychologist, or child guidance center for diagnosis. After tests and symptoms have been evaluated, the proper diagnosis will reveal that this child has learning disabilities resulting from what specialists call minimal brain dysfunction.

Dunn labels the neurologically impaired child as the Strauss-syndrome child and defines the Strausse syndrome in this way:[3]

> Generally, today special educators label a child as fitting the Strauss syndrome when he displays: (1) hyperactivity; (2) incoordination; (3) lack of inhibition; (4) distractibility; and (5) an uneven pattern of learning disabilities, especially in language. Perhaps disturbances of (6) perception and (7) concept formation should also be mentioned but these are more difficult for teachers to observe.

---

[2]"Who Is This Child?" *The TR Times* (Teaching Resources, an Educational Service of the *New York Times*, 334 Boylston Street, Boston, Massachusetts 02116), Vol. 1, No. 1, February, 1967, abstracted from an article by Eileen F. Lehman and Robert E. Hall in *American Education*, April, 1966, a publication of the U. S. Department of Health, Education, and Welfare, Office of Education.

[3]Lloyd M. Dunn, "Minimal Brain Dysfunction: A Dilemma for Educators," in Edward C. Frierson and Walter B. Barbe, Editors, *Educating Children with Learning Disabilities: Selected Readings* (New York: Appleton-Century-Crofts, Inc., 1967), p. 121.

Dunn offers this description of a child with the Strauss syndrome:[4]

Ed is a ten-year-old boy without a motor handicap other than clumsiness. His speech is fairly distinct. Ed's intelligence quotient score is 80. His teacher complains that he talks incessantly, constantly interrupts the class with irrelevant remarks. He has a strong need for attention and thus bothers other children who are working by knocking things off their desks, by hiding their pencils, and by hitting them on the head. His learning patterns are very uneven. It is nearly impossible to settle him down to academic work because he cannot concentrate on one thing for any length of time. In fact, he is at the mercy of any idea which occurs to him, or any environmental event which reaches him.

Signor describes what he calls the "hyperactive child syndrome."[5] Five-year-old Tommy was such a child. In a group of children he tended to become over-excited, throw tantrums, or get into fights. Even though he was bright and curious, he could not concentrate on a project for any length of time. He had difficulty with finer motor coordination such as that required for printing and painting. His restlessness and short attention span were problems in the kindergarten. He didn't finish his work, and he roamed about the room distracting others.

Problems of Perception and Neurological Impairment

Children have many problems which affect their ability to read. These problems can be physical, emotional, or cultural. Most often there is a combination of factors. Disorders of a perceptual and neurological nature are often misunderstood by the average teacher. What is probably the most frequent cause of learning difficulties, although it is perhaps the least widely recognized of all, is a disturbance of the child's perceptual abilities—his visual perception, his auditory perception, his kinesthetic perception, or a combination of these.

Frostig has divided visual perception into five component parts:

1. Deficiency in visual-motor coordination results in difficulty in cutting, pasting, drawing, and in learning how to write. The child also displays clumsiness, and even dressing himself can be difficult.
2. Deficiency in perceptual constancy results in inadequate recognition of and adaptation to the environment. The child may learn to recognize a number, letter, or word in one particular form or context but fail to recognize it when seen in a different manner. Learning to read or work with symbols in any way poses many problems.
3. Deficiency in perception of position in space results in difficulty in understanding what is meant by the words up and down, in and out, before and behind, etc. Difficulty becomes apparent in academic tasks—letters, words, phrases, numbers, and pictures appear

---

[4]*Ibid.*, p. 118.
[5]*Op. cit.*, p. 2.

distorted and confusing. He may be able to pronounce the sounds *p a t* in "pat" but when he blends them together they may come out "tap." He perceives *b* as *d, p* as *q, saw* as *was,* and *24* as *42.* This makes it difficult if not impossible to learn to read, write, spell, or to do arithmetic.

4. Deficiency in perception of spatial relationships leads to many difficulties in academic learning. They may make impossible the proper perception of the sequence of letters in a word, remembering the sequences of processes involved in long division or understanding graphs.

5. Disability in perception of figure-ground is characterized by inattentive and disorganized behavior, inability to shift attention from one stimulus to another, inability to stay within lines or to form letters correctly, inability to find the place on a page, or words in the dictionary, inability to solve familiar problems on the crowded page in his workbook. Children with such difficulties literally cannot find anything, even when it is right in front of their noses.[6]

Suggestions for Teaching the Neurologically Impaired Child

From the definition of the Strauss-syndrome child already given, it is clear that teachers must be prepared to deal with the behaviors of hyperactivity and distractibility, perseveration, meticulousness, withdrawal tendencies, compulsive behavior, abstract concepts, and language disabilities.

Hyperactivity and Distractibility

The child may be seated at the front of the room, separating him as far as possible from classmates (without isolating him from the group). The room decoration should be minimal, perhaps limited to one wall or area. A quiet corner completely devoid of distracting stimuli where the child can sit when he is particularly excited or irritable may help. Special worksheets containing small amounts of material omitting extraneous illustrations or designs may be less distracting and enhance learning to attend. The teacher should keep his appearance plain and avoid non-essential jewelry. Perhaps the child can decide on a reminding device to help keep him in his seat.

Some youngsters develop hysterical reactions to stressful situations. The alert teacher tries to anticipate such situations and to prevent them as much as possible.

Hyperactive children require a teacher with patience and sympathetic understanding of their problems. This teacher will provide materials which will help slow down and channel their random motor movements. The children will be able to construct many of their own learning devices through such activities as cutting, pasting, sorting, etc. When purpose-

---

[6]Marianne Frostig, *Administration and Scoring Manual, Developmental Test of Visual Perception* (Palo Alto, California: Consulting Psychologists Press, 1966), p. 5.

fully engaged, these children tend to become calmer. Calmer behavior leads to gradually improved habits of attending, increased success experiences, and greater interest in the acquisition of academic skills.

Perseveration

Vary the ongoing task with one that is completely different, keeping a pleasantly persuasive attitude. Or provide new materials in easy reach to encourage the child's responses. At the same time, encourage the child to "branch out"—to generalize from the first task. These boys and girls must be specifically taught to do these things.

Meticulousness

Keep the learning assignment short with time limits. This requires careful diagnosis of functioning levels—including attention span to be sure that the task is an appropriate one. The teacher may be able to encourage attending and interacting by using the operant conditioning technique. Tangible rewards for completion of simple tasks under conditions previously agreed upon are sometimes helpful in establishing the pattern of behavior the teacher desires. Oral work should be emphasized in preference to written but at all times avoid overstimulation and failure in oral expression as well as in written expression.

Withdrawal Tendencies

Be sympathetic. Include the child as a part of the group. Any attempt at group socialization must be carefully controlled by the teacher. It is well to recognize those children with a high social quotient or ability to adapt to differences in behavior.

The teacher then manipulates the situation so that communication takes place, for example, "John and Billy, will you please put these notices in their envelopes?" The teacher should strive, at all times, for achieving insight in learning tasks by concretizing them through visual, tactile, and auditory devices.

Compulsive Behavior

It is probably desirable to abandon the phonics method of reading for a child who analyzes compulsively in letter-by-letter elements but has difficulty in blending them into synthesized words.

Abstract Words

Concepts must be broken down into isolated compartmentalized learning. Concrete representations of numbers and letters, color cues, etc., are helpful in securing insight into small learning. Keying new tasks to what the child is capable of performing will help to insure that his responses will more nearly always be correct. In self-tutoring activities, the correct answer should be immediately available. Overlearning is important. Responses need to become automatic after insight is achieved. Separate knowledges should "chain" upon each other in sequential steps until whole concepts are learned.

Language Disabilities

This is probably the most common language disorder of children. These children are unable to perceive and/or accurately record the symbols of the printed page. They cannot interpret written language in the way that unaffected children are able to comprehend it. There are certain remedial approaches which are very effective with these disabled children. Many exercises in proper discrimination of left-right direction will be helpful for those who have visuo-spatial difficulties and do a great deal of letter and word reversal. Shapes and sizes must be perceived. The child will benefit by being taught to look for letter details within a word.

Tactual experiences with letter contours can be gained through using wooden letters upon which sandpaper surfaces are pasted. The child's memory for letter recognition is reinforced through the sense of touch. Tracing the word also reinforces memory through the use of muscle or kinesthetic sense. Through writing, tactual and kinesthetic experiences, he becomes aware of letter details.

Another effective method is presenting the word with one or two letters left out. As the child fills in blanks and finds that he is right, he is forced to become aware of the missing details.

To enhance instruction for neurologically impaired children:

1. The classes should be small;
2. The room should contain a minimum of distracting stimuli;
3. Activities must be paced at the child's capacity for sustained participation with frequent periods of guided and supervised large muscle play, like bicycle riding or running;
4. Maximum permissiveness will be exercised to permit children to leave the classroom and run about the playground to release mounting tensions;
5. Group discipline must be firm and setting clearly defined limits is essential;
6. Children must not be permitted to regularly and habitually experience failure.

Success will build self-esteem and enhance his ability to try harder the next time.

In making shifts of attention from one type of work to another, be aware of the child's difficulties in such shifting and help him by waiting for his attention, asking specifically if he is following, move close to him and either put your hand lightly on his shoulder or help him put away material or get new materials ready.

Drugs may be prescribed either to control impulsive behavior or to make it possible for the child to hold his attention on a topic for longer periods of time.

II.   CHILDREN WITH EMOTIONAL DISTURBANCES

Letting Angry Feelings Come Out

When the standards others have set for the child do not match his own natural way of growing up in his own good time, there are conflicts to be met. Too much "no, no!"; too much "You're a big boy now"; too much "Give that to your little sister!"; too much "I'm not going to let go of you until you apologize to your grandmother!"—these build up anger, resentment, hostility, and hate. These moments of "bad feelings" against another child or any adult must not be pushed deep down inside; they need to come out. Was it not Shakespeare who said, "If there's no one else to talk to, it's better to tell your mad feelings to the picture on the wall than to keep them bottled up inside you"?

If the child tries to let his feelings come out in his paintings, the teacher must not say, "Oh, don't paint such an unhappy picture. Start again and make a nice one."[7] Children can pound nails, hit punching bags, tackle dummies, and work out some of these feelings. If the child can express his feelings well enough, he may spank the doll, put it in the stove, willing to burn it up, flush it down the toilet, stomp on it, or otherwise try to mutilate it. The teacher should keep as neutral as possible. She should not say, "Oh! the nice dolly. You must be nice to him."[8] The neutral response to the child's expressions of "I hate him" is "You don't like the doll (or whoever the doll represents at the moment) very well today, do you?"

Emotional Disturbance in the Classroom

If the teacher has a student who is obviously emotionally disturbed, it is her responsibility to assist the remaining students in a subtle manner to accept the defiant child as part of the group. "Individual differences" in educational jargonese applies not only to academic work. As each child differs in academic ability, so he differs in background experiences that cause him to respond to any situation in a unique manner. Therefore, each child must be accepted, with his strong points and his weak-

---

[7]Hymes, *Understanding Your Child,* (Englewood Cliffs: Prentice-Hall, Inc., 1952), p. 147.

[8]*Ibid.,* p. 149.

nesses, as a person having worth and dignity as a human being. The teacher has the responsibility of encouraging individuality insofar that his behavior does not impinge on the rights of others.

According to national figures, in a class of 35 students the teacher can expect, on the average, two to five students in her class to show symptoms of some sort of exceptionality. How she handles the exceptional child in her room depends upon her educational background and her personal maturity.

The teacher should try to discover the cause of the deviant behavior. The following classification lists distress signals, and offers suggestions for teacher response.

Emotional disturbance may generally be categorized in four types of behavior.

Aggression

Aggression manifests itself in temper tantrums; bullying; teasing; destroying property of others; being physically abusive to other children; interrupting and disrupting classroom routine; stealing or lying.

To help the children with certain of these behaviors, the teacher may:

1. Have a corner set aside that is neutral and non-distracting;
2. Separate the child from the group during periods of active aggressive behavior;
3. Be accepting but firm; be matter-of-fact, business-like, and *fair*;
4. Anticipate aggressive behavior and help the child regain control or select alternate behavior;
5. Set up minimum standards of expected behavior *with* the child, then when corrective measures are taken, the child knows it is his own standard that he has violated;
6. Provide acceptable outlets for tensions that build up aggression: modeling clay, punching bags, non-destructible toys.

Anxiety

The anxious child is the one who cries easily; is timid; is afraid to tackle new tasks; is over-anxious about grades; cannot accept less than his understanding of your standards.

To help the child who is anxious, the teacher should

1. Maintain warm rapport with the child;
2. Attempt to build self-confidence on successive successes;
3. Reassure, but not coddle;
4. Minimize stress over grades;
5. Be able to discipline in a kind way, but be firm;

6. Not allow student to become overly dependent on the teacher for security;
7. Maintain a sense of proportion; this is business-like friendliness;
8. Ask for responses in class when the child will be successful.

Withdrawal

Withdrawing behavior describes the child who daydreams; prefers to be alone; does not seek company of anyone; has few friends, maybe only one with whom he can feel intimacy.

To help the child who withdraws, the teacher can plan specifically to

1. Bring the child into class activities when he is able to handle it emotionally;
2. Make sure that class activities are varied between quiet and active work;
3. Help the child develop interest in school work by varying teaching techniques to include games; giving responsibility in group projects; calling on the child to respond when you know he can be successful.

Bizarre Behavior

Bizarre behavior may be unpredictable behavior; nonsense language responses; or the need to go through "ritual" before any action is taken.

If this symptom persists beyond firm but kind teacher response, the teacher must feel obligated to seek professional help through the school psychologist or the school social worker.

WHAT'S BOTHERING DAVID?

David was in the fourth grade when his teacher suggested to his mother that he needed special help with his reading. Since his school provided no special help, he was enrolled in a private reading clinic for one session a week. It was the middle of the school year and David had just had his tenth birthday.

The reading clinician found that he could read for instruction at the beginning third grade level, he knew most of the 220 Dolch Basic Sight Words, and his spelling was adequate for beginning third grade. He could not discriminate many sounds on the McKee phonics inventory, making many errors in the vowel section. He had difficulty determining that such pairs of words as *puddle-puzzle, clean-cling* were *different* and *not the same.* He passed the vocabulary item of the Binet Intelligence Test at age 12, and since he was just ten, the clinician felt confident he had at least average intelligence.

After several sessions of developing rapport, trying some writing of original paragraphs, completing exercises in the easy levels of SRA Reading for Understanding, Junior Edition,* and enjoying some easy oral reading, the clinician began to feel that reading really wasn't David's problem.

David had read books in the Deep Sea Adventures series until he was now reading *Frogmen in Action* (Third Grade Level) and was thoroughly enjoying the books. He was anxious to get each new one in the series.

It was David's strange mannerisms—not bizarre really, but different— the fear of not doing well, and the inability to sit still—these behaviors bothered his clinician the most. She invited him to talk often by leading into conversations that might reveal what he was thinking or feeling.

One day when David was reading, he began to squirm in his seat and his arms were covered with goosepimples. Then he said that every time he started to read, something gave him "the chills."

The clinician gave David opportunity to discuss the problem by answering with neutral comments, asking questions that might provide further explanation, or restating some of David's observations. The following running commentary is a report of David's report about "shivering" and having the "chills" when he reads. His ability to discuss his feelings at such length suggests that this is a serious problem to him and that he does need to clear up his feelings before he will be able to apply his best efforts in the reading situation.

I try to hold my hand in a fist to keep from having the shivers. Then I cross my feet and try to hold them still. Then I get nervous and make more mistakes. And then I can't read at all. I don't know why this happens when I read. When I was in second grade, the lady in the administration building [diagnostic testing service] said that the stories weren't interesting. But that's not it.

. . . .

I really do want to read. I just get the shivers. Lisa and Jamie [little sister and little brother] holler and that gets me, too. But now, my mother and I read early in the morning and it's better. But I still get the shivers.

. . . .

Well, a long time ago when I was in kindergarten, I don't really think the teacher liked me. She used to say, "Why can't you act like Mark [a big brother]?" But I never did know how I'd acted. Then, one day, you know, she always made us put our heads down, and rest. But one day, she said when we came in, "You've all been so good today, you don't have to put your heads down and rest." Then, all of a sudden, she said, "David Carr, put your head down on that desk and rest." I knew it was me, but I couldn't figure it out. You know, I still don't know what I did or why she made me put my head down.

---

*Science Research Associates, Inc., 259 East Erie St., Chicago, Ill. 60611, 1963.

There's something else that bothers me, too. Sometimes I shut my eyes and when I open them, I don't know where I open them. Once, at ten o'clock in the morning, I closed my eyes at school, and I thought I was at home. Then I had to blink and blink and I was at school. I don't know how I got there, I just remembered crossing the fence. You know that'd happened two times when I was in the car and once when I was playing baseball.

(The clinician asked if he could show how this happened.)

No, I can't just make it happen, but that's the way it happens when it does happen.

. . . .

You know how your eyes are when you first wake up, with a light shining in them. Well, that's what happens and I don't know where I am, except everytime so far, I've been able to blink and think "Where am I?" and then I know. [He made motions—waving with the fingers of one hand—to show that his eyes were flickering.]

(At a session one week later)

You know something real nice happened this week. One evening my dad and I sat out on the patio and talked and talked man to man. We stayed out there till nine-thirty. It sure was neat. He explained to me that my uncle—Uncle Davie—had them, too. [Shivers.] And he still makes funny faces! And even my dad, when he was a kid, and my grandpa had them too. And now me. And I think I know why. Maybe not exactly, and I'm just guessing about this, but my brother is the only one that hasn't had them and he's the only one that hasn't had appendicitis. They all had their appendix out and now I've had it out, too. And now I've got them.

(At a session one week later)

As David was reading, the clinician notices his shoulders were twitching. She said, "Oh, David, have you got the shivers again?" But David, with that strained, faraway look in his eyes, said, "Oh no, I don't have them anymore. My mom and dad both told me just to tell myself I didn't have them and so I do and I don't." But his eyes had a kind of strained, desperate look, that if he didn't keep telling himself, the shivers would come right back.

The clinician began to wonder if a new kind of substitute nervous mannerism might replace the shivers. (If the adult insists the child *not* bite his nails, he *can* pick his nose, and if that is stopped, he *can* twist his hair.)

Why would David be afraid? And of what?

Could there be a neurological basis for the "closing of his eyes and not knowing for a minute where he is"?

If there is a problem with either an organic or psychological base, can the parents help him overcome it by denying the symptoms?

Why would the classroom teacher have referred him for reading? Reading is the most often reported cause of children's failure in school. In a large class, the most obvious behaviors may be unfinished work, inattention, and, as a consequence, some difficulties in reading situations. When the child is doing unsatisfactory school work for any reason, teachers are probably inclined to look first for inability to do activities associated with reading.

The clinician reports that generally, David is an outgoing boy when talking about most things. Physically, he's "a beautiful specimen." And other than laboring over his problem, he's animated about all the things he talks about. When he's reporting something that pleases him, his eyes dance.

"He does have some slight speech problem. I can't really pinpoint what it is. Sometimes he does a great deal of repeating himself, or sometimes he doesn't enunciate clearly, or sometimes he mixes up the syllables in polysyllabic words."

Hewett has found that emotionally disturbed children are usually not ready for "formal" instruction in which skill mastery is the primary objective. He lists *five* prerequisite readiness levels to skill mastery: (1) ability to attend; (2) response to others in learning situations, either signal learning or stimulus-response learning; (3) ability to respond to instructions or to follow directions; (4) exploring the environment meaningfully; and (5) getting along with others—valuing social approval. Beyond these readiness levels, the school expects (6) mastery of skills and (7) achievement.

Hewett summarizes these seven tasks as a hierarchy, the child's difficulties relating to each task, the educational task to be developed, types of learner rewards, and the amount of teacher involvement in structuring child behavior.[9]

The use of programmed instruction and other structural helps, such as the use of the rebus technique in reading context, may be very profitable for teaching emotionally disturbed children.

The rebus technique is one which uses pictorial symbols to represent words in traditional orthography. Rebuses have been used occasionally in the past in children's magazines and books to make the text more readable for children who still have a limited reading vocabulary. The preprimers of the Harper and Row reading series have used rebuses for several words children have not yet learned as sight vocabulary in that reading program. The rebus is used to help the author promote higher

---

[9]Frank M. Hewett, "Educational Engineering with Emotionally Disturbed Children," *Exceptional Children*, 33:461, March, 1967.

TABLE 20.1.   Description of the Hierarchy of Educational Tasks

Hierarchy Level	Attention	Response	Order	Exploratory	Social	Mastery	Achievement
Child's Problem	Inattention due to withdrawal or resistance	Lack of involvement and unwillingness to respond in learning	Inability to follow directions	Incomplete or inaccurate knowledge of environment	Failure to value social approval or disapproval	Deficits in basic adaptive and school skills not in keeping with IQ	Lack of self motivation for learning
Educational Task	Get child to pay attention to teacher and task	Get child to respond to tasks he likes and which offer promise of success	Get child to complete tasks with specific starting points and steps leading to a conclusion	Increase child's efficiency as an explorer and get him involved in multisensory exploration of his environment	Get child to work for teacher and peer group approval and to avoid their disapproval	Remediation of basic skill deficiencies	Development of interest in acquiring knowledge
Learner Reward	Provided by tangible rewards (e.g., food, money, tokens)	Provided by gaining social attention	Provided through task completion	Provided by sensory stimulation	Provided by social approval	Provided through task accuracy	Provided through intellectual task success
Teacher Structure	Minimal	Still limited	Emphasized	Emphasized	Based on standards of social appropriateness	Based on curriculum assignments	Minimal

From Frank N. Hewett, "Educational Engineering with Emotionally Disturbed Children," *Exceptional Children*, 33:461, March, 1967. Used with permission.

interest in stories; permits the use of a wider selection of words in the story; and takes advantage of the child's speaking vocabulary.[10]

Rebuses have been suggested as a useful reading system for severely retarded children.

The Peabody Rebus Reading Program, illustrated on the following pages, is primarily intended for use in kindergartens and in first grades and with some children having marginal learning abilities. Three books are now available but teachers could stop the Rebus Reading Program after using only one, or after using two, or after using all three. According to Woodcock, the first rebus book will have presented most of the readiness work prior to beginning pre-primer level instruction; the second rebus book will have presented most of the skills necessary to begin primer level instruction; and if book three is presented, most children can move easily into the primer level of other reading programs. The Peabody Rebus Reading Program uses the rebus as a link between spoken language and reading print and is organized in programmed text format.[11] The rebus vocabulary for books one and two and four reading frames are presented on pages 486 and 487.

The Emotionally Disturbed Child in the Classroom

Asquith, Donaher, and Barton have described one emotionally disturbed little girl in this way:[12]

> . . . She is hyperactive, interrupts, cries easily, has temper tantrums and is utterly unpredictable from one moment to another. Recently she climbed on top of her desk and screamed and threw books, crayons, and paper all over the room.

Suggestions for the Classroom Teacher:

1. The child should be kept in the regular classroom as much as possible . . . even if for only a few minutes at a time.

    The use of programmed materials, paced at the child's performance level, is recommended. Some teachers have used the rebus technique in easy reading successfully.

2. There should be a movable screen in the classroom that can be used to partition off a small corner or working space and shut out stimuli. This is carefully interpreted to the child as a provision to make it easy for him to work and *not as a punishment*. The teacher can explain that "Some people need a quiet place where they won't be disturbed if they are to get anything done."

---

[10]Mabel O'Donnell, *et al.*, Teacher's Edition of Preprimers One and Two, *The Alice and Jerry Basic Reading Program*, (New York: Harper and Row, 1966), p. 21.

[11]Richard W. Woodcock, *Teacher's Guide, The Peabody Rebus Reading Program*, (Circle Pines, Minnesota 55014: American Guidance Service, Inc., 1969), p. 71.

[12]Melrose Asquith, Mrs. Robert Donaher, and Clifford Barton, "I Have an Emotionally Disturbed Child in My Classroom," *Grade Teacher*, 85:77-80, April, 1968.

REBUS VOCABULARY — BOOKS ONE AND TWO

a	a		can		have		run
	airplane		car		here		see
	and		cat		house		sit
	are		chair	I	I		table
	at		coat		in		the
	ball		come		is		they
	banana		dog		it	3	three
	big		down		little		to
	bird		eat		look		tree
	black	5	five		me	2	two
	blue		floor		my		under
	boat	4	four		no		up
	book		girl		on		walk
	box		go		one		what
	boy		green		play		with
	brown		ground		red		yellow
	cake		hat		ride		yes

From Richard W. Woodcock, *Teacher's Guide: Introducing Reading, Books One and Two*, The Peabody Rebus Reading Program, (Circle Pines, Minnesota: American Guidance Service, Inc., 1967), Back Cover.

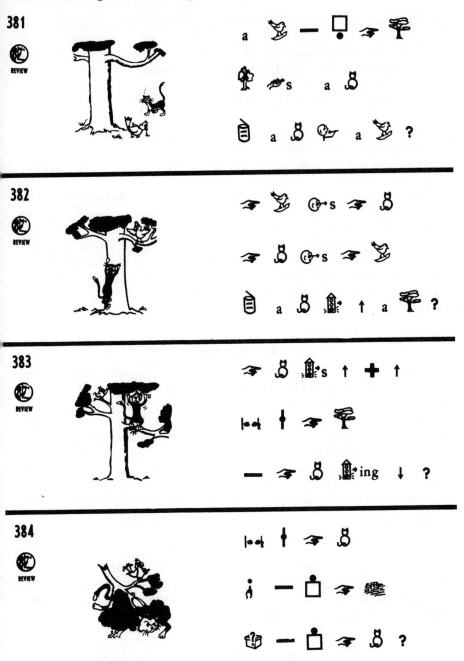

From Richard W. Woodcock, *Introducing Reading—Book Two*, Peabody Rebus Reading Program, (Circle Pines, Minnesota: American Guidance Service, 1967), frames 381-384.

3. The teacher must become skilled in sizing up children's moods early in the day. If a disturbed child is having a bad day, keep him in your line of vision all day long. On his bad days, make a special effort to support him by any of these behaviors carried out casually:
   a. close physical proximity;
   b. gently massage his shoulder and neck muscles as you pass his desk;
   c. talk to him . . . even if he doesn't respond;
   d. set reasonable limits and then hold firmly to them;
   e. check his medical record; ask his family doctor if he has regular medication.

Channels of communication are very important so that everyone who may have useful information has a way to share it with others who badly need it. The teacher—the principal—the family doctor—the school nurse—the social worker—the parents—the neurologist—the school psychologist . . . and if indicated, the psychiatrist. And these people in their academic disciplines have not all learned to talk "the same language" so it is necessary to exchange ideas sufficiently to learn how to work together and how to share information in a useful way.

III. SUMMARY

Special problems of children who are neurologically handicapped or emotionally disturbed have been reviewed in this chapter. It is apparent that most beginning teachers will need expert help and supervision in working with children with these problems. With patience and calmness, many teachers are able to help such children function in regular classes by tailoring their program to fit individual, specific needs.

Although not presented in this chapter, it is extremely important for the teacher to develop the ability to recognize his own emotional needs as well as the child's emotional needs and to be able to separate the two.

SUGGESTED ACTIVITIES

Visit a reading clinic and (1) observe children with special problems being tutored; (2) interview the reading clinician and learn (a) causes of the difficulty, (b) diagnosis (medically, psychologically, educationally), (c) remediation planned.

READING REFERENCES

AXLINE, VIRGINIA. *Dibs* (Boston: Houghton Mifflin, 1967).
AXLINE, VIRGINIA. *Play Therapy* (Boston: Houghton Mifflin, 1947).

BARUCH, DOROTHY. *New Ways in Discipline* (New York: McGraw-Hill, 1949).

BENDER, LAURETTA. *A Visual Motor Gestalt Test and Its Clinical Use* (New York: The American Orthopsychiatric Association, 1938), 165 pp.

BLOM, GASTON E. "Psychoeducational Aspects of Classroom Management," *Exceptional Children*, 32:377-384, February, 1966.

Board of Education of the City of New York. *The Emotionally Disturbed Child: A Bibliography* (Board of Education, Publication Sales, 110 Livingston Street, Brooklyn 1, New York, 1964).

DUBNOFF, BELLE, GEORGE FARGO, and DONALD WEISS. "Aspects of Perceptual Training with Brain Injured and Emotionally Disturbed Children as Related to Reading," *Twenty-Fifth Yearbook, Claremont College Reading Conference* (Claremont, California: Claremont University College, 1961).

EPHRON, BEULAH K. *Emotional Difficulties in Reading* (New York: The Julian Press, 1953).

FABIAN, ABRAHAM. "Reading Disability: An Index of Pathology," *American Journal of Orthopsychiatry*, 24:319-329, April, 1955.

FRIERSON, EDWARD, and WALTER BARBE. *Educating Children With Learning Disabilities* (New York: Appleton-Century-Croft, 1967).

HARING, NORRIS, and E. PHILLIPS. *Educating Emotionally Disturbed Children* (New York: McGraw-Hill, 1962).

HARRIS, ALBERT J. *How to Increase Reading Ability*, 4th Edition (New York: David MacKay, 1961), pp. 249-260, "Lateral Dominance"; pp. 243-248, "Other Physical Conditions"; and pp. 264-275, "Emotional Problems in Reading."

HAY, LOUIS, and SHIRLEY COHEN. "Perspectives for a Classroom for Disturbed Children," *Exceptional Children*, 33:577-580, April, 1967.

HERMANN, KNUD. *Reading Disability: A Medical Study of Word Blindness and Related Handicaps* (Springfield: Charles C. Thomas, 1959).

HEWETT, FRANK M. "Educational Engineering with Emotionally Disturbed Children," *Exceptional Children*, 33:459-470, March, 1967.

HEWETT, FRANK M. *The Emotionally Disturbed Child in the Classroom* (Boston: Allyn and Bacon, 1968).

HEWETT, FRANK M. "A Hierarchy of Competencies for Teachers of Emotionally Handicapped Children," *Exceptional Children*, 33:7-12, September, 1966.

LONG, NICHOLAS. *Conflict in the Classroom* (San Francisco: Wadsworth, 1965).

McDONALD, ARTHUR S. "Intellectual Characteristics of Disabled Readers at the High School and College Levels," *Journal of Developmental Reading*, 7:97-101, Winter, 1964.

MILLER, NANDEEN. "Teaching an Emotionally Disturbed, Brain Injured Child," *The Reading Teacher*, 17:460-465, March, 1964.

PIMM, JUNE B., and GORDON McCLURE. "Working with Emotionally Disturbed Children in the Public School Setting," *Exceptional Children*, 33:653-655, May, 1967.

ROBECK, MILDRED C. "Intellectual Strengths and Weaknesses Shown by Reading Clinic Subjects on the WISC," *Journal of Developmental Reading*, 7:120-129, Winter, 1964.

SILVER, ARCHIE A., and ROSA A. HAGIN. "Specific Reading Disability: Follow-up Studies," *American Journal of Orthopsychiatry*, 34:95-102, January, 1964.

SILVER, ARCHIE A., and ROSA A. HAGIN. "Maturation of Perceptual Functions in Children with Specific Reading Disability, *The Reading Teacher*, 19:253-260, January, 1966.

SMITH, DONALD E. P., and PATRICIA M. CARRIGAN. *The Nature of Reading Disability* (New York: Harcourt, Brace & World, Inc., 1959).

STAUFFER, RUSSELL. "Certain Basic Concepts in Remedial Reading," *Elementary School Journal*, 51:334-342, February, 1951. Reports a case study in which the Fernald Kinesthetic Technique was used. Reprinted in W. B. Barbe, *Teaching Reading: Selected Materials* (New York: Oxford University Press, 1965), pp. 351-358.

STRANG, RUTH. *Diagnostic Teaching of Reading* (New York: McGraw-Hill, 1964), Chapter 9: "Physical Factors in Reading Diagnosis," pp. 163-186.

STRANG, RUTH. *Understanding and Helping the Retarded Reader* (Tucson: University of Arizona Press, 1965), Section 2: "Pupils with Emotional Problems."

STUDHOLME, JANICE M. "Group Guidance with Mothers of Retarded Readers," *The Reading Teacher*, 17:528-530, April, 1964. Reports attitudes held by six mothers of retarded readers and changes in their attitudes before and after attendance in group guidance sessions at a college reading center during the times when their sons were given reading instruction.

TIFT, KATHARINE F. "The Disturbed Child in the Classroom" *NEA Journal*, 57:12-14, March, 1968.

ZINTZ, MILES V. *Corrective Reading* (Dubuque: William C. Brown Co., Publishers, 1966).

21

Evaluation in the Reading Program

Some type of evaluation is the means by which the teacher determines the success or lack of it in his teaching efforts. Evaluation is an on-going process whereby the teacher determines (1) the extent to which his objectives have been met, (2) the need for corrective and remedial teaching, and (3) the extent of review and reinforcement to be included in the reading program. Evaluation will be both *formal,* in the use of standardized measures of achievement, and *informal,* in the use of subjective judgment, opinions of both students and teacher, and keeping records of desired behaviors registered in knowledges, attitudes, and skills. Evaluation, especially the informal measures, involve much more than testing cognitive learning and achievement of specific study skills. Keeping a record of the types of library books read during the year, using such a technique as *My Reading Design,* is a good source for evaluating growth of interests. Having scheduled periods, preferably with groups of ten or twelve students, to discuss books or stories read, with the teacher utilizing higher levels of questioning and affective behaviors involved is a good way to evaluate growth in interpretive abilities and in verbal fluency. If the reading program has been based on a prescribed set of behavioral objectives from the beginning, in which the teacher has already phrased the resulting behavior to be expected if the objectives are met, then final evaluation will be very specific as a planned part of the total program in reading.

Evaluation presupposes that goals have been defined so that results can later determine if they have been achieved. Three steps in evaluation include[1]

1. Formulation of objectives to be used. These objectives must be defined clearly in terms of specific behaviors to be achieved.

---

[1]Joseph Crescimbeni, "The Need for Diagnostic Evaluation," *Education,* 88: 161, November-December, 1967.

2. Identification of sources of evidence. Teachers get this evidence through: rating scales, methods of observation, questionnaires, classroom tests, standardized tests, and projective drawings.
3. Interpretation of results. Final outcomes must be interpreted in terms of behavioral objectives established initially.

Evaluation in the reading program will include the use of (1) standardized reading tests; tests provided by publishers of graded series of readers to be used as each book is finished, semi-formal tests such as those provided by *My Weekly Reader* or the Student Record Book of the SRA laboratories; (2) the written work of children, in writing summaries of stories read, original essays, or answers to questions; (3) the oral work of children, in reading aloud both to the teacher and to groups of children, measuring progress by using the tape recorder to collect samples of reading aloud early in the year to compare with samples from the same children later in the year, and talking about the books and stories read; (4) the use of informal check lists to evaluate individual children from time to time with respect to accuracy in oral reading, attitudes toward reading, and efficiency in silent reading; (5) other informal techniques, including: (a) sociometric tests will help the teacher to evaluate the extent of personal interaction in the group; (b) anecdotal records filed chronologically throughout the year will provide the teacher bases for judging progress or lack of it in the child's total growth; (c) the children's self-evaluation will be helpful in determining the extent to which they feel their school year is successful or profitable to them; and (d) teachers evaluation of cognitive *and* affective growth; and (6) making profiles that evaluate many skills and abilities.

I. STANDARDIZED READING TESTS

A test becomes standardized by administering it to large numbers of subjects of given age and grade status so that the examiner can determine the "expected" performance of boys and girls under given circumstances in taking such a test. Results of such a test are most easily interpreted in percentile ranks. The percentile rank is determined by the percent of the total number of children who took the test who perform less well than a given score. For example, if 1,000 children in fifth grade complete a given reading test, the middle score, the rank of the 500th person, is the fiftieth percentile. Naturally the scores of fifth graders will tend to cluster around a given average score. This means that the difference between the fortieth and sixtieth percentiles may be a very small number of raw score points. However, the differences in raw score points between given percentiles (deciles) may get greater as the distribution of raw scores is tabulated for the high and low extremes of the distribution. The seventieth (70th) percentile represents the raw score below which seventy per cent of the students scored.

The second percentile is the level below which only two per cent of all the students in a given grade scored.

It is especially important for the classroom teacher to find out which students can perform especially well, those who perform in the "middle-third" of the distribution, and those who perform poorly on standardized tests. With this information, the teacher can begin to accumulate many kinds of informal diagnostic information to try to provide instruction in reading skills that will be challenging but not too difficult. The teacher should expect, in a fifth grade class, for example, to find one or two children performing at seventh or eighth grade level in reading ability and one or two performing no better than first or second grade reading ability. (See Chapter 2). Ability to administer individually an oral reading test provides the teacher with some much-needed information for planning a child's work for the year. This is why it is so important for the teacher to do informal reading inventories as early in the school year as is possible. (See Chapter 3). For those few boys and girls with many reading deficiencies, the teacher may wish to administer a standardized oral reading tests as a pre- and post-test of reading ability to measure progress during the school year. The Gilmore Oral Reading Test, published by Harcourt, Brace & World, is one of the easiest of such tests to administer, can be completed with a child in fifteen to twenty minutes, and yields a grade placement score for accuracy in mechanics, a grade placement score in comprehension, and a rating for rate of reading. (See test summary, page 494). The Durrell Analysis of Reading Difficulty, also from Harcourt, Brace & World, and the new Gray's Oral Reading Test, by Bobbs-Merrill, are more diagnostic in nature but can be administered by any classroom teacher who studies the manual of directions carefully and practices following the directions as written. (See cover pages of record booklets on pp. 495-496). The Botel Reading Inventory, Follett Publishing Company, using word recognition and word opposites tests, helps teachers place students at appropriate levels of difficulty.

Standardized silent reading tests for use in elementary schools are readily available. The Gates-MacGinitie Reading Tests, Teacher's College Press, as a complete revision of the Gates Reading Tests, are carefully graduated in difficulty levels and can be used with separate answer sheets to provide for much easier scoring by teachers. A test summary sheet is shown on page 497. The Nelson Reading Test, Houghton Mifflin, was also revised in 1962 and can also be scored on separate answer sheets or on self-marking answer sheets. The Silent Reading Diagnostic Tests, Lyons and Carnahan, provide the teacher with very useful diagnostic information and the results can be presented concisely on a profile provided in the test booklet. (See profile, page 498). Selected oral and written standardized tests are listed below:

NAME_____

TEST SUMMARY   Form C

PARA-GRAPH	ACCURACY		COMPREHENSION	RATE	
	ERRORS	10 MINUS NO. ERRORS	NO. RIGHT (OR CREDITED)	WORDS IN ¶	TIME IN SEC.
1				24	
2				45	
3				50	
4				73	
5				103	
6				117	
7				127	
8				161	
9				181	
10				253	
	ACC. SCORE (TOT. "10 MINUS NO. ER-RORS" COLUMN)		COMP. SCORE (TOT. NO. RIGHT OR CREDITED)	(1) NO. WORDS READ*	
				(2) TIME IN SEC.*	
STANINE				(1) ÷ (2)	X 60
GRADE EQUIV.				RATE SCORE (WPM)	
RATING					

*Do **not** count "ceiling" paragraph or paragraphs below "basal."

COMMENTS:

Reproduced from Gilmore, John V. and Eunice C. Gilmore, *Gilmore Oral Reading Test,* Copyright 1968 by Harcourt, Brace and World, Inc., Reproduced by special permission.

Durrell Analysis of Reading Difficulty

NEW EDITION

INDIVIDUAL RECORD BOOKLET

BY Donald D. Durrell *Professor of Education and Director of Educational Clinic, Boston University*

NAME _____   DATE _____

SCHOOL _____   EXAMINER _____

AGE _____ GRADE _____   REPORT TO _____

DATE OF BIRTH _____   ADDRESS _____

Profile Chart

GRADE	READING ANALYSIS TESTS							ADDITIONAL TESTS							AGE
	Reading		Listen-ing	Flash Words	Word Analysis	Spell-ing	Hand-writing	Durrell-Sullivan				Revised Stanford-Binet				
	Oral	Silent						Capacity		Achievement						
								Word	Para.	Word	Para.	Vocab.	M.A.			
H																12-0
6.5 M																11-8
L																11-4
6.0																11-2
H																11-0
5.5 M																10-8
L																10-4
5.0																10-2
H																9-11
4.5 M																9-8
L																9-5
4.0																9-2
H																9-0
3.5 M																8-8
L																8-5
3.0																8-2
H																8-0
2.5 M																7-9
L																7-5
2.0																7-3
H																7-0
1.5 M																6-9
L																6-6
Record scores here →																

EXAMINER'S RECORD BOOKLET

for the

GRAY ORAL READING TEST

FORM A

Name _Charles_   Grade _6_   Age _12_

School _Lincoln Elementary_   Teacher _Smith_   Sex _M_

City _____   State _____

Examiner _Dale Smith_   Date _5-3-68_

SUMMARY

Passage Number	No. of Errors	Time (in Seconds)	Passage Scores	Comprehension
1.	0	8	9	1
2.	0	16	9	4
3.	0	17	9	4
4.	2	28	5	3
5.	5	36	1	2
6.	8	38	0	2½
7.	7	60	0	2½
8.	6	59	0	2½
9.	9	57	0	2½
10.				
11.				
12.				
13.				
Total Passage Scores			33	
Grade Equivalent			4.1	

TYPES OF ERRORS

1.	Aid	
2.	Gross Mispronunciation	7
3.	Partial Mispronunciation	4
4.	Omission	9
5.	Insertion	5
6.	Substitution	4
7.	Repetition	8
8.	Inversion	

OBSERVATIONS
(Check statement and circle each part)

_____ Word-by-word reading
_____ Poor phrasing
_____ Lack of expression
_____ Monotonous tone
_____ Pitch too high or low; voice too loud, too soft, or strained
_____ Poor enunciation
_____ Disregard of punctuation
_____ Overuse of phonics
_____ Little or no method of word analysis
_____ Unawareness of errors
_____ Head movement
_____ Finger pointing
_____ Loss of place

COMMENTS: _Reads slowly at times. Reads with his teeth clenched (?). When asked if he liked to read he said, "I really don't like reading because it's hard to pronounce the words and I don't understand it so it doesn't give me any fun."_

THE **BOBBS-MERRILL** COMPANY, INC.
A SUBSIDIARY OF HOWARD W. SAMS & CO., INC.
Publishers • INDIANAPOLIS • NEW YORK

HAND-SCORED EDITION

Name __*Ivan*__
 (LAST) (FIRST)

Birth date _____ Boy _X_ Girl _____
 (MONTH, DAY, YEAR)

Grade _*6th grade*_ Testing date *5-9-1968*

Teacher _____

School _*Buena Vista*_

City _____

GATES –
MacGINITIE
READING TESTS

D FORM 3

SURVEY D, FORM 3

Speed & Accuracy
Vocabulary
Comprehension

□□□■■■□□□□□□

TEACHERS COLLEGE PRESS
TEACHERS COLLEGE
COLUMBIA UNIVERSITY
NEW YORK

To the Teacher:
BE SURE to follow the directions in the Manual (included in each test package) when giving these tests. The directions will tell you how to explain the tests and how to work the sample items with the students. Allow the exact time specified in the Manual.

DIRECTIONS: Read sample paragraph S 1. Under it are four words. Find the word that best answers the question.

> **S1.** Mary pulled and tried to turn the knob. She could not turn it. It was a cold day to be locked outside. What was Mary trying to open?
>
> box   bag   (door)   safe

The word **door** is the best answer to the question. Draw a line under the word **door**.

Now read paragraph S2. Find the word below the paragraph that best completes the paragraph, and draw a line under it.

> **S2.** The huge animals walked slowly, swinging their trunks from side to side. They had big floppy ears and long white tusks. These animals were
>
> tigers   deer   lions   (elephants)

The word **elephants** best completes paragraph S2. You should have drawn a line under the word **elephants**.

On the next two pages are more paragraphs like these samples. When you are asked to turn the page, read each paragraph and find the word below it that best answers the question or completes the paragraph. Draw a line under the best word. Mark only *one* word for each paragraph. Do the paragraphs in the order in which they are numbered: 1, 2, 3, etc. If you can't answer a question, go on to the next one. Work as fast as you can without making errors.

		Number right			
COMPREHENSION	Number right	47	57	76	9.5
VOCABULARY	Number right	39	57	76	8.4
SPEED & ACCURACY	Number right	23	53	62	8.9
	Number attempted	24	52	58	8.1
		Raw score	Standard score	Percentile score	Grade score

© 1964 by Teachers College, Columbia University
Printed in U.S.A.

10   9   8   7   6   5   4   3

Reproduced from Gates-MacGinitie Reading Tests, Primary C, Form 1. Copyright 1964 by Teacher's College, Columbia University, New York. Reproduced by permission.

Silent Reading Diagnostic Tests
GRAPHIC PROFILE

Name _____ School _____

Grade _____ Teacher _____ Date _____

Grade Equivalent

BASIC DATA	Pupil Score	1.5	2.0	2.5	3.0	3.5	4.0	4.5	5.0	5.5	6.0	6.5	7.0	7.5	8.0
Grade in School															
Chronological Grade															
Reading Expectancy															
READING ABILITIES															
Vocabulary															
Literal Comprehension															
Creative Comprehension															
Average Reading															
WORD-RECOGNITION SKILL (Tests 1 and 2)															
Total Right (1 + 2)		11	21	29	38	49	60	65	70	75	77	80	82	84	
Words in Isolation (1)		12	17	23	29	37	42	45	47	49	51	52	53	54	
Words in Context (2)		1	5	7	10	15	18	21	23	25	26	28	30		
ERROR PATTERN (1 + 2)															
Total Omitted (1 + 2)		37	29	17	7	4	1								
Total Errors (1 + 2)		31	29	28	27	22	17	15	13	10	7	4	2	1	
Error Type (1 + 2) — Initial		9	8	7	6	5	4	3	3	2	2	1	1	0	
Error Type (1 + 2) — Middle		10	9	7	6	5	4	3	2	1	1	0			
Error Type (1 + 2) — Ending		8	7	7	6	6	5	5	4	3	2	2	1	0	
Error Type (1 + 2) — Orientation		8	7	7	6	6	5	4	3	2	2	1	0		
RECOGNITION TECHNIQUES (Tests 3, 4, and 5)															
Total Right (3 + 4 + 5)		19	23	27	32	38	44	50	55	58	60	69	78	83	85
Visual-Structural Analysis (3)		3	6	7	8	9	10	12	13	14	16	20	26	28	30
Syllabication (4)		8	11	13	15	17	19	20	21	22	23	25	26	28	30
Word Synthesis (5)		4	6	7	9	12	14	17	19	20	22	25	28	30	
PHONIC KNOWLEDGE (Tests 6, 7, and 8)															
Total Right (6 + 7 + 8)		39	45	51	58	63	66	68	71	73	75	78	83	85	88
Beginning Sounds (6)		9	14	17	20	22	23	23	24	25	26	27	28	29	30
Ending Sounds (7)		8	10	12	15	17	19	20	21	22	23	25	27	28	30
Vowel and Consonant Sounds (8)		16	20	22	23	24	24	25	25	26	26	27	28	29	30
		1.5	2.0	2.5	3.0	3.5	4.0	4.5	5.0	5.5	6.0	6.5	7.0	7.5	8.0

Grade Equivalent

Individually Administered Reading Tests for Classroom Teachers

1. Botel Reading Inventory. Tests word recognition, word opposites, listening, and phonic ability. 1010 West Washington Blvd., Chicago, Illinois: Follett Publishing Company.
2. Durrell Analysis of Reading Difficulty. Tests oral and silent reading, listening comprehension, word analyis, phonetic ability, writing and spelling. (New York: Harcourt, Brace & World, 1955).
3. Gilmore Oral Reading Test. Ten reading paragraphs of increasing difficulty. Yields separate accuracy of reading mechanics and level of comprehension scores. (New York: Harcourt, Brace & World, 1968).
4. Gray's Oral Reading Test. Thirteen paragraphs of increasing difficulty. (Indianapolis, 6, Indiana: Bobbs Merrill Company, Inc., 1963).

Standardized Silent Reading Tests for Elementary School Reading Programs

1. California Reading Tests. Separate tests for lower primary, primary, elementary, junior high, and advanced grades. Tests vocabulary and comprehension. (Research Park, Monterrey California: California Test Bureau, 1957).
2. Gates-MacGinitie Reading Tests. Tests vocabulary and comprehension in primary grades; vocabulary, comprehension and speed in upper grades. Primary A: Grade 1; Primary B: Grade 2; Primary C: Grade 3; Survey D: Grades 4, 5, 6; and Survey E: Grades 7, 8, 9. May be machine or hand scored. (New York: Bureau of Publications, Teachers College, Columbia University, 1965).
3. Iowa Tests of Basic Skills. The reading test may be obtained separately from the battery in a reusable booklet. Tests paragraph comprehension and vocabulary. (Boston: Houghton Mifflin Co.).
4. Nelson Reading Test. For Grades 3-9. Timed. Thirty minutes working time. Ten minutes vocabulary; twenty minutes paragraph comprehension. (Boston: Houghton Mifflin, Co., 1962).
5. Silent Reading Diagnostic Reading Tests. Tests word recognition, left-to-right orientation, syllabication, root words, auditory discrimination, and word synthesis. Provides profile for each child. (Lyons and Carnahan, 2500 Prairie Avenue, Chicago 16, Illinois).
6. Stroud-Hieronymus Primary Reading Profiles for Grades 1 and 2. Tests auditory association, word recognition, word attack skills, and reading comprehension. (Boston: Houghton Mifflin Co.).

II. CHILDREN'S WRITTEN WORK

There are several means by which the classroom teacher can obtain from children their written expression which conveys how well they read, how well they can think about and use what they read, and how they feel about the material read, or how they feel about the job of reading.

Teachers often obtain from children early in the year an original paragraph describing an enjoyable summer vacation incident. It would be well for teachers to help children delimit the topic about which they wish to write and not use such global titles as "What I Did last Summer" or "My Summer Vacation," since he needs to be helped to delineate specifics and describe them in concrete terms.

Writing a summarizing paragraph about a lesson is a difficult assignment in the elementary school and boys and girls need help and guidance in arriving at the main point and two or three supporting details and how to write a paragraph that follows the suggestion in Chapter 8 about understanding the anatomy of a paragraph.

When the primary objective is for the young child to express a good idea on paper, the teacher should accept the idea and not judge accuracy in mechanics harshly. After the ideas are on paper, they can be edited as seems necessary to an individual teacher. If teachers insist primarily on capital letters, periods, and margins and indentations, then they may get well-ordered paragraphs without ideas.

A fourth grade boy kept a diary for several weeks when his teacher found that he needed help to *think about* and *write* even one complete sentence. A section of his diary is reproduced on the next page. The reader will note that he almost always writes down the *topic* of his sentence and then begins the sentence he is planning to write. (See page 502)

A fourth grade girl wrote the two book reports included here after she had read the books and discussed them with her remedial reading teacher. (See page 501)

III.   THE ORAL READING OF CHILDREN

Oral reading should have three major aspects in the elementary classroom. In the primary grades on a day-to-day basis the child must read aloud so that the teacher knows how successful he is in learning all the basic sight words which he must master in order to read anything. In the higher grades, there must also be the necessary testing of the ability to read well orally. The teacher will find samples of each child's oral reading useful in order to evaluate with an individual child how well or how poorly he reads and to map out a reading improvement program with him. Such individual oral reading samples can be very useful in parent conferences, too, to point out to parents exactly how well, and at what grade level, a given child reads orally. This first use of oral reading in the classroom is as a testing or evaluation instrument.

Little Black
A   Pony

There once was a pony and a
boy. One day the boy ~~is~~ rode
on a big hores. The boy's pony
was sad. One day he rode on the
horse. There ~~is~~ was a ~~it~~ tree thuck on
the ~~rode~~ the big horse jumped over
     road
the tree ~~it~~ truck but when the
pony jumped over the tree trunk
he got his foot ~~it~~. the pony
     caught
ran a way one morning. The boy
jumped on the horse and went ~~after~~
after his pony. The horse went broke
~~a~~ acrosed some frosan water. it ~~brook~~
his pony got him out. Now the
pony was happy.
Butternut Bill and the
     Big Pumpkin

It was almost time for the fair.
Butternut Bill was going to
take a pumpkin. His Granny
was working to take something
to the fair too. Lazy Daisy
~~brock~~ Butternut Bills pumpkin..
Granny's hen unrattled her work
so they toke a pumpkin pie.

broke   ravel

3/15/68 I like planes. They are fun. To ride in I went to D.C. in one. It was fun we left at 2:30 in D. and got in Alb. at 3:00.

3/16/68 Cars I like cars I like racing cars. I like when they go fast. And I like old old cars too.

3/18/68 fish I like fish they are swim in my room. We have two fish a little one and a big one.

3/22/68 Jon is a French boy. I play with him all day long. He can talk French only. He likes to ride bikes all day.

3/23/68 Arithmetic I like arithmetic it is easy. to do. Today we did some arithmetic like these one's $7)\overline{7935}$ $60-$ I got a B in arithmetic. $\frac{420}{5)\overline{60}}$

3/25/68 Spelling I like spelling it is easy too. We get easy words to spell. I got a B in it too.

3/26/68 Reading I like reading I got a C in it. I like the teacher who teaches me. She is good very good.

3/27/68 Blackbeard's Ghost I saw it Saturday night. It was funny show. It was at Hiland Theater.

3/28/68 I got up at 6:00 and now it is 6:35 right this very min. It is fun to get up at 6:00. I can do my work in 35 min.

The second major use of oral reading in a classroom should be the pleasurable sharing of interesting passages, motivating the reading of good books, and firmly establishing the belief that books are treasures of interesting information to share and to enjoy. If the teacher is a good oral reader (See Chapter 11), the boys and girls can easily be motivated to also share interesting anecdotes, jokes, witticisms, and informational materials that add documentary evidence to former classroom argumentation and debate on issues.

The third use of oral reading is the necessary presentation of evidence to prove a point, to settle an argument, or to give the evidence that a line of reasoning is supported by the authorities.

Both of the latter two uses of oral reading are audience situations wherein only the reader has the information being shared.

IV. CHECK LISTS AND QUESTIONNAIRES

The teacher should be continuously learning more and more about the boys and girls he teaches. How well or how poorly they perform in reading must be equated with the home environment in which they live, the emotional stability of the adults in their lives, the socio-economic level of the home, the *pressures* from outside the child exerted to "guarantee" his academic success, and other so-called intangibles in his day-to-day living. Yet, every day the teacher must make decisions about each child as he performs as an integral part of his total classroom.

In the affective domain, the teacher is concerned about:

How does the teacher feel about George?
How does George feel about the teacher?
How does George feel about himself in relation to all other people?
How do George's parents feel about George?
How do the other children in the room feel about George?

In the cognitive domain, the teacher is concerned about:

How well does George perform on a standardized reading test?
How well can he read aloud?
How well can he read silently?
How well does he retain what he has read?

The teacher can prepare a check list of items that will measure all of the above behaviors to some degree. Such a check list could be edited or extended as the teacher uses it.

The following items might constitute a check list of reading behaviors for the classroom teacher:

1. Reads with understanding
2. Applies phonics skills
3. Reads independently
4. Finishes assignments
5. Reads well orally
6. Uses independent study time efficiently
7. Follows directions
8. Understands reading assignments
9. Pronounces new words efficiently
10. Works well in small groups
11. Brings in new information from outside of school
12. Is embarrassed in front of class
13. Reads in too soft a voice to be heard
14. Misses little words (basic sight words)
15. Reads in a monotone.

V.   OTHER INFORMAL TECHNIQUES IN EVALUATION

For too long, teachers have thought of evaluation as a measurement of cognitive growth. When a unit of work was finished, the test should determine whether the child had absorbed all the facts the teacher had emphasized. There are many other ways, of course, in which the teacher can estimate permanent learning in the cognitive domain. More important, however, is the present day effort to measure growth in affective areas of behavior. Developing appropriate leadership-followership qualities; identifying children who are always on the periphery in social situations: finding out how the child feels about his success or lack of it; and planning for teacher judgment about the cognitive and affective changes in child behavior are all areas of concern in the present day school.

Sociometrics

A sociogram is a chart showing the social interaction among the members of a group at a given time. Sociograms help to visualize social status of the members of the group. Through the construction of a sociogram, a teacher can determine cliques, most popular children, isolates, and leaders. Restructuring the room environment, through such activities as assigning a leader to work with an isolate on a worthwhile project, the teacher may be able to effect a real change in children's behavior over a period of time. Teachers do not discuss the results of the sociogram with the boys and girls; he never indicates to them who is the reject, the isolate, or the most popular. Neither does he naively urge popular children to be "nice" to neglected ones. Teachers will find many sources of specific information about how to construct the socio-gram. A few such sources are

1. JOHN U. MICHAELIS, *Social Studies for Children in a Democracy,* (Englewood Cliffs, New Jersey: Prentice-Hall, Inc., 1956), pp. 164-166.
2. MILES V. ZINTZ, *Corrective Reading,* (Dubuque, Iowa 52001: William C. Brown Co., Publishers, 1966), pp. 173-178.

Anecdotal Records

Anecdotal records are brief descriptions of specific instances of behavior. The anecdote is not a superficial comment made about the child by the teacher; rather, it is a description of a specific behavior of the child. It may be made more meaningful by citing exact comment or conversation of the child. Well thought out anecdotal records become very helpful when the teacher holds parent-teacher conferences. The behavior journal can be organized simply so that the teacher's comments can be recorded easily and chronologically. Michaelis presents an excerpt from a behavior journal for a fourth grade boy about whom the teacher's greatest concern is to help him learn better how to work with others:[2]

Behavior Journal		
Name: Walter Doe	Class: Miss Smith	Grade: IV
Date	Incidents	Comments
9-21	Did not share the picture with others.	Needs help in carrying out standards.
10-2	Helped to make rules for using materials; shared only a few tools.	Group chart may help. Seemed to understand reason for sharing; needs to work with one or two children.
10-19	Discussed need for sharing with others.	
11-2	Worked with David in preparing a report.	Growth is evident; must place in small group of 3 or 4 as a next step.

Anecdotal records begin to have value as soon as the teacher has recorded enough specific behaviors so that threads or patterns of behavior begin to become evident.

<hr>

[2]John U. Michaelis, *Social Studies for Children in a Democracy,* (Englewood Cliffs, N. J.: Prentice-Hall, Inc., 1956), p. 413.

Children's Evaluation of Themselves

Self-evaluation should guide children in developing self-direction. Increased ability to analyse their own strengths and weaknesses, successes and failures, skills and abilities, should improve their abilities in the problem-solving approach to all problems, and develop the ability to set purposes and evaluate end results in mature behavior.

Children need guidance if they are to learn better how to evaluate themselves. Checklists, charts, and development of work standards can provide this guidance.

Children can, with the help of the teacher, prepare guidelines for improving study and work habits. The following group chart is illustrative of a set of guidelines for improving work habits.

Can I answer YES?

1. Do I do my own work?
2. Do I finish whatever I begin?
3. Do I listen to directions?
4. **Do I return materials I have used?**
5. Do I work quietly without asking too many questions?

Teacher's Evaluation

The teacher could check on his own behavior in teaching reading by asking himself questions such as the following:

1. Do I introduce new words and new concepts to teach their meanings?
2. Do I provide for review and reinforcement after initial teaching?
3. Do I have IRI results to show that each child is reading at a level where he understands at least 75% of the ideas in the materials and makes no more than five errors in 100 running words?
4. Do I have to tolerate too many interruptions from children working independently when teaching a directed reading lesson? (If so, is the material that the children are studying too difficult?)
5. Does any child still need a marker when he reads? If so, is there a justifiable reason for it?
6. Does any child still move his lips when reading silently?
7. Do my boys and girls see purpose in their work and is the climate a constructive one?

VI. PROFILES EVALUATE MANY SKILLS AND ABILITIES

A profile is any type of graphic aid that portrays many measures of knowledges, skills, or abilities so that in one picture, the observer is provided at a quick glance strengths and weaknesses, or high, average, and low scores. By comparing above and below median scores, one can quickly conclude whether strengths outweigh weaknesses or vice versa.

The profiles of two individuals are presented on the following page. Both are eighth graders and fifteen years old. One has a Mental Age of only nine years-six months while the other has a mental age equal to his chronological age. The one with normal intelligence is a non-reader *but* with sufficient capacity to read at grade level. The other has a fourth grade reader level which is approximately equal to his level of mental ability. The second is not retarded in reading since he is reading as well as his mental ability indicates. It is clear that the reading teacher needs two entirely different programs for these two students. One needs an intense remedial reading program while the other needs an adapted reading program to provide efficient teaching of skills at the level he can read with understanding.

For the teacher who administers the basic reading tests that accompany the series of basal readers, the summary sheet is a kind of profile of the individual child—and of the whole class. In the sub-test scores, C.A., I.Q., and class rating shown on the Summary Sheet for the *New Times and Places* Reading Test, the teacher has the necessary information to analyze the consistency or inconsistency of results in terms of the expected performance for a given child. In the event of serious discrepancies, the teacher needs to refer the child to the guidance department for more definitive testing. (See page 509)

Valett has provided a profile for the different types of items in the revised Stanford Binet Test. In the profile pictured below, the teacher, with the help of the counselor, can circle all items passed beyond the child's established basal age and look for strengths or weaknesses in general comprehension, visual-motor ability, arithmetic reasoning, memory and concentration, vocabulary and verbal fluency, and in judgment and reasoning. The profile is presented on page 509.

VII. SUMMARY

Evaluating how efficiently the teacher is teaching and how effectively the child is learning is basic to any successful reading program. It will do no good for the teacher to plan and teach a reading lesson if the child cannot profit from that instruction. He will fail to achieve the objective that the teacher has in mind if the material is too difficult, if the concepts necessary for interpreting the story are not understood, or if he is emotionally distressed for reasons which may or may not relate to school. The myriad of factors which cause all children to differ from each other was summarized in Chapter 2. Because this is true, the teacher must develop skill in diagnosing on a day-to-day basis so that all of his teaching is diagnostic teaching.

Johnson and Kress have emphasized this need[3]

---

[3]Marjorie Seddon Johnson and Roy Kress, *Informal Reading Inventories*, (Newark, Delaware: International Reading Association, 1965), pp. 42-43.

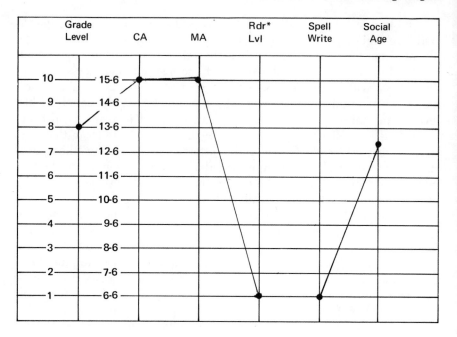

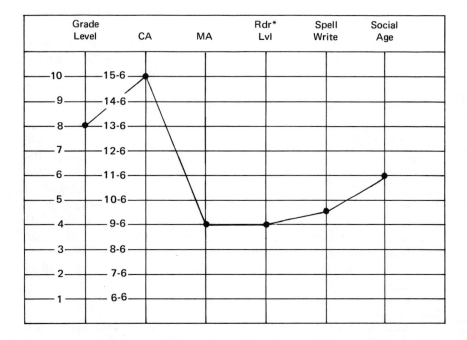

CLASS SUMMARY SHEET FOR BASIC READING TEST

Grade_____ School_____

City_____ State_____

Date of Test_____ Teacher_____

Name of Intelligence Test Used_____

to accompany

THE NEW **Times and Places**

NAME	AGE		I. Q.	SCORE ON TEST							TOTAL	RATING
				I	II	III	IV	V	VI	VII		
	Years	Months		Sentence Meaning	Sensory-Imagery	Relationships	Generalization	Word Meaning	Word Analysis	Dictionary Skills		

From Basic Reading Test to accompany *The New Times and Places,* Gray, Monroe, Artley and Arbuthnot, (Glenview, Ill.: Scott, Foresman & Co., 1955).

A PROFILE FOR THE STANFORD BINET (L-M)

Item Classifications by Robert E. Valett

INSTRUCTIONS: Draw a vertical line through the year for the obtained basal age. Circle all test items passed beyond this level.

SUBJECT'S NAME: _____ CA: _____ MA: _____ IQ Range: _____ Grade: _____ Date of Test: _____

TEST CONSTRUCTS Year:	2	2-6	3	3-6	4	4-6	5	6	7	8	9	10	11	12	13	14	AA	SA I	SA II	SA II
GENERAL COMPREHENSION	3 A 6	1 2 6		6	4 6 A	4 6			2 4 5	4 5 A			6	3 6	4	5	5 6 7	6	3	2 4
VISUAL-MOTOR ABILITY	1 4	A	1 3 5 6	2 5			1 2 4 6 A	6	3	1 3	2	1	A	A		A				
ARITHMETIC REASONING							4				5					4 A	2 4	2	4	
MEMORY & CONCENTRATION	2	5	4 A		2 A	5			6 A	2 6	3 6	6	1 4	4 A	3 6		4	6	6	
VOCABULARY & VERBAL FLUENCY	5 6 A	3 4	2	4	1		3	A		1	4 A 3 5	1 3 5 6	3	1 5 6	2 5		1 3 8	1 3 5	1	1 3 A
JUDGMENT & REASONING		1	1 2 3 A	3 5	1 2 3 A	5 6	2 3 5 A	1 2 4 5	3 4	1 2 4 A	2 4	2 2 4 5 6 A	2	1 4 5 A	2 4 5 6 A	2 3 4 5 6 7 A	2 6 A	2 3 4 5 6 A	2 4 5 6 A

○ Copyright, 1965, by R. E. Valett. It is a violation of copyright law to reproduce this form by any process. Distributed by Consulting Psychologists Press, Inc., 577 College Avenue, Palo Alto.

CONSULTING PSYCHOLOGISTS PRESS
577 College Avenue   Palo Alto, California 94306

From A Profile for the Stanford-Binet (L-M) by Robert Vallett, copyright 1965, published by Consulting Psychologists Press.

Diagnostic teaching should pervade all classroom activities, both group and individual. The classroom teacher's ability to interpret each child's abilities and needs in developmental reading using an informal reading inventory will increase with practice. This sophistication builds confidence and permits the teacher skills so that he no longer need think of *the* informal reading inventory as a single instrument. Rather, if the content area in question is elementary science, an IRI measuring skills and abilities in this subject is possible. Or social studies, or mathematics. Teachers no longer need to infer instructional reading levels in any subject area.

In this way, diagnostic teaching is carried on throughout the school day with day-by-day evaluations of pupils' performances. Continuous diagnosis of weaknesses and strengths and teaching to overcome weaknesses by building on strengths is, indeed, diagnostic teaching.

Hamachek has reported types of comments made by poor teachers that are not made by good teachers as well as types of comments made by good teachers not made by poor ones:[4]

Characteristic Comments Made by Poor But Not by Good Teachers:

Are you working hard? . . . Aren't you ever going to learn that word? . . . Everyone sit up straight, please. . . . I'm afraid you're confused. . . . No, that's wrong. . . . Oh dear, don't you know that? . . . Oh, sit down. . . . Say something.

(Nearly one hundred different expressions were listed. Note the overtones of frustration, futility, and impatience which are implied throughout).

Characteristic Comments Made by Good But Not by Poor Teachers:

Aha, that's a new idea. . . . Are you going to accept that as an answer. I should like more proof. . . . Do you suppose you could supply a better word? . . . Can you prove your statement? . . . Don't you really think you could? . . . I'm not quite clear on that—think a moment. . . . Let's stick to the question. . . . Probably my last question wasn't a good one.

(There was a long list of such expressions. Note the emphasis on challenging the student, on pushing and encouraging him to go beyond where he may be at the moment.)

Busy classroom teachers need ways of keeping records that are as concise and simple as possible. Each one will develop the technique for keeping notes, anecdotes, and needed information to make it as useful as possible. The form on the next page has been prepared to

---

[4]Don E. Hamachek, *Motivation in Teaching and Learning.* The "What Research Says to the Teacher" Series, NEA, 1201 Sixteenth Street, N.W., Washington, D. C. 20036, 1968, pp. 12-13.

Summary of information about reading for each child in my class:

Name of child	IRI Oral Reading	IRI Silent Reading	IRI Capacity Level	Standardized Reading test[1]	Phonetic Skills[2]	Vocabulary Sight Words	Vocabulary Standard Tests[3]	Spelling Ability[4]	Other Information
1.									
2.									
3.									
4.									
5.									
6.									
7.									
8.									
9.									
10.									
11.									
12.									

1. Name of test. _____ .   2. Name of test. _____ .

3. Name of test. _____ .   4. How determined. _____

show how a teacher might summarize on one sheet of paper some of the important data about the boys and girls in one group in the class. If results of an individual intelligence test are available, that information might be included. If a group intelligence test has been administered by the classroom teacher, the probability of the results being invalid for the lower half of the class are so great that the teacher might indicate on the abbreviated record only categories such as high, above average, average, below average.

SUGGESTED ACTIVITIES

1. Administer a standardized reading test to a small group of children in the room where you teach or for the grade level you hope to teach. Analyze the results and write your interpretation.

2. Make a sociogram for the class based on choices for working together on reading and writing activities. Evaluate the positions on the sociogram of the best and poorest readers in the class.

3. The teacher can devise subjective ways to compare his evaluation with a child's self-evaluation and compare both evaluations with objective measures of achievement. What does the child expect of himself? Does this correspond to the idea of the self-fulfilling prophecy?

READING REFERENCES

AUSTIN, MARY C., CLIFFORD L. BUSH, and MILDRED H. HUEBNER, *Reading Evaluation,* (New York: Ronald Press, 1961).

BARRETT, THOMAS C., Editor, *The Evaluation of Children's Reading Achievement,* Perspectives in Reading No. 8, (Newark, Delaware 19711: International Reading Association, 1967).

GRAY, LILLIAN, *Teaching Children to Read,* (New York: The Ronald Press Company, 1963), Chapter 15: "Evaluating Pupil Progress in Reading," pp. 414-431.

JOHNSON, MARJORIE SEDDON, and ROY A. KRESS, Editors, *Corrective Reading in the Classroom,* Perspectives in Reading No. 7, (Newark, Delaware 19711: International Reading Association, 1967).

RAUCH, SIDNEY J., "A Checklist for the Evaluation of Reading Programs," *The Reading Teacher,* 21:519-522, March, 1968.

TINKER, MILES A., and CONSTANCE M. McCULLOUGH, *Teaching Elementary Reading,* Third Edition, (New York: Appleton-Century-Crofts, Inc., 1968), Chapter 17: "Appraisal of Reading Growth," pp. 339-362.

WITTY, PAUL A., ALMA M. FREELAND, and EDITH H. GROTBERG, *The Teaching of Reading,* (Boston: D. C. Heath, 1966), Chapter 17: "Evaluation of Development in Reading," pp. 373-396.

22

Teaching Reading
in Proper Perspective

Throughout the text, emphasis has been given to the extent of differences in children's learning. All the principles of learning that cause groups of boys and girls to become more different instead of more alike as they progress through the school are in direct contradiction to the organization by chronological age level and the inflexible patterns deeply habituated in all schools today. Having copies of the same textbook for every child in the class is just the opposite of a flexible pattern to encourage teachers to provide for many levels of ability within the class. What is the classroom teacher to do?

In planning his reading program, (see Chapter 4) it was suggested that inexperienced teachers would rely much more heavily on basal readers and their corresponding manuals to keep several reading groups progressing in the sequential development of reading skills. More experienced teachers will feel confident to work within broader limits of individualized reading and language experience types of reading and writing. However, they too will rely on organized, sequenced basal-reader lessons for some children in small groups according to the developmental reading needs of the class.

In perspective, how can the classroom teacher keep up with each child in his room if they are nearly all doing different things? Is the atmosphere one of noise and chaos? How will the building principal react to this?

Probably the teacher will not wish to keep up with ten or more separate reading groups day after day when they are all in basal reading series dependent upon the teacher for guidance. Yet, with some well-planned lessons that include individualized reading for those who really want to read, individualized work-type lessons for those who need planned, guided seatwork, most of the children can work independently

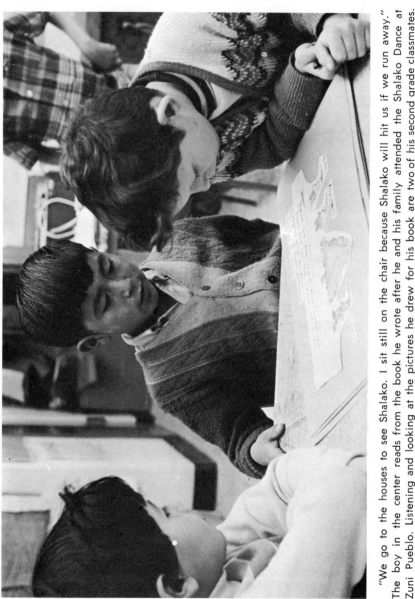

"We go to the houses to see Shalako. I sit still on the chair because Shalako will hit us if we run away." The boy in the center reads from the book he wrote after he and his family attended the Shalako Dance at Zuni Pueblo. Listening and looking at the pictures he drew for his book are two of his second grade classmates. Photo by Khanlian. Courtesy of Albuquerque Public Schools.

for much of an hour that the teacher may have scheduled for reading in his daily program.

The informal reading inventory discussed in detail in Chapter 3, and the use of Dolch Basic Sight Words as a diagnostic instrument in revealing word recognition problems in Chapter 17 constitute two of the classroom teachers' most valuable tools for diagnostic teaching in primary reading.

I. DIAGNOSTIC TEACHING OF READING

Diagnostic teaching of reading requires the acceptance and application of these principles.

1. Children are indivisible entities.
2. No learning takes place without a motive. If it isn't important *to the child,* he won't learn very efficiently.
3. There is *not necessarily any relationship* between disabled readers and intelligence.
4. Differences within the group get greater as children progress through the grades.
5. Each child has his own optimum time for learning.
6. No two children can learn the same thing in the same amount of time with the same amount of practice.
7. No child is inherently lazy. If he acts that way, there has to be a reason why.
8. Most everything that is learned must be reviewed from time to time or it will be forgotten.
9. When an objective is stated behaviorally for the child, the teacher can determine if the objective was achieved.

Some teachers do violate these principles. And all recognize problems in applying them in their day-to-day work. Discussed below are anecdotes reporting teacher behavior.

Parent-Teacher Communication

The second grade teacher showed the following duplicated letter to her student teacher early in the school year and explained that the second graders were "too far behind" in reading.

Dear Parent:

The attached list of 175 words were taught last year in first grade. In second grade, your child will be expected to know them. Please see that your child knows all of these words so that he can do the work in the second grade.

Your child's teacher
Mary Smith

Did all children learn 175, and only 175, service words in first grade? Does forgetting during the summer constitute any problem? Is second grade only for people who have already learned 175 words? Or, can a child be in second grade and know very few sight words?

If Miss Smith has a "usual" heterogenous group of thirty children about seven years old, she should expect to find the whole range of differences inherent in the intellectual, psychological, physical, and social growth of children at this chronological age. Such children, while in first grade, became "more different" and not "more alike." Their growth in emotional stability and independence varied with each set of parents who applied "individual" quantities of over-indulgence, acceptance, rejection, neglect, punishment, or tender-loving care. For the teacher to assume that parents can or will teach their child a basic sight vocabulary, is to assume their "know-how" in methodology is equal to that of the teacher. Sadly, this is occasionally true! The letter tells parents nothing about how to proceed, nothing of the necessity that learning the words must be a meaningful, rewarding kind of experience, nor of the psychological danger of trying to coerce the child into learning.

If the teacher were teaching diagnostically in second grade, she would find out early in the year how many of the 175 sight words each child knew, and arrange her room in such a way that numbers of sub-groups could start reading experiences on the basis of how many words they now know and make progress from that point. Some children might learn best with more auditory help with hearing phonetic elements in words, others with more writing practice of sentences containing words they have learned, others with more easy, oral reading practice, and still others with special attention directed to letters or words often confused ("b" and "d", "n" and "m", "was" and "saw", "and" and "said"). The teacher should expect varying degrees of emotional, social, and intellectual maturity and, as a "professional", she should expect to know how to accomplish this job better than most parents.

The fact that a student teacher recevied the "letter to parents" from her "supervisor" suggests to the young student teacher that this represents "good" teaching practice.

Because a good teacher knows that children need a great deal of easy reading practice to become good readers, she would do well to ask young children to carry home their textbook *after* she has taught them *all* the new words, and hope the mother or father will be a good listener and encourage the child in his oral reading practice. Because parents are *not* oriented in teaching methodology, the teacher still needs to send a letter to the parents. Such a letter might read:

Dear Parent:

Bill has read all of *Peanuts, the Pony*[1] at school and knows all the new words. Of course, he needs much practice to become a good reader. Will you please listen attentively while he reads aloud for you so you can enjoy the story together? After he has read for you, please sign your name below and let *Bill* return the letter to me.

Thank you for your kind cooperation,
Miss Smith

Bill has read *Peanuts, the Pony* aloud, and we enjoyed it together.

Parent _____

Helping Child Work at His Instructional Level All Day Long

Mrs. Walker has been a sixth grade teacher for many years. She has many "beautiful" bulletin boards that she has "used" many times. Her room is clean, efficient, and very quiet. She organizes the work of her student teacher so that the student teacher will learn to perform exactly the way Mrs. Walker performs. This observer believes that such effort will perpetuate indefinitely some very bad practices.

In a culturally deprived, low-socioeconomic area of the city, Mrs. Walker has grouped her twenty-seven sixth graders into three reading groups. About one-third read from a first semester fifth grade reader; another third read from a first semester fourth reader; and the final third read from a first semester second reader. The final third includes a variety of types of reading problems needing carefully tailored "individual" solutions, but each day they have a superficially motivated, directed reading lesson following the manual written for second graders.

A great paradox is that for spelling class, they each study the list of words for the week in *My Word Study Book*, Book Six. For perhaps more than half of the class, this contains a list of words they cannot pronounce and for which they lack many meanings. One condemning end-result in this practice from the mental health point of view is the destruction of ego and devaluation of self when the teacher asks "How many perfect papers?" on the Friday test and looks approvingly at the two or three who always raise their hands. To all those who fail, the admonition to "study harder" or to "write each word ten times" reveals that this teacher does not follow the practice of teaching diagnostically. No child has a *need* for any spelling words he cannot *pronounce and use* in his writing. His level of difficulty in spelling can hardly be greater than his ability to read.

In this same sixth grade, every student used the regular sixth grade arithmetic textbook and every day *all* tried to learn the same mathematics skills in the same amount of time with the same amount of practice.

---

[1]Pre-primer, *Our Animal Story Series*, (Boston: D. C. Heath).

Grouping at instructional reading levels makes possible providing study activities all day long which the child can do successfully. This is one of the advantages of the self-contained classroom.

Perhaps one way to emphasize the extent of differences in the self-contained classroom is to talk about "The Many Faces of Reading."

The Many Faces of Reading

The illustration on page 519 is an attempt to picture the many and varied attitudes toward the reading act in the primary classroom. All classroom teachers teaching heterogenous groups of boys and girls are sure to have enrolled occasionally the one who comes from a foreign language background; the fearful chlid; the child who is already convinced he can't learn; the child who is emotionally disturbed and can't think logically about his immediate problems; the child who thinks that right-to-left direction is as appropriate for reading as is left-to-right; the child who uses all kinds of excuses when the words are difficult but he doesn't want to admit it. Then there are those children who always know all the words; those who have read many interesting stories before they get to the class; those who delight in good reading ("Gee, that's a neat story!"); and those who overwork the expression, "I'm so bored!" A few children have been told emphatically that they have never been taught phonics and that the lack of phonics knowledge is the only reason they are not good readers. From this conglomerate, the teacher must build constructively to find ways to group within the class, ways to identify and develop leadership for groups, and varied activities to make reading fun to do from many different points of view.

II. UNANSWERED QUESTIONS ABOUT THE TEACHING OF READING

Teaching reading diagnostically requires both ability and judgment on the part of the teacher. Below are twenty questions, fairly typical of many other possible questions, for which answers need be sought.

1. How will I organize my room for reading in the fall when school starts?
2. How can I get some kind of grouping established early in the year?
3. How will I explain to mothers or other teachers what I am doing?
4. What will my basic organization be: basal reader, individualized reading, or language-experience?
5. What will each child be reading at his instructional level all the rest of the school day?
6. How can I make sure he is not expected to write and spell words he cannot read?
7. How will I make a daily lesson plan that incorporates everything? (Independent seatwork to last long periods of time)

THE MANY FACES of READING

8. Making reading plans for different kinds of groups: Those who *do* almost all read at grade level or above; those in a normal distribution in the achievement range; and those where the achievement is below grade level for almost everyone.
9. Have I made reading just *one* of the parts of a language arts curriculum?
10. The disadvantaged, the culturally different, or the non-standard user of English needs special teaching. How do I teach them diagnostically?
11. The student for whom English is a foreign language, the culturally different child—do I know how to teach English to him first?
12. Accept and respect the course of study for all children but live fairly with the specific children in my classroom—how do I do this?
13. The child *never* just all of a sudden "catches on" to reading. Do I know how to find out what is wrong?
14. If children want to do well, to follow the principles of growing toward maturity, do I know how to find out what is wrong in case of trouble?
15. No teacher can know all the answers. There has to be support from many disciplines. How can I find answers outside the classroom?
16. Will I make sure the child has a good year to grow on *in my room* and let next year take care of itself?
17. Will I know what to tell parents who ask, "Does the school teach phonics?"
18. Should the school provide programmed material for independent seatwork? What materials?
19. What is dyslexia? Can I help the child who has it?
20. When should a child repeat a grade in the elementary school?

Hunter[2] writes that there are some teachers who still feel that regardless of what a child has learned or has failed to learn they must use the book of the grade level to which he is assigned. Such attitude could hardly be less productive or more inefficient. The appropriate course for teachers, Hunter says, is marked by relevant and provocative diagnostic questions.

> Professional know-how enables us to ask three important diagnostic questions which lead the way to productive learning. The first is, What is the body of *knowledge* for which society says the school is responsible? The second is concerned with the *knower* who must assimilate that knowledge. The Third question is concerned with the *process of knowing*. These questions are interrelated so that the correct answer to any one will further the other two. Conversely, an incorrect answer to one will seriously impede progress in all three areas, and may result

[2]Madeline C. Hunter, "You—as a Diagnostician," *The Instructor,* 76: 31, 126, February, 1967.

in learning failure. Success in the teaching-learning act is directly proportional to the teacher's professional competence in dealing diagnostically with these three categories: knowledge, the knower, and the process of knowing.[3]

English says[4]

. . . the textbook in its present form is outdated, expensive, and inefficient. The assumptions underlying its present usage are false; they do not explain or foster learning in depth or promote student inquiry . . . The removal of legal straitjackets (textbooks) will provide the freedom necessary to arrive at modern education in a time when "modern" is woefully out of date.

But Mr. Soghomonian, in his response to Mr. English, says[5]

There are good and bad textbooks, easy-to-read ones, and hard-to-understand ones. But the major fault, the core of the problem, is not the text *per se*, but that too many teachers have made the text an icon. Therein lies the monster. The text is not protoplasm; the teacher is. The classroom text is inert, as is any tool. It hardly seems fair to criticize the tool and not the operator.

III. SELF-FULFILLING PROPHECIES

Does the teacher's expectations as to his pupil's performance affect that performance? Currently, the answer is *"yes."*

Rosenthal and Jacobson[6] found that when teachers in an elementary school were told that certain children would do especially well, even though they were really picked at random, those children showed significantly greater gains than others during the school year. The effect of expectations was even greater at the primary levels than with the intermediates!

In subjective teacher descriptions of these designated children at the end of the year, teachers thought they had better chances of success, were significantly more interesting and curious, and somewhat more adjusted and affectionate.

Two questions follow: (1) How much does the teacher's attitude toward the child have to do with how successfully he learns to read? and (2) How much are the results of educational research done by teachers affected by the favorable or unfavorable expectation of the teacher beforehand?

---

[3]*Ibid.*, p. 31.
[4]Fenwick English, "The Textbook—Procrustean Bed of Learning," *Phi Delta Kappan*, 48: 395, April, 1967.
[5]Sam Soghomonian, "The Textbook—Tarnished Tool for Teachers," *Phi Delta Kappan*, 48: 395, April, 1967.
[6]"Science and the Citizen," *Scientific American*, 217: 54 +, November, 1967. Reported from Robert Rosenthal and Lenore Jacobson; "Self-Fulfilling Prophecies," *Psychological Reports*, 19 (1): 115-118, 1966.

Self-Esteem

Coopersmith[7] studied behavior patterns in a group of boys, ages ten to twelve, to evaluate qualities that build self-confidence and feelings of personal worth. Expectation of success, motivation to achieve, initiative and dealing with anxieties are behaviors necessary in developing positive self-esteem. Coopersmith found that the opinion a child has of himself is a very significant component of his behavior.

High self-esteem is indicated by academic or social success, confidence, optimism, originality, and parents who are generally strict and consistent in enforcement of rules. Low self-esteem is indicated by conviction of inferiority, fear of social encounters, self-consciousness, sensitivity to criticism, lack of confidence, remaining in the shadows, and listening, not participating.

The interrelationship between self-esteem and level of aspiration needs to be studied and evaluated carefully. If Coopersmith's study is valid, the crucial role of primary teachers is underscored and re-emphasized. The young child who experiences personal failure his first two or three years of school may be fitting into a behavior pattern of low self-esteem with all the negative behaviors that this suggests.

IV. PREVENTION IS BETTER THAN REMEDIATION

The early identification of difficulties in the school learning situation could prevent much of the painful correction that now takes place in special remedial teaching situations. As was emphasized in the chapter on readiness, the basic idea in evaluation before formal reading should be to study the child's status in school with respect to physical, intellectual, emotional, and social readiness for the complex task of learning to read. Formal reading instruction should be carefully delayed for the child who is immature and can profit from pre-reading development in any of these four major areas.

By the end of the first day of school, in a heterogeneous group of thirty children, there are those individuals who have not completely achieved the objective the teacher had in mind in each of several areas of the school curriculum. In truth, then, one can say that there is remedial work to be done from the first day. The teacher must be alert to failure symptoms in any child—whether he is failing in the area of cognition—learning all the facts the teacher has in mind, the area of affect—developing confidence in himself as a person and acquiring the necessary self-esteem, or in the psychomotor area—being able to demonstrate all the necessary motor skills related to the successful completion of academic tasks.

---

[7]Stanley Coopersmith, "Studies in Self-Esteem," *Scientific American*, 218: 96-102ff., February, 1968.

When the failure symptom first appears is the time when the alert teacher searches for ways to re-direct the child's efforts so that he will experience successes—and by rehabilitating in an area of weakness preparing the child for continuous growth.

Diagnostic teaching is the technique of teaching each child the specific skills he has not mastered but must know before he can progress in the sequence to more difficult learning.

Diagnostic teaching starts with the child—each unique one—with his range of competencies, concerns, and enthusiasms; with his own unique self-concept, learning style, aspirations; who can learn only in his own personal way. Learning for each child is a highly affective personal experience.

Dorris M. Lee reminds us[8]

> Diagnostic teaching employs procedures that are based on the findings of experience and research about children and learning, those that can be effective in attaining the goals of the school, and those that recognize unique personal values.

Olsen and Kelley emphasize special needs of lower-class children in school. Olsen says[9]

> We have yet to face the fact that lower-class children are socialized in ways that are quite different from those of the middle-class. We have yet to take full account of the differing value patterns, attitudes, and beliefs with which the lower-class child comes to school. The child brings the reality of his own life into the classroom, and to be effective the school must admit that reality. I suggest that the central challenge that the slum child presents to the school is not only the disadvantages that he brings with him. His challenge to us is much more profound than this. His ambitions, his hopes, his desires, his attitudes toward authority, education, success, and school, his fears, his habits, his hates —in short, his basic orientation toward life—are, in many ways, so different from ours that we do not understand him nor does he understand us.

And Kelley reminds us[10]

> The child born and raised in a lower-class setting derives his perceptions and values, attitudes and habits of living in a cultural setting that teaches, rewards, and reinforces his way of life. His way of perceiving, behaving, and becoming is distinctly different from the school culture.

---

[8]Dorris M. Lee, *Diagnostic Teaching*, (1201 Sixteenth Street, N.W., Washington, D. C. 20036; Department of Elementary-Kindergarten-Nursery Education, National Education Association, 1966).

[9]James Olsen, "Challenge of the Poor to the Schools," *Phi Delta Kappan*, 47: 79, October, 1965.

[10]Earl C. Kelley, *Perceiving, Behaving, Becoming, A New Focus on Education*, (Association for Supervision and Curriculum Development, NEA, 1201 Sixteenth Street, N.W., Washington 6, D. C., 1962.

Finally, the profession needs teachers with the determination which Hunt gives Aunt Cordelia when she explains why she must continue to teach the rural school near her farm:

> Aunt Cordelia didn't really have to teach for a livelihood; the income from the farm was sufficient for her needs, and the modest salary she received for each month of the school year was not the incentive which brought her back to her desk year after year. Her reason for teaching was actually the belief that no one else would do the work quite as well, would understand the backgrounds of these children whose parents she had taught when she was young. There was never a doubt in Aunt Cordelia's mind but that *her* teaching was the best to be had, and she would have felt that she was denying something beyond price to the handful of country children who sat in her classroom if she allowed a younger or a less dedicated woman to take over.[11]

READING REFERENCES

AUSTIN, MARY C., and COLEMAN MORRISON, *The Torch Lighters, Tomorrow's Teachers of Reading*, (Cambridge, Massachusetts: Harvard University Press, 1961).

CHALL, JEANNE S., *Learning to Read: The Great Debate*, (New York: McGraw-Hill Book Company, 1967). "Conclusions and Recommendations," pp. 305-314.

ENGLISH, FENWICK, "The Textbook—Procrustean Bed of Learning," *Phi Delta Kappan*, 48:393-395, April, 1967.

HEILMAN, ARTHUR W., *Principles and Practices of Teaching Reading*, Second Edition, (Columbus, Ohio: Charles E. Merrill Books, Inc., 1967), Chapter 17: "Improving Teaching," pp. 525-548.

International Reading Association, (P. O. Box 695, Newark, Delaware 19711).
    a. Proceeding of the Annual Convention.
    b. *The Reading Teacher* Magazine, eight issues per year.
    c. *The Journal of Reading*, eight issues per year.
    d. *The Reading Research Quarterly.*
    e. *Perspectives in Reading.*

LEE, DORRIS M., *Diagnostic Teaching*, (1201 Sixteenth Street, N.W., Washington, D. C. 20036; Department of Elementary-Kindergarten-Nursery Education, National Education Association, 1966).

MANOLAKES, GEORGE, "Instructional Practices in Reading: An Assessment for the Future," in A. J. Mazurkiewicz, *New Perspectives in Reading Instruction*, (New York: Pitman Publishing Corporation, 1964), pp. 96-111.

SOGHOMONIAN, SAM, "The Textbook—Tarnished Tool for Teachers?" *Phi Delta Kappan*, 48:395-396, April, 1967.

STRANG, RUTH, CONSTANCE McCULLOUGH, and ARTHUR TRAXLER, *The Improvement of Reading*, Fourth Edition, (New York: McGraw-Hill, 1967), "Synthesis of Controversial Issues," pp. 503-514.

---

[11]Irene Hunt, *Up a Road Slowly*, (Chicago: Follett Publishing Company, 1966), p. 21.

Bibliography

ADAMS, FAY, LILLIAN GRAY, and DORA REESE. *Teaching Children to Read.* The Ronald Press, Second Edition, 1957.

Adult Reading. See Henry, Nelson B., Editor, NSSE Yearbook.

ANDERSON, VERNA. *Reading and Young Children.* New York: Macmillan, 1968.

ANDERSON, VERNA, *et al. Reading in the Language Arts.* Second Edition. New York: Macmillan, 1968.

AUSTIN, MARY C., and COLEMAN MORRISON. *The First R.* The Harvard Report on Reading in Elementary Schools. New York: The Macmillan Co., 1963. 262 pp.

BAGFORD, JACK. *Phonics: Its Role in Teaching Reading.* Iowa City, Iowa: Sernoll, Inc., 1967. 80 pp.

BAMMAN, HENRY A., URSULA HOGAN, and CHARLES E. GREENE. *Reading Instruction in the Secondary Schools.* New York: Longmans, Green and Co., 1961. 266 pp.

BARBE, WALTER. *Educator's Guide to Personalized Reading Instruction.* Englewood Cliffs, New Jersey: Prentice-Hall, Inc., 1961.

BARBE, WALTER B. Editor. *Teaching Reading: Selected Materials.* New York: Oxford University Press, 1965. 444 pp.

BETTS, EMMETT ALBERT. *Foundations of Reading Instruction, with Emphasis on Differentiated Guidance.* New York: American Book Company, 1954. 757 pp.

BLAIR, GLENN MYERS. *Diagnostic and Remedial Teaching.* New York: The Macmillan Company, 1956. 409 pp.

BOND, G., and LEO J. BRUECKNER. *The Diagnosis and Treatment of Learning Difficulties.* New York: Appleton-Century-Crofts, Inc., 1955. 424 pp.

BOND, G., and MILES TINKER. *Reading Difficulties, Their Diagnosis and Correction.* Second Edition. New York: Appleton-Century-Crofts, 1967.

BOND, GUY L., and EVA BOND WAGNER. *Teaching the Child to Read.* Fourth Edition. New York: The Macmillan Co., 1966. 404 pp.

BOTEL, M. *How to Teach Reading.* State College, Pa.: Pennsylvania Valley Publishers, Inc., 1959.

BROGAN, PEGGY, and LORENE K. FOX. *Helping Children Read.* New York: Holt, Rinehart, and Winston, 1961. 330 pp.

525

Carpenter, Helen McCracken (ed.). *Skill Development in the Social Studies.* 33rd Yearbook, National Council of the Social Studies. 1201-16th St., N.W., Washington 36, D. C., National Council for the Social Studies, 1963. 332 pp.

Carter, Homer L. J., and Dorothy J. McGinnis. *Teaching Individuals to Read.* Boston: D. C. Heath, 1962. 229 pp.

Causey, Oscar S. (ed.). *The Reading Teacher's Reader.* New York: The Ronald Press Company, 1958. 339 pp.

Chall, Jeanne S. *Learning to Read: The Great Debate.* McGraw-Hill, 1967.

Cohn, Stella M., and Jack Cohn. *Teaching the Retarded Reader, A Guide for Teachers, Reading Specialists, and Supervisors.* New York: The Odyssey Press, Inc., 1967. 174 pp.

Conroy, Sophie C. (ed.). *Specifics for You: A Corrective Reading Handbook.* Brooklyn, New York: Faculty Press, 1961. 73 pp.

Cordts, Anna D. *Phonics for the Reading Teacher.* New York: Holt, Rinehart, and Winston, Inc., 1965. 270 pp.

Crosby, Muriel (ed.). *Reading Ladders for Human Relations.* Fourth Edition. Washington, D. C.: American Council on Education, 1963. 242 pp.

Cutts, Warren G. *Modern Reading Instruction.* New York: Center for Applied Research in Education, 1964. 118 pp.

Cutts, Warren G. (ed.). *Teaching Young Children to Read.* U. S. Office of Education, Department of Health, Education and Welfare. Washington 25, D. C., 1964. 134 pp.

Dallmann, Martha. *Teaching the Language Arts in the Elementary School.* 135 South Locust Street, Dubuque, Iowa 52001, 1966. 342 pp.

Darrow, Helen, and V. M. Howe. *Approaches to Individualized Reading.* New York: Appleton-Century-Crofts, 1960.

Dawson, Mildred A., and Henry A. Bamman. *Fundamentals of Basic Reading Instruction.* Second Edition. New York: David MacKay Co., Inc., 1963. 325 pp.

DeBoer, J. J., and Martha Dallmann. *The Teaching of Reading.* Revised Edition. New York: Holt, Rinehart, and Winston, Inc., 1964. 422 pp.

Dechant, Emerald V. *Improving the Teaching of Reading.* Englewood Cliffs, New Jersey: Prentice-Hall, Inc., 1964. 568 pp.

de Hirsch, Katrina, Jeannette Jefferson Jansky, and William S. Langsford. *Predicting Reading Failure.* New York: Harper and Row, 1966. 144 pp.

Della-Piana, Gabriel M. *Reading Diagnosis and Prescription: An Introduction.* New York: Holt, Rinehart, and Winston, Inc., 1968. 240 pp.

Development in and Through Reading. See Henry, Nelson B. (ed.), NSSE Yearbook.

Dolch, E. W. *A Manual for Remedial Reading.* Champaign, Illinois: Garrard Press, 1945. 464 pp.

————. *Problems in Reading.* Garrard Press, 1947. 373 pp.

————. *Teaching Primary Reading.* Garrard Press, 1951. 458 pp.

Downing, John. *The Initial Teaching Alphabet Explained and Illustrated.* New York: The Macmillan Company, 1964.

Draper, Marcella, and Louise H. Schwietert. *A Practical Guide to Individualized Reading.* Publication No. 40. City of New York: Board of Education, Bureau of Educational Research, 1960. 158 pp.

DURKIN, DOLORES. *Phonics and the Teaching of Reading.* Bureau of Publications, Teachers College, Columbia University, New York: 27, New York, 1965. 100 pp.

DURR WILLIAM K. *Reading Instruction: Dimensions and Issues.* A Book of Readings. Boston: Houghton Mifflin Co., 1967. 359 pp.

DURRELL, DONALD D. *Improving Reading Instruction.* Yonkers-on-Hudson. New York: World Book Co., 1956. 402 pp.

EPHRON, BEULAH K. *Emotional Difficulties in Reading.* New York: The Julian Press, Inc., 1953.

FERNALD, GRACE. *Remedial Techniques in Basic School Subjects.* McGraw-Hill Book Co., 1943.

FITZGERALD, JAMES A., and PATRICIA G. FITZGERALD. *Fundamentals of Reading Instruction.* Milwaukee: The Bruce Publishing Co., 1967.

FLESCH, RUDOLF. *Why Johnny Can't Read and What You Can Do About It.* New York: Harper Brothers, 1955.

FRIERSON, EDWARD C., and WALTER B. BARBE. *Educating Children with Learning Disabilities.* A Book of Readings. New York: Appleton-Century-Crofts, 1967. 502 pp.

FRIES, CHARLES C. *Linguistics and Reading.* New York: Holt, Rinehart, and Winston, Inc., 1963. 265 pp.

GANS, ROMA. *Fact and Fiction About Phonics.* Indianapolis: The Bobbs-Merrill Co., 1963. 107 pp.

—————. *Common Sense in Teaching Reading.* Indianapolis: The Bobbs-Merrill Co., Inc., 1963. 414 pp.

—————. *Guiding Children's Reading Through Experience.* Teachers College, Columbia: Bureau of Publications, 1941. 86 pp.

GATES, A. I. *The Improvement of Reading.* Macmillan, 1947. 657 pp.

GRAY, LILIAN. *Teaching Children to Read.* Third Edition. New York: The Ronald Press Company, 1963. 446 pp.

GRAY, W. S. (ed.). *Classroom Techniques in Improving Reading.* Supplemental Educational Monograph, No. 69. Chicago 37, Illinois: The University of Chicago Press, 1949. 246 pp.

GRAY, W. S. *On Their Own in Reading.* Second Edition. Scott Foresman, 1960. 248 pp.

HAFNER, LAWRENCE. *Improving Reading in Secondary Schools, Selected Readings.* New York: The Macmillan Company, 1967. 445 pp.

HARRIS, ALBERT J. *Effective Teaching of Reading.* New York: David MacKay Co,. Inc., 1962. 387 pp.

—————. *How to Increase Reading Ability.* New York: David MacKay Company, 1961, 625 pp.

—————. *Readings on Reading Instruction.* New York: David MacKay Company, Inc., 1963. 466 pp.

HEILMAN, ARTHUR W. *Phonics in Proper Perspective.* Columbus, Ohio: Charles E. Merrill Books, Inc., 1964. 103 pp.

—————. *Principles and Practices of Teaching Reading.* Second Edition. Columbus, Ohio: Charles E. Merrill Books, Inc., 1967.

HENRY, NELSON B. (ed.). *Adult Reading.* Vol. 55, Part II, NSSE Yearbook. Chicago: University of Chicago Press, 1956. 279 pp.

—————. *Development In and Through Reading.* NSSE Yearbook. Chicago: University of Chicago Press, 1961. 60th Yearbook, Part I. 406 pp.

—————. *Reading in the Elementary School.* NSSE Yearbook, Vol. 48, Part II. Chicago: University of Chicago Press, 1949. 350 pp.

HERR, SELMA E. *Phonics: Handbook for Teachers.* Los Angeles: E. R. A. Publishers, 1961.

HERMANN, KNUD. *Reading Disability, A Medical Study of Word Blindness and Related Handicaps.* Springfield, Illinois: Charles C. Thomas, Publisher, 1959. 182 pp.

HESTER, KATHLEEN B. *Teaching Every Child to Read.* Second Edition. New York: Harper and Row, 1964. 384 pp.

HILDRETH, GERTRUDE. *Teaching Reading.* New York: Holt, Rinehart, and Winston, Inc., 1958. 612 pp.

HOLMES, JACK A., and HARRY SINGER. *Speed and Power of Reading in High School.* Cooperative Research Monograph No. 14. Office of Education. U. S. Department of Health, Education, and Welfare, 1966. 183 pp.

HOWES, VIRGIL M., and HELEN FISHER DARROW. *Reading and the Elementary School Child: Selected Readings.* New York: Macmillan, 1968. 480 pp.

International Reading Association, Box 695, Newark, Delaware 19711. *Perspectives in Reading.* 1964-1968.
  1. College-Adult Reading Instruction.
  2. Reading Instruction in Secondary Schools.
  3. Children, Books and Reading.
  4. Developing Study Skills.
  5. First Grade Reading Programs.
  6. Corrective Reading in the High School Classroom.
  7. Corrective Reading in the Elementary School.
  8. The Evaluation of Children's Reading Achievement.
  9. Organizing for Individual Differences.
  10. Evaluating Books for Children and Young People.

International Reading Association. *Proceedings of the Annual Convention.* Newark, Delaware: International Reading Association.
  Vol. 1. Better Readers for Our Times, 1956.
  2. Reading in Action, 1957.
  3. Reading for Effective Living, 1958.
  4. Reading in a Changing Society, 1959.
  5. New Frontiers in Reading, 1960.
  6. Changing Concepts of Reading Instruction, 1961.
  7. Challenge and Experiment in Reading, 1962.
  8. Reading As an Intellectual Activity, 1963.
  9. Improvement of Reading Through Classroom Practice, 1964.
  10. Reading and Inquiry, 1965.
  11. Vistas in Reading, 1966.
  12. Forging Ahead in Reading, 1967.
  13. Reading and Realism, 1968.

Iowa Elementary Teacher's Handbook, Vol. II. *Reading.* The Printing Office, State of Iowa, 1943.

KING, MARTHA L., BERNIECE D. ELLINGER, and WILLAVENE WOLF. *Critical Reading. A Book of Readings.* Philadelphia: J. B. Lippincott Company, 1967. 480 pp. Fifty selected articles.

KOTTMEYER, W. *Handbook of Remedial Reading.* Webster Publishing Co., St. Louis, 1959. Second Edition.

LANCASTER, LOUISE. *Introducting English: An Oral-Pre-Reading Program for Spanish-Speaking Primary Pupils.* Boston: Houghton Mifflin Co., 1966. 294 pp.

LARRICK, NANCY. *A Teacher's Guide to Children's Books.* Columbus, Ohio: Charles E. Merrill Books, Inc., 1960. 316 pp.

LEE, DORIS M., and R. VAN ALLEN. *Learning to Read Through Experience.* Second Edition. New York: Appleton-Century-Crofts, 1963. 146 pp.

LEFEVRE, CARL A. *Linguistics and the Teaching of Reading.* New York: McGraw-Hill Book Co., 1964.

LONG, NICHOLAS J., WILLIAM C. MORSE, and RUTH G. NEWMAN. *Conflict in the Classroom: The Education of Emotionally Disturbed Children.* Belmont, California: Wadsworth Publishing Co., Inc., 1965. 515 pp.

LORETAN, JOSEPH O., and SHELLY UMANS. *Teaching the Disadvantaged.* New York: Teachers College Press, Columbia University, 1966. 242 pp.

MANUEL, HERSCHEL T. *Spanish-Speaking Children of the Southwest, Their Education and the Public Welfare.* Austin: University of Texas Press, 1965. 222 pp.

MARKSHEFFEL, NED D. *Better Reading in the Secondary School.* New York: The Ronald Press, 1966. 272 pp.

MAZURKIEWICZ, ALBERT J. *New Perspectives in Reading Instruction, A Book of Readings.* New York: Pitman Publishing Corporation, 1964. 574 pp.

MCCRACKEN, G. *The Right to Learn.* Chicago: Henry Regnery, 1959.

MCKEE, PAUL. *Reading: A Program of Instruction for the Elementary School.* Boston: Houghton Mifflin Co., 1966. 498 pp.

————. *The Teaching of Reading in the Elementary School.* Houghton Mifflin, 1948. 622 pp.

MCKIM, MARGARET. *Guiding Growth in Reading.* Macmillan, 1955. 528 pp.

MCKIM, MARGARET G., and HELEN CASKEY. *Guiding Growth in Reading in the Modern Elementary School.* Second Edition. New York: The Macmillan Co., 1963. 454 pp.

MIEL, ALICE. *Individualizing Reading Practices.* New York: Bureau of Publications, Teachers College, Columbia University, 1958.

MONROE, MARION, and BERNICE ROGERS. *Foundations for Reading.* Chicago: Scott, Foresman and Co., 1964. 208 pp.

MONEY, JOHN (ed.). *The Disabled Reader. Education of the Dyslexic Child.* Baltimore: The John Hopkins Press, 1966. 420 pp.

————. *Reading Disability, Progress and Research Needs in Dyslexia.* Baltimore: The John Hopkins Press, 1966. 222 pp.

NSSE Yearbook. See Henry, Nelson B., editor.

NEWTON, J. ROY. *Reading in Your School.* New York: McGraw-Hill Book Co., Inc., 1960. 297 pp.

OTTO, WAYNE, and RICHARD A. MCMENEMY. *Corrective and Remedial Teaching. Principles and Practices.* Boston: Houghton Mifflin Co., 1966. 377 pp.

Perspectives in Reading. International Reading Association, Box 695, Newark, Delaware 19711. See International Reading Association.

POLLACK, M. F. W., and JOSEPHINE A. PIEKARZ. *Reading Problems and Problem Readers.* New York: David MacKay Co., 1963.

Reading in the Elementary School. See Henry, Nelson B., (ed.). NSSE Yearbook.

REEVES, RUTH. *The Teaching of Reading in Our Schools.* A Macmillan Guidebook for Parents. New York: The Macmillan Co., 1966. 120 pp.

ROBINSON, FRANCIS P. *Effective Reading.* New York: Harper and Brothers, Publishers, 1962.

ROBINSON, H. ALAN (ed.). *Meeting Individual Differences in Reading.* Supplemental Educational Monograph, No. 94. Chicago 37, Illinois: The University of Chicago Press, 1964. 246 pp.

ROBINSON, HELEN M. *Why Pupils Fail in Reading*. Chicago: University of Chicago Press, 1946. 257 pp.

ROSWELL, FLORENCE, and GLADYS NATCHEZ. *Reading Disability: Diagnosis and Treatment*. New York: Basic Books, Inc., 1964. 248 pp.

RUSSELL, DAVID. *Children Learn to Read*. Second Edition. Ginn, 1961.

RUSSELL, D., and ETTA KARP. *Reading Aids Through the Grades*. Teachers College: Bureau of Publications, 1951.

RUSSELL, DAVID, and ELIZABETH F. RUSSELL. *Listening Aids Through the Grades*. One Hundred Ninety Listening Activities. Bureau of Publications, Teachers College, Columbia University, New York 27, New York, 1959. 108 pp.

SCHELL, LEO M., and PAUL C. BURNS. *Remedial Reading: An Anthology of Sources*. Boston: Allyn and Bacon, 1968. 468 pp. Fifty-five selected articles.

SCHICK, GEORGE B., and BERNARD SCHMIDT. *A Guidebook for the Teaching of Reading*. Chicago: Psychotechnics Press, 1966. 135 pp.

SCHONELL, FRED J. *Psychology and Teaching of Reading*. New York: Philosophical Library, 1961.

SCHUBERT, DELWYN G., and THEODORE L. TORGERSON. *Improving Reading Through Individualized Correction*. Second Edition. 135 So. Locust Street, Dubuque, Iowa: William C. Brown Company, Publishers, 1968.

SHANE, HAROLD G., and JUNE GRANT MULRY. *Improving Language Arts Instruction Through Research*. 1201 Sixteenth St., N.W., Washington 6, D. C.: Association for Supervision and Curriculum Development, NEA, 1963. 153 pp.

SHAW, PHILLIP B. *Effective Reading and Learning*. Thomas Y. Crowell Company, New York, 1955. 447 pp.

SMITH, DONALD E. P., and PATRICIA M. CARRIGAN. *The Nature of Reading Disability*. New York: Harcourt, Brace & World, 1959. 149 pp.

SMITH, HENRY P., and EMERALD V. DECHANT. *Psychology in Teaching Reading*. Englewood Cliffs, New Jersey: Prentice-Hall, Inc., 1961.

SMITH, NILA BANTON. *American Reading Instruction, Its Development and Its Significance in Gaining a Perspective on Current Practices in Reading*. Newark, Delaware: International Reading Association, 1965. 449 pp.

—————. *American Reading Instruction*. Newark: International Reading Association, (1934), 1965.

—————. *Read Faster and Get More from Your Reading*. Englewood Cliffs, New Jersey: Prentice-Hall, Inc., 1958. 393 pp.

—————. *Reading Instruction for Today's Children*. Englewood Cliffs, New Jersey: Prentice-Hall, Inc., 1963. 594 pp.

SPACHE, GEORGE D. *Reading in the Elementary School*. Second edition. Boston: Allyn and Bacon, Inc., 1969.

—————. *Toward Better Reading*. Champaign, Illinois: Gerrard Publishing Co., 1963.

STAHL, STANLEY S., JR. *The Teaching of Reading in the Intermediate Grades*. William C. Brown Publishers, 135 South Locust Street, Dubuque, Iowa 52001, 1965. 110 pp.

STAIGER, RALPH, and DAVID A. SOHN (eds.). *New Directions in Reading*. New York: Bantam Books, 1967.

STAUFFER, RUSSELL G. *Directing Reading Maturity As a Cognitive Process*, (New York: Harper and Row, 1969).

—————. *Teaching Reading As a Thinking Process*. (New York: Harper and Row, 1969).

STERN, CATHERINE, and TONI S. GOULD. *Children Discover Reading: An Introduction to Structural Reading.* New York: Random House, 1965.

STRANG, RUTH. *Diagnostic Teaching of Reading.* New York: McGraw-Hill Book Co., 1964. 314 pp.

STRANG, RUTH (ed.). *Understanding and Helping the Retarded Reader.* Tucson: University of Arizona Press, 1965. 118 pp.

STRANG, RUTH and DOROTHY KENDALL BRACKEN. *Making Better Readers.* Boston: D. C. Heath and Company, 1957. 367 pp.

STRANG, RUTH, CONSTANCE MCCULLOUGH, and A. E. TRAXLER. *The Improvement of Reading.* Fourth Edition. New York: McGraw-Hill Book Company, 1967. 564 pp.

STRICKLAND, RUTH. *The Language of Elementary School Children: Its Relationship to the Language of Reading Textbooks and the Quality of Reading of Selected Children.* Bloomington, Indiana: Bureau of Educational Studies and Testing, School of Education, Indiana University, 1962.

TERMAN, SIBYL, and CHARLES C. WALCUTT. *Reading: Chaos or Cure.* New York: McGraw-Hill Book Company, Inc., 1958. 285 pp.

THOMPSON, LLOYD J. *Reading Disability: Developmental Dyslexia.* Springfield, Illinois: Charles C. Thomas, 1966.

TINKER, MILES A. *Bases for Effective Reading.* Minneapolis: University of Minnesota Press, 1965.

TINKER, MILES, and CONSTANCE MCCULLOUGH. *Teaching Elementary Reading.* Third Edition. New York: Appleton-Century-Crofts, Inc., 1968.

TOOZE, RUTH. *Your Children Want to Read.* Englewood Cliffs, New Jersey: Prentice-Hall, Inc., 1957. 222 pp.

VEATCH, JEANNETTE. *Individualizing Your Reading Program.* New York: G. P. Putnams Sons, 1959.

————. *Reading in the Elementary School.* 15 East 26th Street, New York 10, New York: The Ronald Press Company, 1966. 535 pp.

WALCUTT, C. C. *Tomorrow's Illiterates.* Boston: Little, Brown and Company, 1961.

WEISS, M. JERRY. *Reading in the Secondary School, A Book of Readings.* New York: The Odyssey Press, Inc., 1961. 464 pp.

WILSON, ROBERT M. *Diagnostic and Remedial Reading, For Classroom and Clinic.* Columbus, Ohio: Charles E. Merrill Books, Inc., 1967. 260 pp.

WILSON, ROBERT M., and MARYANNE HALL. *Programmed Word Attack for Teachers.* Columbus: Charles E. Merrill Books, Inc., 1968. 63 pp.

WITTY PAUL. *How to Become a Better Reader.* 259 East Erie St., Chicago: Science Research Associates, Inc., 1959. 304 pp.

WITTY, PAUL A., ALMA MOORE FREELAND, and EDITH H. GROTBERG. *The Teaching of Reading: A Developmental Process.* Boston: D. C. Heath and Company, 1966. 435 pp.

WITTY, PAUL, and DAVID KOPEL. *Reading and the Educative Process.* Ginn, 1939.

WOOLF, MAURICE D., and JEANNE A. WOOLF. *Remedial Reading, Teaching and Treatment.* New York: McGraw-Hill Book Company, Inc., 1957. 424 pp.

YOAKAM, GERALD A. *Basal Reading Instruction.* New York: McGraw-Hill Book Company, Inc., 1955. 357 pp.

ZINTZ, MILES V. *Corrective Reading.* 135 S. Locust St., Dubuque, Iowa: William C. Brown Co. Publishers, 1966. 380 pp.

Name Index

Topical Index